MW01015012

Criminal Law

Criminal Law

Concepts and Practice

THIRD EDITION

Ellen S. Podgor
GARY R. TROMBLEY FAMILY WHITE-COLLAR CRIME RESEARCH PROFESSOR
PROFESSOR OF LAW
STETSON UNIVERSITY COLLEGE OF LAW

Peter J. Henning
PROFESSOR OF LAW
WAYNE STATE UNIVERSITY LAW SCHOOL

Andrew E. Taslitz
PROFESSOR OF LAW
AMERICAN UNIVERSITY WASHINGTON COLLEGE OF LAW

Alfredo Garcia
PROFESSOR OF LAW
ST. THOMAS UNIVERSITY SCHOOL OF LAW

CAROLINA ACADEMIC PRESS
Durham, North Carolina

ISBN: 978-1-61163-013-8
LCCN: 2013943668

Carolina Academic Press
700 Kent Street
Durham, North Carolina 27701
Telephone (919) 489-7486
Fax (919) 493-5668
www.cap-press.com

Printed in the United States of America

Dedicated To:

Cheryl L. Segal

Molly, Alexandra, and Grace

To the memory of my wise and warm Uncle, Eugene Taslitz

To Cindy, Christina, James, and Catherine

And of course to all of our students.

PREFACE

Crime, and the law related to the prosecution of offenders, is one of the most widely covered and discussed topics in society today. Media coverage is pervasive of both crimes and the prosecutions that result from them, ranging from the innumerable fictional programs devoted to every conceivable aspect of the criminal justice system to YouTube videos showing actual criminal trials. Daily newspapers and local news shows devote substantial coverage to local crimes, while the seemingly endless parade of celebrity run-ins with the law, some as trivial as a traffic ticket while others involving charges of murder, are fodder for breathless coverage in tabloids and weekly magazines. The criminal law is perhaps the most widely followed area in the legal landscape, and crime touches all segments of society.

While the media is quick to label a person as guilty or innocent, the process of determining actual guilt is far more complex. The role of the criminal lawyer, both the prosecutor and the defense attorney, is far different from what is portrayed in television shows or movies, and the law of crimes involves many difficult conceptual and policy issues. One important question in the application of the criminal law is whether the government targets certain groups for a disproportionate level of enforcement, or does not take into consideration the particular circumstances of the defendant's race, gender, sexual orientation, social status, or economic situation in deciding whether conduct constitutes a crime. The criminal law cannot be divorced from the social setting in which it occurs, and media stereotypes can feed perceptions of criminality that are not otherwise supported.

The starting point for any criminal prosecution is determining whether to bring criminal charges and what crime a person will then be charged with, which in turn requires that statutes be reviewed to see if the conduct at issue comes within the parameters of what the legislature has determined to be a criminal offense. Today, the criminal law is, first and foremost, a creature of the legislature, but it is based on a long history of judicial interpretation, known as the common law. The interplay between statutes and the common law gives rise to many difficult interpretive issues in determining the scope of criminal liability.

In addition to the statutes, and perhaps more importantly, the prosecution and defense of criminal charges involves something very important: *evidence*. Whether one believes that the punishment for an offense should be more or less harsh, or whether certain conduct should or should not be subject to a sanction imposed by the government, a particular criminal case requires that each side gather and interpret information that can be presented in court to determine whether the defendant is guilty of a crime. A statute indicates what the legislature has determined, in advance, will constitute a crime. It is the application of that provision to the proof that each side will offer for its position that determines whether a person will be found guilty of a crime. In fact, most criminal prosecutions end well in advance of a trial, by an agreement known as a plea bargain. Even that determination, however, requires that the government, through its investigatory agencies and prosecutorial units, and the defendant, working with a lawyer, ascertain what evidence is available before deciding whether to enter into the agreement.

Quite simply, the criminal law is about a process by which evidence is gathered, organized, analyzed, and, if necessary, presented to a trier of fact to determine whether a defendant has committed a crime. While evidence can be a term of art related to a complex set of rules for use in a trial, its broader meaning is intended here. Evidence can be anything, from a statement or scream to a computer-generated model, that assists in explaining what happened in a course of events. In a criminal case, a key piece of evidence can be a person's statement to a police officer, a strand of hair that allows for DNA testing, or a document describing an apparently ordinary business transaction. Whatever the evidence is, it must be fit within the framework of a criminal statute to determine whether there is enough information to determine whether or not a crime occurred, and if so, who is responsible for it.

The focus of this book is on both sides of the criminal law equation: the *principles* of the law of crimes and the *proof* of the criminal violation. The determination of whether a person is guilty of a crime is the key question in every case, and an issue in all prosecutions is whether there is sufficient evidence to convict a person of a crime charged. What constitutes the type of evidence that will be important to that determination, and whether there is enough evidence to meet the requirements of the statutory definition of a crime, is the primary focus of the lawyers on both sides.

This casebook consists of cases, problems, case studies, and supplemental notes that concentrate primarily on how a particular crime can be proven, the defenses available to that crime, and the tools that are available to lawyers to assist in the process of prosecuting and defending a case. The materials consider the theoretical underpinnings of the criminal law to give a clearer understanding of why the law adopts a particular approach to conduct. It places criminal law in a real setting, one with issues of race and gender.

Lawyers are trained to represent clients, whether the client be society or an individual defendant, and use their abilities to interpret statutes and organize evidence to evaluate how to best represent the client's interests. The casebook is a means to develop those skills in the context of one area of the law, but the reader would be mistaken to view the criminal law as a hermetically-sealed set of legal rules that have no effect on other areas. Lawyers deal with evidence in every area of legal practice, ranging from estate planning to corporate law to real estate finance. Even if a lawyer never represents a client in a criminal case, principles from the criminal law have an impact on how a lawyer and client will (and should) act.

Some of the problems in the casebook are drawn from the facts of actual cases, although in many instances changes have been made to make them more useful tools for analyzing the law and how it might be applied using different legal principles. Below is a list of the problems that are based on actual cases for readers who may wish to see how a court dealt with an issue:

Chapter 1   Problem 1: *United States v. Holmes*, 26 F.Cas. 360 (E.D. Pa. 1842).

Chapter 2   Problem 4: *United States v. Hevelock,* 619 F.3d 1091 (9th Cir. 2010), 664 F.3d 1284 (9th Cir. 2012)(en banc).

Problem 5: *Belay v. District of Columbia*, 860 A.2d 365 (D.C. 2004).

Problem 6: *State v. Wells*, 965 So. 2d 834 (Fla. Dist. Ct. App. 2007).

Chapter 4   Problem 9: *United States v. X-Citement Video*, 513 U.S. 64 (1993).

Problem 12:*Loftus v. District of Columbia,* 51 A.3d 1285 (D.C. 2012).

Chapter 5   Problem 14: *Bullock v. State*, 775 A.2d 1043 (Del. 2001).

Problem 15: *People v. Harding*, 506 N.W.2d 482 (Mich. 1993).

Chapter 6:   Problem 17: *State v. Gerbasio,* 2008 WL 2415083 (N.J. Super Ct. App. Div. 2008).

Problem 18: *United States v. DeJohn*, 368 F.3d 533 (6th Cir. 2004).

Chapter 8   Problem 25: *Commonwealth v. Thomas*, 656 A.2d 514 (Pa. Super. Ct. 1995).

Problem 26: *State v. Elliott*, 411 A.2d 3 (Conn. 1979).

Problem 27: *People v. Carter*, 2005 WL 3500873 (Mich. Ct. App. 2005).

Problem 29: *King v. Commonwealth*, 368 S.E.2d 704 (Va. App. 1988).

Chapter 9 Case Study Four: *Lewis v. Wilkinson*, 307 F.3d 413 (6th Cir. 2002).

Chapter 10 Problem 32: People v. Dadon, 640 N.Y.S.2d 425 (N.Y. Crim. Ct. 1996).

Problem 34: People v. Kelly, 2012 WL 3965150 (Cal. Ct. App. 2012)

Problem 35: State v. Long, 830 So. 2d 552 (La. Ct. App. 2002).

Problem 36: *State v. Office of the Public Defender*, 285 P.3d 622 (N.M. 2012)

Chapter 11 Problem 37: *Collier v. State*, 846 N.E.2d 340 (Ind. Ct. App. 2006).

Problem 38: *State v. Mayteko*, 53 S.W.3d 666 (Tenn. 2001).

Problem 40: *People v. Acosta*, 609 N.E.2d 518 (N.Y. 1992).

Chapter 14 Problem 47: *People v. Genoa*, 470 N.W.2d 447 (Mich. Ct. App 1991).

Chapter 15 Problem 48: *State v. Gardner*, 397 A.2d 1372 (Del. 1979).

Problem 49: HAW. REV. STAT. § 703-309(1) and *State v. Dowling*, 263 P.3d 116 (Haw. Ct. App. 2011)

Chapter 16 Problem 51: *Hair v. State*, 17 So. 3d 804 (2009).

Problem 52: *State v. Norman*, 378 S.E.2d 8 (N.C. 1989).

Problem 54: *Commonwealth v. Haddock*, 704 N.E.2d 537 (Mass. App. Ct. 1999).

Problem 55: *State v. Weddell*, 43 P.3d 987 (Nev. 2002).

The authors' goal in putting together this casebook was to focus on the staples of criminal cases: issues related to how the government goes about proving a crime, the process of statutory interpretation, and the elements of criminal defenses. To that end, we have chosen cases and problems with an eye toward their usefulness in teaching about how the evidence of a crime, or lack thereof, affects the application of the criminal law. Moreover, we chose, by and large, current cases that reflect the approach of courts today. While some "old favorites" familiar to all law students are in the casebook, we opted largely for cases decided since 2000 because they are illustrative of how judges approach cases today and push the law into new areas.

The process of putting together a casebook involves the assistance and support of a number of individuals and institutions beyond the named authors. We would like to express our appreciation to Professors Roger Clark, Bruce Green, and Mae C. Quinn, as well as the following for helping to bring this third edition into being:

Ellen S. Podgor: Thanks go to Stetson University College of Law, former Dean Darby Dickerson and Associate Dean Terri Radwan and present Dean Christopher M. Pietriszkiewicz for their support. Thanks also go to research assistants Ross Felsher, Gordon Kirsch, and Adam Labonte, and the many students at Stetson who caught errors from the prior editions. Thanks also go to Abraham, Hans and Sarah who stayed with me while I worked on this edition, often in the wee hours of the morning. I am particularly grateful to my three co-authors Peter Henning, Andy Taslitz, and Al Garcia, who lightened this project with nicknames and laughter, and of course, incredibly thoughtful contributions.

Peter Henning: Wayne State University Law School provided very generous support throughout all the editions of this book. I appreciate the continuing assistance of Olive Hyman, who provided much help and encouragement. I also am grateful to my family for putting up with me turning our dining room into a repository of all things criminal when I stack piles of cases throughout the house. It is a true joy to work with Ellen Podgor, Andy Taslitz, and Al Garcia on the book – they are an inspiration.

Andrew Taslitz: My thanks to Monika Arvelo, LaShanta Johnson, and Debbie Kim for their awesome research assistance; to Howard University School of Law and American University Washington College of Law, for their support of this project; to my wife, Patricia Sun, Esq., who makes all things worthwhile; to my dogs, B'lanna and Odo, who warm the cockles of my heart; to my sister, Ellen Duncan, who taught me to read and thus made this book possible; to my secretary Gay Kirsch, for obvious reasons; to my dad for teaching me discipline; and to the memory of my mom, who unleashed me on an unsuspecting world. But a special thanks to my three co-authors, Ellen Podgor, Peter Henning, and Alfredo Garcia, whose warmth, smarts, creativity, love of teaching, and good humor have made contributing to the writing of this book a sheer joy!

Alfredo Garcia. My thanks to St. Thomas University School of Law and to my co-authors, three wonderful colleagues, scholars, and teachers, who deserve most of the credit for this endeavor.

                                                                                June, 2013

Acknowledgments

Excerpts from the following books and articles appear with the kind permission of the copyright holders:[a]

Anne M. Coughlin, Sex and Guilt, 84 Virginia Law Review 1 (1998). Reprinted by permission of the Virginia Law Review and Anne M. Coughlin.

Susan Estrich, Rape, 95 Yale Law Journal 1087 (1986). Reprinted by permission of Susan Estrich.

Model Penal Code, Copyright 1985 by the American Law Institute. Reprinted with permission. All rights reserved.

Eugene Milhizer, Justification and Excuse: What They Were, What They Are, and What They Ought to Be, 78 St. John's Law Review 725 (2004). Reprinted by permissions of St. John's Law Review and Eugene Milhizer.

Richard E. Redding, Why It Is Essential to Teach About Mental Health Issues in Criminal Law (And a Primer on How to Do It), 14 Washington University Journal of Law & Policy 407 (2004). Reprinted with permission of the Washington University Journal of Law & Policy and Richard E. Redding.

Andrew E. Taslitz, Rape and Culture of the Courtroom (New York: New York University Press, 1999). Copyright (c) 1999 New York University. Used with permission.

Lalenya Weintraub Siegel, Note, The Marital Rape Exemption: Evolution to Extinction, 43 Cleveland State Law Review. 351 (1995). Reprinted by permission of the Cleveland State Law Review and Lalenya Weintraub Siegel.

---

[a] Case citations in the text, the footnotes of judicial opinions, and in the writings of commentators have been omitted without so specifying. Footnotes in judicial opinions and articles are also omitted without specifying. Numbered footnotes are from the original source; lettered footnotes are written by the authors of this casebook. Asterisks and brackets are used to designate omissions from the original materials.

SUMMARY OF CONTENTS

TABLE OF CONTENTS

PART ONE. GENERAL FOUNDATIONS OF CRIMINAL LAW

PART TWO. ELEMENTS OF A CRIME

PART THREE. PROOF

PART FOUR. CRIMES

PART SIX. DEFENSES

PART ONE
GENERAL FOUNDATIONS OF CRIMINAL LAW

Chapter 1
Principles of Punishment

§ 1.01 Generally

The study of criminal law starts near the end of the criminal process: at sentencing, long after a defendant has been arrested, charged, tried (or plead guilty), and convicted. The reason it is started at the end is that all of criminal law relates to punishment. The reasons why society imposes a particular punishment — incarceration, monetary fine, probation, or other restrictions — on a specific defendant are the same reasons why certain behavior is criminalized in the first place, rather than relying on the civil justice system to deter wrongful conduct or leaving it entirely unregulated by the law. Criminal law statutes and the defenses to crimes are designed to implement the purpose of punishing wrongful conduct that is designated a "crime."

The reason why society designates certain conduct as criminal matters not only in setting criminal justice policy, but also in day-to-day criminal law practice; it is of vital importance to both prosecution and defense counsel. Understanding punishment, therefore, is the only way to understand the point of all that precedes it.

§ 1.02 Theories of Punishment

The Queen v. Dudley and Stephens
Queen's Bench Division
(1884-85) LR 14 Q.B.D. 273

LORD COLERIDGE, C.J., GROVE AND DENMAN, JJ., POLLOCK AND HUDDLESTON, BB.

INDICTMENT for the murder of Richard Parker on the high seas within the jurisdiction of the Admiralty.

At the trial before Huddleston, B., at the Devon and Cornwall Winter Assizes, November 7, 1884, the jury, at the suggestion of the learned judge, found the facts

1

of the case in a special verdict which stated "that on July 5, 1884, the prisoners, Thomas Dudley and Edward Stephens, with one Brooks, all able-bodied English seamen, and the deceased also an English boy, between seventeen and eighteen years of age, the crew of an English yacht, a registered English vessel, were cast away in a storm on the high seas 1600 miles from the Cape of Good Hope, and were compelled to put into an open boat belonging to the said yacht. That in this boat they had no supply of water and no supply of food, except two [one] 1b. tins of turnips, and for three days they had nothing else to subsist upon. That on the fourth day they caught a small turtle, upon which they subsisted for a few days, and this was the only food they had up to the twentieth day when the act now in question was committed. That on the twelfth day the remains of the turtle were entirely consumed, and for the next eight days they had nothing to eat. That they had no fresh water, except such rain as they from time to time caught in their oilskin capes. That the boat was drifting on the ocean, and was probably more than 1000 miles away from land. That on the eighteenth day, when they had been seven days without food and five without water, the prisoners spoke to Brooks as to what should be done if no succour came, and suggested that some one should be sacrificed to save the rest, but Brooks dissented, and the boy, to whom they were understood to refer, was not consulted. That on the 24th of July, the day before the act now in question, the prisoner Dudley proposed to Stephens and Brooks that lots should be cast who should be put to death to save the rest, but Brooks refused to consent, and it was not put to the boy, and in point of fact there was no drawing of lots. That on that day the prisoners spoke of their having families, and suggested it would be better to kill the boy that their lives should be saved, and Dudley proposed that if there was no vessel in sight by the morrow morning the boy should be killed. That next day, the 25th of July, no vessel appearing, Dudley told Brooks that he had better go and have a sleep, and made signs to Stephens and Brooks that the boy had better be killed. The prisoner Stephens agreed to the act, but Brooks dissented from it. That the boy was then lying at the bottom of the boat quite helpless, and extremely weakened by famine and by drinking sea water, and unable to make any resistance, nor did he ever assent to his being killed. The prisoner Dudley offered a prayer asking forgiveness for them all if either of them should be tempted to commit a rash act, and that their souls might be saved. That Dudley, with the assent of Stephens, went to the boy, and telling him that his time was come, put a knife into his throat and killed him then and there; that the three men fed upon the body and blood of the boy for four days; that on the fourth day after the act had been committed the boat was picked up by a passing vessel, and the prisoners were rescued, still alive, but in the lowest state of prostration. That they were carried to the port of Falmouth, and committed for trial at Exeter. That if the men had not fed upon the body of the boy they would probably not have survived to be so picked up and rescued, but would within the four days have died of famine. That the boy, being in a much weaker condition, was likely to have died before them. That at the time of the act in question there was no sail in sight, nor any reasonable prospect of relief. That under these circumstances there appeared to the prisoners every probability that unless they then fed or very soon fed upon the boy or one of themselves they would die of starvation. That there was no appreciable chance of saving life except by killing some one for the others to eat. That assuming any necessity to kill anybody, there was no greater necessity for killing the boy than any of the other three men." But whether upon the whole matter by the jurors found the killing of Richard Parker by Dudley and Stephens be felony and murder the jurors are ignorant, and pray the advice of the Court thereupon, and if upon the whole matter the Court shall be of opinion that the killing of Richard Parker be felony and murder, then the jurors say that Dudley and Stephens were each guilty of felony and murder as alleged in the indictment.

The learned judge then adjourned the assizes until the 25th of November at the Royal Courts of Justice. On the application of the Crown they were again adjourned to the 4th of December, and the case ordered to be argued before a Court consisting of five judges. * * *

LORD COLERIDGE, C.J.

The two prisoners, Thomas Dudley and Edwin Stephens, were indicted for the murder of Richard Parker on the high seas on the 25th of July in the present year. They were tried before my Brother Huddleston at Exeter on the 6th of November, and, under the direction of my learned Brother, the jury returned a special verdict, the legal effect of which has been argued before us, and on which we are now to pronounce judgment.

* * * From these facts, stated with the cold precision of a special verdict, it appears sufficiently that the prisoners were subject to terrible temptation, to sufferings which might break down the bodily power of the strongest man, and try the conscience of the best. Other details yet more harrowing, facts still more loathsome and appalling, were presented to the jury, and are to be found recorded in my learned Brother's notes. But nevertheless this is clear, that the prisoners put to death a weak and unoffending boy upon the chance of preserving their own lives by feeding upon his flesh and blood after he was killed, and with the certainty of depriving *him* of any possible chance of survival. The verdict finds in terms that "if the men had not fed upon the body of the boy they would *probably* not have survived," and that "the boy being in a much weaker condition was *likely* to have died before them." They might possibly have been picked up next day by a passing ship; they might possibly not have been picked up at all; in either case it is obvious that the killing of the boy would have been an unnecessary and profitless act. It is found by the verdict that the boy was incapable of resistance, and, in fact, made none; and it is not even suggested that his death was due to any violence on his part attempted against, or even so much as feared by, those who killed him. Under these circumstances the jury say that they are ignorant whether those who killed him were guilty of murder, and have referred it to this Court to determine what is the legal consequence which follows from the facts which they have found . . .

[The Court discussed the necessity defense, which is considered in Chapter 17.] The Court then proceeded to pass sentence of death upon the prisoners.

NOTES AND QUESTIONS

1. **When to Punish**. The nineteenth-century murder prosecution of Dudley and Stephens in England is one of the most famous criminal law cases in history. Who, if anyone, deserves to be punished in the case of *Dudley and Stephens*? What purposes will punishment serve? Should the severity of the punishment factor into whether conduct should constitute a crime?

2. **What Is a "Crime."** What is it that makes some forms of conduct a crime–and therefore amenable to punishment–rather than a civil wrong to be remedied through private litigation? Professor Hart analyzed the question in this way:

> What distinguishes a criminal from a civil sanction and all that distinguishes it, it is ventured, is the judgment of community condemnation which accompanies and justifies its imposition. * * * [A "crime"] is not simply anything which a legislature chooses to call a "crime." It is not simply antisocial conduct which public officers are given a responsibility to suppress. It is not simply any conduct to which a legislature chooses to attach a "criminal" penalty. It is conduct which, if duly shown to have taken place, will incur a formal and solemn pronouncement of the moral condemnation of the community.

Henry M. Hart, Jr., *The Aims of the Criminal Law*, 23 L. & CONTEMP. PROBS. 401 (1958). If Professor Hart's analysis is correct, does the conduct of Dudley and Stephens deserve moral condemnation?

Theories of Punishment

Though courts and theorists disagree, the prevailing view is that the criminal law, and thus punishment, serves these sometimes competing purposes:

A. **Deterrence**: The idea of deterrence is that individuals will not commit crimes for fear of suffering the same punishment that a current defendant has suffered *(general deterrence)*, and that this defendant will avoid future crimes because he or she too fears additional punishment *(specific deterrence)*.

Deterrence is considered a *utilitarian theory*, that is, one justified primarily by preventing future harms. A wrongdoer's mental state may matter because it helps society decide how much punishment is needed for deterrence. For example, someone who wants to kill others, and indeed enjoys doing so, may require a very severe punishment to be deterred, while someone who kills accidentally may require a very light punishment to be motivated to exercise greater care for human life in the future.

B. *Rehabilitation*: Rehabilitation is also considered a *utilitarian theory*. It is premised upon the idea that society has an obligation to punish an individual in a way that makes him or her a better person and a better citizen tomorrow. It encompasses a belief that individuals with free will are capable of changing and contributing to society positively. The essence of rehabilitation is reform of the individual.

C. *Isolation*: A variation on deterrence focuses on isolating wrongdoers from law-abiding persons. While one is in prison, he cannot harm others, at least those outside the prison. This is not pure deterrence because it does not require the defendant to change his behavior from fear or redemption. Instead, the idea is that the defendant cannot hurt others simply because he or she is locked up for past misconduct. This theory is sometimes referred to as incapacitation.

D. *Education*: Punishing wrongdoers for the evil that they commit educates the rest of the populace in what rules society considers most sacred and important, what value it holds, what procedures it sees as fair, and how it values individuals and groups. In this respect it serves as a general deterrent. Educating the individual, however, is a form of rehabilitation.

E. *Retribution*: Unlike the utilitarian principles discussed above, retributive justifications supposedly look to the past rather than the future, the goal being to ensure that the individual gets what he or she deserves. To a pure retributivist, it is irrelevant that the death penalty might not deter the murderer from committing future acts and might not deter similar potential evildoers. What matters is that a wrong that has been done must be punished.

There are many different sorts of justifications for *retributive theory*. One is the idea that the miscreant must "pay the debt to society" ("just deserts"). All members of society implicitly contract to restrain themselves from certain benefits they might gain without law, such as from stealing from others. When one member breaks this contract, that individual is unjustly enriched, and justice requires that he or she repay a debt in a way equivalent to what has been taken. Just repaying money is not sufficient, first, because certain crimes (any involving violence) do not involve money; second, because, even where money is taken, something intangible is taken as well: our sense of security. Only punishment, therefore, imposes the correct sort of cost on the offender that equalizes the scales.

A variant on retributive theory is *communicative retributivism*. The idea here is that right-deprivations help to define the fundamental equal worth of all human beings. When someone denies another a right, they are treating that other person as worth less. For example, a robber implicitly sends the message to a victim, that he or she can use force to deny the victim rights of property and safety to obtain what the robber desires. Such a message of diminishment leads to victim anger that demands retribution to be sated, a righting of the scales that brings the robber down a peg to make clear that he or she is of no more value than the victim. But if the victim's pain is also seen as harmful to society (*e.g.*, making us all more afraid to go out at night and all feel subject to diminishment, or all angry because a fundamental value we as a society share is that each member deserves respect), then society feels indignant and wants to send the message as a society that it values the victim as an equal to all others.

The idea of shared responsibility might also merit mitigating a defendant's punishment when that punishment is too extreme and does not send a message of equal worth but rather degrades the offender by making that person worth less than the rest of society. Communicative retributivism looks not only to injuries to victims and to society as a whole, but also to groups that may suffer special harm from individual crimes, for example, racial or ethnic or religious groups. The theory is both backward-looking — what did the victim deserve for his past wrong — and forward-looking — how does punishment help to reaffirm social bonds and fundamental social values and rules so that society will in the future better promote recognition of everyone's equal worth.

When using retributive theories, what the defendant deserves turns on a combination of the wrongfulness of the act, the degree of harm caused, and the mental state at the time of the offense. A willful killer sends a more degrading message of another's worthlessness, for example, than does an accidental killer, and is thus more evil. As Professor Finkelstein states: "[w]e are normally inclined to think of conduct as morally wrongful because it is harmful, rather than the other way around. It thus seems more plausible to say that the reason we punish certain acts and the reason those acts are wrongful is the same, namely that the conduct inflicts harm." Claire Finkelstein, *Positivism and the Notion of an Offense*, 99 CAL. L. REV. 335 (2000).

NOTES AND QUESTIONS

1. ***Race and Gender.*** Critical thought can also be applied to modify each of these justifications for punishment. Thus, critical race theorists seek to learn from the disparate impact of criminal laws on racial groups and from the differing

experiences of racial groups. Feminism does the same sort of thing based on gender.

2. ***Tort Versus Crime.*** Civil tort law and criminal law have different purposes. For example, where tort law can serve individual retributive needs, criminal law serves society's retributive needs.

Tort law (damages and injunctions) does not work against the poor (who have no money to pay) or even at times against the rich, who may see damages as a predictable cost of doing business. Also, where it is hard to uncover wrongs, wrongdoers will be deterred only if they fear that if they do fall into the small percentage of those who are caught, they will have to pay an enormous cost such as imprisonment.

Another distinction between torts and crimes is that tort law addresses primarily harms to individuals while criminal law addresses harms to the people as a whole. Thus an aggravated assault harms everyone's sense of safety and commitment to certain deeply shared values that hold society together, requiring criminal punishment, but we also permit a tort suit by an individual for damages he or she suffered at the assailant's hands. Both sorts of suits might serve deterrent functions, but in theory each is deterring a different sort of harm, and in practice both might be necessary to deter adequately at times (*e.g.*, criminal actions against white collar criminals as individuals but a tort suit against their corporation to discourage corporate tolerance of, or willful blindness toward, such individual criminal activity).

PROBLEM ONE

A small passenger boat sailing in the North Atlantic struck an iceberg and sank. The passengers and crew escaped in two lifeboats, which became separated. In one boat was nine members of the crew and thirty-two passengers. The lifeboat began to sink slowly when a leak developed. Although the crew and passengers were able to bail out much of the water, the leak worsened and the waves threw so much water into the boat that it was on the verge of being swamped. The senior officer on the lifeboat ordered the crew members to throw male passengers out of the boat in order to save it. Over the next hour, six men were thrown overboard, some of whom resisted violently, and none were found alive. No member of the crew was ejected from the lifeboat, nor any women or children. The senior officer ordered that if a man's wife were on the lifeboat, he should not be thrown overboard. After being rescued the next morning, all agreed that they would have drowned during the night if a number of people had not been thrown overboard, although it is not clear exactly how many it would have been necessary to remove to save the lifeboat.

Is it appropriate to charge the senior officer with murder for the death of the six men thrown overboard? Should other crew members who participated in throwing the men overboard also be charged with murder? If the senior officer was charged and convicted of first degree murder, which is punishable by life in prison without parole or death, what punishment should the prosecutor seek? What arguments should defense counsel make to mitigate the punishment? What evidence should the court consider in deciding the appropriate punishment?

PROBLEM TWO

Prosecutors often have limited funding and cannot prosecute all of the crimes that occur in the jurisdiction. They have discretion to pick and choose the crimes that they wish to pursue, although they cannot use their discretion in a way that uses impermissible criteria, such as race. Assume that a federal prosecutor has two possible defendants, but because of limited funding can only proceed against one of these two. Potential defendant A is a wealthy hotel owner who failed to pay a significant amount of money in taxes, but the amount is less than two percent of the total amount that is due that year. There is likely to be significant coverage of the case in the local media. Potential defendant B waits tables in a restaurant and fails to report a large amount of the tips received on the tax return. The amount of money due the government is small, but it constitutes over one-third of the person's income that year. Which of these two individuals would you prosecute? How would punishment theories come into play in making your decision? Does the availability of a civil enforcement proceeding to recover unpaid taxes affect your decision about which defendant to charge?

§ 1.03 Determining the Appropriate Sentence

State v. Jensen
46 P.3d 536 (Idaho Ct. App. 2002)

PERRY, Chief Judge:

Vicki A. Jensen appeals from her judgment of conviction and fixed life sentence imposed upon her plea of guilty to first degree murder.* * *

In July 1999, Jensen's husband left her and moved into an apartment with the victim in this case and the victim's three-year-old daughter. Jensen was distraught and became obsessed with winning her husband back. Jensen, a registered nurse, devised a plan to kill the victim by injecting her with a lethal dose of insulin. Jensen enlisted the help of her niece and her niece's ex-boyfriend to carry out the plan.

On the morning of September 9, 1999, Jensen and her accomplices entered the victim's apartment after Jensen's husband left for work. While one of her accomplices restrained the victim, Jensen injected a lethal dose of insulin into the victim's arm. To make it appear as though the victim died of a drug overdose, Jensen also injected the victim with methamphetamine and placed methamphetamine in the victim's purse. For approximately one hour, Jensen and her accomplices watched the victim suffer from the effects of the insulin and waited for her to die. When Jensen was satisfied that the victim would not survive, Jensen and her accomplices fled the apartment, leaving the victim's young daughter alone with her dying mother.

* * * Pursuant to a plea agreement, Jensen pled guilty to first degree murder, and the state dismissed the conspiracy charge and withdrew its notice of intent to seek the death penalty. After a hearing, at which both the state and Jensen presented evidence, Jensen was sentenced to a determinate life term in prison. * * * Jensen appeals, claiming that her sentence was excessive. * * *

An appellate review of a sentence is based on an abuse of discretion standard. * * * Where a sentence is not illegal, the appellant has the burden to show that it is unreasonable, and thus a clear abuse of discretion. * * * A sentence may represent such an abuse of discretion if it is shown to be unreasonable upon the facts of the case. * * * A sentence of confinement is reasonable if it appears at the time of sentencing that confinement is necessary "to accomplish the primary objective of protecting society and to achieve any or all of the related goals of deterrence, rehabilitation or retribution applicable to a given case." * * * Where an appellant contends that the sentencing court imposed an excessively harsh sentence, we conduct an independent review of the record, having regard for the nature of the offense, the character of the offender and the protection of the public interest. * * *

1. Nature of the offense

First, we examine the nature of Jensen's offense. In this case, we are presented with the calculated and senseless murder of the mother of six young children. The record before us demonstrates that Jensen, distraught over the breakup of her marriage, cold-bloodedly devised a plan to kill the victim. The plan was to gain entrance to the victim's apartment, restrain her, and inject her with insulin and methamphetamine. * * * As a registered nurse, Jensen knew that injecting the victim with insulin when the victim did not need it would be fatal and virtually undetectable . . . * * *

In order to carry out her plan, Jensen sought the help of two accomplices. Jensen provided money to her niece and instructed her to buy the methamphetamine that Jensen would ultimately inject into the victim. Jensen instructed her niece's ex-boyfriend to obtain a firearm for use in intimidating and overpowering the victim. Jensen purchased disguises so that she and her accomplices would not be recognized. On the night before the murder, Jensen's two accomplices spent the night at Jensen's home where all three rehearsed their roles in the murder several times.

The next morning, Jensen and her two accomplices drove to the victim's apartment and waited for Jensen's husband to leave for work. The three entered the victim's apartment and restrained the victim. The record reflects that the victim begged Jensen not to inject her with methamphetamine because she was allergic to it. Despite the victim's pleas for mercy, Jensen injected the victim with insulin and methamphetamine. Jensen then watched the victim suffer for almost an hour, until she was satisfied that the victim could not call for help and would die soon. Jensen could have reversed the effects of the insulin and prevented the victim's death at any time during that hour. Jensen then fled the apartment with her two accomplices and left the victim's three-year-old daughter alone to watch her mother die.

Based on the foregoing, the district court concluded that the circumstances surrounding the murder were so egregious that a determinate life sentence was necessary. The district court stated that, although the sentence imposed was necessary to properly punish Jensen and to protect society, the sentence was also necessary so that the heinous nature of Jensen's crime would not be depreciated. Upon review of the record, we conclude that Jensen has failed to show that the district court abused its discretion in that regard.

2. Character of the offender

Next, we examine Jensen's character. The information contained in Jensen's presentence investigation report (PSI) and in the addenda to Jensen's PSI reveals that Jensen was raised in a stable, supportive home. Jensen was a good student, achieving average and above-average grades during junior high and high school. Upon graduation from high school in 1987, Jensen married her high school boyfriend and they had a child together. In 1990, Jensen and her first husband divorced.

In 1988, Jensen enrolled in nursing school. Jensen graduated with an associate's degree in nursing in 1990 and subsequently became licensed as a registered nurse. During her nursing career, Jensen worked at various hospitals and care centers. Her co-workers described her as a very capable worker who was caring and dependable. One supervisor described Jensen as "very jolly and positive about her work." That supervisor also commented that Jensen exhibited good nursing intuition and was upbeat and efficient.

Jensen's family and friends described her as a fun-loving person and a devoted wife and mother. According to Jensen's family members, it was Jensen's devotion to her second husband that caused her to commit the present offense. After marrying her second husband in 1993, Jensen converted to her husband's religion and became very active in her new church. One of Jensen's church callings was as a Cub Scout den mother and church leaders described Jensen as a fun, effective, and committed den mother to the boys in the group. Jensen became so immersed in the beliefs of her new church that she centered her life on her husband, often excluding others close to her. Jensen desperately wanted to have a child with her husband but her pregnancy attempts were unsuccessful. When her husband left, Jensen was devastated. She cried uncontrollably and stopped taking care of herself physically. She became obsessed with getting her husband back. Ultimately, when Jensen discovered that her husband was living with the victim, she became enraged and plotted to murder the victim. Those who knew Jensen indicated that, although Jensen was obsessed with getting her husband back, committing the murder was uncharacteristic of her.

A neuropsychological examination performed on Jensen in anticipation of sentencing indicated that she was intellectually average. Jensen's scores on the examination reflected that she had good attention and concentration abilities. Under some circumstances, however, Jensen did not show good judgment or decision-making. Jensen showed a strong tendency to be more intuitive than analytical and logical, indicating to the examiner that in highly charged emotional situations, Jensen was apt to make poor decisions. The examiner further determined that, despite the nature of the offense Jensen committed, Jensen did not present evidence of an antisocial personality disorder.

Consistent with the assessment of the neuropsychological examination, the record reflects that Jensen engaged in threatening or intimidating behavior when confronted with certain situations. At Jensen's sentencing hearing, Jensen's husband testified of an incident that occurred approximately two years before the murder in the present case, when his first wife succeeded in increasing his monthly child support payments after his attempt to get custody of his children failed. Jensen's husband stated that Jensen became very upset and angry, threatening to kill his first wife in the same manner as the victim in this case — by injecting her with insulin. Jensen's husband further stated that Jensen brought syringes home from work to carry out her threat but that he had disposed of them in a dumpster.

In addition, Jensen's husband testified that both before and after the murder, Jensen stalked him and insisted on communicating with him in any way possible. Several months after the murder, Jensen's husband testified that Jensen came to an apartment he shared with another woman to talk to him. Afraid that the other woman may arrive home while Jensen was there, he and Jensen went for a drive. Jensen asked him if their marriage was over, and he responded that it was. Jensen threatened that if she could not have him, nobody would. The woman who was living with Jensen's husband at that time also testified at Jensen's sentencing hearing. She testified that, after the murder, Jensen called the woman on her cell phone and inquired as to the whereabouts of Jensen's husband. When the woman refused to tell her, Jensen stated that she had a right to know where her husband was and how he was doing. Jensen then related several personal facts about the woman's life that she had never shared with Jensen, such as the address and description of the woman's previous home, the name of the woman's son, how old the woman's son was, and where he went to school. The woman testified that she felt threatened by Jensen's call because she did not know how Jensen obtained her cell phone number, and Jensen would not have known such facts about her without doing some investigation.

At sentencing, the district court found that Jensen was completely devastated by her husband's desertion. After recognizing Jensen's anguish, the district court questioned why Jensen, an intelligent person with strong family support, would use her intelligence and experience to commit such a heinous offense. Jensen's use of her nursing and medical knowledge to commit a coldly calculated murder is particularly disturbing. Despite the neuropsychological examination's assessment that Jensen was unlikely to reoffend and had potential for rehabilitation, the district court determined that the egregious nature of Jensen's crime, coupled with Jensen's conduct before and after the murder, justified a determinate life sentence. Having reviewed the record in this case, we conclude that the record supports the district court's determination and that no abuse of discretion has been shown.

3. Protection of public interest

The appellate courts of this state have noted that * * * the seriousness of a homicide offense mandates a punishment in the form of a substantial prison sentence. * * * A substantial sentence in this regard reflects society's condemnation of a defendant's conduct, deters other members of society from engaging in similar conduct, and protects society from future crime. * * * A sentence need not serve all the sentencing goals or weigh each one equally. * * * Indeed, the primary consideration in sentencing is, and presumptively always will be, the good order and protection of society. All other factors are, and must be, subservient to that end. * * *

The gravity of the offense in this case, as shown by the circumstances, is sufficiently egregious to justify a severe measure of retribution and deterrence. Moreover, as the district court found, Jensen displayed a pattern of threatening and intimidating behavior, particularly toward those who became involved with her husband. Given Jensen's escalating pattern of violence, society must be protected from her.

The sentence imposed in this case is harsh. As our Supreme Court has noted, a fixed or determinate life sentence is a serious penalty, and should not be imposed lightly. * * * In *State v. Eubank*, 759 P.2d 926 (Idaho Ct. App. 1988), this Court stated:

> [A] fixed life sentence may be deemed reasonable if the offense is so egregious that it demands an exceptionally severe measure of retribution and deterrence, or if the offender so utterly lacks rehabilitative potential that imprisonment until death is the only feasible means of protecting society. Unfortunately, in making these determinations, a judge has complete information only in regard to retribution and deterrence, ... The judge must attempt to predict the defendant's future response to rehabilitative programs and the degree of risk he might pose to society if eventually released.

* * * Having thoroughly reviewed the record on appeal, we conclude that Jensen's offense was so egregious that it demanded an exceptionally severe measure of retribution and deterrence, regardless of Jensen's potential for rehabilitation. Accordingly, we hold that the district court did not abuse its discretion in imposing a determinate life sentence in this case. * * *

NOTES AND QUESTIONS

1. ***Determining the Sentence.*** What punishment goals does the court use in the *Jensen* case? How does an examination of the "nature of the offense," "character of the offender," and the "protection of the public interest," fit into setting an appropriate sentence that will meet the punishment goals? Should the fact that the victim was the mother of six children play a role in the sentence received by the defendant? Should the fact that the accused had nursing skills be something that is considered by the court?

2. ***The Sentencing Process.*** After a defendant is convicted or enters a plea of guilty, the next step in the process is the preparation of a presentence report (PSR), usually by an office of the court, such as the Probation Office, that will form the basis for the court's sentencing decision. The PSR is a crucial document because it includes significant information beyond that available from the trial or the defendant's admissions at a plea hearing. In most jurisdictions, a probation officer will interview the defendant to gather information on, *inter alia*, the person's

family, work, and educational history, financial situation, and criminal record. The PSR will also include information from the investigative agents, prosecutors, and victims, and in some cases the defendant's family and friends. The goal is to give the judge a broad array of information to determine the appropriate sentence.

Once the PSR is complete, the parties review it and can raise objections to the information contained in the report. If necessary, the court can hold an evidentiary hearing in order to resolve any factual disputes between the prosecutor and defendant. Before the court imposes a sentence, the parties have an opportunity to present information and arguments to the judge regarding the appropriate sentence. In the most serious cases involving the possible imposition of the death penalty, the sentencing phase can take days. Once each side has had the opportunity to speak, the judge imposes the sentence and the defendant, if sentenced to a term of imprisonment, will be transferred to the jurisdiction's prison authorities for the commencement of the sentence.

3. ***Role of the Lawyer in the Sentencing Process***. The role of the lawyers in the sentencing phase is nearly as important as during the adjudication of guilt. Although prosecutors should only seek an appropriate sentence, often the government is requesting a sentence above what is being requested by defense counsel. In determining the appropriate punishment, the sentencing judge can consider information from a variety of sources, and the procedures for determining the sentence are in many instances not circumscribed by the strict rules of evidence in place for a criminal trial.

4. ***Burden of Proof.*** In the *Jensen* case, the judge considered evidence from a wide variety of sources, including a psychological examination of Jensen and testimony from her ex-husband and his new girlfriend. At the sentencing, the judge's findings do not have to be "beyond a reasonable doubt" — the usual standard for proving a defendant guilty — but the more lenient "preponderance of the evidence" standard, that it is more likely than not that the fact exists or conduct occurred. Note that the sentencing judge, and the Idaho Supreme Court, accepted as true that Jensen stalked her ex-husband and spoke with the new girlfriend about items in her past that had never been shared with Jensen. The government did not charge Jensen with any crimes related to this conduct, but the court could consider it in the process of deciding the sentence. The wider range of information relevant to sentencing makes it imperative that the lawyers for both sides prepare for the post-conviction portion of the case as well as they do for the adjudication of guilt.

5. ***Standard of Review***. The *Jensen* court reviewed the trial judge's decision under the "abuse of discretion" standard. This is the most deferential standard by which a higher court reviews the decision of a lower court that involves factual determinations based on the testimony of witnesses and introduction of evidence. Because the testimony of Jensen's ex-husband and his new girlfriend required the court to consider the credibility of the witnesses, the appellate court will not interfere with

the trial judge's conclusions unless they appear to be highly unreasonable. A judge's legal, as opposed to factual, determinations are reviewed more closely by the appellate court because those decisions do not require the reviewing court to consider issues related to the credibility of witnesses or the weight of the evidence based on observation of a trial proceeding or evidentiary hearing.

6. *Punishment of Dudley and Stephens.* At the sentencing of Dudley and Stephens [p. 1], what arguments should defense counsel make to avoid a sentence of death? What evidence should the court consider? Is the background of the victim relevant to the decision regarding the appropriate punishment? Consider the following description of the sentencing of Dudley and Stephens:

> After the opinion was read and handed down, Sir Henry James, the Attorney General, prayed the court that the sentences be imposed upon Dudley and Stephens. Dudley and Stephens were called to the bench and Lord Coleridge spoke, "You have been convicted of murder. What have you to say why the Court should not give you judgment to die?" In a low voice, Dudley said, "I throw myself on the mercy of the court." Lord Coleridge took the unusual action of not downing his black cap, then passed sentence on Dudley and Stephens, intoning:
>
>> You have been convicted of the crime of wilful murder, though you have been recommended by the jury most earnestly to the mercy of the Crown; a recommendation in which, as I understand, my learned brother who tried you concurs, and in which we all unanimously concur. It is my duty, however, as the organ of the Court, to pronounce on you the sentence of the law, and that sentence is that to the crime of which you have been convicted, you be taken to the prison where you came, and that, on a day appointed for the purpose of your execution you there be hanged by the neck until you be dead.

Joseph J. Simeone, *"Survivors" of the Eternal Sea: A Short True Story*, 45 ST. LOUIS U. L.J. 1123 (2001). The sentence was commuted a short time after the trial by the Home Office to six months' imprisonment, and they were released a year and a day after the ill-fated voyage began.

7. *Factfinding Strategy in Sentencing*. In some jurisdictions an indeterminate sentence may be given to a defendant. For example, if the statute provides for a sentence of one to five years, the parole board would have the discretion as to when the defendant gets released. In other sentencing regimes, in which a judge has wide discretion to sentence a defendant anywhere between the statutory minimum and maximum sentences, the judge engages in a kind of factfinding. Based on pre-sentence and probation officer reports, or witnesses sometimes called by the defense or by the prosecution, and on victim impact statements, a judge must make

decisions about the defendant's character, his or her likely recidivism, the chances of rehabilitation, the general deterrent value of the sentence in discouraging future crimes by other potential offenders, and a host of other facts relevant to choosing a wise sentence, one best serving the purposes of criminal punishment.

In jurisdictions following sentencing guidelines, matters get more complex. Guidelines usually require a more express sort of factfinding. For example, whether an offender "visibly" posseses a gun, what was the precise amount of cocaine in his or her possession, and whether the individual cooperated with the police after arrest in solving related or other crimes are all determinations that the sentencing judge may make, determinations that may raise or lower the seriousness of offense scores, thus affecting the range of the sentences recited in the guidelines. In many jurisdictions, however, guidelines are just that, merely sources of guidance, not binding on the judge but meant to encourage uniformity in sentencing similarly-situated offenders, though in some states judges must justify their reasons for guidelines departures. But in other jurisdictions, the guidelines are *mandatory*, with few deviations permitted. Where guidelines sentencing is purportedly mandatory, judicial factfinding may violate the right to trial by jury declared in the Sixth Amendment to the United States Constitution. In *Blakely v. Washington*, 542 U.S. 296 (2004), the high Court suggested that:

> any and every fact that increases a defendant's effective maximum sentence must now be admitted by the defendant or found by a jury beyond a reasonable doubt. In other words, *Blakely* suggests that the U.S. Constitution does not permit judges to find facts [other than any record of prior convictions] that increase applicable sentences, even though nearly all modern sentencing reforms have made judges central and essential sentencing factfinders. Consequently, the ramifications of *Blakely* for modern sentencing reforms—and for past, present, and future sentences —cannot be overstated.

Douglas Berman, *The Roots and Realities of Blakely,* 19 CRIM. J. 56 (2005).

Blakely involved a challenge to a sentence under Washington State's guidelines, but the parallels between those and the federal ones seemed so strong that many analysts predicted that the federal guidelines would also be found constitutionally defective. That is precisely what happened in *United States v. Booker*, 543 U.S. 296 (2005). As a remedy, however, for the violation, the Court invalidated only those portions of the guidelines and of the federal authorizing statute that made the guidelines mandatory. In effect, the federal guidelines are now merely advisory, thus curing any constitutional infirmity. In dissent, Justice Stevens, joined by Justice Souter and, on most of the dissent, by Justice Scalia, argued that the guidelines were not on their face unconstitutional, and only mandatory guidelines would adequately serve the goal of uniform sentencing, as Congress intended. The guidelines would, however, be *unconstitutionally applied*, therefore, if the relevant factfinding continued to be done by the sentencing judge. The only proper remedy, argued the dissenters, would be to leave the guidelines as they are but to mandate jury involvement in factfinding that might raise the potential sentence.

8. *Collateral Consequences.* There can be many collateral consequences resulting from a criminal conviction. For example a collateral consequence of a felony conviction could be the defendant's loss of voting rights. Convictions for sex offenses can result in the individual being placed on a sex offender registration list. In white collar crime cases, collateral consequences can include the loss of a license, such as a license to practice law or medicine. See *National Inventory of Collateral Consequences of Conviction*, available at http://www.abacollateral consequences.org/.

PROBLEM THREE

Mici was arrested after swinging a beer bottle at a patron in a bar with whom Mici was having an argument. Mici is a graduate of Central University and got into an argument with the victim about the merits of various local colleges. The victim, a graduate of State University, shouted, "I hear you don't even need a room temperature SAT to get into Central," and Mici responded by swinging the bottle at the victim, who ducked out of the way. Mici's actions were observed by two off-duty police officers, who promptly took Mici to jail. After retaining a lawyer, Mici agrees to plead guilty to simple assault, which carries a punishment of a sentence up to one year in the county jail. Mici will be meeting shortly with a probation officer, who will prepare a presentence report for the judge who will decide the sentence. How will the prosecution and defense attorney use the following information in the preparation of the report and in an argument to the court prior to sentencing:

- Mici was convicted for being a minor in possession of alcohol while in college, which Mici explains was after a particularly rowdy party.

- The victim, Kale, was convicted a year earlier for resisting arrest for forcibly pushing aside a police officer who was trying to remove Kale from a sports bar at which Kale had an argument with a patron about local college basketball teams.

- Mici has been employed as a bank loan officer for three years and will complete an MBA in three semesters.

- Mici recently broke up from a long-time relationship with Dale and Dale has sued Mici for removing a plasma television from Dale's apartment that Dale claims was a gift from Mici.

What steps should the defense attorney take prior to a sentencing hearing to maximize the chances of a more lenient sentence for Mici? What witnesses, if any, should the government call at the sentencing hearing? How is this information relevant to the appropriate sentence for the crime? If asked, what sentence should the prosecutor and defense counsel recommend to the court?

§ 1.04 Sentencing Under the Federal Guidelines

Until the early 1980s, most states and the federal government operated under an indeterminate sentencing system, by which the legislature established a maximum term of imprisonment for a crime, and the sentencing judge imposed the sentence that he or she determined was most appropriate without exceeding the maximum authorized sentence. In many states, a parole system developed that allowed the penal authorities to release a prisoner before the completion of a sentence if the person behaved appropriately while incarcerated and did not appear to be a threat to society. The Supreme Court summarized the operation of the indeterminate sentencing system in *Mistretta v. United States*, 488 U.S. 361 (1989):

> For almost a century, the Federal Government employed in criminal cases a system of indeterminate sentencing. Statutes specified the penalties for crimes but nearly always gave the sentencing judge wide discretion to decide whether the offender should be incarcerated and for how long, whether he should be fined and how much, and whether some lesser restraint, such as probation, should be imposed instead of imprisonment or fine. This indeterminate-sentencing system was supplemented by the utilization of parole, by which an offender was returned to society under the "guidance and control" of a parole officer.

> Both indeterminate sentencing and parole were based on concepts of the offender's possible, indeed probable, rehabilitation, a view that it was realistic to attempt to rehabilitate the inmate and thereby to minimize the risk that he would resume criminal activity upon his return to society. It obviously required the judge and the parole officer to make their respective sentencing and release decisions upon their own assessments of the offender's amenability to rehabilitation. As a result, the court and the officer were in positions to exercise, and usually did exercise, very broad discretion. This led almost inevitably to the conclusion on the part of a reviewing court that the sentencing judge "sees more and senses more" than the appellate court; thus, the judge enjoyed the "superiority of his nether position," for that court's determination as to what sentence was

appropriate met with virtually unconditional deference on appeal. The decision whether to parole was also "predictive and discretionary." *Morrissey v. Brewer*, 408 U.S. 471 (1972). The correction official possessed almost absolute discretion over the parole decision. * * *

Congress delegated almost unfettered discretion to the sentencing judge to determine what the sentence should be within the customarily wide range so selected. This broad discretion was further enhanced by the power later granted the judge to suspend the sentence and by the resulting growth of an elaborate probation system. Also, with the advent of parole, Congress moved toward a "three-way sharing" of sentencing responsibility by granting corrections personnel in the Executive Branch the discretion to release a prisoner before the expiration of the sentence imposed by the judge. Thus, under the indeterminate-sentence system, Congress defined the maximum, the judge imposed a sentence within the statutory range (which he usually could replace with probation), and the Executive Branch's parole official eventually determined the actual duration of imprisonment.

A concern expressed about indeterminate sentencing was that the term of imprisonment ostensibly imposed on a defendant did not reflect the actual amount of time a person would actually serve for an offense. Pressure for "truth in sentencing" and greater clarity up-front regarding the actual term of imprisonment led to changes in sentencing. A number of states and the federal government adopted sentencing guidelines to create a measure of uniformity in the decision regarding the appropriate sentence. For example, in the federal system, the 1984 Sentencing Reform Act's "basic objective was to enhance the ability of the criminal justice system to combat crime through an effective, fair sentencing system. To achieve this end, Congress first sought honesty in sentencing." Congress also "sought reasonable uniformity in sentencing by narrowing the wide disparity in sentences imposed for similar criminal offenses committed by similar offenders." Finally, Congress sought "proportionality in sentencing through a system that imposes appropriately different sentences for criminal conduct of differing severity."

Traditionally, the judiciary had complete authority to impose punishment so long as the sentence did not exceed that authorized by the legislature. Since the early 1980s, however, legislatures sought more control over sentencing by, *inter alia*, adopting statutes requiring mandatory minimum sentences and authorizing the adoption of sentencing guidelines that limit the discretion of the courts. As the legislatures diminished the power of the judges, they increased the power of prosecutors who, because of their authority to decide what crime to charge, can effectively decide the sentence a defendant is likely to receive upon conviction.

The following case is illustrative of how the federal courts are approaching sentencing in light of recent Supreme Court cases.

United States v. Crawford
520 F.3d 1072 (9th Cir. 2008)

McKEOWN, Circuit Judge:

Antonio Feliciano Crawford raises a number of sentencing issues that have now been answered by the spate of recent sentencing decisions by the Supreme Court and this court. * * * Crawford was convicted by a jury of two counts of distribution of heroin and distribution of crack cocaine, in violation of 21 U.S.C. § 841(a)(1). He was sentenced to 210 months' imprisonment * * *. The sentence was at the bottom of the applicable Guidelines range of 210 to 262 months.

Crawford's conviction was affirmed on direct appeal in June 2004. Several weeks later, and before our mandate issued, the Supreme Court decided *Blakely v. Washington*, 542 U.S. 296 (2004), which held that in the context of mandatory state sentencing guidelines, the Sixth Amendment right to a jury trial prohibited judges from enhancing criminal sentences based on facts other than those decided by the jury or admitted by the defendant. After *Blakely*, Crawford asked us to recall our previous mandate. While this motion was pending, the Supreme Court issued its opinion in *United States v. Booker*, 543 U.S. 220 (2005), where it held, among other things, that the Sentencing Guidelines were merely advisory, not mandatory, and that appellate courts should review sentences for "reasonableness." In August 2005, we vacated Crawford's sentence and remanded his case for re-sentencing in light of *Booker* * * *.

New counsel was appointed for Crawford and the parties re-briefed the sentencing issues. The district court held another sentencing hearing and imposed the same sentence as before. Crawford appealed his re-sentencing, but his case and others were deferred pending resolution of *United States v. Carty*, 462 F.3d 1066 (9th Cir. 2006), which itself was deferred until after the Supreme Court decided several sentencing cases, among them *Rita v. United States*, 127 S.Ct. 2456 (2007) (holding that appellate courts may presume the reasonableness of within-Guidelines sentences), and *Gall v. United States*, 128 S.Ct. 586 (2007) (holding that appellate courts must review all sentences, within and without the Guidelines range, under a deferential abuse-of-discretion standard). On the same day it decided *Gall*, the Court held in *Kimbrough v. United States* that the Guidelines for crack cocaine, like all others under *Booker*, are advisory only, and "it would not be an abuse of discretion for a district court to conclude when sentencing a particular defendant that the crack/powder [cocaine] disparity yields a sentence 'greater than necessary' to achieve [18 U.S.C.] § 3553(a)'s purposes, even in a mine-run case." 128 S.Ct. 558 (2007). Crawford's sentence was within the Guidelines, and so we can now decide his appeal based on *Rita* * * *.

Crawford argues that the district court erred in imposing a sentence within the Guidelines after declaring its view that such sentences are presumptively reasonable. Though the Supreme Court in *Rita* held that appellate courts may presume that a sentence is reasonable when a district court judge's discretionary decision accords with the sentence the Sentencing Commission deems appropriate in most cases, the Court emphasized that such a presumption was limited to the standard on appeal. See *Rita* ("We repeat that the presumption before us is an appellate court presumption. Given our explanation in *Booker* that appellate 'reasonableness' review merely asks whether the trial court abused its discretion, the presumption applies only on appellate review."

The district court here did not presume the reasonableness of a Guidelines sentence with respect to Crawford's case but, rather, presciently forecasted *Rita*'s holding, while citing to *Booker* and acknowledging other circuits that had already adopted the rule *Rita* would eventually espouse:

> [W]e all recognize that now, the sentencing guidelines are advisory. They're not mandated. We are required to consult them, calculate-the career offender provision under Chapter 4 of the guidelines is advisory *
> * * But as I've said before and I'll say now, in view of the *Booker /FanFan* cases, which require us to look at the guidelines, consult them, calculate the appropriate guideline sentence, that the standard of review on appeal is reasonable if the court feels that-and some of the circuits have said-specifically held that a guideline sentence, unless there's some real reason to vary from it, is presumptively reasonable; and I think that that makes sense.

This statement must be viewed in the context of the entire sentencing hearing. We must distinguish the district court's comment on some circuits' adoption of the presumption for appellate review, a statement made in passing, from the thorough process the court went through in determining the appropriateness of Crawford's sentence, which was done within the framework established by Booker and reinforced by *Rita*, *Gall*, and *Kimbrough*. See *Kimbrough* (the Guidelines are "the starting point and the initial benchmark"); *Gall* (the Guidelines are to be kept in mind throughout the process). The district court neither misapprehended the sentencing framework nor adopted a presumption of reasonableness.

To comply with the requirements of *Booker*, a district court must sufficiently consider the Guidelines, as well as the other factors listed in § 3553(a). The district court here more than met *Booker*'s requirements. The sentencing colloquy and explanation were detailed and thoughtful. The district court then properly applied the § 3553(a) factors alongside the Guidelines, noting that it must look "not only

[at] the recommendations contained in the advisory guidelines, but * * * at the whole picture. And the criteria that we do look at are set forth in 18 USC 3553(a)."[a]

The judge first analyzed § 3553(a)(3) ("kinds of sentences available") and § 3553(a)(4)(A) ("kinds of sentence and the sentencing range established for-the applicable category of offense committed by the applicable category of defendant as set forth in the guidelines") and discussed how, in previously considering Crawford's sentence, he had felt that a potential maximum life sentence was too high and had adjusted it accordingly, taking into account Crawford's acceptance of responsibility. The judge then considered § 3553(a)(1) ("the nature and circumstances of the offense and the history and characteristics of the defendant") and found drug trafficking to be "probably one of the most serious crimes that confronts society at this time," commenting that there was "good reason to believe" that Crawford had been affiliated with gangs and may even have been a participant in a drive-by shooting. Considering § 3553(a)(2)(A) and § 3553(a)(2)(C) ("the need for the sentence imposed to reflect the seriousness of the offense, to promote respect for the law, and to provide just punishment for the offense" and "to protect the public from further crimes of the defendant"), the judge also reflected on the need for the sentence imposed as promoting "[r]espect for the law," and protecting the public, observing the necessary reliance of the distribution schemes of "high-level dealers" on "street dealers," such as Crawford.

With regard to § 3553(a)(2)(B) (the need for the sentence "to afford adequate deterrence to criminal conduct"), the court observed that Congress has created harsh penalties in order to deter such activity because of its ruinous effects on individuals and communities. Finally, with respect to § 3553(a)(2)(D) ("to provide the defendant with needed educational or vocational training, medical care, or other correctional treatment in the most effective manner"), the court then took into

---

[a] The court, in determining the particular sentence to be imposed, shall consider –

(1) the nature and circumstances of the offense and the history and characteristics of the defendant;
(2) the need for the sentence imposed--
   (A) to reflect the seriousness of the offense, to promote respect for the law, and to provide just punishment for the offense;
   (B) to afford adequate deterrence to criminal conduct;
   (C) to protect the public from further crimes of the defendant; and
   (D) to provide the defendant with needed educational or vocational training, medical care, or other correctional treatment in the most effective manner;
(3) the kinds of sentences available;
(4) the kinds of sentence and the sentencing range established for--
   (A) the applicable category of offense committed by the applicable category of defendant as set forth in the guidelines * * *.

account the need for rehabilitation, remarking to Crawford that he was "encouraged" that Crawford felt he was changing his life, and that he hoped Crawford would continue "to act appropriately while * * * incarcerated, earn maximum good time, and participate in the 500-hour drug treatment program" once eligible to do so.

After reviewing these factors, the judge concluded,

> in view of all the factors taken into account-your criminal history background, your long use and selling of drugs — and I emphasize long period of time selling drugs here in this community, your associations and your other activities — they all indicate that a reasonable sentence, taking into account not only the advisory guidelines of 3553, is the sentence that was imposed; and that's the 210 months. And I'm not going to change anything.

In light of the advisory Guidelines and the relevant sentencing factors in § 3553, the district court committed no error in its thorough and sympathetic consideration of Crawford's case.

§ 1.05 Proportionality

The Eighth Amendment provides, "Excessive bail shall not be required, nor excessive fines imposed, nor cruel and unusual punishments inflicted." This incorporates the basic proportionality requirement that is reflected in most theories of criminal punishment, that the sanction imposed on the defendant be commensurate with the crime. While the well-known adage that "the punishment should fit the crime" is easily — and often — expressed, in practice it is quite difficult to apply. The Supreme Court has struggled to determine the contours of this constitutional protection, which involves the interplay of the legislature's prerogative to determine appropriate sentences for a crime and the judiciary's need to protect defendants from attempts to exact excessive retribution. The Court adopted the following three-factor test in *Solem v. Helm*, 463 U.S. 277 (1983), to assess whether a punishment is "cruel and unusual" for being disproportionate: "(i) the gravity of the offense and the harshness of the penalty; (ii) the sentences imposed on other criminals in the same jurisdiction; and (iii) the sentences imposed for commission of the same crime in other jurisdictions."

A recent approach to sentencing in the states involves increasing substantially the punishment for repeat offenders. One of the first such statutes is the California "Three Strikes and You're Out" law, which requires that when a defendant is convicted of a felony, and has previously been convicted of a "serious" or "violent" felony, then the sentence imposed under the three strikes law shall include a five year enhancement. If the defendant has two prior serious or violent felonies, then the minimum term of imprisonment is 25 years. *Cal. Penal Code Ann. § 667*. Under California law, some offenses can be charged as either felonies and misdemeanors. These statutes are known as "wobblers" for purposes of the Three Strikes law. Certain types of theft offenses are wobblers, and the California law treats them presumptively as a felony. The prosecutor must include the prior felony in the charges and prove that the defendant was in fact convicted. Prosecutors have discretion to charge a wobbler as a felony or misdemeanor in deciding whether to seek an enhanced sentence, and the trial court has similar discretion to reduce a felony wobbler conviction to a misdemeanor to avoid the Three Strikes law. Similarly, the trial court can vacate a prior felony conviction if the judge determines that, based on the defendant's background, character, and prospects, he falls "outside the [statutory] scheme's spirit, in whole or in part * * * " *People v. Williams*, 948 P.2d 429 (Cal. 1998).

The question whether the California law violated the Eighth Amendment reached the Supreme Court in **Ewing v. California**, 538 U.S. 11 (2003). The Court recited the following facts regarding the case:

> On parole from a 9-year prison term, petitioner Gary Ewing walked into the pro shop of the El Segundo Golf Course in Los Angeles County on March 12, 2000. He walked out with three golf clubs, priced at $399 apiece, concealed in his pants leg. A shop employee, whose suspicions were aroused when he observed Ewing limp out of the pro shop, telephoned the police. The police apprehended Ewing in the parking lot. * * *

> * * * Ewing was paroled in 1999. * * * Only 10 months later, Ewing stole the golf clubs at issue in this case. He was charged with, and ultimately convicted of, one count of felony grand theft of personal property in excess of $400. * * * As required by the three strikes law, the prosecutor formally alleged, and the trial court later found, that Ewing had been convicted previously of four serious or violent felonies for the three burglaries and the robbery in the Long Beach apartment complex. * * *

> At the sentencing hearing, Ewing asked the court to reduce the conviction for grand theft, a "wobbler" under California law, to a misdemeanor so as to avoid a three strikes sentence. * * * Ewing also asked the trial court to exercise its discretion to dismiss the allegations of some or all of his prior serious or violent felony convictions, again for purposes of avoiding a three strikes sentence. * * * In the end, the trial judge determined that the grand theft should remain a felony. The court also ruled that the four prior strikes for the three burglaries and the robbery in Long Beach should stand. As a newly convicted felon with two or more "serious" or "violent" felony convictions in his past, Ewing was sentenced under the three strikes law to 25 years to life.

The Justices could not decide on an analysis of the three strikes law that garnered support from a majority of the Court, a familiar pattern in this area. Consider the following approaches of the Justices and ask which, if any, best reflects the protection afforded by the Eighth Amendment.

1. Justice O'CONNOR delivered the decision upholding the sentence and an opinion for a plurality of the Court (Chief Justice REHNQUIST and Justice KENNEDY joined her opinion):

    When the California Legislature enacted the three strikes law, it made a judgment that protecting the public safety requires incapacitating criminals who have already been convicted of at least one serious or violent crime. Nothing in the Eighth Amendment prohibits California from making that choice. To the contrary, our cases establish that "States have a valid interest in deterring and segregating habitual criminals."

    In weighing the gravity of Ewing's offense, we must place on the scales not only his current felony, but also his long history of felony recidivism. Any other approach would fail to accord proper deference to the policy judgments that find expression in the legislature's choice of sanctions. In imposing a three strikes sentence, the State's interest is not merely punishing the offense of conviction, or the "triggering" offense: "[I]t is in addition the interest . . . in dealing in a harsher manner with those who by repeated criminal acts have shown that they are simply incapable of conforming to the norms of society as established by its criminal law." To give full effect to the State's choice of this legitimate penological goal, our proportionality review of Ewing's sentence must take that goal into account.

    Ewing's sentence is justified by the State's public-safety interest in incapacitating and deterring recidivist felons, and amply supported by his own long, serious criminal record. Ewing has been convicted of numerous misdemeanor and felony offenses, served nine separate terms of incarceration, and committed most of his crimes while on probation or parole. His prior "strikes" were serious felonies including robbery and three residential burglaries. To be sure, Ewing's sentence is a long one. But it reflects a rational legislative judgment, entitled to deference, that offenders who have committed serious or violent felonies and who continue to commit felonies must be incapacitated.

2. Justice SCALIA (concurring in the result upholding the sentence):

    Proportionality — the notion that the punishment should fit the crime — is inherently a concept tied to the penological goal of retribution. "[I]t becomes difficult even to speak intelligently of 'proportionality,' once deterrence and rehabilitation are given significant weight,"— not to mention giving weight to the purpose of California's three strikes law: incapacitation.

3.   Justice THOMAS (concurring in the result upholding the sentence):

In my view, the Cruel and Unusual Punishments Clause of the Eighth Amendment contains no proportionality principle.

4.   Justice STEVENS (Justices BREYER, GINSBURG, and SOUTER joined his dissenting opinion):

The Eighth Amendment succinctly prohibits "excessive sanctions." Faithful to the Amendment's text, this Court has held that the Constitution directs judges to apply their best judgment in determining the proportionality of fines, see, e.g., *United States v. Bajakajian*, 524 U.S. 321 (1998), bail, see, e.g., *Stack v. Boyle*, 342 U.S. 1 (1951), and other forms of punishment, including the imposition of a death sentence, see, e.g., *Coker v. Georgia*, 433 U.S. 584 (1977). It "would be anomalous indeed" to suggest that the Eighth Amendment makes proportionality review applicable in the context of bail and fines but not in the context of other forms of punishment, such as imprisonment. *Solem v. Helm*. Rather, by broadly prohibiting excessive sanctions, the Eighth Amendment directs judges to exercise their wise judgment in assessing the proportionality of all forms of punishment.

5.   Justice BREYER (Justices GINSBURG, SOUTER, and STEVENS joined his dissenting opinion):

[I]t is important to consider whether special criminal justice concerns related to California's three strikes policy might justify including Ewing's theft within the class of triggering criminal conduct (thereby imposing a severe punishment), even if Ewing's sentence would otherwise seem disproportionately harsh.

I concede that a bright-line rule would give legislators and sentencing judges more guidance. But application of the Eighth Amendment to a sentence of a term of years requires a case-by-case approach. And, in my view, like that of the plurality, meaningful enforcement of the Eighth Amendment demands that application — even if only at sentencing's outer bounds.

A case-by-case approach can nonetheless offer guidance through example. Ewing's sentence is, at a minimum, 2 to 3 times the length of sentences that other jurisdictions would impose in similar circumstances. That sentence itself is sufficiently long to require a typical offender to spend virtually all the remainder of his active life in prison. These and the other factors that I have discussed, along with the questions that I have asked along the way, should help to identify "gross disproportionality" in a fairly objective way — at the outer bounds of sentencing.

In *Ewing*, the four dissenting Justices and the three Justices in the plurality seem to agree that the Eighth Amendment contains some measure of proportionality, but they disagree on how strictly it should be applied. One can infer from this that the Eighth Amendment requires that the sentence be proportionate to the crime, but how that is applied in a particular case is quite hard to gauge.

§ 1.06 Capital Punishment

Roper v. Simmons
543 U.S. 551 (2005)

Justice KENNEDY delivered the opinion of the Court.

* * * At the age of 17, when he was still a junior in high school, Christopher Simmons, the respondent here, committed murder. About nine months later, after he had turned 18, he was tried and sentenced to death. There is little doubt that Simmons was the instigator of the crime. Before its commission Simmons said he wanted to murder someone. In chilling, callous terms he talked about his plan, discussing it for the most part with two friends, Charles Benjamin and John Tessmer, then aged 15 and 16 respectively. Simmons proposed to commit burglary and murder by breaking and entering, tying up a victim, and throwing the victim off a bridge. Simmons assured his friends they could "get away with it" because they were minors.

The three met at about 2 a.m. on the night of the murder, but Tessmer left before the other two set out. (The State later charged Tessmer with conspiracy, but dropped the charge in exchange for his testimony against Simmons.) Simmons and Benjamin entered the home of the victim, Shirley Crook, after reaching through an open window and unlocking the back door. Simmons turned on a hallway light. Awakened, Mrs. Crook called out, "Who's there?" In response Simmons entered Mrs. Crook's bedroom, where he recognized her from a previous car accident involving them both. Simmons later admitted this confirmed his resolve to murder her.

Using duct tape to cover her eyes and mouth and bind her hands, the two perpetrators put Mrs. Crook in her minivan and drove to a state park. They reinforced the bindings, covered her head with a towel, and walked her to a railroad trestle spanning the Meramec River. There they tied her hands and feet together with electrical wire, wrapped her whole face in duct tape and threw her from the bridge, drowning her in the waters below.

By the afternoon of September 9, Steven Crook had returned home from an overnight trip, found his bedroom in disarray, and reported his wife missing. On the same afternoon fishermen recovered the victim's body from the river. Simmons, meanwhile, was bragging about the killing, telling friends he had killed a woman "because the bitch seen my face."

The next day, after receiving information of Simmons' involvement, police arrested him at his high school and took him to the police station in Fenton, Missouri. They read him his *Miranda* rights. Simmons waived his right to an attorney and agreed to answer questions. After less than two hours of interrogation, Simmons confessed to the murder and agreed to perform a videotaped reenactment at the crime scene.

The State charged Simmons with burglary, kidnaping, stealing, and murder in the first degree. As Simmons was 17 at the time of the crime, he was outside the criminal jurisdiction of Missouri's juvenile court system. He was tried as an adult. At trial the State introduced Simmons' confession and the videotaped reenactment of the crime, along with testimony that Simmons discussed the crime in advance and bragged about it later. The defense called no witnesses in the guilt phase. The jury having returned a verdict of murder, the trial proceeded to the penalty phase.

The State sought the death penalty. As aggravating factors, the State submitted that the murder was committed for the purpose of receiving money; was committed for the purpose of avoiding, interfering with, or preventing lawful arrest of the defendant; and involved depravity of mind and was outrageously and wantonly vile, horrible, and inhuman. The State called Shirley Crook's husband, daughter, and two sisters, who presented moving evidence of the devastation her death had brought to their lives.

In mitigation Simmons' attorneys first called an officer of the Missouri juvenile justice system, who testified that Simmons had no prior convictions and that no previous charges had been filed against him. Simmons' mother, father, two younger half brothers, a neighbor, and a friend took the stand to tell the jurors of the close relationships they had formed with Simmons and to plead for mercy on his behalf. Simmons' mother, in particular, testified to the responsibility Simmons demonstrated in taking care of his two younger half brothers and of his grandmother and to his capacity to show love for them.

During closing arguments, both the prosecutor and defense counsel addressed Simmons' age, which the trial judge had instructed the jurors they could consider as a mitigating factor. Defense counsel reminded the jurors that juveniles of Simmons' age cannot drink, serve on juries, or even see certain movies, because "the legislatures have wisely decided that individuals of a certain age aren't responsible enough." Defense counsel argued that Simmons' age should make "a huge difference to [the jurors] in deciding just exactly what sort of punishment to make." In rebuttal, the prosecutor gave the following response: "Age, he says. Think about age. Seventeen years old. Isn't that scary? Doesn't that scare you? Mitigating? Quite the contrary I submit. Quite the contrary."

The jury recommended the death penalty after finding the State had proved each of the three aggravating factors submitted to it. Accepting the jury's recommendation, the trial judge imposed the death penalty. * * *

[Simmons unsuccessfully challenged his conviction and the death penalty in state and federal courts.] After these proceedings in Simmons' case had run their course, this Court held that the Eighth and Fourteenth Amendments prohibit the execution of a mentally retarded person. *Atkins v. Virginia,* 536 U.S. 304 (2002). Simmons filed a new petition for state postconviction relief, arguing that the reasoning of *Atkins* established that the Constitution prohibits the execution of a juvenile who was under 18 when the crime was committed.

The Missouri Supreme Court agreed. * * *

We granted certiorari, and now affirm.

The Eighth Amendment provides: "Excessive bail shall not be required, nor excessive fines imposed, nor cruel and unusual punishments inflicted." The provision is applicable to the States through the Fourteenth Amendment. *Furman v. Georgia,* 408 U.S. 238 (1972). As the Court explained in *Atkins,* the Eighth Amendment guarantees individuals the right not to be subjected to excessive sanctions. The right flows from the basic "'precept of justice that punishment for crime should be graduated and proportioned to [the] offense.'" (quoting *Weems v. United States,* 217 U.S. 349 (1910)). By protecting even those convicted of heinous crimes, the Eighth Amendment reaffirms the duty of the government to respect the dignity of all persons.

The prohibition against "cruel and unusual punishments," like other expansive language in the Constitution, must be interpreted according to its text, by considering history, tradition, and precedent, and with due regard for its purpose and function in the constitutional design. To implement this framework we have established the propriety and affirmed the necessity of referring to "the evolving standards of decency that mark the progress of a maturing society" to determine which punishments are so disproportionate as to be cruel and unusual. *Trop v. Dulles,* 356 U.S. 86 (1958).

In *Thompson v. Oklahoma,* 487 U.S. 815 (1988), a plurality of the Court determined that our standards of decency do not permit the execution of any offender under the age of 16 at the time of the crime. The plurality opinion explained that no death penalty State that had given express consideration to a minimum age for the death penalty had set the age lower than 16. The plurality also observed that "[t]he conclusion that it would offend civilized standards of decency to execute a person who was less than 16 years old at the time of his or her offense is consistent with the views that have been expressed by respected professional organizations, by other nations that share our Anglo-American heritage, and by the leading members of the Western European community." The opinion further noted that juries imposed the death penalty on offenders under 16 with exceeding rarity; the last execution of an offender for a crime committed under the age of 16 had been carried out in 1948, 40 years prior.

Bringing its independent judgment to bear on the permissibility of the death penalty for a 15-year-old offender, the *Thompson* plurality stressed that "[t]he reasons why juveniles are not trusted with the privileges and responsibilities of an adult also explain why their irresponsible conduct is not as morally reprehensible as that of an adult." According to the plurality, the lesser culpability of offenders under 16 made the death penalty inappropriate as a form of retribution, while the low likelihood that offenders under 16 engaged in "the kind of cost-benefit analysis that attaches any weight to the possibility of execution" made the death penalty ineffective as a means of deterrence. With Justice O'Connor concurring in the judgment on narrower grounds, the Court set aside the death sentence that had been imposed on the 15-year-old offender.

The next year, in *Stanford v. Kentucky,* 492 U.S. 361 (1989), the Court, over a dissenting opinion joined by four Justices, referred to contemporary standards of decency in this country and concluded the Eighth and Fourteenth Amendments did not proscribe the execution of juvenile offenders over 15 but under 18. The Court noted that 22 of the 37 death penalty States permitted the death penalty for 16-year-old offenders, and, among these 37 States, 25 permitted it for 17-year-old offenders. These numbers, in the Court's view, indicated there was no national consensus "sufficient to label a particular punishment cruel and unusual." A plurality of the Court also "emphatically reject[ed]" the suggestion that the Court should bring its own judgment to bear on the acceptability of the juvenile death penalty.

The same day the Court decided *Stanford,* it held that the Eighth Amendment did not mandate a categorical exemption from the death penalty for the mentally retarded. *Penry v. Lynaugh,* 492 U.S. 302 (1989). In reaching this conclusion it stressed that only two States had enacted laws banning the imposition of the death penalty on a mentally retarded person convicted of a capital offense. According to the Court, "the two state statutes prohibiting execution of the mentally retarded, even when added to the 14 States that have rejected capital punishment completely, [did] not provide sufficient evidence at present of a national consensus."

Three Terms ago the subject was reconsidered in *Atkins*. We held that standards of decency have evolved since *Penry* and now demonstrate that the execution of the mentally retarded is cruel and unusual punishment. The Court noted objective indicia of society's standards, as expressed in legislative enactments and state practice with respect to executions of the mentally retarded. When *Atkins* was decided only a minority of States permitted the practice, and even in those States it was rare. On the basis of these indicia the Court determined that executing mentally retarded offenders "has become truly unusual, and it is fair to say that a national consensus has developed against it."

The inquiry into our society's evolving standards of decency did not end there. The *Atkins* Court neither repeated nor relied upon the statement in *Stanford* that the Court's independent judgment has no bearing on the acceptability of a particular punishment under the Eighth Amendment. Instead we returned to the rule, established in decisions predating *Stanford*, that "the Constitution contemplates that in the end our own judgment will be brought to bear on the question of the acceptability of the death penalty under the Eighth Amendment." Mental retardation, the Court said, diminishes personal culpability even if the offender can distinguish right from wrong. The impairments of mentally retarded offenders make it less defensible to impose the death penalty as retribution for past crimes and less likely that the death penalty will have a real deterrent effect. Based on these considerations and on the finding of national consensus against executing the mentally retarded, the Court ruled that the death penalty constitutes an excessive sanction for the entire category of mentally retarded offenders, and that the Eighth Amendment "places a substantive restriction on the State's power to take the life of a mentally retarded offender."

Just as the *Atkins* Court reconsidered the issue decided in *Penry,* we now reconsider the issue decided in *Stanford.* The beginning point is a review of objective indicia of consensus, as expressed in particular by the enactments of legislatures that have addressed the question. This data gives us essential instruction. We then must determine, in the exercise of our own independent judgment, whether the death penalty is a disproportionate punishment for juveniles.

The evidence of national consensus against the death penalty for juveniles is similar, and in some respects parallel, to the evidence *Atkins* held sufficient to demonstrate a national consensus against the death penalty for the mentally retarded. * * * Since *Stanford,* six States have executed prisoners for crimes committed as juveniles. In the past 10 years, only three have done so: Oklahoma, Texas, and Virginia. In December 2003 the Governor of Kentucky decided to spare the life of Kevin Stanford, and commuted his sentence to one of life imprisonment without parole, with the declaration that "[w]e ought not be executing people who, legally, were children." *Lexington Herald Leader*, Dec. 9, 2003, p. B3. By this act the Governor ensured Kentucky would not add itself to the list of States that have executed juveniles within the last 10 years even by the execution of the very defendant whose death sentence the Court had upheld in *Stanford v. Kentucky.*

* * * Five States that allowed the juvenile death penalty at the time of *Stanford* have abandoned it in the intervening 15 years — four through legislative enactments and one through judicial decision. * * * The number of States that have abandoned capital punishment for juvenile offenders since *Stanford* is smaller than the number of States that abandoned capital punishment for the mentally retarded after *Penry;* yet we think the same consistency of direction of change has been demonstrated. Since *Stanford,* no State that previously prohibited capital punishment for juveniles has reinstated it. This fact, coupled with the trend toward abolition of the juvenile death penalty, carries special force in light of the general popularity of anticrime legislation, and in light of the particular trend in recent years toward cracking down on juvenile crime in other respects. Any difference between this case and *Atkins* with respect to the pace of abolition is thus counter-balanced by the consistent direction of the change.

* * * Petitioner cannot show national consensus in favor of capital punishment for juveniles but still resists the conclusion that any consensus exists against it. Petitioner supports this position with, in particular, the observation that when the Senate ratified the International Covenant on Civil and Political Rights (ICCPR), Dec. 19, 1966, 999 U.N.T.S. 171 (entered into force Mar. 23, 1976), it did so subject to the President's proposed reservation regarding Article 6(5) of that treaty, which prohibits capital punishment for juveniles. This reservation at best provides only faint support for petitioner's argument. First, the reservation was passed in 1992; since then, five States have abandoned capital punishment for juveniles. Second, Congress considered the issue when enacting the Federal Death Penalty Act in 1994, and determined that the death penalty should not extend to juveniles. The reservation to Article 6(5) of the ICCPR provides minimal evidence that there is not now a national consensus against juvenile executions. * * *

A majority of States have rejected the imposition of the death penalty on juvenile offenders under 18, and we now hold this is required by the Eighth Amendment. * * *

Three general differences between juveniles under 18 and adults demonstrate that juvenile offenders cannot with reliability be classified among the worst offenders. First, as any parent knows and as the scientific and sociological studies respondent and his *amici* cite tend to confirm, "[a] lack of maturity and an underdeveloped sense of responsibility are found in youth more often than in adults and are more understandable among the young. These qualities often result in impetuous and ill-considered actions and decisions." *Johnson.* It has been noted that "adolescents are overrepresented statistically in virtually every category of reckless behavior." Arnett, *Reckless Behavior in Adolescence: A Developmental Perspective*, 12 DEVELOPMENTAL REV. 339 (1992). In recognition of the comparative immaturity and irresponsibility of juveniles, almost every State prohibits those under 18 years of age from voting, serving on juries, or marrying without parental consent.

The second area of difference is that juveniles are more vulnerable or susceptible to negative influences and outside pressures, including peer pressure. This is explained in part by the prevailing circumstance that juveniles have less control, or less experience with control, over their own environment.

The third broad difference is that the character of a juvenile is not as well formed as that of an adult. The personality traits of juveniles are more transitory, less fixed.

These differences render suspect any conclusion that a juvenile falls among the worst offenders. * * * The reality that juveniles still struggle to define their identity means it is less supportable to conclude that even a heinous crime committed by a juvenile is evidence of irretrievably depraved character. From a moral standpoint it would be misguided to equate the failings of a minor with those of an adult, for a greater possibility exists that a minor's character deficiencies will be reformed. * * *

In *Thompson,* a plurality of the Court recognized the import of these characteristics with respect to juveniles under 16, and relied on them to hold that the Eighth Amendment prohibited the imposition of the death penalty on juveniles below that age. We conclude the same reasoning applies to all juvenile offenders under 18.

Once the diminished culpability of juveniles is recognized, it is evident that the penological justifications for the death penalty apply to them with lesser force than to adults. We have held there are two distinct social purposes served by the death penalty: "retribution and deterrence of capital crimes by prospective offenders." *Atkins.* As for retribution, we remarked in *Atkins* that "[i]f the culpability of the average murderer is insufficient to justify the most extreme sanction available to the State, the lesser culpability of the mentally retarded offender surely does not merit that form of retribution." The same conclusions follow from the lesser culpability of the juvenile offender. Whether viewed as an attempt to express the community's moral outrage or as an attempt to right the balance for the wrong to the victim, the case for retribution is not as strong with a minor as with an adult. Retribution is not proportional if the law's most severe penalty is imposed on one whose culpability or blameworthiness is diminished, to a substantial degree, by reason of youth and immaturity.

As for deterrence, it is unclear whether the death penalty has a significant or even measurable deterrent effect on juveniles, as counsel for the petitioner acknowledged at oral argument. In general we leave to legislatures the assessment of the efficacy of various criminal penalty schemes. Here, however, the absence of evidence of deterrent effect is of special concern because the same characteristics that render juveniles less culpable than adults suggest as well that juveniles will be less susceptible to deterrence. In particular, as the plurality observed in *Thompson,* "[t]he likelihood that the teenage offender has made the kind of cost-benefit analysis that attaches any weight to the possibility of execution is so remote as to be virtually nonexistent." To the extent the juvenile death penalty might have residual deterrent effect, it is worth noting that the punishment of life imprisonment without the possibility of parole is itself a severe sanction, in particular for a young person.

In concluding that neither retribution nor deterrence provides adequate justification for imposing the death penalty on juvenile offenders, we cannot deny or overlook the brutal crimes too many juvenile offenders have committed. * * * Given this Court's own insistence on individualized consideration, petitioner maintains that it is both arbitrary and unnecessary to adopt a categorical rule barring imposition of the death penalty on any offender under 18 years of age.

We disagree. The differences between juvenile and adult offenders are too marked and well understood to risk allowing a youthful person to receive the death penalty despite insufficient culpability. An unacceptable likelihood exists that the brutality or cold-blooded nature of any particular crime would overpower mitigating arguments based on youth as a matter of course, even where the juvenile offender's objective immaturity, vulnerability, and lack of true depravity should require a sentence less severe than death. In some cases a defendant's youth may even be counted against him. In this very case, as we noted above, the prosecutor argued Simmons' youth was aggravating rather than mitigating. * * *

Drawing the line at 18 years of age is subject, of course, to the objections always raised against categorical rules. The qualities that distinguish juveniles from adults do not disappear when an individual turns 18. By the same token, some under 18 have already attained a level of maturity some adults will never reach. For the reasons we have discussed, however, a line must be drawn. The plurality opinion in *Thompson* drew the line at 16. In the intervening years the *Thompson* plurality's conclusion that offenders under 16 may not be executed has not been challenged. The logic of *Thompson* extends to those who are under 18. The age of 18 is the point where society draws the line for many purposes between childhood and adulthood. It is, we conclude, the age at which the line for death eligibility ought to rest.

Our determination that the death penalty is disproportionate punishment for offenders under 18 finds confirmation in the stark reality that the United States is the only country in the world that continues to give official sanction to the juvenile death penalty. This reality does not become controlling, for the task of interpreting the Eighth Amendment remains our responsibility. Yet at least from the time of the

Court's decision in *Trop,* the Court has referred to the laws of other countries and to international authorities as instructive for its interpretation of the Eighth Amendment's prohibition of "cruel and unusual punishments."

As respondent and a number of *amici* emphasize, Article 37 of the United Nations Convention on the Rights of the Child, which every country in the world has ratified save for the United States and Somalia, contains an express prohibition on capital punishment for crimes committed by juveniles under 18. United Nations Convention on the Rights of the Child, Art. 37, Nov. 20, 1989, 1577 U.N.T.S. 3, 28 I.L.M. 1448, 1468-1470 (entered into force Sept. 2, 1990). No ratifying country has entered a reservation to the provision prohibiting the execution of juvenile offenders. Parallel prohibitions are contained in other significant international covenants. See ICCPR, Art. 6(5), 999 U.N.T.S., at 175 (prohibiting capital punishment for anyone under 18 at the time of offense) (signed and ratified by the United States subject to a reservation regarding Article 6(5), as noted, *supra,* at 1194); American Convention on Human Rights: Pact of San Jose, Costa Rica, Art. 4(5), Nov. 22, 1969, 1144 U.N.T.S. 146 (entered into force July 19, 1978) (same); African Charter on the Rights and Welfare of the Child, Art. 5(3), OAU Doc. CAB/LEG/ 24.9/49 (1990) (entered into force Nov. 29, 1999) (same).

Respondent and his *amici* have submitted, and petitioner does not contest, that only seven countries other than the United States have executed juvenile offenders since 1990: Iran, Pakistan, Saudi Arabia, Yemen, Nigeria, the Democratic Republic of Congo, and China. Since then each of these countries has either abolished capital punishment for juveniles or made public disavowal of the practice. In sum, it is fair to say that the United States now stands alone in a world that has turned its face against the juvenile death penalty.

Though the international covenants prohibiting the juvenile death penalty are of more recent date, it is instructive to note that the United Kingdom abolished the juvenile death penalty before these covenants came into being. The United Kingdom's experience bears particular relevance here in light of the historic ties between our countries and in light of the Eighth Amendment's own origins. The Amendment was modeled on a parallel provision in the English Declaration of Rights of 1689, which provided: "[E]xcessive Bail ought not to be required nor excessive Fines imposed; nor cruel and unusual Punishments inflicted." 1 W. & M., ch. 2, § 10, in 3 ENG. STAT. AT LARGE 441 (1770). As of now, the United Kingdom has abolished the death penalty in its entirety; but, decades before it took this step, it recognized the disproportionate nature of the juvenile death penalty; and it abolished that penalty as a separate matter. In 1930 an official committee recommended that the minimum age for execution be raised to 21. Parliament then enacted the Children and Young Person's Act of 1933, 23 Geo. 5, ch. 12, which prevented execution of those aged 18 at the date of the sentence. And in 1948, Parliament enacted the Criminal Justice Act, 11 & 12 Geo. 6, ch. 58, prohibiting the execution of any person under 18 at the time of the offense. In the 56 years that have passed since the United Kingdom abolished the juvenile death penalty, the weight of authority against it there, and in the international community, has become well established.

It is proper that we acknowledge the overwhelming weight of international opinion against the juvenile death penalty, resting in large part on the understanding that the instability and emotional imbalance of young people may often be a factor in the crime. The opinion of the world community, while not controlling our outcome, does provide respected and significant confirmation for our own conclusions.

Over time, from one generation to the next, the Constitution has come to earn the high respect and even, as Madison dared to hope, the veneration of the American people. See THE FEDERALIST No. 49, p. 314 (C. Rossiter ed.1961). The document sets forth, and rests upon, innovative principles original to the American experience, such as federalism; a proven balance in political mechanisms through separation of powers; specific guarantees for the accused in criminal cases; and broad provisions to secure individual freedom and preserve human dignity. These doctrines and guarantees are central to the American experience and remain essential to our present-day self-definition and national identity. Not the least of the reasons we honor the Constitution, then, is because we know it to be our own. It does not lessen our fidelity to the Constitution or our pride in its origins to acknowledge that the express affirmation of certain fundamental rights by other nations and peoples simply underscores the centrality of those same rights within our own heritage of freedom.

Justice O'CONNOR, dissenting.

The Court's decision today establishes a categorical rule forbidding the execution of any offender for any crime committed before his 18th birthday, no matter how deliberate, wanton, or cruel the offense. Neither the objective evidence of contemporary societal values, nor the Court's moral proportionality analysis, nor the two in tandem suffice to justify this ruling.

Although the Court finds support for its decision in the fact that a majority of the States now disallow capital punishment of 17-year-old offenders, it refrains from asserting that its holding is compelled by a genuine national consensus. Indeed, the evidence before us fails to demonstrate conclusively that any such consensus has emerged in the brief period since we upheld the constitutionality of this practice in *Stanford v. Kentucky*.

Instead, the rule decreed by the Court rests, ultimately, on its independent moral judgment that death is a disproportionately severe punishment for any 17-year-old offender. I do not subscribe to this judgment. Adolescents *as a class* are undoubtedly less mature, and therefore less culpable for their misconduct, than adults. But the Court has adduced no evidence impeaching the seemingly reasonable conclusion reached by many state legislatures: that at least *some* 17-year-old murderers are sufficiently mature to deserve the death penalty in an appropriate case. Nor has it been shown that capital sentencing juries are incapable of accurately assessing a youthful defendant's maturity or of giving due weight to the mitigating characteristics associated with youth.

On this record — and especially in light of the fact that so little has changed since our recent decision in *Stanford* — I would not substitute our judgment about the moral propriety of capital punishment for 17-year-old murderers for the judgments of the Nation's legislatures. Rather, I would demand a clearer showing that our society truly has set its face against this practice before reading the Eighth Amendment categorically to forbid it.

Justice SCALIA, dissenting.

In urging approval of a constitution that gave life-tenured judges the power to nullify laws enacted by the people's representatives, Alexander Hamilton assured the citizens of New York that there was little risk in this, since "[t]he judiciary ... ha[s] neither FORCE nor WILL but merely judgment." THE FEDERALIST No. 78 (C. Rossiter ed.1961). But Hamilton had in mind a traditional judiciary, "bound down by strict rules and precedents which serve to define and point out their duty in every particular case that comes before them." Bound down, indeed. What a mockery today's opinion makes of Hamilton's expectation, announcing the Court's conclusion that the meaning of our Constitution has changed over the past 15 years — not, mind you, that this Court's decision 15 years ago was *wrong,* but that the Constitution *has changed.* The Court reaches this implausible result by purporting to advert, not to the original meaning of the Eighth Amendment, but to "the evolving standards of decency" of our national society. It then finds, on the flimsiest of grounds, that a national consensus which could not be perceived in our people's laws barely 15 years ago now solidly exists. Worse still, the Court says in so many words that what our people's laws say about the issue does not, in the last analysis, matter: "[I]n the end our own judgment will be brought to bear on the question of the acceptability of the death penalty under the Eighth Amendment." The Court thus proclaims itself sole arbiter of our Nation's moral standards — and in the course of discharging that awesome responsibility purports to take guidance from the views of foreign courts and legislatures. Because I do not believe that the meaning of our Eighth Amendment, any more than the meaning of other provisions of our Constitution, should be determined by the subjective views of five Members of this Court and like-minded foreigners, I dissent. * * *

In determining that capital punishment of offenders who committed murder before age 18 is "cruel and unusual" under the Eighth Amendment, the Court first considers, in accordance with our modern (though in my view mistaken) jurisprudence, whether there is a "national consensus," that laws allowing such executions contravene our modern "standards of decency." *Trop.* We have held that this determination should be based on "objective indicia that reflect the public attitude toward a given sanction" — namely, "statutes passed by society's elected representatives." *Stanford v. Kentucky.* As in *Atkins v. Virginia*, the Court dutifully recites this test and claims halfheartedly that a national consensus has emerged since our decision in *Stanford*, because 18 States — or 47% of States that permit capital punishment — now have legislation prohibiting the execution of offenders under 18, and because all of four States have adopted such legislation since *Stanford*.

Words have no meaning if the views of less than 50% of death penalty States can constitute a national consensus. * * * Though the views of our own citizens are essentially irrelevant to the Court's decision today, the views of other countries and the so-called international community take center stage.

The Court begins by noting that "Article 37 of the United Nations Convention on the Rights of the Child, which every country in the world has ratified *save for the United States* and Somalia, contains an express prohibition on capital punishment for crimes committed by juveniles under 18." The Court also discusses the International Covenant on Civil and Political Rights (ICCPR), which the Senate ratified only subject to a reservation that reads:

The United States reserves the right, subject to its Constitutional restraints, to impose capital punishment on any person (other than a pregnant woman) duly convicted under existing or future laws permitting the imposition of capital punishment, including such punishment for crime committed by persons below eighteen years of age.

Unless the Court has added to its arsenal the power to join and ratify treaties on behalf of the United States, I cannot see how this evidence favors, rather than refutes, its position. That the Senate and the President — those actors our Constitution empowers to enter into treaties, see Art. II, § 2 — have declined to join and ratify treaties prohibiting execution of under-18 offenders can only suggest that *our country* has either not reached a national consensus on the question, or has reached a consensus contrary to what the Court announces. That the reservation to the ICCPR was made in 1992 does not suggest otherwise, since the reservation still remains in place today. It is also worth noting that, in addition to barring the execution of under-18 offenders, the United Nations Convention on the Rights of the Child prohibits punishing them with life in prison without the possibility of release. If we are truly going to get in line with the international community, then the Court's reassurance that the death penalty is really not needed, since "the punishment of life imprisonment without the possibility of parole is itself a severe sanction," gives little comfort.

It is interesting that whereas the Court is not content to accept what the States of our Federal Union *say,* but insists on inquiring into what they *do* (specifically, whether they in fact *apply* the juvenile death penalty that their laws allow), the Court is quite willing to believe that every foreign nation — of whatever tyrannical political makeup and with however subservient or incompetent a court system — in fact *adheres* to a rule of no death penalty for offenders under 18. Nor does the Court inquire into how many of the countries that have the death penalty, but have forsworn (on paper at least) imposing that penalty on offenders under 18, have what no State of this country can constitutionally have: a *mandatory* death penalty for certain crimes, with no possibility of mitigation by the sentencing authority, for youth or any other reason. I suspect it is most of them. To forbid the death penalty for juveniles under such a system may be a good idea, but it says nothing about our system, in which the sentencing authority, typically a jury, always can, and almost always does, withhold the death penalty from an under-18 offender except, after considering all the circumstances, in the rare cases where it is warranted. The foreign authorities, in other words, do not even speak to the issue before us here.

More fundamentally, however, the basic premise of the Court's argument — that American law should conform to the laws of the rest of the world — ought to be rejected out of hand. In fact the Court itself does not believe it. In many significant respects the laws of most other countries differ from our law — including not only such explicit provisions of our Constitution as the right to jury trial and grand jury indictment, but even many interpretations of the Constitution prescribed by this Court itself. The Court-pronounced exclusionary rule, for example, is distinctively American. England, for example, rarely excludes evidence found during an illegal search or seizure and has only recently begun excluding evidence from illegally obtained confessions. Canada rarely excludes evidence and will only do so if admission will "bring the administration of justice into disrepute." The European Court of Human Rights has held that introduction of illegally seized evidence does not violate the "fair trial" requirement in Article 6, § 1, of the European Convention on Human Rights.

The Court has been oblivious to the views of other countries when deciding how to interpret our Constitution's requirement that "Congress shall make no law respecting an establishment of religion . . ." Amdt. 1. Most other countries — including those committed to religious neutrality — do not insist on the degree of separation between church and state that this Court requires. * * *

The Court should either profess its willingness to reconsider all these matters in light of the views of foreigners, or else it should cease putting forth foreigners' views as part of the *reasoned basis* of its decisions. To invoke alien law when it agrees with one's own thinking, and ignore it otherwise, is not reasoned decision-making, but sophistry. * * *

NOTES AND QUESTIONS

1. *Post-***Roper***.* In *Kennedy v. Louisiana*, 554 U.S. 407 (2008), the Supreme Court held that the Eighth Amendment prohibited the imposition of a death penalty "for the rape of child where the crime did not result, and was not intended to result, in the death of the victim." In *Graham v. Florida*, 560 U.S. 48 (2010), the Supreme Court held that it would violate the Eighth Amendment to give a juvenile offender a sentence of life without the possibility of parole in a non-homicide case.

2. *Aggravating Factors.* The Summary on Aggravating Factors of the Constitution Project's Death Penalty Initiative states:

> The death penalty must be reserved for the most culpable of offenders. Limiting the death penalty better promotes the purpose of proportional punishment while reducing the risks of error. There should be only five factors rendering a murderer eligible for capital punishment and jurisdictions should exclude from death eligibility those cases in which eligibility is based solely upon felony murder.

The recommended "five factors rendering a murderer eligible for capital punishment" are:

> 1. The murder of a peace officer killed in the performance of his or her official duties when done to prevent or retaliate for that performance.

> 2. The murder of any person (including but not limited to inmates, staff, visitors) occurring at a correctional facility.

> 3. The murder of two or more persons regardless of whether the deaths occurred as the result of the same act or of several related or unrelated acts, as long as a) the deaths were the result of either an intent to kill more than one person, or b) the defendant knew the act or acts would cause death or create a strong probability of death or great bodily harm to the murdered individuals or others.

> 4. The intentional murder of a person involving the infliction of torture. In this context, torture means the intentional and depraved infliction of extreme physical pain for a prolonged period of time prior to the victim's death; depraved means that the defendant relished the infliction of extreme physical pain upon the victim, evidencing debasement or perversion, or that the defendant evidenced a sense of pleasure in the infliction of extreme physical pain.

> 5. The murder by a person who is under investigation for, or who has been charged with or has been convicted of, a crime that would be a

felony, of anyone involved in the investigation, prosecution, or defense of that crime, including, but not limited to, witnesses, jurors, judges, prosecutors, and investigators.

In discussing the growth of aggravating factors the Project set forth guiding principles that included within them that "[a]ggravators should seek to avoid racial or class bias." The study noted that:

[t]hese criteria implicate public safety and reinforce the most central of public norms, as opposed to protecting against private pain or enforcing deterrence. There is little support for the view that the death penalty deters crime, and this Committee is unconvinced by the few, flawed studies to the contrary.

Death penalty statutes contain a number of factors for a jury to consider in deciding whether to impose capital punishment on a defendant. The California statute provides:

In determining the penalty, the trier of fact shall take into account any of the following factors if relevant:

(a) The circumstances of the crime of which the defendant was convicted in the present proceeding and the existence of any special circumstances found to be true pursuant to Section 190.1.

(b) The presence or absence of criminal activity by the defendant which involved the use or attempted use of force or violence or the express or implied threat to use force or violence.

(c) The presence or absence of any prior felony conviction.

(d) Whether or not the offense was committed while the defendant was under the influence of extreme mental or emotional disturbance.

(e) Whether or not the victim was a participant in the defendant's homicidal conduct or consented to the homicidal act.

(f) Whether or not the offense was committed under circumstances which the defendant reasonably believed to be a moral justification or extenuation for his conduct.

(g) Whether or not defendant acted under extreme duress or under the substantial domination of another person.

(h) Whether or not at the time of the offense the capacity of the defendant to appreciate the criminality of his conduct or to conform his conduct to the requirements of law was impaired as a result of mental disease or defect, or the affects of intoxication.

(i) The age of the defendant at the time of the crime.

(j) Whether or not the defendant was an accomplice to the offense and his participation in the commission of the offense was relatively minor.

(k) Any other circumstance which extenuates the gravity of the crime even though it is not a legal excuse for the crime.

CAL. PENAL CODE § 190.3. The Supreme Court found that § 190.3(a) directing the jury to consider the circumstances of the crime in deciding whether to impose the death penalty was proper in *Tuilaepa v. California*, 512 U.S. 967 (1994). The Court stated, "[t]he circumstances of the crime are a traditional subject for consideration by the sentencer, and an instruction to consider the circumstances is neither vague nor otherwise improper under our Eighth Amendment jurisprudence."

3. *Victim Impact Statements.* A controversial issue in the criminal justice system is whether victims — or in the case of murders, the family of the victim — should be permitted to speak at sentencing and influence the decision regarding the punishment to be imposed. In *Booth v. Maryland*, 482 U.S. 496 (1987), the Supreme Court held that victim impact statements were irrelevant in cases involving capital punishment, but the Court reversed that position in *Payne v. Tennessee*, 501 U.S. 808 (1991), holding that such evidence is "surely relevant in determining [a defendant's] blameworthiness."Although many states permit such evidence, consider the following cautionary discussion in a concurring opinion in the Mississippi Supreme Court.

In *State v. Bernard*, 608 So.2d 966 (La. 1992), the Louisiana Supreme Court allowed the use of some evidence about the victim and the impact of the crime in determining whether to impose the death penalty, but offered the following caution:

Informing the jury that the victim had some identity or left some survivors merely states what any person would reasonably expect and can hardly be viewed as injecting an arbitrary factor into a sentencing hearing. But the more detailed the evidence relating to the character of the victim or the harm to the survivors, the less relevant is such evidence to the circumstances of the crime or the character and propensities of the defendant. And the more marginal the relevance of the victim impact evidence, the greater is the risk that an arbitrary factor will be injected into the jury's sentencing deliberations. Drawing a bright line in this area is very difficult
* * *

In *People v. Lewis*, 140 P.3d 775 (Cal. 2006), the California Supreme Court stated, "[u]nless it invites a purely irrational response from the jury, the devastating effect of a capital crime on loved ones and the community is relevant and admissible as a circumstance of the crime * * * "

4. ***Hate Crimes.*** Hate crimes are those motivated by negative attitudes toward a group. A "motivation" is the reason why someone has a mental state. For example, a common law larceny is the trespassory taking and carrying away the personal property of another *with intent permanently to deprive*. The motive (the reason for intending permanent deprivation) for the larceny might be greed, or it might be revenge against the home's occupant. Motives are generally not elements of the crime but are evidence helpful in convincing the jury to believe that all elements of the crime occurred. But with hate crimes, the motive *is* an element of the crime. In some states, the motive must be hatred of the group (e.g., hatred or animus toward a particular race). In other states, the motive could be a belief that a stereotypical characteristic of the group member makes him or her more vulnerable to the crime. An example of the latter might be a defendant who robs someone he believes to be of Asian ancestry because of a stereotyped belief that Asians or Asian-Americans are passive and thus less likely to resist. If a theft were motivated by hatred of the property's owner because of his race (in some jurisdictions) or a belief that the owner will not resist or report the crime because of his race (in other jurisdictions), that would be a hate crime. Jurisdictions vary in the groups included but often extend the statute to animus or stereotyping based on race, ethnicity, religion, and sexual orientation. A hate crime might be a truly independent crime or might simply increase the sentence of another crime motivated by hatred or stereotyping.

5. ***Constitutionality of Hate Crimes***. In the view of some critics of hate crimes legislation, hate crimes are unconstitutional invasions of free speech rights under the First Amendment to the United States Constitution. The critics' argument is that these crimes essentially add punishment based on expression of a political belief, namely, that some groups are inferior to others. The topic is complex, but the United States Supreme Court has upheld some hate crimes legislation against such attacks while striking down other such legislation, so crafting of these statutes to meet constitutional restrictions is important. See, e.g., *Virginia v. Black*, 538 U.S. 343 (2003) (statute banning cross-burning with intent to intimidate was facially constitutional but jury instruction that an intent to intimidate could be presumed from public cross-burning was unconstitutional).

CASE STUDY ONE

The plight of the Jena 6 made headlines throughout the nation, even leading to a congressional hearing on the subject. The term, the "Jena 6," refers to six African-American students at Jena High School in Jena, Louisiana, who were expelled from school and charged with attempted second degree murder and conspiracy to commit murder for what the students' supporters have called a "school yard brawl." Five of the Jena 6 were juveniles at the time of the assault, though the prosecutor chose to proceed against the one student thus far tried and convicted, Mychal Bell, as an adult, the transfer to adult court having been done without a hearing. Although Louisiana's appellate courts ultimately sent Bell's case back to juvenile court, a major victory for Bell, he was nevertheless sentenced to an 18-month term as a juvenile.

Jena High is a mostly white school, and the schoolyard violence in question may have stemmed from a dispute over the "white tree," a large oak tree under which only white students sat. A black student had asked and received a school official's permission to sit under the tree. Shortly thereafter, students and school authorities found three hangman's nooses dangling from the tree. Several black students responded by sitting under the tree, leading to scuffles, followed by a school assembly at which the local prosecutor, Reed Walters, spoke. At this assembly, Walters allegedly said, specifically to the black students, "I can be your friend or your worst enemy. I can end your lives [and/or make your lives disappear] with the stroke of a pen."

In the ensuing months, school officials put Jena High on lockdown, its main academic building thereafter burning down in what investigators deemed an act of arson. The school principal had recommended that the three white students found to have hung the nooses be expelled, but the school board reduced the punishment to a three-days-long suspension. Meanwhile, when Robert Bailey, who would later become one of the Jena 6, sought to attend a party, a white male attacked Bailey. The Jena prosecutor charged Bailey's assailant with simple battery, his sentence mere probation. The very next day, when Bailey and some of his friends entered a grocery store, a white man named Matt Windham grabbed a shotgun from his truck, purportedly to use on Bailey. Bailey and his friends wrestled the gun away from Windham and took it to the police, reporting the incident. To their surprise, however, authorities charged Windham's victims with robbery and assault for the theft of the firearm.

Only two days after the shotgun incident, the school fight that led to charges against the Jena 6 broke out at Jena High. This fight resulted in a white student, Justin Barker, being knocked unconscious and treated at the local hospital for a concussion, a swollen eye, and a number of cuts and bruises. The hospital released him after two hours, and he purportedly attended a class-ring ceremony that evening. Witnesses conflict over who started the fight and whether some of the Jena

6 were even involved. Authorities eventually charged Barker with possessing a firearm in an arms-free zone for bringing a loaded rifle to Jena High, but the courts released him on $5000 bond. Police arrested the Jena 6, however, for the assault on Barker. Authorities first charged the Jena 6 with aggravated second-degree battery, with the complaint later being amended to include the charges of second-degree murder and conspiracy to commit second-degree murder. The courts ordered bond imposed on each of the Jena 6, ranging from a low of $70,000 to a high of $138,000, a sharp contrast to Barker's relatively meager bond.

Bell's conviction as an adult left him facing a potential sentence of 22 years in prison. His trial counsel, according to his supporters, was ineffective, failing, among other things, to call witnesses in Bell's defense, to question or object to many jurors who admitted having formed prejudgments about the case, and to make serious protests to assure diversity on what turned out to be an all white jury.

The Jena 6 prosecutor published an op-ed piece in several leading national newspapers defending his actions in the case. He argued that the law prohibited him from bringing hate crimes charges against the white students who hung the nooses on the tree, while the law correspondingly required him to proceed against the black students, particularly Mychal Bell, as adults, seeking extremely harsh punishments. Other writers have challenged the accuracy of his legal analysis.

1. Should Reed Walters have charged Mychal Bell with aggravated assault (assume that it is defined as purposely causing serious bodily injury to another), simple assault (assume that it is defined as purposely causing ordinary bodily injury to another or causing serious bodily injury negligently), attempted second degree murder (wanting to and trying to kill another), conspiracy to murder (agreeing to kill another), some of these charges, all of them, or none of them?

2. Assume that a Louisiana statute read: "Any crime of violence committed because of the victim's race, gender, ethnicity, or religion shall be raised to a first degree felony subject to a maximum of thirty years in prison if the underlying crime is less than a first-degree felony." Should Reed Walters have charged Mychal Bell under this hate crimes statute? Should he have so charged Matt Windham? Could Walters have charged the students who hung the nooses on the "white tree" under this statute? If not, could he have charged those students under a "terroristic threats" statute — one making it a crime to threaten another with bodily or serious bodily injury, either with the intention of so inflicting such injury or merely with putting the victim in fear of such injury?

3. Should Walters have charged Bell as an adult, as Walters in fact did, or instead have charged Bell as a juvenile? Assume for purposes of this question

that Bell had one prior juvenile conviction for a simple assault on school grounds.

4. Would the maximum sentence that could have been imposed on Bell in adult court have been a fair one in light of the purposes of sentencing and of the criminal law in an indeterminate sentencing jurisdiction? Was the ultimate juvenile court sentence more or less fair than the initial sentence in adult court?

5. Should it be relevant to what sentence Bell receives that whites involved in these events received no punishment or very light punishments next to that given to Bell? Why or why not?

6. Should Robert Bailey have been charged with robbery (theft from the person or immediate presence of another by force or its threat) or assault for the incident involving wrestling over the shotgun?

7. Was Justin Barker properly charged for bringing a loaded weapon to school, a weapon that may have been involved in an assault? What, if any, further information would you need to answer this question, and from which witnesses, and by what means, would you collect the necessary information?

8. Was the bond imposed on Barker fair? How about the bond imposed on each of the Jena 6? Was the disparity between the bond imposed on Barker and on the Jena 6 justifiable?

9. Should the whole collection of cases have been handled by the criminal justice system, by school disciplinary procedures, by neither, or by both?

10. Do you see any ethical problems with the prosecutor's purported speech to the student assembly? His charging decisions? His decision to proceed in adult court? The sentences that he sought?

11. If you had been the prosecutor, how would you have handled the entire incident to best achieve the goals of the criminal law?

12. If you had been Bell's counsel, how would you have handled his case?

Chapter 2
Criminal Statutes

§ 2.01 The Basics of a Criminal Prosecution

The following is a basic overview of the steps in a criminal prosecution from the point when the authorities become aware of criminal activity through the adjudication of guilt — including review of a conviction by an appellate court — after which the convicted defendant will receive the punishment imposed by the court.

1. **The Investigation**: Usually conducted by police investigators who gather evidence, arrest the defendant(s), and recommend charges to the prosecutor. For certain complex crimes, such a computer crime or large-scale frauds, a unit of the state or federal government devoted to the investigation of these crimes will undertake the task of gathering evidence and analyzing it.

2. **The Charge**: Whether the government will charge a person with a crime is ultimately determined by the prosecutor, sometimes through a *grand jury* handing up the formal accusatory document (*indictment*) or the prosecutor filing the requisite documents to initiate a prosecution (*information*). At this point the formal judicial process commences, and the defendant will be represented by counsel — including appointed counsel if the person cannot afford to retain a lawyer — at all "critical stages" of the proceeding.

3. **Pre-Trial Motions**: The determination of preliminary issues by the court that will affect the ultimate prosecution of the case, such as: (a) exclusion of evidence (e.g, *Miranda* and the exclusionary rule); (b) a request to dismiss the charges for insufficient evidence or failure to charge a crime, which will frequently require the court to interpret the statute the defendant is charged with violating. With regard to the sufficiency of the government's evidence, courts will conduct a *preliminary hearing* to review whether there is *probable cause* that the defendant committed the offense.

4. **Trial**: The Constitution entitles a defendant to a jury trial if he can be incarcerated on a charge for more than 6 months for the offense. A defendant can waive a jury trial if the prosecution agrees, in which case the judge hears the case as the trier-of-fact. For most minor offenses, the court will decide the case.

5. **Plea Bargain**: The government and the defendant — through counsel — can agree to a plea bargain under which a defendant will plead guilty to certain charges, often in exchange for a lower sentence than would be imposed if the case went to trial and a conviction resulted. The agreement requires the defendant to waive the right to trial and proceed immediately to sentencing. The government may demand as a condition of the plea bargain that the defendant cooperate in its investigation by identifying other wrongdoers against whom the defendant will testify if the government initiates or continues other prosecutions. Sentencing may be postponed until the defendant fulfills the bargain to testify against others.

6. **The Jury Instruction**: This is the statement of the law given to the jury at the end of the trial. The instructions usually originate from counsel for both sides, although courts often follow model jury instructions, and the judge ultimately decides what to tell the jury. Among other things, the jury instruction will contain a description of the elements of the crime that the jury must find beyond a reasonable doubt, and a description of the legal requirements for a defense offered by the defendant if there is sufficient evidence to require giving the instruction.

7. **Motion for a Judgment of Acquittal**: This is similar to a summary judgment or directed verdict in a civil case, but only a defendant can seek to have the case dismissed for insufficient evidence. The Constitution prohibits granting a directed verdict of guilty or informing the jury that it must find a particular fact existed.

8. **Double Jeopardy**: The Constitution provides that a defendant may not be put "twice in jeopardy" for the same offense, so that if a person is found "not guilty" of a charge, then the government may not pursue that charge in a second proceeding, regardless of the strength of its evidence. An important exception to this rule is the Dual Sovereignty Doctrine, which permits a different state or the federal government to prosecute a person for the same crime so long as the state or federal government has *jurisdiction* over the offense. For example, Terry Nichols was tried by both federal and Oklahoma courts for the deaths that occurred in connection with the Oklahoma City bombing in 1996. The double jeopardy protection is the source of the jury's power to nullify the law because its not guilty verdict is unreviewable by the court. If the defendant is found guilty, then he can appeal any errors in the trial (e.g., improper jury instructions, insufficient evidence, etc.) and the sentence to a higher court for further review.

9. **The Basis for an Appeal**: The defendant convicted of a crime must demonstrate a legal error in the trial or pre-trial procedure, which is usually based on:

a.　**Insufficient evidence** - when the government fails to present sufficient evidence of the defendant's guilt.

b.　**Improper jury instruction** - when the court gives an improper definition of the crime or interpretation of the statute.

c.　**Evidentiary challenges** - when evidence is improperly admitted or the court excluded evidence relevant to the case.

d.　**Constitutional challenge** - when the statute, charges, jury instruction, or pre-trial or trial procedure deprived the defendant of a constitutional right.

The usual remedy for a legal error at trial that substantially affected the outcome is a new trial, although if the government fails to introduce sufficient evidence of guilt then a "not guilty" verdict must be entered. The government cannot appeal a not guilty verdict returned by a jury, but if a court dismisses a charge before trial, or grants a judgment of acquittal after the jury returns a guilty verdict, then the government is allowed to appeal. The government can appeal sentencing issues, although a jury decision not to impose a death sentence cannot be reviewed.

§ 2.02 Statutory Basis of Criminal Law

1.　**Criminal Statutes.** The determination of what constitutes a "crime" has evolved from the judicial formulation of the common law of offenses to an extensive statutory-based system of laws enacted by the legislatures, enforced by prosecutors, and interpreted by the courts. Each state, the federal government, and many local governments adopt criminal laws that regulate almost all aspects of public conduct, and many private acts and relationships.

While the common law developed a fairly small number of broad offenses, statutes imposing criminal sanctions take up multiple volumes of the state and federal codes and often address very narrow types of conduct, circumstances, or transactions. Moreover, many of the statutes overlap, so that what would appear to be a single criminal act can result in multiple charges. For example, a fraudulent scheme could result in numerous charges if there were multiple contacts with potential victims or separate transfers of funds. A newer type of statute involves criminal enterprises — such as the federal RICO provision — that require proof that the defendants engaged in a series of criminal acts, and a violation is separate from the underlying offenses used to prove the enterprise.

Crimes are usually divided into two categories: felonies and misdemeanors. This may be provided for in the statute defining the offense — for example, dividing larceny according to the value of the property taken — or by the maximum punishment that may be imposed. The classification of crimes as felonies or misdemeanors can be important for application of a "three strikes" statute, such as the one in California at issue in *Ewing v. California* [p. 24]. The type of crime may also be important for collateral consequences triggered by a conviction, such as the loss of voting rights, professional licenses, and the right to own a firearm.

Another division of crimes frequently seen is when an offense is termed *malum in se* or *malum prohibitum*. These labels mean that the conduct is wrongful in itself — *in se* — or wrongful through legislative prohibition. Many record-keeping and regulatory statutes are considered *malum prohibitum* while traditional crimes of violence and theft — murder, rape, larceny — are viewed as inherently wrongful. While this distinction arose in the common law, today the categories are often important in determining what type of "bad" intent, if any, must be proven to establish criminal liability. As a general matter, *malum prohibitum* crimes can have a lower intent, or even require no proof of intent, known as a "strict liability" offense.

While almost all criminal law in the United States is statutory, the common law roots of crimes remains important to understanding how the law works. Although it is rare that a state recognizes a separate common law crime that is not also defined by a statute, legislatures often adopt broadly written laws incorporating common law terminology. Even more modern crimes unknown to the common law, such as carjacking, are informed by the common law roots of the criminal law.

2.   **The Model Penal Code.** One of the most important statutory developments in the criminal law was the promulgation of the Model Penal Code (MPC) in 1962. Drafted by the American Law Institute (ALI), the MPC has been widely influential in the states in drafting their own penal statutes. Many states have adopted portions of the MPC, and courts frequently refer to its approach as a basis for interpreting criminal statutes that are not drawn specifically from that source. Judge Lynch described the impact of the MPC:

> As all criminal law scholars understand, the Model Penal Code is one of the great intellectual accomplishments of American legal scholarship of the mid-twentieth century. In many ways, it marks the culmination of a project of re-interpreting and systematizing the common law of crimes that began with Wechsler and Michael's *A Rationale of the Law of Homicide*, [37 COLUM. L. REV. 701 (1937)], * * * itself recently celebrated as one of the most important law review articles of the last 100 years. Surveying

hundreds of years of common-law evolution in the criminal law, identifying underlying principles, and formulating rules that represented the best of the thinking of judges who had grappled over that period with the violent and destructive results of the unruly passions of humankind, the drafters of the Code, marshaled by the incredible energy, formidable intelligence, and sheer will of the great Herbert Wechsler, developed an intellectually coherent approach to this mass of material, and created a body of rules not only doctrinally consistent, but drafted for easy adoption by legislative bodies.

Gerard E. Lynch, *Revising the Model Penal Code: Keeping It Real*, 1 OHIO ST. J. CRIM. L. 219 (2003).

3. **Interpreting Statutory Language.** Criminal statutes are a reflection of a legislative decision to designate an act, and an accompanying intent in most cases, as a violation of the social order that deserves punishment. The legislature uses broad terms to describe in general the types of conduct that will constitute such a violation and, in a few instances, what defenses a person may raise to show that a violation did not occur or should not be punished. When a law is written to cover a multitude of situations — such as a statute providing that "Murder is the unlawful killing of a human being with malice aforethought" — virtually every word of the statute will have to be defined to determine what conduct in fact violates the law. This process, known as statutory interpretation, is at the heart of the criminal law today. Criminal prosecutions require that each participant in the process — prosecutor, defense lawyer, defendant, judge, and jury — understand what the law means. It is the task of the prosecutor to charge only those crimes that violate the statute, and the defense lawyer must ascertain whether the defendant's conduct in fact violated the identified statute. The judge must determine whether the prosecutor's decision to charge a crime was correct, and then state the law properly to the jury so that the jurors can apply the law to the facts.

Statutory interpretation is about understanding the words of a statute. There are many theories of statutory interpretation, and courts are frequently criticized for not adhering to a single approach to interpreting statutes and for sometimes reaching seemingly inconsistent results when they interpret the same words differently. For example, the Supreme Court interpreted the word "willfully" in *Bryan v. United States*, 524 U.S. 184 (1997), to mean "the defendant acted with an evil-meaning mind, that is to say, that he acted with knowledge that his conduct was unlawful" for a violation of a firearm statute. In *Ratzlaf v. United States*, 510 U.S. 135 (1994), it held that a statute punishing a defendant who "willfully" violated the currency reporting rules required proof that the defendant know that his conduct violated the particular statute rather than just that he knew it was generally unlawful. While there were good reasons for interpreting the statutes differently, it is not particularly helpful to lawyers and judges who need to interpret statutes prohibiting "willful" misconduct when, as the Court pointed out in *Bryan*, "[t]he word 'willfully' is sometimes said to be 'a word of many meanings' whose construction is often dependent on the context in which it appears."

Courts frequently state that their interpretation reflects the intent of the legislature in enacting the statute to reach (or not reach) a particular harm or conduct that the legislature deemed criminal. How does a court determine the intent of the legislature in determining the meaning of a statute? Consider the following description of how courts approach the issue of legislative intent:

> [There are] two different ways of thinking about statutory interpretation. The first is "archeological": the meaning of a statute is set in stone on the date of its enactment, and it is the interpreter's task to uncover and reconstruct that original meaning. * * *

> The second way to think about statutory interpretation is "nautical." At the risk of overextending a metaphor, it may be described as follows. Congress builds a ship and charts its initial course, but the ship's ports-of- call, safe harbors and ultimate destination may be a product of the ship's captain, the weather, and other factors not identified at the time the ship sets sail. This model understands a statute as an on-going process (a voyage) in which both the shipbuilder and subsequent navigators play a role. The dimensions and structure of the craft determine where it is capable of going, but the current course is set primarily by the crew on board. (Of course, Congress may send subsequent messages to the ship or change the waters in which the ship is sailing.)

T. Alexander Aleinikoff, *Updating Statutory Interpretation*, 87 MICH. L. REV. 20 (1988).

Statutory interpretation of criminal statutes requires that the lawyers (and judge) focus first on whether the words should be construed broadly or narrowly. As a general matter, the defense lawyer wants the operative terms of a statute defined as narrowly as possible in order to argue, or present a defense, that the defendant's conduct fell outside the statutory prohibition. The prosecutor, not surprisingly, frequently seeks a broader interpretation of the words to encompass an array of conduct that usually includes the particular defendant's actions. Understanding the words of a statute is important to both sides because the scope of the provision at issue will affect what proof the government will need to introduce to secure a conviction and what defenses and arguments can be advanced to defeat the charge.

4. **Studying Criminal Statutes.** Although every jurisdiction's statutory scheme will share common features with other jurisdictions, each has its own unique statutes and rules for applying those provisions. While many types of statutes will arise in the course of this book, for ease of reference the basic contrast will be drawn between the "common law" approach of statutes and crimes with the Model Penal Code's. Common law jurisdictions have codified (*i.e.*, made into statutes) the crimes that were previously created by judges through decisions in individual cases. Since that codification, legislatures have added new crimes to reflect changing needs. It is important to understand that there is no single common law code available for study, and so statements about the common law are in reality discussions of how many — often most — jurisdictions following this approach would decide an issue. The MPC is such a unified code, and it is studied because it adopts a systematic approach to the criminal law that is often markedly different from the approach of the common law. A commonly asked question by students is, "Do we need to know both the common law and the MPC?" The answer is "Yes" because the criminal law is not a unified set of statutes and encompasses different approaches that are reflected — albeit incompletely — in decisions applying the common law and the MPC.

§ 2.03 Interpreting Criminal Statutes

A. Defining the Crime

A legal term of art can have a significant effect on the interpretation of criminal statutes. In the following cases, consider how the common law term "asportation" plays a role in the interpretation of California and Iowa statutes that both involve the theft, or attempted theft, of vehicles.

People v. Lopez
79 P.3d 548 (Cal. 2003)

CHIN, J.

The crime of carjacking requires the "felonious taking" of a motor vehicle. (Pen.Code, § 215.) Similarly, the crime of robbery requires the "felonious taking" of personal property. (§ 211.) California courts, following common law, have long held that the "taking" element of robbery requires that a defendant gain possession of the victim's property and asport or carry it away. Does the felonious taking element of the crime of carjacking, like robbery, require asportation or movement of the motor vehicle? We conclude that it does. Because the Court of Appeal came to a contrary decision, we reverse that court's judgment.

On July 1, 1999, Wa Vue Yang was seated inside his van in a parking lot when defendant approached him and offered to sell him a watch. When Yang replied that he had a watch, defendant pulled out a gun and shot at the ground. He pointed the gun at Yang and ordered him out of his van. Yang complied, but left his keys in the ignition. Defendant sat in the van and threw his backpack onto the passenger seat. As Yang began to leave, he remembered that he had left some checks inside the van. Deciding that defendant's weapon was an air gun, Yang's fear subsided. He returned to the van to retrieve his checks. Defendant pointed his gun at Yang and pulled the trigger twice, but the gun did not fire. Defendant fled from the van and left his backpack, containing identification, in the van. * * *

[Lopez was found guilty of a number of offenses, including carjacking, and, because he had prior felonies, the court sentenced him to a substantial term of imprisonment under California's "Three Strikes and You're Out" law. A successful challenge to the carjacking conviction may result in a substantially lower sentence under the "Three Strikes" law.]

Carjacking is defined as "the *felonious taking* of a motor vehicle in the possession of another, from his or her person or immediate presence, or from the person or immediate presence of a passenger of the motor vehicle, against his or her will and with the intent to either permanently or temporarily deprive the person in possession of the motor vehicle of his or her possession, accomplished by means of force or fear." (§ 215, subd. (a), italics added.)

Robbery is defined as "the *felonious taking* of personal property in the possession of another, from his person or immediate presence, and against his will, accomplished by means of force or fear." (§ 211, italics added.)

* * * [Defendant] argues that, because the Legislature used the same "felonious taking" phrase in defining carjacking, it intended that the phrase be given the same meaning as the analogous provision in the robbery statute. Following the common law crime of larceny, California courts have construed the taking element of robbery to include two necessary elements: caption or gaining possession of the victim's property and asportation or carrying away the loot. (*People v. Hill* (1998) 72 Cal.Rptr.2d 656). The Attorney General responds that the Legislature created a new crime of carjacking, which, although resembling the crime of robbery in some respects, is a separate crime with meaningful differences. Although we agree with the Attorney General that "[t]he analogy between robbery and carjacking is imperfect" (*People v. Hill* (2000) 98 Cal.Rptr.2d 254), "[t]here is no evidence the Legislature intended to adopt a 'felonious taking' requirement different from that for robbery."

In construing a statute, our role is to ascertain the Legislature's intent so as to effectuate the purpose of the law. In determining intent, we must look first to the words of the statute because they are the most reliable indicator of legislative intent. If the statutory language is clear and unambiguous, the plain meaning of the statute governs. * * *

Section 215, subdivision (a), requires the "taking" of a motor vehicle. Defendant claims that the plain meaning of the word "taking" requires proof of asportation. However, terms such as "asportation," "carries or drives away," or "movement" do not appear in the statute. The plain meaning of "taking" does not necessarily impute an asportation requirement. In contrasting "taking" from "carrying away," one commentator noted that "A *taking* occurs when the offender secures dominion over the property, while a carrying away requires some slight movement away of the property." (3 LaFave, *Substantive Criminal Law* (2003) Larceny — Taking and Carrying Away, § 19.3, p. 74, italics added.) Thus, we must look to extrinsic sources to determine legislative intent.

The Legislature created the crime of carjacking in 1993. Prior to the enactment of section 215, the forcible taking of a motor vehicle was charged and prosecuted as a second degree robbery. The legislative history reveals the underlying purpose for creating the new crime of carjacking: "According to the author [of the legislative bill]: [¶] There has been *considerable increase in the number of persons who have been abducted*, many have been subjected to the violent taking of their automobile and some have had a gun used in the taking of the car. This relatively 'new' crime appears to be as much thrill-seeking as theft of a car. If all the thief wanted was the car, *it would be simpler to hot-wire the automobile without running the risk of confronting the driver*. People have been killed, seriously injured, and placed in great fear, and this calls for a strong message to discourage these crimes. Additionally law enforcement is reporting this new crime is becoming the initiating rite for aspiring gang members and the incidents are drastically increasing. [¶] Under current law there is no carjacking crime per se and many carjackings cannot be charged as robbery because it is difficult to prove the intent required of a robbery offense (to permanently deprive one of the car) since many of these gang carjackings are thrill seeking thefts. There is a need to prosecute this crime." (Assem. Com. on Pub. Safety, Analysis of Sen. Bill No. 60 (1993-1994 Reg. Sess.) July 13, 1993, p. 1, italics added.)

Thus, the legislative history demonstrates that carjacking was made a separate offense because of perceived difficulties with obtaining convictions under the robbery statute. In addition, because of the potentially violent nature of the taking and growing frequency of the crime, the Legislature made the punishment for carjacking greater than that for second degree robbery.

As the Attorney General asserts, there are significant differences between the crimes of carjacking and robbery. First, carjacking requires either an intent to permanently or temporarily deprive; robbery requires an intent to permanently deprive. As reflected above, the Legislature changed the intent requirement of carjacking "to close a potential loophole."

Second, "[u]nlike robbery, which requires a taking from the person or immediate presence of the possessor (§ 211), the Legislature expanded the taking element to a taking from the person or immediate presence of either the possessor or any passenger. (§ 215, subd. (a).)" * * *

Third, robbery can involve any type of personal property, while carjacking involves only vehicles. * * *

Nevertheless, the carjacking statute's language and legislative history — reflected in the author's explanation for the new crime — demonstrate that carjacking is a direct offshoot of robbery and that the Legislature modeled the carjacking statute on the robbery statute. The definition in the carjacking statute (§ 215, subd. (a)) tracks the language in the robbery statute (§ 211). * * *

The carjacking statute itself reflects the overlap between carjacking and robbery. It states, "This section shall not be construed to supersede or affect Section 211. A person may be charged with a violation of this section and Section 211. However, no defendant may be punished under this section and Section 211 for the same act which constitutes a violation of both this section and Section 211." (§ 215, subd. (c).) * * *

When legislation has been judicially construed and a subsequent statute on a similar subject uses identical or substantially similar language, the usual presumption is that the Legislature intended the same construction, unless a contrary intent clearly appears. Moreover, if a term known to the common law has not otherwise been defined by statute, it is assumed that the common law meaning was intended. Because the "felonious taking" in the crime of robbery has an established meaning at common law and the same "taking" language appears in the carjacking, robbery, and unlawful taking or driving of a vehicle statutes, we presume that the Legislature intended the same meaning, unless a contrary intent clearly appears.

* * * [The] Attorney General * * * argues that because carjacking is "more nearly a crime against the person than a crime against property" * * * movement of the vehicle is unrelated to the serious potential for harm to the victim, and thus is not required. Using the facts of this case as illustration, he claims that a defendant who gains possession and control of a vehicle using threats of violence, exposes the victim to the same risks, irrespective of whether the vehicle moves. However, the legislative history indicates that the Legislature was specifically concerned with the "considerable increase in the number of persons who have been abducted" in their vehicles and the associated danger to the driver or passenger. * * * Indeed, the facts in *Hill* illustrate the increased risks involved with abductions

during a carjacking. There, defendant took the victim's car and drove off with the victim and her seven-month-old daughter still in the car. The infant was unbuckled from her carseat, and rolled around the front seat as the vehicle moved. Given the unique nature of the taking and the identical threat of violence and serious potential for harm to all occupants of the car, we analogized the crime of carjacking with kidnapping and found no reason in logic or policy for the Legislature to have precluded an infant from being a victim of a carjacking.

The Attorney General admits that by limiting section 215 to one specific type of property, a motor vehicle, the Legislature focused on criminal conduct akin to hijacking that preys on victims in vulnerable circumstances. Nevertheless, he is correct that a completed carjacking occurs whether the perpetrator drives off with the carjacking victim in the car or forcibly removes the victim from the car before driving off. The inherent dangers and risk of harm to the victim is the same whether the perpetrator drives off or remains stationary after forcibly removing the victim from the vehicle. The Attorney General further argues that the purpose of an asportation requirement in larceny and robbery is to provide an external and observable manifestation of the wrongdoer's possession and control over the property. Unlike robbery of personal property, in which dispossession is made by physically removing the property from the victim's possession, the forcible removal or expulsion of the victim from his van and defendant's entry into that van perfected the caption requirement, without the need for the observable act of moving the van. Thus, he posits that the legislative concern with abductions means only that movement of the vehicle should be a sufficient, but not a necessary condition for carjacking.

Although the Attorney General's arguments are reasonable, we agree with defendant that they are policy arguments reserved for the Legislature. As it stands, based on the language of the statute and its legislative purpose, carjacking adapts and expands specific elements of robbery to address increasing auto theft incidents by perpetrators who may not intend to permanently deprive possession of the vehicle, but whose criminal acts nevertheless heighten the risk of harm to a broader range of victims than were covered under the existing crime of robbery. Thus, the Legislature expanded the taking element to include takings from either the possessor or any passenger, including an infant, but neither the words of the carjacking statute nor the legislative history indicates that the Legislature intended to alter the meaning of "felonious taking" with respect to the requirement of asportation. The legislative history is replete with comparisons between robbery and the new crime of carjacking. Noting the deficiencies in charging and prosecuting a carjacking under the robbery statute, the Legislature affirmatively adjusted the carjacking elements—as distinct from robbery—to include a taking from a passenger, even one without a possessory interest, and to include an intent to temporarily deprive a person of possession of the motor vehicle. (§ 215, subd. (a).) Yet the legislative history is silent as to whether the Legislature intended to further distinguish the crime of carjacking from the crime of robbery by eliminating the asportation requirement. In the absence of a contrary intent, we presume that in adopting the phrase, "felonious taking," from the robbery statute, the Legislature intended that those same words within section 215 be given the same construction.

[The court found the defendant's conduct punishable as an attempted carjacking.]

State v. Donaldson
663 N.W.2d 882 (Iowa 2003)

STREIT, Justice.

Is a person guilty of theft if he breaks into another's car and engages the entire electrical system, save the engine? Specifically, the question on appeal is whether Dean Lester Donaldson possessed or controlled another's van when he broke into it, dismantled the steering column, and manipulated the ignition switch, turning on the radio and lighting the "check engine" sign on the dashboard. After a trial, Donaldson was convicted of second-degree theft. The district court overruled Donaldson's motion for a judgment of acquittal. Donaldson argues there were insufficient facts to show he possessed the van to support the charge of theft. Because we find Donaldson took possession or control of another's property with the intent to steal, we affirm. * * *

The State charged Donaldson with second-degree theft pursuant to Iowa Code section 714.1(1) (2001). This statute provides "a person commits theft when" he or she "[t]akes possession or control of the property of another, or property in the possession of another, with the intent to deprive the other thereof." Iowa Code § 714.1(1). * * *

The Iowa theft statute is modeled after the Model Penal Code, with slight variation. Model Penal Code § 223.2 cmt. 2 (1980). Our terms "possession or control" of another's property replace the common law larceny requirements of "caption" and "asportation." See id. § 223.2 cmt. 1. "Caption," or taking, occurred when the actor secured dominion over the property of another. The element of "asportation," or carrying away, was satisfied with even the most slight change in position of the stolen object. At common law, to prove a theft, the State had to show a defendant took the property of another, i.e., secured dominion over it, and carried the property away. Id. § 223.2 cmt. 2.

The asportation requirement was important at common law because if a defendant's actions fell short of causing the object of the theft to move, the defendant was guilty of attempt only. Because a completed larceny was generally a felony whereas attempt was a misdemeanor, significant differences in "procedure and punishment turned on the criminologically insignificant fact of slight movement of the object of theft." In modern criminal law, however, the penal consequences between attempt and a completed theft are so minimal that it has become less important to draw a bright line between the two actions. As such, the element of asportation is no longer necessary.

Iowa, like many other states following the Model Penal Code, has abandoned the common law asportation requirement. See id. § 223.2 (citing Iowa Code § 714.1).[1] Our definition of "theft" under Iowa Code section 714.1 is based on the Model Penal Code. We now define theft as the possession or control of another's property with intent to deprive the owner thereof. The key to our statute is the words "possession or control." In determining the meaning of "possession" and "control," we look to the Model Penal Code for guidance as our statute is modeled after it. The Model Penal Code contemplates "control" of the object to begin when the defendant "use[s] it in a manner beyond his authority." The method of exerting control over the object of the theft is important only insofar as it "sheds light on the authority of the actor to behave as he did." Our statute replaces the common law element of "taking" with "possession." The Model Penal Code provides a person commits theft if he or she "unlawfully takes, or exercises unlawful control over" the property of another. A taking in this sense concerns whether the offender exerted control over the object "adverse to or usurpatory of the owner's dominion." *State v. Victor*, 368 So.2d 711 (La.1979). That is, one possesses an object if he or she secures dominion over it. See Model Penal Code § 223.2 cmt. 2. To summarize the above concepts, "possession or control" begins and a theft is completed when the actor secures dominion over the object or uses it in a manner beyond his authority.

The question before us concerns whether the defendant possessed or controlled the object of the theft. The critical issue, as the statute dictates, is not whether the defendant used or operated the object of the theft. As to Donaldson's conduct, we must determine whether he exercised wrongful dominion or unauthorized control of the van. * * *

The undisputed facts of the case are the following. At approximately 1:30 a.m., Donaldson entered a van owned by Combined Pool & Spa. The owner of the van did not give Donaldson authority or permission to take possession or control of the van. The officer spotted the van located in the parking lot of Combined Pool & Spa and noticed the van's sliding door was partially open. As the officer walked toward

---

[1] Other jurisdictions following the Model Penal Code are Alabama, Arizona, Arkansas, Colorado, Delaware, Hawaii, Illinois, Indiana, Kansas, Kentucky, Maine, Minnesota, Missouri, Montana, Nebraska, New Hampshire, New Jersey, North Dakota, Ohio, Oregon, Pennsylvania, Texas, Utah, Washington, Wisconsin, Michigan, Oklahoma, and West Virginia. See Model Penal Code § 223.2 cmt. 2, n.3

the van, he saw the brake lights flash suggesting someone was inside the van. As the officer approached, Donaldson got out of the driver's side and ran away. The officer called after Donaldson, identified himself as a police officer, and ordered him to stop. Donaldson kept running. When the officer checked the van, he saw the steering column had been forcibly dismantled; there were wires hanging from the column. The ignition switch had been removed. The radio was operating. The "check engine" sign on the dashboard was lit. At trial, one of the officers testified Donaldson had engaged all of the electric systems. After turning on the electric accessory systems in the car, according to the officer, all Donaldson had left to do was engage the starter.

There is no evidence in the record to suggest Donaldson's tearing apart the steering column was intended for any purpose other than to deprive the owner of her possession of the van. Donaldson argues he did not possess or control the van because he did not have the "ability to readily move or remove" it. This, however, is not the test for possession or control. Because we have abandoned the common law asportation requirement, movement or motion of the car is not essential to finding a defendant had possession or control of the car. Our theft statute does not state possession or control is tantamount to "operation" of the object of the theft. To interpret our statute in this manner is to restrict the definition of theft more narrowly than the legislature intended. Given a strict interpretation of the statute, the State only had to show Donaldson had control of the van, i.e., he had dominion over it in a manner inconsistent with his authority. See Model Penal Code § 223.2. We are unwilling to imply an "operation" requirement for certain kinds of property that are normally operated by its possessor.

The mere fact that Donaldson was interrupted by the police officer before he engaged the starter motor does not remove this case from the realm of a completed theft. It is not necessary that the engine was running and the van could have been moved. That is, technical operation of the van is not necessary to find Donaldson exercised wrongful dominion or unauthorized control over the van. * * * Certainly, Donaldson's acts were sufficient to set into motion the steps necessary to power the van. It was not necessary that the engine was actually running. Rather, at the moment Donaldson began to manipulate the electrical wires for the purpose of starting the engine, he exerted complete control over the vehicle.

In sum, the facts before us show Donaldson was using the van owned by another person. He had the power and intention at the given time to exercise unfettered dominion over the van. Donaldson was in a position to exclude all others from the van, for example, by locking it. No one else could have hot-wired the van or started it with a key while Donaldson had control over it. Moreover, he used the van without the owner's consent and in a manner beyond his authority. Donaldson entered the company's van around 1:30 in the morning. He tore apart the steering column. The ignition switch had been removed; wires protruded from the ignition. The brake lights flashed. The radio worked. The "check engine" sign was lit. When the officer approached the van, Donaldson got out of the driver's side and ran away. All of these facts together are sufficient to show Donaldson controlled the van within the meaning of Iowa Code section 714.1(1). As such, the trial court properly denied Donaldson's motion for judgment of acquittal. We affirm.

NOTES AND QUESTIONS

1. ***Legislative Intent***. Why does the California Supreme Court presume the legislature intended to incorporate the common law asportation requirement into the carjacking statute? What evidence does the court cite beyond its presumption of the legislature's intent to apply the common law meaning to the new statute?

2. *Plain Meaning.* Notice how courts look first for the plain meaning of the statute, oftentimes interpreting the words in a statute through use of a dictionary definition. Legislative history may then play a role in statutory interpretation. Changes in a statute can also be used to discern what the legislature meant. For example, adding new words in a statute may express a specific desire of the legislature to expand or limit the statute. Case law, when available, can also provide interpretation of a statute. Precedent is obviously an important part of statutory interpretation. What role should the judiciary play in interpreting a statute? Some maintain that a strict textual approach should be used, while others desire a more "dynamic" approach. What are the pros and cons of the different approaches? Finally, policy consider-ations can play a role in how the judiciary interprets a criminal statute.

3. ***Role of Legislative History***. What role should legislative history have in interpreting a statute? Should floor debates be used to discern the legislature's intent? Is there a legitimate argument in saying that floor debates are not a part of the law itself and therefore should not be considered? If legislative debates are relevant, what about states that do not have the debates transcribed or otherwise available? Should committee reports and the analysis of a bill provided by a legislative research bureau also be considered?

4. ***Other Statutory Interpretation Tools***. In interpreting criminal statutes there are general rules of statutory interpretation that may factor into how to properly interpret a statute. These are:

A. ***Ejusdem Generis***. When general language follows specific terms in a statute, the *ejusdem generis* rule limits the general language to the specific terms. "This maxim is itself an instance of a more general maxim, 'noscitur a sociis' (it is known by its companions). Both the general and the more specific versions indicate that words often take their shape from those around them, and 'ejusdem generis' is frequently invoked to suggest that a phrase which in isolation appears to have a broad scope should be construed more narrowly when considered in its linguistic setting." David L. Shapiro, *Continuity and Change in Statutory Interpretation*, 67 N.Y.U. L. REV. 921 (1992). In *State v. Kahalewai*, 541 P.2d 1020 (Hawai 1975), the court stated:

> Where words of general description follow the enumeration of certain things, those words are restricted in their meaning to objects of like kind and character with those specified . . . This is the rule of ejusdem generis often utilized by the courts in the construction of statutory law. This doctrine is especially applicable to penal statutes, which must be strictly construed.

> Applying this rule, we held in *Rackle* that the term "other deadly or dangerous weapon," as used in HRS s 134-51 (1973 Supp), preceded by the terms "dirk, dagger, blackjack, slug (sic) shot, billy, metal knuckles, (and) pistol," included only instruments which were designed as offensive weapons and therefore could not include a flaregun designed as an emergency signalling device. We subsequently applied the reasoning of *Rackle* to hold that a diver's knife is not a "dangerous weapon."

B. *Statutory Title.* Does the title of the statute provide an indication of what the legislature intended? Some titles will provide a clear indication of the legislation passed. Others, however, may have been used to allow for easier passage in the legislature, such as the USA PATRIOT Act adopted after the September 11 terrorist attacks.

C. *Expressio unius est exclusio alterius.* "The expression of one thing is the exclusion of another." This maxim is used by defendants when a statute contains a list of acts or circumstances and they argue that by enumerating specific items the legislature intended to exclude anything that falls outside the list. As the Supreme Court noted in *United States v. Vonn*, 535 U.S. 55 (2002), "At best, as we have said before, the canon that expressing one item of a commonly associated group or series excludes another left unmentioned is only a guide, whose fallibility can be shown by contrary indications that adopting a particular rule or statute was probably not meant to signal any exclusion of its common relatives." In *United States v. Cabaccang*, 332 F.3d 622 (9th Cir. 2003), the court reversed the defendants convictions for transporting methamphetamine from California to Guam. The statute, 21 U.S.C. § 952(a), states, "It shall be unlawful to import into the customs territory of the United States from any place outside thereof (but within the United States) . . . ." California is within the customs territory of the United States, while Guam as a territory is "within the United States." The Ninth Circuit held that the statute:

[P]rohibits only the transport of drugs from the noncustoms territory to the customs territory — it does not address the drug trade in the reverse direction. Thus in 1970 when Congress crafted § 952(a), it made a deliberate choice not to make the first clause reciprocal — banning the importation of drugs from, for example, Guam to California but not from California to Guam. * * * * Under the interpretive maxim of *expressio unius est exclusio alterius*, we "read the enumeration of one case to exclude another [if] it is fair to suppose that Congress considered the unnamed possibility and meant to say no to it." *Barnhart v. Peabody Coal Co.*, 537 U.S. 149 (2003). That Congress chose to single out only the transport of drugs from the noncustoms territory to the customs territory rather than the transport between the two territories is a strong indication that Congress did not intend § 952(a) to address "importation" in the opposite (i.e., "outbound") direction. We are thus justified in inferring that "items not mentioned were excluded by deliberate choice, not inadvertence." *Barnhart*.

5. ***Rule of Lenity.*** Unique to criminal law is the statutory maxim that criminal statutes should be interpreted narrowly in order to ensure that a defendant is not convicted for a crime about which the person may have been unaware. This is known as the "Rule of Lenity." If a statute is clear on its face, then the rule of lenity is unnecessary. In *United States v. Wiltberger*, 18 U.S. (5 Wheat.) 76 (1820), Chief Justice John Marshall explained its rationale:

> The rule that penal laws are to be construed strictly, is perhaps not much less old than construction itself. It is founded on the tenderness of the law for the rights of individuals; and on the plain principle that the power of punishment is vested in the legislative, not in the judicial department. It is the legislature, not the Court, which is to define a crime, and ordain its punishment.

If the words of a statute offer two possible meanings, and each meaning is both plausible and constitutional, then the court must decide which interpretation it will follow. Lenity controls here, and the court should interpret the statute narrowly in favor of the defendant. Some states have enacted statutes that specify how the rule works. For example, a Florida statute provides: "The provisions of this code and offenses defined by other statutes shall be strictly construed; when the language is susceptible of differing constructions, it shall be construed most favorably to the accused." FLA. STAT. ch. 750.221 (2005).

6. ***International Law.*** In the case of *Small v. United States*, 544 U.S. 385 (2005), the Court was faced with the question of whether a statute that makes it "unlawful for any person . . . who has been *convicted in any court,* of a crime punishable by

imprisonment for a term exceeding one year . . . to . . . possess . . . any firearm," (18 U.S.C. § 922(g)(1)) should include convictions from foreign courts. The Court stated:

> In 1994 petitioner, Gary Small, was convicted in a Japanese court of having tried to smuggle several pistols, a rifle, and ammunition into Japan. Small was sentenced to five years' imprisonment. * * * After his release, Small returned to the United States, where he bought a gun from a Pennsylvania gun dealer. Federal authorities subsequently charged Small under the "unlawful gun possession" statute here at issue. * * * Small pleaded guilty while reserving the right to challenge his conviction on the ground that his earlier conviction, being a foreign conviction, fell outside the scope of the illegal gun possession statute.

> * * * The question before us is whether the statutory reference "convicted in *any* court" includes a conviction entered in a *foreign* court. The word "any" considered alone cannot answer this question. In ordinary life, a speaker who says, "I'll see any film," may or may not mean to include films shown in another city. In law, a legislature that uses the statutory phrase "'any person'" may or may not mean to include "'persons'" outside "the jurisdiction of the state." * * * Thus, even though the word "any" demands a broad interpretation, * * * , we must look beyond that word itself.

> In determining the scope of the statutory phrase we find help in the "commonsense notion that Congress generally legislates with domestic concerns in mind." * * * This notion has led the Court to adopt the legal presumption that Congress ordinarily intends its statutes to have domestic, not extraterritorial, application. * * * That presumption would apply, for example, were we to consider whether this statute prohibits unlawful gun possession abroad as well as domestically. And, although the presumption against extraterritorial application does not apply directly to this case, we believe a similar assumption is appropriate when we consider the scope of the phrase "convicted in any court" here. * * *

> In addition, it is difficult to read the statute as asking judges or prosecutors to refine its definitional distinctions where foreign convictions are at issue. To somehow weed out inappropriate foreign convictions that meet the statutory definition is not consistent with the statute's language; it is not easy for those not versed in foreign laws to accomplish; and it would leave those previously convicted in a foreign court (say of economic crimes) uncertain about their legal obligations. * * *

> These considerations, suggesting significant differences between foreign and domestic convictions, do not dictate our ultimate conclusion. Nor do

they create a "clear statement" rule, imposing upon Congress a special burden of specificity. * * * They simply convince us that we should apply an ordinary assumption about the reach of domestically oriented statutes here — an assumption that helps us determine Congress' intent where Congress likely did not consider the matter and where other indicia of intent are in approximate balance. * * * We consequently assume a congressional intent that the phrase "convicted in any court" applies domestically, not extraterritorially. But, at the same time, we stand ready to revise this assumption should statutory language, context, history, or purpose show the contrary. * * * We have found no convincing indication to the contrary here.

A dissenting opinion by Justice Thomas, joined by Justices Scalia and Kennedy stated:

The Court's innovation is baseless. The Court derives its assumption from the entirely different, and well-recognized, canon against extraterritorial application of federal statutes: "It is a longstanding principle of American law that legislation of Congress, unless a contrary intent appears, is meant to apply only within the territorial jurisdiction of the United States." *EEOC* v. *Arabian American Oil Co.,* 499 U.S. 244, 248 (1991) * * *. But the majority rightly concedes that the canon against extraterritoriality itself "does not apply directly to this case." * * * Though foreign as well as domestic convictions trigger § 922(g)(1)'s prohibition, the statute criminalizes gun possession in this country, not abroad. In prosecuting Small, the Government is enforcing a domestic criminal statute to punish domestic criminal conduct. * * *

The Court never convincingly explains its departure from the natural meaning of § 922(g)(1). Instead, it institutes the troubling rule that "any" does not really mean "any," but may mean "some subset of 'any,'" even if nothing in the context so indicates; it distorts the established canons against extraterritoriality and absurdity; it faults without reason Congress' use of foreign convictions to gauge dangerousness and culpability; and it employs discredited methods of determining congressional intent.

PROBLEM FOUR

Lynn was despondent over the loss of a job and other problems. Lynn wrote a detailed "Manifesto" outlining a planned attack on spectators at a major sporting event the next week that would lead the police to use deadly force against Lynn to stop the attack, resulting in what is known as "suicide by cop." The Manifesto explained why life had become too difficult and asked forgiveness for the pain that attack caused to others. The day before the planned attack, Lynn mailed an envelope containing the Manifesto to a local television station. The next evening, shortly before the sporting event, Lynn had a change of heart and decided not to carry out the attack. After reading the Manifesto, the television station manager notified the police and turned over the contents. Lynn was arrested and charged with violating a federal law, 18 U.S.C. § 876(c), which provides: "Whoever knowingly so deposits or causes to be delivered . . . any communication . . . addressed to any other person and containing any threat to kidnap any person or any threat to injure the person of the addressee or of another" shall be punished by up to five years in prison. Lynn files a motion to dismiss the charge on the ground that the mailing did not come within the statutory prohibition. What argument(s) will defense counsel make that Lynn's conduct did not violate § 876(c), and how will the prosecutor respond? Does it affect the analysis that the Dictionary Act, 1 U.S.C. § 1, provides that "the words 'person' and 'whoever' include corporations, companies, associations, firms, partnerships, societies, and joint stock companies, as well as individuals."?

PROBLEM FIVE

A bicyclist was riding to work one morning. While riding through a crosswalk, a taxi drove directly in front of the bicyclist, and the bicycle hit the cab's rear passenger door. The bicyclist was unharmed by the accident. The taxi driver was charged with one count of failing to yield the right-of-way to a pedestrian in a crosswalk. The criminal statute provides: "When official traffic-control signals are not in place or not in operation, the driver of a vehicle shall stop and give the right-of-way to a pedestrian crossing the roadway within any marked crosswalk or unmarked crosswalk at an intersection." There was no stoplight at the intersection where the accident occurred, and the bicycle was in the crosswalk at the time. A state traffic regulation provides: "A person propelling a bicycle upon and along a sidewalk or while crossing a roadway in a crosswalk shall have all the rights and duties applicable to a pedestrian under the same circumstances, except that the bicyclist must yield to pedestrians on the sidewalk or crosswalk." What argument(s) will defense counsel make that the taxi driver's conduct did not violate statute, and how will the prosecutor respond? Would it change the argument(s) if the person was riding a skate board through the crosswalk when the accident occurred?

B. Vagueness

Columbus v. Kim
886 N.E.2d 217 (Ohio 2008)

PFEIFER, J.

Defendant-appellant Rebecca Kim was convicted of harboring an unreasonably loud or disturbing animal in violation of Columbus City Code 2327.14. Kim argues that Columbus City Code 2327.14 is unconstitutionally vague. We disagree and affirm the decision of the court of appeals.

Kim's neighbor, Joseph Berardi, testified that on May 13, 2004, Kim's dog barked constantly from approximately 4:30 p.m. until approximately 6:00 p.m. Berardi stated that the dog barked so loudly that it could be heard over the sound of his lawn mower and from inside his house with the windows closed and the air conditioning running. Dr. George H. Urham Jr., a veterinarian, testified that on May 13, 2004, he made a house call at the Berardi residence to vaccinate Berardi's dogs and that from just before 5:00 p.m., when he arrived, until just before 6:00 p.m., when he departed, the dog in Kim's yard had barked incessantly.

Kim was charged with violating Columbus City Code 2327.14 by harboring an unreasonably loud or disturbing animal. The trial court concluded that the duration and intensity of the dog's barking were sufficient to establish a violation of Columbus City Code 2327.14 and convicted Kim and imposed a fine of $100 plus costs.

Kim appealed, alleging that the ordinance is unconstitutionally vague. The court of appeals affirmed the decision of the trial court, concluding that Columbus City Code 2327.14 contained sufficient standards to place a person of ordinary intelligence on notice of what conduct the ordinance prohibited.

The court of appeals found its judgment in this case to be in conflict with the judgment of the Eleventh District Court of Appeals in *State v. Ferraiolo* (2000), 748 N.E.2d 584, and certified the record to this court for review and final determination. We determined that a conflict exists on the following issue: "Whether an ordinance that prohibits a person from keeping or harboring an animal which 'howls, barks, or emits audible sounds that are unreasonably loud or disturbing which are of such character, intensity, and duration as to disturb the peace and quiet of the neighborhood or to be detrimental to the life and health of any individual' is unconstitutionally vague on its face and as applied."

Columbus City Code 2327.14(A) states that "[n]o person shall keep or harbor any animal which howls, barks, or emits audible sounds that are unreasonably loud or disturbing and which are of such character, intensity and duration as to disturb the peace and quiet of the neighborhood or to be detrimental to life and health of any individual."

Kim asserts that Columbus City Code 2327.14 is unconstitutionally vague on its face and as applied. In *State v. Anderson* (1991), 566 N.E.2d 1224, quoting *Coates v. Cincinnati* (1971), 402 U.S. 611, we stated that "[i]n order to prove such an assertion, the challenging party must show that the statute is vague 'not in the sense that it requires a person to conform his conduct to an imprecise but comprehensible normative standard, but rather in the sense that no standard of conduct is specified at all.'" In other words, the challenger "must show that upon examining the statute, an individual of ordinary intelligence would not understand what he is required to do" and "must prove, beyond a reasonable doubt, that the statute was so unclear that he could not reasonably understand that it prohibited the acts in which he engaged."

Kim asks us to adopt the reasoning of *Ferraiolo*, in which the owner's conviction for violating an ordinance virtually identical to Columbus City Code 2327.14 was reversed by the court of appeals because it concluded that the ordinance was impermissibly vague. The court of appeals stated that "all dogs will bark or emit audible sounds at one time or another" and that the reasonableness of the noise is a subjective matter that could vary from person to person given their different sensitivities. The court of appeals questioned how anyone can be expected to know whether his dog's barks are of such an intensity and duration as to disturb the peace and quiet of the neighborhood and concluded that the ordinance offered no standard that could be used to determine what constituted a violation.

But *Ferraiolo* is not before us, and it does not control our decision. We conclude that Columbus City Code 2327.14 is not unconstitutionally vague, because it sets forth sufficient standards to place a person of ordinary intelligence on notice of what conduct the ordinance prohibits. The ordinance incorporates an objective standard by prohibiting only those noises that are "unreasonably loud or disturbing." The ordinance provides specific factors to be considered to gauge the level of the disturbance, namely, the "character, intensity and duration" of the disturbance. Further, we recognize that "there are limitations in the English language with respect to being both specific and manageably brief, and it seems to us that although the prohibitions may not satisfy those intent on finding fault at any cost, they are set out in terms that the ordinary person exercising ordinary common sense can sufficiently understand and comply with." *United States Civ. Serv. Comm. v. Natl. Assn. of Letter Carriers, AFL-CIO* (1973), 413 U.S. 548. We conclude that Kim has not proven that Columbus City Code 2327.14 provides "no standard of conduct * * * at all." Accordingly, we hold that Columbus City Code 2327.14 is not unconstitutionally vague on its face.

Nothing in the record suggests that the constant barking of Kim's dog for over one hour was not "unreasonably loud or disturbing" or not "of such a character, intensity and duration as to disturb the peace and quiet of the neighborhood." We are convinced that a person of ordinary intelligence would understand that Columbus City Code 2327.14 prohibits her from allowing her dog to bark nonstop for over an hour at a level that can be heard while using a lawnmower. Kim had not proven "beyond a reasonable doubt, that the statute [is] so unclear that [she] could not reasonably understand that it prohibited the acts in which [she] engaged." *Anderson.*

Accordingly, we conclude that Columbus City Code 2327.14 is not unconstitutionally vague as applied * * * and affirm the judgment of the court of appeals.

NOTES

1. *Clarity.* Statutes are required to be clear. What constitutes sufficient clarity, however, is a matter of judicial interpretation. The basic rule is that a statute cannot be so "vague that men of common intelligence must necessarily guess at its meaning and differ as to its application." *Connally v. General Construction Co.*, 269 U.S. 385 (1926). A court considering a vagueness challenge asks whether a "person of ordinary intelligence" can understand the terms used by the legislature, but not whether the particular defendant in fact knew what the statute means. If a statute is so vague that a broad array of conduct can violate the statute, then the law has given the police and prosecutor unfettered discretion in deciding its application and it is unconstitutional as vague. If a statutory term has been interpreted narrowly by the courts, then the police and prosecutor know what type of conduct will be subject to the law. As such court precedent can play an important part in finding a statute constitutional and not vague.

2. *Reasonableness.* The Ohio Court of Appeals in *Ferraiolo* described how the legislature could have overcome the perceived vagueness problem in the dog barking statute that was identical to the Columbus statute:

> Further guidance needs to be included in such an ordinance. For example, length of time that a dog is barking could be included, as well as certain prohibited hours during a given day. Additionally, perhaps a certain decibel restriction could lend further guidance. In short, an ordinance needs to be crafted so as to provide a person of average intelligence guidelines that could be followed. We acknowledge that this is not a simple task.

Should a legislature be required to provide such a degree of specificity? The term "reasonable" is quite common in both criminal and tort law, so the legislature may view the term as an acceptable shorthand for prescribing conduct without going to the lengths recommended in *Ferraiolo*. One potential problem with the reasonableness standard is the "slippery slope" issue that a court may face in applying this provision. For example, if Ms. Kim's dog had barked loudly for sixty minutes, would that have been unreasonable? Does the time of day or night of barking make a difference?

3. ***Protections Afforded by Prohibiting Vague Statutes.*** A California statute provided that persons who loiter or wander must provide "credible and reliable" identification when requested by a police officer. The Supreme Court, in *Kolender v. Lawson*, 461 U.S. 352 (1983), struck down the statute. The Court emphasized three protections afforded by the vagueness doctrine: (a) to allow people to arrange their conduct so as to steer clear of unlawful acts, (b) to prevent arbitrary and discriminatory enforcement of laws by police officers, judges and juries, and (c) to avoid limiting the freedom of speech and expression.

4. ***Overbreadth***. The doctrine of overbreadth intersects with the principles underlying the First Amendment's protections of freedom of speech, expression, assembly, association and the freedom to travel. Criminal statutes may not infringe on those constitutionally protected rights. Nevertheless, as the Supreme Court has noted, "[r]arely, if ever, will an overbreadth challenge succeed against a law or regulation that is not specifically addressed to speech or to conduct necessarily associated with speech such as picketing or demonstrating." *Virginia v. Hicks* 539 U.S. 113 (2003). In addition, the First Amendment does not protect certain forms of speech: for example, "fighting" words which by their nature "inflict injury or tend to incite an immediate breach of the peace." *Chaplinsky v. New Hampshire*, 315 U.S. 568 (1942). Thus, a criminal statute prohibiting disorderly conduct would not be overbroad if it punished "fighting words" which provoked an "immediate breach of the peace."

PROBLEM SIX

A law enforcement officer reported witnessing a Chevrolet Corvette driving at a high rate of speed. Another vehicle was following behind the Corvette, also at a high rate of speed. The vehicles were not driving side-by-side, and were traveling at a maximum speed of 130 m.p.h. in a 65 m.p.h. zone while weaving through traffic. The vehicles eventually slowed, pulled side-by-side, and then accelerated back to 90 m.p.h. The officer stopped the Corvette and arrested the driver for racing on a highway. The statute prohibiting racing defines it as "the use of one or more motor vehicles in an attempt to outgain or outdistance another motor vehicle, to prevent another motor vehicle from passing, to arrive at a given destination ahead of another motor vehicle or motor vehicles, or to test the physical stamina or endurance of drivers over long-distance driving routes." A violation is punishable by a $500 fine and a one-year suspension of the driver's license. The criminal information states that "the defendant was driving at a high rate of speed with another vehicle." Defendant files a motion to dismiss the charge because the statute is unconstitutionally vague. What arguments will defense counsel make in support of the motion to dismiss, and how will the government respond?

C. Federalism

Jones v. United States
529 U.S. 848 (2000)

Justice GINSBURG delivered the opinion of the Court.

On February 23, 1998, petitioner Dewey Jones tossed a Molotov cocktail through a window into a home in Fort Wayne, Indiana, owned and occupied by his cousin. No one was injured in the ensuing fire, but the blaze severely damaged the home. A federal grand jury returned a three-count indictment charging Jones with arson, 18 U.S.C. § 844(i); using a destructive device during and in relation to a crime of violence (the arson), 18 U.S.C. § 924(c); and making an illegal destructive device, 26 U.S.C. § 5861(f). Jones was tried under that indictment in the Northern District of Indiana and convicted by a jury on all three counts. [Jones received a 35 year prison term and was ordered to pay $77,396.87 to the insurer of the damaged home as restitution.]

Jones unsuccessfully urged, both before the District Court and on appeal to the Seventh Circuit, that § 844(i), when applied to the arson of a private residence, exceeds the authority vested in Congress under the Commerce Clause of the Constitution, Art. I, § 8, cl. 3. Courts of Appeals have divided both on the question whether § 844(i) applies to buildings not used for commercial purposes, and on the constitutionality of such an application. * * *

[The question presented is] whether, in light of *United States v. Lopez,* 514 U.S. 549 (1995) and the interpretive rule that constitutionally doubtful construc-tions should be avoided, see *Edward J. DeBartolo Corp. v. Florida Gulf Coast Building & Constr. Trades Council,* 485 U.S. 568 (1988), 18 U.S.C. § 844(i) applies to the arson of a private residence; and if so, whether its application to the private residence in the present case is constitutional.

Satisfied that § 844(i) does not reach an owner-occupied residence that is not used for any commercial purpose, we reverse the Court of Appeals' judgment.

Congress enacted 18 U.S.C. § 844(i) as part of Title XI of the Organized Crime Control Act of 1970, Pub.L. 91-452, § 1102, 84 Stat. 952, "because of the need 'to curb the use, transportation, and possession of explosives.'" * * * The word "fire," which did not appear in § 844(i) as originally composed, was introduced by statutory amendment in 1982. As now worded, § 844(i) reads in relevant part:

> Whoever maliciously damages or destroys, or attempts to damage or destroy, by means of fire or an explosive, any building, vehicle, or other real or personal property used in interstate or foreign commerce or in any activity affecting interstate or foreign commerce shall be imprisoned for not less than 5 years and not more than 20 years, fined under this title, or both . . . .

We previously construed § 844(i) in *Russell v. United States,* 471 U.S. 858 (1985), and there held that § 844(i) applies to a building "used as rental property." The petitioner-defendant in *Russell* had unsuccessfully attempted to set fire to a two-unit apartment building he owned. He earned rental income from the property and "treated it as business property for tax purposes."* * * Our decision stated as the dispositive fact: "Petitioner was renting his apartment building to tenants at the time he attempted to destroy it by fire." It followed from that fact, the *Russell* opinion concluded, that "[t]he property was . . . being used in an activity affecting commerce within the meaning of § 844(i)." * * *

We now confront a question that was not before the Court in *Russell:* Does § 844(i) cover property occupied and used by its owner not for any commercial venture, but as a private residence. Is such a dwelling place, in the words of § 844(i), "used in . . . any activity affecting . . . commerce"?

In support of its argument that § 844(i) reaches the arson of an owner-occupied private residence, the Government relies principally on the breadth of the statutory term "affecting . . . commerce," * * *, words that, when unqualified, signal Congress' intent to invoke its full authority under the Commerce Clause. But § 844(i) contains the qualifying words "used in" a commerce-affecting activity. The key word is "used." "Congress did not define the crime described in § 844(i) as the explosion of a building whose damage or destruction might affect interstate commerce . . . ."* * * Congress "require[d] that the damaged or destroyed property must itself have been used in commerce or in an activity affecting commerce." * * * The proper inquiry, we agree, "is into the function of the building itself, and then a determination of whether that function affects interstate commerce." * * *

The Government urges that the Fort Wayne, Indiana, residence into which Jones tossed a Molotov cocktail was constantly "used" in at least three "activit[ies] affecting commerce." First, the homeowner "used" the dwelling as collateral to obtain and secure a mortgage from an Oklahoma lender; the lender, in turn, "used" the property as security for the home loan. Second, the homeowner "used" the residence to obtain a casualty insurance policy from a Wisconsin insurer. That policy, the Government points out, safeguarded the interests of the homeowner and the mortgagee. Third, the homeowner "used" the dwelling to receive natural gas from sources outside Indiana. * * *

The Government correctly observes that § 844(i) excludes no particular type of building (it covers "any building"); the provision does, however, require that the building be "used" in an activity affecting commerce. That qualification is most sensibly read to mean active employment for commercial purposes, and not merely a passive, passing, or past connection to commerce. Although "variously defined," the word "use," in legislation as in conversation, ordinarily signifies "active employment." *Bailey v. United States,* 516 U.S. 137 (1995); see also *Asgrow Seed Co. v. Winterboer,* 513 U.S. 179 (1995) ("When terms used in a statute are undefined, we give them their ordinary meaning.").

It surely is not the common perception that a private, owner-occupied residence is "used" in the "activity" of receiving natural gas, a mortgage, or an insurance policy. * * * The Government does not allege that the Indiana residence involved in this case served as a home office or the locus of any commercial undertaking. The home's only "active employment," so far as the record reveals, was for the everyday living of Jones's cousin and his family.

Our decision in *Russell* does not warrant a less "use"-centered reading of § 844(i). In that case, which involved the arson of property rented out by its owner, * * * the Court referred to the recognized distinction between legislation limited to activities "in commerce" and legislation invoking Congress' full power over activity substantially "affecting . . . commerce." The *Russell* opinion went on to observe, however, that "[b]y its terms," § 844(i) applies only to "property that is 'used' in an 'activity' that affects commerce. * * * "The rental of real estate," the Court then stated, "is unquestionably such an activity." * * * Here, as earlier emphasized, the owner used the property as his home, the center of his family life. He did not use the residence in any trade or business.

Were we to adopt the Government's expansive interpretation of § 844(i), hardly a building in the land would fall outside the federal statute's domain. Practically every building in our cities, towns, and rural areas is constructed with supplies that have moved in interstate commerce, served by utilities that have an interstate connection, financed or insured by enterprises that do business across state lines, or bears some other trace of interstate commerce. * * *

Our reading of § 844(i) is in harmony with the guiding principle that "where a statute is susceptible of two constructions, by one of which grave and doubtful constitutional questions arise and by the other of which such questions are avoided, our duty is to adopt the latter." In *Lopez,* this Court invalidated the Gun-Free

School Zones Act, former 18 U.S.C. § 922(q), which made it a federal crime to possess a firearm within 1,000 feet of a school. The defendant in that case, a 12th-grade student, had been convicted for knowingly possessing a concealed handgun and bullets at his San Antonio, Texas, high school, in violation of the federal Act. Holding that the Act exceeded Congress' power to regulate commerce, the Court stressed that the area was one of traditional state concern, * * * and that the legislation aimed at activity in which "neither the actors nor their conduct has a commercial character," * * *

Given the concerns brought to the fore in *Lopez*, it is appropriate to avoid the constitutional question that would arise were we to read § 844(i) to render the "traditionally local criminal conduct" in which petitioner Jones engaged "a matter for federal enforcement." * * * Our comprehension of § 844(i) is additionally reinforced by other interpretive guides. We have instructed that "ambiguity concerning the ambit of criminal statutes should be resolved in favor of lenity," *Rewis v. United States,* 401 U.S. 808 (1971), and that "when choice has to be made between two readings of what conduct Congress has made a crime, it is appropriate, before we choose the harsher alternative, to require that Congress should have spoken in language that is clear and definite," *United States v. Universal C.I.T. Credit Corp.,* 344 U.S. 218 (1952). We have cautioned, as well, that "unless Congress conveys its purpose clearly, it will not be deemed to have significantly changed the federal-state balance" in the prosecution of crimes. * * * To read § 844(i) as encompassing the arson of an owner-occupied private home would effect such a change, for arson is a paradigmatic common-law state crime. * * *

We conclude that § 844(i) is not soundly read to make virtually every arson in the country a federal offense. We hold that the provision covers only property currently used in commerce or in an activity affecting commerce. The home owned and occupied by petitioner Jones's cousin was not so used–it was a dwelling place used for everyday family living. As we read § 844(i), Congress left cases of this genre to the law enforcement authorities of the States.

Our holding that § 844(i) does not cover the arson of an owner-occupied dwelling means that Jones's § 844(i) conviction must be vacated. Accordingly, the judgment of the Court of Appeals is reversed, and the case is remanded for further proceedings consistent with this opinion.

Justice STEVENS, with whom Justice THOMAS joins, concurring.

* * * The fact that petitioner received a sentence of 35 years in prison when the maximum penalty for the comparable state offense was only 10 years,* * * illustrates how a criminal law like this may effectively displace a policy choice made by the State. Even when Congress has undoubted power to pre-empt local law, we have wisely decided that "unless Congress conveys its purpose clearly, it will not be deemed to have significantly changed the federal-state balance." * * *

For this reason, I reiterate my firm belief that we should interpret narrowly federal criminal laws that overlap with state authority unless congressional intention to assert its jurisdiction is plain. * * *

D. Other Constitutional Limitations

1. **Due Process Right to Privacy**. In *Lawrence v. Texas*, 539 U.S. 558 (2003), the Supreme Court ruled unconstitutional a Texas statute that provided: "[a] person commits an offense if he engages in deviate sexual intercourse with another individual of the same sex." The case arose when:

> In Houston, Texas, officers of the Harris County Police Department were dispatched to a private residence in response to a reported weapons disturbance. They entered an apartment where one of the petitioners, John Geddes Lawrence, resided. * * * The officers observed Lawrence and another man, Tyron Garner, engaging in a sexual act. The two petitioners were arrested, held in custody over night, and charged and convicted before a Justice of the Peace.

In reaching its decision that the statute violated the right to privacy guaranteed by the Due Process Clause of the Fourteenth Amendment, the Court overruled its earlier decision in *Bowers v. Hardwick*, 478 U.S. 186 (1985). In discussing the *Bowers* decision the Court stated:

> To say that the issue in *Bowers* was simply the right to engage in certain sexual conduct demeans the claim the individual put forward, just as it would demean a married couple were it to be said marriage is simply about the right to have sexual intercourse. The laws involved in *Bowers* and here are, to be sure, statutes that purport to do no more than prohibit a particular sexual act. Their penalties and purposes, though, have more far- reaching consequences, touching upon the most private human conduct, sexual behavior, and in the most private of places, the home. The statutes do seek to control a personal relationship that, whether or not entitled to formal recognition in the law, is within the liberty of persons to choose without being punished as criminals.

In discussing the presence of anti-sodomy laws enacted by legislatures, the Court found:

> Laws prohibiting sodomy do not seem to have been enforced against consenting adults acting in private. A substantial number of sodomy prosecutions and convictions for which there are surviving records were

for predatory acts against those who could not or did not consent, as in the case of a minor or the victim of an assault. As to these, one purpose for the prohibitions was to ensure there would be no lack of coverage if a predator committed a sexual assault that did not constitute rape as defined by the criminal law. Thus the model sodomy indictments presented in a 19th-century treatise, * * * addressed the predatory acts of an adult man against a minor girl or minor boy. Instead of targeting relations between consenting adults in private, 19th-century sodomy prosecutions typically involved relations between men and minor girls or minor boys, relations between adults involving force, relations between adults implicating disparity in status, or relations between men and animals.

In discussing the effect of criminalizing such conduct, the Court noted the moral stigma attached to it even if there were no prosecutions:

Equality of treatment and the due process right to demand respect for conduct protected by the substantive guarantee of liberty are linked in important respects, and a decision on the latter point advances both interests. If protected conduct is made criminal and the law which does so remains unexamined for its substantive validity, its stigma might remain even if it were not enforceable as drawn for equal protection reasons. When homosexual conduct is made criminal by the law of the State, that declaration in and of itself is an invitation to subject homosexual persons to discrimination both in the public and in the private spheres. The central holding of *Bowers* has been brought in question by this case, and it should be addressed. Its continuance as precedent demeans the lives of homosexual persons.

2. **Ex Post Facto.** The Constitution prohibits ex post facto (after the fact) laws. U.S. CONST., Art. 1, § 9, 10. In *Calder v. Bull*, 3 U.S. 386 (1798), the Court stated:

I will state what laws I consider ex post facto laws, within the words and the intent of the prohibition. 1st. Every law that makes an action, done before the passing of the law, and which was innocent when done, criminal; and punishes such action. 2nd. Every law that aggravates a crime, or makes it greater than it was, when committed. 3rd. Every law that changes the punishment, and inflicts a greater punishment, than the law annexed to the crime, when committed. 4th. Every law that alters the legal rules of evidence, and receives less, or different, testimony, than the law required at the time of the commission of the offence, in order to convict the offender. All these, and similar laws, are manifestly unjust and oppressive. * * *

3. **Bill of Attainder.** The Constitution prohibits Bills of Attainder. U.S. CONST., Art. 1, § 9, 10. "A bill of attainder is special legislation that declares a specific person to be guilty of a crime and subject to punishment without either a trial or conviction." JOSHUA DRESSLER, UNDERSTANDING CRIMINAL LAW 41 (3d ed. 2001).

PART TWO
ELEMENTS OF A CRIME

Chapter 3
Actus Reus

§ 3.01 The Act

Martin v. State
17 So. 2d 427 (Ala. Ct. App. 1944)

SIMPSON, Judge:

Appellant was convicted of being drunk on a public highway, and appeals. Officers of the law arrested him at his home and took him onto the highway, where he allegedly committed the proscribed acts, viz., manifested a drunken condition by using loud and profane language.

The pertinent provisions of our statute are: "Any person who, while intoxicated or drunk, appears in any public place where one or more persons are present, . . . and manifests a drunken condition by boisterous or indecent conduct, or loud and profane discourse, shall, on conviction, be fined" * * *.

Under the plain terms of this statute, a voluntary appearance is presupposed. The rule has been declared, and we think it sound, that an accusation of drunkenness in a designated public place cannot be established by proof that the accused, while in an intoxicated condition, was involuntarily and forcibly carried to that place by the arresting officer. * * *

Conviction of appellant was contrary to this announced principle and, in our view, erroneous. It appears that no legal conviction can be sustained under the evidence, so, consonant with the prevailing rule, the judgment of the trial court is reversed and one here rendered discharging appellant. * * *

Reversed and rendered.

NOTES AND QUESTIONS

1. ***Elements of a Crime.*** In order to find a defendant guilty of a crime, the government must prove each "element" of the offense. Elements of a crime are the components that, when established, permit a finding of criminal liability. The elements of crimes generally fall into four categories: (1) the act (*actus reus*); (2) the mental state (*mens rea*); (3) causation; and, (4) attendant circumstances. In criminal statutes, the elements will usually — but not always — be spelled out in the language of the provision. In addition, there must be a *concurrence of the elements*, which means that they must be present at the same time for the crime to have taken place. For example, the Texas Court of Appeals noted that for a conviction for driving while intoxicated, "There must be a concurrence of the elements for a crime to have been committed. If a person is intoxicated, but sitting in a parked vehicle, then Texas courts have held that the proof was not legally sufficient to convict a defendant for driving while intoxicated, since the person was not driving or operating the vehicle, even though the person was intoxicated." *Chaloupka v. State*, 20 S.W.3d 172 (Tex. Ct. App. 2000).

2. ***Burglary.*** The common law crime of burglary is a good example of how an offense involves different elements that must be established for a conviction. Under the common law, burglary is the (1) breaking and entering (*actus reus*), (2) the dwelling house (attendant circumstance) (3) of another (attendant circumstance) (4) at nighttime (attendant circumstance) (5) with the intent to commit a felony therein (intent). Causation is also required (see Chap. 5). Additionally, these elements must concur, so that a breaking and entering of a home at night would not be a burglary unless the prosecution can establish that the defendant intended to commit a felony *at the moment* of the entry. Many states have adapted common law crimes to more modern circumstances, and in reviewing a statute the same approach to breaking down the crime into its constituent elements is necessary. For example, the Virginia burglary statute provides: "If any person [in the nighttime enters without breaking or in the daytime breaks and enters . . . a dwelling house . . . or at any time breaks and enters . . . any building permanently affixed to realty] with intent to commit larceny, he shall be guilty of statutory burglary." VA. CODE ANN. § 18.2-91. The statute departs from the common law burglary offense by expanding the attendant circumstances and *actus reus* that can constitute the offense, but the elements must still be present at the time of the entry.

3. ***Model Penal Code - Elements.*** Model Penal Code § 1.13(9)-(10) defines an element of an offense as follows:

(9) "element of an offense" means (i) such conduct or (ii) such attendant circumstances or (iii) such a result of conduct as

(a) is included in the description of the forbidden conduct in the definition of the offense; or

(b) establishes the required kind of culpability; or

(c) negatives an excuse or justification for such conduct; or

(d) negatives a defense under the statute of limitations; or

(e) establishes jurisdiction or venue;

(10) "material element of an offense" means an element that does not relate exclusively to the statute of limitations, jurisdiction, venue, or to any other matter similarly unconnected with (i) the harm or evil, incident to conduct, sought to be prevented by the law defining the offense, or (ii) the existence of a justification or excuse for such conduct;

4. **Wrongful Act.** The term *actus reus* is referred to as "the wrongful act." The Model Penal Code states that "[a] person is not guilty of an offense unless his liability is based on conduct which includes a voluntary act or the omission to perform an act of which he is physically capable." See M.P.C. § 2.01(1).

5. **Voluntary Act.** Simply having an act is not sufficient as seen in the *Martin* case. It is essential that the act be a voluntary act. The Model Penal Code specifies certain forms of conduct that will not constitute an act:

The following are not voluntary acts within the meaning of this Section:

(a) a reflex or convulsion;

(b) a bodily movement during unconsciousness or sleep;

(c) conduct during hypnosis or resulting from hypnotic suggestion;

(d) a bodily movement that otherwise is not a product of the effort or determination of the actor, either conscious or habitual.

M.P.C. § 2.01(2).

6. **Unconsciousness.** When is an act considered to be performed in a state of unconsciousness? In *People v. Newton*, 87 Cal. Rptr. 394 (Cal. Ct. App. 1970), the court stated:

Where not self-induced, as by voluntary intoxication or the equivalent * * * unconsciousness is a complete defense to a charge of criminal homicide * * *. "Unconsciousness,"* * * need not reach the physical dimensions commonly associated with the term (coma, inertia, incapability of locomotion or manual action, and so on); it can exist —

and the above-stated rule can apply — where the subject physically acts in fact but is not, at the time, conscious of acting. * * * Thus, the rule has been invoked in many cases where the actor fired multiple gunshots while inferably in a state of such "unconsciousness" * * * including some in which the only evidence of "unconsciousness" was the actor's own testimony that he did not recall the shooting. * * *

Cox v. Director of Revenue
98 S.W.3d 548 (Mo. 2003)

BENTON, Judge.

The circuit court ruled that the Director of Revenue improperly suspended the driving privileges of Steven R. Cox. The Director appeals. * * *

On Saturday, August 15, 1998, at 10:20 p.m., a police officer discovered Cox sleeping or unconscious, sitting in the driver's seat behind the wheel of a vehicle, in the parking lot of a gas station. Cox was the only person in or around the vehicle. The keys were in the ignition, and the motor was running. Seeing the shift lever in "park," the officer knocked on the window.

Awaking, Cox lowered the window. He had a strong odor of an intoxicating beverage on his breath. His eyes were very bloodshot and watery, and he appeared disoriented. The officer noticed a glass of brown liquid between his legs. At the officer's request, Cox turned off the ignition, exited the vehicle, and tried but failed sobriety tests. The officer arrested him for driving while intoxicated. After *Miranda* warnings, Cox answered "Yes" to the form question, "Were you operating the vehicle?". A subsequent breath test revealed a blood alcohol content of .18 of one percent.

The Director suspended Cox's driving privileges pursuant to section 302.505, RSMo Supp.1997. Cox requested a trial de novo in circuit court. The parties stipulated to admission of the Director's records — including the police reports — subject to Cox's objection that they did not show probable cause for the arrest. At the circuit court, Cox argued that the officer did not observe him "operating" or "driving" the vehicle.

Under section 302.505, the Director shall suspend a driver's license if the arresting officer had probable cause to believe the person was driving a vehicle with a blood alcohol concentration of at least ten hundredths (.10) of one percent.

The term "driving" in section 302.505 is defined in section 577.001.1. The meaning of driving is "physically driving or operating a motor vehicle." Section 577.001.1.

Until 1996, the statutory definition was "physically driving or operating or being in actual physical control of a motor vehicle." Section 577.001.1 RSMo 1994. In 1996, the General Assembly removed the phrase "or being in actual physical control of." 1996 Mo. Laws 593, 617. When the legislature amends a statute, that amendment is presumed to change the existing law. By removing "actual physical control" from the statute, the legislature narrowed its scope. A person is not subject to section 302.505 by simply being in actual physical control of a vehicle while intoxicated. The legislature meant to negate the effect of this Court's holding that "actual physical control" occurs when:

> even though the machine merely stands motionless, . . . a person keeps the vehicle in restraint or [is] in a position to regulate its movements.

State v. O'Toole, 673 S.W.2d 25, 27 (Mo.1984), adopting the definition from *Kansas City v. Troutner*, 544 S.W.2d 295, 300 (Mo.App.1976).

The legislature's re-enactment of the terms "driving" and "operating" in section 577.001 emphasizes that both words have distinct meanings. These words are not further defined in chapters 302 or 577. This Court ascertains the legislature's intent by considering the plain and ordinary meaning of the words in the statute. Absent a definition in the statute, the plain and ordinary meaning is derived from the dictionary.

The dictionary defines drive as "to guide a vehicle along or through." *Webster's Third New International Dictionary* 692 (1993). In this case, Cox was not driving the vehicle, which was motionless. He did not guide it along or through anything.

The dictionary defines operate as "to cause to function usually by direct personal effort: work (~ a car)." Cox meets the bright-line test to operate a car, as he caused its motor to function. Once the key is in the ignition, and the engine is running, an officer may have probable cause to believe that the person sitting behind the steering wheel is operating the vehicle. This is true even if that person is sleeping or unconscious.

In this case, the key was in the ignition, the engine was running, and Cox was sitting behind the steering wheel. Based on these stipulated facts, the officer had probable cause to believe that Cox was operating the vehicle. As no other issues were contested, the Director properly suspended Cox's license.

To the extent that *State v. Cross*, 34 S.W.3d 175 (Mo.App.2000), and *Hoyt v. Director of Revenue*, 37 S.W.3d 356 (Mo.App.2000), hold that the act of turning off the ignition is "operating," they are overruled as that act causes a car not to function. * * *

The judgment is reversed, and the case remanded.

WHITE, Judge, dissenting.

* * * I take no issue with the majority's interpretation of "drive." But the 1996 amendment demonstrates that the legislature intended to de-criminalize and remove administrative consequences in situations where an intoxicated person merely sat behind the wheel of a motionless vehicle, even where the driver is in a position to regulate its movements. The majority's interpretation of "operate" ignores that intent.

"When the legislature amends a statute, it is presumed to have intended the amendment to have some effect." The "legislature's action of repeal and enactment is presumed to have some substantive effect such that it will not be found to be a meaningless act of housekeeping." Because the majority opinion effectively interprets "operate" to cover situations that used to apply under the "actual physical control" term, it is contrary to legislative intent. To give effect to the legislative amendment, "operating" must mean more than keeping restrained a motionless vehicle, even while in a position to operate it. * * *

WOLFF, Judge, dissenting.

This is a close case and I appreciate the principal opinion's attempt to clarify the law as to what it means to operate a vehicle. But, on balance, I agree with Judge White's analysis.

No one wants a person in Cox's condition to drive. That means it should be lawful for him to get in his car, run the engine for heat or air-conditioning, and stay put. There is a risk to Cox of carbon monoxide poisoning when he opts to sleep in his car with the engine running. But that hazard is to him only.

The hazard the legislative change appears intended to avoid is the danger to the public of an intoxicated person actually driving a car. The next time an intoxicated person such as Cox is moved to start a car engine for comfort, perhaps he should then crawl into the back seat for his sobering slumber.

NOTES AND QUESTIONS

1. **Unconsciousness:** The law generally requires that a person be conscious of their act to be held liable for it. Note that Cox was "sleeping or *unconscious"* when the officers arrived at his vehicle. Could he have argued unconsciousness as a defense to the act? Would a voluntary act of placing himself behind the wheel of the vehicle while intoxicated negate this argument?

2. **Timing of Act.** A critical issue in determining whether the defendant's act was voluntary relates both to the definition of the offense and the timing of the defendant's act. In *People v. Decina*, 138 N.E.2d 799 (N.Y. 1956), the defendant was charged with "criminal negligence in the operation of a vehicle, resulting in death." Mr. Decina was an epileptic who suffered a seizure while driving a car, causing the vehicle to careen out of control and striking and killing four children. Of course, the defendant claimed the act resulting in the deaths was involuntary, since he was unconscious as a result of the seizure. He was convicted and appealed. The appellate court rejected the defense, on the ground that the defendant was charged with the "operation of the vehicle" resulting in death and Mr. Decina voluntarily operated the vehicle before he suffered the seizure that led to the deaths. Therefore, the court construed the voluntary act in light of the definition of the offense and broadly interpreted the voluntary act as occurring when the defendant chose to drive the car rather than at the time the car struck the children.

3. **Attendant Circumstances.** The statute requires proof of intoxication, which is described as an "attendant circumstance" and not the "act" element of this offense. An attendant circumstance is an element of the crime that is a condition that must be present at the time of the defendant's action — or inaction, as the case may be — that contributes to the determination that the act is deemed a crime. Many crimes involve proof of a particular attendant circumstance, such as the value of an item taken, the time or location of an act, or the amount of illegal substance involved. An attendant circumstance may also determine whether a crime is a felony or misdemeanor. For example, shoplifting an item worth less than $100 may be a misdemeanor, and a felony if it is worth more than that. In *Cox*, the defendant's intoxication is an attendant circumstance and the government's evidence of intoxication in *Cox* is irrefutable, based on his interaction with the officer and the blood-alcohol test.

4. **Corporate Criminal Liability.** In *New York Central & Hudson Railroad v. United States*, 212 U.S. 481 (1909), the Supreme Court held that a corporation is liable under principles of *respondeat superior* for the actions of its employees. Therefore, for corporate criminal liability the government need only prove that the defendant acted for the benefit of the corporation with the requisite intent for the agent's conduct to be imputed to the corporation so that it will be liable for the crime.

§ 3.02 Omission as Actus Reus

West v. Commonwealth
935 S.W.2d 315 (Ky. Ct. App. 1996)

COMBS, Judge.

This is an appeal from final judgments of the Montgomery Circuit Court sentencing each of the appellants to one year imprisonment. The judgments were based upon jury verdicts finding Appellant Russell West guilty of reckless homicide and his co-defendant, Appellant Ann West, guilty of complicity to reckless homicide. Having considered the arguments of counsel, we affirm the convictions.

Prosecution of the Wests, husband and wife, was precipitated by the death of Lillian West, Russell's fifty-four-year-old disabled sister. The Wests were alleged to have caused Lillian's death by their failure to care adequately for her physical needs and to secure the medical assistance she required.

Lillian West was born with Down's Syndrome and a heart ailment. Throughout most of her life, she was cared for by her mother, Rebekah West. In 1979, Lillian and her mother moved in with the appellants. At that time, Lillian participated in activities at Pathway Shelter, a local health organization providing services to mentally handicapped persons. Activities at this day program encouraged Lillian to develop a more independent lifestyle. With appropriate prompting, she could groom herself, participate in vocational training, and function in social settings. In 1983, Rebekah passed away, and Russell and Ann accepted responsibility for Lillian's care. Later, according to Russell, he became concerned that Lillian was being abused in some manner at Pathway Shelter and notified personnel that she would not continue to participate in the program.

Near Thanksgiving, 1992, according to Russell, Lillian became confined to her bed. He testified that it was at this time that her condition began to decline significantly and that she would not eat. On December 31, 1992, Russell delivered Lillian to the emergency room at Mary Chiles Hospital in Montgomery County. The physician tending to Lillian, Dr. David Gagnon, was alarmed by her condition and discussed the situation with Russell. Unnerved by the conversation, Gagnon referred the matter to a local social worker, who undertook an investigation of the circumstances surrounding Lillian's home environment.

On January 17, 1993, Lillian died at University of Kentucky Medical Center. On March 2, 1993, Russell was indicted for manslaughter in the second degree; Ann was indicted as a complicitor. The indictments were consolidated for trial. At trial, medical witnesses recounted Lillian's horrific physical condition, describing numerous decubitus ulcers (pressure or bedsores) in various stages of development (many severe enough to reveal muscle tissue and even bone), severe malnutrition, and the presence of dried tears and feces upon her body. Physicians attributed the cause of death to sepsis and confluent bronchial pneumonia precipitated by the decubitus ulcers. They testified that caretaker neglect led ultimately to Lillian's death.

* * * A person is not guilty of a criminal offense unless:

(1) He has engaged in conduct which [includes] a voluntary act or the omission to perform a duty which the law imposes upon him and which he is physically capable of performing; and

(2) He has engaged in such conduct intentionally, knowingly, wantonly or recklessly as the law may require, with respect to each element of the offense

. . . .

The Wests present identical issues on appeal. First, they maintain that neither of them had a duty to care for Lillian or to provide her with medical assistance. Thus, they conclude, neither of them could be convicted of an offense based upon the failure to provide such care. In a related argument, they note that the reckless homicide statute underlying their convictions does not, by its terms, impose criminal liability based upon an omission or failure to act. Therefore, they assert, the legislature must have envisioned that an *act* would form the basis of a conviction under the reckless homicide statute rather than a mere omission.

People v. Beardsley, 113 N.W. 1128 (Mich. 1907), a commonly cited case, addresses the issue of criminal ramifications arising from the omission to act where one has a duty to take action to preserve the life of another and that omission results in the death of the person to whom the duty is owed. It provides as follows:

The law recognizes that under some circumstances the omission of a duty owed by one individual to another, where such omission results in the death of the one to whom the duty is owing, will make the other chargeable with manslaughter. This rule of law is always based upon the proposition that the duty neglected must be a legal duty, and not a mere moral obligation. It must be a duty imposed by law or contract, and the omission to perform the duty must be the immediate and direct cause of death . . . . (citations omitted).

* * * We agree that before defendants can be found guilty of either reckless homicide or manslaughter, there must exist a legal duty owed by the defendants to the victim. A finding of legal duty is a critical element of the crime charged. As stated in KRS 501.030 and demonstrated by case law, the failure to perform a duty imposed by law may create criminal liability. Clearly, in the case of reckless

homicide or manslaughter, the duty must be found outside the definition of the crime itself. The duty of care imposed may be found in the common law or in another statute. In this case, that duty statutorily is defined at KRS 209.020(6) as follows:

> "Caretaker" means an individual or institution who has the responsibility for the care of the adult as a result of family relationship, or who has assumed the responsibility for the care of the adult person voluntarily, or by contract, or agreement . . . .

The trial court's instructions required the jury to be convinced beyond a reasonable doubt that Russell West was under a duty to provide Lillian with appropriate care and that he had breached that duty of care before liability could be imposed. The Commonwealth presented substantial evidence from which the jury could have concluded that Russell had assumed the duty of care and that Russell was acting in the capacity of "caretaker" as that term is defined by the provisions of KRS 209.020. Accordingly, the trial court did not err by instructing the jury with respect to reckless homicide and complicity to reckless homicide.

In *Jones v. United States*, 308 F.2d 307 (D.C.Cir. 1962), the court stated as follows:

> There are at least four situations in which the failure to act may constitute breach of a legal duty. One can be held criminally liable: first, where a statute imposes a duty to care for another; second, where one stands in a certain status relationship to another; third, where one has assumed a contractual duty to care for another; and fourth, where one has voluntarily assumed the care of another and so secluded the helpless person as to prevent others from rendering aid.

* * * Russell met the last of the *Jones* tests particularly aptly in voluntarily accepting responsibility for Lillian's care *and thereafter isolating her* from contacts that might have resulted in her aid or assistance. Additionally, Kentucky's Protection of Adults statutes impose a duty on adult caretakers to avoid the abuse, neglect, and exploitation of their charges. Contrary to the appellants' suggestions, we find that Russell's duty of care is well-grounded in the law.

* * * For the foregoing reasons, we affirm the judgments of the Montgomery Circuit Court.

NOTES AND QUESTIONS

1. ***"Mere" Moral Obligation.*** *People v. Beardsley*, quoted in *West*, is a leading, if often criticized, decision on whether an omission can constitute the actus reus of an offense. In *Beardsley*, the defendant did not assist his mistress who took an overdose of drugs shortly before the defendant's wife returned from a trip. The Michigan Supreme Court held that a close personal relationship alone was insufficient to create the requisite legal duty, stating that "[t]his rule of law is always based upon the proposition that the duty neglected must be a legal duty, and not a mere moral obligation." Because the defendant and victim were only secret lovers, he did not owe a legal duty to assist her when she took the pills, although he certainly owed her a moral obligation to provide assistance.

The court's language appears to denigrate moral obligations as somehow less worthy than legal obligations. Why is it that the presence or absence of a legal duty determines whether a person is liable for a criminal offense, when there is a clear moral responsibility to care for another person or prevent them from being harmed, at least if there is little risk from assisting the person? If a person hears a child calling for help, but ignores the cry because it would interrupt watching a favorite television program, would anyone hesitate to condemn the person as immoral if the child died or were seriously injured?

2. ***Model Penal Code § 2.01(3).*** The Model Penal Code provides the following provision for when an omission can constitute a voluntary act triggering criminal liability:

> (3) Liability for the commission of an offense may not be based on an omission unaccompanied by action unless:
>
> (a) the omission is expressly made sufficient by the law defining the offense; or
>
> (b) a duty to perform the omitted act is otherwise imposed by law.

It does not describe what types of duties imposed by law can trigger liability, although the commentary notes that "[l]aws defining the obligation of parents toward infant children provide an illustration."

3. ***Criminal Mistreatment.*** An Oregon statute makes it a crime for a person "in violation of a legal duty to provide care for another person, or having assumed the permanent or temporary care, custody or responsibility for the supervision of another person, intentionally or knowingly withholds necessary and adequate food, physical care or medical attention from that other person." OR. REV. STAT. ANN. § 163.205(a). It further provides that a legal duty "includes but is not limited to a

duty created by familial relationship, court order, contractual agreement or statutory or case law." In *State v. Baker-Krofft*, 239 P.3d 226 (Or. 2010), the Oregon Supreme Court explained that the statute is violated "only if the person with the duty to provide care withholds or keeps back food, physical care, or medical attention . . . ; that is, the statutes rest on the premise that the actor keeps back something (food, physical care, or medical attention) from a person who would not otherwise be able to obtain it for him or herself." The court found that the danger to a defendant's children from "some electrical devices and a space heater positioned on a stack of straw in a chicken coop in the backyard posed potential fire hazards" but did not constitute mistreatment. In *State v. Drown*, 263 P.3d 1057 (Or. Ct. App. 2011), the Oregon Court of Appeals upheld the defendant's conviction for failing to provide vision care for a child who was legally blind and could not see to read.

4. ***Good Samaritan Statutes.*** If the definition of a crime is premised on "conduct which, if duly shown to have taken place, will incur a formal and solemn pronouncement of the moral condemnation of the community," [p. 4] then should society condemn the conduct of someone who fails to assist another in need when there is no appreciable risk to them? Should it at least be considered a crime when someone fails to report the problem to the authorities? See Joshua Dressler, "*Some Brief Thoughts (Mostly Negative) About 'Bad Samaritan' Laws*" 40 SANTA CLARA L. REV. 971 (2000) (discussing the problems with using "Good Samaritan" laws to correct morally reprehensible conduct).

5. ***Duty to Aid.*** Some states have enacted statutes requiring a duty to aid. Consider the Vermont "Duty to Aid the Endangered Act":

> A person who knows that another is exposed to grave physical harm shall, to the extent that the same can be rendered without danger or peril to himself or without interference with important duties owed to others, give reasonable assistance to the exposed person unless that assistance or care is being provided by others.

VT. STAT. ANN tit. 12, § 519(a) (2004). A violation of the statute will result in a $100 fine. Is that punishment sufficient, especially if the person unaided dies?

6. ***Creation of the Danger.*** Courts do recognize a legal duty to report crimes or dangerous situations when the defendant is the cause of the danger and the failure to report results in a death that was preventable. In *State v. Montana Thirteenth Judicial District Court*, 995 P.2d 951 (Mont. 2000), the Montana Supreme Court reviewed a motion to dismiss a negligent homicide prosecution involving a defendant who stabbed the man she was living with, and then failed to call for medical assistance. The defendant claimed that the victim, who died from the wound she inflicted, was abusive so that her use of force against him was justified

as a form of self-defense, and therefore she had no duty to call for medical assistance. The court stated:

> Whether inflicted in self-defense or accidentally, a wound that causes a loss of blood undoubtedly places a person in some degree of peril, and therefore gives rise to a legal duty to either 1) personally provide assistance; or 2) summon medical assistance . . . when a person justifiably uses force to fend off an aggressor, that person has no duty to assist her aggressor in any manner that may conceivably create the risk of bodily injury or death to herself, or to other persons. This absence of a duty necessarily includes any conduct that would require the person to remain in, or return to, the zone of risk created by the original aggressor. We find no authority that suggests that the law should require a person, who is justified in her use of force, to subsequently check the pulse of her attacker, or immediately dial 9-1-1, before retreating to safety.

PROBLEM SEVEN

Jeffrey, who is seventeen years old, witnesses his long-time friend follow a seven-year old girl into the restroom in a restaurant. Jeffrey sees them in a stall but does nothing. A short time later, the girl's body is discovered, and the evidence shows she was sexually-molested. Jeffrey later states that he did not report what he saw to the police because he saw "nothing criminal." He offered the information of what he saw only after his friend was charged with the homicide of the young girl. When asked later why he did not contact the police earlier, he said that "did not want to be the one that takes away my best friend's last day." Should Jeffrey be charged with a crime? Did he commit an act? Should the legislature make his conduct a sufficient act or omission to act for purposes of a crime?

§ 3.03 Possession as Actus Reus

State v. Winsor
110 S.W.3d 882 (Mo. Ct. App. 2003)

ROBERT G. ULRICH, Judge.

* * * Appellant was charged with one count of the Class C felony of possession of a controlled substance on the premises of a county jail. He waived his right to jury trial, and the case was tried before a judge on August 15, 2002. The parties filed a joint stipulation of facts and submitted the case solely on the basis of these facts without presenting any additional evidence at trial. * * * The trial court found Appellant guilty of possession of controlled substance on the premises of the Callaway County Jail. The court sentenced Appellant to three years in the Department of Corrections but suspended execution of sentence and placed him on five years probation. This appeal followed.

Appellant raises one point on appeal. He claims that the trial court erred in convicting him under section 221.111, RSMo 2000, because the evidence which consisted solely of stipulated facts was insufficient to support a conviction in that there was no evidence that Appellant's conduct in possessing the marijuana found in the waistband of his shorts on the premises of the county jail was a voluntary act as defined under section 562.011, RSMo 2000. * * *

Appellant was charged with and convicted of possession of a controlled substance on the premises of a county jail. Section 221.111.1 governs that offense and provides, in pertinent part:

> 1. No person shall knowingly deliver, attempt to deliver, have in his possession, deposit or conceal in or about the premises of any county jail or other county correctional facility:
>
>> (1) Any controlled substance as that term is defined by law, except upon the written prescription of a licensed physician, dentist, or veterinarian;

Under section 562.011.1, RSMo 2000, "a person is not guilty of an offense unless his liability is based on conduct which includes a voluntary act." A voluntary act is defined by section 562.011 as:

> 2. A "voluntary act" is
>
>> (1) A bodily movement performed while conscious as a result of effort or determination; or
>
>> (2) An omission to perform an act of which the actor is physically capable.
>
> 3. Possession is a voluntary act if the possessor knowingly procures or receives the thing possessed, or having acquired control of it was aware

of his control for a sufficient time to have enabled him to dispose of it or terminate his control.[a]

Appellant claims that possession of a controlled substance is inadequate, by itself, to satisfy the elements of the offense. He contends that not only must he have voluntarily possessed marijuana while located on the county jail premises but that he must also have voluntarily been on the county jail's premises. Appellant asserts that his possession of marijuana on county jail premises does not constitute a voluntary act because he was taken onto the county jail's premises against his will. Thus, he claims that a crucial element of the offense is lacking. * * *

A paucity of applicable case law addressing the issue of a voluntary act exists in Missouri. Appellant cites *Martin v. State* [p. 81] as support for his first ground, that the voluntary presence on the county jail premises of the person charged is a crucial element of the crime for which he stands convicted. In *Martin*, the defendant was drinking in his home when police officers seized him, transported him to a public highway and arrested him for public drunkenness. He was later convicted for public drunkenness. The statute defining public drunkenness punished "[a]ny person who intoxicated or drunk . . . appears in any public place . . . and manifests a drunken condition." The Alabama Court of Appeals reversed the conviction because the defendant's presence on the public highway was involuntary. Although reversal was appropriate in *Martin,* it is not appropriate in this case because the voluntary presence of Appellant on county jail premises was not an element of the offense. * * * Rather, Appellant was convicted for his voluntary conduct of possessing a controlled substance in or about the county jail. Appellant's willful possession of a controlled substance itself constitutes the requisite voluntary act. His secreting the substance in or about the county jail, regardless of whether he was present voluntarily, satisfies evidentiary requirements to support the conviction. * * *

Appellant claims that it was not his own conduct that resulted in his presence on the county jail's premises but the arresting officer's conduct in transporting him there. This argument lacks merit because, as noted above, the offense for which Appellant was charged does not require Appellant's voluntary presence on the premises. The statute only requires his voluntary possession of a controlled substance while in or about the county jail.

For his third and final ground in support of his claim that his possession of a controlled substance on county jail premises was not a voluntary act because he

---

[a] The Model Penal Code in § 2.01(4) states that, "Possession is an act, within the meaning of this Section, if the possessor knowingly procured or received the thing possessed or was aware of his control thereof for a sufficient period to have been able to terminate his possession." Ed.

was transported to the county jail against his will, * * * Appellant contends that the statute mandates a voluntary presence at the county jail before he can be convicted under section 221.111. His argument is unavailing. Appellant misconstrues the term "voluntary act" as it applies to the offense of possession of a controlled substance in or about county jail premises. Section 221.111.1(1) prohibits the voluntary act of possessing a controlled substance in or about county jail premises not the act of being involuntarily present on the premises.

Not only does Appellant misconstrue the application of "voluntary act" to the offense charged in this case, but he also applies the wrong definition. Appellant's act of possessing a controlled substance on county jail premises was a voluntary act because he "[had] acquired control of it [and] was aware of his control for a sufficient time to have enabled him to dispose of it or terminate his control." * * *

Subsection 3 provides that possession can be sufficient as a voluntary act. This is needed since possession is not necessarily a bodily movement nor an omission.

To adhere to Appellant's argument would not give effect to the Legislature's intent in enacting subsection three of the statute. "[E]very word, clause, sentence, and provision of a statute must have effect.... [I]t will be presumed that the legislature did not insert idle verbiage or superfluous language in a statute."* * * Because subsection three specifically relates to possession, it governs whether Appellant's conduct in this case constituted a voluntary act.

Whether Appellant's presence on the county jail's premises was voluntary or against his will is irrelevant for purposes of determining whether he committed the offense. To adopt the interpretation of this statute suggested by Appellant would prevent the arrest and conviction of inmates for crimes committed on the jail premises because inmates are not voluntarily present at the jail. "Construction of statutes should avoid unreasonable or absurd results." * * * For that reason, Appellant's interpretation of the statute is not adopted. * * *

A reasonable fact-finder could find on the basis of the evidence presented that Appellant willfully possessed a controlled substance in or about the county jail. For that reason, Appellant's sole point on appeal is denied.

NOTES AND QUESTIONS

1. *Voluntariness.* Could this case have been resolved differently if the focus were on the voluntariness of the defendant's introduction of the substance at the jail as opposed to his possession of the drugs? In *State v. Trippetts*, 43 P.3d 455 (Or. Ct.

App. 2002), the court reversed a conviction for supplying contraband in a jail. The court stated:

> The commentary to the Model Penal Code makes clear that the mere fact that defendant voluntarily possessed the drugs before he was arrested is insufficient to hold him criminally liable for the later act of introducing the drugs into the jail. Rather, to satisfy ORS 161.095(1), the involuntary act must, at a minimum, be a reasonably foreseeable or likely consequence of the voluntary act on which the state seeks to base criminal liability. * * * On these facts, no reasonable juror could find that the introduction of contraband into the jail was a reasonably foreseeable consequence of possessing it.

2. *Involuntarily Brought to Jail*. In *People v. Ross*, 76 Cal.Rptr.3d 477 (Cal. Ct. App. 2008), the California Court of Appeals rejected the defendant's argument that she did not "bring" a firearm into the jail because she was under arrest and brought involuntarily to the facility. The court stated:

> The legislative intent is to deter persons from knowingly bringing deadly weapons into a jail, irrespective of whether they are under arrest or not. Pursuant to respondent's interpretation, the statute would have no deterrent effect as to arrestees who were involuntarily transported to jail. They could knowingly bring deadly weapons into jail with impunity, even though they had deliberately misled law enforcement or correctional officials by denying possession of any weapons.

The Washington Court of Appeals took the opposite approach in *State v. Eaton*, 177 P.3d 157 (Wash. Ct. App. 2008), when it stated "we presume that when the legislature enacted [the possession statute] it did not intend the unlikely, absurd, or strained consequence of punishing a defendant for his involuntary act."

3. *Possession and Control*. Many possession statutes require proof that the defendant actually possess the item, or at least have the ability to exercise dominion or control over the item. How much evidence is sufficient to establish the defendant's dominion or control?

Watson v. State
877 So.2d 914 (Fla.Dist.Ct.App. 2004)

KLEIN, J.

* * * After obtaining a warrant, the police entered the bedroom of an apartment of appellant's grandmother. The officers, when they entered the bedroom, observed

the appellant lying on a bed. Appellant's cousin was standing next to a dresser. They found crack cocaine on top of the dresser and in a dresser drawer.

Appellant's cousin pled guilty to possessing the cocaine with intent to sell. At appellant's trial, the cousin testified that only he lived in the bedroom, and that he had placed the drugs on the dresser and in the drawer while appellant was sleeping in one of the two beds in the bedroom. He further testified that appellant was asleep when the police entered the bedroom and that appellant was not aware of the drugs.

The grandmother testified that the cousin lived in the bedroom, but that the appellant did not, although he was a frequent visitor. She saw him asleep in the bedroom when the police entered. There was no evidence that the appellant lived in the bedroom, had control of it, or was aware of the presence of illegal drugs.

Appellant correctly argues that the state, in order to prove constructive possession under these facts, had to demonstrate that he had control or dominion over the room, citing *Brown v. State*, 428 So.2d 250 (Fla.1983). Although *Brown* is distinguishable on its facts, *Brown* cited with approval *Taylor v. State*, 319 So.2d 114 (Fla.Dist.Ct.App. 1975), in which it was held that a defendant who did not have control or joint control of the premises, but was only a visitor, could not be convicted of possession, unless there was evidence of control over the drugs. Similarly, in *Brooks v. State*, 501 So.2d 176 (Fla.Dist.Ct.App. 1987), we held that a visitor in a bedroom occupied by another could not be guilty of possession of drugs unless there was evidence that the visitor had dominion and control over the drugs.

The state does not disagree with these cases, but contends that the jury could have found from the evidence that the appellant was more than a visitor, emphasizing that it was his grandmother's apartment, that he was there almost every day, and he was sleeping in one of the beds. We disagree that this evidence was sufficient and accordingly reverse the conviction.

§ 3.04 Status or Condition

Robinson v. California
370 U.S. 660 (1962)

MR. JUSTICE STEWART delivered the opinion of the Court.

A California statute makes it a criminal offense for a person to "be addicted to the use of narcotics." * * * This appeal draws into question the constitutionality of that provision of the state law, as construed by the California courts in the present case.

The appellant was convicted after a jury trial in the Municipal Court of Los Angeles. The evidence against him was given by two Los Angeles police officers. Officer Brown testified that he had had occasion to examine the appellant's arms one evening on a street in Los Angeles some four months before the trial.* * * The officer testified that at that time he had observed "scar tissue and discoloration on the inside" of the appellant's right arm, and "what appeared to be numerous needle marks and a scab which was approximately three inches below the crook of the elbow" on the appellant's left arm. The officer also testified that the appellant under questioning had admitted to the occasional use of narcotics.

Officer Lindquist testified that he had examined the appellant the following morning in the Central Jail in Los Angeles. The officer stated that at that time he had observed discolorations and scabs on the appellant's arms, and he identified photographs which had been taken of the appellant's arms shortly after his arrest the night before. Based upon more than ten years of experience as a member of the Narcotic Division of the Los Angeles Police Department, the witness gave his opinion that "these marks and the discoloration were the result of the injection of hypodermic needles into the tissue into the vein that was not sterile." He stated that the scabs were several days old at the time of his examination, and that the appellant was neither under the influence of narcotics nor suffering withdrawal symptoms at the time he saw him. This witness also testified that the appellant had admitted using narcotics in the past.

The appellant testified in his own behalf, denying the alleged conversations with the police officers and denying that he had ever used narcotics or been addicted to their use. He explained the marks on his arms as resulting from an allergic condition contracted during his military service. His testimony was corroborated by two witnesses.

The trial judge instructed the jury that the statute made it a misdemeanor for a person "either to use narcotics, or to be addicted to the use of narcotics * * * * That portion of the statute referring to the 'use' of narcotics is based upon the 'act' of using. That portion of the statute referring to 'addicted to the use' of narcotics is based upon a condition or status. They are not identical. * * * To be addicted to the use of narcotics is said to be a status or condition and not an act. It is a continuing offense and differs from most other offenses in the fact that [it] is chronic rather than acute; that it continues after it is complete and subjects the offender to arrest at any time before he reforms. The existence of such a chronic condition may be ascertained from a single examination, if the characteristic reactions of that condition be found present."

The judge further instructed the jury that the appellant could be convicted under a general verdict if the jury agreed *either* that he was of the "status" *or* had committed the "act" denounced by the statute. * * * "All that the People must show is either that the defendant did use a narcotic in Los Angeles County, or that while in the City of Los Angeles he was addicted to the use of narcotics * * *

The broad power of a State to regulate the narcotic drugs traffic within its borders is not here in issue. * * * Such regulation, it can be assumed, could take a variety of valid forms. A State might impose criminal sanctions, for example, against the unauthorized manufacture, prescription, sale, purchase, or possession of narcotics within its borders. In the interest of discouraging the violation of such laws, or in the interest of the general health or welfare of its inhabitants, a State might establish a program of compulsory treatment for those addicted to narcotics. * * *

It would be possible to construe the statute under which the appellant was convicted as one which is operative only upon proof of the actual use of narcotics within the State's jurisdiction. But the California courts have not so construed this law. Although there was evidence in the present case that the appellant had used narcotics in Los Angeles, the jury were instructed that they could convict him even if they disbelieved that evidence. The appellant could be convicted, they were told, if they found simply that the appellant's "status" or "chronic condition" was that of being "addicted to the use of narcotics." And it is impossible to know from the jury's verdict that the defendant was not convicted upon precisely such a finding. * * *

This statute, therefore, is not one which punishes a person for the use of narcotics, for their purchase, sale or possession, or for antisocial or disorderly behavior resulting from their administration. It is not a law which even purports to provide or require medical treatment. Rather, we deal with a statute which makes the "status" of narcotic addiction a criminal offense, for which the offender may be prosecuted "at any time before he reforms." California has said that a person can be continuously guilty of this offense, whether or not he has ever used or possessed any narcotics within the State, and whether or not he has been guilty of any antisocial behavior there.

It is unlikely that any State at this moment in history would attempt to make it a criminal offense for a person to be mentally ill, or a leper, or to be afflicted with a venereal disease. A State might determine that the general health and welfare require that the victims of these and other human afflictions be dealt with by compulsory treatment, involving quarantine, confinement, or sequestration. But, in the light of contemporary human knowledge, a law which made a criminal offense of such a disease would doubtless be universally thought to be an infliction of cruel and unusual punishment in violation of the Eighth and Fourteenth Amendments. * * *

We cannot but consider the statute before us as of the same category. In this Court counsel for the State recognized that narcotic addiction is an illness. * * *

Indeed, it is apparently an illness which may be contracted innocently or involuntarily * * * We hold that a state law which imprisons a person thus afflicted as a criminal, even though he has never touched any narcotic drug within the State or been guilty of any irregular behavior there, inflicts a cruel and unusual punishment in violation of the Fourteenth Amendment. To be sure, imprisonment for ninety days is not, in the abstract, a punishment which is either cruel or unusual. But the question cannot be considered in the abstract. Even one day in prison would be a cruel and unusual punishment for the "crime" of having a common cold.

We are not unmindful that the vicious evils of the narcotics traffic have occasioned the grave concern of government. There are, as we have said, countless fronts on which those evils may be legitimately attacked. We deal in this case only with an individual provision of a particularized local law as it has so far been interpreted by the California courts. Reversed.

MR. JUSTICE DOUGLAS, concurring.

While I join the Court's opinion, I wish to make more explicit the reasons why I think it is "cruel and unusual" punishment in the sense of the Eighth Amendment to treat as a criminal a person who is a drug addict. * * *

The impact that an addict has on a community causes alarm and often leads to punitive measures. Those measures are justified when they relate to acts of transgression. But I do not see how under our system *being an addict* can be punished as a crime. If addicts can be punished for their addiction, then the insane can also be punished for their insanity. Each has a disease and each must be treated as a sick person. * * *

MR. JUSTICE HARLAN, concurring.

I am not prepared to hold that on the present state of medical knowledge it is completely irrational and hence unconstitutional for a State to conclude that narcotics addiction is something other than an illness nor that it amounts to cruel and unusual punishment for the State to subject narcotics addicts to its criminal law. Insofar as addiction may be identified with the use or possession of narcotics within the State (or, I would suppose, without the State), in violation of local statutes prohibiting such acts, it may surely be reached by the State's criminal law. But in this case the trial court's instructions permitted the jury to find the appellant guilty on no more proof than that he was present in California while he was addicted to narcotics. Since addiction alone cannot reasonably be thought to amount to more than a compelling propensity to use narcotics, the effect of this instruction was to authorize criminal punishment for a bare desire to commit a criminal act. * * *

MR. JUSTICE CLARK, dissenting.

The Court finds § 11721 of California's Health and Safety Code, making it an offense to "be addicted to the use of narcotics," violative of due process as "a cruel and unusual punishment." I cannot agree. * * *

In the instant case the proceedings against the petitioner were brought under the volitional-addict section. There was testimony that he had been using drugs only four months with three to four relatively mild doses a week. At arrest and trial he appeared normal. His testimony was clear and concise, being simply that he had never used drugs. The scabs and pocks on his arms and body were caused, he said, by "overseas shots" administered during army service preparatory to foreign assignment. He was very articulate in his testimony but the jury did not believe him, apparently because he had told the clinical expert while being examined after arrest that he had been using drugs, as I have stated above. The officer who arrested him also testified to like statements and to scabs–some 10 or 15 days old–showing narcotic injections. There was no evidence in the record of withdrawal symptoms. * * * I would affirm the judgment.

MR. JUSTICE WHITE, dissenting.

* * * I am not at all ready to place the use of narcotics beyond the reach of the States' criminal laws. I do not consider appellant's conviction to be a punishment for having an illness or for simply being in some status or condition, but rather a conviction for the regular, repeated or habitual use of narcotics immediately prior to his arrest and in violation of the California law. As defined by the trial court, * * * addiction *is* the regular use of narcotics and can be proved only by evidence of such use. To find addiction in this case the jury had to believe that appellant had frequently used narcotics in the recent past. * * * California is entitled to have its statute and the record so read, particularly where the State's only purpose in allowing prosecutions for addiction was to supersede its own venue requirements applicable to prosecutions for the use of narcotics and in effect to allow convictions for use where there is no precise evidence of the county where the use took place. * * *

NOTE

In **Powell v. Texas,** 392 U.S. 514 (1968), the defendant was convicted under a Texas statute that provided, "[w]hoever shall get drunk or be found in a state of intoxication in a public place, or at any private house except his own, shall be fined not exceeding one hundred dollars." The Supreme Court, per Justice Marshall, distinguished *Robinson* and upheld the conviction over a defense of cruel and unusual punishment stating:

> On its face the present case does not fall within that holding, since appellant was convicted, not for being a chronic alcoholic, but for being in public while drunk on a particular occasion. The State of Texas thus has not sought to punish a mere status, as California did in *Robinson*; nor has it attempted to regulate appellant's behavior in the privacy of his own home. Rather, it has imposed upon appellant a criminal sanction for public behavior which may create substantial health and safety hazards, both for appellant and for members of the general public, and which offends the moral and esthetic sensibilities of a large segment of the community. This seems a far cry from convicting one for being an addict, being a chronic alcoholic, being 'mentally ill, or a leper * * *

Chapter 4
Mens Rea

§ 4.01 Specific Intent-General Intent

United States v. Cortes-Caban
691 F.3d 1 (1st Cir. 2013)

LYNCH, Chief Judge.

We are presented with highly troubling instances of abuses of police power, including the disturbing practice, conducted by certain members of the Mayagüez Drugs and Narcotics Division of the Puerto Rico Police Department, of planting evidence and conducting illegal searches and seizures in violation of the Fourth Amendment.

[Ten officers were charged in a two-count indictment with (1) conspiracy to violate the civil rights of defendants arrested after evidence was planted, and (2) conspiracy to possess with intent to distribute controlled substances. The distribution statute, 21 U.S.C. § 841(a)(1), provides in relevant part: "it shall be unlawful for any person knowingly or intentionally – 1) to manufacture, distribute, or dispense, or possess with intent to manufacture, distribute, or dispense, a controlled substance; or (2) to create, distribute, or dispense, or possess with intent to distribute or dispense, a counterfeit substance." Three officers – Santiago, Cortés, and Domínguez – were convicted for conspiracy to distribute drugs and challenge their conviction on that count.]

The Black Box and the Nefarious Use of its Contents by Certain Police Officers

The underlying criminal acts at issue in this case may be traced back—like so many Pandora-released evils—to a box.

Appellants, members of the Puerto Rico Police Department's Mayagüez Drugs and Narcotics Division (the "Division"), were convicted of fabricating criminal cases against citizens through the planting of controlled substances, leading to such citizens' wrongful arrests based on the fabricated evidence. Several appellants asserted that this was done to meet a department-required weekly quota of arrests.

From 2005 to 2007, Lieutenant Dennis Muñiz served as the director of the Division. He participated and assisted in overseeing this fabrication practice. At trial, Muñiz, testifying as a government witness, stated that the drugs used by the officers for purposes of fabrication typically were stored in a metal black box that generally was under the care and custody of Santiago, a supervisor in the Division. It was Santiago's practice to store the box in a file cabinet in his office. The box contained a mélange of contraband, including crack, cocaine, heroin, aluminum strips, drug paraphernalia, and ammunition rounds. Such contraband was given to agents prior to their execution of a search warrant or other intervention to ensure that an arrest would ensue. Testimony at trial confirmed that Muñiz and Santiago specifically instructed officers to plant drugs if a search or intervention was not "positive," i.e., did not produce valid grounds for arrest. [The court recounted 10 instances in which arrests were made after illegal narcotics were planted at the scene.]

* * * Defendants' conduct here falls within the language of the statute. The jury found that the defendants agreed, voluntarily and knowingly, to take the drugs, either from the black box in Santiago's office or from one another, and to intentionally transfer, and so distribute, those drugs to the victims' persons or property in their proximity. They did this so that the drugs would be "discovered" by officers, giving cause for the victims' arrest. The defendants' acts of transferring the drugs amongst each other and to the victims constitutes an intent to distribute the drugs under § 841(a)(1), which results in a transfer of possession of a controlled substance, in other words, a "distribution."

Specific Intent to Distribute

We turn to the defendants' argument that the evidentiary record does not support a conspiracy with the object of possessing controlled substances with an intent to distribute under 21 U.S.C. §§ 841(a)(1).

As said, specific intent requires a showing that the defendant intended the proscribed outcome as his purpose. In the context of a charge of conspiracy to "possess with intent to ... distribute" controlled substances, 21 U.S.C. § 841(a)(1), the relevant specific intent the defendants must have is a specific intent "to distribute" the controlled substances. The evidence is that there was a transfer of drugs between the officers followed by the planting of drugs to facilitate arrests, which amounts to distribution; it follows that the intent to take those actions satisfies the specific intent requirement of the statute.

The relevant intent here is the "intent to distribute." The dissent argues that because the officers' intent was to fabricate cases by planting evidence, the officers cannot have had the specific intent to distribute the drugs. This argument conflates the specific intent to distribute required by the statute with the very different question of the ultimate objective. Only the former is an element of the statute; the ultimate objective is not a part of the statutory test. That this was Congress's intent is shown not only because there is no reference to the ultimate objective as a matter of statutory language, but also because Congress decided not to make buying or selling elements of the offense. What matters as to specific intent is that the defendant intended to transfer the drugs to someone else.

The dissent also suggests that specific intent to distribute the drugs requires that the defendant intend to either further the incidence of drug abuse or intend to introduce or circulate the drugs into society's illicit drug market channels. This is not the test for specific intent under § 841, and no court has so held. * * *

We conclude that the verdict here was supported by a plausible rendition of the evidence, taken as a whole and in the light most favorable to the prosecution, and so we do not disturb the jury's verdict. We acknowledge that our result is driven by the plain language of the statute and its history, and that Congress may not have anticipated this precise scenario in writing the statute. If Congress disagrees with this outcome, it is free to amend the statute. The defendants' convictions under count two are affirmed. * * *

We are both disturbed and disheartened by the incidents underlying this appeal. Appellants, as police officers, held positions of authority that society regards with admiration and respect, and which it trusts to safeguard our freedoms, not infringe upon them; to protect us from harm, not be the instigator thereof; and to stand the post, not be the cause for the watch. As often echoed, with great power comes great responsibility,[34] and appellants showed themselves susceptible to corruption's tarnishing influence often found lapping at the shores of such power. Simply put, appellants disregarded the honorable integrity of their guardian role, and civil liberties were dealt the tragic blow. We can express no greater disapproval or remorse than this: we are saddened and indignant that today, it falls to us to assume the role of guarding the guardians.

TORRUELLA, Circuit Judge, dissenting [in part].

* * * [M]y colleagues and I agree that the record supports the government's allegations as to count one, *i.e.,* that appellants' actions in planting drugs for the purpose of fabricating criminal cases constitutes a violation of 18 U.S.C. § 241. The government's case charged in count two, however, conspiring to possess with intent to distribute a controlled substance in violation of 21 U.S.C. §§ 841(a)(1) & 846, is a horse of another color.

---

[34] Perhaps one of the best known original sources of this phrase is from the comic book, Spider–Man. *See Amazing Fantasy # 15* (Marvel Comics, August 1962). It is also believed to have possibly originated with Voltaire. *See* Voltaire, et al., 48 *Oeuvres de Voltaire* (Lefèvre, 1840).

* * * On carefully considering the distribution statute's mental state requirement, legislative history, and the historical background surrounding its enactment, I believe that my colleagues' conclusion * * * – that the officers' scheme of possessing and illegally planting controlled substances with the sole intent to fabricate grounds for a target's unlawful arrest is tantamount to possession of controlled substances with an intent to distribute – asks far too much of both Congress's purpose in creating such legislation and the statute's expressly-stated specific intent requirement. * * *

It is a fundamental principle that the trier of fact generally must assess both a defendant's actions and mind-set, splitting a crime into two parts: the *actus reus* of the crime (a physical act or omission, the performance (or lack thereof) of which the legislature has deemed unlawful), and the *mens rea* of the person committing the crime (the defendant's intent or mental state at the time of the crime). When assessing mental intent, courts generally distinguish between two kinds: general and specific.

The former (general intent) requires a showing that a defendant intended to perform a certain act. His mental intent, however, need only be to perform the physical act itself, that is, the *actus reus* of a crime; he need not possess any intent to violate the law.

In contrast, where specific intent is required, a heightened mental state is a *sine qua non*. The government must show not only that a defendant had a general intent to perform a particular act, but also, that he possessed a corresponding mental state when executing such acts. That is, that the defendant performed the offending acts with the specific purpose of producing the law's legally forbidden result, or the desired outcome of executing the *actus reus* was in fact to violate the law.

Notably, § 841(a)(1) is not a crime of general intent, but rather, of specific intent.

Thus, the government shoulders the burden of establishing that the defendants here had the particular purpose of committing the unlawful act of narcotics distribution when in possession of the controlled substances. While there is evidence in the record to support the defendants' possession of controlled substances, no evidence supports the finding that their intent when receiving drugs from "the box" and planting them in their targets' residences was for any other purpose than fabricating false cases.

It is well-accepted that specific intent – an intangible concept – may be established by either direct or circumstantial evidence. Given the challenges presented in proving an individual's subjective mental state, both this court and our sister courts have recognized that a specific intent to distribute controlled substances may be inferred from various factors. These factors include, among others, (1) the quantity of drugs in a defendant's possession, (2) the purity of the drugs at issue, (3) the quantity of cash on a defendant, (4) the manner in which the drugs were packaged, (5) the presence of drug paraphernalia, (6) the lack of any evidence showing a defendant used or consumed the type of drug seized, (7) the presence of firearms, (8) a defendant's history of participation in drug distribution, or (9) a combination of the above. Notably, such precedent for establishing a specific intent to distribute involves factors not present here. Although such cases and their corresponding principles remain relevant for purposes of our analysis, none fall into the more narrow factual scope of our case: police officers planting drugs in order to frame their marks and generate grounds justifying an arrest. ***

Accepting *arguendo* that the officers' physical acts here of planting evidence constitute drug distribution, the only evidence from which the jury could infer an intent to distribute was from the alleged act of distribution itself. I believe such a conclusion in this case presents a two-fold problem.

First, where specific intent is a distinct element of a crime (as here), such element must be proved separately from the actual commission of the crime itself. Thus, even if the officers' case fabrication actions constituted drug distribution as such, the government cannot rest upon this evidence alone to confirm whether the officers held the requisite statutory intent to distribute. Such evidence, while unquestionably relevant, still must be considered in light of the surrounding circumstances.

And secondly, the "surrounding circumstances" of this case consist of the highly disturbing practice of police officers fabricating cases by planting evidence. The officers' constant and unchanging intent—including while driving to the targets' residences, entering their homes, and placing the controlled substances in a location for subsequent seizure—was to create an illusion of law enforcement, that is, catching their victims in a seemingly illegal act, and using the illusion as a justification for an unlawful arrest. The controlled substances here were simply the officers' instrument of choice that they played to their victims' downfall.
The reality is that the officers could have selected from a variety of instruments—swapping narcotics for firearms, ammunition rounds, or even endangered animals—and still have held the same intent (fabricating a case against a target and creating grounds for their arrest) while performing the same physical acts of driving to a home, temporarily depositing their instrument-of-choice in a location, and subsequently retrieving it. I find this to be a noteworthy point.

In reviewing other precedent in which an intent to distribute has been inferred from varying factors such as drug quantity, drug purity, or presence of drug paraphernalia, a switching of drugs with another item would have changed the question of intent entirely. And yet here, if the officers could have executed the same acts with different objects (*i.e.*, not controlled substances) and still satisfied the same intent and achieved the same overall objective, I must ask: how can the officers have held the requisite intent to distribute controlled substances, if without such substances, their intent would have remained the same?

For the officers here to have held an intent to distribute, the court (as it has) would have to accept that an intent to physically pass, move, or pick-up a controlled substance is all that is needed to be shown to establish an intent to distribute * * *. But this, in effect, emasculates the specific intent requirement of § 841(a)(1) such that the crime is degraded to one requiring only a general intent, an unacceptable result under established law. Were § 841(a)(1) the latter, then an intent to perform the *actus reus* of a crime would suffice for liability to attach. But as we have noted, the crime of possession with intent to distribute is one of specific intent requiring a specific *mens rea*.

Having carefully considered the plain language of the statute, I fail to understand the majority's conclusion, the upshot of which dilutes a specific intent crime's mental state requirement to nothing more than a general intent showing.

NOTES

1. ***Common Law Approach.*** At common law crimes were divided into two categories: specific intent and general intent. Specific intent is the higher level, requiring proof that the defendant had a particular state of mind that involved the commission of the offense. General intent is lower, requiring proof that the defendant engaged consciously in the act that constitutes the offense, but the government need not prove that the defendant sought a particular result or was fully conscious that he was committing a crime. Needless to say, the distinction between the two intents is a fine one. In *United States v. Bailey*, 444 U.S. 394 (1980), the Supreme Court summarized the distinction as follows:

> Few areas of criminal law pose more difficulty than the proper definition of the mens rea required for any particular crime. In 1970, the National Commission on Reform of Federal Criminal Laws decried the "confused and inconsistent ad hoc approach" of the federal courts to this issue and called for "a new departure." Although the central focus of this and other reform movements has been the codification of workable principles for determining criminal culpability, see, e. g., American Law Institute, Model Penal Code §§ 2.01-2.13, a byproduct has been a general rethinking of traditional mens-rea analysis.
>
> At common law, crimes generally were classified as requiring either "general intent" or "specific intent." This venerable distinction, however,

has been the source of a good deal of confusion. As one treatise explained:

> Sometimes "general intent" is used in the same way as "criminal intent" to mean the general notion of mens rea, while "specific intent" is taken to mean the mental state required for a particular crime. Or, "general intent" may be used to encompass all forms of the mental state requirement, while "specific intent" is limited to the one mental state of intent. Another possibility is that "general intent" will be used to characterize an intent to do something on an undetermined occasion, and "specific intent" to denote an intent to do that thing at a particular time and place."

W. LaFave & A. Scott, *Handbook on Criminal Law* § 28 (1972) (footnotes omitted).

2. ***Specific Intent/General Intent.*** The difference between specific and general intent can be confusing, as clear lines are often not drawn. Consider the common law burglary statute:

> Breaking and entering the dwelling house of another, at nighttime, with the intent to commit a felony therein.

This is a specific intent crime because the government must prove the defendant's intent to commit a crime at the time of the breaking and entering. If the "intent to commit a felony therein" were omitted, than this would be a general intent crime. Rape, in a jurisdiction where it is defined as "forcible non-consensual sexual intercourse by a man with a woman not his wife," would also be a general intent crime. There is no "extra" mental state requiring the offender to have the purpose to bring about some state of affairs. To redefine rape as a specific intent crime, there would have to be a further mental state added, such as "with the intent to cause serious bodily injury." This does not mean that the rapist is actually required to cause such injury. Having the "intent to cause the serious bodily injury" in rape, just as having an "intent to commit a felony therein" with burglary, is sufficient to make the crime one of specific intent. Absent the added language or the "extra" mental state, the crime is one of general intent. The distinction between general and specific intent crimes can be important in jurisdictions that use a common law approach for the quality of evidence the government must submit and the defenses available to a charge.

§ 4.02 The Model Penal Code

A. Model Statute

§ 1.13. General Definitions

In this Code, unless a different meaning plainly is required: * * *

(2) "act" or "action" means a bodily movement whether voluntary or involuntary;

(3) "voluntary" has the meaning specified in Section 2.01;

(4) "omission" means a failure to act;

(5) "conduct" means an action or omission and its accompanying state of mind, or, where relevant, a series of acts and omissions;

(6) "actor" includes, where relevant, a person guilty of an omission;

(7) "acted" includes, where relevant, "omitted to act"; * * *

(11) "purposely" has the meaning specified in Section 2.02 and equivalent terms such as "with purpose," "designed" or "with design" have the same meaning;

(12) "intentionally" or "with intent" means purposely;

(13) "knowingly" has the meaning specified in Section 2.02 and equivalent terms such as "knowing" or "with knowledge" have the same meaning;

(14) "recklessly" has the meaning specified in Section 2.02 and equivalent terms such as "recklessness" or "with recklessness" have the same meaning;

(15) "negligently" has the meaning specified in Section 2.02 and equivalent terms such as "negligence" or "with negligence" have the same meaning;

(16) "reasonably believes" or "reasonable belief" designates a belief that the actor is not reckless or negligent in holding.

§ 2.02. General Requirements of Culpability.

(1) *Minimum Requirements of Culpability.* Except as provided in Section 2.05, a person is not guilty of an offense unless he acted purposely, knowingly, recklessly or negligently, as the law may require, with respect to each material element of the offense.

(2) *Kinds of Culpability Defined.*

　(a) *Purposely.* A person acts purposely with respect to a material element of an offense when:

　　　(i) if the element involves the nature of his conduct or a result thereof, it is his conscious object to engage in conduct of that nature or to cause such a result; and

　　　(ii) if the element involves the attendant circumstances, he is aware of the existence of such circumstances or he believes or hopes that they exist.

　(b) *Knowingly.* A person acts knowingly with respect to a material element of an offense when:

　　　(i) if the element involves the nature of his conduct or the attendant circumstances, he is aware that his conduct is of that nature or that such circumstances exist; and

　　　(ii) if the element involves a result of his conduct, he is aware that it is practically certain that his conduct will cause such a result.

　(c) *Recklessly.* A person acts recklessly with respect to a material element of an offense when he consciously disregards a substantial and unjustifiable risk that the material element exists or will result from his conduct. The risk must be of such a nature and degree that, considering the nature and purpose of the actor's conduct and the circumstances known to him, its disregard involves a gross deviation from the standard of conduct that a law-abiding person would observe in the actor's situation.

　(d) *Negligently.* A person acts negligently with respect to a material element of an offense when he should be aware of a substantial and unjustifiable risk that the material element exists or will result from his conduct. The risk must be of such a nature and degree that the actor's failure to perceive it, considering the nature and purpose of his conduct and the circumstances known to him, involves a gross deviation from the standard of care that a reasonable person would observe in the actor's situation.

(3) *Culpability Required Unless Otherwise Provided.* When the culpability sufficient to establish a material element of an offense is not prescribed by law, such element is established if a person acts purposely, knowingly or recklessly with respect thereto.

(4) *Prescribed Culpability Requirement Applies to All Material Elements.* When the law defining an offense prescribes the kind of culpability that is sufficient for the commission of an offense, without distinguishing among the material elements thereof, such provision shall apply to all the material elements of the offense, unless a contrary purpose plainly appears.

(5) *Substitutes for Negligence, Recklessness and Knowledge.* When the law provides that negligence suffices to establish an element of an offense, such element also is established if a person acts purposefully, knowingly or recklessly. When recklessness suffices to establish an element , such element also is established if a person acts purposely or knowingly. When acting knowingly suffices to establish an element, such element also is established if a person acts purposely.

(6) *Requirement of Purpose Satisfied if Purpose is Conditional.* When a particular purpose is an element of an offense, the element is established although such purpose is conditional, unless the condition negatives the harm or evil sought to be prevented by the law defining the offense.

(7) *Requirement of Knowledge Satisfied by Knowledge of High Probability.* When knowledge of the existence of a particular fact is an element of an offense, such knowledge is established if a person is aware of a high probability of its existence, unless he actually believes that it does not exist.

(8) *Requirement of Wilfulness Satisfied by Acting Knowingly.* A requirement that an offense be committed wilfully is satisfied if a person acts knowingly with respect to the material elements of the offense, unless a purpose to impose further requirements appears.

(9) *Culpability as to Illegality of Conduct.* Neither knowledge nor recklessness or negligence as to whether conduct constitutes an offense or as to the existence, meaning or application of the law determining the elements of an offense is an element of such offense, unless the definition of the offense or the Code so provides.

(10) *Culpability as Determinant of Grade of Offense.* When the grade or degree of an offense depends on whether the offense is committed purposely,

knowingly, recklessly or negligently, its grade or degree shall be the lowest for which the determinative kind of culpability is established with respect to any material element of the offense.

NOTE AND QUESTION

How does the common law approach differ from the Model Penal Code (MPC) approach? In *Bailey* [p. 108], the court stated:

This ambiguity [in distinguishing between specific and general intent] has led to a movement away from the traditional dichotomy of intent and toward an alternative analysis of mens rea. This new approach, exemplified in the American Law Institute's Model Penal Code, is based on two principles. First, the ambiguous and elastic term "intent" is replaced with a hierarchy of culpable states of mind. The different levels in this hierarchy are commonly identified, in descending order of culpability, as purpose, knowledge, recklessness, and negligence. Model Penal Code § 2.02. Perhaps the most significant, and most esoteric, distinction drawn by this analysis is that between the mental states of "purpose" and "knowledge." As we pointed out in *United States v. United States Gypsum Co.*, 438 U.S. 422 (1978), a person who causes a particular result is said to act purposefully if "'he consciously desires that result, whatever the likelihood of that result happening from his conduct,'" while he is said to act knowingly if he is aware "'that that result is practically certain to follow from his conduct, whatever his desire may be as to that result.'"

B. Purposely

Vermont v. Trombley
807 A.2d 400 (Vt. 2002)

Defendant Matthew Trombley appeals his aggravated assault conviction, claiming several errors in the court's jury instructions. Defendant contends that (1) the court improperly instructed the jury to consider whether defendant acted either "purposely" or "knowingly" when defendant was charged with only "purposely" inflicting serious bodily harm * * * .

Defendant was charged with aggravated assault under 13 V.S.A. § 1024(a)(1). The charge read: "[defendant] was then and there a person who purposely caused serious bodily injury to another, to wit: George Demarais, by knocking some teeth out by repeatedly punching Mr. Demarais in violation of 13 V.S.A. § 1024(a)(1)." The jury convicted defendant of aggravated assault.* * *

Defendant first argues that the jury charge was improper because it instructed the jury to consider whether defendant acted either "purposely" or "knowingly" when defendant was charged with only "purposely" inflicting serious bodily harm. The trial court judge instructed the jury as follows:

"To commit the offense purposely means that [defendant] acted with the conscious purpose of causing serious bodily injury or that he acted under circumstances where he was practically certain that his conduct would cause serious bodily injury."

Defendant argues that because the information charged defendant with only "purposely" causing serious bodily injury, the additional charge regarding whether he acted knowingly allowed the jury to improperly consider and weigh evidence going to whether the defendant acted under circumstances where he was practically certain his conduct would cause serious bodily injury. Defendant argues that a proper jury instruction would have told the jury that to convict defendant it had to find that it was defendant's conscious objective to inflict serious bodily injury on Demarais; if defendant only acted under circumstances where he was practically certain his conduct would result in serious bodily injury to Demarais, the jury could not convict him.

Criminal liability is normally based upon the concurrence of two factors: "an evil-meaning mind" and "an evil-doing hand." *Morissette v. United States*, 342 U.S. 246 (1952). We recognize that one of criminal law's most basic principles is that "a person is not criminally liable for causing a bad result if he or she did not have some culpable mental state with respect to that result." * * * In the instant case, we must examine the mental element, or mens rea, required for conviction under § 1024(a)(1). If the jury instructions failed to charge the proper mental state required for a conviction under aggravated assault, we would find error.

At common law, crimes generally were classified as requiring either "general intent" or "specific intent." This distinction, however, has been the source of much confusion, and in the 1970's a reform movement of sorts began to replace this traditional dichotomy with an alternative analysis of mens rea. The American Law Institute's Model Penal Code exemplifies this new approach. The Code delineates four kinds of culpability: purposely, knowingly, recklessly, and negligently. Model Penal Code § 2.02(2)(a)-(d). In doing so, it abandoned the "specific intent" — "general intent" terminology prevalent in traditional criminal law. W. LaFave, *Criminal Law* § 3.5(e)(2000). * * *

In Act No. 222 of the 1971 Adjourned Session, the Vermont General Assembly enacted 13 V.S.A. § 1024(a)(1), which states that a person is guilty of aggravated assault if he attempts to cause serious bodily injury to another, or causes such injury purposely, knowingly or recklessly under circumstances manifesting extreme indifference to the value of human life. This language is borrowed from the Model Penal Code. We have noted that although the rationale of the Code is not binding on this Court, it is indicative of what the General Assembly intended in adopting the legislation modeled on the Code. * * *

Defendant argues that since the Legislature adopted the Model Penal Code language, which makes a distinction between "purposely" and "knowingly," and because he was charged with only "purposely" causing serious bodily injury, it was erroneous to instruct the jury on the mens rea of "knowingly." We agree.

The modern approach under the Code defines separately the mental states of "purpose" and "knowledge," because there are several areas of the law where it may be critical to distinguish between one's objective and one's knowledge. For example, when a defendant is charged with treason, the government must demonstrate that the defendant acted with a purpose or objective to aid the enemy. *United States v. Bailey*, 444 U.S. 394 (1980). In addition, a heightened mental state in the inchoate offenses of attempt and conspiracy "separates criminality itself from otherwise innocuous behavior." *Id.* (citing Model Penal Code § 2.02, Comments, p. 125 (Tent. Draft No. 4, 1955)). Finally, "the statutory and common law of homicide often distinguishes, either in setting the 'degree' of the crime or in imposing punishment, between a person who knows that another person will be killed as a result of his conduct and a person who acts with the specific purpose of taking another's life." * * * We too conclude that it is important to distinguish between a person who knows another may be seriously injured because of his conduct and a person who acts with the specific purpose of seriously injuring another.

Because the defendant was charged with only "purposely" causing serious bodily injury, the trial court's instruction on the mens rea of "knowingly" was erroneous. We find, however, that beyond a reasonable doubt that error was harmless.

Defendant posits that his conscious objective was not to inflict serious bodily injury, but rather to defend himself against Demarais's knife attack and that the jury instruction on knowingly prevented the jury from considering only this conscious objective. Defendant's argument is premised on the notion that when considering whether defendant had formed the conscious objective to inflict serious bodily injury on Demarais, the jury may also consider defendant's justification for inflicting serious bodily injury. Defendant's attempt to infect the jury's deliberation on his mens rea with consideration of his possible self-defense justification is misplaced. Properly argued, self-defense stipulates that while defendant indeed committed the act, he was nevertheless justified in defending himself, and is not, therefore, guilty of any crime. Defendant bears the burden of producing evidence of his justification. 2 P. Robinson, *Criminal Law Defenses* § 132, at 99 (1984). Defendant's mens rea is not properly considered along with defendant's possible justification for defending himself.

The trial court's inclusion of "knowingly" in the jury instructions was harmless error in the instant case because defendant's own assertion of self-defense established that he acted with the purpose of inflicting serious bodily injury on Demarais. Assuming defendant's only motivation for punching Demarais was to defend himself against Demarais's attack, it was still his primary conscious objective to inflict serious bodily injury in order to achieve that goal. Given that there was a separate jury charge on defendant's claim of self-defense, the jury was properly afforded the opportunity to consider any justification for defendant's actions. While defendant appropriately raises a question as to whether the court erred in failing to distinguish between "purposely" and "knowingly," we do not find defendant's rationale — that this error precluded the jury's consideration of any self-defense justification — persuasive.

NOTE

Even if the trial court makes a mistake, an appellate court is not required to overturn the conviction because it may find that the error was "harmless," *i.e.*, it did not affect the outcome of the trial. Even errors that involve constitutional rights can be found harmless. As the Supreme Court is fond of stating, "[T]he Constitution entitles a criminal defendant to a fair trial, not a perfect one." *Delaware v. Van Arsdall*, 475 U.S. 673 (1986). In *Trombley*, the Vermont Supreme Court determined that including "knowingly" was legally incorrect, but that the defendant effectively admitted that he acted purposely when he argued that his attack on Demarais was in self-defense, which means that it is unlikely the error had any effect on the jury's decision to convict.

C. Knowingly

United States v. Youts
229 F.3d 1312 (10th Cir. 2000)

SEYMOUR, Chief Judge:

Abner Youts appeals from an adverse jury verdict. As the parties' oral arguments showed, the events leading up to his criminal conviction under 18 U.S.C.

§ 1992 for wrecking a train are unusual and give rise to a number of interesting parallels in modern folk music. We begin with the facts.

"He made that freight train boogie, as he rolled down the line."[1]

In the early morning hours of January 10, 1994, after an evening of misadventure, Abner Youts and Richard Nesbitt needed a ride home. The pair set out on foot and ended up at the Union Pacific Railyard in Wichita, Kansas, where they boarded two idling locomotives that were connected together. After playing with the controls, they figured out how to move the trains back and forth. Mr. Youts remarked to Mr. Nesbitt that, as a boy, he had always loved trains and wanted to be an engineer. Mr. Youts then decided to drive the train home.

Upon arriving at a point on the tracks approximately half a block from his house, Mr. Youts stopped the train, let Mr. Nesbitt off, and decided to send the train back through town. He put the train into reverse at full throttle and disembarked. The train got as far as a curve in the tracks in downtown Wichita. The normal speed for this curve is ten miles per hour. The driverless train took it at fifty-six miles per hour and derailed. One locomotive car ended up lying in the street and the other landed on its side in the dirt next to the tracks. Although no one was hurt, the derailment caused Union Pacific and the City of Wichita a total of $ 234,145 in damage and clean-up costs.

As a result of anonymous tips to the Wichita Crimestoppers hotline, investigating authorities learned Mr. Nesbitt and Mr. Youts may have been involved in the offense. Eventually, Mr. Nesbitt gave a confession that detailed their activities on the evening in question and the two men were each indicted on one count of violating 18 U.S.C. § 1992, the federal train wreck statute. Mr. Nesbitt pled guilty and agreed to testify against Mr. Youts. The case against Mr. Youts was tried before a jury, which found him guilty. He was sentenced to 46 months in prison and ordered to pay $ 234,145 in restitution.

This appeal followed. Mr. Youts raises three claims: first, he contends the statute required a showing of specific intent to wreck the train, and the evidence of his specific intent was insufficient to support the jury's determination of guilt; second, he asserts that evidence of his other crimes was improperly admitted; and third, he argues that the district court mishandled an allegation of juror misconduct. For the reasons discussed below, we deny each of these claims. * * *

Although we review a challenge to the sufficiency of the evidence de novo, we do so while viewing the evidence and the reasonable inferences to be drawn therefrom in the light most favorable to the government. * * * We will reverse

---

[1] John Denver, *Choo Choo Ch'Boogie, on* ALL ABOARD (Sony/Wonder 1997).

"'only if no rational trier of fact could have found the essential elements of the crime beyond a reasonable doubt.'" * * *

The federal train wreck statute punishes anyone who "*willfully* derails, disables, or wrecks any train, engine, motor unit, or car used, operated, or employed in interstate or foreign commerce by any railroad." 18 U.S.C. § 1992 (emphasis added). Mr. Youts contends the statute should be read to require proof of a specific intent to disable, derail, or wreck the train. He argues there was no evidence he actually wanted the train to wreck. Rather, he maintains the evidence indicated that he took the train on impulse and that he meant to return it to the station when he was finished.

Section 1992 requires a showing of "willfulness." The term "willful" is frequently used in criminal statutes, but it has a less than clear statutory and common law history. In response to the ambiguity of such common law terms, the Model Penal Code delineated four categories of culpable mens rea, corresponding to actions taken purposely, knowingly, recklessly, or negligently. MODEL PENAL CODE § 2.02(2)(a)-(d). The Model Penal Code parallels many judicial decisions in declaring that knowing conduct is sufficient to establish willfulness. See id. § 2.02(8) ("A requirement that an offense be committed wilfully is satisfied if a person acts knowingly with respect to the material elements of the offense . . ."); see also *United States v. M.W.*, 890 F.2d 239 (10th Cir. 1989) (holding that, for purposes of federal arson statute, "'willfully and maliciously' includes acts done with the knowledge that burning of a building is the practically certain result") * * *

In addition, the legislative history of section 1992 indicates Congress did not intend the statute to contain a specific intent requirement. A House Committee Report on the legislation recommended that the words "and maliciously" be stricken after "willfully," because the committee believed "that the words would place too great a burden on the prosecution of an offense under the bill." *Making it a Crime to Wreck or Attempt to Wreck a Train Engaged in Interstate Commerce*, H.R. REP. NO. 76-2175 (3d Sess. 1940). "Maliciously," like willfully, is a nebulous term. In this context, however, it indicates a heightened level of culpability akin to specific intent. Congress rejected this requirement, and removed the language from the bill. Consequently, the willfulness language in section 1992 is best understood as a knowledge requirement.

"A person acts knowingly with respect to a material element of an offense when[,] . . . if the element involves a result of his conduct, he is aware that it is practically certain that his conduct will cause such a result." MODEL PENAL CODE § 2.02(2)(b)(ii). *Cf. id.* § 2.02(2)(a)(i) ("A person acts purposely with respect to a material element of the offense when[,] . . . if the element involves ... a result [of his conduct], it is his conscious object . . . to cause such a result."). The natural, probable consequences of an act can satisfactorily evidence the state of mind accompanying it. That showing has been met here. The natural, probable, and practically certain consequence of sending a driverless locomotive down curving tracks at full speed will be the result punished by the statute.

In holding that section 1992 does not require specific intent to wreck a train, we are in agreement with every other appellate court to consider this issue * * * Mr. Youts knowingly set in motion — literally and figuratively — the events which caused the train to wreck. That is all section 1992 requires. We hold that the jury was presented with sufficient evidence to find Mr. Youts guilty. * * * AFFIRMED.

D.   Recklessly

People v. Hall
999 P.2d 207 (Colo. 2000)

Justice BENDER delivered the Opinion of the Court.

We hold that Nathan Hall must stand trial for the crime of reckless manslaughter. While skiing on Vail mountain, Hall flew off of a knoll and collided with Allen Cobb, who was traversing the slope below Hall. Cobb sustained traumatic brain injuries and died as a result of the collision. The People charged Hall with felony reckless manslaughter.

At a preliminary hearing to determine whether there was probable cause for the felony count, the county court found that Hall's conduct "did not rise to the level of dangerousness" required under Colorado law to uphold a conviction for manslaughter, and the court dismissed the charges. On appeal, the district court affirmed the county court's decision. The district court determined that in order for Hall's conduct to have been reckless, it must have been "at least more likely than not" that death would result. Because the court found that "skiing too fast for the conditions" is not "likely" to cause a another person's death, the court concluded that Hall's conduct did not constitute a "substantial and unjustifiable" risk of death. Thus, the district court affirmed the finding of no probable cause.

The charge of reckless manslaughter requires that a person "recklessly cause[] the death of another person." § 18-3-104(1)(a), 6 C.R.S. (1999). For his conduct to be reckless, the actor must have consciously disregarded a substantial and unjustifiable risk that death could result from his actions. * * *

We hold that under the particular circumstances of this case, whether Hall committed the crime of reckless manslaughter must be determined by the trier of fact. Viewed in the light most favorable to the prosecution, Hall's conduct — skiing straight down a steep and bumpy slope, back on his skis, arms out to his sides, off-balance, being thrown from mogul to mogul, out of control for a considerable distance and period of time, and at such a high speed that the force of the impact between his ski and the victim's head fractured the thickest part of the victim's skull — created a substantial and unjustifiable risk of death to another person. A reasonable person could infer that the defendant, a former ski racer trained in skier safety, consciously disregarded that risk. * * *

On April 20, 1997, the last day of the ski season, Hall worked as a ski lift operator on Vail mountain. When he finished his shift and after the lifts closed, Hall skied down toward the base of the mountain. The slopes were not crowded.

On the lower part of a run called "Riva Ridge," just below where the trail intersects with another called "North Face Catwalk," Hall was skiing very fast, ski tips in the air, his weight back on his skis, with his arms out to his sides to maintain balance. He flew off of a knoll and saw people below him, but he was unable to stop or gain control because of the moguls.

Hall then collided with Cobb, who had been traversing the slope below Hall * * * Hall's blood alcohol level was .009, which is less than the limit for driving while ability impaired. A test of Hall's blood for illegal drugs was negative.

[After conducting a preliminary hearing to review the evidence], the county court considered whether there was sufficient evidence to find probable cause that Hall recklessly caused Cobb's death. The county court reviewed other Colorado manslaughter cases where courts found substantial and unjustified risks of death resulting from conduct such as firing a gun at a person or kicking an unconscious person in the head. The court found that Hall's conduct — which the court characterized as skiing "too fast for the conditions"— did not involve a substantial and unjustifiable risk of death and "does not rise to the level of dangerousness required under the current case law" to sustain a count of manslaughter. Because Hall's conduct did not, in the court's view, involve a substantial and unjustifiable risk of death, the court found that the prosecution failed to provide sufficient proof that Hall acted recklessly. The county court therefore dismissed the manslaughter count.

* * * To provide background for our explanation of recklessness, we review the history of culpable mental states. Depending on the specific crime charged and the jurisdiction, juries might be instructed to determine whether the defendant acted with "'felonious intent,' 'criminal intent,' 'malice aforethought,' 'guilty knowledge,' 'fraudulent intent,' 'wilfulness,' 'scienter,' . . . or 'mens rea,' to signify an evil purpose or mental culpability." *Morissette v. United States*, 342 U.S. 246 (1952). * * *

To demonstrate that Hall committed the crime of manslaughter, the prosecution must provide sufficient evidence to show that the defendant's conduct was reckless. § 18-3-104(1)(a). Thus, we focus on describing the mental state of recklessness and determining whether Hall's conduct meets that definition. * * *

As Colorado's criminal code defines recklessness, "A person acts recklessly when he consciously disregards a substantial and unjustifiable risk that a result will occur or that a circumstance exists." § 18-1-501(8). Thus, in the case of manslaughter, the prosecution must show that the defendant's conduct caused the death of another and that the defendant:

1) consciously disregarded

2) a substantial and

3) unjustifiable risk that he would

4) cause the death of another.

We hold that whether a risk is unjustifiable must be determined by assessing the nature and purpose of the actor's conduct relative to how substantial the risk is. Finally, in order for conduct to be reckless, the risk must be of such a nature that its disregard constitutes a gross deviation from the standard of care that a reasonable person would exercise.

As well as being substantial, a risk must be unjustifiable in order for a person's conduct to be reckless. Whether a risk is justifiable is determined by weighing the nature and purpose of the actor's conduct against the risk created by that conduct. See MPC, § 2.02, cmt. at 125 (Tentative Draft No. 4) * * * .

If a person consciously disregards a substantial risk of death but does so in order to advance an interest that justifies such a risk, the conduct is not reckless. For example, if a surgeon performs an operation on a patient that has a seventy-five percent chance of killing the patient, but the patient will certainly die without the operation, then the conduct is justified and thus not reckless even though the risk is substantial.

In addition to the separate analyses that are applied to determine whether a risk is both "substantial" and "unjustified," the concept of a "substantial and unjustifiable risk" implies a risk that constitutes a gross deviation from the standard of care that a reasonable law-abiding person would exercise under the circumstances. Both the Model Penal Code and the New York Code, which the General Assembly followed in drafting the Colorado criminal code, expressly define a "substantial and unjustifiable risk" as one that is a gross deviation from the reasonable standard of care. See MPC, § 2.02 at 226; N.Y. Penal Law, § 15.05. A substantial and unjustifiable risk must constitute a "gross deviation" from the reasonable standard of care in order to justify the criminal sanctions imposed for criminal negligence or reckless conduct, as opposed to the kind of deviation from the reasonable standard of care that results in civil liability for ordinary negligence.[12]

* * * In addition to showing that a person created a substantial and unjustifiable risk, the prosecution must demonstrate that the actor "consciously disregarded" the risk * * * Although recklessness is a less culpable mental state than intentionally or knowingly, it involves a higher level of culpability than criminal negligence. * * * [T]he court may infer that the defendant was subjectively aware of that risk, but the court cannot hold the defendant responsible if she were actually unaware of a risk that a reasonable person would have perceived.

Hence, in a reckless manslaughter case, the prosecution must prove that the defendant acted despite his subjective awareness of a substantial and unjustifiable risk of death from his conduct. Because absent an admission by the defendant such awareness cannot be proven directly, * * *.

The final element of recklessness requires that the actor consciously disregard a substantial and unjustifiable risk of a particular result, and in the case of manslaughter the actor must risk causing death to another person. The risk can be a risk of death to another generally; the actor does not have to risk death to a specific individual. * * *

[W]e must consider the facts in the light most favorable to the prosecution and we must draw all inferences against the defendant. Furthermore, the prosecution does not have to satisfy the much higher burden of proof necessary to convict Hall of reckless manslaughter. Rather, it need only establish sufficient evidence so that a reasonably prudent and cautious person could entertain the belief that Hall committed the crime.

* * * Hall was out of control and unable to avoid a collision with another person. All the witnesses said Hall was not traversing the slope and that he was skiing straight down the fall line. Hall was back on his skis, with his ski tips in the air and his arms out to his sides to maintain balance. Allen said that Hall was bounced around by the moguls on the slope rather than skiing in control and managing the bumps. * * * Obviously, this opinion does not address whether Hall is ultimately guilty of any crime. Rather, we hold only that the People presented sufficient evidence to establish probable cause that Hall committed reckless

---

[12] We note that both criminal negligence and recklessness require that the actor's conduct involve a "gross deviation" from the standard of care that a reasonable person would exercise under the circumstances in each case. Thus, the same risk will suffice for either criminally negligent or reckless conduct. However, the standards are sufficiently distinct to justify unequal penalties because in the case of reckless conduct the actor must be aware of the risk he creates, while criminally negligent conduct requires only that he failed to perceive the risk.

manslaughter, and the court should have bound Hall's case over for trial. * * * Thus, we remand this case to the district court for trial.

————————————

NOTES AND QUESTIONS

1. **Criminal Recklessness.** Should the prosecutor have charged this case as a criminal action? What is the key fact that shows Hall's conduct was reckless? Is it his status as a ski instructor, the presence of alcohol, conditions on the ski slope at the time of the collision, or his making a jump at a high rate of speed where others may be present? If the case proceeds to trial, should defense counsel call Hall as a witness? If one had similar facts and the accused had a reputation among the other ski instructors as "a guy who skis on the edge" and who participates in "extreme sports" as a hobby, should the defendant be called as a witness?

2. **Standard of Review.** The *Hall* case is at the pre-trial stage. The Colorado Supreme Court in *Hall* considered the evidence in the light most favorable to the government. The reason is that the dismissal of the charges is the equivalent of a grant of summary judgment, so appellate review of the facts is made in the light most favorable to the losing party below, in this case the prosecution. Note that the court is careful to point out that its analysis is not a factual resolution of the case.

E. Negligently

State v. Larson
103 P.3d 524 (Mont. 2004)

Justice JIM REGNIER delivered the Opinion of the Court.

Defendant Mark Theodore Larson (Larson) was convicted by a jury * * * on one count of negligent homicide, a felony, and one count each of the following misdemeanors: driving under the influence, speeding and failure to wear a seatbelt. Larson appeals his convictions. We affirm.

* * * The State's evidence at trial showed during the evening hours of November 10 and early morning hours of November 11, 2001, Larson and two college friends, Morgan and Clare, were drinking in his vehicle and in various bars and residences in the Conrad and Dutton area.

At about 3:30 a.m., Larson was driving his pickup at a high rate of speed south on the frontage road between Conrad and Brady when it veered off the right shoulder of the road surface near the beginning of a left curve. Larson pulled the pickup back onto the asphalt surface but overcorrected, sending his pickup across the highway and into the ditch on the left side of the highway. At that point, the car flipped multiple times, ejecting all three passengers, who were not wearing seatbelts.

The State's expert, Lynn Kurtz, of the state crime lab, testified analysis of Larson's blood sample taken three hours after the accident showed a blood alcohol concentration of 0.12%. Kurtz also testified concerning the effects of alcohol on an individual's ability to operate a motor vehicle, stating alcohol impairs an individual's ability to drive.

* * * At the conclusion of the trial but before deliberations, the parties submitted proposed jury instructions to the District Court. During the settling of jury instructions, Larson objected to the State's Instruction 19 which defined criminal negligence as follows:

> A person acts negligently with respect to the death of a human being or to a circumstance when an act is done with a conscious disregard of the risk that death of a human being will occur or that the circumstance exists or when the person disregards a risk of causing the death of another human being which the person should be aware that the result will occur or that the circumstance exists.

> The risk must be of a nature and degree that to disregard it involves a gross deviation from the standard of conduct that a reasonable person would observe in the actor's situation. "Gross deviation" means a deviation that is considerably greater than lack of ordinary care.

Larson objected to the instruction on the grounds the word "consciously" should have been inserted before the word "disregards" in defining criminal negligence. The court rejected Larson's objection, stating, "I believe the Court's Instruction is the definition, as provided by the Statute."

* * * Larson argues the District Court erred when it lowered the standard of proof required under the statutory scheme defining criminal negligence. Larson maintains the instruction for criminal negligence given to the jury should have included the word "consciously" as it related to the individual's disregard for a known risk. Larson contends by omitting the modifying adverb "consciously" before the word "disregards," the District Court lowered the standard of proof as required under the Criminal Code.

The State counters the District Court properly instructed the jury on the definition of criminal negligence. The State asserts the existing statutory definition given to the jury provided an adequate means of distinguishing criminal negligence from ordinary negligence. The State contends the instruction given to the jury made clear the standard on which to judge Larson's disregard of the risk involved as well as his gross deviation from a reasonable standard of conduct.

A person commits negligent homicide if the person negligently causes the death of another human being. A person acts negligently with respect to a result or circumstance, "when the person consciously disregards a risk that the result will occur or that the circumstance exists or when the person disregards a risk of which the person should be aware that the result will occur or the circumstance exists." Section 45-2-101(42), MCA. Further, the risk "must be of a nature and degree that to disregard it involves a gross deviation from the standard of conduct that a reasonable person would observe in the actor's situation." The term "gross deviation" is defined by the statute as meaning "a deviation that is considerably greater than lack of ordinary care."

This Court has previously decided mental state is not at issue in negligent homicide cases. *State v. Gould*, 704 P.2d 20 (Mont. 1985). In *Gould*, we held the defendant's proposed instruction referred improperly to the necessity of acting with the mental state of "consciously" as an element of the offense of negligent homicide. We deemed such instruction improper. Similarly, Larson's proposed instruction included the term "consciously," as used in § 45-2-101(42), MCA, to define criminal negligence. Unlike deliberate homicide however, which requires the offense be committed purposely or knowingly, negligent homicide does not require such purpose and knowledge. Negligent homicide only requires a gross deviation from a reasonable standard of care. Further, we have held criminal negligence can arise as a result of intoxication. Larson's mental state at the time he was driving his car is not at issue. Instead, the issue is whether the driving of a car while intoxicated was a gross deviation from the standard of reasonable care. It is difficult to imagine that conduct, which included drinking both beer and whiskey over many hours, disregarding the prevailing notion that drinking and driving is dangerous, and then getting behind the wheel of a vehicle and driving down an isolated county road at a speed in excess of the speed limit, could not be classed as a gross deviation that is considerably greater than the lack of ordinary care.

* * * We hold the jury was adequately instructed on negligence and the elements of the offense charged. Under the given instructions, if the jury believed Larson's account of the accident, they could have found in his favor. However, it was the jury's duty to determine which account of the accident, the State's or Larson's, they believed more credible and worthy of belief. Where the jury is adequately instructed, no error occurs in refusing a proposed instruction which is already covered. Here, the jury was fully instructed and Larson had a full opportunity to argue the merits of his defense. Accordingly, we hold the District Court properly instructed the jury on the definition of criminal negligence.

* * * Larson argues the State's evidence at trial was insufficient to support the jury's determination he was impaired by alcohol at the time of the accident. Larson

maintains the inference of impairment resulting from his 0.12% blood alcohol concentration was rebutted by other evidence indicating the accident was caused by a momentary lapse of attention while driving on a dangerous road.

* * * We conclude the State provided sufficient evidence of Larson's impairment to support Larson's conviction for negligent homicide and driving under the influence. Here, the State presented evidence Larson drank a substantial amount of alcohol during the evening and morning hours before the accident. Further, Larson admitted to EMTs and officers at the hospital he had consumed a considerable amount of alcohol. The State also showed Larson drove his pickup at a high rate of speed off the shoulder of the highway, causing the pickup to roll over and eject all three passengers. The State's expert witness testified the driving ability of anyone with a blood alcohol concentration of 0.08% or more is impaired or diminished. The jury in this case also heard testimony Larson's blood alcohol concentration was 0.12% two hours after the accident and four hours after he had stopped drinking.

We cannot know precisely why or how the jury reached its decision to convict Larson. We only know Larson presented his theory that other mitigating factors may have caused the accident, and the jury apparently rejected it. We hold, therefore, sufficient evidence exists to support Larson's convictions. * * *

PROBLEM EIGHT

Jess is driving an automobile within the speed limit on a sunny day. Jess passes through a crosswalk and — because of the blinding sun — does not see Lynn in the crosswalk in a wheelchair. Jess' car hits and kills Lynn. If the jurisdiction had a statute that made the "reckless killing of a human being" a crime, did Jess act recklessly? Should Jess be considered to have acted negligently? If Jess had been going five miles over the speed limit, would that change the level of intent? At what point does a person pass from acting negligently to recklessly? If Jess had been intoxicated, what would be the appropriate level of *mens rea* to charge an offense under the Model Penal Code?

---

§ 4.03 Proving Intent

Holloway v. United States
526 U.S. 1 (1999)

Justice STEVENS delivered the opinion of the Court.

Carjacking "with the intent to cause death or serious bodily harm" is a federal crime.[1] The question presented in this case is whether that phrase requires the Government to prove that the defendant had an unconditional intent to kill or harm in all events, or whether it merely requires proof of an intent to kill or harm if necessary to effect a carjacking. Most of the judges who have considered the question have concluded, as do we, that Congress intended to criminalize the more typical carjacking carried out by means of a deliberate threat of violence, rather than just the rare case in which the defendant has an unconditional intent to use violence regardless of how the driver responds to his threat.

A jury found petitioner guilty on three counts of carjacking, as well as several other offenses related to stealing cars. In each of the carjackings, petitioner and an armed accomplice identified a car that they wanted and followed it until it was parked. The accomplice then approached the driver, produced a gun, and threatened to shoot unless the driver handed over the car keys.[3] The accomplice testified that

---

[1] [T]he statute provides:

"Whoever, *with the intent to cause death or serious bodily harm* takes a motor vehicle that has been transported, shipped, or received in interstate or foreign commerce from the person or presence of another by force and violence or by intimidation, or attempts to do so, shall—

"(1) be fined under this title or imprisoned not more than 15 years, or both,

"(2) if serious bodily injury (as defined in section 1365 of this title, including any conduct that, if the conduct occurred in the special maritime and territorial jurisdiction of the United States, would violate section 2241 or 2242 of this title) results, be fined under this title or imprisoned not more than 25 years, or both, and

"(3) if death results, be fined under this title or imprisoned for any number of years up to life, or both, or sentenced to death." 18 U.S.C. § 2119 (emphasis added).

[3] One victim testified that the accomplice produced his gun and threatened, "Get out of the car or I'll shoot." Another testified that he said, "Give me your keys or I will shoot you right now."

the plan was to steal the cars without harming the victims, but that he would have used his gun if any of the drivers had given him a "hard time." When one victim hesitated, petitioner punched him in the face, but there was no other actual violence.

The District Judge instructed the jury that the Government was required to prove beyond a reasonable doubt that the taking of a motor vehicle was committed with the intent "to cause death or serious bodily harm to the person from whom the car was taken." After explaining that merely using a gun to frighten a victim was not sufficient to prove such intent, he added the following statement over petitioner's objection:

> In some cases, intent is conditional. That is, a defendant may intend to engage in certain conduct only if a certain event occurs.

> In this case, the government contends that the defendant intended to cause death or serious bodily harm if the alleged victims had refused to turn over their cars. If you find beyond a reasonable doubt that the defendant had such an intent, the government has satisfied this element of the offense. . . .

* * * The specific issue in this case is what sort of evil motive Congress intended to describe when it used the words "with the intent to cause death or serious bodily harm" in the 1994 amendment to the carjacking statute. More precisely, the question is whether a person who points a gun at a driver, having decided to pull the trigger if the driver does not comply with a demand for the car keys, possesses the intent, at that moment, to seriously harm the driver. In our view, the answer to that question does not depend on whether the driver immediately hands over the keys or what the offender decides to do after he gains control over the car. At the relevant moment, the offender plainly does have the forbidden intent.

The opinions that have addressed this issue accurately point out that a carjacker's intent to harm his victim may be either "conditional" or "unconditional." The statutory phrase at issue theoretically might describe (1) the former, (2) the latter, or (3) both species of intent. Petitioner argues that the "plain text" of the statute "unequivocally" describes only the latter: that the defendant must possess a specific and unconditional intent to kill or harm in order to complete the proscribed offense. To that end, he insists that Congress would have had to insert the words "if necessary" into the disputed text in order to include the conditional species of intent within the scope of the statute. Because Congress did not include those words, petitioner contends that we must assume that Congress meant to provide a federal penalty for only those carjackings in which the offender actually attempted to harm or kill the driver (or at least intended to do so whether or not the driver resisted).

We believe, however, that a commonsense reading of the carjacking statute counsels that Congress intended to criminalize a broader scope of conduct than attempts to assault or kill in the course of automobile robberies. As we have repeatedly stated, "the meaning of statutory language, plain or not, depends on context." *Brown v. Gardner*, 513 U.S. 115 (1994). When petitioner's argument is considered in the context of the statute, it becomes apparent that his proffered construction of the intent element overlooks the significance of the placement of that element in the statute. The carjacking statute essentially is aimed at providing a federal penalty for a particular type of robbery. The statute's mens rea component thus modifies the act of "tak[ing]" the motor vehicle. It directs the factfinder's attention to the defendant's state of mind at the precise moment he demanded or took control over the car "by force and violence or by intimidation." If the defendant has the proscribed state of mind at that moment, the statute's scienter element is satisfied.

Petitioner's reading of the intent element, in contrast, would improperly transform the mens rea element from a modifier into an additional actus reus component of the carjacking statute; it would alter the statute into one that focuses on attempting to harm or kill a person in the course of the robbery of a motor vehicle. Indeed, if we accepted petitioner's view of the statute's intent element, even Congress' insertion of the qualifying words "if necessary," by themselves, would not have solved the deficiency that he believes exists in the statute. The inclusion of those words after the intent phrase would have excluded the unconditional species of intent–the intent to harm or kill even if not necessary to complete a carjacking. Accordingly, if Congress had used words such as "if necessary" to describe the conditional species of intent, it would also have needed to add something like "or even if not necessary" in order to cover both species of intent to harm. Given the fact that the actual text does not mention either species separately — and thus does not expressly exclude either — that text is most naturally read to encompass the mens rea of both conditional and unconditional intent, and not to limit the statute's reach to crimes involving the additional actus reus of an attempt to kill or harm. * * *

[I]t is reasonable to presume that Congress was familiar with the cases and the scholarly writing that have recognized that the "specific intent" to commit a wrongful act may be conditional. The facts of the leading case on the point are strikingly similar to the facts of this case. In *People v. Connors*, 253 Ill. 266 (1912), the Illinois Supreme Court affirmed the conviction of a union organizer who had pointed a gun at a worker and threatened to kill him forthwith if he did not take off his overalls and quit work. The court held that the jury had been properly instructed that the "specific intent to kill" could be found even though that intent was "coupled with a condition" that the defendant would not fire if the victim complied with his demand. That holding has been repeatedly cited with approval by other courts and by scholars. * * * The core principle that emerges from these sources is that a defendant may not negate a proscribed intent by requiring the victim to comply with a condition the defendant has no right to impose; "[a]n intent to kill, in the alternative, is nevertheless an intent to kill."

This interpretation of the statute's specific intent element does not, as petitioner suggests, render superfluous the statute's "by force and violence or by intimidation" element. While an empty threat, or intimidating bluff, would be sufficient to satisfy the latter element, such conduct, standing on its own, is not enough to satisfy § 2119's specific intent element.[13] In a carjacking case in which the driver surrendered or otherwise lost control over his car without the defendant attempting to inflict, or actually inflicting, serious bodily harm, Congress' inclusion of the intent element requires the Government to prove beyond a reasonable doubt that the defendant would have at least attempted to seriously harm or kill the driver if that action had been necessary to complete the taking of the car.

In short, we disagree with petitioner's reading of the text of the Act and think it unreasonable to assume that Congress intended to enact such a truncated version of an important criminal statute.[14] The intent requirement of § 2119 is satisfied when the Government proves that at the moment the defendant demanded or took control over the driver's automobile the defendant possessed the intent to seriously harm or kill the driver if necessary to steal the car (or, alternatively, if unnecessary to steal the car). Accordingly, we affirm the judgment of the Court of Appeals.

Justice SCALIA, dissenting.

* * * I dissent from that holding because I disagree with the following, utterly central, passage of the opinion: "[A] carjacker's intent to harm his victim may be either 'conditional' or 'unconditional.' * * * I think, to the contrary, that in customary English usage the unqualified word "intent" does not usually connote a purpose that is subject to any conditions precedent except those so remote in the speaker's estimation as to be effectively nonexistent—and it never connotes a purpose that is subject to a condition which the speaker hopes will not occur.* * * "Intent" is "[a] state of mind in which a person seeks to accomplish a given result

---

[13] In somewhat different contexts, courts have held that a threat to harm does not in itself constitute intent to harm or kill. In *Hairston v. State*, 54 Miss. 689 (1877), for example, the defendant in an angry and profane manner threatened to shoot a person if that person stopped the defendant's mules. The court affirmed the defendant's conviction for assault, but reversed a conviction of assault with intent to commit murder, explaining that "we have found no case of a conviction of assault with intent to kill or murder, upon proof only of the levelling of a gun or pistol." * * *

[14] We also reject petitioner's argument that the rule of lenity should apply in this case. We have repeatedly stated that "[t]he rule of lenity applies only if, after seizing everything from which aid can be derived, . . . we can make no more than a guess as to what Congress intended." * * *

through a course of action." *Black's Law Dictionary* 810 (6th ed.1990). One can hardly "seek to accomplish" a result he hopes will not ensue.

The Court's division of intent into two categories, conditional and unconditional, makes the unreasonable seem logical. * * * Conditional intent is no more embraced by the unmodified word "intent" than a sea lion is embraced by the unmodified word "lion."

If I have made a categorical determination to go to Louisiana for the Christmas holidays, it is accurate for me to say that I "intend" to go to Louisiana. And that is so even though I realize that there are some remote and unlikely contingencies — "acts of God," for example — that might prevent me. * * * It is less precise, though tolerable usage, to say that I "intend" to go if my purpose is conditional upon an event which, though not virtually certain to happen (such as my continuing to live), is reasonably likely to happen, and which I hope will happen. I might, for example, say that I "intend" to go even if my plans depend upon receipt of my usual and hoped-for end-of-year bonus.

But it is not common usage — indeed, it is an unheard-of usage — to speak of my having an "intent" to do something, when my plans are contingent upon an event that is not virtually certain, and that I hope will not occur. When a friend is seriously ill, for example, I would not say that "I intend to go to his funeral next week." I would have to make it clear that the intent is a conditional one: "I intend to go to his funeral next week if he dies." The carjacker who intends to kill if he is met with resistance is in the same position: He has an "intent to kill if resisted"; he does not have an "intent to kill." No amount of rationalization can change the reality of this normal (and as far as I know exclusive) English usage. The word in the statute simply will not bear the meaning that the Court assigns.

NOTES AND QUESTIONS

1. *Direct and Circumstantial Evidence.* The evidence available to establish a defendant's guilt for an offense is usually divided into two categories: "direct" and "circumstantial." Direct evidence generally consists of physical evidence, eyewitness statements, and statements by the defendant. In contrast, circumstantial evidence can be anything that allows a reasonable juror to infer a fact that is relevant to the prosecution. "Circumstantial evidence tends to prove a fact in issue by proving other events or circumstances which afford a basis for reasonable inference by the jury of the occurrence of the fact in issue." *State v. Evans*, 62 P.3d 220 (Kan. 2003). Circumstantial evidence plays its most important role in proving the defendant's intent when the prosecution does not have any statements from the defendant about his state of mind at the time the offense occurred. "It is an

elementary principle of law that intent may be proved by circumstantial evidence; that the element of intent can rarely be shown by direct evidence; and it may be shown by reasonable inference arising from the circumstances surrounding the act." *State v. Yabusaki*, 570 P.3d 844 (Hawaii 1977). For example, an eyewitness may see a defendant hurrying away from a dead body and throw what appears to be a handgun into the bushes. If the victim was shot at close range, is there proof that the defendant intended to kill the victim? The eyewitness testimony and other evidence, such as forensic proof that the victim was shot at close range, can support a finding that the defendant specifically intended to kill the victim.

2. ***Natural and Probable Consequences.*** Inferring intent from circumstantial evidence requires a jury to decide whether the circumstances reflect the requisite mens rea, sometimes in the face of a defendant's denial that he acted with that intent. One means of making the requisite inference is the "natural and probable consequences" doctrine: "In reaching its conclusion, the jury may infer that a person intends the natural and probable consequences of his actions and a defendant's statements as to his intentions are not binding on the jury if his acts demonstrated a contrary intent." *State v. Cooper*, 561 N.W.2d 175 (Minn. 1997). For example, in *Youts*, [p. 116] the court found that it was so clear that putting a train in reverse and then leaping out was so likely to result in destruction of the train that the defendant must have known, despite his denial. Although the jury may infer the requisite intent by finding that the defendant intended a particular result because it is a natural and probable consequence of his action, the court must be careful to instruct the jury that such a finding is not a necessary result, i.e., a defendant's guilt may not be presumed. In *Sandstrom v. Montana*, 442 U.S. 510 (1979), the Supreme Court found that an instruction to the jury that "the law presumes that a person intends the ordinary consequences of his voluntary acts" violated the defendant's due process right to have the government prove all the elements of the crime beyond a reasonable doubt.

3. ***Sufficient Evidence of Intent.*** "This court has long held that circumstantial evidence 'may be a thoroughly satisfactory basis for conviction of the highest crimes.'" *Commonwealth v. Guy*, 803 N.E.2d 707 (Mass. 2004). That said, an appellate court reviewing a conviction will scrutinize a case based *solely* on circumstantial evidence more closely because "a conviction based on circumstantial evidence may stand only where the facts and circumstances disclosed by the circumstantial evidence form a complete chain which, in light of the evidence as a whole, leads so directly to the guilt of the accused as to exclude, beyond a reasonable doubt, any reasonable inference other than that of guilt." *State v. Wahlberg*, 296 N.W.2d 408 (Minn. 1980).

4. ***Defendant's Testimony.*** The best source of proof of what was in the defendant's mind at the time of the alleged crime would be — not surprisingly — the defendant. Can the government call the defendant as a witness to testify as to what he was thinking? The Fifth Amendment provides a privilege against self-incrimination that

prevents a person from being compelled to testify against themselves, and that prevents the government not only from calling a defendant to testify at trial, but also prohibits commenting on a defendant's failure to testify at trial as circumstantial proof of the defendant's guilt. Therefore, circumstantial evidence may be all the government has available to show the defendant's intent. When the defendant does testify the prosecution can show that the testimony is inconsistent with prior statements or the evidence introduced at trial, and in some instances may be able to bring in prior misconduct by the defendant to show he should not be believed.

5. *False Testimony.* A defendant charged with a specific intent crime can be strongly tempted to testify falsely or wish to present witnesses who will testify falsely in the hope of securing an acquittal. There is no dispute that defense counsel may not call witnesses who intend to commit perjury. ABA Model Rules of Professional Conduct, Rules 1.2, 3.3, 3.4. Counsel for the defense is presented with some competing ethical concerns when it is his or her client that has testified falsely on the witness stand. Jurisdictions do not always resolve this issue in a uniform manner. See ABA Model Rules of Professional Conduct, Rules 3.4. See also *Nix v. Whiteside*, 475 U.S. 157 (1986).

6. *Elements Requiring Intent.* It is often necessary to decide which elements of the statute will have a mens rea requirement. The level of mens rea for each of the elements in a statute may not be the same. Consider the following case:

State v. Worthy
746 A.2d 1063 (N.J. Super. Ct. App. Div. 2000)

HAVEY, Presiding Judge Appellate Division.

Defendant was convicted by a jury of third-degree criminal restraint pursuant to N.J.S.A. 2C:13-2, which provides in pertinent part that "[a] person commits a crime of the third degree if he knowingly: a. Restrains another unlawfully in circumstances exposing the other to risk of serious bodily injury. . . ." We agree with defendant that the jury instruction given here did not make clear that the requisite mental state of "knowledge" applies to all material elements of the offense, including the risk of serious bodily injury to the victim. We therefore reverse and remand for further proceedings.

The State presented evidence that sixteen-year old K.B., the alleged victim, had been defendant's friend since her childhood. During their long friendship, they communicated daily. They "went for rides" and defendant often took K.B. shopping.

On November 28, 1996, at approximately 11:30 p.m., K.B. and her friend, Wakeen Conover, walked towards Conover's vehicle, which was parked in front of K.B.'s sister's house on James Street in Lakewood. K.B. got into the passenger seat of the vehicle. When defendant suddenly appeared and got into the driver's seat, Conover ran back into the house. K.B. testified that she attempted to jump out of the vehicle, but was restrained by defendant. Defendant then drove the vehicle away at approximately thirty-five to forty miles per hour while K.B.'s feet were scraping along the street.

K.B.'s brother chased defendant in his own vehicle. According to Brown, during the chase his vehicle reached a speed of up to fifty-five miles per hour. He testified that defendant's vehicle made a "sharp" turn "all the way in the other lane" before coming to a stop.

According to K.B., during the chase she asked to be returned to her sister's home. Defendant responded that he would do so once her brother-in-law, who was also following them, stopped the chase. K.B. testified that defendant proceeded throughout the neighborhood at approximately twenty-five to thirty miles per hour for approximately thirty minutes. Defendant was "calm" and "under control" and insisted that he intended to return K.B. to her sister's home.

Eventually, defendant stopped the vehicle one block behind K.B.'s sister's home. Defendant and K.B. then walked around the neighborhood with defendant holding K.B.'s hand. Her attempts to run away were unsuccessful. They returned to the vehicle, drove by K.B.'s sister's home and noticed that police officers were present. Defendant then parked one block from K.B.'s sister's house and walked away.

K.B. acknowledged that she was testifying because her parents threatened that if she did not, a warrant would be issued for her arrest. She admitted that on the day of the episode she had been with defendant earlier and that defendant had paged her on her beeper. She also acknowledged that after the episode she explained to the police and the prosecutor's office that defendant had not threatened her or forced her "to do anything" while they were in the vehicle.

Defendant testified that on the day of the incident K.B. attempted to page him. She later called him and gave him directions to her sister's house. When defendant arrived at the house, he got into Conover's vehicle with K.B. The vehicle was running and in gear and began to "buck just like a horse" while his left leg was still outside the vehicle. He asked K.B. to get into the car and close the door for her safety. During the "bucking," the vehicle did not exceed seven miles per hour.

While driving through the neighborhood, a relative of defendant told him that the police were looking for him. When he proceeded toward K.B.'s sister's house, K.B. told him not to stop. He therefore parked the vehicle one block from the house, walked away and presented himself to the Lakewood Police Department.

The trial court instructed the jury as follows:

Now, Mr. Worthy is accused of violating a statute which reads in pertinent part as follows: A person is guilty of criminal restraint if he knowingly restrains another unlawfully in circumstances exposing the other to the risk of serious bodily injury. In order for you to find Mr. Worthy guilty of this offense, the State must prove the essential elements of the offense beyond a reasonable doubt, and those essential elements are as follows:

One, the State must prove that Brian Worthy *knowingly restrained* [K.B.];

And, two, that the *restraint was known* by Brian Worthy *to be unlawful*;

And, three, the restraint was under circumstances exposing [K.B.] to the risk of serious bodily injury.

Now, I've used the terms restraint, knowingly, unlawfully, and serious bodily injury.

After defining "knowingly," the court summarized as follows:

[T]he State must prove the following elements beyond a reasonable doubt:

One, that Mr. Worthy *knowingly restrained* [K.B.].

Restraint means to confine, limit, or restrict one's liberty;

Two, that the *restraint was known* by Mr. Worthy *to be unlawful*. The term unlawful means it was accomplished by restraint, by force, threat, or deception;

And, *three*, that the restraint was under circumstances exposing [K.B.] to the risk of serious bodily injury.

At the close of the instruction, defense counsel took issue with the trial court's failure to make clear that the requisite mental state of knowledge applied to all three elements. * * *

Defense counsel [later] repeated his objection, arguing that it was his view that the model jury charge followed by the trial court did not make clear that the mental state of "knowledge" applied to all elements of the offense. The court noted the objection and overruled it.

We agree with defendant that the jury instruction was erroneous and a reversal is required. As noted earlier, the criminal restraint statute provides that "[a] person commits a crime of the third degree if he *knowingly*: a. Restrains another unlawfully in circumstances exposing the other to risk of serious bodily injury. . . ." (Emphasis added). Because "knowingly" is part of the introductory sentence of the statute, the Legislature no doubt intended that the "knowing" mental state applies to each of the elements in subparagraph a; that is, he knowingly restrains, he knows the restraint is unlawful, and knows that the restraint is under circumstances exposing the victim to serious bodily injury.

The Legislature's intent is also clear from the legislative history of the statute. According to the Model Penal Code, after which our criminal restraint statute is modeled, criminal restraint was intended to provide an "intermediate offense between kidnapping and false imprisonment." Model Penal Code § 212.2 comment 2 (Official Draft and Revised Comments 1980). The offense is distinguished from kidnapping "either by the lack of substantial removal or confinement, as required for the greater offense, or by the absence of any of the specified kidnapping purposes." It is distinguished from false imprisonment in that criminal restraint requires that the unlawful restraint occur under circumstances creating a risk of serious harm. The Model Penal Code's formulation is intended to punish "one who is *aware* of the risk" involved. Model Penal Code, § 212.2 comment 2 (emphasis added). Consequently, "[s]ection 212.2 requires proof that the accused acted *knowingly*. Thus [the actor] must have been *aware* that he was restraining his victim, that the restraint was unlawful, *and* that it exposed the victim to physical danger." (emphasis added).

Further, any ambiguity as to whether "knowingly" was intended to apply to each element of the offense is clarified by reference to other provisions of the Criminal Code. N.J.S.A. 2C:2-2a provides that "[e]xcept as provided in subsection c.(3) of this section, a person is not guilty of an offense unless he acted purposely, *knowingly*, recklessly or negligently, as the law may require, with respect to each material element of the offense." (Emphasis added).

In addition, N.J.S.A. 2C:2-2c(1) provides that "[w]hen the law defining an offense prescribes the kind of culpability that is sufficient for the commission of an offense, without distinguishing among the material elements thereof, such provision *shall apply to all the material elements of the offense*, unless a contrary purpose plainly appears." (Emphasis added). Subparagraph 2c(1) was intended to "assist in resolution" of precisely the type of ambiguity we have here, namely "the statement of a particular culpability requirement in the definition of an offense in such a way that it is unclear whether the requirement applies to all the elements of the offense or only to the element that is immediately introduced." Thus, "[t]he Code proceeds in the view that if a particular kind of culpability has been articulated at all by the Legislature, as sufficient with respect to any element of the offense, the normal probability is that it was designed to apply to all material elements. Hence this construction is required, unless a "contrary purpose plainly appears." When a distinction is intended, as it often is, proper drafting ought to make it clear.

This approach is consistent with the established rule of construction providing that courts are "enjoined to construe penal statutes strictly and to construe ambiguous language against the State." *State v. Galloway*, 628 A.2d 735 (N.J. 1993). We therefore hold that a jury instruction on criminal restraint must make clear that the mental state of knowledge applies to all material elements of the offense, including the risk of serious bodily injury to the victim. * * *

With a proper instruction the jury could well have found that defendant's conduct constituted a knowing and unlawful restraint, but that he had not knowingly exposed the victim to the risk of serious bodily injury. "A person acts knowingly with respect to a result of his conduct if he is aware that it is practically certain that his conduct will cause such a result." N.J.S.A. 2C:2-2b(2). Defendant testified that when he entered the vehicle it was already in gear. It began to "buck just like a horse" while his left leg was still outside the vehicle. He then asked K.B. to "[s]hut the door. You're going to hurt yourself[,]" suggesting concern for her safety because of the erratic nature of the vehicle's movement. According to defendant, at the time the vehicle was "buck[ing]" he was proceeding at approximately six to seven miles per hour and during the ensuing drive he was proceeding at approximately twenty miles per hour before he dropped off K.B. K.B. testified that [she] attempted to explain to the police that defendant had not threatened her or forced her "to do anything." On these facts, the jury may have concluded defendant was not aware that it "was practically certain" that his conduct exposed K.B. to the risk of serious bodily injury.

Reversed and remanded for a new trial.

PROBLEM NINE

Tracy operates a kiosk at a local shopping mall where Tracy develops photographs from digital cameras and memory cards. A customer attaches the camera or card to a reader, which downloads the pictures the customer selects and within one hour the photographs are printed. A customer can return to pick up the prints, or Tracy will send them by overnight delivery for a small additional charge. Nicki brings a digital camera to Tracy's kiosk and orders 15 pictures to be sent to an address provided. The computer downloads the pictures and then prints them.

Tracy takes the pictures from the printer and places them in an envelope without ever looking at them. Tracy gives the envelope to the delivery service that evening. A short time later, police execute a search warrant at Nicki's house and seize the pictures and envelope from Tracy. All 15 pictures depict young children engaging in sexually-explicit acts. Tracy is charged with violating the following statute:

> Any person who knowingly transports, ships, mails, or otherwise delivers, including electronic transmission by computer, any visual depiction, if (A) the producing of such visual depiction involves the use of a minor engaging in sexually explicit conduct; and (B) such visual depiction is of such conduct; shall be imprisoned not less than five years and not more than twenty years.

What argument will defense counsel make that Tracy did not violate the law, and how will the government respond?

§ 4.04 Willful Blindness

Rice v. State
766 A.2d 663 (Md. Ct. Spec. App. 2000)

EYLER, Judge.

* * * William Thomas Rice, appellant, was convicted in a court trial of driving while his license was suspended, in violation of § 16-303(c) of the Transportation Article ("TA"), speeding, failing to obey a stop sign, and failing to display a registration card on demand. Appellant was sentenced to one weekend in the Howard County Detention Center and was fined $500 on the driving while suspended conviction. * * *

Appellant's trial was held on July 18, 2000. The State called Officer Thomas Rukamp, of the Howard County Police Department, who testified that on September 24, 1999, at 11:20 p.m., he was on patrol in a marked police cruiser on Ducketts Lane, near Karas Walk, in Howard County. He saw the driver of a black car speed down Karas Walk, fail to stop for a stop sign, make a U-turn, and speed back down Karas Walk in the direction from which he had come. Officer Rukamp followed the driver, who continued to speed. Eventually, the driver turned into the driveway of the house at 6192 Karas Walk. Officer Rukamp pulled into the driveway behind the black car and turned on his emergency lights. The driver jumped out of the car, ran to the front door of the house, and banged on it, yelling to be let in. The door opened and he ran inside.

* * * During Officer Rukamp's testimony, the State moved into evidence, without objection, a computer print-out of appellant's driving record, from the

MVA [Motor Vehicle Administration]. The record shows that on March 18, 1998, appellant's driver's license was suspended for refusal to submit to a breathalyzer test. That suspension was withdrawn on July 15, 1998. On January 28, 1999, appellant was charged with driving under the influence of alcohol. He was tried and convicted of that charge on June 2, 1999, and was assessed eight points. Thereafter, on August 5, 1999, the MVA sent appellant a letter notifying him that unless he requested a hearing in ten days of the date the letter was mailed, his driver's license would be suspended. This notice of suspension letter was sent by certified mail. On August 20, 1999, appellant's license was suspended for six months. On August 30, 1999, the certified notice of suspension letter to appellant was returned to the MVA by the United States Postal Service. * * *

Appellant testified in his own defense. He admitted driving on the night in question, but stated that he had not known, at that time, that his driver's license was suspended. * * * According to appellant, his wife did not tell him about any correspondence for him from the MVA, and during the pertinent time frame he did not receive any mail at the Karas Walk address. Also, at some unspecified point in time, appellant's wife went to Virginia for three weeks, and was not collecting the mail at the Karas Walk address. Appellant went to that house "very seldom" and "wasn't concerned about too much in the mail." He happened to be at the house on the night in question because it was "the first night that [he and his] wife . . . had been back together." Finally, appellant stated that he "had no idea" after the court proceeding of June 2, 1999, that his license was going to be suspended.

[The trial judge discredited the defendant's testimony, stating: "And it is ignorance and it is intentional ignorance to just say, well, ghee [sic], I didn't get the mail. He's not saying anyone usurped the mail, he's simply saying that I didn't get it, and that is not satisfactory. * * * The Court enters a guilty finding to driving on a suspended license. I find that the evidence is sufficient to sustain that even if he didn't hear it from his attorney and that can't be introduced because that's attorney/client privilege, unless it was part of an actual record which the State hasn't produced, but the fact of the matter is, Defendant has been suspended before as shown by the record and he's not a novice in these kind of proceedings."]

Appellant contends that the evidence was insufficient to sustain his conviction because it could not support a finding of the mens rea – i.e., criminal intent – element of the crime of driving while suspended. Specifically, he argues that there was no evidence that on the night in question he knew that his driver's license was suspended; therefore, there was no evidence to support a finding that he intended to drive while his license was suspended. He maintains that the standard of proof of mens rea in a driving while suspended case is actual knowledge, of which there was no proof here; and that, even if deliberate ignorance or willful blindness is sufficient to show knowledge, the evidence was insufficient to support such a finding. He relies upon *State v. McCallum*, 583 A.2d 250 (Md. 1991), in advancing that argument.

The State, also citing *McCallum*, acknowledges that there was no evidence of actual knowledge in this case, *i.e.*, that appellant had obtained possession of the suspension letter and had read its contents. The State responds, however, that deliberate ignorance or willful blindness is a proper standard of proof of knowledge in a driving while suspended case, and that the proof in this case met that standard.

In a concurring opinion [in *McCallum*], Judge Chasanow, expressing the belief that, for the guidance of the trial court, the Court of Appeals "should . . . elaborate on the mens rea that would be necessary to convict," explained that the criminal intent required for the offense of driving while suspended "is knowledge rather than intent. Unquestionably, McCallum intended to drive. The issue is whether McCallum had 'knowledge' that his driving privileges were suspended, and thus, his mental state must be assessed." Judge Chasanow further explained that knowledge in this context can be "actual knowledge," meaning "an actual awareness or an actual belief that a fact exists," or "deliberate ignorance or willful blindness," which is to say that a person "believes that it is probable that something is a fact, but deliberately shuts his or her eyes or avoids making reasonable inquiry with a conscious purpose to avoid learning the truth." "Deliberate ignorance requires a conscious purpose to avoid enlightenment; a showing of mere negligence or mistake is not sufficient. Also, deliberate ignorance is a form of knowledge, not a substitute for knowledge. Therefore, if McCallum actually believed that his driver's license was not suspended, he could not be guilty of the offense."

The notice of suspension letter in this case was sent by the MVA by certified mail, return receipt requested, because by statute, the letter was required to be served in that fashion. Ordinarily, and unless a statute provides otherwise, the MVA may serve notice by mail by sending it first class, postage prepaid. As we have explained, however, under TA § 16-404(b)(2)(i), if a notice of suspension for an accumulation of points is to be served by mail, it must be sent certified mail, return receipt requested. When a letter is sent by certified mail, return receipt requested, the United States Postal Service delivers to the addressee a green card stating that the certified letter is at the post office, and giving the name of the sender. The letter itself is not delivered; rather, the addressee (or, if it is not restricted delivery, someone else) must go to the post office to claim it, and must sign a return receipt for it. If no one claims the letter at the post office within 15 days, the United States Postal Service returns it to the sender.

Keeping in mind Judge Chasanow's description of "deliberate ignorance" as "a form of knowledge, not a substitute for knowledge," we think that it would make little sense to conclude that the only form of knowledge of an impending suspension under TA § 16-404-(b)(1)(i) sufficient to establish the mens rea for the offense of driving while suspended is actual knowledge gained from receipt of a suspension letter sent by certified mail. If that were the case, the certified mail requirement of that statute would make service by mail useless and ineffectual in virtually every case in which a person's privilege to drive was legitimately subject to suspension. A person having reason to think that his driving privilege was being threatened with suspension would have no incentive to go to the post office to collect his certified letter; to the contrary, he would have every incentive to avoid doing so because by not collecting the certified letter, he could claim lack of knowledge and thereby insulate himself from a successful prosecution for driving while suspended. It would make no difference that his lack of knowledge was self-imposed. Nor would it make any difference that, given his already existing awareness that his right to drive might be subject to suspension, the delivery of a green card informing him that the MVA had a letter for him at the post office was tantamount to being placed on actual knowledge that what he had thought likely now was imminent.

We see no meaningful distinction between the state of knowledge of an impending driver's license suspension that a person gains from reading a certified letter from the MVA to that effect and the state of knowledge of an impending driver's license suspension that a person gains when, having reason to believe that his privilege to drive may be in jeopardy, he learns that the post office is holding a certified letter for him from the MVA. In the latter situation, the person knows enough about the likely contents of the MVA letter that his unexplained failure to obtain it from the post office is "deliberate ignorance" or "willful blindness."

In this case, there was ample evidence of knowledge on appellant's part sufficient for the court to find, beyond a reasonable doubt, the intent element of the offense of driving while suspended. As the court pointed out, appellant was not a novice in matters pertaining to the MVA. He had had his driving privileges suspended in the past. On June 2, 1999, he was assessed 8 points upon being convicted of driving while under the influence. It is immaterial whether appellant was informed by the court that assessed those points that the law requires the MVA to notify a person who has accumulated 8 points that, absent a request for a hearing, his license will be suspended. "[E]veryone is presumed to know the law regardless of conscious knowledge or lack thereof, and [is] presumed to intend the necessary and legitimate consequences of [his] actions in its light." *Benik v. Hatcher*, 750 A.2d 10 (Md. 2000). Once appellant was convicted of DUI and had 8 points assessed against him, he had reason to believe that the MVA would take action to suspend his driving privilege.

NOTES

1. ***Ostrich Instruction.*** Judge Posner noted that willful blindness or the "ostrich instruction" should only be given in cases in which the defendant's knowledge of the underlying conduct is at issue:

The most powerful criticism of the ostrich instruction is, precisely, that its tendency is to allow juries to convict upon a finding of negligence for crimes that require intent. Robbins, *The Ostrich Instruction: Deliberate Ignorance as a Criminal Mens Rea*, 81 J. CRIM. L. & CRIMINOLOGY 191 (1990). The criticism can be deflected by thinking carefully about just what it is that real ostriches do (or at least are popularly supposed to do). They do not just fail to follow through on their suspicions of bad things. They are not merely careless birds. They bury their heads in the sand so that they will not see or hear bad things. They deliberately avoid acquiring unpleasant knowledge. The ostrich instruction is designed for cases in which there is evidence that the defendant, knowing or strongly suspecting that he is involved in shady dealings, takes steps to make sure that he does not acquire full or exact knowledge of the nature and extent of those dealings. A deliberate effort to avoid guilty knowledge is all the guilty knowledge the law requires. "[T]o know, and to want not to know because one suspects, may be, if not the same state of mind, the same degree of fault." *AMPAT/Midwest, Inc. v. Illinois Tool Works Inc.*, 896 F.2d 1035 (7th Cir.1990). A good example of a case in which the ostrich instruction was properly given is *United States v. Diaz*, 864 F.2d 544 (7th Cir.1988). The defendant, a drug trafficker, sought "to insulate himself from the actual drug transaction so that he could deny knowledge of it," which he did sometimes by absenting himself from the scene of the actual delivery and sometimes by pretending to be fussing under the hood of his car.

United States v. Giovannetti, 919 F.2d 1223 (7th Cir. 1990). In *United States v. Black*, 530 F.3d 596, 604 (7th Cir. 2008), Judge Posner rejected an argument of an improper ostrich instruction being given to the jury and noted in his decision:

The first is whether an "ostrich" instruction should have been given. The reference of course is to the legend that ostriches when frightened bury their head in the sand. It is pure legend and a canard on a very distin-guished bird. Zoological Society of San Diego, *Birds: Ostrich*, www.sandiegozoo.org/animalbytes/t-ostrich.html (visited June 12, 2008) ("When an ostrich senses danger and cannot run away, it flops to the ground and remains still, with its head and neck flat on the ground in front of it. Because the head and neck are lightly colored, they blend in with the color of the soil. From a distance, it just looks like the ostrich has buried its head in the sand, because only the body is visible"). It is too late, however, to correct this injustice.

2. *Global Tech.* In *Global-Tech Appliances, Inc., et al. v. SEB S.A.*, 131 S.Ct. 2060 (2011), the Supreme Court examined the concept of willful blindness in the context of a patent infringement case. The Court stated:

\

The doctrine of willful blindness is well established in criminal law. Many criminal statutes require proof that a defendant acted knowingly or willfully, and courts applying the doctrine of willful blindness hold that defendants cannot escape the reach of these statutes by deliberately shielding themselves from clear evidence of critical facts that are strongly suggested by the circumstances. The traditional rationale for this doctrine is that defendants who behave in this manner are just as culpable as those who have actual knowledge. * * *

It is also said that persons who know enough to blind themselves to direct proof of critical facts in effect have actual knowledge of those facts. See *United States v. Jewell,* 532 F.2d 697, 700 (C.A.9 1976) (en banc). This Court's opinion more than a century ago in *Spurr v. United States,* 174 U.S. 728, 19 S.Ct. 812, 43 L.Ed. 1150 (1899), while not using the term "willful blindness," endorsed a similar concept. The case involved a criminal statute that prohibited a bank officer from "willfully" certifying a check drawn against insufficient funds. We said that a willful violation would occur "if the [bank] officer purposely keeps himself in ignorance of whether the drawer has money in the bank." * * * Following our decision in *Spurr,* several federal prosecutions in the first half of the 20th century invoked the doctrine of willful blindness. Later, a 1962 proposed draft of the Model Penal Code, which has since become official, attempted to incorporate the doctrine by defining "knowledge of the existence of a particular fact" to include a situation in which "a person is aware of a high probability of [the fact's] existence, unless he actually believes that it does not exist." ALI, Model Penal Code § 2.02(7) (Proposed Official Draft 1962). Our Court has used the Code's definition as a guide in analyzing whether certain statutory presumptions of knowledge comported with due process. * * * And every Court of Appeals—with the possible exception of the District of Columbia Circuit, * * * has fully embraced willful blindness, applying the doctrine to a wide range of criminal statutes.

Given the long history of willful blindness and its wide acceptance in the Federal Judiciary, we can see no reason why the doctrine should not apply in civil lawsuits for induced patent infringement under 35 U.S.C. § 271(b). * * *

While the Courts of Appeals articulate the doctrine of willful blindness in slightly different ways, all appear to agree on two basic requirements: (1) the defendant must subjectively believe that there is a high probability that a fact exists and (2) the defendant must take deliberate actions to avoid learning of that fact. * * * We think these requirements give willful blindness an appropriately limited scope that surpasses recklessness and negligence. Under this formulation, a willfully blind defendant is one who takes deliberate actions to avoid confirming a high probability of wrongdoing and who can almost be said to have actually known the critical facts. See G. Williams, Criminal Law § 57, p. 159 (2d ed. 1961) ("A court can properly find wilful blindness only where it can almost be said that the defendant actually knew"). By contrast, a reckless defendant is one who merely knows of a substantial and unjustified risk of such wrongdoing, see ALI, Model Penal Code § 2.02(2)(c) (1985), and a negligent defendant is one who should have known of a similar risk but, in fact, did not, see § 2.02(2)(d).

The test applied by the Federal Circuit in this case departs from the proper willful blindness standard in two important respects. First, it permits a finding of knowledge when there is merely a "known risk" that the induced acts are infringing. Second, in demanding only "deliberate indifference" to that risk, the Federal Circuit's test does not require active efforts by an inducer to avoid knowing about the infringing nature of the activities.

PROBLEM TEN

Dr. Browne operates a family practice clinic in a rural community, and some of Dr. Browne's patients are covered by Medicare/Medicaid. Mickey, the office manager, tells J.C., the clinic's accountant, that the government has been slow in making payments for Medicare/Medicaid patients, causing the clinic to fall behind in paying its bills. J.C. tells Mickey that a number of doctors submit claims for a greater amount than the government would pay for the work performed, so that, when the government does finally pay, the doctor receives a larger payment. According to J.C., at the end of the year, Dr. Browne can reimburse the government for any amounts greater than what the clinic should have been paid. J.C. says, "Look, you should hold on to their money, they shouldn't hold on to yours. As long as you pay them back, who loses?" Over the next 6 months, Mickey has Dr. Browne sign 50 Medicare/Medicaid claims on behalf of the clinic to be submitted to the government for reimbursement. On a few occasions, Dr. Browne asks Mickey to make sure that the claim is correct, and Mickey replies, "Don't worry, Doc, you're just getting what you deserve. We'll straighten things out later if we have to." A routine audit of Dr. Browne's reimbursement claims for that year by the Department of Health & Human Services shows that 10 claims were inflated or sought reimbursement for procedures that were never actually performed on a patient. After Mickey receives immunity and agrees to testify, the federal government charges Dr. Browne with 10 counts of submitting false Medicare/Medicaid claims. The relevant statute makes it a felony for any person to "knowingly submit or cause to be submitted false or fictitious claims for reimbursement for the purpose of obtaining money, property, or anything of value." Has Dr. Browne acted with the requisite intent? What arguments will the prosecution and defense make?

§ 4.05 Transferred Intent

State v. Fennell
531 S.E.2d 512 (S.C. 2000)

Justice WALLER:

John Bennett Fennell (appellant) was indicted for the murder of one man and the assault and battery with intent to kill (ABIK) of a second man. A jury found him guilty but mentally ill on both charges. He was sentenced to life in prison for murder and twenty years for ABIK. We affirm.

Appellant was diagnosed as suffering from paranoid schizophrenia in 1984. Appellant's illness led to the loss of his job as an accountant, a divorce, and his decision to move from Columbia back to Chester County to live with his elderly mother. Appellant joined the Chester Civitan Club and was appointed to oversee its "candy box" program. He was responsible for collecting money from boxes left in stores, replenishing the candy, and making deposits. He took the job very seriously and usually performed it well.

In fall 1996, William R. Thrailkill, the owner of a home remodeling business and a Civitan Club member also involved in the candy box program, and appellant had a dispute about an empty candy box at a local store. The argument angered and upset appellant.

At a Civitan Club meeting at a restaurant about two weeks later, neither appellant nor Thrailkill initially appeared upset. Appellant approached Thrailkill to discuss the candy box matter again as Thrailkill, his son, and other members formed a line at the buffet. Thrailkill refused to discuss it and made a disparaging remark that angered appellant. Appellant immediately left the room and retrieved a .38-caliber revolver from his car. Appellant strode back into the restaurant, declaring he was "going to kill that son of a bitch." He emptied his gun at Thrailkill, striking him with five shots. Thrailkill died at a hospital two months later from complications caused by his injuries.

A stray bullet struck Elihue Armstrong, a semi-retired grocer and barber who was standing nearby, in the right arm and chest. Armstrong survived the injuries. Appellant told a psychiatrist that he did not intend to injure Armstrong.

Appellant moved for a directed verdict on the ABIK charge. Appellant asserted that the State had failed to prove he intended to kill Armstrong, and the doctrine of transferred intent did not apply. The judge denied the motion.

Did the trial judge err in refusing to direct a verdict on the ABIK charge because the doctrine of transferred intent is inapplicable when the intended victim is killed and a stray bullet injures — but does not kill — an unintended victim?

* * *Appellant contends the trial judge erred in refusing to direct a verdict in his favor on the ABIK charge. The doctrine of transferred intent does not apply because any intent was "fully satisfied" by the death of Thrailkill (the intended victim); therefore, nothing was left to transfer to Armstrong (the unintended victim). Furthermore, appellant argues, the doctrine is inapplicable because the harm appellant intended to inflict on Thrailkill (death) was not identical to the harm inflicted on Armstrong (injury). We disagree.

Criminal liability normally is based upon the concurrence of two factors: the defendant's criminal intent and the actual, physical act constituting the offense. * * * A defendant may not be convicted of a criminal offense unless the State proves beyond a reasonable doubt that he acted with the criminal intent, or mental state, required for a particular offense. * * *

Appellant's first argument is easily resolved. Some have observed, as the prosecutor did at appellant's trial, that "malice follows the bullet." Such explanations, as well as the term "transferred intent" itself, are somewhat misleading. The defendant's mental state, or mens rea, whatever it may be at the time he allegedly commits a criminal act, is contained within the defendant's brain when he commits the act. That mental state never leaves the defendant's brain; it is not "transferred" from the defendant's brain to another person or place. A more apt description might be that the mental state is like a spotlight emanating from its source–the defendant's mind — to its target — the intended victim.

Nor is that mental state in limited supply. The mental state "spotlight" is not extinguished at the moment a bullet strikes and kills the intended victim, such that there is no mental state left upon which to convict an unintended victim who also is injured or killed.* * *

The more difficult question is the one presented by the facts of this case and appellant's second argument. Is it appropriate to use the doctrine of transferred intent — admittedly a legal fiction — to transfer appellant's alleged mental state with regard to Thrailkill, the intended victim who was killed, to Armstrong, the unintended victim who was injured but not killed? To pursue our analogy, the jury ordinarily may not unilaterally shift the defendant's mental state "spotlight" from one person to another. The jury simply must determine whether that spotlight existed, i.e., was it "on" or "off." The question in this case is whether it is appropriate to allow the jury to place its collective hand upon the "spotlight" of appellant's mental state and adjust the imaginary beam so that it encompasses not only Thrailkill, but also Armstrong in order to convict appellant of ABIK. Answering that question requires consideration of transferred intent cases decided by this Court and the role of the doctrine in our criminal law.

This Court in several cases has held that a defendant may be found guilty of murder or manslaughter in a case of bad or mistaken aim under the doctrine of transferred intent. In the classic case, the defendant intends to kill or seriously injure one person, but misses that person and mistakenly kills another. Although the defendant did not act with malice toward the unintended victim, the defendant's criminal intent to kill the intended victim (i.e., his mental state of malice) is transferred to the unintended victim. "If there was malice in [defendant's] heart, he was guilty of the crime charged, it matters not whether he killed his intended victim or a third person through mistake." * * *

The unintended victim in the cases cited above was killed by the defendant. The Court has not decided a case such as the present one in which the intended victim was killed and the unintended victim was injured, but not killed.

Some courts decline to resort to the doctrine of transferred intent when they are convinced this legal fiction is not needed to hold the defendant criminally liable for his acts. * * *

We conclude that our criminal laws, unlike those of some other jurisdictions, make it necessary to impose the doctrine of transferred intent in this case. South Carolina recognizes three levels of assault: the offense of simple assault and battery, the offense of assault and battery of a high and aggravated nature (ABHAN), and the offense of ABIK. * * *

Our holding is consistent with the approach taken by other jurisdictions. "When a defendant contemplates or designs the death of another, the purpose of deterrence is better served by holding that defendant responsible for the knowing or purposeful murder of the unintended as well as the intended victim." * * *

The doctrine of transferred intent applies only in the situation of the same intended harm inflicted on an unintended victim. * * * The intent to assault and batter the police officer cannot be transferred to the property damage since the harm caused was different from the type of harm intended. * * * [State v.]Bryant [447 S.E.2d 852 (1994)] may be read to say the doctrine of transferred intent is inapplicable when the harm caused (injury to property) is different from the type of harm intended (injury to a person). Thus, the case at hand is distinguishable from Bryant because appellant intended to harm one person and in the process harmed another person. On the other hand, Bryant could be read to say that intent is not transferable when the harm caused (injuring a person) is different from the type of harm intended (killing a person). Under that interpretation, appellant's intent would not be transferable.

We find the former interpretation more appropriate than the latter, and so we distinguish appellant's case from *Bryant*. A coincidental damaging of property while intending to harm a person simply presents a different situation than harming one person while intending to harm another person. * * *

We hold that the doctrine of transferred intent may be used to convict a defendant of ABIK when the defendant kills the intended victim and also injures an unintended victim. We affirm appellant's ABIK conviction and the twenty-year sentence. * * * AFFIRMED.

NOTES

1. *Model Penal Code.* Transferred intent is a common law doctrine that was adopted by the Model Penal Code and fit within its gradations of intent. Section 2.03 provides:

> (2) When purposely or knowingly causing a particular result is an element of an offense, the element is not established if the actual result is not within the purpose or the contemplation of the actor unless:
>
> > (a) the actual result differs from that designed or contemplated, as the case may be, only in the respect that a different person or different property is injured or affected or that the injury or harm designed or contemplated would have been more serious or more extensive than that caused; or
> >
> > (b) the actual result involves the same kind of injury or harm as that designed or contemplated and is not too remote or accidental in its occurrence to have a [just] bearing on the actor's liability or on the gravity of his offense.
>
> (3) When recklessly or negligently causing a particular result is an element of an offense, the element is not established if the actual result is not within the risk of which the actor is aware or, in the case of negligence, of which he should be aware unless:
>
> > (a) the actual result differs from the probable result only in the respect that a different person or different property is injured or affected or

that the injury or harm would have been more serious or more extensive than that caused; or

(b) the actual result involves the same kind of injury or harm as the probable result and is not too remote or accidental in its occurrence to have a [just] bearing on the actor's liability or on the gravity of his offense.

2. ***Exceptions to Transferred Intent.*** Several exceptions to the transferred intent doctrine have developed in the law.

(a) Although the so-called "bad shot" cases are the paradigm example of transferred intent, cases of misidentification have been found unacceptable. Thus, aiming at a person and instead hitting the person next to the individual is usually considered to be transferred intent. In contrast, aiming at a person thinking they are someone else is considered misidentification and may not be considered to be a *transferred intent.* This does not mean that in the case of misidentification that a person is excused from liability for the criminal conduct. Rather, it means that they will be liable for the intent that they had.

(b) Further, some courts reject cases where the accused can be charged with a crime against the intended victim. This does not preclude charging the defendant with a crime against the second unintended victim, it just means that in determining the crime to be charged against the second individual, the doctrine of transferred intent will not be used.

(c) If the legislature has clearly precluded use of the doctrine of transferred intent, then the issue will be resolved by the statute's wording and transferred intent will not be permitted.

(d) It also has been held not to apply if a completely different harm is caused (e.g., intended to kill dog but strikes human instead). Again, this does not mean that the perpetrator of the wrong is excused from criminal conduct. It merely means that the doctrine of transferred intent is not used as the basis for determining the mens rea of the accused.

3. ***Statutory Transferred Intent.*** Some states have codified the transferred intent doctrine in much less detail than the Model Penal Code. For example, Texas has the following provision:

(b) A person is nevertheless criminally responsible for causing a result if the only difference between what actually occurred and what he desired, contemplated, or risked is that:

(1) a different offense was committed; or

(2) a different person or property was injured, harmed, or otherwise affected.

TEX. PENAL CODE ANN. § 6.04 (2002). The Texas Court of Appeals explained the statute's rationale:

> Though section 6.04(b) is titled transferred intent, it is somewhat of a misnomer because the concept does not address intent or any other mens rea. Rather, it depicts an effort by the legislature to criminalize an act that resulted in a different offense than the accused intended to commit. Section 6.04(b) transfers the mens rea of a contemplated, but incomplete, offense to the offense actually committed by mistake or accident. The rationale is that public policy demands that persons engaged in criminal activity not be exonerated "merely because they accidentally commit a different offense than originally contemplated." Therefore, the intent to commit the contemplated offense transfers to the offense in fact committed.

Loredo v. State, 130 S.W.3d 275 (Tex. App. 2004).

PROBLEM ELEVEN

Jane's boyfriend Seth tells her he wants to end the relationship because "I see my life moving in a different direction." A few days later, Jane sees Seth with Wilma, a co-worker, entering a movie theater holding hands. When Jane confronts Wilma the next day, Wilma says that she and Seth have been dating for about a month. Jane becomes enraged and screams, "Stay away from him or I'll kill you!" After she calms down, Jane sends an e-mail to her co-workers apologizing for her behavior. Two days later, Jane observes Wilma getting into Seth's car in front of their office building. Jane calls out, "Seth, I still love you and want you back." Seth smiles and waves, and then he and Wilma drive off. Later that evening, while driving down Main Street, Jane notices that Seth and Wilma are in the vehicle in front of her. She speeds up and rams the back of Seth's car twice, shouting out, "It's a rough ride with Wilma." When Jane hits Seth's car a third time, he loses control of the vehicle, crosses into on-coming traffic, and hits a truck head-on. Wilma is killed in the accident and Seth is seriously injured.

The jurisdiction adopted the intent provisions of the Model Penal Code. What is Jane's intent regarding Wilma's death? What is Jane's intent regarding Seth's injury? Can her intent regarding Wilma be transferred to Seth?

§ 4.06 Strict Liability

People v. Nasir
662 N.W.2d 29 (Mich. Ct. App. 2003)

HOLBROOK, Jr., P.J.

Defendant appeals as of right from his jury trial conviction of possessing or using counterfeit tax stamps, M.C.L. § 205.428(6). Defendant was sentenced to 18 to 120 months' imprisonment. We reverse and remand for a new trial.

In April 1999, two Michigan State Police officers assigned to the State Police Tobacco Tax Unit conducted an administrative inspection of the Ridgeway Party Store. Defendant, the store manager, was the only employee present. Upon examination, one of the officers determined that counterfeit tax stamps were affixed to a number of the tobacco products being sold.

Defendant requested that the jury be instructed as follows on the elements of the offense of possessing or using counterfeit cigarette tax stamps: "The elements of the offense with which the defendant is charged are these: (1) possession of counterfeit stamps; or (2) use of counterfeit stamps; (3) knowledge on defendant's part that the stamps are counterfeit; (4) a specific intent on defendant's part to violate the Michigan Tobacco Tax Act." The prosecution opposed this proposed instruction, arguing that the statute creates a strict-liability offense. The court agreed, and instructed the jury that the prosecution had to prove beyond a reasonable doubt that defendant possessed or used a counterfeit stamp at the Ridgeway Party Store without the authorization of the Michigan Department of Treasury.

Of central importance to this appeal is the issue whether the Legislature intended to dispense with a mens rea or fault requirement when creating this offense. While strict-liability offenses are generally disfavored, *United States v. United States Gypsum Co.*, 438 U.S. 422 (1978), the Legislature's authority to create strict-liability offenses is firmly rooted. As with all questions of statutory interpretation, when determining whether a statute imposes strict liability, our primary goal is to determine and effectuate the Legislature's intent. "The starting place for the search for intent is the language used in the statute." *Bio-Magnetic Resonance, Inc. v. Dep't of Pub. Health*, 593 N.W.2d 641 ([Mich. Ct. App.] 1999). MCL 205.428(6) reads:

> A person who manufactures, possesses, or uses a stamp or manufactures, possesses, or uses a counterfeit stamp or writing or device intended to replicate a stamp without authorization of the department, or a licensee who purchases or obtains a stamp from any person other than the department, is guilty of a felony and shall be punished by imprisonment

for not less than 1 year or more than 10 years and may be punished by a fine of not more than $50,000.00.

Clearly, the statute does not include a fault element. The single reference to intent does not come in the context of describing a particular mens rea. Rather, it is used to identify the type of writing or device prohibited under the statute, i.e., a writing or device designed to replicate an authentic stamp. The failure to include a fault element in a statute does not end the inquiry, however. As our Supreme Court observed in *People v. Lardie*, [551 N.W.2d 656 (Mich. 1996)], "In interpreting a statute in which the Legislature has not expressly included language indicating that fault is a necessary element of a crime, this Court must focus on whether the Legislature nevertheless intended to require some fault as a predicate to finding guilt." Courts commonly consider the following factors when making such an examination.

First and foremost, courts consider whether the statute at issue is a codification of the common law. "[W]here mens rea was a necessary element of the crime at common law, [we] will not interpret the statute as dispensing with knowledge as a necessary element." The crime of possessing or using counterfeit tax stamps is not a creature of the common law. Defendant argues that it derives from the common-law crime of forgery, and thus should include a mens rea element. We disagree. While elements of forgery inform M.C.L. § 205.428(6), it is at its heart a revenue statute, designed to assure that tobacco taxes levied in support of Michigan schools are not evaded.

MCL 205.428(6) is a revenue provision, not a public welfare law. The statute is not designed to place the burden of protecting the public welfare on an "otherwise innocent" person, *United States v. Dotterweich*, 320 U.S. 277 (1943), who is in a position to prevent an injury to the public welfare "with no more care than society might reasonably expect . . . ." While the regulation of the sale and consumption of cigarettes is a public health concern, this statute only tangentially touches on these matters. In 1997, the Tobacco Products Tax Act, M.C.L. § 205.421 et seq., was amended in order to deal with what was identified as the substantial and widespread smuggling of cigarettes into Michigan in order to circumvent the tax levied on each pack of cigarettes. To combat this problem, the Legislature enacted a tax stamp program, 1997 PA 187, which included the creation of the offense in issue.

We also believe that the punishment provided for in the statute and the danger that conviction poses to a defendant's reputation is severe. * * * Violation of M.C.L. § 205.428(6) is a felony punishable by a maximum term of imprisonment of ten years and a possible fine of up to $50,000. With some obvious and notable exceptions, this is not the type of punishment typical of public welfare offenses. See *Staples v. United States*, 511 U.S. 600 (1994) (observing that the Court's conclusion that a mens rea requirement should be read into the statute in issue is supported by the fact that the potential term of imprisonment for violation of the statute is ten years). Further, the statute mandates a prison term of not less than one year. Additionally, while not quantifiable, we believe the damage the proscribed punishment could potentially inflict to a defendant's reputation is more in keeping with the notion that such a defendant is guilty of some level of fault greater than what typically accompanies a strict-liability offense. "After all, 'felony' is, as we noted in distinguishing certain common-law crimes from public welfare offenses, '"as bad a word as you can give to man or thing.""' *Id.*

Connected to the severity of the potential punishment is the real possibility that to read the statute as not including a mens rea element would lead to the criminaliza-tion of "a broad range of apparently innocent conduct." *Liparota v. United States*, 471 U.S. 419 (1985). For example, because the statute punishes possession of counterfeit tax stamps, a strict reading of the statute would render criminal the possession by a retail customer of a pack of cigarettes bearing a counterfeit tax stamp. We do not believe that the Legislature intended that this potential problem would be regulated solely by prosecutorial discretion.

We also do not believe that the potential harm to the public at large is of such severity that we should presume the Legislature intended to impose liability without fault. In observing that the immediate harm attendant to a violation of M.C.L. §205.428(6) is basically the loss of potential revenue, we do not intend to minimize the effect of that harm. We simply note that it is not the type of immediate harm to the public welfare that is common to many strict-liability offenses. For example, the prospective immediate harm imposed by the sale of adulterated food is both widespread and potentially devastating to the people and families injured by the contaminated food.

Finally, we do not believe that prosecutors would face an oppressive burden if the statute were read to include a fault element. Unlike traffic law violations, we do not see the potential number of prosecutions arising from this statute to be overwhelmingly large. Nor do we believe that proving a fault element would be so difficult that strict liability should be imposed. Proving an actor's state of mind is difficult in virtually all criminal prosecutions. Indeed, this recognized difficulty has led to the rule that "minimal circumstantial evidence is sufficient" to establish a defendant's state of mind. We do not believe that proving that a defendant charged with violating M.C.L. § 205.428(6) had a certain state of mind is so difficult that it cannot be established through minimal circumstantial evidence.

Accordingly, we hold that knowledge is an element of the offense of which defendant stands convicted. Therefore, in order to establish that a defendant is guilty of possessing or using counterfeit tax stamps, the prosecution must prove that (1) the defendant possessed or used (2) a counterfeit stamp, or a writing or device intended to replicate a stamp, (3) that the defendant possessed or used the counterfeit tax stamp, or a writing or device intended to replicate a stamp, with knowledge that the stamp, writing, or device was not an authentic tax stamp, and (4) that the defendant acted without authorization of the Michigan Department of Treasury. We do not believe that the Legislature intended that the offense contain a specific intent element, nor do we believe that a defendant need act with knowledge that the defendant does so without the authorization of the Michigan Department of Treasury. We also conclude that any potential due process problem is remedied by the inclusion of the above fault element in the prima facie case.

Accordingly, we reverse and remand for a new trial.

METER, J. (dissenting).

I respectfully dissent because I believe that applying M.C.L. § 205.428(6) according to its plain meaning best effectuates the Legislature's intent. I would affirm.

The primary goal of judicial interpretation of statutes is to ascertain and give effect to the intent of the Legislature. As noted in *People v. Venticinque*, 586 N.W.2d 732 (Mich. 1998), the Legislature is presumed to have intended the meaning it plainly expressed. If the plain and ordinary meaning of the language in a statute is clear, judicial construction is generally not permitted.

As noted by the majority, M.C.L. § 205.428(6) clearly does not include an element of intent or knowledge. Given that many other criminal statutes do include elements of intent or knowledge, I conclude that the Legislature was aware of the consequences of the language employed in M.C.L. § 205.428(6) and consciously chose to enact a statute creating a strict-liability crime. See, generally, *People v. Ramsdell*, 585 N.W.2d 1 (Mich. Ct. App. 1998). In *Ramsdell*, this Court rejected the defendant's contention that an element of knowledge be imputed to the crime of being a prisoner in possession of contraband, M.C.L. § 800.281(4). Significantly, the Court stated:

> The word "knowingly" is absolutely absent from the statute as enacted by the Legislature and signed into law by the Governor.

> Defendant's position implicitly suggests that that Legislature did not know quite what it was doing when it enacted M.C.L. § 800.281(4) . . . . We disagree; the Legislature is presumed to be aware of the consequences of the use, or omission, of language when it enacts the laws that govern our behavior.

As noted in *People v. Lardie*, 551 N.W.2d 656 (Mich. 1996), states may punish certain acts or omissions regardless of the actor's intent. Given this recognized authority of the Legislature to enact strict-liability crimes, and given the clear absence of an element of intent or knowledge from the statute at issue in this case,

I see no reason to contravene the plain meaning of the statute and the clear legislative intent by imputing an additional element to the crime in question.

* * * [T]he majority contends that an element of knowledge must be imputed to M.C.L. § 205.428(6) because the statute is not a public welfare law, because it exposes a defendant to severe punishment, because it has the potential to criminalize a broad range of apparently innocent conduct, and because the burden on prosecutors to prove guilty knowledge would not be oppressive. In response, I note that providing funding for schools, which the Tobacco Products Tax Act, M.C.L. § 205.421 et seq., does, is indeed a matter of public welfare, and requiring prosecutors to prove guilty knowledge would increase the chances of fraudulent avoidance of the tax. Moreover, while the penalty under M.C.L. § 205.428(6) is potentially severe, I note that in *People v. Motor City Hosp. & Surgical Supply, Inc.*, 575 N.W.2d 95 (Mich. Dist. App. 1997), this Court upheld a strict-liability crime despite a potential punishment of four years' imprisonment and a $30,000 fine. Accordingly, a potentially severe penalty does not automatically mandate the imputation of an intent or knowledge element to a strict-liability crime. With regard to the notion that M.C.L. § 205.428(6) potentially punishes a range of apparently innocent conduct, I note simply that this argument could be made in the context of any strict-liability offense. For example, the statute at issue in *Ramsdell* punishes a prisoner for possessing contraband even if the prisoner did not know the true nature of the item he possessed. I do not find the majority's argument a persuasive reason for ignoring the clear legislative intent expressed in M.C.L. § 205.428(6). * * *

Because I conclude that M.C.L. § 205.428(6) should be enforced as written, and because I find no merit to the additional issues defendant raises on appeal, I would affirm.

NOTES

1. ***Model Penal Code***. The Model Penal Code provides:

§ 2.05. When Culpability Requirements Are Inapplicable to Violations and to Offenses Defined by Other Statutes; Effect of Absolute Liability in Reducing Grade of Offense to Violation.

(1) The requirements of culpability prescribed by Sections 2.01 and 2.02 do not apply to:

(a) offenses that constitute violations, unless the requirement involved is included in the definition of the offense or the Court determines that its application is consistent with effective enforcement of the law defining the offense; or

(b) offenses defined by statutes other than the Code, insofar as a legislative purpose to impose absolute liability for such offenses or with respect to any material element thereof plainly appears.

(2) Notwithstanding any other provision of existing law and unless a subsequent statute otherwise provides:

(a) when absolute liability is imposed with respect to any material element of an offense defined by a statute other than the Code and a conviction is based upon such liability, the offense constitutes a violation; and

(b) although absolute liability is imposed by law with respect to one or more of the material elements of an offense defined by a statute other than the Code, the culpable commission of the offense may be charged and proved, in which event negligence with respect to such elements constitutes sufficient culpability and the classification of the offense and the sentence that may be imposed therefor upon conviction are determined by Section 1.04 and Article 6 of the Code.

The Model Penal Code defines violations in § 1.04(5) as:

An offense defined by this Code or by any other statute of this State constitutes a violation if it is so designated in this Code or in the law defining the offense or if no other sentence than a fine, or fine and forfeiture or other civil penalty is authorized upon conviction or if it is defined by a statute other than this Code that now provides that the offense shall not constitute a crime. A violation does not constitute a crime and conviction of a violation shall not give rise to any disability or legal disadvantage based on conviction of a criminal offense.

2. *Public Welfare Offenses.* The Supreme Court has found that it is constitutionally permissible for the legislature to enact a law that imposes criminal punishment when the violation involves protection of the public welfare without requiring proof of the defendant's intent. In *Staples v. United States*, 511 U.S. 600 (1994), the Court noted that "such offenses involve statutes that regulate potentially harmful or injurious items," such as addictive drugs or hazardous materials like asbestos. In deciding whether the government must prove a defendant's mens rea, the Court stated that "we essentially have relied on the nature of the statute and the particular character of the items regulated to determine whether congressional silence concerning the mental element of the offense should be interpreted as dispensing with conventional mens rea requirements." But there is at least one type of intent required even for a

strict liability crime – proof that the defendant knows that the hazardous item is being possessed. The Court explained:

> By interpreting such public welfare offenses to require at least that the defendant know that he is dealing with some dangerous or deleterious substance, we have avoided construing criminal statutes to impose a rigorous form of strict liability. True strict liability might suggest that the defendant need not know even that he was dealing with a dangerous item. Nevertheless, we have referred to public welfare offenses as "dispensing with" or "eliminating" a mens rea requirement or "mental element," and have described them as strict liability crimes. While use of the term "strict liability" is really a misnomer, we have interpreted statutes defining public welfare offenses to eliminate the requirement of mens rea; that is, the requirement of a "guilty mind" with respect to an element of a crime. Under such statutes we have not required that the defendant know the facts that make his conduct fit the definition of the offense.

The Court found that the statute at issue in *Staples*, involving possession of an automatic weapon, required proof of the defendant's knowledge that it had been modified so that it constituted an automatic weapon. Unlike other items that can be viewed as inherently dangerous, "the fact remains that there is a long tradition of widespread lawful gun ownership by private individuals in this country" and "despite their potential for harm, guns generally can be owned in perfect innocence." On the other hand, in *United States v. Freed*, 401 U.S. 601 (1971), involving possession of a hand grenade, the Court found that the statute was a strict liability provision as "a regulatory measure in the interest of the public safety, which may well be premised on the theory that one would hardly be surprised to learn that possession of hand grenades is not an innocent act."

3. ***The Prosecution's Burden.*** When a statute imposes strict liability, then the prosecutor need not prove the defendant's state of mind at the time of the violation. This eases considerably the prosecution's burden of proof because once it establishes that the defendant committed the actus reus of the offense, then liability is imposed immediately without the need to infer any particular level of intent. When a court interprets a statute as requiring some proof of intent, as the court did in *Nasir*, then the defendant can mount a defense to the charge, even if it is only a general intent. Note that the determination of whether a statute contains an intent element or is a strict liability provision is an exercise in statutory interpretation.

4. ***Strict Liability Elements.*** Certain crimes may require intent, but have elements within the crime for which no intent need be proven for liability. The most common crime that contains a "strict liability element" is statutory rape, which is sexual intercourse with a person under the age of consent. In some jurisdictions, if the age of consent is 16, then a defendant who has sexual relations with a 15-year old will have committed the crime, regardless of whether the person knew of the victim's

age and, more importantly, even if the person's mistake regarding age is entirely reasonable. Other examples of elements of crimes for which there is usually no intent are venue (*i.e.* the location of the offense), the status of the victim (*e.g.* the victim is a police officer or government employee), and the nature of the weapon.

PROBLEM TWELVE

Tracy pleaded guilty to driving while impaired (DWI) and was sentenced to pay a $1,000 fine and perform 50 hours of community service. Under the state's Motor Vehicle Code, the license of a person guilty of a DWI is automatically suspended for six months. The person is eligible to file a petition with the Secretary of State to have the driver's license reinstated after the six-month suspension and completion of all the terms of the sentence imposed by the court. A defendant sentenced to community service must submit a form to the court clerk's office signed by a supervisor at the location where it was performed attesting to completion of the required hours. Tracy completed the community service and submitted the signed form, and was told by the court clerk that it would be sent to the Secretary of State. Tracy believed that was all that was necessary for the driver's license to reinstated, and did not submit a petition to the Secretary of State. A year after the DWI, Tracy was stopped for speeding. The officer ran a check on the driver's license and discovered that it was still suspended. Tracy is charged with operating after suspension (OAS), a misdemeanor. A statute in the jurisdiction provides: "Any individual found guilty of operating a motor vehicle during the period for which the individual's license is revoked or suspended, or for which the right to operate is suspended or revoked, shall, for each such offense, be fined not to exceed $5,000 or imprisoned for not more than 1 year, or both." At trial, Tracy's lawyer asks the court to instruct the jury that the government was required to prove Tracy knew, or had reason to know, the license was suspended at the time of the traffic stop. The government argues that the proposed instruction is improper because the OAS statute is a strict liability offense. What arguments will the defense make that the instruction is proper, and how will the prosecutor respond? Would it affect the analysis if a different statute required the court to impose a minimum 30-day jail sentence for an OAS conviction if the license was suspended or revoked because of a prior DWI conviction?

---

§ 4.07 Mistake

A. Mistake of Fact

State v. Contreras
167 P.3d 966 (N.M. Ct. App. 2007)

SUTIN, Chief Judge:

* * * Defendant [Anthony Contreras] checked into a Motel 6 at 3:30 one afternoon and paid for a room. He was assigned Room 125 and was given a plastic key card, but the key card did not have a room number on it. Defendant was very intoxicated when he checked in and he left his identification at the front desk. At 4:45 p.m., the police were called to the Motel 6 because someone had thrown a heavy trash can through the window of Room 121. Room 121 was four doors down from Room 125. When Officer Salbidrez arrived, he went into Room 121 and began to give verbal commands to the person inside. Defendant came out from the bathroom area. He did not have his shoes on and he was obviously intoxicated. Defendant initially responded to the officer with obscene remarks, although when told that he was under arrest, he offered to pay for the window. The officer found nothing broken or damaged in the room, other than the broken window, and nothing had been stolen. Defendant's key card was found on the ground outside of Room 121. The officer confirmed that the key opened Room 125. Defendant was indicted on one charge of breaking and entering, contrary to Section 30–14–8(A) and one charge of criminal damage to property, contrary to Section 30–15–1.

Defendant did not testify at trial. He did not present any evidence. No witness testified as to any statements made by Defendant about why he broke the window or whether he thought he had permission to be in Room 121. Based on the evidence presented in the State's case, Defendant requested an instruction on mistake of fact and argued that he showed his identification, paid for a room, had permission to go into a room, thought he was entering the room he had a right to be in, and made a mistake. He argued that this mistake of fact negated the mental state accompanying entry without permission, which is an element of breaking and entering and, therefore, did not commit the crime of breaking and entering, even if he would have been guilty of a different crime based on breaking the window. Defendant's requested mistake-of-fact instruction * * * read as follows.

> Evidence has been presented that the defendant believed that he had a right to enter the motel room. The burden is on the state to prove beyond a reasonable doubt that the defendant did not act under an honest and reasonable belief in the existence of those facts. If you have a reasonable doubt as to whether the defendant's action resulted from a mistaken belief of those facts, you must find the defendant not guilty.

Defendant also requested that the instruction on the elements of breaking and entering required the State to prove beyond a reasonable doubt that (1) he "entered a motel room without permission"; (2) "[t]he entry was obtained by the breaking of a window"; and (3) he "did not act under a mistake of fact [,] i.e. that he entered without permission[.]" The district court refused to give the instruction and concluded that the evidence was not sufficient to support the instruction. The court indicated that direct evidence was not required, but that a mistake could not be inferred, and Defendant would have to prove more than what the evidence showed. The court further stated that there was no evidence of what Defendant believed and thus denied Defendant's request regarding the mistake-of-fact instruction. * * *

Defendant argues that the district court erred in refusing to instruct on mistake of fact. The State argues that the evidence was insufficient to show that Defendant had an honest and reasonable belief that he was in the correct room or that he went into the wrong room by mistake. The State also argues that the jury was not required to find a specific mental state as an element of breaking and entering, and that the general intent instruction that was given to the jury was adequate. In addition, the State argues that its case offered no evidence that Defendant thought he had permission to "break into either room." This latter argument is off-issue. The issue is not whether Defendant believed that he had permission to break into a room, but whether he believed he had permission to enter the room, because the lack of permission to enter is an element of breaking and entering.

Generally, a mental state can be proved by circumstantial evidence. "If the State may prove a defendant's state of mind through circumstantial evidence, then common sense dictates that a defendant may attempt to prove his state of mind through circumstantial evidence as well." *Williams v. State*, 915 P.2d 371 (Okla. 1996). Evidence supporting a defense theory can be introduced in either the defendant's case or the State's case.

The evidence in favor of giving the mistake-of-fact instruction in the present case includes that defendant was very intoxicated; Defendant paid for a room and was thus authorized to enter a room; nothing was stolen; Defendant took his shoes off and was in the bathroom in Room 121, from which it can be inferred that he was using the room as one for which he had paid; Defendant's key card for Room 125 was on the ground outside near Room 121, from which it can be inferred that he had attempted to use it to enter Room 121; and the key card did not have a room number on it. Viewing this evidence in the light most favorable to giving a mistake-of-fact instruction, a reasonable jury could conclude that Defendant believed that he had permission to enter the room that he entered. The belief element in the mistake-of-fact instruction requires that Defendant had subjective or actual knowledge of permission to enter Room 121.

The defense of mistake of fact also requires the defendant's mistake to be honest and reasonable. The issue of whether that mistake was honest and reasonable should, generally, be a question for the jury. As such, we hold that there was sufficient evidence to submit an instruction on mistake of fact to the jury.

The State also argues that, even without a mistake-of-fact instruction, the jury was properly instructed because the general intent instruction sufficiently covered the mental state required to convict Defendant of breaking and entering. If we correctly understand the State's argument, it is contending that even if there were sufficient evidence to support a mistake-of-fact instruction, such instruction was unnecessary as a matter of law because the general intent instruction was sufficient to properly instruct the jury. The general intent instruction in this case read:

> In addition to the elements of breaking and entering ..., the state must prove to your satisfaction beyond a reasonable doubt that the defendant acted intentionally when he committed the crime charged. A person acts intentionally when he purposely does an act which the law declares to be a crime, even though he may not know that his act is unlawful. Whether the defendant acted intentionally may be inferred from all the surrounding circumstances, such as the manner in which he acts, the means used, his conduct and any statements made by him.

Defendant disagrees with the State. He contends that an essential element of breaking and entering is knowledge on his part that he did not have permission to enter Room 121. Therefore, because the jury was not instructed on this essential element of breaking and entering, the district court erred when it refused his requested mistake-of-fact instruction. Mistake of fact is a defense when it negates "the existence of the mental state essential to the crime charged." *State v. Fuentes*, 577 P.2d 452 (N.M. Ct. App.1978). The trial court need not give a mistake of fact instruction where the intent element of the crime is adequately defined by the other instructions given by the trial court. We determine the mental state required for the commission of a particular crime by looking at legislative intent. We then look to the jury instructions to determine whether they properly instructed on the requisite mental state.

Under Section 30–14–8(A), breaking and entering "consists of the unauthorized entry of any . . . dwelling or other structure, . . . where entry is obtained by . . . the breaking . . . of any part of the . . . dwelling or other structure[.]" When a statute is silent as to criminal intent, as Section 30–14–8(A) is, it is well settled that we presume criminal intent unless it is clear from the statute that the legislature intended to omit the mens rea element. A single statute may require proof of different mental states for different elements of the crime. General intent is only the intention to make the bodily movement which constitutes the act which the crime requires.

* * * [W]e believe that Section 30–14–8(A) evinces more than just one requisite intent. In the present case, there are three elements, namely, entering, doing so without permission, and entering by breaking the window. As to entering and breaking the window, those are intended physical acts, bodily movements, to which the general intent instruction clearly applies. However, we do not see how the general intent instruction can logically apply to the fact of lack of permission to enter. Unless strict liability applies, lack of permission requires recognition of circumstances that produce a mental state of knowledge. We agree with Defendant that the mental state which accompanies the "without permission" element of breaking and entering is knowledge of the lack of permission. In our view, the second mental state, namely, knowledge, is necessary with respect to the permission element of breaking and entering, and the general intent instruction did not adequately instruct the jury on that second mental state. In the present case, no instruction relating to knowledge was given to the jury. Thus, there was no instruction that properly instructed on that requisite mental state. Under the circumstances, Defendant was entitled to a mistake-of-fact instruction in order to attempt to defend by negating the mental state of knowledge that he did not have permission to enter Room 121. Thus, we hold that the district court erred when it refused Defendant's requested mistake-of-fact instruction. * * *

We reverse and remand for a new trial based on the denial of Defendant's requested jury instruction on mistake of fact.

NOTES

1. ***General and Specific Intent***. A claim of mistake as a defense to a charge must negate an element of the offense, and most often it goes to the defendant's intent to commit the offense. Under the common law, a defendant's claimed mistake for a specific intent crime did not have to be reasonable, only that the defendant had a subjective mistake that negated the intent element of the offense. In contrast, for a general intent crime, the defendant's claimed mistake must be a reasonable one, *i.e.* a mistake that a person of ordinary care and prudence would make in similar circumstances. In *Contreras*, the court viewed the knowledge aspect of the lack of permission element as involving a general intent, so the defendant's burden would be higher because the jury must first determine whether he actually had the mistaken belief, and then that the mistake was one a reasonable person would make. If the jury finds that the proffered mistake was unreasonable, and there is sufficient evidence to establish general intent, then the defendant will be convicted. A claim of mistake is often called a "defense" to the crime, but in reality it is an assertion by the defendant that the prosecution has not proven the intent element of the offense. For a strict liability crime, mistake is irrelevant because intent is not an element of the crime.

2. ***Theory of the Case Instruction.*** A defendant is entitled to a "theory of the case" instruction if there is sufficient evidence to support the defense position and it is consistent with the law. In determining whether to give the instruction, the court construes the evidence in the light most favorable to the defendant, and, as *Contreras* shows, the defendant need not introduce evidence apart from the prosecution's case-in-chief to qualify for an instruction. The instruction is a means for the defense to respond to the charging document, which is usually read to the jury and may even be provided during the deliberations. Although the court should instruct the jury on a defense theory if there is a basis for it, the jury need not be given a separate instruction if the other instructions, considered in their entirety, adequately cover the defense theory.

B. Mistake of Law

Cheek v. United States
498 U.S. 192 (1991)

Justice WHITE delivered the opinion of the Court.

* * * Petitioner John L. Cheek has been a pilot for American Airlines since 1973. He filed federal income tax returns through 1979 but thereafter ceased to file returns. * * * He also claimed an increasing number of withholding allowances — eventually claiming 60 allowances by mid-1980 — and for the years 1981 to 1984 indicated on his W-4 forms that he was exempt from federal income taxes. In 1983, petitioner unsuccessfully sought a refund of all tax withheld by his employer in 1982. Petitioner's income during this period at all times far exceeded the minimum necessary to trigger the statutory filing requirement.

* * * He was charged with six counts of willfully failing to file a federal income tax return for the years 1980, 1981, and 1983 through 1986, in violation of [26 U.S.C.] § 7203. He was further charged with three counts of willfully attempting to evade his income taxes for the years 1980, 1981, and 1983 in violation of 26 U.S.C. § 7201. * * *

At trial, the evidence established that between 1982 and 1986, petitioner was involved in at least four civil cases that challenged various aspects of the federal income tax system. * * * In all four of those cases, the plaintiffs were informed by the courts that many of their arguments, including that they were not taxpayers within the meaning of the tax laws, that wages are not income, that the Sixteenth Amendment does not authorize the imposition of an income tax on individuals, and that the Sixteenth Amendment is unenforceable, were frivolous or had been repeatedly rejected by the courts. During this time period, petitioner also attended at least two criminal trials of persons charged with tax offenses. In addition, there was evidence that in 1980 or 1981 an attorney had advised Cheek that the courts had rejected as frivolous the claim that wages are not income.

Cheek represented himself at trial and testified in his defense. He admitted that he had not filed personal income tax returns during the years in question. He testified that as early as 1978, he had begun attending seminars sponsored by, and following the advice of, a group that believes, among other things, that the federal tax system is unconstitutional. Some of the speakers at these meetings were lawyers who purported to give professional opinions about the invalidity of the federal income tax laws. Cheek produced a letter from an attorney stating that the Sixteenth Amendment did not authorize a tax on wages and salaries but only on gain or profit. Petitioner's defense was that, based on the indoctrination he received from this group and from his own study, he sincerely believed that the tax laws were being unconstitutionally enforced and that his actions during the 1980-1986 period were lawful. He therefore argued that he had acted without the willfulness required for conviction of the various offenses with which he was charged.

In the course of its instructions, the trial court advised the jury that to prove "willfulness" the Government must prove the voluntary and intentional violation of a known legal duty, a burden that could not be proved by showing mistake, ignorance, or negligence. The court further advised the jury that an objectively reasonable good-faith misunderstanding of the law would negate willfulness, but mere disagreement with the law would not. The court described Cheek's beliefs about the income tax system and instructed the jury that if it found that Cheek "honestly and reasonably believed that he was not required to pay income taxes or to file tax returns," * * * , a not guilty verdict should be returned.

* * * At the end of the first day of deliberation, the jury sent out [a] note saying that it [] could not reach a verdict because "'we are divided on the issue as to if Mr. Cheek honestly & reasonably believed that he was not required to pay income tax.'" * * * When the jury resumed its deliberations, the District Judge gave the jury an additional instruction. This instruction stated in part that "an honest but unreasonable belief is not a defense and does not negate willfulness," * * * and that "advice or research resulting in the conclusion that wages of a privately employed person are not income or that the tax laws are unconstitutional is not objectively reasonable and cannot serve as the basis for a good faith misunderstanding of the law defense." * * * The court also instructed the jury that "persistent refusal to acknowledge the law does not constitute a good faith misunderstanding of the law." * * * Approximately two hours later, the jury returned a verdict finding petitioner guilty on all counts.

Petitioner appealed his convictions, arguing that the District Court erred by instructing the jury that only an objectively reasonable misunderstanding of the law negates the statutory willfulness requirement. The United States Court of Appeals for the Seventh Circuit rejected that contention and affirmed the convictions. 882 F.2d 1263 (7th Cir. 1989) * * *

The general rule that ignorance of the law or a mistake of law is no defense to criminal prosecution is deeply rooted in the American legal system. * * * Based on the notion that the law is definite and knowable, the common law presumed that every person knew the law. This common-law rule has been applied by the Court in numerous cases construing criminal statutes.* * *

The proliferation of statutes and regulations has sometimes made it difficult for the average citizen to know and comprehend the extent of the duties and obligations imposed by the tax laws. Congress has accordingly softened the impact of the common-law presumption by making specific intent to violate the law an element of certain federal criminal tax offenses. Thus, the Court almost 60 years ago interpreted the statutory term "willfully" as used in the federal criminal tax statutes as carving out an exception to the traditional rule. This special treatment of criminal tax offenses is largely due to the complexity of the tax laws. * * *

* * * Willfulness, as construed by our prior decisions in criminal tax cases, requires the Government to prove that the law imposed a duty on the defendant, that the defendant knew of this duty, and that he voluntarily and intentionally violated that duty. We deal first with the case where the issue is whether the defendant knew of the duty purportedly imposed by the provision of the statute or regulation he is accused of violating, a case in which there is no claim that the provision at issue is invalid. In such a case, if the Government proves actual knowledge of the pertinent legal duty, the prosecution, without more, has satisfied the knowledge component of the willfulness requirement. But carrying this burden requires negating a defendant's claim of ignorance of the law or a claim that because of a misunder-standing of the law, he had a good-faith belief that he was not violating any of the provisions of the tax laws. This is so because one cannot be aware that the law imposes a duty upon him and yet be ignorant of it, misunderstand the law, or believe that the duty does not exist. In the end, the issue is whether, based on all the evidence, the Government has proved that the defendant was aware of the duty at issue, which cannot be true if the jury credits a good-faith misunderstanding and belief submission, whether or not the claimed belief or misunderstanding is objectively reasonable.

In this case, if Cheek asserted that he truly believed that the Internal Revenue Code did not purport to treat wages as income, and the jury believed him, the Government would not have carried its burden to prove willfulness, however unreasonable a court might deem such a belief. Of course, in deciding whether to credit Cheek's good-faith belief claim, the jury would be free to consider any admissible evidence from any source showing that Cheek was aware of his duty to file a return and to treat wages as income, including evidence showing his awareness of the relevant provisions of the Code or regulations, of court decisions rejecting his interpretation of the tax law, of authoritative rulings of the Internal Revenue Service, or of any contents of the personal income tax return forms and accompanying instructions that made it plain that wages should be returned as income.

We thus disagree with the Court of Appeals' requirement that a claimed good-faith belief must be objectively reasonable if it is to be considered as possibly negating the Government's evidence purporting to show a defendant's awareness of the legal duty at issue. Knowledge and belief are characteristically questions for the factfinder, in this case the jury. Characterizing a particular belief as not objectively reasonable transforms the inquiry into a legal one and would prevent the jury from considering it. It would of course be proper to exclude evidence having no relevance or probative value with respect to willfulness; but it is not contrary to common sense, let alone impossible, for a defendant to be ignorant of his duty based on an irrational belief that he has no duty, and forbidding the jury to consider evidence that might negate willfulness would raise a serious question under the Sixth Amendment's jury trial provision. * * * It is common ground that this Court, where possible, interprets congressional enactments so as to avoid raising serious constitutional questions. * * *

It was therefore error to instruct the jury to disregard evidence of Cheek's understanding that, within the meaning of the tax laws, he was not a person required to file a return or to pay income taxes and that wages are not taxable income, as incredible as such misunderstandings of and beliefs about the law might be. Of course, the more unreasonable the asserted beliefs or misunderstandings are, the more likely the jury will consider them to be nothing more than simple disagreement with known legal duties imposed by the tax laws and will find that the Government has carried its burden of proving knowledge. * * *

Cheek asserted in the trial court that he should be acquitted because he believed in good faith that the income tax law is unconstitutional as applied to him and thus could not legally impose any duty upon him of which he should have been aware. * * *

We do not believe that Congress contemplated that such a taxpayer, without risking criminal prosecution, could ignore the duties imposed upon him by the Internal Revenue Code and refuse to utilize the mechanisms provided by Congress to present his claims of invalidity to the courts and to abide by their decisions.* * * Of course, Cheek was free in this very case to present his claims of invalidity and have them adjudicated, but like defendants in criminal cases in other contexts, who "willfully" refuse to comply with the duties placed upon them by the law, he must take the risk of being wrong.

We thus hold that in a case like this, a defendant's views about the validity of the tax statutes are irrelevant to the issue of willfulness and need not be heard by the jury, and, if they are, an instruction to disregard them would be proper. For this purpose, it makes no difference whether the claims of invalidity are frivolous or have substance. It was therefore not error in this case for the District Judge to instruct the jury not to consider Cheek's claims that the tax laws were unconstitutional. However, it was error for the court to instruct the jury that petitioner's asserted beliefs that wages are not income and that he was not a taxpayer within the meaning of the Internal Revenue Code should not be considered by the jury in determining whether Cheek had acted willfully.* * *

For the reasons set forth in the opinion above, the judgment of the Court of Appeals is vacated, and the case is remanded for further proceedings consistent with this opinion. * * *

Justice SOUTER took no part in the consideration or decision of this case. [The concurring opinion of Justice SCALIA is omitted here.]

Justice BLACKMUN, with whom Justice MARSHALL joins, dissenting.

It seems to me that we are concerned in this case not with "the complexity of the tax laws," * * * but with the income tax law in its most elementary and basic aspect: Is a wage earner a taxpayer and are wages income?

The Court acknowledges that the conclusively established standard for willfulness under the applicable statutes is the "'voluntary, intentional violation of a known legal duty.'" * * * That being so, it is incomprehensible to me how, in this day, more than 70 years after the institution of our present federal income tax system with the passage of the Income Tax Act of 1913, * * * any taxpayer of competent mentality can assert as his defense to charges of statutory willfulness the proposition that the wage he receives for his labor is not income, irrespective of a cult that says otherwise and advises the gullible to resist income tax collections. One might note in passing that this particular taxpayer, after all, was a licensed pilot for one of our major commercial airlines; he presumably was a person of at least minimum intellectual competence.

The District Court's instruction that an objectively reasonable and good-faith misunderstanding of the law negates willfulness lends further, rather than less, protection to this defendant, for it adds an additional hurdle for the prosecution to overcome. Petitioner should be grateful for this further protection, rather than be opposed to it.

This Court's opinion today, I fear, will encourage taxpayers to cling to frivolous views of the law in the hope of convincing a jury of their sincerity. If that ensues, I suspect we have gone beyond the limits of common sense.

While I may not agree with every word the Court of Appeals has enunciated in its opinion, I would affirm its judgment in this case. I therefore dissent.

NOTES AND QUESTIONS

1. *Is* **Cheek** *Sui Generis*? In *Ratzlaf v. United States*, 510 U.S. 135 (1994), the Court found it necessary to analyze a currency reporting and structuring statute that required proof of "willfulness." The Court stated:

> On the evening of October 20, 1988, defendant-petitioner Waldemar Ratzlaf ran up a debt of $160,000 playing blackjack at the High Sierra Casino in Reno, Nevada. The casino gave him one week to pay. On the due date, Ratzlaf returned to the casino with cash of $100,000 in hand. A casino official informed Ratzlaf that all transactions involving more than $10,000 in cash had to be reported to state and federal authorities. The official added that the casino could accept a cashier's check for the full amount due without triggering any reporting requirement. The casino helpfully placed a limousine at Ratzlaf's disposal, and assigned an employee to accompany him to banks in the vicinity. Informed that banks, too, are required to report cash transactions in excess of $10,000, Ratzlaf purchased cashier's checks, each for less than $10,000 and each from a different bank. He delivered these checks to the High Sierra Casino.

> Based on this endeavor, Ratzlaf was charged with "structuring transactions" to evade the banks' obligation to report cash transactions exceeding $10,000; this conduct, the indictment alleged, violated 31 U.S.C. § 5322(a) and 5324(3). The trial judge instructed the jury that the Government had to prove defendant's knowledge of the banks' reporting obligation and his attempt to evade that obligation, but did not have to prove defendant knew the structuring was unlawful. Ratzlaf was convicted, fined, and sentenced to prison * * * .

> Undoubtedly there are bad men who attempt to elude official reporting requirements in order to hide from Government inspectors such criminal activity as laundering drug money or tax evasion. But currency structuring is not inevitably nefarious. Consider, for example, the small business operator who knows that reports filed under 31 U.S.C. § 5313(a) are available to the Internal Revenue Service. To reduce the risk of an IRS audit, she brings $9,500 in cash to the bank twice each week, in lieu of transporting over $10,000 once each week. That person, if the United States is right, has committed a criminal offense, because she structured

cash transactions "for the specific purpose of depriving the Government of the information that Section 5313(a) is designed to obtain." * * * Nor is a person who structures a currency transaction invariably motivated by a desire to keep the Government in the dark. But under the Government's construction an individual would commit a felony against the United States by making cash deposits in small doses, fearful that the bank's reports would increase the likelihood of burglary, or in an endeavor to keep a former spouse unaware of his wealth.

Courts have noted "many occasions" on which persons, without violating any law, may structure transactions "in order to avoid the impact of some regulation or tax." * * * In current days, as an *amicus* noted, countless taxpayers each year give a gift of $10,000 on December 31 and an identical gift the next day, thereby legitimately avoiding the taxable gifts reporting required by 26 U.S.C. § 2503 (b) * * * .

In light of these examples, we are unpersuaded by the argument that structuring is so obviously "evil" or inherently "bad" that the "willfulness" requirement is satisfied irrespective of the defendant's knowledge of the illegality of structuring. Had Congress wished to dispense with the requirement, it could have furnished the appropriate instruction * * * .

2. ***Environmental Statutes.*** Should this doctrine also apply to environmental statutes that are complicated? In *United States v. Overholt*, 307 F.3d 1231 (10th Cir. 2002), the court distinguished the position taken in *Ratzlaf* when applied to environmental cases stating that:

> [W]e strongly doubt that as the federal government has sought to protect the environment by imposing more and more restrictions on those handling dangerous chemicals, Congress has intended to reduce the burden on such persons to inform themselves of what the law requires. In short we have no reason to believe that the word "willful" in 42 U.S.C. §§ 300h-2(b)(2) requires proof of knowledge of the regulation allegedly violated.

3. ***Due Process.*** In *Lambert v. California*, 355 U.S. 225 (1957), the Supreme Court considered a challenge to a Los Angeles Municipal Code, providing "that it shall be unlawful for 'any convicted person' to be or remain in Los Angeles for a period of more than five days without registering; it requires any person having a place of abode outside the city to register if he comes into the city on five occasions or more during a 30-day period; and it prescribes the information to be furnished the Chief of Police on registering." Each day's failure to register was a separate offense. The defendant challenged this registration law as a violation of her right to due process of law because she was unaware of the statutory requirement. The Court stated:

Appellant, arrested on suspicion of another offense, was charged with a violation of this registration law. The evidence showed that she had been at the time of her arrest a resident of Los Angeles for over seven years. Within that period she had been convicted in Los Angeles of the crime of forgery, an offense which California punishes as a felony. Though convicted of a crime punishable as a felony, she had not at the time of her arrest registered under the Municipal Code. * * * The case was tried to a jury which found appellant guilty. The court fined her $250 and placed her on probation for three years. * * *

The registration provision, carrying criminal penalties, applies if a person has been convicted "of an offense punishable as a felony in the State of California" or, in case he has been convicted in another State, if the offense "would have been punishable as a felony" had it been committed in California. No element of willfulness is by terms included in the ordinance nor read into it by the California court as a condition necessary for a conviction.

We must assume that appellant had no actual knowledge of the requirement that she register under this ordinance, as she offered proof of this defense which was refused. The question is whether a registration act of this character violates due process where it is applied to a person who has no actual knowledge of his duty to register, and where no showing is made of the probability of such knowledge.

We do not go with Blackstone in saying that "a vicious will" is necessary to constitute a crime, * * * for conduct alone without regard to the intent of the doer is often sufficient. There is wide latitude in the lawmakers to declare an offense and to exclude elements of knowledge and diligence from its definition. * * * But we deal here with conduct that is wholly passive–mere failure to register. It is unlike the commission of acts, or the failure to act under circumstances that should alert the doer to the consequences of his deed. . . . The rule that "ignorance of the law will not excuse" * * * is deep in our law, as is the principle that of all the powers of local government, the police power is "one of the least limitable." On the other hand, due process places some limits on its exercise. Engrained in our concept of due process is the requirement of notice. Notice is sometimes essential so that the citizen has the chance to defend charges. Notice is required before property interests are disturbed, before assessments are made, before penalties are assessed. Notice is required in a myriad of situations where a penalty or forfeiture might be suffered for mere failure to act.* * *

Registration laws are common and their range is wide. * * * We believe that actual knowledge of the duty to register or proof of the probability of such knowledge and subsequent failure to comply are necessary before a conviction under the ordinance can stand. As Holmes wrote in THE COMMON LAW, "A law which punished conduct which would not be blameworthy in the average member of the community would be too severe for that community to bear." * * * Its severity lies in the absence of an opportunity either to avoid the consequences of the law or to defend any prosecution brought under it. Where a person did not know of the duty to register and where there was no proof of the probability of such knowledge, he may not be convicted consistently with due process. Were it otherwise, the evil would be as great as it is when the law is written in print too fine to read or in a language foreign to the community.[a]

4. **Sex Offender Registration Laws.** A number of states now require that persons convicted of certain sex offenses must register with local authorities and provide an updated address whenever they move. Can such a statute impose criminal liability without a mens rea element? In *State v. White*, 590 S.E.2d 448 (N.C. Ct. App. 2004), the North Carolina Court of Appeals held that the state's sex offender registration statute, which requires a person covered by the act to notify the local sheriff within ten days, was a strict liability provision, thereby precluding defendant from raising a mistake defense. Is that consistent with *Lambert*? The Arkansas, Connecticut, and Illinois Supreme Courts have also interpreted their sex offender registration statutes to be strict liability provisions. *Adkins, v. State*, 371 Ark. 159 (Ark. 2007); *State v. T.R.D.*, 942 A.2d 1000 (Conn. 2008); *State v. Molnar*, 857 N.E.2d 209 (Ill. 2006). The Florida Supreme Court held that the sex offender registration law, which did not contain any reference to intent, required proof of the defendant's actual knowledge of the duty to register: "[T]he due process requirements explained in *Lambert* would apply if we did not find a knowledge requirement in the statutes * * * As the Court did in *Lambert*, we agree that ordinarily moving one's residence would not give rise to the belief that a crime was being committed absent some express knowledge to the contrary." *State v. Giorgetti*, 868 So.2d 512 (Fla. 2004). In *People v. Lopez*, 140 P.3d 106 (Colo. Ct. App. 2006), the Colorado Court of Appeals relied on *Lambert* in finding that the sex offender registration statute required proof of a defendant's knowledge even though the statute did not incorporate any intent element. A number of statutes include a knowledge element for failure to register or maintain proper registration. ALASKA STAT. § 11.56.840; DEL.CODE ANN. tit. 11, § 4120; UTAH CODE ANN. § 77-27-21.5(14); VA.CODE ANN. § 18.2-472.1; WASH. REV.CODE § 9A.44.130(11). The presence of a knowledge element means that a defendant can offer a good faith defense that he did not know registration was required, or that he believed he had done so successfully, which would not be available for a strict liability offense.

---

[a] Justice FRANKFURTER, joined by Justices HARLAN and WHITTAKER stated in dissent, "I feel confident that the present decision will turn out to be an isolated deviation from the strong current of precedents — a derelict on the waters of the law."

C. Mistake of Fact and Law — Model Penal Code

MODEL PENAL CODE

§ 2.04. Ignorance or Mistake.

(1) Ignorance or mistake as to a matter of fact or law is a defense if:

(a) the ignorance or mistake negatives the purpose, knowledge, belief, recklessness or negligence required to establish a material element of the offense; or

(b) the law provides that the state of mind established by such ignorance or mistake constitutes a defense.

(2) Although ignorance or mistake would otherwise afford a defense to the offense charged, the defense is not available if the defendant would be guilty of another offense had the situation been as he supposed. In such case, however, the ignorance or mistake of the defendant shall reduce the grade and degree of the offense of which he may be convicted to those of the offense of which he would be guilty had the situation been as he supposed.

(3) A belief that conduct does not legally constitute an offense is a defense to a prosecution for that offense based upon such conduct when:

(a) the statute or other enactment defining the offense is not known to the actor and has not been published or otherwise reasonably made available prior to the conduct alleged; or

(b) he acts in reasonable reliance upon an official statement of the law, afterward determined to be invalid or erroneous, contained in (i) a statute or other enactment; (ii) a judicial decision, opinion or judgment; (iii) an administrative order or grant of permission; or (iv) an official interpretation of the public officer or body charged by law with responsibility for the interpretation, administration or enforcement of the law defining the offense.

(4) The defendant must prove a defense arising under Subsection (3) of this Section by a preponderance of evidence.

NOTES AND QUESTIONS

1. *Official Statements of Law.* If a defendant relies on an Attorney General's Opinion, is this an official statement of law? What if he or she relies on the opinion

of a local prosecutor that a court later interprets differently when a new prosecutor takes office? Can mistake of law be premised upon the advice of one's counsel? In *United States v. Cross*, 113 F. Supp. 2d 1253 (S.D. Ind. 2000), the court stated that the defense is "rarely available" and found it unavailable "as a defense to federal charges, specifically including the operation of an illegal gambling business and money laundering charges in this case, when the claimed reliance is upon a statement or conduct by a state or local official rather than an appropriate federal official."

2. *Negligence.* Can mistake of fact or mistake of law be used with a crime involving negligence? Would the answer be different with respect to the common law and the Model Penal Code? See Model Penal Code§ 2.04(1)(a). Is this consistent with the holding in *State v. Cavness*, 911 P.2d 95 (Hawaii Ct. App. 1996), where the court stated:

> [I]f a person is ignorant or mistaken as to a matter of fact . . . the person's ignorance or mistake will, in appropriate circumstances, prevent the person from having the requisite culpability with respect to the fact . . . as it actually exists. For example, a person who is mistaken (either reasonably, negligently, or recklessly) as to which one of a number of similar umbrellas on a rack is the person's and who takes another's umbrella should be afforded a defense to a charge of theft predicated on either intentionally or knowingly taking the property of another . . . . A reckless mistake would afford a defense to a charge requiring intent or knowledge — but not to an offense which required only recklessness or negligence. Similarly, a negligent mistake would afford a defense to a charge predicated on intent, knowledge, or recklessness — but not to an offense based on negligence.

3. *Distinguishing Mistakes.* The defendant in *Cheek* was permitted to advance a defense that he did not understand the requirements of the Internal Revenue Code to negate his intent, could this have been considered a mistake of fact? Is there a clear distinction between a mistake of fact and one of law, especially when one's understanding–or misunderstanding–of legal rights can play a significant role in how one acts? See *United States v. Barker*, 546 F.2d 940 (D.C. Cir. 1976).

PROBLEM THIRTEEN

Kim needed money for an upcoming vacation, so Kim went to a pawn shop and obtained a loan for $500 secured by a ring worth over $5,000 that belonged to Kim's great-grandmother. Kim signed a form that stated in small print at the bottom: "Failure to repay the loan, with all accrued interest, within 30 days gives the lender the right to take ownership of the collateral securing the loan and sell it, keeping all proceeds with no obligation to remit any funds to the borrower." After the vacation, Kim was so swamped at work that Kim forgot about reclaiming the ring until the following month. Kim went to the pawn shop with the money to repay the loan, including the interest, and asked to see the ring. The owner showed it to Kim and said, "Look, you didn't repay the loan within 30 days so I own it now. Read the paperwork. If you want it back, it'll cost you $6,500." Kim said "the ring is mine" and then grabbed it, threw the money on the counter to repay the loan, and ran out of the store. The owner called the police, who arrested Kim a few miles from the pawn shop on the way home. Kim was charged with larceny, which requires the government to prove the taking and carrying away of property from another with the specific intent to steal it from the person who possessed it. Kim's attorney moves to dismiss the charge, arguing that Kim believed the ring was owned by the individual once the loan was repaid. What argument will the government make that Kim's mistake is irrelevant to the charge? Does it make a difference that courts have held the pawn shop's form is not an enforceable contract if the borrower tenders full payment within a reasonable period?

CASE STUDY TWO

On January 21, 2012, a fire broke out in Marzipan, a nightclub on the second floor of a two-story building in downtown Miami, Florida. A charitable fundraiser was being held that night for invited guests only. The guests were not required to pay to enter, but the hope was to generate enough good-will with the Miami elite to encourage them to give large sums of money to a foundation for feeding the homeless, at least after the cost of sponsoring the event had been deducted from any charitable contributions received. Although the club owner, Jamie, cared deeply about the plight of the homeless, Jamie also hoped that sponsoring the charitable event would give the club good press that it sorely needed to help to reverse its sharply declining popularity. There were three fire exits, each with separate staircases to the street, and one main entrance, also having a staircase to the street. Someone, however, had placed chains and locks across all three fire exit doors so that they could not open. All the patrons, smelling smoke and finding the other doors blocked, ran to the main entrance and stairway, trampling each other in an effort to escape. Although most ultimately got out of the building alive and uninjured, four customers were trampled to death by the crowd. A forensics expert wrote a report stating that if even only two of the three fire exits had been open, likely no one would have died from trampling.

A Florida statute declares that it is a felony of the third degree "to prevent safe ingress and egress from any building used for commercial purposes." The statute had been passed as the result of a 2009 incident in which a pedestrian sky-bridge across the lobby of a major new hotel had collapsed, crushing several guests, but more being killed and injured from trampling when there proved to be too few means for quick exit from the lobby. Moreover, because the only exit was via a revolving door, in the rush to leave several people got their feet caught in the door, causing serious foot injuries. Such injuries had happened on normal, everyday hotel business days. A whistleblower in the architect's firm had told the building's owner that cheap materials had been used in the skybridge, and it was at a very high risk of collapsing and should be dismantled before the building opened. The owner was in debt from paying for the construction and needed a quick cash inflow, so the owner ignored the whistleblower's warning, opened the hotel, and people died.

A third degree felony is punishable by no less than five and no more than twenty years in prison. Some legislators objected that this was too high a penalty for an unintended or unknowing causation of physical harm. Others argued that the hotel owner had been told of the almost certain collapse of the building so that the conduct being reached was knowingly dangerous after all. But still others argued that even negligent endangerment merited such high punishment and thus supported the bill. The bill, of course, ultimately passed.

Against the advice of counsel, Jamie admitted to the police to having barred one of the fire exit doors. But Jamie said that this was done because a customer had told Jamie that one of the stone stairs in that stairwell had literally collapsed that morning and was dangerous. The stair could not be repaired before the fundraiser, and Jamie had previously once been told by a fire department official that two fire exit stairwells, when combined with the main exit, should be sufficient for customer safety. But Jamie denied having blocked the other two exits and insisted to not knowing how they became blocked. Jamie's fingerprints were found, however, on the locks and chains on each of the three fire exit doors. The police did not check for other fingerprints. The police also discovered a one-inch deep, one-inch wide chip missing from one stair in the staircase that Jamie admitted blocking but did not find any stair had collapsed or was in such disrepair as to create a serious danger to customers. Jamie also had been fined once before (about two years earlier) for blocking all three fire exits, which Jamie had done because some customers would use them to leave without paying their accumulated food and drink bills; this happened well before the third degree felony egress statute had been adopted. Jamie told the police that every fire inspection since that time had been passed and that Jamie scrupulously avoided blocking more than one exit precisely because the earlier fining incident led to an understanding of the danger. Jamie further admitted to not having inspected any of the stairwells or fire exit doors before or during the charitable benefit.

Jamie did remember, however, seeing Lynn in the crowd outside the nightclub during the blaze. Lynn had been a cook at the club but was fired when Jamie accused Lynn of stealing money. Unable to get an appropriate reference, Lynn proved also unable to find a chef's job at a similarly high salary and blamed Jamie for this underemployment. Jamie produced text messages and Facebook postings from Lynn containing vague threats to "get even" with Jamie for "ruining my life." But Lynn refused to talk to the police, and they chose not to investigate Lynn further, even though Lynn was quite drunk when questioned shortly after the fire. Although Jamie insisted that Lynn must have blocked the other two doors, it was Jamie whom the police arrested on homicide charges and on a charge of violating the third degree felony statute prohibited preventing safe ingress and egress.

(1) If in a common law jurisdiction, what is the likelihood that Jamie will be convicted of the felony preventing egress charge?

(2) What if the jurisdiction defines four types of homicide, which are, in descending order of seriousness:

    (a) purposeful unlawful killing;

    (b) knowing unlawful killing;

    (c) reckless unlawful killing; and

    (d) negligent unlawful killing.

Of what degree of homicide, if any, will Jamie likely be convicted? How would this differ in a Model Penal Code jurisdiction?

(3) If a prosecutor believed Jamie's story, that Lynn had been the one who had blocked the two remaining unblocked fire exits, what further investigation would be necessary to build a case against Lynn? Of what crimes, if any, could Lynn be convicted of under the law recited above?

(4) Does Jamie's story about Lynn create a risk of mistaken prosecution against Harris? How would the defense make use of that theory at Jamie's trial? Could the defense make use of this story in persuading the prosecution not to proceed against Jamie?

Chapter 5
Causation

For crimes that require a specific result, such as death or financial harm, the government must prove beyond a reasonable doubt that the defendant caused the particular harm as an element of the offense. There are two components to causation. The first is cause-in-fact, which requires the government to prove that but for the actions of the defendant the result would not have happened when it happened. The second causation requirement is that the defendant be the proximate cause of the result. In the criminal law context, proximate cause is a means to determine whether the defendant, as a matter of fairness, should be held liable for the criminal activity. Proximate cause limits the actual or "but for" causation to that which is directly related to the act.

§ 5.01 Cause-in-Fact

State v. Lane
444 S.E.2d 233 (N.C. Ct. App. 1994)

ARNOLD, Chief Judge:

On the evening of 17 September 1990, nineteen-year-old defendant and his two cousins, Steve Coor and Rodney Coor, left defendant's home * * * and walked around the corner to a Jet Service Station to purchase some beer. On their way home, defendant and Steve Coor turned around to observe Rodney walking with and talking to a highly intoxicated white male, who was staggering along Grantham Street, a four-lane highway otherwise known as Business Route 70.

Steve Coor testified that he told the man with Rodney to be careful in the street. The man responded by swearing and making gestures. Steve and Rodney saw defendant swing at the man, and saw the man fall on the cement on the edge of Grantham Street. Defendant, Rodney and Steve continued to walk home.

At 9:48 p.m., Sergeant M.A. Cruthirds of the Goldsboro Police Department responded to a call regarding a white male lying in the road at one corner of Grantham Street. Sergeant Cruthirds discovered Gregory Linton lying in the road, three feet from the curb. * * * Rescue personnel arrived at the scene. Cruthirds applied pressure behind Linton's ear to which Linton responded by trying to remove Cruthirds' hand. After determining that there was no sign of injury, and that Linton was only intoxicated, the rescue team left, and Sergeant Cruthirds took

Linton into custody and placed him in the Wayne County jail for public drunkenness.

Linton was taken to the hospital the following day * * * around 4:30 p.m. He was unconscious. He had a blood alcohol concentration level of .34 percent on the breathalyzer scale at the approximate time of his arrival at the hospital. Linton died at 6:30 p.m. An autopsy revealed no external injuries, but did reveal a subdural hematoma on the right side of the brain, a swollen brain, brain contusions or bruises, pneumonia on the lungs, and fatty change of the liver, which is most commonly caused by alcohol abuse. In the medical examiner's opinion, Linton died as a result of blunt force injury to the head.

Defendant was indicted and tried for involuntary manslaughter. The jury returned a verdict of guilty. After finding the aggravating factors outweighed the mitigating factors, defendant received the maximum sentence of ten years imprisonment. Defendant appeals.

Defendant's first assignment of error raises the question of whether the State's evidence was sufficient to show that defendant's act of hitting Gregory Linton was both the actual and legal cause of his death. * * *

In considering a motion to dismiss, the trial court must determine whether substantial evidence of each element of the offense exists. * * * The trial court must consider the evidence in the light most favorable to the State, thereby giving the State the benefit of every reasonable inference that might be drawn therefrom.***

Involuntary manslaughter is "the unintentional killing of a human being without malice, proximately caused by (1) an unlawful act not amounting to a felony nor naturally dangerous to human life, or (2) a culpably negligent act or omission." * * * The State must prove that defendant's action was the cause-in-fact (actual cause) and the proximate cause (legal cause) of the victim's death to satisfy the causation element. * * * Defendant contends that the State failed to prove the causation element.

First, defendant contends that the State failed to present substantial evidence that his punch was the cause-in-fact of Linton's death because (1) the State's theory was that as a result of defendant's punch Linton banged his head on the pavement, yet the evidence showed that Linton did not fall on his head, or bang it against the pavement as a result of being hit by defendant, and (2) it is impossible to prove beyond a reasonable doubt that the trauma which triggered the decedent's brain hemorrhage was defendant's punch, and not some other factor which could have occurred either before or after the incident.

There is evidence in the record, contrary to defendant's contentions, from which a reasonable jury could find that defendant's punch was the actual cause of the blunt force injury to the head, leading directly to Linton's death. First, it should be noted that the State's theory at the time of defendant's motion to dismiss was not limited to whether the decedent's head struck the pavement. Therefore, while it appears from the record that Linton's head did not strike the pavement, it can be reasonably inferred that defendant's punch was the cause-in-fact of decedent's death. Steve Coor testified that he saw defendant swing at Linton "around the head." The medical examiner testified that the decedent's swollen brain could have been a response to either a blow to the head or a response to the head striking some object. This is reasonable evidence to support the conclusion that defendant's punch to the head was a cause-in-fact of decedent's death. Furthermore, defendant's second contention that decedent *could* have suffered trauma to the head in a manner other than defendant's assault is speculative. There is no evidence in the record to substantiate defendant's suggestion that decedent *may* have lost his balance sometime before he encountered defendant, that he *may* have fallen again sometime after he was hit, or that he *may* have fallen in his jail cell.

[The court also found that there was sufficient evidence of proximate cause and upheld the conviction.]

NOTES AND QUESTIONS

1. *Generally.* The issue of causation comes up most frequently in homicide prosecutions, in which the exact cause of the victim's death may be at issue. The unavailability of the victim's testimony in homicide cases can make it much more difficult to demonstrate that the defendant's actions resulted in the death, especially if there are no other witnesses to the conduct. In a robbery, on the other hand, the victim can identify the defendant as the person who used force or a threat to obtain property from the victim, so that the key issue is not whether the victim was robbed, but whether the defendant in fact is the person who committed the crime or whether force or a threat was employed. The relationship between the defendant's conduct and the result is often clear from the facts, or causation may not be an issue when the defendant concedes that he committed the act but has a defense to the charge (*e.g.* self defense). In other cases, causation will be unclear because the link between the defendant and the victim is not immediately apparent, or there may be conduct by a second actor — including the victim — that is also a cause of the harm. Simply because a person is a cause-in-fact of a result, however, is not sufficient to trigger criminal liability.

2. *Terminology.* A host of different terms are used to describe the actual cause. One finds the terms "but-for-cause," "sine qua non," and "factual cause."

3. *Circumstantial Evidence.* In *Lane*, it does not appear that the defendant testified. The government's evidence consisted of the eyewitness testimony of the two individuals who observed the defendant swing at the victim's head, and the medical testimony on the cause of death. In viewing the evidence in determining whether it was sufficient, the court examines "the evidence in the light most favorable to the State, thereby giving the State the benefit of every reasonable inference that might be drawn therefrom." [See Chap. 6].

4. *Conditions.* A condition is not considered part of the actual cause. An example of a condition might be that one would not charge the mother of a perpetrator of a crime for the crime of her child merely because she gave birth to this child. Although one could say that "but for" the birth of the child the crime would not have been committed, that does not mean a parent is automatically guilty for the crimes of their children. This is called a condition.

5. *Concurrent Sufficient Causes.* What if more than one person beats the victim, who dies from the blows? Can any of them be charged with a crime if there were multiple blows? The answer is yes under the doctrine of concurrent sufficient causes if the blows of each could have caused the death of the victim. For example, an Alabama statute provides: "A person is criminally liable if the result would not have occurred but for his conduct, operating either alone or concurrently with another cause, unless the concurrent cause was sufficient to produce the result and the conduct of the actor clearly insufficient." ALA. CODE 1975 § 13A-2-5(a).

6. *Obstructed Cause.* If a person shoots someone but does not cause life-threatening injuries, the person is not criminally liable for murder if a different person later causes the victim's death. This is known as an obstructed cause and it precludes the initial perpetrator from suffering consequences beyond the crime that he or she committed.

7. *Accelerating a Result.* Consider the situation when the first person injures the victim, who will die in a relatively short period of time from the injury, and then a second person inflicts a fatal injury that causes the victim to die immediately. Can both persons be held liable for the homicide, even though there is only one victim? In fact, both can be found to be the cause of death if the individual would have died from the first injury and the second person merely accelerated that death. Everyone will die, so it is theoretically possible for a defendant to argue that he should not be held responsible for a result that was going to take place at some point. The law, however, holds a person liable for causing a death at a particular point in time before the victim otherwise would have died, so that if a person kills someone shortly before they were going to die anyway, then by accelerating death the person is liable for the killing. Acceleration requires specific proof of when the victim would have died, to establish the liability of the first defendant, and then how the second defendant's conduct caused the otherwise inevitable death to occur earlier.

Consider in the following case whether the prosecution's proof was sufficient for both defendants:

Oxendine v. State
528 A.2d 870 (Del. 1987)

HORSEY, Justice:

Defendant, Jeffrey Oxendine, Sr., appeals his conviction in trial by jury in Superior Court of manslaughter * * *[1] in the beating death of his six-year-old son, Jeffrey Oxendine, Jr. Oxendine was sentenced to twelve years' imprisonment.[2] On appeal, Oxendine's principal argument is that the Trial Court committed reversible error by denying his motion for a judgment of acquittal on the issue of causation. Specifically, he argues that the State's medical testimony, relating to which of the codefendants' admittedly repeated beatings of the child was the cause of death, was so vague and uncertain as to preclude his conviction of any criminal offense.* * *

The facts may be summarized as follows: On the morning of January 18, 1984, Leotha Tyree, Oxendine's girlfriend, who lived with him, pushed Jeffrey into the bathtub causing microscopic tears in his intestines which led to peritonitis. During a break at work that evening, Oxendine telephoned home and talked to Jeffrey, who complained of stomach pains. When Oxendine returned home from work, he saw bruises on Jeffrey and knew that Tyree had beaten the child during the day. Although Jeffrey continued to complain of a stomachache, he apparently did not tell his father how or when he received the bruises.

The next morning at approximately 7:30 a.m., Oxendine went into Jeffrey's bedroom and began screaming at him to get up. A neighbor in the same apartment building testified to hearing sounds coming from the room of blows being struck, obscenities uttered by a male voice, and cries from a child saying, "Please stop, Daddy, it hurts." After hearing these sounds continue for what seemed like five to ten minutes, the witness heard a final noise consisting of a loud thump, as if someone had been kicked or punched "with a great blow."

Later that day, Jeffrey's abdomen became swollen. When Oxendine arrived home from work at about 5:00 p.m., Tyree told him of Jeffrey's condition and

---

[1] "A person is guilty of manslaughter when: (1) He recklessly causes the death of another person."

[2] Codefendant, Leotha Tyree, was also convicted in the same trial of manslaughter in the death of Jeffrey Oxendine, Jr. and was sentenced to nine years' imprisonment. On direct appeal, this Court has affirmed her conviction. *Tyree v. State*, Del.Supr., 510 A.2d 222 (1986).

urged him to take Jeffrey to the hospital. Oxendine, apparently believing that Jeffrey was exaggerating his discomfort, went out, bought a newspaper, and returned home to read it. Upon his return, Tyree had prepared to take Jeffrey to the hospital. En route, Jeffrey stopped breathing; and was pronounced dead shortly after his arrival at the hospital.

In order to convict Oxendine of manslaughter, the State had to show that his conduct caused Jeffrey's death. 11 Del.C. § 261 defines causation as the "antecedent but for which the result in question would not have occurred." 11 Del.C. § 261. At trial, the State's original theories of causation were, alternatively, (1) a "combined direct effect," or (2) an "aggravation" theory.

During its case-in-chief, the State called medical examiners Dr. Inguito and Dr. Hameli, who both testified that Jeffrey's death was caused by intra-abdominal hemorrhage and acute peritonitis, occurring as a result of blunt force trauma to the front of the abdomen. Similarly, each pathologist identified two distinct injuries, one caused more than twenty-four hours before death, and one inflicted less than twenty-four hours before death.

Dr. Inguito could not separate the effects of the two injuries. In his view, it was possible that both the older and more recent hemorrhage could have contributed to the death of the child, but he was unable to tell which of the hemorrhages caused the death of the child. Dr. Inguito could not place any quantitative value on either of the hemorrhages nor could he state whether the fresh hemorrhage or the older hemorrhage caused the death. The prosecutor never asked, nor did Dr. Inguito give, an opinion on whether the second hemorrhage accelerated Jeffrey's death.

Dr. Hameli, on the other hand, was of the opinion that the earlier injury was the underlying cause of death. According to him, the later injury, i.e., the second hemorrhage, "was an aggravating, and probably some factors [sic] contributing," but it was the earlier injury that was the plain underlying cause of death.

The prosecutor, however, did explicitly ask Dr. Hameli if the second injury accelerated Jeffrey's death. The relevant portion of the testimony is as follows:

Prosecutor: Dr. Hameli, within a reasonable degree of medical certainty and in your expert opinion, did the second hemorrhage accelerate this child's death?

Hameli: I do not know. If you are talking about timewise–I assume that's what you are talking about, exploration.

Prosecutor: You cannot give an opinion of that area; is that correct?

Hameli: No.

Oxendine moved for judgment of acquittal at the end of the State's case-in-chief. The Trial Court, however, denied his motion.

As part of her case, codefendant Tyree called Dr. Hofman, a medical examiner, who disagreed about the number of injuries. He perceived only one injury inflicted about twelve hours before death. Subsequently, the prosecutor asked Hofman the following hypothetical question that assumed two blows when Hofman only testified as to one blow:

> **Prosecutor**: In your expert medical opinion within a reasonable degree of medical certainty, if this child, given his weakened state as a result of the significant trauma to his abdominal cavity, suffered subsequently another blunt force trauma to the same area, would it accelerate this child's death?

> **Hofman**: My opinion, as in a general statement, not knowing this child, it certainly would have an impact on shortening this child's life.

> **Prosecutor**: Is then, therefore, your answer yes?

> **Hofman**: Yes.

At the end of trial, Oxendine again moved for judgment of acquittal. The Trial Court denied the motion and instructed the jury on the elements of recklessness, causation and on various lesser included offenses. The ultimate and only theory of causation on which the jury was charged was based on "acceleration." The Trial Court instructed the jury that "[a] defendant who causes the death of another . . . is not relieved of responsibility for causing the death if another later injury accelerates, that is, hastens the death of the other person. Contribution without acceleration is not sufficient." As previously noted, the jury returned verdicts of manslaughter against Oxendine and Tyree.

In this case, the evidence established that Oxendine inflicted a nonlethal injury upon Jeffrey after his son had, twenty-four hours earlier, sustained a lethal injury from a previous beating inflicted by Tyree. Thus, for Oxendine to be convicted of manslaughter in this factual context, the State was required to show for purposes of causation under 11 Del.C. § 261 that Oxendine's conduct hastened or accelerated the child's death. The Superior Court correctly instructed the jury that "[c]ontribution [or aggravation] without acceleration is insufficient to establish causation." We do not equate aggravation with acceleration. It is possible to make the victim's pain more intense, i.e., aggravate the injury, without accelerating the time of the victim's death. Thus, in terms of section 261, and as applied to defendant, the relevant inquiry is: but for his infliction of the second injury, would the victim have died when he died? If the second injury caused his son to die any sooner, then defendant, who inflicted the second injury, would be deemed to have caused his son's death within the definition of section 261.

A finding of medical causation may not be based on speculation or conjecture. A doctor's testimony that a certain thing is possible is no evidence at all. His opinion as to what is possible is no more valid than the jury's own speculation as to what is or is not possible. Almost anything is possible, and it is improper to allow a jury to consider and base a verdict upon a "possible" cause of death. Therefore, a doctor's testimony can only be considered evidence when his conclusions are based on reasonable medical certainty that a fact is true or untrue.

The State's expert medical testimony, even when viewed in the light most favorable to the State, was (1) insufficient to sustain the State's original theories of causation (a "combined direct effect" or an "aggravation" theory); and (2) insufficient to sustain the State's ultimate theory of causation ("acceleration") on which the court instructed the jury. Both of the State's expert witnesses, Dr. Inguito and Dr. Hameli, were unable to state with any degree of medical certainty that the second injury contributed to the death of the child. Dr. Inguito could only testify that it was possible that both the older and more recent hemorrhage could have contributed to the death of the child. As for Dr. Hameli, he testified that the second injury independent of the first injury could have caused death but probably would not cause death. Furthermore, Dr. Hameli explicitly stated that he could not give an opinion as to whether the second injury accelerated Jeffrey's death. Similarly, Dr. Inguito was neither asked nor did he offer an opinion about acceleration.

The record establishes that the only theory of causation under which the State submitted the case to the jury was the acceleration theory. * * * The State concedes that when it closed its case-in-chief it did not have a prima facie case to support acceleration. Therefore, even though the State could, based on Dr. Hofman's testimony, establish a prima facie case of acceleration at the end of the trial, Oxendine's conviction of manslaughter must be set aside for insufficiency of the evidence to establish that his conduct accelerated Jeffrey's death.

Furthermore, even if the State's evidence was sufficient to sustain its original theories of causation, we could not affirm Oxendine's conviction because the jury was not instructed on either of these theories. Although the State may submit alternate theories of causation to the jury, if supported by the evidence, it must establish in its case-in-chief a prima facie basis for each theory that goes to the jury.[4] In this case, the State did not maintain alternate theories throughout the trial. The State abandoned and completely changed its section 261 theories of causation after it closed its case-in-chief. The ultimate and only theory ("acceleration") on

---

[4] This practice is often employed in murder cases when the State is unsure as to what type of murder, i.e., intentional, second degree, felony murder, etc., has taken place.

which the court instructed the jury was different and not compatible with the State's original theories of causation that it attempted to establish during its case-in-chief. As previously noted, acceleration is not synonymous with either aggravation or the combined effects of two injuries. Thus, when the State was unable to establish at the end of its case-in-chief a prima facie case for acceleration, its case for manslaughter failed.

It is extremely "difficult to be objective about the death of a child. . . . Those responsible ought to be punished. Nevertheless, there must be proof as to who, if anyone, inflicted the injuries that resulted in death." * * * "Reprehensible and repulsive as the conduct of the defendant is, nevertheless it is not proof of manslaughter." * * *

The Trial Court, however, properly denied Oxendine's motion for judgment of acquittal at the close of the State's case because its medical testimony was sufficient for a rational trier of fact to conclude beyond a reasonable doubt that Oxendine was guilty of the lesser included offense of assault in the second degree, 11 Del.C. § 612(1). Therefore, we reverse Oxendine's conviction of manslaughter and remand the case to Superior Court for entry of a judgment of conviction and resentence of defendant for the lesser included offense of assault in the second degree.

Notes and Questions

1. *Expert Medical Testimony.* When the cause of death or the time when it occurred is not clear, then the government will have to introduce the testimony of an expert — usually the coroner or a pathologist — to explain the medical facts surrounding the death. The defendant can introduce his own experts to testify regarding their conclusions regarding the death, and it will be up to the jury to determine which expert's testimony to credit in deciding whether the defendant was the cause-in-fact of the death. Note the standard for the expert's testimony: "a reasonable medical certainty." As the *Oxendine* court stated, "Almost anything is possible, and it is improper to allow a jury to consider and base a verdict upon a 'possible' cause of death." The first doctor (Inguito) could not separate out the two injuries, and therefore could not offer an opinion as to which defendant caused Jeffrey's death. The second doctor (Hameli) concluded that Tyree's blow caused Jeffrey's death, but could not offer an opinion regarding whether Oxendine's blow accelerated the death.

2. *Alternate Theories of Causation.* In footnote 4 in *Oxendine*, the Delaware Supreme Court noted that the prosecutor had different theories of causation, and that it needed to introduce sufficient evidence of each theory for the jury to convict

the defendant. When the prosecutor first began putting together the case, there were a number of different possible theories of causation. Should a prosecutor be allowed to present different theories and allow a jury to select the one that best suits the case? Was the prosecutor poorly prepared for the trial by not having the medical experts clearly address the issue of causation? Should the government make its theory clear from the beginning of the trial, so that the defendant is not surprised?

3. *Sufficiency of the Evidence*. Why was Oxendine's manslaughter conviction reversed when Tyree's medical expert, Hofman, did testify that Oxendine's blow to Jeffrey shortened his life? The reason is that the prosecutor did not introduce sufficient evidence in its *case-in-chief* on the causation element, and therefore the manslaughter charge should have been dismissed at that point in time. [See Chap. 6]. At the end of the prosecution's evidence, the prosecution had not introduced any evidence that Oxendine's blow caused Jeffrey's death, either directly or under an acceleration theory, nor had it introduced any evidence to support another theory of causation, such as concurrent sufficient causes or that Oxendine assisted Tyree (or vice-versa). Therefore, the charge must be dismissed, although the evidence was sufficient to establish an assault, which is called a lesser-included offense.

MODEL PENAL CODE § 2.03

§ 2.03. Causal Relationship Between Conduct and Result; Divergence Between Result Designed or Contemplated and Actual Result or Between Probable and Actual Result.

(1) Conduct is the cause of a result when:

(a) it is an antecedent but for which the result in question would not have occurred; and

(b) the relationship between the conduct and result satisfies any additional causal requirements imposed by the Code or by the law defining the offense.

(2) When purposely or knowingly causing a particular result is an element of an offense, the element is not established if the actual result is not within the purpose or the contemplation of the actor unless:

(a) the actual result differs from that designed or contemplated, as the case may be, only in the respect that a different person or different property is injured or affected or that the injury or harm designed or contemplated would have been more serious or more extensive than that caused; or

(b) the actual result involves the same kind of injury or harm as that designed or contemplated and is not too remote or accidental in its occurrence to have a [just] bearing on the actor's liability or on the gravity of his offense.

(3) When recklessly or negligently causing a particular result is an element of an offense, the element is not established if the actual result is not within the risk of which the actor is aware or, in the case of negligence, of which he should be aware unless:

(a) the actual result differs from the probable result only in the respect that a different person or different property is injured or affected or that the probable injury or harm would have been more serious or more extensive than that caused; or

(b) the actual result involves the same kind of injury or harm as the probable result and is not too remote or accidental in its occurrence to have a [just] bearing on the actor's liability or on the gravity of his offense.

(4) When causing a particular result is a material element of an offense for which absolute liability is imposed by law, the element is not established unless the actual result is a probable consequence of the actor's conduct.

§ 5.02 Proximate Cause

State v. Lamprey
821 A.2d 1080 (N.H. 2003)

DUGGAN, J.

The defendant, Nancy Lamprey, appeals a jury verdict from the Superior Court finding her guilty of one count of manslaughter, one count of misdemeanor reckless conduct, and four counts of first-degree assault, in connection with a motor vehicle crash that occurred on September 14, 2000 * * * .

The record supports the following facts. The defendant operated a child daycare center in her home. For a number of years, she cared for pre-school-age children during the day and provided after-school care to school-age children. The defendant would meet the school-age children in the afternoon at the bus stop where the school bus dropped them off, sometimes walking to the bus stop and other times driving her pickup truck. When the defendant drove the truck, the children routinely rode back to her house in the truck bed. According to testimony at trial, on one occasion not long before the accident, a parent saw children riding in the bed of the defendant's truck and complained to her.

On September 14, 2000, the defendant drove her truck to the bus stop and picked up six children. Three of the children were six years old and three were ten years old. At the bus stop, she opened the gate to the bed of the truck and all six children climbed into the bed. No child seats or safety belts were in place in the truck bed.

On the drive to the defendant's home, the truck left the road and struck a tree. All six children suffered injuries, and one of the children, Katie Silva, died.

According to the State, the accident occurred while the defendant was driving so-called "swervies" to entertain the children. When performing swervies, the defendant would steer the truck back and forth in a zigzag pattern. The State introduced testimony from three children that the defendant was doing swervies just before the accident, as well as testimony by police officers about tire marks they observed on the road leading to the site of the accident. According to expert testimony for the State, no mechanical problem with the truck contributed to the accident. The defendant stated she did not remember doing swervies on the day of the accident but, if she did so, it was because there was a dog in the road. She contended that a mechanical defect in the truck caused an unexpected acceleration resulting in the accident. She also argued that the tire tracks were too contaminated by other vehicles for the State's witnesses to have drawn reliable conclusions.

We first address whether the trial court's jury instruction on causation conflicts with New Hampshire law by defining too restrictively the circumstances in which an intervening cause warrants acquittal. Causation is an element of both manslaughter, and first-degree assault. To establish causation, the State needed to prove not only that the prohibited result would not have occurred but for the conduct of the defendant, but also that the defendant's conduct was the legal (or proximate) cause of the prohibited result.

The scope and wording of jury instructions is generally within the sound discretion of the trial court, and any allegations of error will be evaluated by interpreting the disputed instructions in their entirety, as a reasonable juror would have understood them, and in light of all the evidence in the case. Reversal of a jury verdict is unwarranted when a jury charge fairly covers the issues and law of a case.

The instruction given by the trial court was, in pertinent part, as follows:

[T]he State must prove that the actions of the defendant directly caused Katie Silva's death and serious bodily injuries to the other children. A legal cause of death and/or serious bodily injuries is a cause that is a direct and substantial factor in bringing about that death and/or injuries. It is not merely a possible cause or a contributing cause of death and contributing cause of injuries. It must be the predominant cause without which the results would not have occurred. Because there can be more than one cause of death and/or injuries, the State does not have to prove that the defendant's conduct was the sole cause of the victim's death and/or injuries. However, the State does have to prove that the victim's death and/or injuries were a direct result of the defendant's actions; stated in a different way, that the defendant's conduct was a substantial factor in causing Katie Silva's death or the serious bodily injuries to the other children. . . .

Now the defendant claims that a vehicle malfunction caused the vehicle to speed up resulting in a loss of control. It is up to you to determine whether this happened and, if so, if it is a supervening or alternate cause of Katie Silva's death in the manslaughter charge and the serious bodily injuries in the first degree assault charges. The causal link required between the defendant's acts and the death and/or the serious bodily injuries is not proved if the intervening cause is the sole substantial cause of such death and/or injuries. The State must prove beyond a reasonable doubt that the acts of the defendant remain a substantial cause of the death and/or injuries. The element of causation is satisfied if the State proves beyond a reasonable doubt that the acts of the defendant remained the substantial cause of the death and/ or injuries.

Under the instructions given by the trial court, the element of legal causation is defeated by an intervening cause only when the intervening cause amounts to the "sole substantial cause" of the prohibited result. First, she argues that the language provided by the trial court failed to instruct the jury on legal causation in accordance with *State v. Seymour*, 673 A.2d 786 (N.H. 1996), and second, that the standard for defeating legal causation provided by the trial court was appropriate for cases involving responsive intervening causes and inappropriate for coincidental intervening causes such as the instant case.

First, we address whether the jury instruction was in accord with *Seymour*. The trial court in *Seymour* stated that "a legal cause is the cause without which the event would not have occurred, and the predominating cause, a substantial factor from which the event follows as a natural, direct and immediate consequence." Here, the jury instruction described legal causation using the following language:

a cause that is a direct and substantial factor in bringing about that death and/or injuries . . . not merely a possible cause or a contributing cause. . . . It must be the predominant cause without which the results would not have occurred. . . . [T]he State [must] prove that the victim's death and/or injuries were a direct result of the defendant's actions. . .

While the language used by the trial court in *Seymour* is preferable, the jury instruction in this case made clear that the legal cause must be the predominant cause and a substantial factor in bringing about the prohibited result. Further, the instruction that the prohibited result must be the "direct result" of the defendant's actions is substantially the same as the "natural, direct and immediate consequence" instruction in *Seymour*. We conclude that the jury instruction provided by the trial court, considered as a whole, adequately stated the relevant law as set forth in *Seymour*.

Second, we address whether the "sole substantial cause" standard used by the trial court is the correct standard for legal causation under New Hampshire law in cases involving coincidental intervening causes. The "sole substantial cause" standard for legal causation has previously been used in criminal negligence cases. See *State v. Soucy*, 653 A.2d 561 (N.H. 1995). As the defendant points out in her brief, the trial court applied the "sole substantial cause" standard of *Soucy*, "though Lamprey's case involved no question of medical malpractice."

* * * [T]he defendant argues that the "sole substantial cause" language of *Soucy* should be limited largely to "medical malpractice intervening causes." The defendant argues that an intervening cause that is a coincidence — a cause that occurs simultaneously with the defendant's act — should be treated differently from an intervening act that is a response to the defendant's prior act. She contends that when the intervening cause is a response to the defendant's act, as in *Soucy*, a greater degree of culpability is appropriate because the defendant's act placed the victim in danger of the subsequent act (e.g., medical negligence) occurring. However, when the intervening cause is coincidental (such as the alleged unexpected acceleration in this case), the defendant argues that a lesser degree of culpability is appropriate because the intervening cause arose independently of the defendant's acts.

To apply this distinction, the defendant argues that the jury should have been instructed that there is no legal causation when an intervening cause contributes to the resulting death or injury. Under the defendant's proposed instruction, the defendant should be acquitted if there exists a coincidental intervening cause which itself is a "but for" cause of the accident, even if the coincidental intervening cause is not the sole substantial cause of the accident. The defendant does not cite, nor are we aware of, any New Hampshire cases in which we have made such a distinction.

The defendant, citing Professor LaFave's criminal law treatise and the Model Penal Code, provides two examples of tests that could be applied in cases of coincidental intervening causes, both of which incorporate some form of foreseeability test. "If the intervening cause is merely a coincidence rather than (as with medical treatment) a response, then the question is whether it was foreseeable." LaFave, [CRIMINAL LAW] § 3.12(g); see also Model Penal Code and Commentaries § 2.03 (1985) (acquittal appropriate where prohibited result is "too remote or accidental in its occurrence" when compared to defendant's act).

However, the jury instruction proposed by the defendant at trial contained no such foreseeability test. As she states in her brief, the defendant "asked the court to instruct the jury that the intervening cause in this case–the mechanical defect producing unintended acceleration–would defeat the element of causation if the jury believed that the mechanical defect 'contributed to' the accident." Thus, even if we were to agree that the tests set forth by LaFave and the Model Penal Code should apply, the instruction proposed by the defendant before the trial court is substantially different.

Moreover, we believe that the defendant's proposed instruction makes an unwarranted distinction in degrees of criminal culpability. Often the risk of a particular kind of contributing coincidental intervening cause is the very risk that made the conduct reckless in the first place. For example, if one were to pick up a loaded handgun, ensure that the safety is engaged, aim at a bystander and pull the trigger, it does not follow that a mechanical failure of the safety should exculpate the defendant if he kills the bystander. Yet, under the instruction proposed by the defendant, a jury would be instructed that if it found the intervening cause to be coincidental and if that cause contributed to the resulting death, then the jury should return a verdict of not guilty. We believe the "contributed to" standard, as proposed by the defendant, would be an inappropriate test to determine criminal culpability. We hold that the "sole substantial cause" instruction given by the trial court, and set forth in *Soucy*, is the correct standard under New Hampshire law as applied to the facts of this case. * * *

Affirmed.

NOTES AND QUESTIONS

1. ***Criminal Law and Tort Law***. Although some of the terminology used in criminal law is identical to that found in the law of torts, such as the term proximate cause, the analysis is more narrow in the criminal law case.

2. ***Intervening Causes.*** To say that the language used to describe proximate cause in criminal law is confusing is an understatement. The issue of proximate cause is usually described as a duality of intervening causes that might cut-off a defendant's liability for a harm, with causes on one side sufficient while those on the other are insufficient. "The general rule is that the intervening conduct of a third party will relieve a defendant of culpability only if such an intervening response was not reasonably foreseeable." *Commonwealth v. Askew*, 536 N.E.2d 341 (Mass. 1989).

3. ***Independent and Dependent Intervening Causes.*** Courts sometimes categorize intervening causes into independent and dependent intervening causes. "A defendant may be relieved of criminal liability for a victim's death if an independent" intervening cause has occurred, meaning an act of an independent person or entity that destroys the causal connection between the defendant's act and the victim's injury and, thereby becomes the cause of the victim's injury." *State v. Pelham* [p. 189]. This can be contrasted with a dependent intervening cause, which does not relieve the accused of criminal liability. "If an intervening cause is a normal and reasonably foreseeable result of defendant's original act the intervening act is 'dependent.'"*People v. Cervantes,* 29 P.3d 225 (Cal. 2001).

4. ***Model Penal Code.*** The Model Penal Code § 2.03(2)(b) and (3)(b) expresses the application of proximate cause as a judgment of responsibility by the jury in deciding whether the particular result was "not too remote or accidental in its occurrence to have a just bearing" on liability. Is the law reduced to a jury deciding that it will "know it when it sees it"?

5. **De Minimis** *Causes.* The cause must be more than a "trifle." "To be considered the proximate cause of the victim's death, the defendant's act must have been a substantial factor contributing to the result, rather than insignificant or merely theoretical." *People v. Briscoe*, 112 Cal.Rptr.2d 401, 413-14 (Cal. Ct. App. 2001).

PROBLEM FOURTEEN

At 6:25 p.m., Bernie was traveling from Newark, Delaware westward on Route 40 when the traffic light at an intersection turned yellow. Ali was waiting in the left-turn lane on eastbound Route 40, facing a red arrow while preparing to cross Route 40 and travel north on Pleasant Valley Road. Bernie increased the automobile's speed when the light turned yellow. Ali entered the intersection against the red signal and pulled in front of Bernie, who hit Ali's car broadside and killed Ali instantly. An officer questioning Bernie at the scene detected the odor of alcohol and noted that Bernie's eyes were glassy. Bernie admitted to drinking three beers earlier in the afternoon. Bernie failed two field sobriety tests, including the portable breathalyzer test. A blood test of Bernie two hours after the accident showed a blood-alcohol level of .079, below the legal intoxication level by .001, and Bernie was not cited for drunk driving. The police accident reconstruction expert filed the following report with the prosecutor's office:

Bernie faced a yellow light when proceeding through the intersection and Ali faced a solid red arrow when attempting to cross Route 40 onto Pleasant Valley Road. Bernie clearly had the right of way at the time of the accident. Only 300 feet separated the two vehicles when Ali initially pulled out onto Route 40 and Bernie spanned this distance in three seconds. A normal person can perceive and react to a danger in 1 ½ seconds. At fifty-five mph, a driver would travel 120 feet before perceiving and reacting to a danger and would travel another 260 feet before the car could come to a complete stop. At the point of impact, Ali was traveling slightly above 11 mph while Bernie was traveling approximately 77 mph. Markings on the road indicated that Bernie steered right in an attempt to avoid the collision. Bernie's speed and consumption of alcohol likely contributed to the accident, although a primary contributing circumstance of the collision was Ali passing through a red light.

In determining whether to file charges against Bernie, assess whether the prosecution will be able to establish that Bernie was the proximate (or legal) cause of Ali's death.

State v. Pelham
824 A.2d 1082 (N.J. 2003)

LaVecchia, J.

* * * The facts of the horrific car accident in which defendant, Sonney Pelham, was involved are summarized from the trial record. On the evening of December 29, 1995, William Patrick, a sixty-six-year-old lawyer, was driving his Chrysler LeBaron in the right lane of northbound Route 1 in South Brunswick. At approximately 11:42 p.m., a 1993 Toyota Camry driven by defendant struck the LeBaron from behind. The LeBaron sailed over the curb and slid along the guardrail, crashing into a utility pole before it ultimately came to rest 152 feet from the site of impact. The Camry traveled over a curb and came to rest in a grassy area on the side of the highway.

Two nearby police officers heard the collision and rushed to the scene. The officers found Patrick, still wearing his seatbelt, unconscious and slumped forward in the driver's seat. The rear of the LeBaron was crumpled through to the rear tire and the backseat, and the convertible top was crushed. Patrick was making "gurgling" and "wheezing" sounds, and appeared to have difficulty breathing.***

At the accident scene, Officer Heistand smelled an odor of alcohol on defendant's breath, and noted that he was swaying from side to side and front to back. He had no injuries, but was "belligerent." Heistand believed defendant was intoxicated. Three field sobriety tests were conducted. Defendant failed all three. He was placed under arrest for driving while intoxicated, transported to the police station, and later taken to Robert Wood Johnson for a blood alcohol test. * * * Experts assessed his BAC between .19 and .22 at the time of the accident.

Patrick's condition was critical on his arrival at [the hospital.] * * * The catastrophic injuries Patrick experienced made it virtually impossible for him to breathe on his own. * * * He was placed on a ventilator. Within five days of the accident, Patrick experienced "Adult Respiratory Distress Syndrome," a diagnosis indicating that his lungs had begun to fail. * * *

On March 13, 1996, Patrick was transferred to the Kessler Institute for Rehabilitation (Kessler), because it specialized in the care of patients with spinal cord injuries. When he arrived, Patrick was unable to breathe on his own, and was suffering from multi-organ system failure. * * *.

While at Kessler, Patrick also was monitored by psychiatric staff. He presented as depressed, confused, uncooperative, and not engaged psychologically. At times he was "hallucinating," even "psychotic." The staff determined that he was "significantly" brain injured. Nonetheless, Patrick was aware of his physical and cognitive disabilities. During lucid moments, he expressed his unhappiness with his situation, and, on occasion, tried to remove his ventilator.

Patrick improved somewhat during the month of April, but then his condition rapidly regressed. By early May, severe infections returned, as well as pneumonia. It was undisputed at trial that Patrick had expressed to his family a preference not to be kept alive on life support. Because of his brain damage, his lack of improvement, and his severe infections Patrick's family decided to act in accordance with his wishes and remove the ventilator. He was transferred to Saint Barnabas Medical Center and within two hours of the ventilator's removal on May 30, 1996, he was pronounced dead. The Deputy Middlesex County Medical Examiner determined that the cause of death was sepsis and bronchopneumonia resulting from multiple injuries from the motor vehicle accident.

Defendant was charged with first-degree aggravated manslaughter * * *. Defense counsel filed a motion to dismiss the indictment, contending that the removal of the ventilator constituted an independent intervening cause that insulated defendant from criminal liability. The trial court held that the removal of life support was not an intervening cause and denied the motion. * * *

Consistent with its earlier stated intention, the trial court included in its jury charge on causation an instruction concerning intervening cause and a victim's determination to remove life support. On those points, the trial court instructed the jury as follows:

* * * Let me now instruct you on what an intervening cause is and what it's not. An intervening cause is a cause which breaks the original chain

of causation. In that regard you have heard testimony that on May 30, 1996 William Patrick was taken off the ventilator pursuant to his wishes and that he died several hours later. I instruct you that the removal of life supports, in this case a ventilator, is not a sufficient intervening cause to relieve the defendant of criminal liability. In other words, the removal of life supports from Mr. Patrick who is not brain dead was not a sufficient intervening cause to relieve Mr. Pelham from criminal liability.[2]

If you find that the defendant's actions set in motion the victim's need for life support the causal link between the defendant's actions and the victim's death is not broken by the removal or refusal of life support as long as you find that the death was the natural result of the defendant's actions.

The jury acquitted defendant of aggravated manslaughter, but convicted him of the lesser-included offense of second-degree vehicular homicide. He was sentenced to a custodial term of seven years with a mandatory parole ineligibility period of three years. In the appeal from his conviction, defendant argued, among other points, that the trial court erred in instructing the jury that removal of life support was not an intervening cause if death was the "natural result" of defendant's actions. * * *

The causation requirement of our Code contains two parts, a "but-for" test under which the defendant's conduct is "deemed a cause of the event if the event would not have occurred without that conduct" and, when applicable, a culpability assessment. *State v. Martin*, 573 A.2d 1359 (N.J. 1990) Under the culpability assessment,

[w]hen the actual result is of the same character, but occurred in a different manner from that designed or contemplated [or risked], it is for the jury to determine whether intervening causes or unforeseen conditions lead to the conclusion that it is unjust to find that the defendant's conduct is the cause of the actual result. Although the jury may find that the defendant's conduct was a "but-for" cause of the victim's death . . . it may nevertheless conclude ... that the death differed in kind from that designed or contemplated [or risked] or that the death was too remote, accidental in its occurrence, or dependent on another's volitional act to justify a murder conviction. [*Martin.*]

---

[2] We do not approve of language in the last two sentences of this paragraph. Nonetheless, reviewing the charge as a whole, we believe that the jury did not misunderstand its obligation to determine the factual question concerning causation in this case, namely, whether Patrick's death resulted from the natural progression of his accident injuries and their complications.

Our Code, like the Model Penal Code (MPC), does not identify what may be an intervening cause. Instead, the Code "deals only with the ultimate criterion by which the significance of such possibilities ought to be judged." Removal of life support, as it relates to causation, should be judged only by the criteria of the Code, assuming that the law recognizes the possibility that removal can be an intervening cause. * * *

"Intervening cause" is defined as "[a]n event that comes between the initial event in a sequence and the end result, thereby altering the natural course of events that might have connected a wrongful act to an injury." *Black's Law Dictionary* (7th ed.1999). Generally, to avoid breaking the chain of causation for criminal liability, a variation between the result intended or risked and the actual result of defendant's conduct must not be so out of the ordinary that it is unfair to hold defendant responsible for that result. Wayne R. LaFave & Austin W. Scott, Jr., *Handbook on Criminal Law* § 35 (1972). A defendant may be relieved of criminal liability for a victim's death if an "independent" intervening cause has occurred, meaning "an act of an independent person or entity that destroys the causal connection between the defendant's act and the victim's injury and, thereby becomes the cause of the victim's injury." *People v. Saavedra-Rodriguez*, 971 P.2d 223, 225-26 (Colo. 1998) (explaining Wharton's rule on intervening cause); see generally Charles E. Torcia, 1 *Wharton's Criminal Law* § 26 (15th ed.1993) (stating that independent intervening cause that defendant cannot foresee is sufficient to relieve defendant of criminal responsibility for homicide). The question we address, then, is whether the removal of the victim's life support may constitute, as a matter of law, an "independent intervening cause," the significance of which a jury may evaluate as part of a culpability analysis.

The longstanding, clear policy of this State recognizes the constitutional, common-law, and now statutorily based right of an individual to accept, reject, or discontinue medical treatment in the form of life supporting devices or techniques. An ill or injured person has that personal right and is free to exercise it, at his or her discretion, directly or through a family member or guardian acting in accordance with the person's wishes. In other words, a person's choice to have himself or herself removed from life support cannot be viewed as unexpected or extraordinary. * * *

Removal of life-sustaining treatment is a victim's right. It is thus foreseeable that a victim may exercise his or her right not to be placed on, or to be removed from, life support systems. Because the exercise of the right does not break unexpectedly, or in any extraordinary way, the chain of causation that a defendant initiated and that led to the need for life support, it is not an intervening cause that may be advanced by the defendant. The question is whether it was impermissible for the trial court to have so instructed the jury. The Appellate Division viewed the trial court's instruction as, in effect, directing a verdict for the prosecution because the instruction constituted an improper comment on the quality of the evidence.

That, the court concluded, impermissibly invaded the province of the jury. We disagree.

Causation is a factual determination for the jury to consider, but the jury may consider only that which the law permits it to consider. The purpose of the charge to the jury is to inform the jury on the law and what the law requires. * * * Therefore, although the trial court must be careful not to suggest that it is directing a verdict on causation, here, the court's instruction viewed in its entirety informed the jury that it could not consider the victim's removal from life support as an intervening cause of his death so long as the death was the natural result of defendant's actions. That is, if defendant's actions set in motion the victim's need for life support, without which death would naturally result, then the causal link is not broken by an unforeseen, extraordinary act when the victim exercises his or her right to be removed from life support and thereupon expires unless there was an intervening volitional act of another, such as gross malpractice by a physician.***

In conclusion, we hold that there was no error in instructing the jury that a victim's decision to invoke his right to terminate life support may not, as a matter of law, be considered an independent intervening cause capable of breaking the chain of causation triggered by defendant's wrongful actions. The judgment of the Appellate Division is reversed and the matter remanded to the trial court for reinstatement of the judgment of conviction.

ALBIN, J., dissenting.

"Hard facts make bad law" is an old saw and an apt description of the resolution of this appeal. * * * After the passage of five months during which his condition continued to deteriorate, Patrick, in accordance with his wishes, was taken off a ventilator, and died several hours later. * * *

Proof of causation is an element of every criminal offense and, until today, was no different from other elements that must be submitted to the jury. The New Jersey Code of Criminal Justice (Code) reserves to the jury the ultimate authority to determine whether intervening circumstances break the chain of causation of criminal culpability. In this case, the Code required the jury to determine whether the manner of Patrick's death, which followed from the voluntary removal of life support, was "too remote, accidental in its occurrence, or dependent on another's volitional act to have a just bearing on the actor's liability or on the gravity of his offense." The general and broad language of that provision was intended to apply to the infinite number of variables that arise in the unique circumstances of each new case, including that of this defendant. Causation was a matter that the jury should have been trusted to decide correctly.

Instead, the majority ignores the statutory language that governs this case and imports into the law of causation its own moral and philosophical preferences as it departs from the bedrock principle that a judge cannot direct a verdict against a defendant on an element of an offense, even where evidence of guilt appears overwhelming. The majority has carved from the Code's broad language on causation an inflexible rule that, in all cases, a victim's termination of medical care to support life may never be considered an independent intervening circumstance capable of breaking the chain of causation. The majority has come to that conclusion because it finds that the victim's removal of life-sustaining treatment is always foreseeable.

I object not so much to the wisdom of that new rule of law, as to its failure to find any support in the text of the Code. The Code's drafters left to the jury the commonsense judgment of distinguishing those cases in which intervening circumstances "would have a just bearing on the actor's liability or on the gravity of his offense." Our jurisprudence has traditionally deferred to the jury the delicate and difficult task of deciding the facts on which a defendant's guilt or innocence depends. * * *

NOTE

Under the common law, a defendant could not be charged with a homicide if the victim did not die within a year and a day of the wrongful conduct causing the death. The "year-and-a-day rule" has been abolished in most states either judicially or by the state legislature. The Michigan Supreme Court, in overturning the rule, explained:

> The advances of modern medical science, by extending life and by providing strong evidence of the cause of death, have undermined the wisdom of the irrebuttable presumption that the death of one who expires more than a year and a day after receiving an injury was not caused by the injury.... The presumption was wooden and arbitrary from the beginning, since it prevented a murder conviction even in those rare cases when causation could be proved. Now, when medical causation can be proven with much greater frequency and certainty, the old rule is simply too often demonstrably wrong to be upheld.

People v. Stevenson, 331 N.W.2d 143 (Mich. 1982).

The rationale for retaining the rule is that it provides certainty in the law by allowing juries to determine causation based upon a clear cut rule.

PROBLEM FIFTEEN

Chris walked up to Kylie, took out a gun and said, "Give me your wallet." Finding only one dollar in the wallet, Chris shot Kylie once in the heart and then threw Kylie headfirst into a sewer. Chris was charged and convicted for armed robbery and assault with intent to commit murder, and is serving a 30 year prison term. Kylie survived the attack, and four years later — after numerous surgeries, implantation of a pacemaker, and medication — appeared to be leading a normal life. At a family picnic, Kylie played half-court basketball for almost half an hour. After the game, Kylie got into an argument with a cousin and they began to wrestle until Kylie began having convulsions. Kylie died shortly thereafter. Dr. Lee, Kylie's physician, described Kylie as a "time bomb," subject to death if involved in any physical activity or emotional upset that pushed the heart too strenuously. Dr. Lee stated that if Kylie had avoided strenuous exercise, Kylie would have lived longer. According to Dr. Lee, the chance of a person in Kylie's condition living five years was less than fifty percent; the chance of living another ten years was less than five percent. Dr. Lee also stated that playing basketball was "almost suicide for Kylie." An autopsy revealed that the cause of death was a result of the permanent damage to Kylie's heart caused by the gunshot wound inflicted by Chris. Assuming the jurisdiction does not apply the year-and-a-day rule, can the government prove that Chris is the actual and proximate cause of Kylie's death? If so, can Chris be charged with murder after the prior conviction for robbery and assault?

PART THREE
PROOF

Chapter 6
Concurrence and Proof of the Elements

§ 6.01 Concurrence

The elements of the offense must all concur. Thus, in most cases one cannot form the intent after the act occurs, and if an act or attendant circumstance is an element of the crime, then the government must prove that it existed at the time of the offense. Consider the following two jury instructions:

> In the [crime[s]] [and] [allegation[s]] charged in Count[s] _____, _____ and _____ [or which [is a] [are] lesser crime[s] thereto], [namely,] _____, _____ and _____, there must exist a union or joint operation of act or conduct and a certain specific intent in the mind of the perpetrator. Unless this specific intent exists the [crime] [or] [allegation] to which it relates [is not committed] [or] [is not true].

California Jury Instructions–Criminal 3.31 (2004).

———————

Wyoming Criminal Pattern Jury Instruction — 3.501 Concurrence of Act and Specific Intent states:

> To constitute the crime charged there must be a union of two essential elements, an act forbidden by law and a specific intent.

> Specific intent means more than the general intent to commit the act. To prove a crime which involves specific intent, the prosecution must prove beyond a reasonable doubt:

> (1) That the defendant did the act charged; and

201

(2) That he did it with the specific intent described in the crime charged. The specific intent must be proved beyond a reasonable doubt as any other fact in the case.

Reilly v. Wyoming, 55 P.3d 1259 (Wyo. 2002).

PROBLEM SIXTEEN

Jody and Tomi plan to rob a bank by pretending to have a bomb. As part of the plan, they will steal a car to drive to the bank. The morning of the robbery, they see a BMW parked in a driveway with its engine running and driver's door open, but apparently no one in the car. Jody quickly gets into the idling BMW, pulls out of the driveway and begins to drive down the street. Suddenly, a man emerges from the house at which the BMW was parked and runs down the street screaming, "Don't take my baby!" Jody looks in the back seat and sees an infant in a child car seat. Jody pulls over to the curb, steps out of the car and shoves a hand into the left pocket of the jacket Jody is wearing. As the man approaches the BMW, Jody points at him with the pocket and shouts, "Stop right there. If you come any closer some one will get hurt." The man stops and says, "Please just let me take the baby." Jody says, "All right, but no funny stuff." The man removes the child from the BMW and walks back toward the house. Jody gets into the BMW and begins to drive away when two police cars pull in front of the BMW. Jody is arrested, and a search at the scene shows that Jody had a gun in the left coat pocket. Jody is charged with (1) false imprisonment and (2) carjacking. The state has enacted the Model Penal Code's false imprisonment statute, which provides, "A person commits a misdemeanor if he knowingly restrains another unlawfully so as to interfere substantially with his liberty." The carjacking statute states:

> Whoever, with the intent to cause death or serious bodily harm, takes a motor vehicle from the person or presence of another by force and violence or by intimidation, or attempts to do so, is guilty of a felony punishable by up to 15 years imprisonment.

Jody files a pretrial motion to dismiss the charges. What arguments will Jody make in a motion to dismiss the carjacking charge? What arguments will Jody make in a motion to dismiss the false imprisonment charge? How will the government respond to these arguments?

§ 6.02 Proof Beyond a Reasonable Doubt

The cornerstone of the criminal justice system is that the government must prove all the elements of the charged offense "beyond a reasonable doubt." In *Davis v. United States*, 160 U.S. 469 (1895), the Supreme Court stated:

> Strictly speaking, the burden of proof, as those words are understood in criminal law, is never upon the accused to establish his innocence, or to disprove the facts necessary to establish the crime for which he is indicted. It is on the prosecution from the beginning to the end of the trial, and applies to every element necessary to constitute the crime.

The Supreme Court made it explicit in *In re Winship*, 397 U.S. 358 (1970), that proof beyond a reasonable doubt applies in every criminal prosecution:

> The reasonable-doubt standard plays a vital role in the American scheme of criminal procedure. It is a prime instrument for reducing the risk of convictions resting on factual error. The standard provides concrete substance for the presumption of innocence–that bedrock "axiomatic and elementary" principle whose "enforcement lies at the foundation of the administration of our criminal law." * * *

A. Reasonable Doubt

United States v. Jackson
368 F.3d 59 (2d Cir. 2004)

LEVAL, Circuit Judge.

* * * The defendant was found guilty at a trial conducted on November 5 and November 6, 2001. Special Agent Matthew White of the United States Bureau of Alcohol, Tobacco and Firearms (the "ATF") was the principal government witness. He testified that, in carrying out his duties, which included investigating illegal possession of firearms by convicted felons, he and other agents of the ATF went on September 7, 1999 to Jackson's apartment in the Bronx and asked him whether he had any firearms or ammunition, whereupon Jackson showed them a safe containing a quantity of ammunition. The agents seized the ammunition.

To prove that Jackson was a previously convicted felon, the government offered a certified copy of a judgment of the New York Supreme Court for New York County (Manhattan) showing that on January 11, 1984, a person named Aaron Jackson was convicted of unlawful possession of a weapon and of a controlled substance. The government offered no further evidence connecting the defendant to the 1984 conviction. The defendant neither testified nor called witnesses in his defense. On summation, defense counsel argued for the first time that the government had failed to prove that the Aaron Jackson named in the certificate of conviction might be someone other than the defendant on trial. The jury found the defendant guilty.

The test for determining a challenge to the sufficiency of the evidence asks whether a "rational trier of fact could have found the essential elements of the crime beyond a reasonable doubt." *Jackson v. Virginia*, 443 U.S. 307 (1979). The evidence, in other words, must be of such persuasive quality that a jury could reasonably find the essential elements beyond a reasonable doubt on the basis of that evidence.

The first question we face is whether a fact-finder, given the evidence presented at trial of a 1984 conviction record of a person named Aaron Jackson, could reasonably conclude beyond a reasonable doubt from that evidence alone that the 1984 conviction was of the defendant, Aaron L. Jackson. We do not see how such a degree of confidence could possibly be justified by this evidence. There was no reason to believe the defendant was the only person so named. The name Jackson is quite common, and the first name Aaron, which is of biblical origin, is also quite common. New York is a city of nearly eight million inhabitants, plus a huge number of additional visitors.

If A were to speak of an acquaintance in the City of New York named Aaron Jackson, and B responded, "Why, yesterday in New York City I met a person named Aaron Jackson," one could not be reasonably certain that they were speaking of the same individual. And if B's response were, "Eighteen years ago in New York City I met someone named Aaron Jackson," the likelihood would be even smaller that the two Aaron Jacksons were one and the same. * * *

A conclusion cannot be reached with sufficient confidence to satisfy the beyond-reasonable-doubt standard that two separate episodes involving persons of similar features relate to the same person unless the similarities are sufficiently distinctive to make it highly improbable that the two observed persons could be other than the same. Thus, where two separately observed individuals share a highly distinctive feature in common, such as identical DNA or identical fingerprints, we can conclude beyond reasonable doubt that they must be the same person because of well-established scientific information that a particular structure of DNA and a particular fingerprint configuration occur in only one individual. However, when the points of similarity are less unique or distinctive, more similarities are required before the probability of identity between the two becomes convincing. * * * A conclusion of identity cannot be made beyond a reasonable doubt unless experience, or statistics (if admissible), teach it is far more likely, given the similarities, that the two are the same person, than that they are two different people. The evidence must make it highly improbable that two different people are involved.

No such judgment can be made with any reasonable degree of confidence from two observations, eighteen years apart, of persons with the not-unusual name of Aaron Jackson, in a city with a population exceeding eight million. The government offered no evidence that the two Aaron Jacksons were of the same race, or of similar height, coloring, fingerprint configuration, or even general physical description. There was no showing of the previously convicted Aaron's age. There was no showing that he was a resident of New York, much less that he lived at the same address as the defendant, or that the two shared any other significantly narrowing features. The jury had no reason to believe that the name Aaron Jackson is of sufficiently rare incidence in New York City to make it improbable that an individual of that name convicted in 1984 was the person now on trial before them eighteen years later. We cannot characterize it as highly improbable that two different persons were involved. In short, on this evidence, a jury could not reasonably conclude beyond a reasonable doubt that the two Aaron Jacksons were the same.

The government invites us to adopt a special rule of conditional sufficiency. The rule the government advocates would be that where a prior conviction is an essential element of the crime charged, a court certificate of conviction of a similarly named person will be deemed to satisfy the beyond-reasonable-doubt standard if the defendant offers no evidence in rebuttal. ("The rule simply provides that, where the Government produces evidence of the prior felony conviction in the form of a certified copy of the judgment in the defendant's name, and there is no evidence to the contrary," the evidence will be found legally sufficient. Government's Brief at 23.) * * *

We must reject the rule proposed by the government. No such rule exists in this circuit. We see no reason for such a rule. Furthermore, such a rule could not easily be reconciled with fundamental constitutional principles found by the Supreme Court to be embodied in the Due Process Clause of the Fifth Amendment–the presumption of innocence, and the related requirement of proof beyond a reasonable doubt to sustain a criminal conviction.

While we do not rest our decision on the constitutional ground, we begin by discussing the constitutional cases that bear on the question. In a series of decisions primarily in the 1970s, the Supreme Court made clear that the presumption of innocence and the requirement of proof beyond a reasonable doubt, long recognized as fundamental principles of criminal law, are imbedded in the Fifth Amendment's command that "no person shall . . . be deprived of . . . liberty . . . without due process of law." Taken together, these principles mandate that, in order to secure a criminal conviction, the prosecution must present evidence establishing the defendant's guilt beyond a reasonable doubt and that, if it fails to do so, the defendant is entitled to acquittal without having to offer evidence in his defense.

In *In re Winship*, 397 U.S. 358 (1970), the Supreme Court held that "the Due Process Clause protects the accused against conviction except upon proof beyond a reasonable doubt of every fact necessary to constitute the crime with which he is charged." The Court noted that this requirement dates "at least from our early years as a Nation" and had been expressed in similar form "from ancient times." The Court reasoned that "use of the reasonable-doubt standard is indispensable to command the respect and confidence of the community in applications of the criminal law. It is critical that the moral force of the criminal law not be diluted by a standard of proof that leaves people in doubt whether innocent men are being condemned." * * *

The Court has recognized that the presumption of innocence requires that the accused be acquitted so long as the government has not proved every element of the offense beyond a reasonable doubt, without any requirement that the accused offer evidence (or indeed lift a finger) in his defense. * * * It is * * * a tenet of our criminal law that "[i]f the prosecution fails in its case-in-chief to present evidence establishing a prima facie case for conviction, the defense is entitled to a directed acquittal without the necessity of ever producing its own evidence." LaFave, Israel, & King, 1 CRIMINAL PROCEDURE § 1.4(d) (2d ed.2004). * * *

The government further argues that failure to accept its argument would be tantamount to adopting a rule that prior convictions can be proved only by "direct evidence such as fingerprints." Government Brief at 26. This misunderstands the issue. We in no way suggest that "direct" evidence is needed to prove a defendant's prior conviction. * * *

The government also argues that, even if the similarity of name between the defendant and the certificate of conviction was insufficient, the defendant's identity as the person convicted in 1984 was sufficiently corroborated by other evidence. The government points to the fact that both Aaron Jacksons possessed firearms (as the 1984 conviction was in part for Possession of a Weapon, 3rd Degree, while the present defendant was shown to have ammunition in his safe at his residence).*** The possession of weapons is not a rarity in New York City. If both Aaron Jacksons owned something unusual — a blue parrot, a rhesus monkey, or a green Maserati — the coincidence of such unusual details would add more substantially to the likelihood that the two were the same; but ownership of firearms, it appears, is no more unusual in New York City than ownership of a pet, or a car. There is nothing improbable about two different persons, each named Aaron Jackson, each owning firearms in New York City eighteen years apart. * * *

It may well be that the government's attorneys (and the court) were surprised when the defendant contested the issue of his prior conviction. Such issues are often stipulated (or in any event not contested). * * * Having neither received, nor even clearly requested, a stipulation taking the issue out of contention, the government had no reason to expect to be excused from its constitutional obligation to prove every essential element of the crime beyond a reasonable doubt, as in every other case.

We are left in the unhappy position of being required to reverse a conviction notwithstanding our knowledge that the defendant is guilty. That is the consequence of being governed by the rule of law.

NOTES AND QUESTIONS

1. *Policy Rationales*. Why did the court let Jackson go free when it acknowledged at the end of the opinion that he was in fact guilty? If the judges know he is guilty and the jury convicted him, then how can reversal of the conviction be considered just? In *Winship*, Justice Harlan stated in his concurrence, "I view the requirement of proof beyond a reasonable doubt in a criminal case as bottomed on a fundamental value determination of our society that it is far worse to convict an innocent man than to let a guilty man go free." This is a paraphrase of a statement by Lord Blackstone that "the law holds that it is better that ten guilty persons escape than that one innocent suffer."

2. *Burden of Production/Burden of Persuasion.* There are two burdens on the government in proving "every fact necessary to constitute the crime": the burden of production and the burden of persuasion. The burden of production requires the government to introduce sufficient evidence that the defendant committed the crime to permit the trier of fact to make the ultimate determination of guilt. This is usually referred to as the "sufficiency of the evidence," that there be enough evidence from which a rational juror could find the defendant guilty of the charged offense. The burden of persuasion is encapsulated in the "beyond a reasonable doubt standard," which means the government must prove the defendant committed the crime to such an extent that none of the jurors harbor a sufficient doubt.

3. *Differing Views on Burden of Production.* Jurisdictions differ on what they mean by the "burden of production." Some mean the burden of merely producing "some evidence" that an element of a crime, claim, or defense exists. Others mean sufficient evidence to enable a reasonable jury to find that the element exists by whatever is the burden of persuasion for that element. For example, if the burden of persuasion on an entrapment defense's elements is by a preponderance of the evidence, and if the defense has the burden of production on each of the elements, then the defense would have to present sufficient evidence to enable a reasonable jury to find by a preponderance of the evidence that each of the elements of

entrapment exists. It is irrelevant whether the judge is so persuaded; all that matters is whether some reasonable jury could be convinced by a preponderance. This latter approach to the burden of production clearly requires more than "some evidence" for the burden to be met.

4. *Defendant's Role.* A defendant need not offer any defense. It has long been established that the burden of proof rests with the prosecution. See *Davis v. United States*, 160 U.S. 469 (1895).

5. *Affirmative Defenses.* In footnote 7 of the *Jackson* opinion, the court noted that:

> In *Mullaney v. Wilbur*, 421 U.S. 684, 95 S.Ct. 1881, 44 L.Ed.2d 508 (1975), the Supreme Court struck down a Maine statute which, as interpreted by the Maine Supreme Court, required a defendant charged with murder to prove by a preponderance of the evidence that the defendant acted in the heat of passion on sudden provocation in order to reduce the murder to manslaughter. The Court found the statute unconstitutional in shifting a burden from the prosecution to the defendant. In light of *Winship*, the court ruled that where malice aforethought is an element of the offense, the Due Process Clause requires the prosecution to prove the absence of heat of passion beyond a reasonable doubt.

In the case of *Patterson v. New York,* 432 U.S. 197 (1977), however, the Court distinguished *Mullaney* by holding that the prosecution did not have to prove an affirmative defense. The Court stated that "[p]roof of the non-existence of all affirmative defenses has never been constitutionally required; and we perceive no reason to fashion such a rule in this case and apply it to the statutory defense at issue here." Thus, if the legislature designates an element as an affirmative defense, the legislature does not have to require the state prove that element. The legislature does have the option of having the state prove this affirmative defense, but there is no due process violation if proof is left to the defense. How far can the legislature go in making an element an affirmative defense? Can they designate substantial elements of an offense as affirmative defenses and lessen the prosecution's burden?

6. *Affirmative Defenses that Negate an Element of the Offense.* In the case of *United States v. Kloess*, 251 F.3d 941 (11th Cir. 2001), the Court considered the role of the government with respect to affirmative defenses and stated:

> There has been a twentieth-century trend toward requiring the government to bear the burden of persuasion on certain affirmative defenses. An examination of the cases reveals, however, "a quite divided jurisprudence, without any clear default rule as to how affirmative defenses generally should be treated." *United States v. Dodd*, 225 F.3d 340 (3d Cir. 2000).

There is agreement, however, on one sort of affirmative defense. Any defense which tends to negate an element of the crime charged, sufficiently raised by the defendant, must be disproved by the government. * * * Section 1515(c) provides such an affirmative defense. To violate Section 1512(b)(3), the defendant must knowingly act with the specific intent to hinder or delay the communication to the court of the commission of a federal offense or probation violation. * * * In order to convict a defendant under Section 1512(b)(3), the government must prove that the defendant acted with an improper purpose. * * * Section 1515(c) provides a complete defense to the statute because one who is performing bona fide legal representation does not have an improper purpose. His purpose — to zealously represent his client — is fully protected by the law. Section 1515(c), therefore, constitutes an affirmative defense which negates an element of the offense stated in Section 1512(b)(3).

* * * A defendant-lawyer seeking the safe harbor of Section 1515(c) must affirmatively show that he is entitled to its protection. This is a minimal burden. Evidence tending to show that the defendant is a licensed attorney who was validly retained to perform the legal representation which constitutes the charged conduct is sufficient to raise an inference of innocent purpose. Any requirement to do more would unconstitutionally shift the burden to the defendant to prove his innocence by negating an element of the statute–the required mens rea. This the Constitution forbids. * * *

Once the Section 1515(c) defense has been fairly raised, the government must undertake to prove its case, including the requisite improper purpose, by adducing evidence that the charged conduct did not constitute lawful, bona fide representation. * * * The defendant is entitled to rebut the government's proof. * * *

In view of the foregoing, we hold that Section 1515(c) constitutes an affirmative defense to the crime stated in 18 U.S.C. § 1512(b)(3). Although the burden of raising Section 1515(c) as a defense is on the defendant, the burden of proof as to its non-applicability is always on the government. * * *

7. *Circumstantial Evidence.* Proof beyond a reasonable doubt can be premised upon circumstantial evidence. The government needs to introduce sufficient proof so that a reasonable juror could find the defendant guilty beyond a reasonable doubt, but not that the evidence *compels* such a conclusion. It does not denigrate the standard of proof that one observer might find the defendant guilty while another would not, each with a reasonable basis for that conclusion. There is no requirement that the finding reach the level of scientific or philosophical certitude. Consider the issue of circumstantial evidence as it arises in the following case:

People v. Solmonson
683 N.W.2d 761 (Mich. Ct. App. 2004)

PER CURIAM.

Defendant appeals by right his convictions following a jury trial of operating a motor vehicle while under the influence of intoxicating liquor [OUIL] or while having an alcohol content of 0.10 * * *; operating a motor vehicle while his license was suspended or revoked, second offense; and possessing open intoxicants in a motor vehicle on a highway. [Defendant received a sentence of two-to-ten years for the third OUIL offense.] * * *

The testimony at trial established that the police found defendant unconscious in the driver's seat of a Chevrolet Cavalier station wagon with an open can of beer between his legs at 3:45 a.m. The car was parked just outside the white fog lines but was still on the road pavement. Although the engine was off, the keys were in the ignition and the engine was still warm. Defendant was alone but there were five full cans of cold beer on the passenger seat and one empty can in the back. The police found no one else in the area.

When two deputy sheriffs woke defendant and identified themselves, defendant replied, "You guys are f___ing ass holes." The deputies testified that defendant tried to turn the ignition key but one of the deputies prevented him from doing so. Defendant failed sobriety tests of reciting the alphabet and counting backwards. Defendant told the deputies that, "This is bullshit," and to just take him to "f___ing jail." Defendant also told the deputies that he was coming from a neighboring county, where he had been working, that he had started drinking at 6:00 p.m. that night, and that he had consumed six beers. Both deputies testified without objection that defendant never denied being the driver of the Cavalier. [A blood test showed that defendant had a blood alcohol level of .21, and the legal limit at that time was .10.] * * *

Defense counsel acknowledged that defendant was drunk and belligerent, and that defendant's driver's license was revoked, but he also claimed defendant was not operating the vehicle. Defense counsel theorized that someone else had driven defendant to where the police found him but he presented no evidence to support this theory. Defendant did not testify.

Defendant * * * argues that insufficient evidence supported his convictions. We disagree. * * * We must view the evidence in a light most favorable to the prosecution and determine whether a rational trier of fact could have found all the elements of the offense proved beyond a reasonable doubt. All the elements of an offense may be proved beyond a reasonable doubt by circumstantial evidence and reasonable inferences therefrom. Further, when reviewing claims of insufficient evidence, this Court must make all reasonable inferences and resolve all credibility conflicts in favor of the jury verdict. "Even in a case relying on circumstantial evidence, the prosecution need not negate every reasonable theory consistent with the defendant's innocence, but need merely introduce evidence sufficient to convince a reasonable jury in the face of whatever contradictory evidence the defendant may provide." *People v. Hardiman*, 646 N.W.2d 158 (Mich. 2002).

Defendant relies on *People v. Wood*, 538 N.W.2d 351 (Mich. 1995), and *People v. Burton*, 651 N.W.2d 143 (Mich. Ct. App. 2002), to argue that he was not "operating" the parked car when the police found him unconscious in the driver's seat, and there was reasonable doubt that he drove to that location while intoxicated. Defendant's reliance on *Wood* and *Burton* is misplaced. In *Wood* our Supreme Court limited *People v. Pomeroy* (On Rehearing), 355 N.W.2d 98 (Mich. 1984), which held, "a person sleeping in a motionless car cannot be held to be presently operating a vehicle while sleeping." In *Burton* the prosecutor charged that defendant was attempting to drive while intoxicated at the time the police found him unconscious in his lawfully parked vehicle with its engine running. This Court held that the prosecution failed to prove its theory that the unconscious defendant specifically intended to operate the vehicle while intoxicated at some point in the future but the police intervened before he could do so. But here, the prosecutor did not claim that the evidence established defendant was operating the vehicle at the point the police found him unconscious or that the police found defendant attempting to operate a vehicle while intoxicated. Here, the prosecutor argued that the evidence at trial presented a compelling circumstantial case that defendant had driven while intoxicated to the location where the police found him.

Although defense counsel argued below that someone else drove defendant to where the police found him, he presented no evidence at trial to support that theory. Moreover, the prosecution need not disprove all theories consistent with defendant's innocence; it need only introduce sufficient evidence to convince a reasonable jury of its theory of guilt despite the contradictory theory or evidence a defendant may offer. Also, the trial court specifically instructed the jury regarding the element of "operating" that a person "sleeping in a motionless car . . . cannot be held to be presently operating a vehicle." Thus, because jurors are presumed to follow the trial court's instructions, the jury must have concluded from the circumstantial evidence and reasonable inferences that the prosecutor met his burden of proving defendant was operating the vehicle in an intoxicated state before the police arrived. Because this Court must draw all reasonable inferences in favor of the jury verdict, defendant's conviction must be affirmed.

NOTES AND QUESTIONS

1. *Appellate Review.* In considering a defendant's challenge to a guilty verdict on the ground that the government did not introduce sufficient evidence to establish guilt beyond a reasonable doubt, the appellate court reviews the evidence in the light most favorable to the government, with all inferences drawn from the facts proven at trial in favor of the guilty verdict. As the Supreme Court stated, "It is not for us to weigh the evidence or to determine the credibility of witnesses. The verdict of a jury must be sustained if there is substantial evidence, taking the view most favorable to the Government, to support it." *Glasser v. United States*, 315 U.S. 60 (1942). A challenge to the sufficiency of the evidence is very difficult to win because the burden of proof now shifts to the defendant to establish that no reasonable juror could have found him guilty, with all inferences from circumstantial evidence running in the government's favor. Although appellate courts reverse convictions for insufficient evidence, it is comparatively rare.

2. *Insufficient Evidence.* The rare case of reversal for insufficient evidence is often found in situations where the evidence is extremely weak and the case is premised solely on circumstantial evidence. For example, in the case of *State v. Jones*, 516 N.W.2d 545 (Minn. 1994), the court stated:

> Respondent argued in the court of appeals that the evidence presented at trial was insufficient to convict him. In this case there was no direct evidence linking respondent to the shooting of Blair. This court has held that a conviction based entirely on circumstantial evidence merits stricter scrutiny than convictions based in part on direct evidence. *State v. Scharmer*, 501 N.W.2d 620 (Minn.1993). In such cases "the circumstantial evidence must do more than give rise to suspicion of guilt; 'it must point unerringly to the accused's guilt.'" *Scharmer*. Although we decline to require that a jury instruction including this standard be given, we wish to reaffirm that the standard of appellate review for circumstantial evidence cases remains as we have previously stated it, that "[c]ircumstantial evidence in a criminal case is entitled to as much weight as any other kind of evidence so long as the circumstances proved are consistent with the hypothesis that the accused is guilty and inconsistent with any rational hypothesis except for that of guilt." *State v. Pilcher*, 472 N.W.2d 327 (Minn.1991). Further, we have said that on appeal a conviction based on circumstantial evidence may stand "only where the facts and circumstances disclosed by the circumstantial evidence form a complete chain which, in light of the evidence as a whole, leads so directly to the guilt of the accused as to exclude, beyond a reasonable doubt, any reasonable inference other than that of guilt." *State v. Wahlberg*, 296 N.W.2d 408 (Minn.1980).

MODEL PENAL CODE § 1.12

§ 1.12. Proof Beyond a Reasonable Doubt; Affirmative Defenses; Burden of Proving Fact When Not an Element of an Offense; Presumptions.

(1) No person may be convicted of an offense unless each element of such offense is proved beyond a reasonable doubt. In the absence of such proof, the innocence of the defendant is assumed.

(2) Subsection (1) of this Section does not:

(a) require the disproof of an affirmative defense unless and until there is evidence supporting such defense; or

(b) apply to any defense that the Code or another statute plainly requires the defendant to prove by a preponderance of evidence.

(3) A ground of defense is affirmative, within the meaning of Subsection (2)(a) of this Section, when:

(a) it arises under a section of the Code that so provides; or

(b) it relates to an offense defined by a statute other than the Code and such statute so provides; or

(c) it involves a matter of excuse or justification peculiarly within the knowledge of the defendant on which he can fairly be required to adduce supporting evidence.

(4) When the application of the Code depends upon the finding of a fact that is not an element of an offense, unless the Code otherwise provides:

(a) the burden of proving the fact is on the prosecution or defendant, depending on whose interest or contention will be furthered if the finding should be made; and

(b) the fact must be proved to the satisfaction of the Court or jury, as the case may be.

(5) When the Code establishes a presumption with respect to any fact that is an element of an offense, it has the following consequences:

(a) when there is evidence of the facts that give rise to the presumption, the issue of the existence of the presumed fact must be submitted to the jury, unless the Court is satisfied that the evidence as a whole clearly negatives the presumed fact; and

(b) when the issue of the existence of the presumed fact is submitted to the jury, the Court shall charge that while the presumed fact must, on all the evidence, be proved beyond a reasonable doubt, the law declares that the jury may regard the facts giving rise to the presumption as sufficient evidence of the presumed fact.

(6) A presumption not established by the Code or inconsistent with it has the consequences otherwise accorded it by law.

PROBLEM SEVENTEEN

Odo ended a dating relationship with Jaylin acrimoniously. A short time later, a Domestic Violence Final Restraining Order (an "FRO") was entered against Jaylin that included, among many other restrictions, one that prohibited Jaylin "from being at Odo's place of employment." Odo and Jaylin had both worked at the Bigfish Grill for over two years before they began dating. Jaylin no longer works there. The Bigfish Grill shares a parking lot for its patrons and/or employees with other businesses in the area. Approximately six weeks after the issuance of the FRO, Frank, the kitchen manager of the Bigfish Grill, stepped outside to smoke a cigarette shortly after closing when Frank saw Jaylin speaking to two other servers from a car. The car was parked in the shared parking lot about eighty feet from the entrance to the restaurant. Frank was unaware that the FRO prohibited Jaylin from being at Odo's place of employment, and Frank spoke with Jaylin for about ten minutes. During the conversation, Jaylin got out of the car and walked with Frank to the sidewalk area directly outside of the front of the Bigfish Grill, about ten feet from the front door. Odo was not working at the restaurant that evening, and two days later when Frank told Odo about speaking with Jaylin, Odo contacted the police to complain that Jaylin was coming to the restaurant. Jaylin is charged with knowingly violating the FRO, which is punishable by up to one year in jail. Jaylin admits to the police of having knowledge of the FRO and not being allowed to go to the Bigfish Grill, and Jaylin also admits to speaking with Frank outside the restaurant that evening. What argument will the defense make that Jaylin cannot be found guilty beyond a reasonable doubt of knowingly violating the FRO, and how will the government respond?

B. Defining Reasonable Doubt

State v. Rimmer
250 S.W.3d 12 (Tenn. 2008)

GARY R. WADE, J.

On November 7, 1998, Michael Dale Rimmer (the "Defendant"), a white male, was convicted of theft, aggravated robbery, and the first degree murder of the victim, Ricci Ellsworth. A Shelby County jury imposed the death sentence. * * *

During the middle 1980's, the Defendant had an on-again-off-again romantic relationship with the victim. They started dating sometime after the victim obtained a divorce in 1977 from her first husband, Donald Eugene Ellsworth, by whom she had two children. At the time, the victim was apparently struggling with a drinking problem and Ellsworth was experiencing drug problems. Later, after his relationship with the victim had come to an end, the Defendant was indicted for the aggravated assault and rape of the victim and the first degree burglary of her residence. In 1989, he entered pleas of guilt to each charge and was sentenced to the Department of Correction.

During his incarceration, the victim often accompanied the Defendant's mother, Sandra Rimmer, on visits to the prison. Because the victim participated in a religious program that ministered to inmates from about 1988 to 1992, she saw the Defendant regularly. According to the Defendant's mother, the victim and the Defendant displayed an affection for each other during the prison visits. Despite this purported renewal of their relationship, however, there was evidence that during this period of time, the Defendant informed two inmates, Roger LeScure and William Conaley, of his desire to kill the victim upon his release from the prison. He even described to LeScure how he intended to dispose of her body. The Defendant explained to the inmates that he blamed the victim for his incarceration and was entitled to money from her.

The Defendant was released by the Department of Correction in October of 1996 and began work at an auto body repair shop in Memphis. By that time, the victim, who was employed as a night auditor at the Memphis Inn, had remarried Donald Ellsworth and had experienced some success in controlling her alcohol problems.

On February 7, 1997, the victim was scheduled to begin her shift at 11:00 p.m. Her husband awakened her and kissed her goodbye. She drove to the hotel in her 1989 Dodge Dynasty. The only access to her office was through a door, which was locked, or through a small opening in the glass security window. Several hotel guests saw the victim at her office desk between 1:00 and 2:00 a.m. Before 2:00

a.m., one of the guests noticed a "dark-maroonish brown" car that had been backed into an area near the hotel entrance. Although it was raining at the time, the trunk was open.

At about 2:30 a.m., Raymond Summers, a railroad supervisor with CSX Transportation, drove to the hotel when the management service was unable to make telephone contact with a work crew, which was staying there overnight. Because no one was at the front desk, Summers entered the office area. When he heard the sound of water running in the office restroom, he looked inside and discovered blood splatters on the sink, the wall, the toilet bowl, and some towels. He reported his findings to Shelby County officers who were leaving a nearby Denny's Restaurant. The officers notified Linda Spencer, the hotel manager, who lived on the premises. When they investigated, they discovered signs of a struggle in the office area. There were "puddles" of blood throughout the restroom. The sink was cracked, and the lid had been ripped off the commode. Police found the victim's purse. There was a trail of blood approximately thirty-nine feet long that led from the restroom, through the equipment room, office, reception area, and to the vending space. The trail ended on the curb outside the night entrance, indicating that the victim may have been dragged from the restroom to the curb. Some $600 in cash was missing from the register, and three sets of sheets had been taken from the equipment room. Officer Robert Moore of the Memphis Police found a green cigarette lighter under a bloody towel and discovered the victim's gold ring between the office and the bathroom.

Sergeant Robert Shemwell of the homicide department testified that during the investigation the police questioned Richard Rimmer, the Defendant's brother, and Richard Rimmer's ex-girlfriend, Joyce Frazier. According to Sergeant Shemwell, the Defendant appeared at his brother's house during the morning hours after the murder. The Defendant's car was muddy and so were his shoes. The back seat of the car appeared to be wet. There was a shovel inside. The Defendant had asked Richard Rimmer, who was a carpet cleaner, if he knew how to get blood out of carpet. Richard Rimmer admitted that sometime after he had learned of the victim's disappearance, he disposed of the shovel in a dumpster.

The police learned that the Defendant left Memphis without taking the last paycheck he was due from his employer. He gave no notice of his departure. He also left without taking his work tools or the clothing he had stored in the room he occupied.

On March 5, 1997, Michael Adams, a Johnson County, Indiana deputy, stopped the Defendant, checked the license plate number on the Honda, and determined that the vehicle had been reported as stolen in early January. The Defendant was arrested for possession of a stolen vehicle and public intoxication. He registered .06 on a blood-alcohol test. A receipt in the vehicle indicated that the Defendant was in Myrtle, Mississippi on the day after the victim's disappearance. Receipts from

Florida, Missouri, Wyoming, Montana, California, Arizona, and Texas with dates ranging from February 13, five days after the police were alerted of the crime, to March 3, 1997, two days before the Defendant's arrest, were found in the vehicle.

There were blood stains on the carpet and on a seat belt in the back seat of the Honda. Subsequent testing of the stains in the car revealed that the DNA from the blood was consistent with the bloodline of the victim's mother, Marjorie Floyd, who lived in Florence, Alabama. It was also consistent with the blood type of the victim, as compared through a sample previously taken from a pap smear. Frank Baetchel, the FBI forensic expert who performed the tests, also examined a bloody hotel towel found at the Memphis Inn, concluding that the blood sample matched the stains found inside the Honda. * * *

During the course of the investigation, the police had explored numerous leads. One report indicated that between 1:45 and 2:00 a.m., James Darnell, along with Dixie Roberts, saw two white males at the Memphis Inn. It was dark and the weather was rainy. He said that both men had blood on their knuckles and appeared to have been fighting. Darnell told officers that one of the men, who he believed to be a clerk, was behind the hotel window and appeared to be giving change to the other. Darnell inferred that the clerk was trying to get the other man, who was "very drunk," to leave. Darnell also saw a dark-colored car "backed in front of the night entrance." Darnell, when shown a photographic line-up, was unable to identify the Defendant as one of the two men. Two composite drawings were made of these individuals, based on Darnell's descriptions. * * *

The Defendant next takes issue with the jury instruction defining "reasonable doubt." He argues that the definition lowered the burden of proof, in violation of the due process clause in the United States Constitution * * *. The trial court instructed the jury as follows:

Reasonable doubt is that doubt engendered by an investigation of all the proof in the case and an inability after such investigation to let the mind rest easily upon the certainty of guilt. Reasonable doubt does not mean a doubt that may arise from possibility. Absolute certainty is not demanded by the law.

The Defendant specifically calls our attention to the words "[r]easonable doubt does not mean a doubt that may arise from possibility." He argues that this sentence lowered the burden of proof from guilt beyond a reasonable doubt.

In *Cage* [*v. Louisiana*, 498 U.S. 39 (1990)], the United States Supreme Court held unconstitutional an instruction equating reasonable doubt with "actual substantial doubt" and "grave uncertainty." The Court held that "[w]hen those statements are then considered with the reference to 'moral certainty,' rather than evidentiary certainty, it becomes clear that a reasonable juror could have interpreted the instruction to allow a finding of guilt based on a degree of proof below that required by the Due Process Clause."

In *Victor v. Nebraska*, 511 U.S. 1 (1994), the Supreme Court considered the definition of reasonable doubt given in the trial of two criminal defendants from two state courts. Jurors in the first case were told that they must have "an abiding conviction, to a moral certainty, of the truth of the charge" in order to meet the reasonable doubt standard. In the second case, the instruction provided that a reasonable doubt is "an actual and substantial doubt" and that the jury must have "an abiding conviction, to a moral certainty, of the guilt of the accused." The Supreme Court concluded that while they would not "condone" the use of the term "moral certainty," the instructions were distinguishable from those given in *Cage* because the jurors were instructed to base their verdict on the evidence rather than any other factor which might conceivably allow a conviction on a standard lower than reasonable doubt. Further, the Court stated that "instructing the jurors that they must have an abiding conviction of the defendant's guilt does much to alleviate any concerns that the phrase 'moral certainty' might be misunderstood in the abstract."

The specific instruction under review comes from the Tennessee Pattern Jury Instructions for criminal trials. T.P.I.Crim. 2.03 (5th ed.2000). As we have previously noted, pattern jury instructions are only suggestions for a trial court because they are "not officially approved by this Court or by the General Assembly and should be used only after careful analysis." *State v. Hodges*, 944 S.W.2d 346 (Tenn.1997). Thus, pattern jury instructions are not entitled to any particular deference on review. Still, this Court has previously upheld the constitutionality of a similar instruction. *State v. Hall*, 976 S.W.2d 121 (Tenn.1998). In fairness, however, the focus in *Hall* was on the use of the phrase "moral certainty" and whether that implied a lesser standard of proof required by the State. The Defendant complains that "[r]easonable doubt does not mean a doubt that may arise from possibility" is ambiguous terminology. He asserts that the jury might have understood the instruction to permit a conviction on insufficient evidence.

Jury instructions must be reviewed in their entirety. Phrases may not be examined in isolation. The sentence preceding the phrase at issue explains that reasonable doubt is the inability to "let the mind rest easily upon the certainty of guilt" after reviewing all the facts. The sentence following directs that absolute certainty of guilt is not required. In context, a fair interpretation is that reasonable doubt does not mean a doubt that may arise from mere possibility no matter how improbable.

Further, in order to determine whether there was harm to the Defendant by an ambiguous erroneous instruction, we must consider "whether the ailing instruction by itself so infected the entire trial that the resulting conviction violates due process." *Cupp v. Naughten*, 414 U.S. 141 (1973). * * * One ambiguous term does not necessarily constitute error:

> [J]urors do not sit in solitary isolation booths parsing instructions for subtle shades of meaning in the same way that lawyers might. Differences among them in interpretation of instructions may be thrashed out in the deliberative process, with commonsense understanding of the instructions in the light of all that has taken place at the trial likely to prevail over technical hairsplitting.

Hodges. By the application of this standard, we do not find a reasonable likelihood that the jury applied the burden of proof in an unconstitutional way.

Although this jury instruction did not result in a denial of due process in this context, we acknowledge the language of this particular instruction may not be helpful. As such, we discourage the further use of this instruction.

NOTES AND QUESTIONS

1. ***Defining "Beyond a Reasonable Doubt"***. Jurisdictions vary widely in how they define "beyond a reasonable doubt." Most jurisdictions refuse to translate the term into mathematical terms, such as "95% confidence in a defendant's guilt." Some common instructions given the jury include that the term does "not require proof to a mathematical certainty" and that any doubts "must be based in reason and evidence, not speculation." On the other hand, different formulations are used to impress upon the jury the importance of the task before them and the heavy burden that is placed on the state. Constitutional challenges are often mounted on void-for-vagueness grounds or claiming that the instruction misleads the jury into thinking the burden is too low. These challenges sometimes succeed, far more often fail. An example here would be the instructions considered in *Victor v. Nebraska*, 511 U.S. 1 (1994), and discussed in the *State v. Rimmer* case, *supra*.

Some jurisdictions refuse to allow counsel, in arguments to the jury, to discuss the definition of reasonable doubt. See *United States v. Glass*, 846 F.2d 386 (7th Cir. 1988). Also consider this common formulation in some courts: "You have a reasonable doubt if it is the kind of doubt that would make you hesitate in a matter of grave importance in your personal life, such as in the decision whether to marry." Is this formulation sufficiently clear and accurate to survive constitutional challenge? Some prosecutors object that this formulation in fact sets the standard too high because many people might hesitate over a decision whether to marry but do it anyway and are thereafter confident in their choice. The available empirical evidence suggests that the vagueness of the standard leads different jurors and juries to interpret how much confidence they must have in the prosecution's proof very differently. What is clear, though it is rarely explained to the jury this way, is that the standard is higher than a preponderance of the evidence (a term meaning "more likely than not") and higher than "clear and convincing evidence" (another term whose definition is elusive but, if we sought to include a mathematical translation, probably requires confidence in the range of 60-75%).

2. *Jury Nullification*. There is no right to have the jury instructed on jury nullification. In many states the jury decides the facts of the case and the judge instructs the jury that they must follow the law. Although there is no right to explain to juries that they can disregard the law, juries sometimes use their power to decide the facts to reject the law in the jurisdiction. Some states even provide for juries to consider the law. For example, in *Holden v. State*, 788 N.E.2d 1253 (Ind. 2003), Justice Rucker stated:

> Article I, Section 19 of the Indiana Constitution provides "In all criminal cases whatever, the jury shall have the right to determine the law and the facts." Holden argues the trial court erred in refusing to give an instruction advising the jury, among other things, "[w]hile this provision does not entitle you to return false verdicts, it does allow you the latitude to refuse to enforce the law's harshness when justice so requires." Holden's argument is inspired at least in part by a Law Review article written by the author of this opinion. See Honorable Robert D. Rucker, *The Right to Ignore the Law: Constitutional Entitlement Versus Judicial Interpretation*, 33 VAL. U.L.REV. 449 (1999). Tracing the history of the doctrine that allowed juries to determine both the law and the facts in criminal cases, the article reached several conclusions. One conclusion was that "an instruction telling the jury that the constitution intentionally allows them latitude to 'refuse to enforce the law's harshness when justice so requires' would be consistent with the intent of the framers and give life to what is now a dead letter provision."

> The general thrust of the article is that Article I, Section 19 amounts to a constitutionally permissible form of jury nullification. That is, under the Indiana Constitution the jury has the right to return a verdict of not guilty despite the law and the evidence where a strict application of the law would result in injustice and violate the moral conscience of the community. Although jury nullification has been variously defined, this is its central tenet. See, e.g., Jeffrey Abramson, WE, THE JURY 57 (1994) (defining nullification as the jurors' "right to refuse to enforce the law against defendants whom they believe in good conscience should be acquitted"); Clay S. Conrad, JURY NULLIFICATION: THE EVOLUTION OF A DOCTRINE 7 (1998) (defining nullification as the jurors' "right to refuse to convict if they believe that a conviction would be in some way unjust"); Irwin A. Horowitz, et al., *Jury Nullification: Legal and Psychological*

Perspectives, 66 BROOK. L.REV. 1207, 1208 (2001) (defining the term as the "power to acquit defendants despite evidence and judicial instructions to the contrary" and noting that its purpose is to "return an acquittal when strict interpretation of the law would result in an injustice and violate the moral conscience of the community").

It is historically accurate to say that a jury's right in a criminal case to "determine the law and the facts" has a long and distinguished history that can be traced from medieval England through the seditious libel trial of New York publisher John Peter Zenger. It is also true that early case authority in this state stood for the proposition that the jury's law determining function meant that the jury could "disregard" the instructions of the trial court. However, on closer examination it appears that the right to disregard the trial court's instructions has never been equated as a right to disregard "the law." * * *

Although there may be some value in instructing Indiana jurors that they have a right to "refuse to enforce the law's harshness when justice so requires," the source of that right cannot be found in Article I, Section 19 of the Indiana Constitution. This Court's latest pronouncement on the subject is correct: "[I]t is improper for a court to instruct a jury that they have a right to disregard the law. Notwithstanding Article 1, Section 19 of the Indiana Constitution, a jury has no more right to ignore the law than it has to ignore the facts in a case." *Bivins v. State*, 642 N.E.2d 928 (Ind.1994). The trial court in this case properly refused to give Holden's tendered instruction.

See also Paul Butler, *Racially Based Jury Nullification: Black Power in the Criminal Justice System*, 105 Yale L.J. 677 (1995).

3. ***Ethics***. Both the prosecution and defense are bound by ethical rules in their presentation of evidence. Although these rules are set forth by the particular jurisdiction, states often adopt the rules promulgated by the American Bar Association. Consider this American Bar Association Model Rule of Professional Conduct, Rule 3.8, setting forth some of the ethical rules for prosecutors:

The prosecutor in a criminal case shall:

(a) refrain from prosecuting a charge that the prosecutor knows is not supported by probable cause;

(b) make reasonable efforts to assure that the accused has been advised of the right to, and the procedure for obtaining, counsel and has been given reasonable opportunity to obtain counsel;

(c) not seek to obtain from an unrepresented accused a waiver of important pretrial rights, such as the right to a preliminary hearing;

(d) make timely disclosure to the defense of all evidence or information known to the prosecutor that tends to negate the guilt of the accused or mitigates the offense, and in connection with sentencing, disclose to the defense and to the tribunal all unprivileged mitigating information known to the prosecutor, except when the prosecutor is relieved of this responsibility by a protective order of the tribunal; * * *

The Comments to these rules provide additional guidance. For example, the comment to Rule 3.8 states, "A prosecutor has the responsibility of a minister of justice and not simply that of an advocate." Defense counsel can be faced with ethical issues in representing a client when the client desires to testify, but the testimony will not be truthful. See *Nix v. Whiteside*, 475 U.S. 157 (1986). [See Chap. 15]. There is also the ABA Criminal Justice Standards: The Prosecution and Defense Function Standards which provide guidance to attorneys who handle criminal matters.

C. Jury Unanimity

The common understanding of the *petit* jury in a criminal case is twelve citizens who must agree unanimously if a defendant is to be convicted. The unanimity rule has its roots in fourteenth-century England, and was a common feature of criminal trials before the American Revolution. As a matter of constitutional law, however, there is no requirement that a state court jury be comprised of twelve members, nor must the jury reach a unanimous agreement on guilt in order to convict a defendant of an offense. In *Williams v. Florida*, 399 U.S. 78 (1970), the Supreme Court stated, "We hold that the 12-man panel is not a necessary ingredient of 'trial by jury,' and that [the state]'s refusal to impanel more than the six members provided for by Florida law did not violate petitioner's Sixth Amendment rights as applied to the States through the Fourteenth Amendment." In *Apodaca v. Oregon*, 406 U.S. 404 (1972), a plurality of the Justices upheld Oregon's scheme that required at least ten out of twelve votes in favor of conviction to find a defendant guilty, finding that the Sixth Amendment did not require unanimity to find a defendant guilty beyond a reasonable doubt. Six states permit criminal juries of fewer than 12 members, and two allow non-unanimous verdicts in felony cases, although in a case involving the death penalty the jury must be unanimous on a defendant's guilt and punishment.

While the Sixth Amendment does not require a unanimous jury in state court proceedings, it does in federal criminal prosecutions, and a number of states require unanimous jury verdicts in criminal cases. Even in a non-unanimous verdict jurisdiction, what exactly do the jurors have to agree on? While it is easy to say that the government must prove the elements of the crime beyond a reasonable doubt, it is not always clear what constitutes the particulars of the offense that the jury must agree upon. In *State v. Johnson*, 627 N.W.2d 455 (Wis. 2001), the Wisconsin Supreme Court explained how to determine what a jury must agree upon unanimously in reaching its verdict:

> To say that the jury must be unanimous, however, does not explain what the jury must be unanimous about. For this we look to the statutory language defining the crime and its elements. The principal justification for the unanimity requirement is that it ensures that each juror is convinced beyond a reasonable doubt that the prosecution has proved each essential element of the offense. Thus, while jury unanimity is required on the essential elements of the offense, when the statute in question establishes different modes or means by which the offense may be committed, unanimity is generally not required on the alternate modes or means of commission.
>
> Ordinarily, then, the first step in a unanimity challenge is an examination of the language of the statute in order to determine the elements of the crime and whether the legislature has created a single offense with multiple or alternate modes of commission. The point is to determine legislative intent: did the legislature intend to create multiple, separate offenses, or a single offense capable of being committed in several different ways? For example, where the legislature has specified that any of several different mental states will satisfy the intent or mens rea element of a particular crime, unanimity is not required on the specific alternate mental state as long as the jury unanimously agrees that the state has proven the intent element beyond a reasonable doubt.
>
> Federal constitutional due process considerations, however, limit the state's ability to define a crime so as to dispense with the requirement of jury unanimity on the alternate means or modes of committing it. So the second step in the analysis is an evaluation of whether the lack of jury unanimity on the alternate means or modes of commission violates due process. This involves an inquiry into the fundamental fairness and rationality of the legislative choice, starting, however, with a presumption that the legislature has made its determination fairly and rationally.

In *Richardson v. United States*, 526 U.S. 813 (1999), the Supreme Court considered a challenge to a conviction for engaging in a "continuing criminal enterprise" that required the government to prove that the defendant violated the federal drug laws as "part of a continuing series of violations." The trial judge instructed the jury that it had to find at least three violations, but rejected the defendant's request for an instruction requiring the jury to "unanimously agree on which three acts constituted [the] series of violations." The Court reversed the conviction and offered the following analysis of the statutory phrase:

> In this case, we must decide whether the statute's phrase "series of violations" refers to one element, namely a "series," in respect to which the "violations" constitute the underlying brute facts or means, or whether those words create several elements, namely the several "violations," in respect to each of which the jury must agree unanimously and separately. Our decision will make a difference where, as here, the Government introduces evidence that the defendant has committed more underlying drug crimes than legally necessary to make up a "series." (We assume, but do not decide, that the necessary number is three, the number used in this case.) If the statute creates a single element, a "series," in respect to which individual violations are but the means, then the jury need only agree that the defendant committed at least three of all the underlying crimes the Government has tried to prove. The jury need not agree about which three. On the other hand, if the statute makes each "violation" a separate element, then the jury must agree unanimously about which three crimes the defendant committed.
>
> When interpreting a statute, we look first to the language. In this case, that language may seem to permit either interpretation, that of the Government or of the petitioner, for the statute does not explicitly tell us whether the individual violation is an element or a means. But the language is not totally neutral. The words "violates" and "violations" are words that have a legal ring. A "violation" is not simply an act or conduct; it is an act or conduct that is contrary to law. Black's Law Dictionary 1570 (6th ed.1990). That circumstance is significant because the criminal law ordinarily entrusts a jury with determining whether alleged conduct "violates" the law, and, as noted above, a federal criminal jury must act unanimously when doing so. Indeed, even though the words "violates" and "violations" appear more than 1,000 times in the United States Code, the Government has not pointed us to, nor have we found, any legal source reading any instance of either word as the Government would have us read them in this case. To hold that each "violation" here amounts to a separate element is consistent with a tradition of requiring juror unanimity where the issue is whether a defendant has engaged in conduct that violates the law. To hold the contrary is not.

In *Schad v. Arizona*, 501 U.S. 624 (1991), the Court upheld a defendant's conviction for first degree murder for robbing and then strangling the victim. The prosecution offered two theories for convicting the defendant under the state's murder statute: that the defendant engaged in a willful, deliberate, and premedidated killing, or that the killing occurred during the course of and in furtherance of a felony specified in the statute, known as felony-murder (see Chapter 8). A four-Justice plurality concluded that the two mental states for proving first degree murder – willfull, deliberate and premeditated on the one hand and felony-murder on the other – were so close as to be morally equivalent, and therefore did not require the jury to agree unanimously on which mens rea supported the conviction. The plurality opinion stated:

> It is, as we have said, impossible to lay down any single analytical model for determining when two means are so disparate as to exemplify two inherently separate offenses. In the case before us, however, any scrutiny of the two possibilities for proving the *mens rea* of first-degree murder may appropriately take account of the function that differences of mental state perform in defining the relative seriousness of otherwise similar or identical criminal acts. If, then, two mental states are supposed to be equivalent means to satisfy the *mens rea* element of a single offense, they must reasonably reflect notions of equivalent blameworthiness or culpability, whereas a difference in their perceived degrees of culpability would be a reason to conclude that they identified different offenses altogether. Petitioner has made out no case for such moral disparity in this instance.

In an opinion concurring in the result, Justice Scalia disagreed with the pluralities "moral equivalence" approach and offered a historical argument that the two theories of murder had traditionally been considered together without requiring the jury be unanimous on which one supported the conviction, and therefore the Constitution did not require anything further:

> Submitting killing in the course of a robbery and premeditated killing to the jury under a single charge is not some novel composite that can be subjected to the indignity of "fundamental fairness" review. It was the norm when this country was founded, was the norm when the Fourteenth Amendment was adopted in 1868, and remains the norm today. Unless we are here to invent a Constitution rather than enforce one, it is impossible that a practice as old as the common law and still in existence in the vast majority of States does not provide that process which is "due."

PROBLEM EIGHTEEN

Police executed a search warrant at Spencer's apartment, seizing eight one-pound bags of marijuana. While searching a bedroom in the apartment, an officer found an unloaded Glock pistol under a bed and a hunting rifle in the closet. Spencer is charged in U.S. District Court with possession of marijuana with intent to distribute and a violation of 18 U.S.C. § 922(g)(1), which makes it a crime for any person convicted of a felony to possess "any firearm or ammunition." Spencer was convicted two years earlier of felony assault in state court, and a § 922 conviction requires an additional mandatory five-year prison term. At trial, a relative of Spencer testifies that he owns the rifle and had left it at Spencer's apartment after a recent hunting trip. Spencer testifies that the guns were found in a guest bedroom and a friend, Taylor, would spend the night there occasionally and had boasted about owning a Glock. Spencer admits on cross-examination to not knowing Taylor's last name, residence, or telephone number. Defense counsel requests that the judge instruct the jury that it must decide unanimously which weapon the defendant possessed, which the prosecutor opposes. The court asks each side to present its arguments at a hearing in chambers. How should the court decide on the defense request for a unanimity instruction?

§ 6.03 Jurisdiction and Venue

Jurisdiction is the power of a court to hear a case and render a valid decision, while venue concerns the place where a case may be filed or tried. In criminal cases, the Constitution requires that "such trial shall be held in the state where the said crimes shall have been committed . . . ." U.S. CONST. art. III, § 2, cl. 3.

Jones v. State
537 S.E.2d 80 (Ga. 2000)

SEARS, Justice:

Appellant Gary Jones appeals his conviction for felony murder, * * * arguing, among other things, that because the State failed to prove beyond a reasonable doubt that venue for his trial was properly laid in Fulton County, he was denied his constitutional right to be tried in the county in which his crimes allegedly occurred. * * *We hold that, without exception, * * * the State is required in all criminal trials to introduce evidence establishing that venue is properly laid beyond a reasonable doubt. * * *

The evidence of record shows that in August 1995, appellant asked David Zellars to help him buy crack cocaine. Zellars directed appellant to the home of Jerry Zellner and Horace Lawson. At the home, Zellars purchased drugs from

Lawson, and appellant and Zellars then drove away. Later that evening, appellant returned alone to the home. Gunshots were exchanged, and Jerry Zellner and Horace Lawson were killed. Appellant was shot twice during this incident, and sought medical attention at Grady Memorial Hospital in Atlanta. While at Grady, appellant said that he had been kidnapped and robbed by two men, including David Zellars, and forced to drive to the home of Jerry Zellner and Horace Lawson, where appellant was shot. A bullet removed from appellant's body matched the caliber of the rifle that Jerry Zellner was holding when he was fatally shot. Ballistics testing showed that the bullets removed from Jerry Zellner's body could have come from either: (1) a .9 mm pistol, such as the one owned by appellant's wife that was found after the murder discarded along an interstate highway ramp near Grady Hospital, or (2) a .380 pistol, such as the one recovered after the murder from appellant's car.

These facts, supported by evidence introduced at trial, were sufficient to enable rational jurors to conclude beyond a reasonable doubt that appellant was guilty of the crimes for which he was convicted. * * *

Our Georgia Constitution requires that venue in all criminal cases must be laid in the county in which the crime was allegedly committed. Venue is a jurisdictional fact, and is an essential element in proving that one is guilty of the crime charged. "Like every other material allegation in the indictment, [venue] must be proved [by the prosecution] beyond a reasonable doubt." Proof of venue is a part of the State's case, and the State's failure to prove venue beyond a reasonable doubt renders the verdict contrary to law, without a sufficient evidentiary basis, and warrants reversal.

This Court has previously recognized an exception to the rule requiring venue to be proved beyond a reasonable doubt. We have held that in certain situations, mere slight evidence of venue will be sufficient. "Only when the evidence [of venue] is not conflicting and when no challenge to venue is raised at trial will slight evidence be sufficient to prove venue." However, as explained below, close examination of the "slight evidence exception" reveals that, by its own definition, it can never be applied to situations where a criminal defendant pleads not guilty to the charges indicted against him or her and is placed on trial.

The slight evidence exception has two parts and is written in the conjunctive; before slight evidence of venue will be deemed sufficient, venue must not have been challenged and there must be no conflicting evidence regarding venue. The first of these requirements will never be satisfied in a criminal trial, because venue is challenged *whenever* a criminal defendant pleads not guilty to an indictment's charges. The act of pleading not guilty to an indictment is considered by law to be an irrefutable challenge to all the allegations set forth therein, including those allegations pertaining to venue. Hence, when a criminal defendant pleads not guilty, he or she has challenged venue, and the State will not be permitted to invoke the exception permitting it to establish venue with mere slight evidence. Quite to the contrary, whenever a criminal defendant pleads not guilty and is put on trial, the State is placed on notice that at trial, it will be required to establish venue beyond a reasonable doubt. Therefore, by its own definition, the slight evidence exception can never be invoked after a criminal defendant pleads not guilty and is placed on trial.

Once the burden is placed upon the State to establish venue beyond a reasonable doubt, the burden never shifts to the defendant to disprove venue, as it is axiomatic that the evidentiary burden in a criminal prosecution is "upon the State to prove every material allegation of the indictment and every essential element of the crime charged beyond a reasonable doubt." The State may establish venue by whatever means of proof are available to it, and it may use both direct and circumstantial evidence. It must, however, come forth in all criminal prosecutions with evidence to show beyond a reasonable doubt that venue is properly laid.

We acknowledge that Georgia precedent has not always properly construed the slight evidence exception. Both this Court and the Court of Appeals have misapplied the exception to situations where a criminal defendant has appealed a judgment of conviction entered after a jury trial. In accordance with this opinion, these cases shall no longer be followed with regard to their application of the slight evidence exception. We also recognize that, for all practical purposes, our clarification today of the slight evidence exception renders it a nullity. Henceforth, it will not be recognized in any appeal from a judgment of conviction entered after a bench or jury trial in any criminal matter.

In this matter, the appellant pled not guilty to the indictment lodged against him, thereby challenging all the accusations contained therein, including those pertaining to venue. Hence, the State was required to introduce evidence establishing venue beyond a reasonable doubt. Our review of the record shows that the State failed to satisfy this evidentiary burden.

Appellant was tried in the Superior Court of Fulton County, based upon the State's accusation that the murder he stood accused of took place in Fulton County. The record reveals that the City of Atlanta police officers who responded to the shooting patrolled both Fulton and DeKalb Counties. Therefore, the Atlanta Police Department's investigation of the murder does not establish that venue was properly laid in Fulton County.

At trial, the only evidence regarding venue concerned the county in which the murder victims' neighbor lived. The neighbor testified, (1) that his home is located on Evans Drive, (2) that Evans Drive is located in Fulton County, and (3) that his home is located directly across the street from the murder victims' home. However, while this testimony was somewhat relevant to the location of the neighbor's home, it was irrelevant with regard to the locale of the victims' home where the murder took place. It is entirely possible that the neighbor's house is located in one county, while the houses located across the street are sited in an adjoining county. Moreover, a street name, standing alone, is never sufficient to establish venue, because streets frequently run through more than one county.

Accordingly, this being the only evidence of record pertaining to venue, we conclude that the State failed to prove beyond a reasonable doubt that venue for appellant's murder trial was properly laid in Fulton County. It follows that the verdict rendered is contrary to the law, and must be reversed. [The court then discussed why double jeopardy would not preclude a retrial of this case.]

BENHAM, Chief Justice, with whom Justice HUNSTEIN joins, dissenting.

I respectfully dissent to the majority opinion because I believe the evidence in the record was sufficient to support the jury's finding that the state met its burden in establishing venue. Even if we assume that the State is required to establish venue beyond a reasonable doubt, whether the State has met that burden is a question for the jury. * * * As such, it is our duty to uphold the jury's determination on this issue when there is sufficient evidence in the record authorizing a rational trier of fact to make such a finding. * * *

In the instant case, two witnesses testified as to venue. A Fulton County police investigator testified that the crime scene was on Evans Drive, and a neighbor to the victim testified he lived on Evans Drive; that Evans Drive is in Fulton County; and that the crime took place in a house directly across the street from the witness's house. This evidence is more than sufficient to authorize a reasonable jury to find the prosecution proved venue beyond a reasonable doubt. While it is possible that houses that are directly across from one another, or even next door to each other, are in different counties since county lines may be drawn anywhere, there was no evidence in this case to suggest this possibility. Even if one were to speculate, reasonable people may differ as to whether this possibility creates a sufficient doubt under the law with respect to the venue question at hand because it is axiomatic that the majority of houses located opposite each other on a particular street will be located in the same county. * * *

NOTES AND QUESTIONS

1. *Burden of Proving Venue.* Do all states require venue as an element that must be proven beyond a reasonable doubt? In *Turner v. State*, 285 P.2d 459 (Okla. Crim. App. 1955), the court stated, "[i]n a criminal case it is the duty of the prosecution to prove venue, but venue may be established by circumstantial evidence, and venue need not be shown beyond a reasonable doubt." California does not consider venue an element of the offense that need be considered by the

jury, and instead it is solely an issue of law for the court to determine before trial. *See California v. Posey*, 8 Cal.Rptr.3d 551 (Cal. 2004) "([W]e conclude that the rule that venue is a question of fact for the jury should be rejected in favor of a rule that venue is a question of law for determination by the court."). In federal prosecutions, while venue is an element of the offense, a jury need not be instructed to find venue unless "(1) the defendant objects to venue prior to or at the close of the prosecution's case-in-chief, (2) there is a genuine issue of material fact with regard to proper venue, and (3) the defendant timely requests a jury instruction." *United States v. Perez*, 280 F.3d 318 (3d Cir. 2002). If venue is an element of the offense, then why does the defendant have to raise the issue and request the instruction?

2. ***Continuing Crimes.*** For many crimes, especially those involving violence inflicted on a victim, the venue for the crime will be easily determined. It is where the act occurred. In some cases, however, a crime may involve a number of steps, or a defendant's failure to act may constitute the offense. In these situations, the issue of venue may be more difficult to determine. For example, in *Jenner v. State*, 159 So.2d 250 (Fla. Ct. App. 1964):

> a defendant lawfully took possession of boats in Taylor County, Florida, which were then delivered to, and stored in, St. Louis, Missouri, with the owner's consent, for sale. After disputes with the Florida boat company arose, defendant refused to return the boats to the owner in Florida. The state charged the defendant with theft. Defendant contested whether a charge could be brought in Taylor County. The court determined that because defendant had been in lawful possession of the boats when they left Florida, the intent to deprive the owner of its property could not have occurred in Florida but instead occurred, if at all, in Missouri. The court reversed appellant's conviction and remanded for discharge.

Levine v. State, 849 So.2d 455 (Fla. Ct. App. 2003). In some cases, such as prosecutions involving charges of conspiracy, venue may be in more than one location.

3. ***Extraterritorial Jurisdiction.*** When Congress explicitly states within a statute that it intends the statute to cover acts outside the United States, extraterritorial jurisdiction is clear. More common, however, are instances when the statute omits extraterritorial language and the courts are left to discern the intent of Congress. Some courts will refer to international norms to determine if the statute and acts are encompassed within United States jurisdiction. In *United States v. Layton*, 509 F. Supp. 212 (N.D. Cal. 1981),[a] the court discussed applicable international principles:

---

[a] The Ninth Circuit dismissed the appeal for lack of a final judgment. See United States v. Layton, 645 F.2d 681 (9th Cir. 1981).

There are five principles under which the law of nations permits the exercise of criminal jurisdiction by a nation: territorial jurisdiction based on the location where the alleged crime was committed, and including "objective" territorial jurisdiction, which allows countries to reach acts committed outside territorial limits but intended to produce, and producing, detrimental effects within the nation; nationality jurisdiction based on the nationality of the offender; protective jurisdiction based on the protection of the interests and the integrity of the nation; universality jurisdiction for certain crimes where custody of the offender is sufficient; and passive personality jurisdiction based on the nationality of the victim.

PROBLEM NINETEEN

Jackie, a computer science student in a country outside the United States, creates a computer virus that is put into the Internet with the deliberate purpose of showing Jackie's computer science instructor that there are lapses in computer security in defense installations of many countries. The computer virus causes significant monetary damage to defense installations and university computer systems in the United States. Should Jackie be prosecuted in the United States? What if the country where Jackie's act occurred wants to prosecute, which country should have priority? Should it make a difference if the laws in Jackie's home country provide little punishment for this alleged criminal activity? If someone in the United States placed something in the Internet that was considered criminal activity in another country, would the United States allow that person to be prosecuted in that country? What if the conduct was permitted in the United States by the First Amendment of the U.S. Constitution?

Chapter 7
Proving the Case

§ 7.01 Factfinding and Credibility Determinations

This chapter shifts discussion from criminal law to factfinding, from *rules* of law to witness examination at trial. The chapter begins by discussing why facts matter so much, the two types of facts ("raw" and "normative"), the nature of credibility, and the ways to support and challenge it at trial. Next, the chapter discusses in greater depth character evidence and some critical techniques for impeaching witnesses as well as a special focus on the importance of expert evidence in modern criminal trials. The remainder of the chapter considers the role of factfinding in settings other than the trial, including during guilty plea negotiations. Good lawyers are masters of proof as well as law, grand story-tellers and dramatic actors as well as logicians.

A. Trials Determine Facts, Not Law

In most criminal cases, the law is not in dispute. Rather, controversy centers around what the facts are and how the law should apply to them. Factfinding is therefore central to the criminal trial — indeed it is central to civil trials as well and to much other lawyering activity. The facts that must be proven or disproven are those that help to establish or undermine the existence of any of the basic elements of a crime — the act, attendant circumstances, mental state, and result — or to support or attack an affirmative defense.

Facts relevant to any or all elements of a crime or defense might be in controversy. For example, *who* did the criminal act is always an implicit element of every crime. Defense counsel thus might, via cross-examination, try to raise a reasonable doubt about whether a robbery victim had identified the right person. A scared robbery victim, attacked from behind in darkness, would, the defense would maintain, have had little opportunity to see the attacker. Although the defendant cannot constitutionally be required to take the stand under the privilege against self-incrimination, which is recited in the Fifth Amendment to the United States Constitution (indeed the defense cannot be required to present *any* evidence at all), the robbery defendant might nevertheless choose to go further than simply questioning the sufficiency of the prosecution's proof of the elements of the crime. For example, the defendant might also offer an alibi defense, perhaps by calling his or her mother to say that her child was home at the time of the crime. [Chap. 15].

In a date rape case, by contrast, although the prosecution must still offer evidence of the offender's identity, the accused usually will not challenge that he was the one who committed the act of sexual intercourse. Instead, he will challenge another act element — whether he used force — and will certainly challenge whether the alleged victim consented (an attendant circumstance) and whether, even if she did not consent, he knew or (depending upon what mental state the statute specifies) had *any reason to know* of her non-consent.

In a homicide case against a pharmacist for dispensing a fatal overdose of a mislabeled drug, the pharmacist might not challenge prosecution proof that he or she did so, and did so negligently, but the pharmacist might dispute whether the actions *caused* the patient's death, death being the result required by the crime. Thus the pharmacist might offer forensic medical evidence suggesting that the time of death showed that the patient died of a heart attack long before the slow-acting medication could have killed him or her. The prosecution might respond with its own expert opining that the mislabeled drug, and only that drug, triggered the fatal heart attack.

Likewise, any affirmative defense offered will raise factual disputes. For example, if an accused offers a subjective entrapment defense [See Chap. 18], he or she must prove that the police enticed the accused to commit a crime that they otherwise were not predisposed to commit. The accused may, therefore, offer evidence of police pressure on him or her to buy cocaine and of the accused's previously clean criminal record. The prosecution will respond with evidence that the police merely created an opportunity to commit the crime, an opportunity that the accused eagerly took, as is suggested by evidence of a longstanding drug addiction.

B. Two Types of Facts: "Raw" and "Normative"

There are two broad sorts of facts that must be proven at a criminal trial. The first sort are "raw" facts — who did what to whom, when, and why. In a self-defense claim, the dispute might therefore be over whether the accused started the fight (favoring his or her guilt) or instead whether the alleged victim did so (favoring acquittal). The most important raw fact commonly challenged is the criminal's identity. As will be discussed later in this chapter, there have been a spate of recent acquittals of the innocent, those who were wrongly convicted based upon good faith but mistaken eyewitness identifications. A raw fact is something that happened "out there," in the real, observable world of the past, that is, the event either happened or did not. Since it is impossible to travel back in time and observe the crime, factfinder biases; lawyer errors; insufficient, fraudulent, or distorted evidence; poor judgment; and myriad other factors might result in the factfinder making a mistake about what really happened. But, in theory, there is one and only one "right" answer waiting to be found.

The second sort of fact is a "normative" fact, one for which even time travel would not present a single, crystal clear answer. For such instances, the fact finder's values play an especially large role. Mental state determination involves normative facts to varying degrees. Again, imagine traveling back in time to witness a wife shooting her husband. Did she *want* to kill him, or did she merely "know" that he would die? Did she instead want merely to hurt him, but her plans went awry, and, to her horror and surprise, he died? If she did want only to hurt him, was she aware of a risk that she would nevertheless cause his death, or was she entirely oblivious to that risk? Perhaps, instead, her real goal was simply to defend herself because she believed that he was about to kill or maim her? The answers to these questions will affect the degree of homicide of which the wife may be convicted or whether she is convicted at all. Yet, even if present at the shooting, *it would be impossible to read the wife's mind*.

Even if mind reading was possible, it would not settle the question. Human beings can have mixed motives, multiple, complex, subtle, and ambiguous, even paradoxical, thoughts and feelings. We often do not know our own minds, struggling to understand why we did what we did in the past and what it is that we really want for the future. Some of our thoughts are subconscious, affecting our conscious thoughts without our knowing it. Other times we distract ourselves when submerged thoughts break through to the surface, an effort to hide those thoughts from ourselves, for self-deception and rationalization are common experiences in everyone's lives. If we struggle to understand ourselves — drawing on our entire life's experiences — how can we expect less fully-informed mind readers (jurors) to find greater clarity? Just as in introspection, we judge ourselves, bringing our own and our society's moral standards and mores into our crafting an explanation for why we did certain things, so too will observers bring those things to bear on judging our thoughts and feelings.

The normative content of mental state inquiries is stronger still whenever the *mens rea* requirement is negligence. Factfinders are instructed to determine what a "reasonable person" under the circumstance should know or do. Although courts sometimes guide jurors concerning what "circumstances" should be part of the reasonable person's world, not all circumstances are specified, and the term "reasonable" is either undefined or given a thoroughly ambiguous meaning. Jurors are therefore left to draw on their own sense of what is "reasonable," which translates into their sense of what is right and just. There are other sorts of ambiguously-defined mental states, such as having a "depraved heart" or acting in the reasonable "heat of passion," that invite similar normative inquiry.

Yet, even proving normative facts turns on proving raw facts that support normative inferences. If the wife who shot her husband said, "I'm going to kill you for cheating on me," that supports believing that she wanted her husband dead. If instead she said, "One step closer or I'll shoot," that supports a self-defense claim. But different witnesses may recount different versions of what words in fact escaped from the wife's lips. Furthermore, once the factfinder decides what words were said, more must be known about the surrounding circumstances to decide what normative significance the words deserve. A wife who kills her husband for cheating on her may have done so in "cold blood" (possible first degree murder) or "hot blood" (second degree murder or, if the provocation is found reasonable, voluntary manslaughter). What kind of person the wife was (jealous or not, vindictive or not, religious or not) and what kind of relationship she had with her husband (psychologically abusive or not), themselves partly moral judgments, will infuse the jury's decision about the degree of the crime. But the wife's character and the nature and history of her marriage may also be subject to debate, including disputes over whether specific events happened — actions or words that shed light on the nature of the parties and on their relationship.

C. What Is Credibility, and How Can It Be Challenged?

These disputes over what happened and over how events should be interpreted are questions of credibility. "Credibility" judgments are decisions about who is telling the truth or whose tale merits belief. Although a witness might speak an un-truth knowingly, that is, might lie, more often witnesses are mistaken or confused. It is the job of the direct-examiner to build up his or her witness's credibility and of the cross-examiner to undermine it or test the veracity of the statements. Cross-examination usually turns on four broad techniques, captured by the mnemonic "ROTC"— questioning the witness's abilities to Remember, Observe, Tell the Truth, and Communicate.

Memory might be challenged by asking about details: What was the robber wearing? What color was his or her shirt? Prior inconsistent statements might also call memory into question — for example, the witness's saying on the stand that the robber's hair was brown (as is the defendant's) when the witness told the police just after the crime that the robber's hair was red.

The ability to observe may be questioned by exploring obstacles to clear observation. Was the witness wearing glasses at the time of the crime? Was it dark? How far away was the witness from the robbery? Didn't the crime last only ten seconds?

The ability to tell the truth can be challenged by showing that the witness is a liar, that is, that the witness has lied about important things in the past or been convicted of crimes whose nature suggest that this is an untruthful person. A witness might also have a motive to lie, such as would be true of a mother who dearly loves her child testifying in support of the child's alibi defense. Her motive, of course, is to keep the child out of prison. Prior inconsistent statements about major things — things about which someone would not likely be mistaken — also suggest that a witness is a liar. For example, a rape defendant who told the police that he was happily married, when he was in fact acrimoniously divorced and lonely, seems like an outright lie. It is hard to believe that the defendant "forgot" either his marriage or his divorce.

The ability to communicate clearly can be tested by asking a witness to describe something where the accuracy of the descriptions can quickly be verified. If a witness says, "I was only ten feet away from the robbery," you can thus ask the witness to point at an object ten feet away from the witness in the courtroom. If the witness points at the back of the room, that distance can be measured, and, if it turns out to be 50 feet, that suggests that the witness is poor at judging distances and was likely much further from the crime scene than realized.

These are just a few, far from exhaustive, illustrations of how lawyers can seek to guide factfinder credibility judgments. The details of what evidence can be offered to prove an element of a crime or defense or to challenge credibility are governed by each locality's rules of evidence. As this is not an evidence law course, those rules are not reviewed here in detail. The broad outlines, however, though not the many fine points of some important evidentiary doctrines, will be reviewed briefly and the rough contours of some evidentiary rules will be mentioned in future chapters.

D. Illustrating and Practicing Credibility Judgments

1. Background

Factfinder judgments of witness credibility are ordinarily not subject to appellate review. If a jury acquits, the Double Jeopardy Clause of the Constitution prohibits prosecution appeal on any ground. If the jury convicts, the defense ordinarily will be unsuccessful on appeal on an argument that the prosecution's witnesses were not credible or that the defense witnesses, if any, were. Instead, the appellate court ordinarily assumes the credibility of the verdict winner's (the prosecution's) witnesses and makes any plausible inferences that can be drawn in the winner's favor in deciding whether the law was violated. Similar principles of appellate review — limiting appellate re-evaluation of credibility — are at work in appeals from certain types of pre-trial and post-trial hearings and decisions.

In rare instances, however, credibility judgments can be of concern to an appellate court. One such instance involves claims under the Federal Anti-Terrorism and Effective Death Penalty Act of 1996 ("AEDPA") that a state court decision was "based on an unreasonable determination of the facts in light of the evidence presented in the state court proceeding." 28 U.S.C. § 2254 (d)(2). Rephrased, "a federal court may not second-guess a state court's fact-finding process unless, after review of the state-court record, it determines that the state court was not merely wrong but actually unreasonable." *Taylor v. Maddox,* 366 F.3d 992 (9th Cir. 2004).

Study of the AEDPA's procedures is a topic taught in advanced criminal law and procedure courses. But this quirky statute provides an opportunity for examining how judges go about making credibility determinations. In the case excerpted below, the defendant filed a habeas corpus claim — a request to release his body, his "corpus," from prison — in federal court under the AEDPA as he started to serve a life sentence without parole for first-degree felony murder and second-degree robbery. Taylor had filed a motion to suppress evidence — a pretrial motion to exclude certain evidence from trial on the ground that it was obtained by unconstitutional means, in this case in violation of *Miranda v. Arizona,* 384 U.S. 436 (1966). Under *Miranda,* the privilege against self-incrimination requires anyone subjected to custodial interrogation to be warned of certain rights, including the right to remain silent and the right to consult with an attorney before and during questioning. The police may not question someone in custody unless they have given the individual *Miranda* warnings and that person has knowingly, voluntarily, and intelligently waived the *Miranda* rights. If the person does not waive them, he or she may not be questioned. If the person asks for a lawyer, all questioning must stop until he or she meets with an attorney. Taylor claimed that while being questioned by two detectives, he asked for, but did not receive, a lawyer, yet the questioning continued.

The Due Process Clause of the Fourteenth Amendment also prohibits using any "involuntary" confession against an accused at trial, even if *Miranda* has not been violated. The state trial court found as facts that Taylor never requested a lawyer and that the confession was voluntary, thus denying Taylor's motion to suppress his confession on Fifth and Fourteenth Amendment grounds. The trial judge gave a brief oral opinion from the bench declaring, while giving few reasons for doing so, that he believed the detectives' version of the relevant facts and disbelieved Taylor's version. Accordingly, he denied the motion.

After the jury heard Taylor's confession, it convicted him, and he repeatedly contested the suppression judge's factfindings concerning the confession, first through the federal *habeas* process, until reaching the Ninth Circuit. The Ninth Circuit agreed that the state suppression court judge's factfindings were unreasonable within the meaning of the AEDPA and reversed the conviction. The Ninth Circuit remanded the matter to the federal district court to grant a conditional writ of habeas corpus, ordering Taylor's release unless the state of California notified the district court within 30 days of an intention to retry Taylor based on evidence *other than* the confession and actually beginning that retrial within 70 days of issuance of the mandate.

2. *Taylor* Case Facts

Here were the uncontested facts, as described by the Ninth Circuit:

On May 31, 1993, William Shadden was riding his bicycle through a beachside area in Long Beach, California, when two assailants attempted to take it from him. Shadden resisted and the assailants fled. Unwisely, Shadden gave chase and one of the assailants shot Shadden twice, killing him. Three months later, Detectives Craig Remine and William MacLyman, both of the Long Beach Police Department, came to suspect that [then 16 year-old] Leif Taylor had been involved and obtained a search warrant for his apartment. Remine, MacLyman and at least two other law enforcement officers executed the search warrant and an arrest warrant for Taylor at roughly 11:30 pm on September 1, 1993. They found Taylor sleeping on a couch in his living room; his mother, who was his only custodial parent, was apparently absent.

Taylor was startled awake by four men with guns drawn and flashlights trained around the room. Taylor was permitted to dress; he was then handcuffed and driven to the police station. He arrived at the station ten minutes later, was escorted onto an elevator to the third floor and placed in a small interrogation room, where he sat alone for about thirty minutes. By the time Remine and MacLyman entered and began to question Taylor, it was past midnight. For three hours, the detectives interrogated the boy, who was "considerably younger and physically smaller" than they * * * Taylor "was given no food, offered no rest break, and may not have been given any water." Neither Taylor's mother nor an attorney was present to advise him during the questioning. Taylor denied involvement in the crime "[f]or in excess of two and a-half hours," before finally inculpating himself. At the detective's behest, he then memorialized on audio tape his confession and a waiver of his rights under *Miranda v. Arizona*, 384 U.S. 436 (1966). Begun at 3:02 a.m. and completed at 3:13 a.m., the recording was just eleven minutes long; there is no record of the earlier two-and-a-half-hours of questioning. This is so because Remine and MacLyman questioned Taylor without turning on the tape recorder eventually used to record his confession — or the hidden recording equipment installed in the interrogation room — until after he had inculpated himself. Remine took notes during the questioning but subsequently disposed of them. There is no videotape, so we cannot see whether Taylor was calm and cool or tearful and agitated nor do we have the audio tape to listen to. Indeed, there is no contemporaneous record at all of what happened during most of the time that Taylor spent in the interrogation room with Remine and MacLyman.

The disputed facts in *Taylor* were two-fold: (1) whether Taylor had repeatedly, or ever, requested an attorney; and (2) whether the detectives had threatened Taylor or otherwise engaged in misconduct to get him to talk. Here, in part, is how the Ninth Circuit addressed the reasonableness of the suppression judge's credibility determinations on these two questions.

Taylor v. Maddox
366 F.3d 992 (9th Cir. 2004)

KOZINSKI, Circuit Judge.

In his testimony at the suppression hearing, Taylor gave a disturbing account of his interrogation. He recalled that he awoke to find a flashlight and a gun pointed at him, and his living room filled with men. As he was handcuffed and placed in a police car, he was not told why he was being arrested. Taylor asked the officer driving the car if he knew the reason for the arrest. The officer said Taylor would be told at the station. Taylor also asked the officer if he "could call . . . [his] mom when . . . [he] got there. [The officer] . . . said that she would be notified for . . . [him]." * * *

Once at the station, Taylor recounted, he was taken on an elevator to an upper floor, where he waited alone in a small interrogation room for about thirty minutes. When Remine and MacLyman arrived, they did not tell him immediately why he had been arrested, asserting instead that he knew why he was there. MacLyman — who Taylor described as "the bigger fellow" — wore a ring inscribed with the police code for murder, "187," which he thrust in Taylor's face, saying, "'Well, you know why you're down here.'" * * * MacLyman then told Taylor he had been arrested in connection with Shadden's killing.

During the questioning that followed, Taylor asked several times to speak to his mother and an attorney named Arthur Close. Taylor was adamant in his assertions at the suppression hearing that he had requested counsel before incriminating himself. For example:

Q: [D]id you ask to speak to anyone?

A: I asked to speak with my attorney. I told . . . [the detectives] I knew an attorney from the outs. I thought maybe I could call him to get some advice, and they told me no, it wouldn't be possible.

Q: Did you ask to speak with anyone else?

A: I then asked, "Well, can I speak with my mother, can I call her?" And they told me, no.

Similarly:

Q: Did you ask to speak to a lawyer?

A: Yes.

Q: And did you ask to speak to a specific lawyer?

A: Yes, I did.

Q: Did you have the telephone number of a lawyer to call?

A: Yes, I did.

Q: And do you remember that telephone number now?

A: I do.

Q: What telephone number is that?

A: Area code 310, 599-6448.

Q: Did you want to talk to these detectives?

A: No, I didn't.

Q: Did you want to talk to Art Close before you talked to the detective?

A: Yes.

Q: Did you try to do that?

A: Yes.

Q: Did somebody prevent you from doing that?

A: Yes.

Q: Who did that?

A: One of the detectives, I can't remember.

Q: How did they prevent you?

A: They told me it wouldn't be possible. They told me just,
        you know, they wanted me to tell them what they wanted
        to hear. They told me just to tell them what happened, and
        they would let me use the phone.

And again:

Q: [After some questioning had elapsed], did you still want to
        speak to your lawyer or a lawyer?

A: Several times, I mentioned to speak to him. And on cross-
        examination by the prosecution:

Q: [The detectives] ... told you you couldn't have an attorney?

A: They didn't tell me I couldn't have one. They told me I couldn't
        make a phone call to one.

Q: You said "I want to call an attorney?"

A: Yes.

Q: * * * You didn't say, you want to call Art?

A: I said I want to call an attorney, and they said who, . . .

In these and other exchanges, Taylor never wavered in his assertion that he
wanted to call a lawyer during his interrogation and asked for access to a phone
in order to do so.

According to Taylor, the detectives denied his requests. Instead, MacLyman
drew long and short lines on a piece of paper, explaining to Taylor that he could
go to jail for the rest of his life (long line) or just until he was twenty-five (short
line), depending on whether he cooperated with the detectives. MacLyman also
coaxed Taylor, saying he knew Taylor didn't kill Shadden deliberately but had
done so unintentionally. Although Taylor steadfastly denied involvement, the
detectives persisted in the questioning and would not permit Taylor to make a
phone call until he told them "the truth."

Taylor became desperate and upset. Concluding that he could clear up the
matter later, Taylor decided to yield to the detectives' insistent demands that he
confess in order to gain access to a phone. He then made the eleven-minute
recording memorializing his *Miranda* waiver and confession. Explaining why he
would give a false confession, Taylor said, * * *

I was just tired, you know. I wanted to get out of that room, for one thing. I was thinking, you know, you know, I am just not knowing what was going on. I am thinking these guys are supposed to be the good guys. I was never involved in any serious crime, so if I just agree with them, get my phone call, I will get it straightened out, I will go home.
* * *

MacLyman, the bête noire in Taylor's account of these events, did not testify at the suppression hearing. Remine, who did testify, related a story very different from Taylor's — or, at least, professed to lack specific recollection on key points in Taylor's story. Remine asserted that Taylor had been advised of his *Miranda* rights immediately after Remine and MacLyman joined him in the interrogation room, and that he had waived his rights at that time by signing the advisement form. Remine did confirm that MacLyman wore a "187" ring and that the interrogation room was on an upper floor in the police station. He denied or could not recall that Taylor appeared emotional during questioning, that Taylor asked to speak with his mother, that MacLyman thrust his "187" ring in Taylor's face, and that MacLyman mapped lines representing potential sentences. Remine also denied that he told Taylor he knew Taylor hadn't intended to kill the victim; he was never asked whether MacLyman made that statement. When asked by defense counsel whether Taylor asked to speak with Close, Remine replied, "I don't recall him making that statement."

Asked by defense counsel if Taylor requested a lawyer *prior* to signing the advisement form, Remine unqualifiedly stated, "No, sir." But when defense counsel asked whether Taylor asked for a lawyer *after* signing the form, Remine ambiguously replied, "Not to my recollection, he did not," and to counsel's repeated inquiry whether Taylor ever asked to speak with a lawyer named Close, Remine hedged, "I don't recall him saying that, no, sir." Remine also denied that Taylor had asked for his mother before questioning and could not recall whether he had asked for his mother during questioning. The prosecutor did not seek to clarify the ambiguities in Remine's testimony, and never asked Remine if Taylor had asked to speak with counsel at any point.

In evaluating the relative credibility of these two sharply differing accounts of the events inside the interrogation room, the state courts treated this as a swearing-contest between Taylor and Remine. The state trial judge simply said that he believed Remine, not Taylor. He purported to give reasons for disbelieving Taylor's account of the interrogation, but his explanation defie[d] rational understanding. * * *

[When Close, the lawyer whom Taylor wanted to contact testified] in [many] respects, [his testimony] substantially corroborated Taylor's story. But Close's testimony also went beyond the scope of Taylor's, for Close testified that "[Taylor] said he requested, by name, to speak to me on the elevator in the police department, prior to the questioning." Close further testified that Taylor was crying and upset during the call and that Taylor provided these details without prompting from Close.

While Close's testimony is based on what Taylor told him during their telephone conversation following the end of the interrogation, it nevertheless corroborates Taylor's account in important respects. To begin with, the record discloses that Taylor called Close at the first available opportunity. Taylor's taped confession ended at 3:13 a.m., and he was thereafter booked — a process that was completed no earlier than 3:55 a.m. Close testified that he received Taylor's call at approximately 4:00 a.m. This confirms Taylor's claim that he wanted to get in touch with Close at the first available opportunity. Moreover, Taylor's call also confirms his claim that he could, in fact, get in touch with a lawyer, even in the middle of the night: He knew Close's home phone number and felt comfortable waking him. Perhaps most important, the details of Taylor's story, as related to Close during their telephone conversation, precisely matched Taylor's testimony at the suppression hearing, precluding the possibility that Taylor had fabricated those details during the eleven months between his confession and the hearing. Finally, Close testified that, during the telephone conversation, Taylor was "in tears and highly agitated." This contradicts Remine's account that Taylor was calm during questioning and confirms Taylor's account of the interrogation as a coercive ordeal. * * *

Because Remine and Taylor gave contradictory accounts of what transpired inside the interrogation room, we start by considering what weight to give Close's testimony. We note that Close's testimony satisfies the customary criteria of reliability: It is direct and precise, internally consistent and plausible. * * * Close did not back-track or equivocate; he did not claim a failure of memory. As a lawyer, Close was doubtless acutely aware of his duty to speak candidly, and of the criminal and professional consequences of failure to do so. Moreover, Close told Taylor that he (Close) would likely be called upon to testify about their conversation; he was thus aware of the need to commit the details of the conversation to memory. His testimony was also confirmed as to two significant details. Close said that one of the officers wore a ring with "187" inscribed on it, as Detective Remine also testified. Further, Detective Remine testified that the interrogation room was on the third floor, thus indirectly confirming Close's testimony that Taylor rode an elevator at the police station. Other details, such as the timing of the call, are consistent with the record. * * * If Close's testimony is to be disbelieved or discounted, it would be on two possible grounds: Either Close committed perjury in coordination with Taylor, or Taylor lied, not only at the suppression hearing, but also when he called the attorney.

There is nothing in the record to suggest that Close would put his license to practice law on the line by perjuring himself in order to support Taylor's story. * * * From what we know of Close and Taylor, the two did not have the kind of personal relationship that might have motivated Close to lie. The prosecution did not attempt to impugn Close's credibility; its entire cross-examination consisted of one question: * * *

> [PROSECUTION]: Mr. Close, I am not quite clear, did [Taylor] tell you "I lied to the police and confessed to them," or did he tell you "I confessed?"

> [CLOSE]: No, he adamantly insisted that he didn't do it, but the only reason he confessed was because he was desirous of making a phone call to his lawyer and his mother. He said that was the reason for the confession. * * *

Neither the state trial court nor the court of appeal found that Close had lied at the suppression hearing, and we find no basis for doing so. * * * Nor do we find plausible the alternative theory for discrediting Close's testimony, namely, that Taylor had fabricated the story of the false confession out of whole cloth by the time he called Close. The record reveals that Taylor has only a low-average IQ. * * * We think it highly improbable that a sixteen-year-old boy, of limited mental acuity and with a minimal police record, * * * had the wherewithal to concoct a tale of police intimidation, filled with graphic details, in the short span between the end of his interrogation and his phone call to Close. Taylor was a teenager without parent, attorney or friend, taken from his home at gunpoint in the dead of night and then questioned at length by two police officers, and thus was particularly vulnerable to the inherently coercive environment in which he found himself. * * * Close, who knew Taylor well, clearly believed the boy was telling the truth.

Further, that Taylor called Close immediately after being given access to a phone means that he had little time in which to fabricate a story with the specific, peculiar details he related, such as the fact that he asked for a lawyer and his mother, that a detective thrust a "187" ring in his face or that the same detective mapped out Taylor's potential fate on a sheet of paper. Moreover, Close's recollection that Taylor was "in tears and highly agitated," * * * underscores how remote a possibility it is that Taylor had the time or mental clarity to calmly fabricate his tale before calling Close. Finally, the story Taylor told Close on September 2, 1993, was in all material respects the same story he told at the suppression hearing on August 17, 1994.

We find it highly plausible that a frightened teenager would ask to speak with a lawyer he knew — or any lawyer — yet, when he is repeatedly denied the right to do so, would eventually give up hope, sign a waiver form and simply give the two adult authorities who stood between him and a phone call what they insisted on. That scenario is far more plausible than the prospect of a boy *not* asking for an attorney throughout his questioning — an attorney whose home phone number he knew by heart — confessing to murder, and then rushing to a phone to call the attorney, concocting an elaborate tale of police misconduct and feigning tears and agitation.

Remine's ambiguous assertions at the suppression hearing that he could not recall whether Taylor had requested counsel during questioning do not adequately contradict Taylor's and Close's testimony on this point. Moreover, even were we to construe Remine's ambiguous responses as affirmative denials that Taylor requested counsel, we would still credit Taylor's claims that he asked for an attorney, as corroborated by Close's virtually unquestioned testimony, over Remine's testimony.

We need not find that Remine perjured himself, although there is ample basis in the record for doing so — such as his repeated invocation of equivocal phrases such as "I don't recall" and "Not to my recollection." Rather, we can attribute Remine's watery testimony to the fallibility of human memory and to inherent limitations on Remine's observations in the early morning hours of September 2. * * * When defense counsel pressed Remine on whether he had "a specific recollection of transporting him yourself?", Remine replied, "*I am almost positive* that's what happened." * * * However, upon checking the record of transportation noted on Taylor's booking slip, Remine was forced to concede, "My mistake, Detective Dagan transported him." * * *

Remine was similarly unclear about the manner in which he and/or MacLyman advised Taylor of his *Miranda* rights. Inquiring about the procedure used to advise Taylor of his rights, defense counsel asked, "In this case did Mr. Taylor read it to himself, or did you read it to him?" * * * Remine replied, "*I don't recall which way it was*. I will say that we turned [it] around, and we read it to him. We turned it around and let him read it, and we read it to him while he was reading it to himself." * * * Defense counsel sought to clarify Remine's answer: "And do you have a specific recollection of doing that?" * * * Remine conceded, "No, sir[,] I do not." * * *

* * * In addition to the potential detrimental effect of time on his memory, Remine was also inherently limited as a witness because he was not present during all the events to which Taylor testified. Remine was not with Taylor during his transportation to the police station when Taylor asked if his mother would be contacted, and he was not with Taylor during Taylor's arrival at the station and elevator ride to the third floor where the interrogation room was located. Thus, Remine's one unambiguous denial to defense counsel that Taylor requested a lawyer — that Taylor did not ask for counsel *prior* to signing the advisement form at the start of questioning — does not contradict Close's testimony that Taylor asked to speak with Close while on the elevator. Further, although present for much of the interrogation, Remine was not with Taylor during the entire period of questioning. Remine explained in response to defense counsel questions that, while either he or MacLyman were with Taylor throughout the interrogation, there were times when one of them was absent. ***

These limitations on Remine's testimony are compounded by the fact that Remine was the *only* state witness at the suppression hearing. The prosecution could have filled the gaps in Remine's memory or ability to observe unfolding events by calling MacLyman to testify, or by calling the officer who transported Taylor and escorted him to the interrogation room. But it did not. The detectives could have fully documented the interrogation by taping it in its entirety or preserving notes of the session. But they did not. Thus, we are compelled to weigh Remine's inherently incomplete and somewhat confused testimony against Taylor's precise account of police misconduct, an account that remained consistent over the course of about a year, and Close's highly corroborative testimony.

In evaluating the relative credibility of Taylor and Remine, we also cannot avoid considering the circumstances under which this interrogation took place. For reasons not disclosed on the record, the two detectives executed the search and arrest warrants just before midnight, rather than at a more appropriate hour. The crime in question had occurred many weeks earlier, so the officers were hardly in hot pursuit. And there is no indication that Taylor was aware he was under suspicion and would attempt to flee the jurisdiction. To the contrary, he was found in his home, sleeping.

The detectives knew Taylor was sixteen. Yet, having arrested Taylor in the middle of the night, and having found him in his home without a parent present, they chose to conduct the interrogation immediately and to carry it on until they got a confession. There is no evidence that the detectives attempted to locate Taylor's mother, nor any suggestion as to the existence of an exigency that required that Taylor be arrested and interrogated at a time when his defenses and ability to think straight were weakened by the lateness of the hour, the absence of a parent and the inherent intimidation of the circumstances. Commencing the interrogation of a teenager after midnight, and pressing it past 3:00 a.m., absent some showing that delay would risk the destruction of evidence or other such harm, creates far too great a risk that a false confession will be extracted, leading to the unjust conviction of an innocent person. * * * Moreover, the very fact that the detectives chose to conduct their interrogation of Taylor in such circumstances, rather than waiting until he had an opportunity to rest and contact his mother, lends plausibility to Taylor's claim that the detectives engaged in hardball tactics to get him to confess before he had a chance to seek the advice of an adult as to how he should proceed. By their unjustified and distasteful actions, Detectives MacLyman and Remine lent credence to Taylor's account of what happened during the three hours that he was trapped by them in the interrogation room. * * *

We find clear and convincing evidence in the record that Taylor, during questioning, asked to speak with a lawyer and with his mother more than once before inculpating himself; that these requests went unheeded; that MacLyman brandished his ring in Taylor's face; and that MacLyman threateningly mapped the potential consequences for Taylor if he did not confess, in a disingenuous effort to persuade Taylor that persisting in his denials would cost him dearly, and the only way to avoid a life sentence would be for him to fess up. * * *

QUESTIONS

1. Do you agree with the Ninth Circuit that the suppression judge's credibility judgments were unreasonable? What arguments did the court make for believing Taylor and disbelieving the officers? Did they give fair considerations to counter arguments?

2. If you were Taylor's counsel at the suppression hearing, what questions would you have asked each of the detectives on cross-examination? Remember that cross-examination can be used to get a witness to admit to facts favorable to your position as well as to facts calling into question the witness's truthfulness or accuracy. Would the questions that you would ask at a jury trial, were the confession admitted at such a trial, be any different from the questions that you would ask at a suppression hearing? If yes, how so, and why?

3. If Taylor chose to take the stand at the suppression hearing, what questions would you, as the prosecutor, ask Taylor to challenge his credibility while supporting the police version of events?

4. Why do you think that the detectives did not tape the entire interrogation process? Could credibility judgments concerning the police be rendered easier by the law's mandating such taping of the whole process?

5. Is it good policy that appellate courts generally do not re-visit trial court and jury credibility determination?

6. Was the suppression court expected to find "raw" or "normative" facts or some combination? Why is the answer to this question significant?

§ 7.02 The Law of Factfinding - Character Evidence

As noted earlier, the law of evidence governs what evidence may be presented, and in what manner, at trial. The ability to prove or disprove facts, to bolster or attack credibility, is thus closely tied to the content of, and lawyers' command of, the rules of evidence. The Federal Rules of Evidence ("FRE") are the governing rules in federal proceedings. Each state has its own evidence codes, though many such codes are modeled after the FRE. This section briefly reviews some of those rules, with a later section focusing on one special set of rules: those involving scientific and other kinds of expert testimony.

A. Act Propensity Evidence

"Character" is, in a very general sense, the kind of person you are — good or evil, strong or weak. A "character trait" is an aspect of your character — a tendency or predisposition to think or act a certain way in a range of particular types of situations. For example, whether someone is punctual or tardy, violent or peaceful, careful or careless, are all character traits. A character trait expresses a statement about the relative, rather than the absolute, probability that a person will think or act a certain way on a particular occasion. To say that someone is "tardy" is, therefore, to say that he or she is more often late for appointments than are most people. This person might, accordingly, not be late most of the time or even very often, but would still be "tardy" if he or she is late more than others. How often most people are late is the "base rate." A tardy person's lateness must exceed this rate if the person is to qualify as tardy.

> *Example 1*: Almost all faculty members at a well-known law school arrive ten minutes "fashionably" late for monthly faculty meetings, making ten minutes per meeting the base rate for lateness. Of the ten regular faculty meetings each year, Professor Robinson also arrives ten minutes late for seven of the meetings, but he is a full half hour late for three of the meetings, thus exceeding the average base rate of ten minutes lateness, thereby justifying labeling Robinson "tardy,"or at least the "tardiest", member of his faculty.

FRE 404 generally prohibits using evidence of character or character traits to prove that a party or witness *acted* consistently with those traits on a particular occasion. The example of Professor Robinson demonstrates the reasons for this prohibition on "act propensity" evidence. Suppose that the President of the University is going to address the law school faculty on an important matter at the February meeting. To impress the President with his faculty's professionalism, the law school dean declares that any faculty member who arrives late for the meeting will pay a fine. Professor Robinson is accused by Professor Jones of arriving late. At a disciplinary hearing, Jones testifies that he saw Robinson arriving one-half hour late, while Robinson denies arriving even one second past the appointed time. To prove that Robinson was late for *this meeting,* Jones calls several senior faculty members to the stand, who testify that Robinson has, in their experience, been later than any other faculty member in arriving at three out of the ten regularly scheduled meetings each year. Robinson does not challenge the truth of these statements. How probative is this character evidence — that is, how much logical force does it have in proving that Robinson was late for the February meeting?

Remember that Robinson is no later than other faculty members seven out of every ten times, that is, seventy percent of the time. If the past is a good predictor of the future, that might tell us that Robinson will be later than other faculty members more often than they will be extra-late *in the course of a full academic year*, but this tells us little, if anything, about the likelihood that he will be later than will others *for any specific meeting*.

Furthermore, however, once the hearing panel learns that Robinson is a tardy person, the panel might too readily assume that Robinson *must have* been late on this one occasion, though there may be little other proof that this is so. Additionally, if the panel consists of the few faculty members who are consistently timely in attending meetings and who highly value punctuality, the panel may be offended by Robinson's tardiness, judging him as overall a bad person who should be punished for his past, and likely future, wrongs, regardless of whether he committed a wrong in this particular case. Moreover, to allow the panel properly to understand relative probabilities, Robinson might seek to respond with witnesses testifying that almost *all* faculty members are routinely late; he is just somewhat more late than they a few times a year. But allowing these responses, which seems fair, is time-consuming.

Finally, this February meeting is special, different from all others in an important way: the advertised presence of the University President for an important meeting combined with the threat of a fine for stragglers may have dramatically altered the situation — creating a motive for punctuality that was missing in the past. These different circumstances might make any faculty member's past behavior, under radically different conditions, a poor predictor of current behavior. This combination of factors — character's poor value in predicting behavior *on a specific occasion*, the factfinder's inability fully to appreciate that flaw in the evidence and its likely failure to consider base rates and changed circumstances, the human tendency to judge a person as bad overall based on one bad trait (the "devil's horn" effect), the equal human tendency to judge someone's character based on very little evidence, and the sheer consumption of time involved — all support a general prohibition on act propensity uses of character evidence.

B. Mental Propensity and Other Uses of Character

That general prohibition does not make sense, however, for other uses of character evidence. For example, "mental propensity" evidence — using character to prove that someone had a particular mental state on a particular occasion — is not as worrisome as act propensity evidence. One reason is that people often think bad thoughts without acting on them. Although the likelihood of thinking bad thoughts is also a probability judgment, where there is other evidence of the criminal act, character seems, at least in the eyes of the law, still to shed some significant light on the likely associated mental state. Furthermore, precisely because we cannot read people's minds, the need for evidence of mental state is greater than is the need for evidence of action.

> *Example 2*: Ronnie Johnson was caught red-handed shooting and killing Lannie Hammond. The eyewitnesses were impeccable. Ronnie admits to shooting Lannie, but Ronnie claims to have done it in anger, on the spur-of-the-moment, when Ronnie discovered that Lannie had been cheating with Ronnie's spouse, thus making Ronnie guilty at most of second degree murder or voluntary manslaughter at common law. But the state has charged Ronnie with first-degree murder, that is, "willful, deliberate, and premeditated" killing, potentially punishable by death.

Ronnie calls character witnesses to testify that they have known Ronnie for years, and that Ronnie is an extremely peaceful person who never would hurt a fly. Ronnie offers this evidence not to disprove the act of killing — as Ronnie admits that — but to argue that a peaceful person is less likely to plan and premeditate a murder in a deliberate fashion than to strike out suddenly as a cry of pain in a single, highly unusual situation. Such mental propensity evidence would not be barred. Similarly, if the prosecution sought to offer evidence of Ronnie's violent character to show that Ronnie did premeditate the crime, that too would likely not be flatly barred.

Note, however, that if Ronnie denied ever shooting the gun at all, there is a grave danger that a jury would use evidence of Ronnie's violent nature to prove the commission of the act (which proof is prohibited), as well as the mental state. Although the evidence might be logically somewhat helpful for both purposes, most courts would exclude the prosecution's evidence where Ronnie denied being the shooter because of the danger that the jurors will use it in the prohibited, act propensity fashion, that is, to prove that Ronnie shot the gun and did so in part because it is Ronnie's nature to do so as a violent person.

A related concept to the mental propensity idea is the "doctrine of objective chances." The idea here is that, when the accused claims mistake, evidence that he or she has repeatedly *claimed* to make the same mistake in other instances can be used to prove that the accused was in fact *not* mistaken in the case at hand. This doctrine arises most often in date rape cases and in theft offenses in proving the absence of a claimed mistake as to consent or ownership:

> *Example 3*: Bob is charged with raping his date, Tammy. Bob testifies at trial that he was shocked by the charge. He does not dispute that Tammy believes in her own mind that she did not consent. But he says that he mistakenly *believed* that she consented because she never said "no," and he thought that her tears were tears of joy.

The prosecution offers evidence that in nine other instances women with whom Bob had sexual intercourse under very similar circumstances confronted him, asking him how he could dare to rape them. In each instance he expressed shock, declaring that he believed their tears to be tears of joy. None prosecuted Bob because they all feared his wealthy family.

But how many times can we believe that Bob made a mistake and didn't know it? The "objective chances" of his repeatedly making the same mistake are small. This evidence thus suggests that Bob was *not* mistaken in this case, thus knowing full well that Tammy did not consent. Of course, the jury might conclude that Bob is a bad person — a rapist who likely raped again. But the law is not overly concerned about this use of character because Bob concedes the relevant acts, the evidence being used only to prove his mental state at the time of the crime.

> *Example 4*: Andi is caught with forty stolen television sets purchased from a supplier at a cost well below the market price. Andi is charged with knowingly receiving stolen property. Andi's testimony at trial is that Andi thought the supplier could sell so low because the supplier bought in bulk, but that Andi had no idea that the TVs were stolen. The prosecution offers evidence, however, that on twelve prior occasions Andi bought TVs at ridiculously low prices from twelve completely different buyers, even after being warned by a friend in the police department that the TVs sold at such prices must be stolen. Again, how many times must we believe that Andi was mistaken?

There is another use of character to prove mental state that commonly arises when self-defense claims are raised. Self-defense against deadly force in most jurisdictions requires proof that a defendant acted with the actual and reasonable belief that an assailant (soon to be the purported "victim" of a homicide, attempted homicide, or assault) was about to cause the defendant's imminent death or serious bodily injury. A defendant might support a claim with witnesses testifying to the defendant's *belief* that the person attacking had a violent character, so the defendant feared for his or her life and had to shoot first:

> *Example 5*: Ali is charged with killing Pat. Ali raises a self-defense claim, calling witnesses who told Ali before shooting Pat that Pat was an extremely violent, dangerous person with a history of attacking redheads, like Ali, on sight because Pat had a hatred for the "torch-hairs." Ali thus argues justifiable fear of life when seeing Pat moving rapidly toward Ali in a bar, so Ali shot Pat. If offered solely to prove fearful mental state at the time of the crime, this evidence would not fit within the *act* propensity ban. Likewise, the prosecution would be free to offer evidence that Ali was in fact aware that Pat was a peaceful person, so Ali lacked the mental state to establish self-defense.

On the other hand, another element of self-defense is that the defendant was not the first aggressor — an action. If Ali seeks to prove not simply that a belief that Pat was violent but that Pat was *in fact* violent and, therefore, as a violent person was more likely violent — and thus the first aggressor - - *in this case*, that would be an effort to prove an act by Pat by evidence of Pat's character, thus fitting within the character evidence bar on act propensity testimony. A way around this for a defendant like Ali is to offer evidence of a belief about Pat's character to prove mental state but to offer *eyewitness evidence* about who started the fight or threats to establish that Pat, and not Ali, was the first aggressor.

C. Things That Look Like Character But Are Not

1. The Forms of Character Evidence

There are three ways to prove character, three "forms" of character evidence:

1. *Reputation*: Your reputation is what people in the relevant community say about your character.

2. *Opinion*: Someone who knows you well can offer an opinion about a relevant character trait of yours with which they are familiar.

3. Specific Acts: Evidence that you have committed certain actions in the past may suggest that they reflect deeper personality traits.

Example 6: Johnnie, charged with assault, wants to prove that Johnnie is a peaceful person unlikely to commit the crime of attacking another. An exception to the act propensity bar [p.250] permits Johnnie to do so. There are logically three ways to prove a peaceful nature: (1) neighbors testify that Johnnie is well-known in the neighborhood as a peaceful person (reputation); (2) a next-door-neighbor who knows Johnnie particularly well opines that Johnnie is a peaceful person; or (3) another neighbor recounts observing instances where weaker people assaulted Johnnie, but, rather than strike back, Johnnie took the blows in the name of peace (specific acts).

The usual rule, remember, is that you may not use character evidence to prove an action. So, applying this usual rule to Example 6, none of the neighbors should be permitted to testify for Johnnie. But there are several exceptions to the usual rule. One of those exceptions, discussed in more detail shortly, permits the criminal defendant to choose to offer evidence of his good character to disprove his criminal acts in the current case. Thus Johnnie wants to call these neighbors to prove that he is a peaceful person, thus less likely than other sorts of persons to have committed the violent act of assault. The exception applies. But when exceptions like these apply, the only *form* of character evidence permitted is reputation or opinion, not specific acts, evidence. Therefore, Johnnie may in Example 6 call to the stand on his behalf the neighbors in parts (1) and (2) in the example because they will testify respectively to Johnnie's reputation as a peaceful person and to an opinion that Johnnie is peaceful. But Johnnie may not call his final neighbor in part (3) of the example because that neighbor testifies to specific instances where many people might be tempted violence but Johnnie was not.

All three forms of character evidence can be used, however, if offered to prove someone's mental state, not his or her actions. Suppose that Johnnie had raised self-defense in a jurisdiction requiring him to prove that he believed that he was in imminent danger of bodily harm. Johnnie offers evidence that he saw his supposed victim randomly attack other people for no apparent reason on five other occasions. Johnnie therefore feared that his "victim" would mount such an attack on Johnnie when the two exchanged harsh words. This evidence of specific acts is admissible. The acts are not offered to show that Johnnie's alleged assault victim did anything but only that Johnnie *believed* that the victim was about to do something physically harmful to Johnnie. Specific acts offered to show a relevant belief in another's character rather than actions resulting from that character are admissible. Some sorts of evidence also look like character but are not, consequently not being barred by the character evidence rules, as we next explain. These categories include (1) motive, (2) habit, (3) common plan, scheme, or design, (4) "signature" evidence, and (5) "essential element" evidence.

2. Motive

Remember that character evidence is distrusted partly because it refers to *average behavior only*, that is, how we behave *in general* relative to others, so that it is thought to have little value in explaining how we are likely to behave on a specific occasion. But motive evidence by definition concerns a specific relationship between or among two or more people that gives a suspect a reason to think or act in a particular way *on a particular occasion*. Motive is usually proven by specific acts, but motive is not considered character evidence because it is far more probative than character. Motive evidence can be used to prove either the criminal act or the required mental state or both.

Example 7: Jo is charged with killing a spouse, Marti. Evidence is offered that: (1) Jo's business was just about to go bankrupt and (2) Jo convinced Marti — only one week before the death — to raise the coverage of Marti's life insurance policy, in which Marti named Jo as beneficiary, to $2,000,000. These two items of evidence would show that Jo had a strong motive to commit the crime. If Jo's defense is mistaken identification, that is, arguing that someone else did the crime, this evidence of motive to kill Marti — to collect on the life insurance policy — would tend to show that Jo, and no one else, did the dirty deed. If Jo admitted killing Marti but claimed that it was an angry heat of passion killing, this evidence of motive would suggest instead planning, that is, a more serious willful, deliberate, and premeditated killing.

Most standard criminal law texts will say that motive is *never* an element of a crime. Rather, motive is simply circumstantial evidence helping to prove the existence of an element. These assertions are usually correct but are overstated because sometimes "motive" is an element of a crime, though not always so labeled. For example, if motive is defined as *the reason why* an offender thought or acted a certain way in a particular case, then the specific intent portion of every specific intent crime constitutes motive as an element.

Common law burglary was thus defined as:

(1) breaking and entering

(2) the dwelling house

(3) of another

(4) in the nighttime

(5) with intent to commit a crime therein.

Note in this definition that the *reason why* a suspect broke into a home matters. If an offender was a homeless person freezing in the dead of winter, who broke into someone else's home to get warm, that would still be a crime – criminal trespass – but it would not be common law burglary. For both crimes, trespass and burglary, "knowledge" that what you are breaking into is a home not your own is required. But such knowledge, while sufficient for criminal trespass, is not enough for burglary. Burglary requires showing that your motive for breaking into the home was to commit another crime, such as stealing a TV set.

Motive is also sometimes more explicitly made an element of a crime, hate crimes being the classic example. Any ordinary crime done *because of* the victim's race, gender, disability, sexual orientation, or other category listed in a particular state's statute can be elevated to a hate crime. In some states, the "because of" or "by reason of" language means that the offender must have harbored racial or other listed animus toward the victim, such as robbing someone primarily because you hate people of their race and want to make them suffer. In other states, the "because of" or similar language means that the offender must have selected the victim because of his group membership, even if he harbored no group hatred, as may happen if an offender robs only Asian immigrants, not because he dislikes them, but because he buys into racist stereotypes that they are passive and distrust the police, thus suggesting to the offender that these immigrants will be easy targets.

3. Habit

Specific acts can also be used to prove someone's habit. "Habit" is defined in two different ways, depending upon the jurisdiction. Under the frequency or probability theory of habit, habit is a very frequently-repeated response to a very specific stimulus, a response so frequent as to make it a good predictor of behavior. Under the alternative psychological theory, frequency is still required, but in addition the behavior must be semi-automatic so that it is not under the actor's fully conscious control.

> *Example 8*: Andi, charged with homicide, raises an alibi defense. To prove that Andi was home watching television, Andi calls witnesses who testify that Andi is addicted to the TV show, *"24"*, and is home watching it every Monday night 9-10 p.m. without fail. This would be evidence of habit under the frequency theory offered to prove that Andi acted consistently in this case, that is, that Andi was home watching *24* at the time of the crime, the home being many miles away from the crime scene. This evidence, however, would not constitute habit under the semi-automatic theory because watching TV is so clearly within conscious control that Andi easily could have chosen to skip *24* for one night to commit the killing. On the other hand, had Andi been charged with negligent vehicular homicide for causing an accident by changing lanes at high speeds on a highway without signaling, evidence that Andi always used signals would likely also meet the psychological theory of habit because signaling is a behavior that most experienced drivers do semi-automatically, that is, without really thinking about it.

4. Common Plan, Scheme, or Design

Sometimes prior acts that seem unconnected to a particular crime show that the seemingly isolated crime is in fact but one event in a broader scheme. The acts do not therefore show character but rather establish the pattern revealing the larger scheme or plan, that plan often revealing the motive of the one seemingly isolated crime.

> *Example 9:* A sniper has been randomly shooting and killing people in Washington, DC and its nearby suburbs in Maryland and Virginia. After several of the shootings, the sniper sent a note to the police in all three areas threatening to continue the killings unless he received

$2,000,000. The money was not paid, so the killings continued. By the time that the sniper was caught, there were ten shootings, only one of which happened in Virginia. Virginia courts have jurisdiction only over killings that take place in that state, so they try the sniper for the one Virginia attack. However, they offer evidence that he committed the nine other attacks — even though he is not charged with those crimes — to prove that the Virginia attack was part of a giant plot to extort millions of dollars, thus establishing the sniper's motive to commit the Virginia crime.

In some instances, an offender might be charged with crimes committed by other persons, [see Chap. 14] notably when the offender is an "accomplice," meaning that he or she aided the other persons in committing the crimes, making the person legally responsible for those crimes as if he or she had committed them alone. In such instances, evidence of the acts of others is offered not to show that the offender keeps bad company but rather to prove that he or she committed all the charged crimes.

Example 10: Mari wants to rob several banks but needs a gun. Robbie gives Mari a gun to use in the robberies on condition that Robbie gets a portion of the proceeds. Robbie is charged with committing all ten robberies ultimately done by Mari with the same gun, even though Robbie robbed no one. Therefore, evidence of Mari's ten bank robberies can be offered against Robbie at Robbie's trial for robbery on an accomplice liability theory.

5. Signature

The idea here is that some criminals use the same *modus operandi,* the same way of operating in every crime that they commit. The similarities are so stark that the criminal's unusual method is like a "signature," a calling card saying, "I was here."

Example 11: Numerous killings have been taking place in a city. There are few similarities among the killings, but one stark similarity stands out: every victim has a different sign of the zodiac found carved on his or her chest. There is an eyewitness to only one — the first — of the five total killings. When the suspected "zodiac killer" is arrested, that witness identifies Georgi as the killer in the first case. The state argues, however, that whoever did the first killing must have done all the other killings because the same "calling card" — the carved zodiac signs — were left at each killing. Evidence that Georgi did the first killing is thus admissible at Georgi's trials for each of the other four killings to show that Georgi indeed committed those other dastardly deeds.

6. Essential Element of a Crime, Claim, or Defense

Sometimes character is an essential element of a crime, claim, or defense, that is, there is no logical way to prove the element but by proving the offender's character. For such crimes, however, the character evidence is not offered to prove that the accused thought or acted in a particular way on a particular occasion. The element is proven simply by showing the offender's character in itself, so no "act propensity" is involved. Distinguishing character as an "essential element" from character as mere circumstantial evidence of another type of element is tricky. Luckily, essential element analysis matters in this course only in one instance: proving the subjective version of the affirmative defense of entrapment. That defense requires proof of two elements: first, that the government induced the offender to commit the crime; and, second, that he or she was induced to commit a crime that *he or she was not otherwise predisposed to commit*. To identify someone's "predisposition" to do something is but other language meaning their relevant character or personality trait. Subjective entrapment therefore *requires* the defendant to prove good character on a trait relevant to the crime, but fairness then permits the prosecution to respond with evidence of the defendant's bad character.

> *Example 12:* Marion is charged with possessing crack cocaine. Marion testifies at trial that a person acting as an undercover agent for the police kept offering crack cocaine, and that Marion repeatedly turned the person down. Marion relented only when the individual offered to sleep with Marion. Upon the first puff on the crack pipe, police burst into the hotel room and arrested Marion. In support of an entrapment defense, Marion calls witnesses to testify that Marion has never once in life used an illegal drug before this incident. In response, the state calls witnesses who say that they saw Marion smoking crack on numerous occasions.

D. Exceptions to the Act Propensity Bar

Below, in highly simplified form, is a brief review of the most relevant to this course exceptions to the bar on using character evidence to prove act propensity.

1. The Mercy Rule

This rule permits a defendant to choose to offer evidence of a pertinent trait of his or her character — one relevant to disproving one or more of the elements of a crime. It is called the "mercy rule" because it is considered an act akin to mercy to allow a defendant to seek to raise a reasonable doubt about his or her guilt of a crime by proving pertinent good character. The danger for the defendant, however, is that the accused then "opens the door" for the prosecutor's offering evidence of the defendant's bad character to prove that the defendant did indeed commit the criminal act.

> *Example 13:* A defendant charged with a seemingly random assault offers evidence of reputation for peacefulness in the neighborhood to prove that the defendant is not likely to have committed the particular violent act with which he or she is charged. In rebuttal, the prosecution calls witnesses to testify that in their opinion the defendant is a brutal, violent person.

2. A Pertinent Character Trait of the Victim

An accused can also offer evidence of a pertinent bad character trait of the victim. Doing so, however, permits the prosecution both to offer evidence that the victim's relevant character trait was instead a good one *and* that the defendant had a bad character concerning the same trait.

> *Example 14*: Peti is charged with aggravated assault. To prove that Peti acted in self-defense, Peti offers evidence of the victim's violent character, suggesting that the victim, Victory, was the first aggressor. The prosecutor may now respond *both* with evidence that Victory is a peaceful person *and* with evidence that the defendant is a violent person, even though the prosecutor could not have offered either sort of evidence had the defendant not first chosen to attack the victim's character.

In a homicide case only, as opposed to, for example, an assault case, however, the state can offer evidence of the victim's peaceful character even if the defense has not first attacked the victim's character as violent, so long as *some evidence has been offered that the victim was the first aggressor.* Character is not the only way to prove who started a fight. Eyewitness testimony can accomplish the task just as well or even better.

> *Example 15:* Now Peti is charged with murder for killing Victory. The prosecution's first two eyewitnesses testify that defendant Peti started the fight. But the prosecution's third witness, while describing Peti's violence, admits on cross that, as he recalls it, Victory was the first aggressor. The prosecutor can now call witnesses to the stand to testify that Victory was a peaceful person, thus not likely to start a fight. The prosecutor can call these witnesses despite the defense's never once having attacked Victory's character.

3. Impeachment

Character can be offered for act propensity purposes to impeach a witness, the act being that of lying on the stand and the character trait being that of untruthfulness. Once the witness's character for truthfulness is attacked, the opponent can respond with evidence that the victim is a truthful person. There are four types of character evidence that may be used to prove a witness's untruthful character to show that he or she lied on the stand or to rebut those claims:

(i) *Reputation:* Testimony may be offered that people in the witnesses' neighborhood have repeatedly heard from others in the neighborhood that the witness is an untruthful (or truthful) person.

(ii) *Opinion*: Someone who knows the witness well can testify that, in his or her opinion, the witness is a truthful (or untruthful) person.

(iii) *Specific, Unconvicted Acts of Untruthfulness*: Someone testifies to observing specific acts of the witness's lying, even if those acts never resulted in criminal charges or did not constitute crimes. The court has discretion to decide whether the time it would take to prove these acts is worth the candle, that is, whether the acts are so probative of truthfulness or untruthfulness, but so unlikely to anger or confuse the jury, that time spent proving these lies is well worth it. Note that, while specific acts may ordinarily not be used to prove act propensity, they can be so used when impeaching a witness with evidence that he or she is an untruthful person. Evidence of *truthful* acts can be offered to prove truthful character only *after* that character has been attacked.

(iv) *Prior Convictions*: There are two categories of crimes that may be used to impeach a witness:

(a) *Crimen Falsi*: Evidence that a witness has committed a crime involving dishonesty or false statement, regardless of the actual or potential punishment, *shall* be admitted to show that the witness is an untruthful person. These "crimen falsi" crimes can be hard to identify, but the clearest example would be perjury — lying under oath.

(b) *Felonies*: Here, "felonies" means crimes punishable by death or imprisonment in excess of one year under the law under which the witness was convicted. The theory here is that anyone convicted of a serious crime is more likely to be untruthful than are other people, even if the crime did not involve false statements. Thus a witness might be impeached with evidence that he or she was convicted of a crime involving serious violence, such as an aggravated assault. Admission of this evidence is not automatic, the judge again being free to apply a balancing test to decide whether the value of this evidence is substantially outweighed by the dangers of unfairly prejudicing the jury against the witness. When the witness is the defendant, a special balancing test applies that favors exclusion of the evidence, meaning that a very strong showing is required that the probative value is so high as to substantially exceed countervailing dangers like unfair prejudice.

There are a variety of fine points concerning when and how each of these impeachment techniques may be exercised.

Example 16: A prosecution witness testifies to seeing the defendant rob a bank. The defendant responds with evidence that the witness was convicted of perjury — a crimen falsi crime, which must be admitted — and of felony robbery, a non-crimen-falsi crime that *may* be admitted in the exercise of the judge's sound discretion.

E. Special Rules: Rape and Other Sexual Assault Crimes

There are special evidence rules that apply in rape cases and other sexual assault cases. Briefly, "rape shield" statutes generally prohibit, subject to several exceptions, the defense's offering evidence of the alleged victim's "sluttish" character, or opinions that she is a "loose" woman, or evidence of specific prior acts from her sex life to prove that she consented in this case or that she is not credible. FRE 413 and related rules, and similar statutes in many states, on the other hand, permit the prosecution's offering evidence of a defendant's prior offenses of sexual assault (even if he was neither charged with, nor convicted of, them) for any relevant purpose, including that he committed the current rape. [See Chap. 9].

NOTE

The key with respect to these evidence rules is to consider credibility, evidence, and proof as central to all lawyering tasks, to make *how* to prove a case an instinctive inquiry when studying and applying the relevant substantive law, for this is how all practicing criminal lawyers and other litigators must think.

PROBLEM TWENTY

Jaci is charged with burglarizing Mal's home, killing Mal once inside. Jaci plans to take the stand in the defense case to tell a very different story: that Mal invited Jaci to Mal's home and, once there, Mal tried to stab Jaci, falsely accusing Jaci of sleeping with Mal's spouse. In self-defense, Jaci pulled out a knife, stabbing Mal but once, though Mal died as a result. Consider whether each of the following items of evidence should be admitted at, or excluded from, trial:

(1)   Prosecution evidence that Jaci was sleeping with Mal's spouse, that Mal was a wealthy person, and that Mal's spouse promised to marry Jaci upon Mal's death.

(2)   Prosecution evidence, offered in its case-in-chief, that Jaci had a reputation in the neighborhood as a violent person;

(3)   Prosecution evidence in its case-in-chief that Jaci had been convicted of aggravated assault, punishable by up to ten years in prison.

(4)   Prosecution evidence that Mal was a very private person who never invited anyone into Mal's home on a social basis.

(5)   Prosecution evidence that Jaci had married wealthy people twice before, shortly after their spouses had died, then quickly divorced each spouse in exchange for a handsome financial settlement with the person, and that Jaci had long talked of a dream of owning an airline, a dream that would be realized with the money gained from eventually marrying Mal's spouse.

(6)   Prosecution evidence that Jaci used an unusual three-sided knife with a skull and cross-bones on it and that the unknown killers of the prior two spouses used just such a knife.

(7)   Defense evidence, in its case-in-chief, that Mal had repeatedly assaulted friends and neighbors, though they had been too afraid of Mal to prosecute.

(8)   A defense witness testifying that Jaci was, in the witness's opinion, a peaceful person.

(9)   Defense cross-examination of the prosecution's witness in (4) above, asking the witness whether the witness lied about the income on the witness' federal tax returns last year.

(10)   Defense cross-examination of the prosecution's witness in (4) above, asking the witness whether the witness had beaten up a neighbor last year, though the neighbor had never reported the matter to the police.

(11)   Defense cross-examination of the prosecution's witness in (4) above, asking the witness whether the witness had been convicted in the last five years of: [a] perjury; [b] felony robbery; [c] misdemeanor theft of a candy bar.

(12)   Defense evidence that a mutual friend of Jaci and Mal's had told Jaci that Mal had been a Navy seal, trained to kill, and had recently hospitalized several people who angered Mal (none of this information turned out to be true).

§ 7.03 Jury Trials Versus Bench Trials

In theory, the same rules of evidence apply in both jury trials and bench trials (those in which the judge is the factfinder). In practice, in a bench trial, the same judge who rules on evidence motions determines the facts. Thus, a judge who hears evidentiary argument and decides to exclude an item of evidence will still know it exists and must perform the remarkable feat of ignoring that evidence in reaching a verdict.

In a jury trial, however, excluded evidence is never heard by the jury. Moreover, the jury verdict in most jurisdictions must be unanimous, so the jury will hang if even one member has a reasonable doubt, rendering the defense's task in avoiding a conviction easier. Lawyers also usually have some role in jury selection, often being allowed to "voir dire" potential jurors, that is, to ask them questions, ostensibly to determine their ability to be fair, though in fact looking for jurors thought to be more favorable to that lawyer's side. Prosecutors can try to exclude "for cause" some persons whose answers arguably indicate that they could not be fair and can exercise a limited number of peremptory challenges, challenges that need not be justified to the court so long as they do not reflect racial, ethnic, or gender bias. Lawyers thus often believe that they have more ability to choose who shall decide the case in a jury trial than in a bench trial.

Why, then, would a defendant ever choose a bench trial? There are many possible reasons, but among the most important ones are these: (1) the defense might believe that a particular judge is more likely than a jury to acquit; (2) the defense might have a very technical argument unlikely to be emotionally appealing to a jury; (3) the defense might believe that the risk of conviction is high, but no guilty plea could be reached, and the defense believes that, if convicted, the judge will impose a lesser sentence when the accused has saved the trouble of a jury trial, which is much more time-consuming than a bench trial. In some jurisdictions, *both* sides must agree to waive the right to a jury trial. The prosecution might agree for many reasons, including: (1) the prosecution thinks that the chances of conviction are still high before a judge, and the bench trial saves scarce time and money; (2) the prosecution agrees with the defense that the facts are straightforward and that the case will ultimately turn on a legal issue; (3) the prosecution disagrees with the defense's assessment of this judge, believing that in this particular case the judge is more likely than the jury to convict the defendant.

There is, however, one important commonality to both jury and bench trials: conviction or acquittal turns on narrative, on who tells a better, more convincing story. Ample empirical research demonstrates that both judges and juries reason to a verdict by crafting a story that makes sense to them. Good lawyers thus marshal their evidence not so much to build a syllogistic case for their side as to craft a persuasive tale. Good stories match the plots of ones similar to those told in popular culture, with which jurors are already likely to be familiar. Stories define the characters of the players and offer plots that are internally consistent, reflect jurors' likely understanding of human nature, leave no gaps in the tale, and are gripping. It is not enough for the prosecution simply to list the evidence that it believes shows guilt beyond a reasonable doubt or for the defense to list reasons why there is such doubt. Each side, to prevail, must explain what story the evidence supports and why. Creating a good narrative line will thus guide every step of a trial lawyer's preparation. Being a good narrator in turn requires a lawyer steeped in both elite and popular culture, able to spot a good tale as well as to tell a good story. Increasingly, telling such stories turn not only on a silver tongue but also on a golden expert, for jurors live in an age of science and a fascination with TV programs.

§ 7.04 Scientific and Expert Evidence

A. The Importance of Expert Testimony at Trial

Expert testimony, particularly that involving scientific principles, is becoming increasingly important in every serious criminal case. If a warehouse burns down, a Fire Marshall's testimony about burn patterns may be what distinguishes intentional burning of the building — arson — from accident. If a woman is raped by a stranger in an alleyway, DNA testing of semen may be the only evidence linking the defendant to the crime. If a defendant raises an insanity defense, an experienced psychiatrist's opinion that the defendant is a paranoid schizophrenic may mean the difference between conviction and acquittal on grounds of legal insanity. A good lawyer must, therefore, become familiar with the relevant science so that he or she can aid the expert in clearly communicating to the jury and be ready effectively to examine the opposing expert.

DNA profiling is the forensic scientific technique that has received most of the attention by the media. The technique has become so sophisticated that sometimes a single hair found at a crime scene or the residue on a fingerprint can be sufficient to obtain a usable profile. There are now a variety of techniques for DNA profiling. Most of them rely, however, on a few basic facts: (1) DNA is the basic genetic material that determines, in conjunction with environmental factors, each individuals' species and unique or unusual characteristics; (2) DNA is "divided and packaged into chromosomes that reside in the nucleus of individual cells," Frederick R. Biber, *Science and Technology of Forensic DNA Profiling: Current Use and Future Directions*, in DNA AND THE CRIMINAL JUSTICE SYSTEM: THE TECHNOLOGY OF JUSTICE 23, 25 (ed. David Lazzer 2004); (3) about 2% of human DNA accounts for individual differences with sufficient variation to be useful for forensic purposes, the variation being in DNA lengths or sequences ("alleles"); (4) it is this allele variation that enables properly-trained experts to declare a "match" between a DNA sample found at a crime scene and one taken from the defendant.

Usually, the laboratory reaches one of three conclusions: "inclusion" (in common terms, a "match"), "exclusion" (the defendant's DNA was not found in the crime scene sample), or "inconclusive." These are not absolute statements but rather statistical probabilities, for example, permitting an expert at trial to testify that the FBI laboratory had done a comparison between DNA in semen found on Monica Lewinsky's dress and then-President Clinton's DNA and that the expert concluded that the chance that the semen was not the President's was very, very low, "one in 7.87 trillion," a "figure exceeding both the present world population and the number of human beings who have ever populated the world." Edward J. Imwinkelried, *The Relative Priority that Should Be Assigned to Trial Stage DNA Issues, in* TECHNOLOGY OF JUSTICE, *supra,* at 91, 93. Such probability statements may be exaggerated and subject to challenge, but the probabilities are sufficient to enable confident judgments that there is or is not a match between a suspect and a crime scene sample. DNA testing has resulted in numerous recent high-profile exonerations of innocent persons wrongly convicted at trial, many of whom were on death row. Similarly, DNA matches have identified lawbreakers who otherwise might have escaped punishment. Yet the importance of DNA testing is often overstated.

Notably, a match does not necessarily prove that the defendant was the person who did the criminal act. One would expect to find an ex-husband's DNA at his ex-wife's home if he often visits his children there. If she is found dead, the presence of his DNA at the crime scene does not alone show that he was the killer. Analogously, in a date rape case where it is clear that the defendant had sexual intercourse with his alleged victim, the presence of his DNA in semen tells us nothing we do not already know. Guilt turns on whether she consented and, if she did not, whether, at least in many jurisdictions, he should have known that. A DNA match will contribute nothing to resolving the consent and mental state issues.

Usable DNA samples are also often simply not found at the crime scene, and where there is otherwise strong evidence, it may not be worth the expense of DNA testing in a routine case. Even if a sample is found and profiled, there may be no known match in a computer database consisting largely of previously-convicted, or at least previously-arrested, persons' DNA. A suspect will therefore need to be found by other means, though DNA matching may be sought once the suspect is identified.

Often other matching techniques are needed, such as handwriting analysis to show that it was the defendant who falsely signed another's name or bullet analysis to determine whether certain recovered bullet fragments came from the defendant's gun, because no DNA is available at the scene. Furthermore, even when a DNA match is found, juries may still be skeptical. As a leading expert in the area explains:

> Two of the leading students of statistical evidence, David Kaye and Jonathan Kohler, have remarked that "[t]he clearest and most consistent finding" in the studies conducted to date is that laypersons *undervalue* expert testimony of a statistical nature, such as testimony about random match probabilities in DNA cases. In short, the influence of DNA evidence on triers of fact may be more modest than some anecdotes suggest.

Id. at 97. Indeed, in the vast majority of cases using forensic evidence, techniques other than DNA profiling are involved. This observation is not meant to minimize DNA profiling's importance – which is still tremendous – but rather to counsel viewing DNA profiling as but one among many scientific techniques that must be mastered by the criminal trial lawyer.

B. The Dangers of Expert Testimony

Courts and legislatures have increasingly become suspect about the value of scientific and other expert testimony for good reason. First, forensic laboratory error rates are high, most such laboratories being neither accredited for quality by any authoritative body nor employing technicians certified as qualified in their fields. These labs often neither articulate nor enforce written standard protocols setting out the right way to perform tests, nor do they uniformly require examiner proficiency testing in the particular technique in question. Convictions of substantial numbers of innocent persons have been the result.

Lab technicians are indeed often sloppy or incompetent, losing critical evidence and misreporting results. Underfunding and overwork further raise the risk of error, and there have been some major cases recently proven to have involved outright fraud. The most infamous of these cases have taken place in Oklahoma, Montana, Texas, West Virginia, Delaware, Florida, Hawaii,

Kentucky, Nebraska, New Mexico, Ohio, Pennsylvania, and Virginia. Perhaps one of the worst offenders was forensic scientist Fred Zain, originally a "forensic superstar," who found "flecks of blood or smudges of semen where his colleagues found nothing." He was said to possess "phenomenal lab techniques — a unique ability to detect genetic markers in crime scene stains that turned otherwise hopeless cases into prosecution dreams. Zain's magic turned out, however, to be what most magic is — illusion and deception involving massive fraud." A judicial report summarized the wide array of Zain's fraudulent acts:

> (1) overstating the strength of results; (2) overstating the frequency of genetic matches on individual pieces of evidence; (3) misreporting the frequency of genetic matches; (4) reporting that multiple items of evidence have been tested, when only a single item had been tested; (5) reporting inconclusive results as conclusive; (6) repeatedly altering laboratory records; (7) grouping results to create the erroneous impression that genetic markers had been obtained from all samples tested; (8) failing to report conflicting results; (9) failing to conduct or to report conducting additional testing to resolve conflicting results; (10) implying a match with a suspect when testing supported only a match with a victim; and (11) reporting scientifically impossible or improbable results.

In re Investigation of the W. Va. State Police Crime Lab, Serology Div., 438 S.E.2d. 501, 503 (W. Va. 1993) (quoting report of the Special Investigator appointed by the West Virginia Supreme Court to investigate Zain's work).

Zain's outright fraud and the sloppiness of other lab examiners highlights one particular concern about all expert evidence: even if the particular technique used is a sound one based on well-accepted scientific principles, the technique can be mis-applied in an individual case. It is not enough to show that DNA profiling works *in general*. It is also important to show that the technique was done properly *in this case*, subject to proper guarantors of accuracy.

On the other hand, even a technique done correctly is useless if the technique itself or the principles upon which it is based are not scientifically valid. A "principle" is a general statement asserted to be true about the world. A "technique" is a means for applying that principle to individual cases. Thus, for DNA,

Principle: All humans have unique DNA.

Technique or Method: DNA profiling is an accurate means for identifying each person's unique DNA in any individual case, provided that proper protocols were followed.

Case-Specific Application: These protocols were properly followed in defendant Joseph Marsh's case and showed a match.

Conclusion: Joseph Marsh was at the crime scene.

The reliability of even some time-tested techniques like fingerprinting and handwriting analysis has recently been questioned by some courts.

C. The Federal Rules of Evidence

Federal Rule of Evidence 702 requires that all scientific or other expert evidence be shown by the proponent (the one who wants to get the expert's testimony admitted at trial) to be "the product of reliable principles and methods." In *Daubert v. Merrell Dow Pharmaceuticals, Inc.* 509 U.S. 579 (1993), the Court identified the following factors as relevant ones to be weighed in determining whether principle and methods or techniques are reliable ones:

(1) whether the theory and technique are testable, have been tested, and have survived such testing;

(2) whether they have also survived peer review and the gauntlet of the publication process;

(3) whether the potential error rate is known;

(4) whether there are authoritative standards controlling the technique's operation; and

(5) whether the principle or technique has attained widespread acceptance in the relevant field.

Rule 702 also requires that the expert witness be qualified "by knowledge, skill, experience, training, or education, to testify thereto in the form of an opinion or otherwise." The expert must be qualified to give *the particular opinion* that he or she is offering, and the testimony must "assist the trier of fact." Rule 702 also requires, once the principles and methods are proven reliable, that "the witness has applied the principles and methods reliably to the facts of the case." Zain's errors noted above are the clearest example of a showing of reliable *case-specific-application* missing.

PROBLEM TWENTY-ONE

Joni has been charged with murdering Ani. The primary evidence against Joni is that a dog named "Huggy" alerted to Joni at a dog scent lineup. In a dog scent lineup, a trained dog sniffs an item found at a crime scene — here, a hat that fell from the killer's head as the killer fled the crime's location. The dog then sniffs six suspects in a lineup, the suspects selected based upon circumstantial evidence. Thus far the courts have automatically admitted such evidence, refusing to hear expert testimony challenging the reliability of the dog scent lineup, because, citing TV shows like *Lassie*, the courts have concluded that everyone knows that dogs can do these feats, so it would be a waste of time to debate the question. Several experiments have revealed dog error rates ranging between 35% and 85% mistakes in a total of five experiments done by five different researchers. Dog trainers and police canine teams have long widely accepted the reliability of this sort of lineup, though 99 of the 100 lead canine biologists in the nation flatly consider the technique untrustworthy. Leading police canine professional training periodicals have published numerous peer-reviewed articles declaring the technique highly reliable, though five articles by each of the five canine biologists investigating the question have also been published in *Canine Nature*, the leading professional publication in the area. The Association of Police Canine Forensics has published authoritative standards on how to conduct these lineups properly, including: (a) having at least six people in the lineup; (b) using a dog trained for at least six months by a trainer certified by the Association; c) doing the lineups "blind," that is, with the dog handler not knowing who was the suspect. In this case, there were indeed six suspects and Huggy did have a properly certified trainer (though Huggy only completed five of the six months of training), but the lineup was not blind.

1. As defense counsel, how would you convince the trial judge that a suppression hearing is warranted under the state's evidence rules, which track the FRE and the *Daubert* test?

2. What witnesses would you call to the stand and why? What questions would you ask them and why?

3. What arguments will you make to the trial judge and why?

4. What witnesses can you expect the prosecution to call to avoid suppression, and what arguments will they likely raise in support of their position?

5. As a matter of good policy, which side should be successful in this argument, and why?

§ 7.05 Case Planning

A. Defining Case Planning and Why It Is Needed

Because the ultimate goal of any trial lawyer is to persuade the factfinder to find those facts that benefit the lawyers' client, all lawyers must prepare their case with that goal in mind. There is both a technical and an artistic aspect to such preparation. The technical part is that there must be adequate proof of each of the elements of the crime or defense collected by whomever has the burden of persuasion. Correspondingly, the opposing party must consider ways to call into question whether the necessary burden has been met. Whomever bears the burden must prove every element of the crime or defense.

The prosecution always bears the burden of proving every element of the crime beyond a reasonable doubt. Therefore, if the defense can raise a reasonable doubt as to *but one* element of the crime, acquittal will result. Defendants might raise two broad sorts of defenses: failure of proof and affirmative defenses. "Failure of proof" defenses are but ways for the defense to argue that the prosecution has failed to meet its burden of persuasion beyond a reasonable doubt as to some element. For policy reasons, the defense might have the "burden of production" on some such failure-of-proof defenses – usually meaning the burden of producing "some" evidence in support of the defense, a burden that might in some cases be met entirely by cross-examining prosecution witnesses. But, once some such evidence has been produced, the prosecution bears the burden of *disproving* the defense in order to meet its burden of proving every element of the crime beyond a reasonable about.

One example would be mistake of fact. Suppose that a defendant is charged with receiving stolen property, defined in this hypothetical jurisdiction as "receiving movable property knowing that it has been stolen." The case arises when the defendant buys a *"Movado"* (expensive watch) from a street vendor at an absurdly low price. The prosecution's argument is that anyone buying a very expensive brand watch at such a low price *would know that it must have been stolen*, so the jury should believe that this defendant *in fact knew* that the watch was stolen when he bought it. An undercover officer observed the entire transaction and arrested the defendant. On cross-examination by the defense at trial, however, the officer admits to overhearing this conversation between the defendant and the watch vendor:

Defendant: *"Movado."* I never heard of that brand. Is it as good as Radio Store?

Watch Vendor: Even better, but by buying in bulk, and given my low overhead, I can afford to sell it at just below Radio Store prices.

Defendant: What a great deal! I'll take it.

This exchange is clearly "some" evidence that the defendant mistakenly believed that the watch was legally obtained by the vendor rather than being stolen. Having presented some evidence on the point, the accused can argue it in closing to the jury. The prosecution will have to persuade the jury beyond a reasonable doubt that the defendant was not mistaken but rather did know of the stolen status of the watch. Of course, even if the defendant had not presented any evidence of being mistaken, the prosecutor would still have had to have prove beyond a reasonable doubt that the defendant knew that the watch was stolen. But in that circumstance the prosecutor's task would be easier, for the defendant would not be free to argue a mistaken belief; that would raise the likelihood that the jury will assume the absence of mistake and conclude that, since most people under the circumstances would have known that the watch was stolen, this defendant, seeming to be like most people, also in fact knew that the vendor came by the watch illegally.

On the other hand, with "affirmative defenses," the defendant has the burden of persuasion, usually (though not always) by a preponderance of the evidence (the Model Penal Code gives the term "affirmative defense" a special meaning). For example, one definition of legal insanity in some jurisdictions is the condition in which the accused, "by reason of mental disease or defect, lost the ability to know right from wrong or to know the nature and quality of his [or her] actions at the time of the crime." It is not enough that a defendant did not know right from wrong because of a bad upbringing. The accused has the burden of proving *by a preponderance of the evidence* (in most jurisdictions) both a complete inability to tell right from wrong *and* that that inability was caused by a mental disease or defect. The prosecution's role is to raise doubts about whether the defense has met this burden, but it is the accused who has the burden, and, absent adequate proof of all the elements, the defense will not succeed.

B. Elements Charts

Burdens of proof [See Chap. 6] matter here because, in case planning, it is essential to know what elements must be proven and what elements the opponent must prove. One way trial lawyers ensure that they can meet technical legal requirements is to do a chart listing all the elements of each crime and defense, who has the burden of proof, and, under each element, which witnesses the lawyer will offer to prove or disapprove each element and what physical or demonstrative evidence must be brought to the jury's attention through each witness. Here is a simplified version of such a chart prepared by the prosecution in a stranger rape case and just concerning the prosecutor's burden:

Elements of the Crime	Witnesses	Physical Evidence
1. Forcible	a. *Molly, Victim*: to describe being held down. b. Admitting Nurse: to describe victim's injuries	a. Photographs of injuries (Molly or Admitting Nurse) b. Stitches (Admitting Nurse)
2. Non-consensual	a. *Molly*: said "no" b. *Molly's mom*: Molly complained promptly, in tears. c. 911 operator	a. 911 Tape (Molly or call recipient) b. Scar (to display to jury) (Molly)
3. Sexual intercourse	a. Molly b. Lab technician: Semen found c. Admitting Nurse (chain of custody)	
4. By a man	Molly	
5. With a woman	Molly	
6. Not his wife	Molly	

Burden of Persuasion On Each of These Elements: On the Prosecution, Beyond a Reasonable Doubt.

C. Mini-Closing Arguments

The artistic part of case prosecution is coming up with the narrative that you think will most appeal to the jury. The story that you want to tell may not be the only plausible one, but it is the one you most want the jury to believe and that you think they will in fact find credible. Story lines may need to be revised as more is learned about the case, but crafting a story as soon as possible is central to good case planning. Many lawyers thus write a miniature version of their expected closing statement to the jury as early as possible. As evidence is developed, they may repeatedly rewrite that closing.

A closing is the final argument made by each side to the jury. A closing tells a story but also explains what evidence supports your story and undercuts your opponent's tale. Where credibility is in dispute, as it so often is, a closing also explains to the jury why one side's witnesses', and not the other side's, should be believed. At the end of each major portion of this draft closing, the lawyer will list all witnesses and all physical evidence supporting that part of the narrative, for lawyers may ethically tell only stories for which there is supporting evidence. The elements charts and working closing arguments help the lawyer ensure that all necessary evidence will be presented in a persuasive fashion. For each witness, a lawyer can then prepare a list of questions, or, as many more experienced lawyers do, a list of expected answers, that help that witness present the evidence relating to the relevant element and the relevant part of the story in the best light.

PROBLEM TWENTY-TWO

Assume that the motion to suppress evidence is denied in the *Taylor v. Maddox* case [p. 240]. Prepare an elements list and mini-closing argument for the defense, then do the same for the prosecution.

§ 7.06 Investigation

A. Basic Investigation

When a case begins, each side has only a limited idea of what evidence is in fact available. Investigation must be conducted: witnesses interviewed, new witnesses located, scientific tests done, crime scenes examined, photographs taken, and discovery exchanged.

In a run-of-the-mill street crime case, the initial investigation will have been done by the police, who are usually brought to the crime scene as a result of a phone call by the victim or an eyewitness. Ordinarily in such cases, an arrest will result, if at all, only if the suspect is found hiding nearby, fleeing from the police, or as a result of a quick tip that leads them to the offender's hideaway. In more serious cases, even if no suspect is quickly found, the police will look for "stoolies" (street informants) and will conduct forensic testing, such as looking for fingerprints or DNA samples, in an effort to find a suspect.

If a suspect is quickly found, a "showup" may be held on the scene, that is, the suspect may be shown to a victim or witness for the purposes of identification. Whether or not a showup is done, a lineup may be held later, usually meaning about six persons being placed in a line — one of whom is the suspect — to determine whether the victim or an eyewitness recognizes someone in the line as the thief, assailant, rapist, robber, or burglar. The police might also interrogate a suspect upon arrest, provided they *Mirandize* him, and he waives his rights to silence and to an attorney during questioning. The police prepare reports summarizing what witnesses have said, what were the results of lineups, showups, or photospreads, as well as what were the results of forensic tests.

B. Investigating Grand Juries and Subpoenas

In complex cases in which the state suspects a crime but cannot yet prove it or are uncertain who committed it, they may often proceed by way of an investigating grand jury. A "grand jury" is a group of citizens, in many jurisdictions typically 23, who sit to decide whether there is probable cause to indict someone for a crime. A grand jury can subpoena witnesses to testify before it or to produce documents for its examination. In most states, the decision whether there is sufficient evidence in a felony case to proceed to trial is decided by a judge in a "preliminary hearing," the judge deciding whether to issue an "information" stating the charges on which the state may proceed to trial. No grand jury is needed. Nevertheless, even in such states, the prosecution might convene a grand jury because it needs the subpoena power to aid investigation, thus the term "investigating grand jury." A subpoena is a court order, and refusal to appear, to testify, or to produce documents in response to a subpoena subjects the subpoena's addressee to contempt of court, which may result in a fine or imprisonment.

C. Formal Versus Informal Discovery and Witness Interviews

Discovery in most criminal cases in most jurisdictions is usually far more limited than in civil cases. Often the defense will receive at least portions of some of the police reports, though the names and addresses of at least some of the witnesses might be deleted to protect them against threats. For certain defenses, there is "reciprocal discovery," that is, the prosecution must produce information for a defendant *only if* the defendant produces it for the prosecution and vice-versa. Typically, for example, alibi and insanity defenses create reciprocal discovery obligations so that the defense must identify its planned witnesses and the general nature of these defenses for the prosecution, who must then respond by identifying its rebuttal witnesses. Depositions are usually allowed only if a motion requesting them is filed, the need for them is proven, and the court has issued an order permitting them, though a few states allow for routine depositions, even in serious criminal cases. The prosecution must provide all exculpatory material to the defense.

The defense will usually send investigators out to interview any identified prosecution witnesses. Although the witnesses are not obligated to talk to defense counsel, the prosecutor is ethically prohibited from instructing his or her witnesses not to talk to the defense. Defense counsel must also interview the client and locate and interview any potential defense witnesses. For example, potential alibi witnesses must be interviewed to determine whether they can in fact support the defendant's alibi. The defense might also arrange for its own forensic testing and examinations, such as re-testing DNA samples or being examined by a psychiatrist in support of an insanity defense.

Conversations between an attorney and his client are protected from disclosure to the prosecution by the attorney-client privilege. If defense counsel prepares memoranda summarizing witness interviews but commenting on the tactical strengths and weaknesses of the case that follow from those interviews, the contents of the interviews might be qualifiedly protected from disclosure as attorney work product, meaning it must be produced for the other side only if that side demonstrates great need for the evidence.

Ethically, lawyers are generally prohibited from any direct contact with a party or witness who is represented by counsel. Instead, all communications must be between the two lawyers, who may then negotiate whether any direct witness contact is permitted (if it is, usually it will be only in counsel's presence).

D. Using Elements Lists and Mini-Closings to Create Investigation Plans

One way to decide what investigation must be secured is for a lawyer to prepare element lists and a mini-closing based on preliminary investigation (such as police reports and a client interview), then brainstorming about what sorts of witnesses and physical evidence might support each element and each portion of the closing and how to identify the witnesses, learn their story, and get hold of the physical evidence. These speculations and the methods for pursuing them are then noted under each element and after each closing paragraph, and the investigation begins.

PROBLEM TWENTY-THREE

You represent Johnny, who has been charged with rape. Johnny is accused of rape by a hotel employee, Joanna. Joanna met Johnny when he was staying in the hotel. She delivered a drink to Johnny's room and he asked her inside. He then started kissing her, and she kissed back. But next, without asking, he ripped off her panties and as she said "No!" he had sexual intercourse with her. She fled to her mother's home in tears, then reported the incident to the police, and was examined at a hospital, where vaginal abrasions were found. Johnny corroborates her story in almost all respects but says that she never said no and that she consented. Design an investigation plan, first for the prosecution, then for the defense, using elements lists and mini-closing arguments as guides.

§ 7.07 Negotiating Guilty Pleas

Factfinding concerns also hang heavily over parties attempting to negotiate guilty plea agreements. The major task of a negotiator is to convince his or her opponent that the factfinder is more likely than the opponent initially thinks to decide in the negotiator's favor should the case go to trial. No one can be guaranteed of winning at trial, so each side has an incentive to settle, to reach a plea agreement that reduces the risks for both sides. An accused facing a very high potential prison sentence if convicted but a moderate chance of complete acquittal may nevertheless plead guilty in exchange for the certainty of a lower sentence. A prosecutor in the same circumstances may agree to the plea to avoid the risk of an acquittal, of no punishment at all. The higher the perceived risk of conviction, however, the lower the prosecutor's risk of getting nothing by going to trial, so the less the prosecutor will be willing to reduce the sentence via the plea agreement. On the other hand, the higher the risk of *acquittal*, the further down the penalty scale the prosecutor will be willing to go. Each side must thus try to convince the other side that the probabilities of conviction or acquittal favor the negotiator's client.

Such persuasion is effective only if perceived to be done in good faith, that is, if each side makes justified concessions when the evidence calls for it. The adjective "justified" means here supported by sound reasons, for if you concede something without a convincing explanation for doing so, your action will be perceived as weakness, and your opponent will thus believe that he or she can get more and give less by refraining from too readily reaching any deal. Successful negotiations thus *require* an exchange of information about what evidence each side has to offer, what arguments it will make about credibility, and what legal issues it will rely upon. Because no agreement may be reached, each side tries to reveal as little information as possible without being seen as acting in bad faith while getting as much information as possible from the opponent. Information improves each side's ability to craft reasonable settlement terms and aids decisionmaking about trial tactics should the case reach a jury or bench trial.

For defense counsel it is important to remember that no information may be revealed without the consent of the client. It is also important to remember that only the client can consent to the plea agreement.

The information exchanged will primarily be about what evidence will be presented and why it will persuade a jury to decide in your favor. Preparing thoroughly for a negotiation, therefore, also again requires thorough investigation, preparation, and an elements list chart noting supporting evidence, as well as a clear narrative in the form of a miniature draft closing argument. These tools enable a lawyer to sell his or her side's story to the opponent.

Under the Federal Rules of Evidence and most state codes, statements made during plea negotiations *with the prosecutor* are inadmissible at trial, although there are some exceptions. The purpose of this rule is to encourage candid, open negotiations with a high chance of ultimate agreement because guilty pleas save enormous judicial resources in terms of time and money.

CASE STUDY THREE

Quinn's home was burglarized recently. The burglary took place about 2 a.m. Quinn, who is 83 years old and wears prescription glasses for seeing distances, was awakened by sounds in the kitchen that led to a call to the police. Quinn then stepped to the top of the stairs, seeing a person at the bottom (no lights were on, but Quinn shined a flashlight in the person's direction), screaming that this individual should leave the property immediately. Acorn complied, fleeing the house. Quinn found that $500 hidden in the kitchen cookie jar was missing. The police arrived within minutes, and Quinn told the police that the burglar as a neighborhood teenager named Acorn, who had once done some repair work for Quinn in the home. Quinn described Acorn as about 5' 6" in height, red-headed, thin build, white, and wearing a yellow shirt with buttons on the front, a blue denim jacket, and dark blue pants at the time of the burglary.

The police immediately sent a car to pick up Acorn. Not finding Acorn at home, however, they returned to show Quinn eight black-and-white photographs, asking Quinn whether the burglar was one of the individuals in the photos. Quinn said that the photos were very grainy, but that number 3 or 4 was the individual, though Quinn thought that number 3 was much more likely the thief, that is, Quinn said, more likely Acorn. Acorn's face was in fact, however, in photo number 4. Quinn insisted that there was no doubt that Acorn did the crime; it was the pictures that were unclear, not Acorn's memory. Another police team, having received a radio bulletin about the burglary, then called to say that they had just stopped Acorn about 3 blocks from Quinn's home. The police drove Quinn to the street corner where Acorn was being detained and they asked Quinn whether Quinn recognized this individual. As Acorn's color arrest photo would later show, Acorn was then wearing a bright red t-shirt, a blue denim jacket, and black pants. The officers described Acorn's hair as blond with reddish highlights. Quinn said that Acorn was the one, and the police arrested Acorn. Upon searching Acorn incident to arrest, they found a small quantity of cocaine and $550 in the left front pants pocket, money that Acorn blurted out was earned from odd jobs in the neighborhood.

Acorn has just turned age 18. Acorn has one prior arrest for marijuana possession, but the charge was dismissed when Acorn successfully completed pre-trial probation that included drug counseling. Acorn is a straight "A" senior high school student. Acorn has notified the prosecution that Acorn plans to offer an alibi defense at trial. As best the prosecution can glean, Acorn's mom will testify that Acorn was home at the time of the burglary but had awakened her to say that Acorn was getting dressed to go to a late night performance of the Rocky Horror Picture Show with some friends, telling her that the movie played all night long every Friday night, and they thought it would be more fun to go late at night since the movie was a musical comedy horror picture. Acorn just woke her so that she would not worry.

In this common law jurisdiction, sentencing is indeterminate. Acorn has been charged with burglary, grand larceny, and possession of a cocaine, the first charge being subject to a maximum penalty of 20 years imprisonment, the second a maximum term of 5 years imprisonment, and the third a maximum of 10 years imprisonment. There are no statutory minimum penalties. The case has been assigned for trial to Judge Maxi Flood, whose nickname is the "Hanging Judge," though at sentencing Hon. Maxi Flood is known to have a soft spot for drug addicts, whom the judge sees as more ill than evil.

Negotiate an attempted resolution of this case, considering what tactics and strategy to follow for the: (a) the defense; (b) the prosecution.

PART FOUR
CRIMES

Chapter 8
Homicide

§ 8.01 Outline of the Law of Homicide

General Definition of Homicide at Common Law: An unlawful (that is, unjustified or inexcusable) killing of a human being.

General Definition of Murder at Common Law: An unlawful killing done with "malice aforethought," a term of art meaning any of the mental states sufficient for murder listed in numbers 1 and 2 below. Some states do not require "malice" in the ordinary sense of that word. Similarly, there are mental states subsumed by the term "malice aforethought" that do not necessarily require thinking about the killing significantly before the act that causes death takes place. As such, they do not require "aforethought" in the common sense meaning of that word.

General Definition of Manslaughter at Common Law: An unlawful killing that is not done with "malice aforethought," more specifically one done with any of the mental states listed in numbers 3 and 4 below.

The Elements of the Major Forms of Common Law Homicide in Most Jurisdictions:

1. *First Degree Murder* (Potentially Subject to the Death Penalty)

   a. Willful, deliberate, and premeditated (that is, purposely killing while fully appreciating the significance of your actions and thinking about them beforehand; also known as killing in "cold blood"); or

   b. Felony murder as specified by statute; or

   c. Killing by poison or lying in wait.

279

2. *Second Degree Murder*

    a. Any intentional (that is, purposeful or knowing) killing other than first degree murder or voluntary manslaughter (for example, a purposeful killing done while unreasonably in the heat of passion); or

    b. Intentionally (that is, purposeful or knowingly) causing serious bodily injury but where death, though never intended, results; or

    c. Felony murder (if not raised to first degree by statute); or

    d. Depraved heart (or abandoned and malignant heart) murder (a special kind of extremely reckless killing that exhibits indifference to the value of human life).

3. *Voluntary Manslaughter*

A killing that would otherwise be murder but that is mitigated to manslaughter because it was done upon being reasonably provoked into a sudden heat of passion without cooling off where a reasonable person would not have cooled off. Its elements, therefore, are:

    1. mental state that would ordinarily qualify as murder (for example, a purposeful killing);

    2. when the defendant has been provoked by the victim into the heat of passion;

    3. a reasonable person would have been so provoked;

    4. the defendant has not cooled off by the time of the killing; and

    5. a reasonable person would not have cooled off.

4. *Involuntary Manslaughter*

    a. In some jurisdictions, a reckless killing (provided that it is not of the special type of recklessness that elevates the crime to depraved heart murder); in other jurisdictions, a criminally negligent killing; and, in still other jurisdictions, a killing done with ordinary tort negligence; or

    b. Misdemeanor-manslaughter

    c. Imperfect Self-Defense. (There is disagreement as to whether imperfect self-defense belongs in the voluntary or involuntary category).

§ 8.02 Intentional Killings

A. Murder–Willful, Deliberate and Premeditated

CALIFORNIA PENAL CODE

§ 187. Murder defined

(a) Murder is the unlawful killing of a human being, or a fetus, with malice aforethought. (b) [Section (b) exempts certain lawful abortions]

§ 188. Malice defined

Such malice may be express or implied. It is express when there is manifested a deliberate intention unlawfully to take away the life of a fellow creature. It is implied, when no considerable provocation appears, or when the circumstances attending the killing show an abandoned and malignant heart.

When it is shown that the killing resulted from the intentional doing of an act with express or implied malice as defined above, no other mental state need be shown to establish the mental state of malice aforethought. Neither an awareness of the obligation to act within the general body of laws regulating society nor acting despite such awareness is included within the definition of malice.

§ 189. Degrees of murder

All murder which is perpetrated by means of a destructive device or explosive, a weapon of mass destruction, knowing use of ammunition designed primarily to penetrate metal or armor, poison, lying in wait, torture, or by any other kind of willful, deliberate, and premeditated killing, or which is committed in the perpetration of, or attempt to perpetrate, arson, rape, carjacking, robbery, burglary, mayhem, kidnaping, train wrecking, or any act punishable under Section 206, 286, 288, 288a, or 289, or any murder which is perpetrated by means of discharging a firearm from a motor vehicle, intentionally at another person outside of the vehicle with the intent to inflict death, is murder of the first degree. All other kinds of murders are of the second degree. . . .

To prove the killing was "deliberate and premeditated," it shall not be necessary to prove the defendant maturely and meaningfully reflected upon the gravity of his or her act.

MODEL PENAL CODE
ARTICLE 210. CRIMINAL HOMICIDE

§ 210.0. Definitions.

In Articles 210-213, unless a different meaning plainly is required:

(1) "human being" means a person who has been born and is alive;

(2) "bodily injury" means physical pain, illness or any impairment of physical condition;

(3) "serious bodily injury" means bodily injury which creates a substantial risk of death or which causes serious, permanent disfigurement, or protracted loss or impairment of the function of any bodily member or organ;

(4) "deadly weapon" means any firearm or other weapon, device, instrument, material or substance, whether animate or inanimate, which in the manner it is used or is intended to be used is known to be capable of producing death or serious bodily injury.

§ 210.1. Criminal Homicide.

(1) A person is guilty of criminal homicide if he purposely, knowingly, recklessly or negligently causes the death of another human being,

(2) Criminal homicide is murder, manslaughter or negligent homicide.

§ 210.2. Murder.

(1) Except as provided in Section 210.3(1)(b), criminal homicide constitutes murder when

(a) it is committed purposely or knowingly; or

(b) it is committed recklessly under circumstances manifesting extreme indifference to the value of human life. Such recklessness and indifference are presumed if the actor is engaged or is an accomplice in the commission of, or an attempt to commit, or flight after committing or attempting to commit robbery, rape or deviate sexual intercourse by force or threat of force, arson, burglary, kidnaping or felonious escape.

(2) Murder is a felony of the first degree [but a person convicted of murder may be sentenced to death, as provided in Section 210.6].

State v. Thompson
65 P.3d 420 (Ariz. 2003)

BERCH, Justice.

Defendant Larry Thompson challenges the constitutionality of Arizona's first degree murder statute. * * * On May 17, 1999, Thompson shot and killed his wife, Roberta Palma. Several days before the shooting, Palma had filed for divorce, and Thompson had discovered that she was seeing someone else. Just a week before the shooting, Thompson moved out of the couple's home. As he did so, Thompson threatened Palma that, "[i]f you divorce me, I will kill you."

Thompson returned to the couple's neighborhood the morning of May 17. He was seen walking on the sidewalk near the home and his car was spotted in a nearby alley. Two witnesses reported that a man dragged a woman by the hair from the front porch into the home. That same morning, police received and recorded a 9-1-1 call from the house. The tape recorded a woman's screams and four gunshots. The four gunshots span nearly twenty-seven seconds. Nine seconds elapse between the first shot and the third, and there is an eighteen-second delay between the third shot and the fourth.

Police arrived shortly after the call and found Palma dead from gunshot wounds. An autopsy of her body revealed several fresh abrasions, five non-contact gunshot wounds, and one contact gunshot wound.

At trial, Thompson did not deny killing his wife, but claimed that he did so in the heat of passion, making the killing manslaughter or, at most, second degree murder. During closing arguments, Thompson's counsel argued that the crime had occurred in the heat of passion and that Thompson had "simply snapped."

In her closing arguments, the prosecutor argued that the evidence that Thompson premeditated the murder was "overwhelming." She emphasized the timing of the shots and the delay between them. The prosecutor also reminded the jury of Thompson's threat, made a week before the murder, to kill his wife. The prosecutor then argued that Thompson need not actually have reflected, but only had the time to reflect. * * * Nonetheless, the prosecutor referred to circumstantial evidence suggesting that Thompson actually had reflected, but then told the jury it need only decide that Thompson had the time to reflect, not that he actually had reflected.

After closing arguments, the judge instructed the jury regarding premeditation as follows:

"Premeditation" means that the defendant acts with either the intention or the knowledge that he will kill another human being, when such intention or knowledge precedes the killing by any length of time to permit reflection. Proof of actual reflection is not required, but an act is not done with premeditation if it is the instant effect of a sudden quarrel or heat of passion.

The jury found Thompson guilty of first degree murder and the judge sentenced him to life in prison without the possibility of parole. * * *

* * * The statute at issue, Arizona's first degree murder statute, provides that "[a] person commits first degree murder if . . . [i]ntending or knowing that the person's conduct will cause death, the person causes the death of another *with* premeditation." A.R.S. § 13-1105(A)(1). Thompson challenges the constitutionality of the statute, arguing that it renders first degree murder indistinguishable from second degree murder. A person commits second degree murder in Arizona "if *without* premeditation . . . [s]uch person intentionally causes the death of another person." A.R.S. § 13-1104(A)(1). Thus, for the purposes of this appeal, first and second degree murder are indistinguishable except that first degree murder requires premeditation.

According to the definition adopted by the legislature,

"[p]remeditation" means that the defendant acts with either the intention or the knowledge that he will kill another human being, when such intention or knowledge precedes the killing by any length of time to permit reflection. *Proof of actual reflection is not required*, but an act is not done with premeditation if it is the instant effect of a sudden quarrel or heat of passion.

A.R.S. § 13-1101(1).

The question before us is whether this definition of premeditation abolishes the requirement of actual reflection altogether, whether it eliminates the require-ment of direct proof of actual reflection, or whether it substitutes for the necessary proof of actual reflection the mere passage of enough time to permit reflection. The State asserts the third interpretation, that the legislature intended to relieve the State of the burden of proving a defendant's hidden thought processes, and that this definition of premeditation establishes that the passage of time may serve as a proxy for reflection. * * *

Thompson maintains that reducing premeditation to the mere passage of time renders the statute vague and unenforceable because courts have held that actual reflection can occur as quickly as "successive thoughts of the mind." Thus, he argues and the court of appeals agreed, the difference between first and second degree murder has been eliminated. * * *

For most of this state's history, first degree murder explicitly required proof of "premeditation," or actual reflection by the defendant.

Because premeditation involves a defendant's thought processes, the question arose how to prove that a defendant had reflected on the decision to kill. Courts responded by allowing the issue to be proved by circumstantial evidence. Indeed, at one time, the murder statute set forth fact patterns that suggested premeditation: "poison, lying in wait, torture, or when the killing is done in the perpetration or attempt to perpetrate certain felonies. If none of these elements appear, the evidence must show in some manner that the killing was 'wilful, deliberate and premeditated.'"

In 1978, however, premeditation was redefined to mean

that the defendant acts with either the intention or the knowledge that he will kill another human being, when such intention or knowledge precedes the killing by a length of time to permit reflection. An act is not done with premeditation if it is the instant effect of a sudden quarrel or heat of passion.

This definition highlights the time element, speaking, as it does, in terms of intention or knowledge that precedes the killing by enough time to allow reflection and excluding killings that occur as a result of a sudden quarrel. * * *

We have not, until this case, had the opportunity to address the confusion surrounding the issue of premeditation. Thompson urges us to overturn his conviction on the ground that the statute is unconstitutionally vague. The State, on the other hand, argues that the statute is constitutional and that the current definition of premeditation meaningfully distinguishes between first and second degree murder.

We conclude, as did the court of appeals, that if the only difference between first and second degree murder is the mere passage of time, and that length of time can be "as instantaneous as successive thoughts of the mind," then there is no meaningful distinction between first and second degree murder. Such an interpretation would relieve the state of its burden to prove actual reflection and would render the first degree murder statute impermissibly vague and therefore unconstitutional under the United States and Arizona Constitutions.

We are, however, mindful of our duty to construe this statute, if possible, in a way that not only gives effect to the legislature's intent, but also in a way that maintains its constitutionality. * * * [W]e conclude that the legislature intended to relieve the state of the burden of proving a defendant's thought processes by direct evidence. It intended for premeditation, and the reflection that it requires, to mean more than the mere passage of time. * * *

Our decision today distinguishes the element of premeditation from the evidence that might establish that element. Although the mere passage of time suggests that a defendant premeditated–and the state might be able to convince a jury to make that inference–the passage of time is not, in and of itself, premeditation. To allow the state to establish the element of premeditation by merely proving that sufficient time passed to permit reflection would be to essentially relieve the state of its burden to establish the sole element that distinguishes between first and second degree murder.

* * * [O]nly in rare situations will a defendant's reflection be established by direct evidence such as diary entries or statements to others. But the state may use all the circumstantial evidence at its disposal in a case to prove premeditation. Such evidence might include, among other things, threats made by the defendant to the victim, a pattern of escalating violence between the defendant and the victim, or the acquisition of a weapon by the defendant before the killing. In short, the passage of time is but one factor that can show that the defendant actually reflected. The key is that the evidence, whether direct or circumstantial, must convince a jury beyond a reasonable doubt that the defendant actually reflected.

* * * We recognize that premeditation should be defined for the jury. But we also recognize that the statutory definition of premeditation may not explain it in an easily understandable way and, indeed, might mislead the jury. Thus, we disapprove of the use of the phrase "proof of actual reflection is not required" in a jury instruction. * * * We also discourage the use of the phrase "as instantaneous as successive thoughts of the mind." We continue to be concerned that juries could be misled by instructions that needlessly emphasize the rapidity with which reflection may occur. Accordingly, trial judges should, in future cases, instruct juries as follows:

> "Premeditation" means that the defendant intended to kill another human being [knew he/she would kill another human being], and that after forming that intent [knowledge], reflected on the decision before killing. It is this reflection, regardless of the length of time in which it occurs, that distinguishes first degree murder from second degree murder. An act is not done with premeditation if it is the instant effect of a sudden quarrel or heat of passion.

Only when the facts of a case require it should a trial judge instruct the jury, or may the state argue, that "the time needed for reflection is not necessarily prolonged, and the space of time between the intent [knowledge] to kill and the act of killing may be very short." It is the act of premeditation and not the length of time available that determines the question.

This instruction does not mean that the state must rely on direct evidence of premeditation; as we have noted, such evidence is rarely available. Nor does this instruction mean that the state cannot rely on the passage of time between the formation of intent and the act of killing as a fact tending to show premeditation. This instruction merely clarifies that the state may not use the passage of time as a proxy for premeditation. The state may argue that the passage of time suggests premeditation, but it may not argue that the passage of time is premeditation.

In the case before us, the jury was instructed that "proof of actual reflection is not required." We hold that, without further clarification, this instruction was erroneous. The State also argued that it did not have to prove actual reflection, but had to prove only that enough time had elapsed to allow reflection. This, too, was in error. However, the jury was not instructed that actual reflection can occur as instantaneously as successive thoughts of the mind. Moreover, the State presented overwhelming evidence that Thompson actually reflected on his decision to kill his wife, including evidence of threats to kill her a week before the murder, the time that elapsed between each gunshot, and the victim's screams as recorded on the 9-1-1 tape between each gunshot. We conclude beyond a reasonable doubt that the flawed jury instruction and the State's reliance on that instruction did not affect the jury's verdict, and we will not overturn Thompson's conviction and sentence.

RYAN, Justice, Concurring in Part and Dissenting in Part:

* * * Unlike my colleagues, I do not find the legislature's decision to eliminate proof of actual reflection and instead rely, in part, on the passage of enough "time to permit reflection," makes the statute unconstitutional. The definition of premeditation must be read as a whole. And read as a whole, I think the statute adequately distinguishes between an intentional or knowing second degree murder and an intentional or knowing first degree murder. * * *

* * * By using the passage of time as a substitute for actual reflection, while at the same time requiring that a killing not be "the instant effect of a sudden quarrel or heat of passion," the legislature has drawn a discernible line between intentional or knowing first degree murder and intentional or knowing second degree murder. That is all the constitution requires. * * *

NOTES AND QUESTIONS

1. **Common Law Homicide.** At common law, there were two categories of criminal homicide: murder and manslaughter. The mens rea for murder was "malice aforethought," and some states allow for "express" and "implied" malice, such as the California statute. Implied malice involves a killing that results from the defendant's extreme recklessness. This is sometimes referred to as *depraved heart*

murder or murder with an *abandoned and malignant heart*. Express malice requires proof of a specific intent to kill, usually described as a killing that was "willful, deliberate, and premeditated."

2. ***Degrees of Murder.*** Today, the common approach in murder statutes is to provide different degrees of murder, based on the defendant's intent. First degree murder normally requires proof of express malice, while second degree murder involves implied malice, *i.e.* extreme recklessness; in some states, any murder that is not first degree murder falls into the residual category of second degree murder. Other types of first degree murder can involve the status of the victim — such as a law enforcement officer as the victim — or killings in the course of the commission of certain specified felonies, called *felony murder*. This latter category of murder does not require proof of an intent to kill, at least in most states, but only the intent to commit the underlying felony that results in the death of the victim during and in relation to the felony.

3. ***Human Rights Violations.*** Large-scale murders can serve as the basis for human rights violations. For example, in Article Seven of the Rome Statute for the International Criminal Court (http://www.un.org/law/icc/), it provides that a crime against humanity includes murder "when committed as part of a widespread or systematic attack directed against any civilian population, with knowledge of the attack."

4. ***Death.*** The first element of a homicide case is a death. Various issues can arise with this first element: When do you have a death? What happens if a person is being kept on a respirator, are they considered dead for legal purposes? [Chap. 5].

5. ***Killing of a Human Being.*** The common law required the killing of a human being for a murder conviction. What constitutes a human being? At a minimum, the victim must be alive at the time of the *actus reus*, but there is no requirement that the person be conscious, so that killing a comatose patient in a hospital will be a murder. The Model Penal Code requires that the victim be born alive for a murder prosecution, precluding murder prosecutions for an unborn fetus. A number of states have amended their homicide statutes to include the killing of a fetus. See CALIFORNIA PENAL CODE § 187(a) [p. 277]. For example, Florida provides: "[t]he unlawful killing of an unborn quick child, by any injury to the mother of such child which would be murder if it resulted in the death of such mother, shall be deemed murder in the same degree as that which would have been committed against the mother." FLA. STAT. ANN. § 782.09(1).

6. ***Premeditation.*** "In pre-Revolutionary America, William Penn insisted that premeditation be the word used to describe the most culpable murders." Matthew A. Pauley, *Murder by Premeditation*, 36 AM. CRIM. L. REV. 145 (1999). "[M]any states copied the Pennsylvania premeditation/deliberation distinction. Today, in England and in a minority of American states, there is no differentiation of murder

into degrees. But, in most American states, there are degrees of murder, and premeditation remains a very common dividing line between murders of the first and second degree." *Id.*

7. ***Distinguishing Among "Willful, Deliberate, and Premeditated."*** Courts recite the intent level for first-degree murder almost as if it were a mantra without necessarily explaining the terms. As with the burden of proof beyond a reasonable doubt, there is no requirement that the terms be specifically defined for the jury, although courts often do try to distinguish between them. Consider the following proposed instructions to determine whether the terms have distinct meanings:

> Murder of the first degree is murder which is perpetrated by means of any kind of willful, deliberate, and premeditated killing. All three elements — willfulness, deliberation, and premeditation — must be proven beyond a reasonable doubt before an accused can be convicted of first-degree murder. Willfulness is the intent to kill. There need be no appreciable space of time between formation of the intent to kill and the act of killing. Deliberation is the process of determining upon a course of action to kill as a result of thought, including weighing the reasons for and against the action and considering the consequences of the action. A deliberate determination may be arrived at in a short period of time. But in all cases the determination must not be formed in passion, or if formed in passion, it must be carried out after there has been time for the passion to subside and deliberation to occur. A mere unconsidered and rash impulse is not deliberate, even though it includes the intent to kill. Premeditation is a design, a determination to kill, distinctly formed in the mind by the time of the killing. Premeditation need not be for a day, an hour, or even a minute. It may be as instantaneous as successive thoughts of the mind. For if the jury believes from the evidence that the act constituting the killing has been preceded by and has been the result of premeditation, no matter how rapidly the act follows the premeditation, it is premeditated. The law does not undertake to measure in units of time the length of the period during which the thought must be pondered before it can ripen into an intent to kill which is truly deliberate and premeditated. The time will vary with different individuals and under varying circumstances. The true test is not the duration of time, but rather the extent of the reflection. A cold, calculated judgment and decision may be arrived at in a short period of time, but a mere unconsidered and rash impulse, even though it includes an intent to kill, is not deliberation and premeditation as will fix an unlawful killing as murder of the first degree.

Byford v. State, 994 P.2d 700 (Nev. 2000).

There must be not only an intention to kill, but there must also be a deliberate and premeditated design to kill. Such design must precede the killing by some appreciable space of time. But the time need not be long. It must be sufficient for some reflection and consideration upon the matter, for choice to kill or not to kill, and for the formation of a definite purpose to kill. And when the time is sufficient for this, it matters not how brief it is. Whether a deliberate and premeditated design to kill was formed must be determined from all the circumstances of the case.

State v. Patten, 813 A.2d 497 (N.H. 2002).

Coolen v. State
696 So.2d 738 (Fla. 1997)

PER CURIAM.

Coolen was charged with first-degree murder for the stabbing death of John Kellar on November 7, 1992. The evidence introduced at trial revealed the following facts. Kellar and his wife, Barbara Caughman Kellar, went to a pub in Clearwater at approximately 4:30 p.m. and struck up a conversation with Coolen and his girlfriend Deborah Morabito. The two couples drank beer and talked for three or four hours and then went back to the Kellars' home where they continued to party and drink beer in the backyard. According to nine- year-old Jamie Caughman, Barbara's son, the two men fought over a can of beer during the evening.

Coolen and Jamie walked down a nearby dirt road to shoot off fireworks that Coolen had in his van. Coolen then played tag with Jamie in the yard. During the game of tag, Coolen pulled Jamie away from the van door, put him on the ground, took a knife out of his pocket, and warned Jamie not to step on the door again. Jamie told no one about the incident and went into the house to play Nintendo.

John Kellar escorted Morabito into the house so that she could use the bathroom. During their absence, Coolen put his hand down Barbara Kellar's shirt. She pushed Coolen away and did not know where he went. When John Kellar and Morabito returned from the house a few minutes later, they joined Barbara Kellar at the van and the three continued their conversation. Suddenly Coolen pulled John Kellar away and backed him up to the house. John Kellar began to holler and moan as Coolen stabbed him. Barbara Kellar ran to assist her husband when he fell to the ground. She threw her body over his as protection and Coolen struck her several times with a knife. Jamie came outside in time to see John Kellar and Coolen fighting. He saw Coolen stabbing his stepfather and his stepfather trying to push

Coolen away. While Coolen was driving away from the scene, he hit a tree and the Kellars' truck. [Kellar died from six stab wounds, including a deep stab wound to the right chest and one to his right back; he also had defensive stab wounds on his forearm and hand. At the time of death, Kellar's blood alcohol level was .22.]

* * * Coolen was * * * interviewed at the sheriff's office several hours after the stabbing. In that taped interview, which was played to the jury, Coolen admitted stabbing Kellar with the knife found in Morabito's coat. He stated that he had been "playing word games" with Barbara Kellar when John Kellar "copped an attitude." He saw "something silver" in Kellar's hand, thought it was a small handgun that Kellar said he owned, and attacked Kellar to protect himself.

At the close of the State's evidence, defense counsel moved for a judgment of acquittal on the basis that the State had failed to adduce any evidence of premeditation. Defense counsel renewed the motion on the same grounds at the close of all evidence. The court denied the motion both times. The jury returned a verdict of guilty of murder in the first degree as charged. [The judge sentenced Coolen to death.]

* * * For the reasons discussed below, we find the evidence to be insufficient to support Coolen's conviction for first-degree murder.

Premeditation is the essential element which distinguishes first-degree murder from second-degree murder. * * * Premeditation is defined as

> more than a mere intent to kill; it is a fully formed conscious purpose to kill. This purpose to kill may be formed a moment before the act but must exist for a sufficient length of time to permit reflection as to the nature of the act to be committed and the probable result of that act.

While premeditation may be proven by circumstantial evidence, the evidence relied upon by the State must be inconsistent with every other reasonable inference. * ** Where the State's proof fails to exclude a reasonable hypothesis that the homicide occurred other than by premeditated design, a verdict of first-degree murder cannot be sustained. * * *

The State asserts that the following evidence establishes premeditation in the instant case. Barbara Kellar testified that Coolen suddenly attacked Kellar without warning or provocation. Jamie Caughman testified that Coolen had threatened him with the knife earlier in the evening, that he had seen Kellar and Coolen fight over a beer, and that Kellar tried to fend off Coolen during the attack. The State also contends that the deep stab wounds to Kellar's chest and back and the defensive wounds on his forearm and hand are indicative of the premeditated nature of the attack and inconsistent with Coolen's claim of self-defense.

Although this evidence is consistent with an unlawful killing, we do not find sufficient evidence to prove premeditation. Barbara Kellar testified that the two men had not been arguing and that Coolen simply "came out of nowhere" and starting stabbing her husband. Jamie Caughman described an ongoing pattern of hostility between two intoxicated men that culminated in a fight over a beer can. The testimony of these eyewitnesses is contradictory and neither provides sufficient evidence of premeditation. While the nature and manner of the wounds inflicted may be circumstantial evidence of premeditation, * * *, the stab wounds inflicted here are also consistent with an escalating fight over a beer (Jamie Caughman's account) or a "preemptive" attack in the paranoid belief that the victim was going to attack first (Coolen's version). Because the evidence was insufficient to prove premeditation, we reverse the conviction for first-degree murder and vacate the death sentence. * * *

As discussed above, we reverse Coolen's conviction for first-degree murder and vacate his death sentence. However, we find sufficient evidence in the record to sustain a conviction of second-degree murder.

Thus, in accordance with section 924.34, Florida Statutes (1995), this case is remanded to the trial court with instructions to enter a judgment for second-degree murder and to sentence Coolen accordingly. * * *

GRIMES, Justice, dissenting.

I cannot agree that the evidence was insufficient to convict Coolen of premeditated first-degree murder.

In *Sireci v. State,* 399 So.2d 964 (Fla. 1981), this Court said:

Premeditation is a fully-formed conscious purpose to kill, which exists in the mind of the perpetrator for a sufficient length of time to permit of reflection, and in pursuance of which an act of killing ensues. *Weaver v. State,* 220 So.2d 53 (Fla.Ct.App. 1969). Premeditation does not have to be contemplated for any particular period of time before the act, and may occur a moment before the act. *Hernandez v. State,* 273 So.2d 130 (Fla.Ct.App. 1973). Evidence from which premeditation may be inferred includes such matters as the nature of the weapon used, the presence or absence of adequate provocation, previous difficulties between the parties, the manner in which the homicide was committed and the nature and manner of the wounds inflicted. It must exist for such time before the homicide as will enable the accused to be conscious of the nature of the deed he is about to commit and the probable result to flow from it insofar as the life of his victim is concerned. *Larry v. State,* 104 So.2d 352 (Fla. 1958).

Thereafter, in *Penn v. State,* 574 So.2d 1079 (Fla. 1991), we explained:

Premeditation can be shown by circumstantial evidence. Whether or not the evidence shows a premeditated design to commit a murder is a question of fact for the jury.

Without apparent provocation, Coolen rushed over to the victim and stabbed him six times. Two of the stab wounds were defensive and one was in the back. When the victim's wife threw her body over his in order to protect him, Coolen also stabbed her several times.

Cool and calculated — no; but clearly premeditated. How can it be said that the jury could not reasonably conclude that Coolen intended to kill his victim? I respectfully dissent. * * *

Gilbert v. State
487 So.2d 1185 (Fl. Dist. Ct. App. 1986)

WALDEN, J.

Upon trial by jury, Roswell Gilbert was found guilty of the premeditated murder of his wife, Emily, in contravention of section 782.04(1)(a)1, Florida Statutes (1981). He, at age 75, was sentenced to life imprisonment. Under section 775.082, Florida Statutes (1981), there is a mandatory minimum sentence of 25 years. Thus, Mr. Gilbert would be incarcerated until he reached the age of 100 years before he would be eligible for release.

Mr. and Mrs. Gilbert lived together in a Fort Lauderdale condominium. They had been married for 51 years. Emily suffered from osteoporosis and Alzheimer's Disease. Her physician, Dr. Hidalgo, had prescribed Percodan to help alleviate the pain of the arthritis. The dosage was for moderate pain. There is no doubt that she was in pain because of the osteoporosis and sometimes confused because of the Alzheimer's.

At trial, appellant's attorney called a couple of Emily's friends, in addition to Dr. Hidalgo, to testify as to her physical and emotional condition before her death.

On direct examination Lillian Irvin testified that Emily was in a lot of pain because of the arthritis. One day, while Lillian was in her condominium office, Emily came in looking for appellant. She was upset and crying. He was in a condominium meeting, so Lillian called him out of the meeting to come and attend to his wife. When he arrived Emily said, "I'm so sick, I want to die, I'm so sick ... Ros I want to die, I want to die."

On cross-examination Lillian testified that Emily would come down from her tenth floor apartment every day to either look for appellant or walk around the condominium pool. The couple also went out to lunch every day.

Jacqueline Rhodes also testified for the defense. She stated that Emily had deteriorated during the last two years of their acquaintance. She was forgetful at times and in pain because of her back. In Jacqueline's opinion appellant had always been very kind and attentive to his wife.

On one particular occasion, Jacqueline went to the Gilberts' apartment and saw Emily lying on the sofa crying and looking very sick. This struck Jacqueline as particularly indicative of Emily's condition.

Appellant testified in his own defense. He recounted their lives together from the first incident of osteoporosis, which was approximately eight years before her death. As time progressed the arthritis worsened and then Emily began to lose her memory. This was diagnosed as Alzheimer's Disease. The manifestation of Emily's illness which appeared to bother appellant the most was her increased dependence on him.

Appellant then described the events which led up to Emily's death. On March 2, Emily had another bout with osteoporosis. The next day he took her to the hospital. Emily did not want to stay there and became uncooperative and insisted on going home. Finally, appellant decided it was best to take her home. This made Emily feel better.

On March 4, the day of the killing, appellant took Emily out to lunch as usual. When they got back he gave her four Percodan tablets, put her on the sofa and went to a condominium meeting. A few minutes later Emily followed him down to the meeting. Appellant left the meeting and took Emily back to their apartment. As she lay on the sofa, she said, "Please, somebody help me. Please, somebody help me." In his own words this is how appellant killed Emily:

> Who's that somebody but me, you know, and there she was in pain and all this confusion and I guess if I got cold as icewater that's what had happened. I thought to myself, I've got to do it, it's got to be mine, I've got to end her suffering, this can't go on.

> I went in. The gun was up on the top shelf with a clip in it. I loaded it with one shell, pulled the clip out. I don't like to leave loaded guns laying around.

Well, then I shot her in the head. I felt her pulse, I could still feel it. I thought, Oh, my God, I loused it up.

I went back to the shop. This time I was shaking. I wasn't cold as ice at all. Back to the shop, put another round in the gun, came back, put another bullet in her head.

The only comforting thing, the first shot there was no convulsive reaction, just her right hand shook like that fast and her head went over the impacted bullet and it slowly came down, didn't make any noise except her mouth just opened slowly like that and then, you know, I thought it hit so fast she didn't know what happened. Then I felt her pulse. It turned out I was wrong. The pulse keeps going after this episode for a few minutes anyway. I didn't know that. I just thought I had, you know--and the second time I fired I felt the pulse seemed to be gone. So I somehow got to the telephone and called the security guard downstairs and I said, "I just killed my wife," and —

His attorney continued the questioning:

[Mr. Varon:] Ros, why did you use a gun?

[Appellant:] I think poison is a horrible way to die. There's no such thing as instantaneous death with poison. I know nothing about poisons but I know that and I know nothing about poisons, I didn't have any. If I did have any, I wouldn't know how to use it. I'd probably louse it up, just get her terribly sick and that's not going to do any —

Q Ros —

A Firing a shot in the head will cause cessation of all consciousness in one millisecond, one thousandth of a second. I'm sure she didn't even hear the gun go off and I've been asked that question.
....

Q Why did you think that or did you feel that you're the only one that could have ended her suffering?

A Natural conclusion. I can't go to the medical people. They have no cure for Alzheimer's. The osteoporosis was getting worse slowly in time. Everything looked like it was converging to a climax.

Q Ros —

A I couldn't see any other end than her dying. If I put her in a nursing home, well, after that hospital thing I don't think a nursing home would take her. The hospital certainly wouldn't take her.

So I put her in a nursing home and they won't let me stay there and she's separated from me. It would be a horrible death for her. She would die.

Then I can't confide in my friends without getting them involved, you know, in this sort of thing that I did. I couldn't go to the doctor. He is a professional. He is duly bound to report it to the authorities and they would pull me out of the picture.

The whole thing was a mess and the only solution to me was to terminate her suffering. That's all.

Q Now, Ros —

A If I could continue?

Q Yes, please.

A I didn't consider what would happen to me at all. The only important thing was to terminate her suffering. I could take care of whatever happens to me and it's happening right now and that was of no consequence to me.

Sure, I know I was breaking the law but there seems to be things more important than the law, at least to me in my private tragedy. So it's murder. So what?

On cross-examination appellant testified that he had never talked with Emily about killing her and had decided to shoot her from behind so she would not see the gun.

The record reveals that up until the time of her death, Emily was always neat and well-dressed, wearing makeup, jewelry, and coordinated outfits. She also went to the hairdresser every two weeks up until the last week of her life.

Her doctor testified that Emily could have lived for another five to ten years. She was never bedridden or completely incapacitated.

The appellate presentation on behalf of appellant has been skilled, sensitive and innovative. Regardless, the task facing counsel was impossible or insurmountable in light of the uncontroverted facts and the current state of the law. While we will and do affirm, we shall discuss the several points:

Point 1. It is asserted on behalf of appellant that the trial court erred in refusing to give this charge on the word "felonious."

The Court will give you the definition of the word "feloniously" as follows:

Of, pertaining to, or having, the quality of felony. Proceeding from an evil heart or purpose; done with a deliberate intention of committing a crime. Without color of right or excuse. Malignantly; maliciously. Acting with a felonious intent; i.e., acting with intent to commit a felony.

We hold that no error was committed because the matter was adequately and correctly covered by the standard jury instruction on first degree murder which was given. That instruction provided:

In this case, Roswell Ward Gilbert is accused of murder in the first degree. Murder in the first degree includes the lesser crimes of murder in the second degree and manslaughter, all of which are unlawful. A killing that is excusable or was committed by the use of justifiable deadly force is lawful.

If you find Emily Gilbert was killed by Roswell Ward Gilbert, you will then consider the circumstances surrounding the killing in deciding if the killing was murder in the first degree or was murder in the second degree or was manslaughter or whether the killing was excusable or resulted from justifiable use of force, deadly force, that is.

Justifiable homicide: The killing of a human being is justifiable homicide and lawful if necessarily done while resisting an attempt to murder or commit a felony upon the defendant or to commit a felony in any dwelling house in which the defendant was at the time of the killing.

Excusable homicide: The killing of a human being is excusable and therefore lawful when committed by accident and misfortune in doing any lawful act by lawful means with usual ordinary caution and without any unlawful intent or by accident or misfortune in the heat of passion upon any sudden and sufficient provocation or upon a sudden combat without any dangerous weapon being used and not done in a cruel or unusual manner.

I will now instruct you on the circumstances that must be proved before Roswell Ward Gilbert may be found guilty of murder in the first degree or any lesser included crime.

Before you can find the defendant guilty of first degree premeditated murder the State must prove the following three elements beyond a reasonable doubt:

(1) Emily Gilbert is dead;

(2) The death was caused by the criminal act or agency of Roswell Ward Gilbert; and

(3) There was a premeditated killing of Emily Gilbert.

Killing with premeditation is killing after consciously deciding to do so. The decision must be present in the mind at the time of the killing. The law does not fix the exact period of time that must pass between the formation of the premeditated intent to kill and the killing.

The period of time must be long enough to allow reflection by the defendant. The premeditated intent to kill must be formed before the killing. The question of premeditation is a question of fact to be determined by you from the evidence. It will be sufficient proof of premeditation if the circumstances of the killing and the conduct of the accused convince you beyond a reasonable doubt of the existence of premeditation at the time of the killing.

Moreover, the term felonious is mere surplusage. * * * The crime of first degree murder as defined in section 782.04(1)(a)1, Florida Statutes (1981), does not include the definition of "felonious" as proposed by appellant, i.e., involving evil, malicious or malignant motivation or intent.

Finally, it is not reflected how appellant was prejudiced or how the outcome of the trial would have been different but for the exclusion.

[A] judgment will not be reversed for failure to give a particular charge where, as here, on the whole, the charges as given are clear, comprehensive and correct. * * *

Point 2. We hold that no error was committed by refusal of the court to instruct the jury on euthanasia and substituted judgment per these two requested instructions:

DEFENDANT'S REQUESTED INSTRUCTION NO. 4

The Court instructs the jury of the definition of Euthanasia to be:

The act or practice of painlessly putting to death persons suffering from incurable and distressing disease as an act of mercy.

The judge denied this instruction because there was no supporting evidence.* * *

In this case one of the principal defenses interposed by the Defendant, ROSWELL GILBERT, is for what he believed his wife wanted done under the circumstances and that he acted in good faith.

Euthanasia is not a defense to first degree murder in Florida and this court has been furnished with no law or statute to the contrary.

If a requested instruction is not a legal defense then there is no error in refusing it. * * * Having completely considered the written and oral appellate presentation, the judgment of conviction is AFFIRMED.

OWEN, WILLIAM C., Jr., Associate Judge, concurs.

GLICKSTEIN, J. Judge, concurring specially.

I agree in general with the reasoning of the majority, and entirely concur in the result.

Were this not a cause celebre, the opinion might well have read simply, "PER CURIAM AFFIRMED," for none of the appellant's contentions have merit. * * *

* * * I have some concern, also, about the hint in the main opinion that trial courts should be enabled to vary minimum mandatory sentences according to the "kind" of wrongdoer; e.g., hired killer versus misguided mercy killer. I do not favor opening the door to such distinctions.

My thoughts lie with the victim, who was silenced forever by appellant's criminal act. She would be no more dead if a hired gangland killer had pulled the trigger.

Can it be that we feel more comfortable about imposing severe punishment on persons we perceive to belong to a separate tribe, whom we label criminals, than on those we see as members of our own tribe? In fact, we are all members of a common humanity.

The Decalogue states categorically, "Thou shalt not murder." It draws no distinction between murder by members of the middle class and murder by members of an underclass. It draws no distinction between murder by a family member and murder by a stranger. It draws no distinction between murder out of a misguided notion of compassion and murder for hire.

The victims in all such cases are equally dead. If the act was deliberate, the minimum penalty should not vary with the actor's purported motivation.

The concept of permissive mitigation of the minimum penalty based upon a claim the motive for the killing was compassion is even more difficult to accept when the offender is sophisticated, educated and mature, and has enjoyed opportunities in life to make choices.

NOTES AND QUESTIONS

1. *Motive.* What role does motive play in determining the accused mens rea? Are the court decisions in *Coolen* and *Gilbert* consistent? Should other factors be considered in assessing the line between first and second degree murder?

2. *Factors Proving Premeditation.* Consider whether certain types of circumstantial evidence weigh in favor of finding premeditation, as described by the North Carolina Supreme Court in *State v. Jackson*, 343 S.E.2d 814 (N.C. 1986):

> Premeditation and deliberation relate to mental processes and ordinarily are not readily susceptible to proof by direct evidence. Instead, they usually must be proved by circumstantial evidence. Among other circumstances to be considered in determining whether a killing was with premeditation and deliberation are: (1) want of provocation on the part of the deceased; (2) the conduct and statements of the defendant before and after the killing; (3) threats and declarations of the defendant before and during the course of the occurrence giving rise to the death of the deceased; (4) ill-will or previous difficulty between the parties; (5) the dealing of lethal blows after the deceased has been felled and rendered helpless; and (6) evidence that the killing was done in a brutal manner. We have also held that the nature and number of the victim's wounds is a circumstance from which premeditation and deliberation can be inferred.

The California Supreme Court described three general categories of circumstantial evidence that can support a finding of premeditation:

> The type of evidence which this court has found sufficient to sustain a finding of premeditation and deliberation falls into three basic categories: (1) facts about how and what defendant did prior to the actual killing which show that the defendant was engaged in activity directed toward, and explicable as intended to result in, the killing — what may be characterized as "planning' activity"; (2) facts about the defendant's prior

relationship and/or conduct with the victim from which the jury could reasonably infer a "motive" to kill the victim, which inference of motive, together with facts of type (1) or (3), would in turn support an inference that the killing was the result of "a pre-existing reflection" and "careful thought and weighing of considerations" rather than "mere unconsidered or rash impulse hastily executed"; (3) facts about the nature of the killing from which the jury could infer that the manner of killing was so particular and exacting that the defendant must have intentionally killed according to a "preconceived design" to take his victim's life in a particular way for a "reason" which the jury can reasonably infer from facts of type (1) or (2). Analysis of the cases will show that this court sustains verdicts of first degree murder typically when there is evidence of all three types and otherwise requires at least extremely strong evidence of (1) or evidence of (2) in conjunction with either (1) or (3).

People v. Anderson, 447 P.2d 942 (Cal. 1968).

PROBLEM TWENTY-FOUR

Robbie was shot twice in the back of the head with a Glock 9mm pistol and found dead in the trunk of a car that had been abandoned in a wooded area. The vehicle was owned by Robbie. The police went to Robbie's home and found a pool of Robbie's blood on the floor. The police receive an anonymous tip that Terry had planned to meet with Robbie the evening of the shooting to buy drugs. The police interviewed an acquaintance of Terry's who said that Terry often carried a gun, and owned a number of weapons. Terry had a permit to carry a concealed weapon in the jurisdiction. The coroner's report stated that the shooter was approximately four feet away when firing the shots that killed Robbie, and the victim did not have any marks indicating a struggle or any defensive wounds. The police were unable to locate a Glock 9mm pistol after obtaining a search warrant for Terry's apartment and car, although they found other guns, some of which were not registered. The police also discovered ½ pound of 90% pure cocaine hidden in the back of a closet, which was the drug that Robbie usually sold. Terry gave a statement to the police and denied owning a Glock 9mm pistol. On the evening of the shooting, Terry admitted to going to see Robbie to buy drugs, but Robbie became angry when Terry told of being short $3,500 for the purchase. Terry said the additional funds would be available shortly, but Robbie started making threats to get a gun and shoot Terry. This made Terry fearful, and so Terry grabbed the drugs while trying to flee from the house. When Robbie lunged at Terry, Terry reached for a gun on a table, turned and shot Robbie, who was on the floor. Terry said that perhaps Robbie had tripped while trying to reach Terry. After shooting Robbie, Terry admitted to putting the body in the trunk of Robbie's car and driving it out of town to hide it. Terry then walked back to Robbie's house, throwing the gun into a dumpster along the way and then cleaning up any fingerprints that might have been left. Terry admits to the police to purchasing drugs from Robbie on one other occasion nine months earlier, and said they were not enemies.

The prosecutor is considering filing first degree murder charges against Terry. What would be the government's theory of first degree murder, and what evidence supports finding that Terry committed willful, deliberate, and premeditated murder? What arguments can Terry raise to rebut a charge of first degree murder?

B. Murder–Depraved Heart

State v. Doub, III
95 P.3d 116 (Kan. Ct. App. 2004)

GREENE, J.

* * * Following a party for his softball team at a club where he admitted drinking six beers, Doub admitted that his pickup struck two parked vehicles and that he left the scene because he was concerned that he had been drinking. Doub ultimately admitted that, approximately 2 hours after striking the parked cars, he drove his pickup into the rear of a Cadillac in which 9-year-old Jamika Smith was a passenger. According to the State's accident investigator, the collision occurred as Doub's pickup, "going tremendously faster," drove "up on top of [the Cadillac]," initially driving it down into the pavement, and ultimately propelling it off the street and into a tree. Doub offered no aid to the victims, left the scene of the accident, and initially denied any involvement in the collision, suggesting that his pickup had been stolen. Some 15 hours after the collision, Smith died as a result of blunt traumatic injuries caused by the collision.

Approximately 6 months after these events, Doub admitted to a former girlfriend that he had a confrontation with his second ex-wife the evening of the collision, had been drinking alcohol and smoking crack, and had subsequently caused the collision. The girlfriend approached the authorities with Doub's statements, which suggested that Doub left the softball party, caused the collisions with the parked vehicles, left that scene, subsequently consumed the additional alcohol and crack cocaine, and then caused the collision resulting in Smith's death, all within a 2- to 3-hour period.

Doub was charged with: (1) second-degree depraved heart murder. * * * Doub appeals. * * * When the sufficiency of the evidence is challenged in a criminal case, the standard of review is whether, after review of all the evidence, viewed in the light most favorable to the prosecution, the appellate court is convinced that a rational factfinder could have found the defendant guilty beyond a reasonable doubt. * * *

Elements of Second-Degree "Depraved Heart" Murder

K.S.A.2003 Supp. 21-3402 defines second-degree murder as follows:

"Murder in the second-degree is the killing of a human being committed:

(a) Intentionally; or

(b) unintentionally but recklessly under circumstances manifesting extreme indifference to the value of human life."

When the offense is committed pursuant to subsection (b), our courts have employed the common-law nomenclature of "depraved heart" second-degree murder. * * *

In *State v. Robinson,* [934 P.2d 38 (Kan. 1997)], our Supreme Court discussed the requirements for depraved heart murder:

> "Both depraved heart murder and reckless involuntary manslaughter require recklessness--that the killing be done under circumstances showing a realization of the imminence of danger and a conscious disregard of that danger. *Depraved heart murder requires the additional element that the reckless killing occur under circumstances manifesting extreme indifference to the value of human life.*
>
> ....
>
> "We hold that depraved heart second-degree murder requires a conscious disregard of the risk, sufficient under the circumstances, to manifest extreme indifference to the value of human life. *Recklessness that can be assimilated to purpose or knowledge is treated as depraved heart second-degree murder,* and less extreme recklessness is punished as manslaughter. Conviction of depraved heart second-degree murder requires proof that the defendant acted recklessly under circumstances manifesting extreme indifference to the value of human life. This language describes a kind of culpability that differs in degree but not in kind from the ordinary recklessness required for manslaughter." * * *

Overview of Depraved Heart Murder by Vehicle in Other Jurisdictions

The state of mind or *mens rea* required for second-degree murder has been somewhat problematic throughout the history of Anglo-American jurisprudence. As early as 1762, Sir Michael Foster termed the requisite mental state for the common-law offense as a "heart regardless of social duty and fatally bent upon mischief." Foster, CROWN LAW 257 (1762). Since the advent of the automobile in the nineteenth century, many jurisdictions have struggled with the application of second-degree murder statutes in this context, and the debate seems to have been focused largely on whether malice, whether express or implied, should be required. * * * We need not enter this debate, however, since our Supreme Court has determined that the 1993 amendment to the second-degree murder statute eliminated malice as an element of second-degree murder in Kansas. * * * Instead, our focus is the statutory language adopted in Kansas that apparently had its genesis in the Model Penal Code first proposed in 1962, which required killing "recklessly under circumstances manifesting extreme indifference to the value of human life." A.L.I., Model Penal Code § 210.2 (Proposed Official Draft 1962).

Since 1975 the appellate courts of many states have acknowledged that the required state of mind for depraved heart murder can be attributed to the driver of an automobile. * * * Our review of such cases reveals that most jurisdictions with statutory provisions patterned after the Model Penal Code have acknowledged that the offense may be committed by automobile. Cases to the contrary generally construe and apply statutes that retain some requirement of malice. * * *

One commentator surveyed 20 cases between 1975 and 1986 and found the following factors as persuasive of the requisite state of mind:

"1. *Intoxication.* The driver was using alcohol, illegal drugs, or both.

"2. *Speeding.* Usually excessive rates are recorded.

"3. *Near or nonfatal collisions shortly before the fatal accident.* Courts believe that collisions should serve as a warning to defendants that their conduct is highly likely to cause an accident. Failure to modify their driving is viewed as a conscious indifference to human life.

"4. *Driving on the wrong side of the road.* Many cases involve head-on collisions. Included here is illegally passing or veering into oncoming traffic.

"5. *Failure to aid the victim.* The driver left the scene of the accident and/or never attempted to seek aid for the victim.

"6. *Failure to heed traffic signs.* Usually more than once prior to the fatal accident, the driver ran a red light and/or stop sign.

"7. *Failure to heed warnings about reckless driving.* In *Pears v. State,* for example, the court cited as proof of Pears' extreme indifference to life the fact that he continued driving after he had been warned by police officers not to drive because he was intoxicated. In other cases a police pursuit of the driver for earlier traffic violations was an implicit warning that the defendant's driving was dangerous.

"8. *Prior record of driving offenses (drunk or reckless driving or both).* The relevance of a defendant's prior record for reckless or intoxicated driving is, as *United States v. Fleming* pointed out, not to show a propensity to drive while drunk but 'to establish that defendant had grounds to be aware of the risk his drinking and driving while intoxicated presented to others.'"

* * *

Application of these factors seems appropriate to determine whether evidence in a particular case meets the requisite state of mind, but we are mindful that no precise universal definition or exclusive criteria is appropriate. The comments to the Model Penal Code declare that "recklessness" must be of such an extreme nature that it demonstrates an indifference to human life similar to that held by one who commits murder purposely or knowingly, but precise definition is impossible.

"The significance of purpose of knowledge as a standard of culpability is that, cases of provocation or other mitigation apart, purposeful or knowing homicide demonstrates precisely such indifference to the value of human life. Whether recklessness is so extreme that it demonstrates similar indifference is not a question, it is submitted, that can be further clarified. It must be left directly to the trier of fact under instructions which make it clear that recklessness that can fairly be assimilated to purpose or knowledge should be treated as murder and that less extreme recklessness should be punished as manslaughter." A.L.I., Model Penal Code & Commentaries Part II § 210.2, Comment. 4, pp. 21-22 (1980).

The evidence against Doub is particularly damning considering that (a) he admits that his driving was preceded by drinking; (b) he admits that he struck two parked cars and ignored commands to stop because he was concerned that he had been drinking; (c) he then consumed additional alcohol and used crack cocaine; (d) he then resumed driving and caused a fatal collision, due in part to excessive speed; (e) he failed to render aid to the victims; and (f) he fled the scene in order to avoid criminal liability. We conclude that these facts clearly demonstrate an extreme indifference to human life.

Affirmed.

NOTE

It is important to recognize that homicide law distinguishes between ordinary recklessness and "depraved heart" recklessness. The line between the two is important, the former being manslaughter, the latter being murder (at common law, usually second degree). Many states are vague about the dividing line between the two terms, and those that seek to add clarity vary in how they do so. Some states seem to focus on the size of the risk. A substantial but relatively small risk of death would be manslaughter, a large risk murder. Others apparently require in addition to a large risk a defendant's appreciation of just how large is that risk. Still others add yet a third requirement: that the risk stem from an "anti-social motive," a term again undefined but including creating a risk of death to accomplish another crime. For example, assume that a defendant's guard dog attacked and killed his neighbor's three-year-old child. The defendant was aware of the risk and its size, having told the child's parents when they moved in to their property not to let the child wander onto the defendant's property because his guard dog might attack, seriously wounding or even killing the child. But the defendant had a trained attack dog roaming free on his property because he wanted to protect his huge marijuana grow behind his house from poachers. Growing marijuana is a crime, so endangering the child's life to protect the marijuana evidenced an "anti-social motive." Still other jurisdictions adopt a myriad of other tests, such as the apparent multi-factor test in *State v. Doub* above.

The Model Penal Code never uses the words "depraved heart." Instead, the Code declares homicide in section 210.2(b) to be murder when "it is committed recklessly under circumstances manifesting extreme indifference to the value of human life." It is manslaughter under section 210.3 (1)(a) to commit a homicide merely recklessly. Yet the Code never defines the difference between ordinary recklessness and recklessness manifesting extreme indifference to the value of human life. The explanatory notes and comments to the Code do not identify this language change as one of the "innovations" to be made to the common law. The Code's drafters apparently assumed therefore that it worked no substantive change to the common law depraved heart versus manslaughter distinction. If that is so, the extreme versus ordinary recklessness distinction under the MPC may be given meaning by analogizing to the common law depraved heart/ordinary reckless manslaughter distinction. The same sorts of factors as under common law (e.g,, size of the risk, appreciation of its size, and anti-social motive) should thus control, though case law and legislative history in any jurisdiction adopting the MPC's provisions must obviously be consulted to see whether any locality has taken a different approach.

The Model Penal Code also declares that "such recklessness and indifference are presumed if the actor is engaged in or is an accomplice in the commission of, or an attempt to commit, or flight after committing or attempting to commit robbery, rape or deviate sexual intercourse by force or threat of force, arson, burglary, kidnapping or felonious escape." Thus if a defendant commits a burglary and, in the course of doing so, the occupant runs down the stairs to confront the defendant, falling and dying, the defendant is presumed to be guilty of extreme reckless indifference murder. But the presumption is rebuttable. If the defendant can show that he was not reckless as to the risk of ending a human life at all, or was so reckless but did not manifest extreme indifference to the value of human life (perhaps because the risk was relatively small, or he did not appreciate its size), then he is not guilty of murder but only of burglary. Shortly we will study a common law form of murder known as felony murder which, roughly speaking, holds a defendant who kills during the course of a felony strictly liable for murder under certain circumstances. The Model Penal Code does not recognize felony murder (the Code rejects the strict liability aspect of the doctrine) but replaces it with this evidentiary presumption of murder when the death occurred during certain felonies.

While under the right circumstances a killing done with a vehicle can be depraved heart murder, some jurisdictions create a separate charge of "vehicular homicide" or even of "DUI [driving under the influence of alcohol] homicide." These charges are variously named and defined. In some states, merely causing a death while having a certain specified percentage of alcohol in the bloodstream constitutes DUI homicide. Vehicular homicide, often a more serious offense, might require proof of gross or wanton negligence or instead of recklessness.

PROBLEM TWENTY-FIVE

Five children, ages four to eight, were playing on a swing set in the back yard of Bobbi Wright. Wright lived in the end house of a series of row houses in a residential area in the City. Wright's yard was enclosed by a wrought-iron fence. At 6:00 p.m., Tomi, driving in a stolen car, made a left hand turn onto the street with the row houses; there is no evidence that Tomi was speeding. After making the turn, Tomi, in the thirty-six-foot wide street, attempted to make a U-turn. Tomi's car, however, instead jumped the four-inch-high curb, crashed through the wrought-iron fence, ran into the swing set where the children were playing, continued into the neighbor's yard, and did not come to a stop until it hit another vehicle; one child was killed by Tomi's car. Tomi fled from the scene of the accident and was later caught by neighbors. An accident reconstructionist's report states that from the markings on the roadway, Tomi accelerated the automobile while making the U-turn and at no time applied the brakes. A neighbor tells of hearing a car "burning rubber" immediately before the accident. Is this evidence sufficient to establish malice for a second-degree murder charge?

C. Manslaughter

CALIFORNIA PENAL CODE

§ 192. Manslaughter

Manslaughter is the unlawful killing of a human being without malice. It is of three kinds:

(a) Voluntary – upon a sudden quarrel or heat of passion.

(b) Involuntary – in the commission of an unlawful act, not amounting to felony; or in the commission of a lawful act which might produce death, in an unlawful manner, or without due caution and circumspection. This subdivision shall not apply to acts committed in the driving of a vehicle.

(c) [vehicular homicide].

MODEL PENAL CODE

§ 210.3. Manslaughter.

(1) Criminal homicide constitutes manslaughter when:

(a) it is committed recklessly; or

(b) a homicide which would otherwise be murder is committed under the influence of extreme mental or emotional disturbance for which there is reasonable explanation or excuse. The reasonableness of such explanation or excuse shall be determined from the viewpoint of a person in the actor's situation under the circumstances as he believes them to be.

(2) Manslaughter is a felony of the second degree.

People v. Pouncey
471 N.W.2d 346 (Mich. 1991)

MALLETT, Justice.

* * * The defendant-appellee, Ollie Pouncey, was convicted of one count of second-degree murder and one count of possessing a firearm at the time of commission or attempted commission of a felony.

The conviction arose out of an altercation that occurred on May 4, 1987. The defendant and his two friends, Mr. White and Mr. Johnston, were at Mr. White's home. They left Mr. White's house, drove around the corner to the home of Mr. Bland and accused him of stealing Mr. White's car. When Mr. Bland denied stealing the car, the defendant and his friends returned to Mr. White's home. As they pulled into the driveway of Mr. White's home, Mr. Bland, accompanied by his older brother and the victim, Steven Powers, approached.

Mr. Bland repeatedly denied knowing anything about the theft. At this point, Mr. White went into his house and did not come back outside until after the shooting. The defendant, as well as Mr. Johnston, the two Bland brothers, and Mr. Powers, remained outside.

As the argument continued, Mr. Powers threatened to put the defendant "on his head" and called the defendant names. The decedent walked towards the defendant, but Mr. Bland held the decedent back. The defendant said "don't walk up on me." There were no blows struck; indeed, there was no physical contact of any kind between the decedent, the defendant or anyone else. The defendant testified that the decedent was not armed.

After this verbal exchange, the defendant walked into the house. He went to the back of the house and retrieved a gun from a closet. He then came back outside, approximately thirty seconds later, carrying a shotgun. As he was coming out, he instructed Mr. Johnston to hit Mr. Powers with a monkey wrench. Mr. Johnston swung the wrench, but the decedent ducked out of the way. At that point, the defendant fired one shot, hitting Mr. Powers in the abdomen. Mr. Johnston ran home, as did the two Bland brothers, who called the police. The defendant and Mr. White drove off in the defendant's car.

The defendant was charged with first-degree murder and possession of a firearm during the commission of a felony. On the murder charge, the judge instructed the jury on first-degree murder, second-degree murder, involuntary manslaughter, and careless and reckless use of a firearm resulting in death. The judge refused the defendant's request for an instruction on voluntary manslaughter, finding that the evidence offered at trial did not support this offense. On September 22, 1987, the jury found the defendant guilty of second-degree murder and felony-firearm. He was sentenced to a term of ten to fifteen years for the murder conviction and a mandatory term of two years for the felony-firearm conviction.

The Court of Appeals reversed the decision of the trial court and remanded for a new trial. The panel believed there was sufficient evidence of provocation and passion in the record to support an instruction on voluntary manslaughter. The panel based its finding on various witnesses' testimony regarding the argument between the defendant and the decedent. * * * This Court granted leave to appeal * * * to consider whether the trial judge erred in not instructing on voluntary manslaughter, * * *.

It is the duty of the court to "instruct the jury as to the law applicable to the case. . . ." M.C.L. § 768.29; M.S.A. § 28.1052. However, a verdict shall not be set aside where the court fails to instruct on any point of law unless the accused requests such instruction.

It is undisputed that the defense counsel in this case made a proper request for an instruction on voluntary manslaughter. Therefore, the issue before us is whether the trial court's refusal to instruct on voluntary manslaughter was error.

The court's duty to instruct on the law applicable to the case depends on the evidence presented at trial. * * * To determine whether the judge erred in not instructing on voluntary manslaughter, we must ascertain whether there was evidence presented at the defendant's trial which would support a conviction of voluntary manslaughter. * * *

M.C.L. § 750.321; M.S.A. § 28.553 specifies the punishment for the crime of manslaughter. However, it is the common law which defines the crime. Voluntary manslaughter, an intentional killing, has been defined by this Court as follows:

> [I]f the act of killing, though intentional, be committed under the influence of passion or in heat of blood, produced by an adequate or reasonable provocation, and before a reasonable time has elapsed for the blood to cool and reason to resume its habitual control, and is the result of the temporary excitement, by which the control of reason was disturbed . . . then the law, out of indulgence to the frailty of human nature . . . regards the offense as of a less heinous character than murder, and gives it the designation of manslaughter. *Maher v. People,* 10 Mich. 212 (1862).

Murder and manslaughter are both homicides and share the element of being intentional killings. However, the element of provocation which characterizes the offense of manslaughter separates it from murder. Murder and manslaughter are separate offenses, but, as noted above, voluntary manslaughter is a cognate lesser included offense of murder.

The above definition of voluntary manslaughter encompasses several components which comprise the test for voluntary manslaughter: First, the defendant must kill in the heat of passion. Second, the passion must be caused by an adequate provocation. Finally, there cannot be a lapse of time during which a reasonable person could control his passions. * * *

The provocation necessary to mitigate a homicide from murder to manslaughter is that which causes the defendant to act out of passion rather than reason. * * * One commentator interprets the law as requiring that the defendant's emotions be so intense that they distort the defendant's practical reasoning:

> The law does not excuse actors whose behavior is caused by just any . . . emotional disturbance. . . . Rather, the law asks whether the victim's provoking act aroused the defendant's emotions to such a degree that the choice to refrain from crime became difficult for the defendant. The legal

doctrine reflects the philosophical distinction between emotions that only cause choice and emotions so intense that they distort the very process of choosing.

In addition, the provocation must be adequate, namely, that which would cause the reasonable person to lose control. * * * Not every hot-tempered individual who flies into a rage at the slightest insult can claim manslaughter. The law cannot countenance the loss of self- control; rather, it must encourage people to control their passions. * * *

The determination of what is reasonable provocation is a question of fact for the factfinder. * * * However, the judge does play a substantial role. The judge furnishes the standard of what constitutes adequate provocation, i.e., that provocation which would cause a reasonable person to act out of passion rather than reason. When, as a matter of law, no reasonable jury could find that the provocation was adequate, the judge may exclude evidence of the provocation. * * *

A review of the evidence establishes that none of the three prongs necessary for a finding of voluntary manslaughter are present. There is no evidence that the defendant was in a highly inflamed state of mind: he testified that at the time that he went into the house to retrieve the gun, he was not angry. This reveals that the defendant's ability to reason was not blurred by passion; his emotional state did not reach such a level that he was unable to act deliberately. Indeed, he stated that he was not angry at all. Even if he was scared and confused, his decision to retrieve the gun was a deliberate and reasoned act.

Furthermore, the claimed provocation in this case consists only of words, which other courts generally have held do not constitute adequate provocation, *Allen v. United States*, 164 U.S. 492 (1896), and in some instances words alone did not even justify an assault and battery, *Goucher v. Jamieson*, 82 N.W. 663 (Mich. 1900). However, words of an informative nature, rather than mere insults, have been considered adequate provocation. See LaFave & Scott, CRIMINAL LAW § 76. But this is not such a case, for this case involves insulting words, not words of an informational character. Nonetheless, we decline to issue a rule that insulting words per se are never adequate provocation. Instead, we reiterate that what constitutes adequate provocation is a factual question, and on these facts, the provocation was not adequate.

The evidence offered at trial painted a picture of a verbal fracas between six young men. The decedent insulted the defendant, but there were no punches thrown. There was no physical contact of any kind between the defendant, the decedent, or any of the six. The judge was absolutely correct in ruling that as a matter of law there was insufficient evidence to establish an adequate provocation. * * *

Finally, sufficient time passed to constitute a "cooling-off period." After a few insults were exchanged, the defendant went into the house, a safe harbor. There was no evidence that the defendant was compelled to go back outside by anyone. The defendant could have stayed in the house, as did Mr. White. Instead, the defendant chose to retrieve the shotgun from a closet in the back of the house and chose to go back outside. Once outside, shotgun in hand, he instructed Mr. Johnson to hit Mr. Powers with the wrench. When that failed, the defendant shot and killed Mr. Powers.

The evidence adduced at trial would not support finding the defendant guilty of voluntary manslaughter. This is the finding that the trial judge made in deciding not to give the requested instruction on voluntary manslaughter. Because of this, the trial judge was correct in refusing the requested instruction on voluntary manslaughter. To instruct the jury on an offense not supported by the evidence would confuse the jury, and be "a distortion of the factfinding process." * * *

The law of voluntary manslaughter developed as a means of taking into consideration the weaknesses of human beings. Key to any finding of voluntary manslaughter is evidence of adequate provocation that a reasonable factfinder could conclude that the defendant, overcome by emotion, could not choose to refrain from the crime. Adequate provocation does not excuse or justify murder, but rather designates one guilty of manslaughter less culpable than one guilty of murder.*** We reverse the decision of the Court of Appeals.

NOTES AND QUESTIONS

1. *Adequate Provocation.* Under the early English common law, adequate provocation was based on a limited number of rigid categories: "(1) an aggravated assault or battery; (2) mutual combat; (3) commission of a serious crime against a close relative of the defendant; (4) illegal arrest; and (5) observation of spousal adultery." JOSHUA DRESSLER, UNDERSTANDING CRIMINAL LAW § 31.07[B][2] (6th ed. 2012). More recently in *People v. Beltran*, ___ P.3d ___ 2013 WL 2372307 (Cal. 2013), the California Supreme Court stated:

> The Attorney General argues the provocation must be of a kind that would cause an ordinary person of average disposition to kill. We disagree. Nearly one hundred years ago, this court explained that, when examining heat of passion in the context of manslaughter, the fundamental "inquiry is whether or not the defendant"s reason was, at the time of his act, so disturbed or obscured by some passion . . . to such an extent as would render ordinary men of average disposition liable to act rashly or without due deliberation and reflection, and from this passion rather than from judgment." (People v. Logan (1917) 175 Cal. 45, 49 (Logan).) The proper

standard focuses upon whether the person of average disposition would be induced to react from passion and not from judgment.

2. ***Mere Words/Informational Words.*** The court in *Pouncey* notes that generally courts hold that mere words cannot be "adequate provocation." The court, however, does state that courts have found that informational words can serve as adequate provocation. What words might express sufficient information to rise to the level of convincing a jury that there was adequate provocation? In *State v Simonovich*, 688 S.E.2d 67 (N.C. Ct. App. 2010), the North Carolina Court of Appeals rejected a defendant's argument that his wife's statements about continuing to have affairs with other men was sufficient provocation to permit the trial judge to instruct the jury on voluntary manslaughter in a first degree murder prosecution:

> In the case before us, Defendant and Inna were in bed when they began arguing. Defendant testified he was aware of Inna's past relationships with other men and her stated intent to continue that behavior. There was no evidence that Defendant had found Inna in the very act of intercourse, or under circumstances clearly indicating that the act had just been completed, or was severely proximate. There was, therefore, no evidence that Defendant was driven to strangle Inna by a legally recognized heat of passion. To the contrary, Defendant himself testified that he put his hands on Inna's throat because he "simply wanted her to shut up, not to aggravate [him], not to make [him] mad."

> Although Defendant acknowledges that he did not find Inna in the very act of intercourse, or under circumstances clearly indicating that the act had just been completed, or was 'severely proximate, he "requests that [this Court] extend existing case law to consider the evidence of on-going adulterous behavior of a spouse, along with the promise to continue the adulterous intercourse, to be adequate provocation and sufficiently proximate to warrant a voluntary manslaughter instruction." Our Supreme Court has developed longstanding case law governing the range of legally adequate provocations for voluntary manslaughter. Defendant's conduct is clearly not within that range and our Court cannot extend existing case law in the manner requested by Defendant. Because there was no evidence that Defendant was driven to kill Inna by a legally recognized adequate provocation, we find no error in the trial court's refusal to instruct the jury on voluntary manslaughter.

3. ***Reasonable Person.*** Adequate provocation usually uses an objective standard, that being, would a reasonable person be provoked. Some courts, however, have added some subjectivity. For example, a court might look at the reasonable person as if he or she were placed in the actor's situation. Which provides a fairer standard, an objective or subjective test? Consider the following excerpt from *Commonwealth v. Halbert*, 573 N.E.2d 975 (Mass. 1991):

One of the grounds on appeal raised by defendant was that " the judge erred in refusing to instruct the jury on manslaughter where there was evidence of provocation." In affirming the conviction, the court stated:

"Instructions on voluntary manslaughter must be given if there is evidence of provocation deemed adequate in law to cause the accused to lose his self-control in the heat of passion, and if the killing followed the provocation before sufficient time had elapsed for the accused's temper to cool." * * * Provocation is viewed objectively: "the jury must be able to infer that a reasonable person would have become sufficiently provoked." * * * This court has consistently rejected the argument that provocation should be viewed subjectively through the eyes of the accused.* * * In determining whether an instruction is warranted we view the evidence in the light most favorable to the defendant. * * * We conclude that the facts of this case did not warrant an instruction on manslaughter.

The defendant suggests that he was provoked by the victim's homosexual advance, which consisted of the victim's putting his hand on the defendant's knee and asking, "Josh, what do you want to do?" The defendant offered evidence that he was sexually abused as a child and that he was the victim of a homosexual "gang" rape shortly before the night of the murder. While the defendant's history of sexual abuse is tragic, it has no bearing on the question whether the victim's conduct satisfied the objective test of provocation. The issue is: would the victim's nonthreatening physical gesture and verbal invitation have provoked a reasonable person into a homicidal rage?

The victim's question ("Josh, what do you want to do?") was neither insulting nor hostile; it was at most a salacious invitation. Clearly, neither the question nor the accompanying physical gesture (the victim's placing his hand on the defendant's knee) would have been "likely to produce in an ordinary person such a state of passion, anger, fear, fright, or nervous excitement as would eclipse his capacity for reflection or restraint."* * * Because the evidence was insufficient to support a finding of reasonable provocation, the judge did not err in refusing to instruct the jury on voluntary manslaughter. * * *

4. *Sudden Heat of Passion With No Opportunity to Cool Off.* What will be considered sufficient time? In an unreported decision, *State v. Grigsby*, 2001 WL 585685 (Ohio Ct. App. 2001), the court looked at what constitutes an adequate cooling off time to warrant an instruction on voluntary manslaughter and held:

* * * On the morning of August 25, 1999, Grigsby took his girlfriend, Monica Seldon, to her place of employment. The two had been involved in an argument that morning, resulting in Grigsby breaking up with her when he dropped her off at work.

That afternoon, Seldon's friend, Raymond Captain, arrived at her place of work to give her a ride home. Captain's car was parked in front of Seldon's place of employment and the two were sitting in the car, when Grigsby pulled up in Seldon's car. Seldon informed Captain that she would ride home with Grigsby. As Seldon got out of Captain's car and began to gather up her belongings, Grigsby approached the car and attempted to shoot Captain. For some reason, the gun did not discharge. Grigsby then walked around to the front of the vehicle. Grigsby proceeded to shoot Seldon twelve times; ten of the shots were fired after Seldon fell to the ground. Captain exited his car and began to run away, at which time Grigsby turned and fired twice at him. Grigsby then got back in Seldon's car, drove away and disposed of the gun. Upon his arrest, Grigsby admitted that he shot Seldon, but did not recall shooting at Captain.

* * * Grigsby first argues that the trial court erred by denying his request to instruct the jury on Voluntary Manslaughter, a lesser-included offense of Murder. * * * To establish Voluntary Manslaughter, one must show that: (1) there was reasonable provocation; (2) the defendant was in fact provoked; (3) a reasonable man would not have "cooled off" in the time between the provocation and the offense; and (4) the defendant did not in fact "cool off." * * *

Here, Grigsby contends that he was seriously provoked by the fact that he and Seldon argued and broke up in the morning, and by the fact that when he went to pick her up after work, she was in the car with another man. He claims that he was "pissed," and that "it is clear that seeing the mother of one's children in a car with another man shortly after an acrimonious fight in which his relationship was ended would be sufficient" to show serious provocation, and a lack of cooling-off time.

The record shows that Grigsby was aware that Captain and Seldon were merely friends. The only possible provocation shown on this record is the argument that occurred in the morning when Grigsby broke up with Seldon. The crime occurred more than seven hours later. Grigsby has failed to show that a reasonable person would not have cooled off between the time of the fight and the time of the killing. Therefore, we conclude that the trial court did not err in denying the requested instruction. * * *

5. *Lesser-Included Offense Instruction*. The Michigan Supreme Court held in *Pouncey* that there was insufficient evidence of a heat-of-passion defense to require

the trial court to instruct the jury that it could find the defendant guilty of manslaughter. Why does the judge get to decide a factual issue rather than the jury, and when is the court required to give an instruction on a lesser offense? The Minnesota Supreme Court explained the analysis in *Stiles v. State*, 664 N.W.2d 315 (Minn. 2003):

> Our case law on lesser-included offenses mandates that the trial court instruct the jury on the requested offense if the defendant establishes three things: the lesser offense is included in the higher charge, the evidence provides a rational basis for acquitting the defendant of the offense charged, and the evidence provides a rational basis for convicting the defendant on the lesser-included offense. The mandatory nature of the rule acts as a safeguard within our jury system. As the United States Supreme Court has noted, it safeguards against juries who may be improperly predisposed to find defendants guilty by offering the jury alternatives. See *Keeble v. United States*, 412 U.S. 205 (1973) ("[w]here one of the elements of the offense charged remains in doubt, but the defendant is plainly guilty of some offense, the jury is likely to resolve its doubts in favor of conviction"). If, over the course of a trial, evidence develops that would provide a rational basis to acquit on the charged crime, and the defense counsel requests an instruction on a lesser-included offense supported by the evidence, the judge should grant it lest the jury be left with a Hobson's choice between the higher offense or nothing.

6. ***Lesser Included Offenses Defined***. But when is one offense a lesser included offense of another? Once again, the term's definition varies among jurisdictions and may even vary within a single jurisdiction, depending upon the specific offenses involved. A common definition, stated in commonsense terms, is this: one offense is a lesser included offense of another if the greater offense includes all the elements of the lesser offense. For example, common law robbery is often defined as a larceny accomplished by force or its threat from the person or immediate presence of another. Proving robbery thus automatically also proves all the elements of larceny, so larceny is a lesser included offense of robbery. But if the alleged "lesser" offense in fact includes at least one element that the greater one does not, then the lesser offense is not a lesser *included* offense of the greater. For example, in *Carter v. United States*, 530 U.S. 255 (2000), the Court interpreted the federal bank robbery statute as not including the specific intent permanently to deprive another (a departure from the common law definition of ordinary robbery). But the Court concluded that the lesser theft offense did include a specific intent to "steal or purloin," that is, to permanently deprive another. Although bank robbery included most of the same elements as theft, it did not include *all* the elements of theft because bank robbery lacked the specific intent that theft required. Therefore, theft was not a lesser included offense of federal bank robbery. In some jurisdictions, one offense's merely being a lesser included offense of another may entitle the defendant to a jury instruction on that offense upon request. In other

jurisdictions, however, it must also be the case that there is a rational basis for a jury acquitting a defendant on the greater charge before he may receive an instruction on the lesser charge. The reason for this rule is to avoid compromise verdicts, that is, the jury acquitting the defendant of the greater charge, convicting him only of the lesser charge, because of sympathy for the defendant rather than the absence of evidence.

7. **Strategic Choice.** Can a defense lawyer object to an instruction on a lesser-included offense, in the hope that if the jury has only the "Hobson's choice" between a higher charge and acquittal, it will opt not to find the defendant guilty of the charged offense? In *Commonwealth v. Woodward*, 694 N.E.2d 1277 (Mass. 1998), a woman who served as a nanny was charged with second-degree murder in connection with the death of the child for whom she cared. The case, known as the "Nanny Murder Trial," generated substantial publicity. The trial court acceded to defense counsel's request and refused to give the state's proposed involuntary manslaughter instruction as a lesser-included offense to murder. The jury returned a verdict of guilty on the second-degree murder charge, which the trial court then reduced to involuntary manslaughter on the ground that it should have given the lesser-included offense instruction. In reviewing the decision not to give the lesser-included offense instruction, the Massachusetts Supreme Judicial Court stated:

> Authorities elsewhere hold overwhelmingly that the prosecution has a right to jury instructions on lesser included offenses, on request, if the evidence so warrants, in spite of a defendant's objection. As far as we are aware, no jurisdiction that has considered the issue has allowed a defendant to veto a lesser included offense instruction properly requested by the prosecution.

8. **Model Penal Code.** Does the fact that the Model Penal Code approach uses "influence of extreme mental or emotional disturbance," dramatically change the definition of voluntary manslaughter? What if the *Pouncey* and *Grigsby* cases where tried in a MPC jurisdiction, would the results be different? Consider the following case:

People v. White
590 N.E.2d 236 (N.Y. 1992)

MEMORANDUM.

[The Appellate Division] properly concluded, contrary to defendant's contention on this appeal, that the trial court did not err in refusing to instruct the jury on the affirmative defense of extreme emotional disturbance.

In order for defendant to be entitled to such an instruction, a court must determine that sufficient credible evidence has been presented for the jury to find, by a preponderance of the evidence, that the elements of the affirmative defense have been established. The affirmative defense has two components: an objective element requiring sufficient proof that there was a reasonable explanation or excuse for the emotional disturbance, and a subjective element requiring sufficient proof that the conduct was influenced by an extreme emotional disturbance at the time the alleged crime was committed. This appeal centers on the second element.

We note initially that defendant's steadfast claim of innocence cannot defeat his entitlement to the instruction solely because an affirmative defense of extreme emotional disturbance would be inconsistent with an outright denial of involvement in the crime. Here, however, defendant's repeated claims of innocence necessarily impacted upon the sufficiency of the evidence offered to demonstrate that he acted under the influence of extreme emotional disturbance at the time of the homicide.

Viewing the evidence in the light most favorable to the defendant, as we must in considering whether the instruction should have been given, we agree with the Appellate Division that defendant may have met his burden with respect to the first element of the affirmative defense by evidence of a violent and tumultuous relationship with his wife. The fact that defendant had been repeatedly humiliated by her was sufficient to establish the requisite provocation. However, the second element of this defense cannot be inferred from the provocative act itself, which occurred weeks before the homicide.

While the passage of time alone is not sufficient to defeat, as a matter of law, a claim of extreme emotional disturbance, there nevertheless remains the need for some proof that a temporally remote provocative act affected the defendant at the time of the homicide to such a degree that a jury could reasonably conclude that he acted under the influence of an extreme emotional disturbance. This record is barren of any statement of defendant or other witnesses, or any other evidence, establishing the events which immediately preceded the commission of the crime or defendant's state of mind at the time the homicide occurred. Thus, any findings the jury might have made in this respect would have been pure speculation.

Defendant concedes that the evidence upon which he relies to support the subjective element of the affirmative defense is largely circumstantial and focuses primarily on his actions after the homicide. As he testified, after he found his wife dead in their apartment, he washed her body, wrapped it in a bedspread and placed it in a closet in their apartment where it remained, decomposing, for one week, as he went about his daily activities of cleaning and cooking for his stepchildren. He contends that this posthomicide circumstantial evidence of highly abnormal activity, considered in the light of the prior tumultuous relationship with the deceased, is probative of his state of mind at the time of the killing such that the jury could have inferred that he was acting under the influence of an extreme emotional disturbance.

We disagree and conclude that this evidence, which relates solely to defendant's posthomicide conduct, failed to establish the necessary second element of the affirmative defense. Thus, instructing the jury as to the defense, under the circumstances of this case, would have done no more than invite impermissible speculation as to defendant's state of mind at the time of the killing.

Contrary to defendant's contention, neither *People v. Moye*, 489 N.E.2d 736 (N.Y. 1985), nor *People v. Roe*, 542 N.E.2d 610 (N.Y. 1989), requires a different result. In contrast to the paucity of evidence here, in *Moye*, defendant's heinous acts, combined with his numerous statements made to the police and the prosecutor regarding his state of mind and the events that transpired immediately prior to the killing, constituted sufficient evidence of a loss of self-control associated with the affirmative defense of extreme emotional disturbance so as to warrant the charge. In *Roe*, our primary concern was not, as here, defendant's mens rea but whether an objective assessment of the circumstances surrounding defendant's discharge of a shotgun was sufficient to support a finding of the serious risk of death required for depraved indifference murder.

NOTE

The Model Penal Code equivalent to the Common Law's "heat of passion" defense is broader in scope and combines elements of the "diminished responsibility" variant of the insanity defense. Under the Code, a defendant who kills either purposely or knowingly is guilty of manslaughter if she kills the victim while suffering "from an extreme emotional disturbance for which there is a reasonable explanation or excuse." In turn, the reasonable explanation or excuse is subjectively judged "from the viewpoint of a person in the actor's situation under the circumstances as he believes them to be." Contrasting with the heat of passion defense, EED (Extreme Emotional Disturbance) does not require a legally adequate provocation by the victim or that the defendant act in the heat of passion when he commits the homicide. Further, the reasonable explanation or excuse refers to the extreme emotional disturbance and not to the homicide. In effect, the defendant need not furnish a "reasonable explanation or excuse" for the homicide; rather, she must establish that the emotional disturbance was either reasonable or excusable. The MPC merely requires the defendant who asserts the defense to produce evidence that she suffered from EED at the time of killing (see MPC § 1.12 (2)), then the burdens shifts to the prosecution to disprove the defense beyond a reasonable doubt. Most states that have adopted EED, however, require that the defendant prove the defense by a preponderance of the evidence.

PROBLEM TWENTY-SIX

Early one morning, Harper, armed with a revolver, went to the home of Harper's sibling, Avery. The front door was locked, so Harper pushed open the home's kitchen door in order to enter. Once inside, Harper threatened a ten-year old niece with a gun until she told Harper that Avery was upstairs in the bedroom. On the stairway, Harper encountered Avery's spouse, Kai. When Kai saw Harper, Kai ran down the hallway to the back door. Harper pursued Kai down the hall, pointing a gun at Kai. Kai saw that Harper was only a few feet away. Kai then saw Avery come up from behind Harper. Kai called out "Avery." Harper then turned around and shot Avery twice in rapid succession. Harper said nothing during the entire episode. Avery died from the gunshot wounds. Harper was apprehended shortly after the shooting about one half mile away from the house where the shooting occurred.

At trial for the crime of murder, Harper offered into evidence the testimony of a psychiatrist who interviewed the defendant about eleven months after the shooting. The psychiatrist testified that the defendant, at the time of the shooting, was acting under extreme emotional disturbance caused by a combination of child custody problems, the inability to maintain a recently purchased home and an overwhelming fear of Avery. The psychiatrist emphasized the history of conflict between the two siblings, noting that the defendant referred to Avery as a "killer." The defendant told the psychiatrist that at one time Avery took a tire iron from a bus and chased Harper with this tire iron. The defendant stated that this incident was so frightening that it caused Harper to leave the area for a couple of years. The psychiatrist believed that this incident, compounded by the other extenuating circumstances of dealing with child custody problems and the inability to maintain a recently purchased home resulted in the defendant's overwhelming fear of Avery.

Is Harper entitled to a jury instruction on the "heat of passion" defense? Is Harper entitled to a similar instruction on the MPC's extreme emotional disturbance defense?

§ 8.03 Unintentional Killings

GEORGIA PENAL CODE

§ 16-5-3. Involuntary manslaughter

(a) A person commits the offense of involuntary manslaughter in the commission of an unlawful act when he causes the death of another human being without any intention to do so by the commission of an unlawful act other than a felony. A person who commits the offense of involuntary manslaughter in the commission of an unlawful act, upon conviction thereof, shall be punished by imprisonment for not less than one year nor more than ten years.

(b) A person commits the offense of involuntary manslaughter in the commission of a lawful act in an unlawful manner when he causes the death of another human being without any intention to do so, by the commission of a lawful act in an unlawful manner likely to cause death or great bodily harm. A person who commits the offense of involuntary manslaughter in the commission of a lawful act in an unlawful manner, upon conviction thereof, shall be punished as for a misdemeanor.

MODEL PENAL CODE

§ 210.4. Negligent Homicide.

(1) Criminal homicide constitutes negligent homicide when it is committed negligently.

(2) Negligent homicide is a felony of the third degree.

State v. Williams
484 P.2d 1167 (Wash. Ct. App. 1971)

HOROWITZ, J.

Defendants, husband and wife, were charged by information filed October 3, 1968, with the crime of manslaughter for negligently failing to supply their 17-month child with necessary medical attention, as a result of which he died on September 12, 1968. Upon entry of findings, conclusions and judgment of guilty, sentences were imposed on April 22, 1969. Defendants appeal.

The defendant husband, Walter Williams, is a 24-year-old full-blooded Sheshont Indian with a sixth-grade education. His sole occupation is that of laborer. The defendant wife, Bernice Williams, is a 20-year-old part Indian with an 11th grade education. At the time of the marriage, the wife had two children, the younger of whom was a 14-month son. Both parents worked and the children were cared for by the 85-year-old mother of the defendant husband. The defendant husband assumed parental responsibility with the defendant wife to provide clothing, care and medical attention for the child. Both defendants possessed a great deal of love and affection for the defendant wife's young son.

* * * That both defendants were aware that William Joseph Tabafunda was ill during the period September 1, 1968 to September 12, 1968. The defendants were ignorant. They did not realize how sick the baby was. They thought that the baby had a toothache and no layman regards a toothache as dangerous to life. They loved the baby and gave it aspirin in hopes of improving its condition. They did not take the baby to a doctor because of fear that the Welfare Department would take the baby away from them. They knew that medical help was available because of previous experience. They had no excuse that the law will recognize for not taking the baby to a doctor.

The defendants Walter L. Williams and Bernice J. Williams were negligent in not seeking medical attention for William Joseph Tabafunda.

That as a proximate result of this negligence, William Joseph Tabafunda died. * * * Defendants take no exception to findings but contend that the findings do not support the conclusions that the defendants are guilty of manslaughter as charged. The contentions raise two basic issues, (1) the existence of the duty to furnish medical aid charged by the information to be violated and the seriousness of the breach required; and (2) the issue of proximate cause, *i.e.,* whether defendants were put on notice, in time to save the child's life, that medical care was required. Because the nature of the duty and the quality or seriousness of the breach are closely interrelated, our discussion of the first issue involved will embrace both matters.

Parental duty to provide medical care for a dependent minor child was recognized at common law and characterized as a natural duty.* * * In Washington, the existence of the duty is commonly assumed and is stated at times without reference to any particular statute. * * * The existence of the duty also is assumed, but not always defined, in statutes that provide special criminal and civil sanctions for the performance of that duty.* * * On the question of the quality or seriousness of breach of the duty, at common law, in the case of involuntary manslaughter, the breach had to amount to more than mere ordinary or simple negligence — gross negligence was essential.* * * Under these statutes [in Washington] the crime is deemed committed even though the death of the victim is the proximate result of only simple or ordinary negligence.

The concept of simple or ordinary negligence describes a failure to exercise the "ordinary caution" necessary to make out the defense of excusable homicide. * * * Ordinary caution is the kind of caution that a man of reasonable prudence would exercise under the same or similar conditions. If, therefore, the conduct of a defendant, regardless of his ignorance, good intentions and good faith, fails to measure up to the conduct required of a man of reasonable prudence, he is guilty of ordinary negligence because of his failure to use "ordinary caution."* * * If such negligence proximately causes the death of the victim, the defendant, as pointed out above, is guilty of statutory manslaughter.

In the instant case, defendants contend that the only duty to provide medical care for the infant child is the statutory duty set forth in RCW 26.20.030; that the court having concluded that the defendants were not guilty of "willful . . . misconduct," that no duty to furnish medical care was violated and that, accordingly, defendants are not guilty of the crime of statutory manslaughter charged in the information.

RCW 26.20.030 (1) (b) makes it a felony for a person who "willfully omits, without lawful excuse, to furnish necessary . . . medical attendance for his or her child . . ." The words "willfully omits" are, as pointed out in *State v. Russell,* 442 P.2d 988 (1968), used in two senses, namely, (1) "an act or omission done intentionally . . ." or (2) when used in statutes making nonsupport a crime, "an absence of lawful excuse or justification on the part of the accused parent." * * * Hence, RCW 26.20.030 is presumptively violated either because a defendant intentionally omits to furnish necessary medical care, or omits so to do without lawful excuse. * * *

We need not, however, rest our decision solely on the above-mentioned grounds. The information charging statutory manslaughter made no mention of and did not purport to restrict itself to the violation of the duty set forth in RCW 26.20.030 (1) (b). The information charged the violation of "the legal duty of providing necessary . . . medical attention to said . . . minor child . . ." This general language permits reliance upon the existence of the legal duty no matter from what source derived. We have already pointed out that such a parental duty is recognized in the decisions of this state and has been characterized as a natural duty existing independently of statutes. * * * We therefore hold that the violation of the parental duty to furnish medical care to a minor dependent child, the other elements of manslaughter being present, is a sufficient basis on which to rest a conviction of the crime of manslaughter under RCW 9.48.060 and 9.48.150. * * *

In the instant case, however, the defendant husband is not the father of the minor child, nor has he adopted that child. Nevertheless, the evidence shows that he had assumed responsibility with his wife for the care and maintenance of the child, whom he greatly loved. Such assumption of responsibility, characterized in the information as that required of a "guardian and custodian," is sufficient to impose upon him the duty to furnish necessary medical care. * * *

The remaining issue of proximate cause requires consideration of the question of when the duty to furnish medical care became activated. If the duty to furnish such care was not activated until after it was too late to save the life of the child, failure to furnish medical care could not be said to have proximately caused the child's death. Timeliness in the furnishing of medical care also must be considered in terms of "ordinary caution." The law does not mandatorily require that a doctor be called for a child at the first sign of any indisposition or illness. The indisposition or illness may appear to be of a minor or very temporary kind, such as a toothache or cold. If one in the exercise of ordinary caution fails to recognize that his child's symptoms require medical attention, it cannot be said that the failure to obtain such medical attention is a breach of the duty owed. * * * We quite agree that the Code does not contemplate the necessity of calling a physician for every trifling complaint with which the child may be afflicted which in most instances may be overcome by the ordinary household nursing by members of the family; that a reasonable amount of discretion is vested in parents, charged with the duty of maintaining and bringing up infant children; and that the standard is at what time would an ordinarily prudent person, solicitous for the welfare of his child and anxious to promote its recovery, deem it necessary to call in the services of a physician. * * *

* * * Dr. Gale Wilson, the autopsy surgeon and chief pathologist for the King County Coroner, testified that the child died because an abscessed tooth had been allowed to develop into an infection of the mouth and cheeks, eventually becoming gangrenous. This condition, accompanied by the child's inability to eat, brought about malnutrition, lowering the child's resistance and eventually producing pneumonia, causing the death. Dr. Wilson testified that in his opinion the infection had lasted for approximately 2 weeks, and that the odor generally associated with gangrene would have been present for approximately 10 days before death. He also expressed the opinion that had medical care been first obtained in the last week before the baby's death, such care would have been obtained too late to have saved the baby's life. Accordingly, the baby's apparent condition between September 1 and September 5, 1968 became the critical period for the purpose of determining whether in the exercise of ordinary caution defendants should have provided medical care for the minor child.

The testimony concerning the child's apparent condition during the critical period is not crystal clear, but is sufficient to warrant the following statement of the matter. The defendant husband testified that he noticed the baby was sick about 2 weeks before the baby died. The defendant wife testified that she noticed the baby was ill about a week and a half or 2 weeks before the baby died. The evidence showed that in the critical period the baby was fussy; that he could not keep his food down; and that a cheek started swelling up. The swelling went up and down, but did not disappear. In that same period, the cheek turned "a bluish color like." The defendants, not realizing that the baby was as ill as it was or that the baby was in danger of dying, attempted to provide some relief to the baby by giving the baby aspirin during the critical period and continued to do so until the night before the baby died. The defendants thought the swelling would go down and were waiting for it to do so; and defendant husband testified, that from what he had heard, neither doctors nor dentists pull out a tooth "when it's all swollen up like that." There was an additional explanation for not calling a doctor given by each defendant. Defendant husband testified that "the way the cheek looked, ... and that stuff on his hair, they would think we were neglecting him and take him away from us and not give him back." Defendant wife testified that the defendants were "waiting for the swelling to go down," and also that they were afraid to take the child to a doctor for fear that the doctor would report them to the welfare department, who, in turn, would take the child away. "It's just that I was so scared of losing him." They testified that they had heard that the defendant husband's cousin lost a child that way. The evidence showed that the defendants did not understand the significance or seriousness of the baby's symptoms. However, there is no evidence that the defendants were physically or financially unable to obtain a doctor, or that they did not know an available doctor, or that the symptoms did not continue to be a matter of concern during the critical period. Indeed, the evidence shows that in April 1968 defendant husband had taken the child to a doctor for medical attention.

In our opinion, there is sufficient evidence from which the court could find, as it necessarily did, that applying the standard of ordinary caution, *i.e.,* the caution exercisable by a man of reasonable prudence under the same or similar conditions, defendants were sufficiently put on notice concerning the symptoms of the baby's illness and lack of improvement in the baby's apparent condition in the period from September 1 to September 5, 1968 to have required them to have obtained medical care for the child. The failure so to do in this case is ordinary or simple negligence, and such negligence is sufficient to support a conviction of statutory manslaughter. * * * The judgment is affirmed.

NOTES AND QUESTIONS

1. ***Gross or Simple Negligence.*** The *Williams* court states the common law requirement that gross negligence is usually required for an involuntary manslaughter prosecution, while under the Washington statute only ordinary negligence was required. What is the difference between the two standards? In *Mills v. State*, 282 A.2d 147 (Md. Ct. Sp. App. 1971), the Maryland Court of Special Appeals stated that "where a charge of involuntary manslaughter is predicated on negligently doing some act lawful in itself, the negligence necessary to support a conviction must be gross or criminal, viz., such as manifests a wanton or reckless disregard of human life." How is this standard different from depraved heart for second degree murder, or the civil standard of ordinary negligence? In *Williams*, if the common law standard had applied, would the result be different? Could the defendants have been charged with murder based on proof of malice?

2. ***Causation.*** The court in the *Williams* case states that "proximate cause requires consideration of the question of when the duty to furnish medical care becomes

activated." Would the amount of evidence necessary to meet the element of causation differ depending on whether the court uses a standard of gross or simple negligence? [See Chap. 5].

PROBLEM TWENTY-SEVEN

Lou was cooking steaks on a backyard grill at a neighborhood gathering when Lou began to speak with Jamie, a new neighbor. As the two chatted, they began to flirt with one another and Jamie engaged Lou in horseplay by poking Lou with a fork. Lou began poking Jamie back with a steak knife that Lou was holding. The horseplay continued for two minutes, with both laughing as they tried to poke the other gently with the utensil. Lou then stuck Jamie in the abdomen with the steak knife, creating a deep cut that went through the stomach and pierced Jamie's aorta. Jamie collapsed and died in less than five minutes. The jurisdiction follows the common law for homicide offenses, requiring proof of malice for second degree murder, punishable by up to life in prison, and recklessness for involuntary manslaughter, punishable by up to fifteen years in jail. The state also has a negligent homicide statute that requires proof of "ordinary negligence," punishable by up to two years in the county jail. As the prosecutor, what crime (if any) should Lou be charged with for the death of Jamie? If given the opportunity to meet with the prosecutor before any charges are filed, what argument(s) should defense counsel make regarding the appropriate disposition of the matter?

§ 8.04 The Felony Murder Rule

The felony murder rule developed in the United States as a separate means to hold a person liable for a killing. The rule provides that if a person causes the death of another during the course of a felony, or an attempt to commit the felony, then the killing constitutes murder. In a jurisdiction that divides murder into degrees, this type of murder would be in the second degree, although a number of states provide in their homicide statutes that killings during certain specified felonies raise the charge to first degree murder. By 1900, a number of states adopted statutes making a killing during the commission of specified felonies, such as burglary, rape, and robbery, a basis for first degree murder. Guyora Binder, *The Origins of American Felony Murder Rules*, 57 STAN. L. REV. 59 (2004). In recent years, many states have expanded the number of offenses that can trigger liability for first degree murder to include child and spousal abuse. To be held liable for the killing, it does not matter whether the death was intentional, and the government need not prove any level of *mens rea* for the killing, just the intent for the underlying felony (or attempted felony) that led to the death. Thus, even completely unintended or accidental deaths can trigger liability if the killing was during the course of and in furtherance of a felony.

The felony murder rule is often justified as a means to deter people from committing a crime because they may be held liable for murder regardless of whether there was any intent to kill or even injure another. A related argument is that the rule deters felons from committing felonies carelessly or in a dangerous manner since they may be liable for the accidental events that arise during the crime. Critics of the rule argue that it extends liability for murder too far, imposing significant punishment even though the person never intended to do anything more serious than to commit the underlying felony. While courts and commentators have expressed significant hostility toward the felony-murder rule, the legislatures have embraced it in large part because of the ease with which a murder charge can be proved against a defendant who is not entirely appealing.

Hines v. State
578 S.E.2d 868 (Ga. 2003)

FLETCHER, Chief Justice.

While hunting, Robert Lee Hines mistook his friend Steven Wood for a turkey and shot him dead. A jury convicted Hines of felony murder based on the underlying crime of possession of a firearm by a convicted felon, but acquitted him of felony murder based on the underlying felony of misuse of a firearm while hunting.

Hines contends that a convicted felon's possession of a firearm while turkey hunting cannot be one of the inherently dangerous felonies required to support a conviction for felony murder. "The only limitation on the type of felony that may serve as an underlying felony for a felony murder conviction is that the felony must be inherently dangerous to human life." A felony is "inherently dangerous" when it is "'dangerous per se'" or "'by its circumstances create[s] a foreseeable risk of death.'" Depending on the facts, possession of a firearm by a convicted felon can be an inherently dangerous felony.

In *Ford v. State*, [423 S.E.2d 255 (Ga. 1992)] the defendant was a convicted felon who was unloading a handgun when it accidentally discharged, went through the floor, and killed an occupant of the apartment below. A jury convicted Ford for felony murder based on his felonious possession of a firearm. This Court reversed, finding that, because no evidence showed the defendant knew there was an apartment below him or that the victim was present, his possession of a firearm could not support a conviction for felony murder.

In contrast to *Ford,* Hines intentionally fired his shotgun intending to hit his target. He had been drinking before he went hunting, and there was evidence that he had been drinking while hunting. He knew that other hunters were in the area and was unaware of their exact location. He also knew that other people visited the area in which he was hunting. He took an unsafe shot at dusk, through heavy foliage, at a target eighty feet away that he had not positively identified as a turkey. Under these circumstances, we conclude that Hines's illegal possession of a firearm created a foreseeable risk of death. Accordingly, Hines's violation of the prohibition against convicted felons possessing firearms was an inherently dangerous felony that could support a felony murder conviction. * * * Judgment affirmed.

SEARS, Presiding Justice, dissenting.

Because I conclude that circumstances surrounding Hines's commission of the status felony of possessing a firearm were not inherently dangerous within the meaning of our decision in *Ford v. State,* I dissent to the majority's affirmance of Hines's conviction of felony murder.

In *Ford,* this Court held that for a felony to serve as the basis for a felony murder conviction, it had to be inherently dangerous by its very nature or had to be committed under circumstances creating a foreseeable risk of death. We also held that the imputation of malice that justifies the felony murder rule is dependent on the "perpetrator's life- threatening state of mind accompanying [the] commission [of the underlying felony]." In *Ford,* however, we did not specify how to determine whether a particular felony, either by its nature or as it was committed, was inherently dangerous to human life. Because of the severe punishments that accompany a conviction of murder and because it is illogical to impute malice for purposes of felony murder "'from the intent to commit a felony not [foreseeably] dangerous to human life,' I conclude that for purposes of our felony-murder doctrine, a felony is inherently dangerous per se or as committed if it carries" "'a high probability' that [a human] death will result." This standard will ensure that our felony murder rule is not inappropriately expanded by "reducing the seriousness of the act which a defendant must commit in order to be charged with murder."

In the present case, I conclude that the possession of a firearm by Hines was not committed in a fashion that was inherently dangerous and that carried a high probability that death would result. The fact that Hines was hunting, a dangerous sport; the fact that he had been drinking before he went hunting; the fact that he was hunting at dusk; and the fact that he fired a shot when he knew other hunters were in the general area in which he was hunting may establish that Hines was negligent, but do not establish that his acts created a high probability that death to a human being would result, or that he had a "life-threatening state of mind." Moreover, as for the fatal shot, Hines testified that he heard a turkey gobble, that he "saw it fan out," and that he then fired at the object. Even though Hines may not, as stated by the majority, have positively identified his target as a turkey, he had to make a split-second decision regarding his target and concluded, based on hearing a gobble and seeing something "fan out," that the object was a turkey. I cannot conclude that, under these circumstances, the failure of the hunter to identify his target beyond doubt carried a high probability that a human being would be killed or that he acted with a "life-threatening state of mind." The death in this case is clearly a tragic incident, and Hines's conduct before and after the shooting was reprehensible. But the sanction of life in prison for murder should be reserved for cases in which the defendant's moral failings warrant such punishment. Here, the application of the felony murder statute to Hines's actions punishes him more severely than his culpability merits. In this regard, Hines will be serving the same punishment–life in prison–as an arsonist convicted of felony murder who firebombed an apartment that he knew was occupied, causing the death of two young children, and the same punishment as an armed robber convicted of felony murder who entered a store with a firearm and shot and killed a store employee. This result is unwarranted and unnecessary, as Hines could be prosecuted and convicted of an appropriate lesser crime, such as involuntary manslaughter or the misuse of a firearm while hunting.

One final note. Hunting is a time-honored recreational activity encouraged by the State of Georgia and enjoyed by many of our State's citizens. No doubt a number of hunters have probably engaged in negligent hunting practices similar to those in this case. Although I do not condone such careless practices, neither can I agree with subjecting so many hunters to the possibility of spending life in prison when they do not fastidiously follow proper hunting procedures and accidentally shoot a fellow hunter. * * * For the foregoing reasons, I dissent to the majority opinion.

NOTES AND QUESTIONS

1. *Inherently Dangerous.* What test should be used in deciding whether a crime is inherently dangerous? Some courts look at the statute in the abstract and decide whether the offense is inherently dangerous. The California Supreme Court explained in *People v. Burroughs*, 201 Cal. Rptr. 319 (Cal. 1984), why an abstract approach is appropriate:

> In assessing whether the felony is inherently dangerous to human life, we look to the elements of the felony in the abstract, not the particular facts of the case. This form of analysis is compelled because there is a killing in every case where the rule might potentially be applied. If in such circumstances a court were to examine the particular facts of the case prior to establishing whether the underlying felony is inherently dangerous, the court might well be led to conclude the rule applicable despite any unfairness which might redound to the defendant by so broad an application: the existence of the dead victim might appear to lead inexorably to the conclusion that the underlying felony is exceptionally hazardous. We continue to resist such unjustifiable bootstrapping.

Other states look to the facts and circumstances of the underlying felony because the felony murder rule is designed to deter criminals from committing offenses in a reckless fashion. Consider the analysis of the Maryland Court of Appeals in *Fisher v. State*, 786 A.2d 706 (Md. 2001):

> In our view the abstract approach undermines one of the primary purposes of the modern felony murder rule. The modern version of the rule is intended to deter dangerous conduct by punishing as murder a homicide resulting from dangerous conduct in the perpetration of a felony, even if the defendant did not intend to kill. If the felonious conduct, under all of the circumstances, made death a foreseeable consequence, it is reasonable for the law to infer from the commission of the felony under those circumstances the malice that qualifies the homicide as murder. The abstract approach, however, eliminates this inference merely because death is not a necessary consequence of the felony, i.e., because the felony could have been committed in a non-mortally-dangerous manner.

Florida's homicide statute, § 782.04 lists a total of seventeen felonies that qualify as predicate felonies under the felony murder rule and render the actor liable for first degree murder. The felonies listed as qualifying felonies include such felonies as escape, aircraft piracy, trafficking in controlled substances, and other offenses. Furthermore, the statute punishes as "murder in the third degree" any death that occurs when the defendant is engaged in the perpetration or attempted perpetration of a felony not enumerated in the first degree murder category. Therefore, through statutory definition, Florida avoids the ambiguity raised by the "inherently dangerous" felony doctrine.

2. ***Causation.*** Would the defendant's position in *Hines* be better served by the argument that there is no causal relationship with the underlying felony and the crime? Some states do not require any greater proof of causation for a felony murder charge than the defendant setting in motion a chain of events leading to the death, essentially cause-in-fact. For example, the Oklahoma Court of Criminal Appeals held, "The legislature's definition of [felony] murder . . . is a reflection of the policy that one who, by his willful criminal conduct, sets in motion a chain of events so perilous to the sanctity of human life that death results therefrom; must bear the ultimate responsibility for his actions." *Hatch v. State*, 662 P.2d 1377 (Okla. Cr. App. 1983). Other states require a closer connection between the death and the underlying felony. Consider the Connecticut Supreme Court's analysis in *State v. Young*, 469 A.2d 1189 (Conn. 1983):

> [T]he phrase "in furtherance of" was intended to impose the requirement of a relationship between the underlying felony and the homicide beyond that of mere causation in fact, similar to the concept of proximate cause in the law of torts. Primarily its purpose was to limit the liability of a person whose accomplice in one of the specified felonies has performed the homicidal act to those circumstances which were within the contemplation of the confederates to the undertaking, just as the liability of a

principal for the acts of his servant is similarly confined to the scope of the agency.

3. ***Mens Rea***. Does the felony murder rule eliminate proof of mens rea, or does it eliminate proof of mens rea only for the murder? Felony murder is termed a strict liability crime, yet it clearly does not meet the factors used to determine whether a crime falls within that category of offenses. There is a high penalty, a significant stigma, and murder is a common law crime. The "strict liability" comes from the imposition of liability for a crime without requiring proof of the intent to commit that crime, but rather deriving it from the proof of intent for the underlying felony. As described by the Wyoming Supreme Court in *Mares v. State*, 939 P.2d 724 (Wyo. 1997): "The felony murder statute imposes a form of strict responsibility on those perpetrating the underlying felony for killings occurring during the commission of that felony; the intent to kill is not an element of the crime. Even so, the State is not relieved of establishing a mens rea. Rather, the necessary intent the State must prove to convict a person of felony murder is the intent associated with the underlying felony."

Hawaii and Kentucky have abolished felony murder by statute. HAW. REV. STAT. ANN. § 707.701; KY. REV. STAT. ANN. § 507.020. A few states do not permit the simple transfer of the intent for the underlying felony to the murder charge, instead requiring proof of malice for the killing. See *State v. Ortega*, 817 P.2d 1196 (N.M. 1991). In Michigan, once a jury finds the defendant acted with malice, which would be sufficient to prove second-degree murder, it can then convict the defendant of first-degree murder if the malice killing occurred during the course of one of the felonies enumerated in the first-degree murder statute. *People v. Aaron*, 299 N.W.2d 304 (Mich. 1980).

4. ***Proof of Murder***. Prosecutors frequently charge murder under alternative theories, and use felony-murder as a fall-back position in second-degree murder cases. This is because the proof of the underlying felony will often allow the prosecutor to argue that the intent to commit the felony shows the defendant acted with the requisite high degree of recklessness to establish malice for a second-degree murder charge. If the jury does not find malice, it can still convict the defendant of murder based on the proof of the felony. First-degree murder charges based on the felony murder rule permit the prosecutor to bypass the much more difficult intent standard for that crime. Indeed, in many felony murder cases the prosecutor could not prove the defendant acted willfully, deliberately and with premeditation because the death was accidental or otherwise unintended.

5. ***Sentencing.*** In some jurisdictions the court will only permit a defendant to be sentenced on one homicide offense for each person killed. Thus, if the prosecutor charges both murder and felony murder for the same homicide, the case might proceed to trial on both counts, but if found guilty on both counts the judge would sentence only on one of these convictions. Similarly, a few states do not permit

imposition of a sentence for both the felony-murder and the underlying felony offense.

6. ***Misdemeanor-Manslaughter Rule.*** Most states permit a prosecution for manslaughter rather than murder when the death occurs during the commission of an offense that is a misdemeanor rather than a felony. The Model Penal Code suggests abolition of the misdemeanor-manslaughter rule, but not the felony-murder rule. Why the difference? The misdemeanor-manslaughter rule developed as a response to the harshness of the penalty for murder under the common law. See Fred T. Harring, Note, *The Misdemeanor-Manslaughter Rule: Dangerously Alive in Michigan*, 42 WAYNE L. REV. 2149 (1994); see also Rudolph J. Gerber, *The Felony Murder Rule: Conundrum Without Principle*, 31 ARIZ. ST. L.J. 763 (1999).

State v. Contreras
46 P.3d 661 (Nev. 2002) (en banc)

BECKER, J.

* * * This case arises out of an incident at the Roundhouse Motel in Carson City on August 23, 1998. Based on the limited record submitted, it appears that prior to the incident resulting in the charged crimes, respondent Evans was involved in a separate altercation at the motel. The police arrived and investigated that incident. Later that evening, apparently in retaliation for the previous altercation, respondent Evans allegedly gathered the other respondents, and they proceeded back to the motel with metal and wooden clubs. Respondents knocked on a motel room door, and when the door opened, rushed into the room and proceeded to beat Samuel Resendiz and Carlos Lainez. Resendiz died as a result of his injuries.

* * * Respondents filed a motion to dismiss the first-degree felony-murder charge based on the merger doctrine. The district court granted respondents' motion to dismiss the felony-murder charge. The State appeals. * * *

Nevada's statutory scheme has long recognized the felony-murder rule. NRS 200.030(1)(b) defines first-degree felony murder as a murder that is committed in the perpetration or attempted perpetration of certain enumerated crimes, including burglary. The felonious intent involved in the underlying felony is deemed, by law, to supply the malicious intent necessary to characterize the killing as a murder, and because felony murder is defined by statute as first-degree murder, no proof of the traditional factors of willfulness, premeditation, or deliberation is required for a first-degree murder conviction.

In this case, the prosecutor charged both traditional second-degree murder, requiring proof of malicious intent (without premeditation and deliberation), and first-degree felony murder, based on the allegation that the defendants entered the premises "with the intent then and there to apply force and violence" and thereby alleging the felony of burglary. The district court relied on the merger doctrine to dismiss the felony-murder charge, holding that the burglary merged into the homicide because both involved the same intent — the defendants' intent to apply force and violence to the victims.

In so holding, the district court relied on the California Supreme Court's decision in *People v. Wilson* [462 P.2d 22 (Cal. 1969)]. In *Wilson,* the defendant was charged with felony murder based on burglary. The burglary was alleged to have occurred when the defendant broke into his wife's home with the intent to assault her with a deadly weapon. The California court stated:

> [T]he only basis for finding a felonious entry is the intent to commit an assault with a deadly weapon. When, as here, the entry would be nonfelonious but for the intent to commit the assault, and the assault is an integral part of the homicide and is included in fact in the offense charged, utilization of the felony-murder rule extends that doctrine "beyond any rational function that it is designed to serve." We have heretofore emphasized "that the felony-murder doctrine expresses a highly artificial concept that deserves no extension beyond its required application."

The California court concluded that the purpose of the felony-murder rule, to deter felons from killing negligently or accidentally, was not met when the underlying felony has the same general mental purpose as the homicide — to physically harm the victim. Therefore, in *Wilson,* the California Supreme Court merged the two crimes and held that a felony-murder conviction was not appropriate because the intent in committing the burglary was the same as the intent in committing the homicide.

The California Supreme Court's decision in *Wilson* was an extension of the merger doctrine as previously applied by California and other states. California and many other states have applied the merger doctrine as a limitation on felony murder when a prosecutor has attempted to charge felony murder based on a felonious assault or battery that culminates in a homicide. In these cases, the courts have held that the battery merges into the homicide. Absent such merger, virtually every homicide would be felony murder, and the traditional factors of willfulness, premeditation and deliberation would never be required for a first-degree murder conviction. This application of the merger doctrine has not been considered in Nevada because NRS 200.030(1)(b), the felony-murder statute, does not include assault or battery as crimes that support a felony-murder charge.

Not all courts, however, have followed California's approach in felony-murder cases based on burglary with intent to assault. For example, the New York Court of Appeals in *People v. Miller* [297 N.E.2d 85 (N.Y. 1973)] held that any burglary, including one based on intent to assault, justifies application of the felony-murder rule. The New York court's rationale was that homicide is more likely to result when the assault is committed within the victim's home rather than in the street, even if the criminal intent in both locations is the same. The court stated:

> It should be apparent that the Legislature, in including burglary as one of the enumerated felonies as a basis for felony murder, recognized that persons within domiciles are in greater peril from those entering the domicile with criminal intent, than persons on the street who are being subjected to the same criminal intent. . . When the assault takes place within the domicile, the victim may be more likely to resist the assault; the victim is also less likely to be able to avoid the consequences of the assault, since his paths of retreat and escape may be barred or severely restricted by furniture, walls and other obstructions incidental to buildings. Further, it is also more likely that when the assault occurs in the victim's domicile, there will be present family or close friends who will come to the victim's aid and be killed. Since the purpose of the felony-murder statute is to reduce the disproportionate number of accidental homicides which occur during the commission of the enumerated predicate felonies by punishing the party responsible for the homicide not merely for manslaughter, but for murder, the Legislature, in enacting the burglary and felony-murder statutes, did not exclude from the definition of burglary, a burglary based upon the intent to assault, but intended that the definition be "satisfied if the intruder's intent, existing at the time of the unlawful entry or remaining, is to commit *any crime.*"

* * * Although Nevada's statutory scheme is basically the same as California's, and the purpose of the felony-murder statute has been stated to be the same, we find the reasoning of the New York court on this issue more persuasive. The Nevada Legislature has specifically included burglary as one of the crimes that can escalate a homicide to first-degree murder without the necessity of proving premeditation and deliberation. There is a rational basis for including burglary in the felony-murder statute, even when the criminal intent behind the burglary is assault or battery. In *Wilson,* the California court minimizes the impact of the location of an assault. Yet the likelihood of harm to individuals is greater when they are encountered in a dwelling or an enclosed space where escape or outside intervention is less likely than if they are encountered on the street. In the instant case, it certainly appears that the attack in a motel room held greater risk of homicide for the victims than if they had been outside and better able to escape or receive help.

We do not believe it is appropriate to apply the merger doctrine to felony murder when the underlying felony is burglary, regardless of the intent of the burglary. The legislative language is clear, and we are not persuaded that any policy considerations should override the legislature's determination that burglary should be one of the enumerated felonies appropriate to elevate a homicide to felony murder. We, therefore, hold that the district court was incorrect in dismissing the felony-murder charge against the respondents.

SHEARING, J., with whom ROSE and LEAVITT, JJ., agree, dissenting.

I would affirm the judgment of the district court dismissing the first-degree felony-murder charge. The intent required to make the entry into the motel room a burglary, namely, the intent to apply force and violence to the victims, is the same intent that supports the felony-murder charge The felony-murder rule raises a homicide to first-degree murder without requiring the State to prove the traditional first-degree murder elements of willfulness, premeditation, and deliberation. The felonious intent involved in the underlying felony is regarded as sufficient intent to raise the resulting homicide to first-degree murder. When the felonious intent involved in committing the burglary is the same intent involved in the resulting homicide, the felony-murder rule is expanded beyond the reason for its existence. * * *

The California court [in *Wilson*] concluded that the purpose of the felony-murder rule, to deter felons from killing negligently or accidentally, is not met when the underlying felony has the same general mental purpose as the homicide—to physically harm the victim. The court went on to say:

> In [*People v. Ireland*, 450 P.2d 580 (Cal. 1969)], we rejected the bootstrap reasoning involved in taking an element of a homicide and using it as the underlying felony in a second degree felony-murder instruction. We conclude that the same bootstrapping is involved in instructing a jury that the intent to assault makes the entry burglary and that the burglary raises the homicide resulting from the assault to first degree murder without proof of malice aforethought and premeditation. To hold otherwise, we would have to declare that because burglary is not technically a lesser offense included within a charge of murder, burglary constitutes an independent felony which can support a felony-murder instruction. . . . [A] burglary based on intent to assault with a deadly weapon is included in fact within a charge of murder, and cannot support a felony-murder instruction.

* * * Here, when the defendants entered the building with the intent to harm the victims, the purpose of the felony-murder rule was not implicated because the subsequent harm to the victims was not negligent or accidental; harm to the victims was the very reason for the defendants' entry into the motel room. * * * Where, as here, the intent in both the underlying felony and the homicide is the same, application of the felony-murder rule does not further the rule's intended purpose, to prevent accidental or negligent killing, but rather, extends the rule unjustly.

Felony murder itself is an anomaly in that, unlike most felonies, it does not require that the defendant intend the resulting harm; on the contrary, it addresses accidental or unintentional killing. Application of the felony-murder rule when the underlying felony involves the intent to do serious bodily harm defeats the purpose of the rule and unfairly elevates a crime to first-degree murder without requiring the State to prove willfulness, deliberation, and premeditation. The State here has every opportunity to prove second-degree murder.

NOTES

1. ***Merger and First Degree Felony Murder***. If the "do not convict of felony murder where the underlying crime is a violent felony" rule is the most important application of the merger rule but is not itself the merger rule, then what exactly is the merger rule? Here confusion reigns. Courts often recite the rule without defining it, as if its meaning should be clear, and reach a conclusion about its application to a particular set of facts without explaining its underlying reasoning.

The merger rule is stated differently in every jurisdiction where it has been adopted. In *People v. Wilson*, 462 P. 2d 22 (Cal. 1969), discussed in *Contreras*, the California Supreme Court limited felony murder to those situations in which there was an "independent felonious purpose" for the underlying felony. In *People v. Farley*, 210 P.3d 61 (Cal. 2009), the court overturned its holding in *Wilson* when the underlying felony is one of the crimes enumerated for first degree murder. According to the California Supreme Court:

> In enacting section 189, the Legislature did not limit the definition of burglary, or exclude burglaries based upon an intent to assault. Rather, section 189 applies the felony-murder rule to all burglaries. Under section 459, also enacted in 1872, burglary is committed when the defendant "enters any [defined structure] with intent to commit grand or petit larceny or any felony," including assault. Thus, nothing in the language of section 189 supports the application of the merger doctrine to its terms.

Thus, courts disagree over whether a burglary (which does not by definition involve violence) done for the purpose of committing an assault inside the residence should merge or not. A note on terminology: If the felony "merges" into the homicide, then the felony murder rule cannot be applied; if the felony does not merge into the homicide, then the felony murder rule does apply (if all the rule's other limitations are met).

The best way to make sense of this confusion is to view the merger question as one of policy: Would applying the felony murder rule to this specific set of facts best serve, or instead undermine, the purposes of the rule? Answering that question of course requires knowing what is indeed the felony murder rule's purpose. But here too jurisdictions are often murky and disagree among themselves. The most commonly stated purpose is to discourage felons from engaging in their felonies in ways that create more danger to human life than minimally meeting the elements of the felony would otherwise require. In other words, do your felonies carefully. Under this view, the reason we do not punish deaths resulting from violent felonies as felony murder is that the felonies created risks of death or serious bodily injury anyway; they cannot be committed by definition without generating these risks, and the potential sentence is therefore already high. There is no need to add the extra punishment of felony murder to discourage the violence. The penalty already in place for the felony often does the job just fine.

2. *Second Degree Felony Murder*. Unless a statute specifies that a killing during the commission of a specified offense is first degree murder, then it can only be prosecuted as second degree murder. The California Supreme Court rejected application of the merger doctrine to enumerated offenses for first degree murder, it took a much more expansive approach to the doctrine in *People v. Chun*, 203 P.3d 425 (Cal. 2009). The court held that for a charge of second degree felony murder, "When the underlying felony is assaultive in nature . . . we now conclude that the felony merges with the homicide and cannot be the basis of a felony-murder instruction. An 'assaultive' felony is one that involves a threat of immediate violent injury."

The crime of assault can be committed in two ways: by an attempt to commit a battery, or by intentionally placing another person in fear of an imminent battery. Both forms of the offense involve some potential for an unlawful touching, and states have different degrees of the offense based on the potential harm to the victim or the use of a weapon, such as "assault with intent to commit great bodily harm" or "assault with a deadly weapon." Under *Chun*'s analysis, unless the underlying felony is enumerated in the first degree murder statute, then it cannot form the basis for a second degree murder prosecution if it involves a type of crime that comes within the broad category of including assaultive conduct.

The Oklahoma Court of Criminal Appeals took the opposite approach to applying the merger doctrine to second degree felony murder in *Barnett v. State*, 263 P.3d 959 (Okla. 2011), rejecting its application that had been followed in the state for over a century. The court stated:

> The felony crimes of assault and battery, child neglect, caretaker abuse and neglect, operation of a motor vehicle while intoxicated, unlawful possession and use of firearms and explosives, using a vehicle to facilitate intentional discharge of a firearm, and a host of other felonies,

can have deadly consequences. The Legislature is well within reason to define killings during the commission of these dangerous felonies as murder, even when the felony is not "independent" of the act or acts resulting in death. Indeed, it is when such felonies destroy life that they are most deserving of the infamy and punishment of murder. Continued adherence to the merger doctrine. . . would, in many instances, nullify the proper exercise of the Legislature's power to define and punish murder. We will not follow that course.

State v. Sophophone
19 P.3d 70 (Kan. 2001)

LARSON, J.:

This is Sanexay Sophophone's direct appeal of his felony-murder conviction for the death of his co-felon during flight from an aggravated burglary in which both men participated.

The facts are not in dispute. Sophophone and three other individuals conspired to and broke into a house in Emporia. The resident reported the break-in to the police.

Police officers responded to the call, saw four individuals leaving the back of the house, shined a light on the suspects, identified themselves as police officers, and ordered them to stop. The individuals, one being Sophophone, started to run away. One officer ran down Sophophone, hand-cuffed him, and placed him in a police car.

Other officers arrived to assist in apprehending the other individuals as they were running from the house. An officer chased one of the suspects later identified as Somphone Sysoumphone. Sysoumphone crossed railroad tracks, jumped a fence, and then stopped. The officer approached with his weapon drawn and ordered Sysoumphone to the ground and not to move. Sysoumphone was lying face down but raised up and fired at the officer, who returned fire and killed him. It is not disputed that Sysoumphone was one of the individuals observed by the officers leaving the house that had been burglarized. * * *

Sophophone moved to dismiss the felony-murder charges, contending the complaint was defective because it alleged that he and not the police officer had killed Sysoumphone and further because he was in custody and sitting in the police car when the deceased was killed and therefore not attempting to commit or even fleeing from an inherently dangerous felony. His motion to dismiss was denied by the trial court.

* * *Sophophone does not dispute that aggravated burglary is an inherently dangerous felony which given the right circumstances would support a felony-murder charge. His principal argument centers on his being in custody at the time his co-felon was killed by the lawful act of the officer which he contends was a "break in circumstances" sufficient to insulate him from further criminal responsibility.

This "intervening cause" or "break in circumstances" argument has no merit under the facts of this case. We have held in numerous cases that "time, distance, and the causal relationship between the underlying felony and a killing are factors to be considered in determining whether the killing occurs in the commission of the underlying felony and the defendant is therefore subject to the felony-murder rule." * * * Based on the uncontroverted evidence in this case, the killing took place during flight from the aggravated burglary, and it is only because the act which resulted in the killing was a lawful one by a third party that a question of law exists as to whether Sophophone can be convicted of felony murder. * * *

Our cases are legion in interpreting the felony-murder statute, but we have not previously decided a case where the killing was not by the direct acts of the felon but rather where a co-felon was killed during his flight from the scene of the felony by the lawful acts of a third party (in our case, a law enforcement officer). * * *

The two different approaches applicable are succinctly set forth in Comment, *Kansas Felony Murder: Agency or Proximate Cause?*, 48 KAN. L.REV. 1047, 1051-52 (2000), in the following manner:

> There are two basic approaches to application of the felony-murder doctrine: the agency and proximate cause theories. The agency approach, which is the majority view, limits application of the doctrine to those homicides committed by the felon or an agent of the felon. Under such an approach, "[t]he identity of the killer becomes the threshold requirement for finding liability under the felony-murder doctrine." [Rule]

> The proximate cause approach provides that "liability attaches 'for *any* death proximately resulting from the unlawful activity — even the death of a co-felon — notwithstanding the killing was by one resisting the crime.'" Under the proximate cause approach, felony murder may preclude consideration of the deceased's identity, which would make a defendant liable for all deaths caused by others during the crime. Application of the proximate cause varies greatly by jurisdiction because the statutes differ substantially. The proximate cause approach becomes

controversial when the homicide is committed by someone other than the felons, but only a minority of jurisdictions follow this approach.

* * * The leading case adopting the agency approach is *Commonwealth v.. Redline*, 137 A.2d 472 (Pa. 1958), where the underlying principle of the agency theory is described as follows: "In adjudging a felony-murder, it is to be remembered at all times that the thing which is imputed to a felon for a killing incidental to his felony is malice and not the act of killing. The mere coincidence of homicide and felony is not enough to satisfy the felony-murder doctrine."

The following statement from *Redline* is more persuasive for Sophophone:

In the present instance, the victim of the homicide was one of the robbers who, while resisting apprehension in his effort to escape, was shot and killed by a policeman in the performance of his duty. Thus, the homicide was justifiable and, obviously, could not be availed of, on any rational legal theory, to support a charge of murder. How can anyone, no matter how much of an outlaw he may be, have a criminal charge lodged against him for the consequences of the lawful conduct of another person? The mere question carries with it its own answer.

* * * The minority of the states whose courts have adopted the proximate cause theory believe their legislatures intended that any person, co-felon, or accomplice who commits an inherently dangerous felony should be held responsible for any death which is a direct and foreseeable consequence of the actions of those committing the felony. These courts apply the civil law concept of proximate cause to felony-murder situations. * * *

It should be mentioned that some courts have been willing to impose felony-murder liability even where the shooting was by a person other than one of the felons in the so-called "shield" situations where it has been reasoned "that a felon's act of using a victim as a shield in compelling a victim to occupy a place or position of danger constitutes a direct lethal act against the victim." * * *

* * *The overriding fact which exists in our case is that neither Sophophone nor any of his accomplices "killed" anyone. The law enforcement officer acted lawfully in committing the act which resulted in the death of the co-felon. This does not fall within the language of K.S.A. 21-3205 since the officer committed no crime.

* * * Of more assistance to us is our long-time rule of statutory interpretation:

[C]riminal statutes must be strictly construed in favor of the accused. Any reasonable doubt about the meaning is decided in favor of anyone subjected to the criminal statute. The rule of strict construction, however, is subordinate to the rule that judicial interpretation must be reasonable and sensible to effect legislative design and intent. * * *

It appears to the majority that to impute the act of killing to Sophophone when the act was the lawful and courageous one of a law enforcement officer acting in the line of his duties is contrary to the strict construction we are required to give criminal statutes. There is considerable doubt about the meaning of K.S.A. 21-3401(b) as applied to the facts of this case, and we believe that making one criminally responsible for the lawful acts of a law enforcement officer is not the intent of the felony-murder statute as it is currently written. * * *

It does little good to suggest one construction over another would prevent the commission of dangerous felonies or that it would deter those who engage in dangerous felonies from killing purposely, negligently, or accidentally. Actually, innocent parties and victims of crimes appear to be those who are sought to be protected rather than co-felons.

We hold that under the facts of this case where the killing resulted from the lawful acts of a law enforcement officer in attempting to apprehend a co-felon, Sophophone is not criminally responsible for the resulting death of Somphone Sysoumphone, and his felony-murder conviction must be reversed.* * *

ABBOTT, J., Dissenting:

* * * When an issue requires statutory analysis and the statute is unambiguous, we are limited by the wording chosen by the legislature. We are not free to alter the statutory language, regardless of the result. In the present case, the felony-murder statute does not require us to adopt the "agency" theory favored by the majority. Indeed, there is nothing in the statute which establishes an agency approach. The statute does not address the issue at all. The requirements, according to the statute, are: (1) there must be a killing, and (2) the killing must be committed in the commission, attempt to commit, or flight from an inherently dangerous felony. The statute simply does not contain the limitations discussed by the majority. There is nothing in K.S.A. 21-3401 which requires us to adopt the agency approach or that requires Sophophone to be the shooter in this case. The facts in this case, in my opinion, satisfy all of the requirements set forth in K.S.A. 21- 3401(b). * * *

The majority in this case points out that the majority of states have adopted the agency approach when faced with the death of a co-felon. They acknowledge, however, that because statutes vary significantly from state to state, reference to a "majority" rule and a "minority" rule is meaningless. Indeed, an in-depth analysis of the current case law in this area leads me to the following conclusions: (1) While a majority of states would agree with the majority opinion in this case, the margin is slim; (2) many of the states that have adopted the so-called "agency" approach have done so because the statutory language in their state *requires* them to do so;

and (3) several of the states that have adopted the "proximate cause" approach have done so because their statutes are silent on the issue, like Kansas. * * *

In my opinion, our statute is unambiguous and simply does not require the defendant to be the direct cause of the victim's death, nor does it limit application of the felony-murder rule to the death of "innocents." * * *

The majority has opened a Pandora's box and left the law grossly unsettled. It does not take much imagination to see a number of situations where a death is going to result from an inherently dangerous felony and the majority's opinion is going to prevent the accused from being charged with felony murder.

If there is to be a change in the law, it should be by the legislature and not by this court adopting a statutory scheme set forth by the legislatures of other states. I would continue to follow the proximate cause theory of liability for felony murder which holds that criminal liability attaches for any death proximately resulting from the unlawful activity notwithstanding the fact that the killing was by one resisting the crime. * * *

NOTES AND QUESTIONS

1. *"In Furtherance Of."* Another limitation on application of felony murder requires that the death have occurred "in furtherance of" the felony. In jurisdictions applying this limitation, the "in furtherance of" language is linked to the agency theory rather than a proximate cause theory of liability. For example, if a police officer shoots a co-felon in the course of trying to get away with the proceeds from a bank robbery, that shooting was not done "in furtherance" of the bank robbery – to the contrary, the officer wanted to thwart the robbery. So the felony murder rule should not be applied to hold the surviving felon liable for the death of his co-felon because the killing did not advance the goal of robbing the bank.

In *Davis v. Fox*, 735 S.E.2d 259 (W.Va. 2012), the West Virginia Supreme Court rejected the prosecutor's argument that the death of a co-felon, killed by the son of a convenience store owner during a break-in and attempted theft at the store, could be the basis for a felony murder charge against the surviving co-felons even though the murder statute specifically included burglary as an enumerated crime that can lead to a first degree murder charge. The court concluded, "[W]e are convinced that the statutory offense of felony murder remains deeply ensconced in its common-law foundations. And until such time as the Legislature sees fit to further amend West Virginia Code § 61-2-1, we do not accept [the prosecutor]'s argument that the criminal offense of felony murder encompasses every death that occurs in the course of a statutorily-enumerated felony regardless of who causes the death." This is the same outcome achieved by describing this set of facts as governed by an "agency" approach to accomplice liability. But a theory other than felony murder (perhaps depraved heart murder) might apply.

2. *Negligent Omissions*. Can an individual's negligent failure to act in violation of a legal duty be the basis for liability for felony murder if a death occurs because of the omission? That issue was presented in *State v. Small*, 100 So. 3d 797 (La. 2012), when a mother was charged with second degree felony murder based on the underlying crime of neglect of a juvenile after leaving her two small children at home and a fire broke out that killed one of them. The Louisiana Supreme Court overturned her conviction on the ground that the agency theory of felony murder liability would not permit a conviction because there was no direct act that led to the child's death. The court stated,

> We are mindful of the legislature's prerogative to allow a prosecution for second degree murder by including cruelty to juveniles based on criminal neglect as an underlying predicate felony. However, neglect takes many forms, and neglect in the form of lack of supervision simply cannot supply the direct act of killing needed for a second degree felony murder conviction. To the contrary, cases where second degree murder convictions have been affirmed based on an underlying felony of cruelty to juveniles have not involved lack of supervision, but have involved some direct act of negligence which killed the victim . . . An interpretation of the felony murder statute to allow a second degree murder conviction anytime a parent is criminally negligent in failing to supervise her child and the child dies as a result of some intervening act would be contrary to the rule of lenity and could result in unintended consequences.

In a state applying the "proximate cause" theory of felony murder liability, would cruelty to a juvenile based on a negligent failure to protect a child from harm support a conviction for murder?

3. *Statutory Expansion*. Some states have expanded the definition of felony murder to include the death of any person, including a co-felon, that occurs during the commission of the felony, regardless of who actually caused the death, the agency theory of liability. Oklahoma's first degree murder statute provides for felony murder liability in this way:

> A person also commits the crime of murder in the first degree, regardless of malice, when that person *or any other person* takes the life of a human being during, or *if the death of a human being results from*, the commission or attempted commission of murder of another person, shooting or discharge of a firearm or crossbow with intent to kill, intentional discharge of a firearm or other deadly weapon into any dwelling or building * * * , forcible rape, robbery with a dangerous weapon,

kidnapping, escape from lawful custody, first degree burglary, first degree arson, unlawful distributing or dispensing of controlled dangerous substances, or trafficking in illegal drugs.

21 OKLA. STAT. ANN. § 701.7(B) (emphasis added).

PROBLEM TWENTY-EIGHT

Reconsider the facts of Problem Twenty-Four. Can Terry be convicted of felony murder for the death of Robbie? If so, what underlying felony should the prosecutor identify as the basis for the felony murder charge?

PROBLEM TWENTY-NINE

Spencer and Kendal agree to transport drugs for $10,000, with half to be paid immediately and the rest upon delivery. In El Paso, Texas, they are given a car in which 5 kilos of cocaine is hidden in a secret compartment and told to drive it to an address in Saginaw, Michigan. While driving during a heavy thunderstorm, Spencer loses control of the vehicle and it flips over into a ditch. Kendal, who was not wearing a seatbelt at the time of the accident, is thrown from the car and killed. Spencer and Kendal were to deliver the cocaine to Chris, a drug dealer, who would pay them the remaining $5,000. Is Spencer liable under the common law for felony murder for the death of Kendal? If Spencer had died in the accident and Kendal survived, would that change the felony murder analysis? If the accident occurred in a jurisdiction with a provision similar to the Oklahoma felony murder statute, (§ 701.7(B)), what effect would it have on the liability analysis? Assume Chris is arrested with an envelope containing $5,000 at the location where Spencer and Kendal were to deliver the drugs. Can Chris be held liable for felony murder?

Chapter 9
Rape

§ 9.01 Common Law Rape

> At common law, rape was a general intent crime. * * * Blackstone defined rape as "carnal knowledge of a woman forcibly and against her will." Additional requirements, that the victim report the incident promptly, corroboration of the victim's story, and utmost resistance, heightened the proof necessary for a conviction. Generally, a conviction rested on the last of these requirements: how well the woman conveyed her unwillingness to engage in intercourse. * * *

Nicole Fusilli, Notes, *New York State of Mind: Rape and Mens Rea*, 76 ST. JOHN'S L. REV. 603 (2002).

Susan Estrich, *Rape*, 95 YALE L.J. 1087 (1986)

* * *

II. THE DEFINITION OF RAPE: THE COMMON LAW TRADITION

The traditional way of defining a crime is by describing the prohibited act (actus reus) committed by the defendant and the prohibited mental state (mens rea) with which he must have done it. We ask: What did the defendant do? What did he know or intend when he did it?

The definition of rape stands in striking contrast to this tradition, because courts, in defining the crime, have focused almost incidentally on the defendant-and almost entirely on the victim. It has often been noted that, traditionally at least, the rules associated with the proof of a rape charge — the corroboration requirement, the requirement of cautionary instructions, and the fresh complaint rule — as well as the evidentiary rules relating to prior sexual conduct by the victim, placed the victim as much on trial as the defendant. Such a reversal also occurs in the course of defining the elements of the crime. Mens rea, where it might matter, is all but eliminated; prohibited force tends to be defined according to the response of the victim; and nonconsent — the sine qua non of the offense — turns entirely on the victim's response.

But while the focus is on the female victim, the judgment of her actions is entirely male. If the issue were what the defendant knew, thought, or intended as to key elements of the offense, this perspective might be understandable; yet the issue has instead been the appropriateness of the woman's behavior, according to male standards of appropriate female behavior.

To some extent, this evaluation is but a modern response to the longstanding suspicion of rape victims. As Matthew Hale put it three centuries ago: "Rape is . . . an accusation easily to be made and hard to be proved, and harder to be defended by the party accused, tho never so innocent."

But the problem is more fundamental than that. Apart from the woman's conduct, the law provides no clear, working definition of rape. This rather conspicuous gap in the law of rape presents substantial questions of fair warning for men, which the law not so handily resolves by imposing the burden of warning them on women.

At its simplest, the dilemma lies in this: If nonconsent is essential to rape (and no amount of force or physical struggle is inherently inconsistent with lawful sex), and if no sometimes means yes, and if men are supposed to be aggressive in any event, how is a man to know when he has crossed the line? And how are we to avoid unjust convictions?

This dilemma is hardly inevitable. Partly, it is a product of the way society (or at least a powerful part of it) views sex. Partly, it is a product of the lengths to which the law has gone to enforce and legitimize those views. We could prohibit the use of force and threats and coercion in sex, regardless of "consent." We could define consent in a way that respected the autonomy of women. Having chosen neither course, however, we have created a problem of fair warning, and force and consent have been defined in an effort to resolve this problem. * * *

Anne M. Coughlin, *Sex and Guilt,* 84 VA. L. REV. 1 (1998)

* * * I argue that we cannot understand rape law unless we study the doctrine, not in isolation, but in conjunction with the fornication and adultery prohibitions with which it formerly resided and, perhaps, continues to reside. When we recall that the contemporary definition of rape emerged from a system that outlawed these forms of consensual heterosexual intercourse, it seems clear that the official purposes of rape law — and, surely, there were and are many theoretical and practical justifications for the rape prohibition — did not include the protection of sexual autonomy. Contrary to the assumptions of the modern rape critique, influential institutions within that former system decreed that sexuality was a force

so dangerous that it could not safely be left to self-regulation, but rather should be closely confined, by state law, within marital relationships. Far from being positively valued and protected, therefore, the exercise of sexual autonomy was something to be discouraged, even criminalized. Since legal institutions were assigned the task of enforcing both the rape laws and the fornication and adultery laws, it would not be surprising to discover that appellate judges and, presumably, other law enforcement officials found ways to enlist rape doctrine to detect and discipline sexual transgressions by women, as well as by men.

Therefore, I propose that we examine rape law by suspending our understanding that heterosexual intercourse ordinarily is lawful activity and by attempting instead to recapture the ways of thinking about heterosexual intercourse underlying the fornication and adultery laws. In other words, what I suggest is an investigation of rape doctrine that proceeds from the premise that nonmarital heterosexual intercourse is — and should be — criminal misconduct for both men and women. When we consider the regulatory framework from which rape law emerged, this reversal of value is sensible, indeed, necessary, though it may seem absurd at first glance, especially to liberal readers. We inherited the rape crime from a culture in which rape was only one of two basic categories of heterosexual offenses. The other category of offenses consisted of consensual sexual intercourse outside marriage — fornication and adultery — in which the man and the woman were accomplices. The existence of this prohibition on consensual nonmarital sex has a number of important implications, one of which I will explore in this Article and another of which I will notice, briefly, at relevant points herein.

The first set of implications * * * concerns the influence that we would expect the fornication and adultery prohibitions to exert on the development of the substantive definition of rape. How would judges who believed that consensual nonmarital intercourse was a crime define rape? This Article will develop a contentious point: By unearthing our ancestors' belief that all nonmarital intercourse should be criminalized, we may begin to understand, even as we reject, the inclination of courts to approach rape complaints with deep suspicion. Since, under our ancestors' system, the underlying sexual activity in which a rape complainant engaged (albeit, by her own testimony, unwillingly) was criminal misconduct, her complaint logically could be construed as a plea to be relieved of responsibility for committing that crime. A court would be receptive to such a plea only if the woman could establish that, although she had participated in a sexual transgression, she did so under circumstances that afforded her a defense to criminal liability. Significantly, careful examination of rape doctrine reveals that the elements of the rape offense (almost) are a mirror image of the defenses we would expect from women accused of fornication or adultery. Such traditional defensive strategies would include the claim that the woman had committed no actus reus, that she lacked the mens rea for fornication or adultery, or that she had submitted to the intercourse under duress. For example, just as courts allowed perpetrators of nonsexual crimes to interpose a duress defense, so we must assume that they would be willing to excuse those women suspected of fornication or adultery who could prove that their accomplices had forced them to offend under threat of death or grievous bodily harm. According to this account, the features of rape law to which the critics most strenuously object — namely, the peculiar definitions of the nonconsent and force elements of the crime — are better understood as criteria that excuse the woman for committing an illegal sexual infraction, than as ingredients of the man's offense. Curiously, when we acknowledge, rather than ignore or minimize, the long-standing and explicit connection our culture has made between sexual intercourse and criminal guilt, we produce a description of rape law that incorporates a justification for thorough doctrinal reform. That is, if we now are prepared to agree that fornication and adultery no longer should be criminalized — whether because these offenses violate contemporary constitutional guarantees or contemporary moral and political judgments (to the extent that such judgments differ from constitutional guarantees) — then there appears to be no justification for adhering to a definition of rape that treats the rapist's victim as a lawbreaker who must plead for an excuse from criminal responsibility.

§ 9.02 Statutes

ALABAMA

§ 13A-6-61. Rape; first degree[a]

(a) A person commits the crime of rape in the first degree if:

(1) He or she engages in sexual intercourse with a member of the opposite sex by forcible compulsion; or

(2) He or she engages in sexual intercourse with a member of the opposite sex who is incapable of consent by reason of being physically helpless or mentally incapacitated; or

(3) He or she, being 16 years or older, engages in sexual intercourse with a member of the opposite sex who is less than 12 years old.

* * *

---

[a]A 2000 amendment to the statute made it gender-neutral by substituting "person" for "male," inserting "or she" in three places, and substituting "member of the opposite sex" for "female" in three places.

GEORGIA

§ 16-6-1. Rape

(a) A person commits the offense of rape when he has carnal knowledge of:

(1) A female forcibly and against her will; or

(2) A female who is less than ten years of age.

Carnal knowledge in rape occurs when there is any penetration of the female sex organ by the male sex organ. The fact that the person allegedly raped is the wife of the defendant shall not be a defense to a charge of rape.

(b) A person convicted of the offense of rape shall be punished by death, by imprisonment for life without parole, by imprisonment for life, or by imprisonment for not less than ten nor more than 20 years. Any person convicted under this Code section shall, in addition, be subject to the sentencing and punishment provisions of Code Sections 17-10-6.1 and 17-10-7.

(c) When evidence relating to an allegation of rape is collected in the course of a medical examination of the person who is the victim of the alleged crime, the Georgia Crime Victims Emergency Fund, as provided for in Chapter 15 of Title 17, shall be responsible for the cost of the medical examination to the extent that expense is incurred for the limited purpose of collecting evidence.

MAINE

17-A M.R.S.A. § 253. Gross Sexual Assault

1. A person is guilty of gross sexual assault if that person engages in a sexual act with another person and:

A. The other person submits as a result of compulsion, as defined in section 251, subsection 1, paragraph E. Violation of this paragraph is a Class A crime;

B. The other person, not the actor's spouse, has not in fact attained

the age of 14 years. Violation of this paragraph is a Class A crime;
or

C. The other person, not the actor's spouse, has not in fact attained
12 years of age. Violation of this paragraph is a Class A crime.

2. A person is guilty of gross sexual assault if that person engages in a
sexual act with another person and:

A. The actor has substantially impaired the other person's power
to appraise or control the other person's sexual acts by furnishing,
as defined in section 1101, subsection 18, paragraph A, administering or employing drugs, intoxicants or other similar means.
Violation of this paragraph is a Class B crime;

B. The actor compels or induces the other person to engage in the
sexual act by any threat. Violation of this paragraph is a Class B
crime;

C. The other person suffers from mental disability that is reasonably apparent or known to the actor, and which in fact renders the
other person substantially incapable of appraising the nature of the
contact involved or of understanding that the person has the right
to deny or withdraw consent. Violation of this paragraph is a Class
B crime;

D. The other person is unconscious or otherwise physically
incapable of resisting and has not consented to the sexual act.
Violation of this paragraph is a Class B crime;

E. The other person, not the actor's spouse, is under official
supervision as a probationer, a parolee, a sex offender on supervised release, a prisoner on supervised community confinement
status or a juvenile on community reintegration status or is
detained in a hospital, prison or other institution, and the actor has
supervisory or disciplinary authority over the other person.
Violation of this paragraph is a Class B crime;

F. The other person, not the actor's spouse, has not in fact attained
the age of 18 years and is a student enrolled in a private or public
elementary, secondary or special education school, facility or
institution and the actor is a teacher, employee or other official
having instructional, supervisory or disciplinary authority over the
student. Violation of this paragraph is a Class C crime;

G. The other person, not the actor's spouse, has not attained the age of 18 years and is a resident in or attending a children's home, day care facility, residential child care facility, drug treatment center, youth camp licensed under Title 22, section 2495 or similar school, facility or institution regularly providing care or services for children, and the actor is a teacher, employee or other person having instructional, supervisory or disciplinary authority over the other person. Violation of this paragraph is a Class C crime;

H. The other person has not in fact attained the age of 18 years and the actor is a parent, stepparent, foster parent, guardian or other similar person responsible for the long-term care and welfare of that other person. Violation of this paragraph is a Class B crime;

I. The actor is a psychiatrist, a psychologist or licensed as a social worker or purports to be a psychiatrist, a psychologist or licensed as a social worker to the other person and the other person, not the actor's spouse, is a current patient or client of the actor. Violation of this paragraph is a Class C crime;

J. The actor owns, operates or is an employee of an organization, program or residence that is operated, administered, licensed or funded by the Department of Health and Human Services and the other person, not the actor's spouse, receives services from the organization, program or residence and the organization, program or residence recognizes the other person as a person with an intellectual disability or autism. It is an affirmative defense to prosecution under this paragraph that the actor receives services for an intellectual disability or autism or is a person with an intellectual disability, as defined in Title 34-B, section 5001, subsection 3, or autism, as defined in Title 34-B, section 6002. Violation of this paragraph is a Class C crime;

K. The actor owns, operates or is an employee of an organization, program or residence that is operated, administered, licensed or funded by the Department of Health and Human Services and the other person, not the actor's spouse, receives services from the organization, program or residence and suffers from a mental disability that is reasonably apparent or known to the actor. Violation of this paragraph is a Class C crime; or

L. The actor is employed to provide care to a dependent person, who is not the actor's spouse or domestic partner and who is unable to perform self-care because of advanced age or physical or mental disease, disorder or defect. For the purposes of this paragraph, "domestic partners" means 2 unmarried adults who are domiciled together under a long-term arrangement that evidences a commitment to remain responsible indefinitely for each other's welfare. Violation of this paragraph is a Class C crime.

3. It is a defense to a prosecution under subsection 2, paragraph A that the other person voluntarily consumed or allowed administration of the substance with knowledge of its nature, except that it is no defense when:

A. The other person is a patient of the actor and has a reasonable belief that the actor is administering the substance for medical or dental examination or treatment; or

B. The other person is in fact 14 or 15 years of age. * * *

WISCONSIN

§ 940.225. Sexual assault.

(1) FIRST DEGREE SEXUAL ASSAULT. Whoever does any of the following is guilty of a Class B felony:

(a) Has sexual contact or sexual intercourse with another person without consent of that person and causes pregnancy or great bodily harm to that person.

(b) Has sexual contact or sexual intercourse with another person without consent of that person by use or threat of use of a dangerous weapon or any article used or fashioned in a manner to lead the victim reasonably to believe it to be a dangerous weapon.

(c) Is aided or abetted by one or more other persons and has sexual contact or sexual intercourse with another person without consent of that person by use or threat of force or violence.

(2) SECOND DEGREE SEXUAL ASSAULT. Whoever does any of the following is guilty of a Class C felony:

(a) Has sexual contact or sexual intercourse with another person without consent of that person by use or threat of force or violence.

(b) Has sexual contact or sexual intercourse with another person without consent of that person and causes injury, illness, disease or impairment of a sexual or reproductive organ, or mental anguish requiring psychiatric care for the victim.

(c) Has sexual contact or sexual intercourse with a person who suffers from a mental illness or deficiency which renders that person temporarily or permanently incapable of appraising the person's conduct, and the defendant knows of such condition.

(cm) Has sexual contact or sexual intercourse with a person who is under the influence of an intoxicant to a degree which renders that person incapable of appraising the person's conduct, and the defendant knows of such condition.

(d) Has sexual contact or sexual intercourse with a person who the defendant knows is unconscious.

(f) Is aided or abetted by one or more other persons and has sexual contact or sexual intercourse with another person without the consent of that person.

(g) Is an employee of a facility or program under § 940.295(2)(b), (c), (h) or (k) and has sexual contact or sexual intercourse with a person who is a patient or resident of the facility or program. * * *

(3) THIRD DEGREE SEXUAL ASSAULT. Whoever has sexual intercourse with a person without the consent of that person is guilty of a Class G felony. Whoever has sexual contact in the manner described in sub. (5)(b)2. with a person without the consent of that person is guilty of a Class G felony.

(3m) Fourth degree sexual assault. Except as provided in sub. (3), whoever has sexual contact with a person without the consent of that person is guilty of a Class A misdemeanor.

(4) CONSENT. "Consent", as used in this section, means words or overt actions by a person who is competent to give informed consent indicating a freely given agreement to have sexual intercourse or sexual contact. Consent is not an issue in alleged violations of sub. (2) (c), (cm), (d) and (g). The following persons are presumed incapable of consent but the presumption may be rebutted by competent evidence, subject to the provisions of § 972.11 (2):

(b) A person suffering from a mental illness or defect which impairs capacity to appraise personal conduct.

(c) A person who is unconscious or for any other reason is physically unable to communicate unwillingness to an act.

(5) DEFINITIONS * * *

(b) "Sexual contact" means any of the following:

1. Any of the following types of intentional touching, whether direct or through clothing, if that intentional touching is either for the purpose of sexually degrading; or for the purpose of sexually humiliating the complainant or sexually arousing or gratifying the defendant or if the touching contains the elements of actual or attempted battery under § 940.19(1):

a. Intentional touching by the defendant or, upon the defendant's instruction, by another person, by the use of any body part or object, of the complainant's intimate parts.

b. Intentional touching by the complainant, by the use of any body part or object, of the defendant's intimate parts or, if done upon the defendant's instructions, the intimate parts of another person.

2. Intentional penile ejaculation of ejaculate or intentional emission of urine or feces by the defendant or, upon the defendant's instruction, by another person upon any part of the body clothed or unclothed of the complainant if that ejaculation or emission is either for the purpose of sexually degrading or sexually humiliating the complainant or for the purpose of sexually arousing or gratifying the defendant.

3. For the purpose of sexually degrading or humiliating the complainant or sexually arousing or gratifying the defendant, intentionally causing the complainant to ejaculate or emit urine or feces on any part of the defendant's body, whether clothed or unclothed.

(c) "Sexual intercourse" includes the meaning assigned under § 939.22(36) as well as cunnilingus, fellatio or anal intercourse between persons or any other intrusion, however slight, of any part of a person's body or of any object into the genital or anal opening either by the defendant or upon the defendant's instruction. The emission of semen is not required. * * *

(6) MARRIAGE NOT A BAR TO PROSECUTION. A defendant shall not be presumed to be incapable of violating this section because of marriage to the complainant.

(7) DEATH OF VICTIM. This section applies whether a victim is dead or alive at the time of the sexual contact or sexual intercourse.

MODEL PENAL CODE

§ 213.1. Rape and Related Offenses.

(1) **Rape.** A male who has sexual intercourse with a female not his wife is guilty of rape if:

(a) he compels her to submit by force or by threat of imminent death, serious bodily injury, extreme pain or kidnapping, to be inflicted on anyone; or

(b) he has substantially impaired her power to appraise or control her conduct by administering or employing without her knowledge drugs, intoxicants or other means for the purpose of preventing resistance; or

(c) the female is unconscious; or

(d) the female is less than 10 years old.

Rape is a felony of the second degree unless (i) in the course thereof the actor inflicts serious bodily injury upon anyone, or (ii) the victim was not a voluntary social companion of the actor upon the occasion of the crime and had not previously permitted him sexual liberties, in which cases the offense is a felony of the first degree.

(2) **Gross Sexual Imposition.** A male who has sexual intercourse with a female not his wife commits a felony of the third degree if:

(a) he compels her to submit by any threat that would prevent resistance by a woman of ordinary resolution; or

(b) he knows that she suffers from a mental disease or defect which renders her incapable of appraising the nature of her conduct; or

(c) he knows that she is unaware that a sexual act is being committed upon her or that she submits because she mistakenly supposes that he is her husband.

§ 213.2. Deviate Sexual Intercourse by Force or Imposition.

(1) **By Force or Its Equivalent.** A person who engages in deviate sexual intercourse with another person, or who causes another to engage in deviate sexual intercourse, commits a felony of the second degree if:

(a) he compels the other person to participate by force or by threat of imminent death, serious bodily injury, extreme pain or kidnapping, to be inflicted on anyone; or

(b) he has substantially impaired the other person's power to appraise or control his conduct, by administering or employing without the knowledge of the other person drugs, intoxicants or other means for the purpose of preventing resistance; or

(c) the other person is unconscious; or

(d) the other person is less than 10 years old.

(2) **By Other Imposition.** A person who engages in deviate sexual intercourse with another person, or who causes another to engage in deviate sexual intercourse, commits a felony of the third degree if:

(a) he compels the other person to participate by any threat that would prevent resistance by a person of ordinary resolution; or

(b) he knows that the other person suffers from a mental disease or defect which renders him incapable of appraising the nature of his conduct; or

(c) he knows that the other person submits because he is unaware that a sexual act is being committed upon him.

§ 213.3. Corruption of Minors and Seduction.

(1) **Offense Defined.** A male who has sexual intercourse with a female not his wife, or any person who engages in deviate sexual intercourse or

causes another to engage in deviate sexual intercourse, is guilty of an offense if:

(a) the other person is less than [16] years old and the actor is at least [four] years older than the other person; or

(b) the other person is less than 21 years old and the actor is his guardian or otherwise responsible for general supervision of his welfare; or

(c) the other person is in custody of law or detained in a hospital or other institution and the actor has supervisory or disciplinary authority over him; or

(d) the other person is a female who is induced to participate by a promise of marriage which the actor does not mean to perform.

(2) **Grading.** An offense under paragraph (a) of Subsection (1) is a felony of the third degree. Otherwise an offense under this section is a misdemeanor.

§ 213.4. Sexual Assault.

A person who has sexual contact with another not his spouse, or causes such other to have sexual contact with him, is guilty of sexual assault, a misdemeanor, if:

(1) he knows that the contact is offensive to the other person; or

(2) he knows that the other person suffers from a mental disease or defect which renders him or her incapable of appraising the nature of his or her conduct; or

(3) he knows that the other person is unaware that a sexual act is being committed; or

(4) the other person is less than 10 years old; or

(5) he has substantially impaired the other person's power to appraise or control his or her conduct, by administering or employing without the other's knowledge drugs, intoxicants or other means for the purpose of preventing resistance; or

(6) the other person is less than [16] years old and the actor is at least [four] years older than the other person; or

(7) the other person is less than 21 years old and the actor is his guardian or otherwise responsible for general supervision of his welfare; or

(8) the other person is in custody of law or detained in a hospital or other institution and the actor has supervisory or disciplinary authority over him.

Sexual contact is any touching of the sexual or other intimate parts of the person for the purpose of arousing or gratifying sexual desire.

PROBLEM THIRTY

You have just been appointed to the staff of the state Senate Judiciary Committee that is considering rewriting the state's rape statute. The current statute reflects the common law of forcible rape, requiring the government to prove the following elements: (1) sexual intercourse; (2) force and against the victim's will; (3) the victim's lack of consent; and (4) general intent. Consider what the new statute should be titled (e.g. "Rape," "Criminal Sexual Conduct," "Sexual Assault")? What should be the elements of the offense(s). Also consider whether there will be a separate provision for acts involving minors, whether the statute will be gender neutral, and whether there will be different considerations placed into the statute(s) should the accused be married to the victim. Consider whether there are advantages to having different degrees within a rape statute, or whether the statute should define the crime of rape without different levels of conduct and punishment.

NOTE AND QUESTIONS

1. **Mens Rea**. States differ widely in what mental state they require to prove forcible rape (The term "forcible rape" is used here to distinguish it from other kinds, for example, statutory rape, even though modern reforms sometimes delete any requirement of "force" or have lesser crimes when force is not involved). Many states are ambiguous about what mental state is required. Others seem to adopt a strict liability standard, though the primary effect of this appears to be to make juries even more reluctant to find that other elements of the crime, such as non-consent, exist. The majority of states today, however, apply a negligence standard: Should the defendant have known that the person with whom he or she had sexual relations was not consenting? *See* STEPHEN SCHULHOFER, UNWANTED SEX: THE

CULTURE OF INTIMIDATION AND THE FAILURE OF LAW (1998). The common law also implicitly followed a negligence standard, though the common law definition of the crime is silent about mental state. As rape is a general intent crime and mistake of fact is a defense at common law for general intent crimes only if the mistake was both honest (the defendant is not lying in saying he or she was mistaken) and reasonable, it means that a defendant can be guilty only if his mistake was unreasonable, that is, negligent. [See Chap. 4]. The theory behind a negligence standard in this area is that "[t]he injury of an unwanted sexual intrusion is great, and there is a clear need to give the man a reason to pay attention to the woman's wishes." *See id.* at 258.

If negligence as to whether the woman consented is the appropriate *mens rea* requirement for rape, that result seems to create a new conundrum: forcible rape is punished very severely – as severely as some forms of purposeful or knowing murder. Yet when the criminal law imposes liability for negligence, the punishment is usually mild relative to that for more egregious mental states. What justifies harsh punishment in rape cases for an act done with a negligently-held belief where we impose more lenient sentences for negligence with other sorts of crimes?

Professor Andrew E. Taslitz argues that more than ordinary criminal negligence is involved. Rather, there is an element of intention in the sense that negligent beliefs in date rape generally stem from male self-deception: from knowing and not knowing at the same time that the woman is not consenting. How is this possible? One way is for the man to suppress any awareness of the woman's true state of mind, for example, by distracting himself by focusing only on the opportunity to have sex or by rationalizing that she is just acting coy and must really "want it." In this state of mind, the defendant can readily ignore a woman's apparent discomfort or choose to interpret it as a sign of consent, consigning any doubts to a semi-conscious netherworld. Alternatively, the man might be aware of the true state of affairs – or at least of a strong risk that the woman is not consenting – but only at the subconscious level. His subconscious screens this awareness from the conscious mind out of self-interest: if he consciously admitted to himself that the woman did not want to have sex, he would stop, so his subconscious saves him from this unpleasant moral choice. The point is an important one, for, if Professor Taslitz is right, then two things are true: first, that at least some men who testify that they believed the woman was consenting when she in fact was not are consciously telling the truth as they see it; and, second, that their failure to discern what reasonably should have been clear to them is a particularly egregious form of unreasonable belief because, at some less than fully conscious level, they knew exactly what the truth was. *See* Andrew E. Taslitz, *Willfully Blinded: On Date Rape and Self-Deception*, 28 HARV. J. L. & GENDER 381 (2005).

But, if this is all so, what then can be done about it? Any requirement of an actual, subjective mental state would require acquittal. But if the test is an objective one of whether the defendant *should have been consciously aware* of what any non-self-deceiving male would have been, or at least that such a male should have been on notice to make further serious inquiry into the woman's consent or its absence, then this defendant can be held liable — and without any inquiry into his subconscious state of mind in the individual case (a particularly difficult task) — and he deserves punishment more severe than for most other crimes of criminal negligence.

Taslitz offers the following example of potential self-deception at work in a recent infamous case:

> Basketball star Kobe Bryant, as virtually every national newspaper and news broadcast station prominently reported, was charged ... with raping a nineteen-year-old female employee at a Colorado mountain resort. [T]he prosecution ultimately withdrew the criminal charges — apparently for reasons having nothing to do with their credibility....
>
> Investigative reporter Jeffrey Scott Shapiro, in his ... book, *Kobe Bryant: The Game of His Life*, reports that Bryant and his alleged victim — whom Shapiro identifies by the pseudonym "Lilly Fuller"— told the police virtually identical stories, with one major exception: Bryant insists that Lilly never told him "no," while Lilly equally insists that she said "no" firmly and indicated her lack of consent in other ways as well. Shapiro describes the detectives' interview with Bryant on whether Lilly consented, saying:
>
>> When one of the detectives asked . . . [Bryant] whether or not Lilly had ever said "no," Bryant hesitated and said nothing. The detectives in the room sat motionless.
>>
>> "You're not answering the question," one of them said.
>>
>> "I'm thinking," Bryant said, slightly annoyed.
>>
>> Exhaling a deep breath and looking down at his sneakers, Bryant made a variety of frustrated facial expressions and then, after [a full] 30 seconds of pondering the question, he responded.
>>
>> "It was consensual," he said.
>>
>> "What's that mean?" one of the detectives asked, getting frustrated.
>>
>> Bryant said nothing, looking at the two men before him. The detective firmly reiterated the question. "Did she ever say 'no'?"

Bryant paused. "No," he said quietly.

On the one hand, Bryant's defenders have argued for one version of the truth: Lilly lied. She had consented but saw a chance for fame, money, or feeding her ego by crying rape. On the other hand, Bryant's critics interpret his lengthy delay in responding to the detectives' questions to support the very different inference that Bryant, not Lilly, was lying: Lilly had said "no," and Bryant understood that this meant she did not consent, but he proceeded with the sexual encounter nonetheless.

The detectives had yet another interpretation of the interaction between Bryant and Fuller. Explains Shapiro: "For Bryant to have waited that long and still not flatly deny the allegation, instead saying, 'it was consensual,' told investigators that Lilly had likely said 'no,' but that in Bryant's mind, 'no' could have meant 'yes.'" In other words, Bryant told the truth when he said that he honestly believed that Lilly had consented. But he lied about whether she said "no" because he feared, in retrospect, that no one would believe him if he admitted to Lilly's protests. If the detectives are right, the only basis for prosecuting Bryant for the rape would be that Lilly did not in fact consent, and Bryant *reasonably should have known* that he proceeded against her will—assuming, of course, that negligence about whether a woman consented is sufficient culpability to prove rape under Colorado law.

Bryant himself recently came close to admitting that he should have, or at least could have, known that Lilly was not consenting. After a series of technical mishaps resulted in the inadvertent revelation by the court of information that had been ordered sealed, Lilly, expressing a loss of confidence in the fairness of the criminal process, refused to cooperate with that process further. When the criminal case was dismissed, Bryant made the following public statements:

> Although I truly believe[d] this encounter between us was consensual, I recognize now that she did not and does not view this incident the same way I did. After months of reviewing discovery, listening to her attorney, and even her testimony in person, I now understand how she feels that she did not consent to this encounter.

I believe that this quote reveals that Bryant's behavior can be explained by male self-deception.

Id. at 381-84.

2. ***Reasonableness***. How a "reasonable man" should think or behave is generally undefined, leaving to the jury the task of giving the term meaning. *See* Andrew E.

Taslitz, *Patriarchal Stories I: Cultural Rape Narratives in the Courtroom*, 5 S. CAL. REV. L. & WOMEN'S ST. 387 (1995). What factors might a jury consider here? Might a jury decide that a man's ignoring a "no" was consistent with his reasonably believing that she consented under a wide array of surrounding circumstances? *See* SCHULHOFER, *supra* note 1 (calling for "concrete reforms" "to specify which beliefs about consent are reasonable."). Is a reasonableness standard justified by the idea of self-deception, that is, that most date rapists who sincerely believe that they have consent are deluding themselves? *See* p. 349-51, Note 1 (discussing reasonableness as that of a "man not deceiving himself about the woman's likely consent."). Should it be a "reasonable woman's standard, essentially asking, "[w]ould a reasonable woman in the man's position have understood that there was consent?" *See* CAROLINE FORELL & DONNA A. MATTHEWS, A LAW OF HER OWN: THE REASONABLE WOMAN AS A MEASURE OF MAN 223-40 (2000).

3. *Model Penal Code.* The Model Penal Code takes a more subjective approach. The forcible rape statute, section 213.1, is largely silent about mental state, so, under the interpretive principles stated in section 2.02, silence means that the operative mental state is at least recklessness. Recklessness, of course, requires conscious awareness of a substantial and unjustifiable *risk* that the woman was not consenting. The Code thus requires negligence *plus* conscious awareness of the risk. Although this is admittedly a lesser standard than *knowing* that the woman did not consent, a defendant who *should have known better* but was not consciously aware even of the risk of non-consent must be acquitted.

§ 9.03 Force

In re D.B.
53 A.3d 646 (N.H. 2012)

CONBOY, J.

The juvenile, D.B., appeals the Manchester Family Division's finding of delinquency based upon a petition alleging misdemeanor sexual assault. He argues that there was insufficient evidence for the trial court to find that he committed sexual assault against the complainant pursuant to the variant charged. We reverse.

The record supports the following facts. In May 2010, the juvenile and the complainant, also a juvenile, regularly rode the school bus together. On May 19, the juvenile sat next to the complainant on the bus ride home. The complainant testified that during the ride, the juvenile put his hand down her shirt and touched her breasts. She further stated that he put his hand down her pants and "ran it" down to her ankle. The complainant repeatedly told the juvenile to stop, but he did not. She testified that, immediately after the incident, the juvenile [threatened her if she told anyone about the incident.]

A week later, the complainant reported the incident to a guidance counselor. The juvenile was charged with misdemeanor sexual assault, RSA 632–A:4, I(a), and witness tampering, RSA 641:5 (2007). The sexual assault petition alleged that the juvenile "[d]id commit the crime of sexual assault in that he purposefully subjected [the complainant] (15 years old) to sexual contact without her consent by squeezing her breasts and touching her nipples with his hand by overcoming the victim through the actual application of physical force."

The complainant wrote a statement describing the incident and provided it to the police. Although the statement was not admitted into evidence at trial, the complainant agreed, in response to questioning, that in the statement she wrote that when the juvenile reached underneath her clothes, he "squeezed and rubbed" her breasts, and "touched [her] privates and ... rubbed them." She also agreed that in her statement, she described the juvenile's conduct as "hurting" her and being "rough."

In addition to the complainant's testimony, the State presented at trial a surveillance video of the May 19 bus ride. The complainant testified that she did not alert other students on the bus at the time of the incident because she "did not want to get in trouble," "did not want other people to know," and "was in shock."

At the close of the State's case, and at the end of the trial, the juvenile moved to dismiss the sexual assault charge for lack of sufficient evidence. Subsequently, the trial court found the juvenile delinquent on both charges. On appeal, the juvenile challenges only the sexual assault delinquency finding.

The juvenile argues that "[t]he evidence did not justify a rational trier of fact in finding beyond a reasonable doubt that [he] sexually assaulted" the complainant because it failed to demonstrate that he "overcame" her "through the actual application of physical force." * * *

In challenging the sufficiency of the evidence, the juvenile must "prove that no rational trier of fact, viewing all of the evidence and all reasonable inferences from it in the light most favorable to the State, could have found guilt beyond a reasonable doubt." *State v. Oakes*, 13 A.3d 293 (N.H. 2010). We will consider the entire trial record because the juvenile chose to present a case after unsuccessfully moving to dismiss the petitions.

The juvenile first argues that the State failed "to prove that [he] overcame [the complainant] with the actual application of physical force." He contends that the State was required to prove that he exerted physical force apart from that inherent in the sexual contact itself. His argument focuses on the phrase "overcomes the victim through the actual application of physical force," RSA 632–A:2, I(a), and, more specifically, on the term "overcomes" as used in the statute. The State argues that the statute does not require application of force greater than that inherent in the act itself. In the alternative, the State contends that the juvenile used more force than that involved in the act itself, thereby satisfying either construction of the statute.

* * * Under the charged variant of misdemeanor sexual assault, a person is guilty when he "subjects another person who is 13 years of age or older to sexual contact" and "overcomes the victim through the actual application of physical force, physical violence or superior physical strength." RSA 632–A:4, I(a); RSA 632–A:2, I(a). "Sexual contact" is defined as "the intentional touching whether directly, through clothing, or otherwise, of the victim's or actor's sexual or intimate parts, including emissions, tongue, anus, breasts, and buttocks," and includes only the "aforementioned conduct which can be reasonably construed as being for the purpose of sexual arousal or gratification." RSA 632–A:1.

The statute does not set forth the degree of force required to demonstrate that a person "overcomes the victim through the actual application of physical force." Neither does it define the term "overcomes." The general meaning of the term is twofold: it can either mean "to get the better of: SURMOUNT, CONQUER, SUBDUE," *Webster's Third New International Dictionary* 1607, or "to affect or influence so strongly as to make physically helpless or emotionally distraught ...: OVERPOWER, OVERWHELM." Both understandings of the word thus share the connotation "to defeat." As to either understanding of the word, under the plain language of the statutory variant charged here, the actor must "overcome [ ] the victim through the actual application of physical force, physical violence or superior physical strength." Indeed, RSA 632–A:2, I(a) is the only variant under RSA 632–A:2 that requires "the actual application of physical force."

The State relies upon *People v. Premo*, 540 N.W.2d 715 (Mich. Ct. App. 1995), in arguing that our statute requires no greater application of force than that necessary to perform the sexual co-tact itself. However, in concluding that the defendant's pinching of the victim's buttocks "satisfie[d] the force element" of Michigan's statute, which is broader in scope than ours, the court did not address the statute's "overcoming" requirement. Thus, *Premo* is not on point.

The juvenile cites *State v. Simpson*, 582 A.2d 619 (N.H. 1990), as well as cases from other jurisdictions, in support of his argument that, to "overcome by physical force," the actor must use physical force apart from that inherent in the sexual contact. In *Simpson*, we held that the evidence was sufficient to find the defendant guilty of aggravated felonious sexual assault under RSA 632–A:2, I(a) where the victim testified that the defendant fondled her breasts and sexually penetrated "her while physically holding her down." Although *Simpson* does not establish the parameters for the amount of force required to show that a victim was overcome by force, we agree that to sustain a sexual assault charge under RSA 632–A:2, I(a), the evidence must show that the actor applied some degree of force greater than that inherent in the sexual act itself. Cf. *State v. Marshall*, 253 P.3d 1017, 1028 (Ore. 2011) (determining "that, when the state elects to prove the 'forcible compulsion' element of a charge of first-degree sexual abuse by evidence of physical force, it must show that the physical force that the defendant used was greater in degree or different in kind from the simple movement and contact that is inherent in the act of touching the intimate part of another" and the force "was sufficient to compel the victim to submit to or engage in the sexual contact, against the victim's will"); *State v. Lynch*, 19 A.3d 51, 57 (R.I. 2011) (stating that "to prove first-degree sexual assault by force or coercion ... 'proof of force beyond that which is used in the consummation of the act is required' ").

To read the statute as requiring no greater force than that inherent in the sexual contact itself would make this variant applicable to any and all sexual assault allegations, essentially rendering meaningless the "physical force" and "overcoming" requirements. This we decline to do. Therefore, the legislature's use of the phrase "overcomes the victim through the actual application of physical force" in RSA 632–A:2, I(a) means that the State must prove the use of actual physical force, and not simply lack of consent, to support a delinquency finding under this variant. The State is not required, however, to prove that the victim resisted. The legislature did not require a sexual assault victim to resist and we will not add language to the statute that the legislature did not see fit to include.

Here, the complainant's direct testimony indicated that the juvenile put his hand down her shirt and touched her breasts. She further stated that the juvenile put his hand down her pants and "ran it" down to her ankle. This evidence, however, fails to describe in what way the juvenile overcame her with the actual application of physical force. Nor does the surveillance video support the State's position. In fact, the video shows no movement consistent with the juvenile engaging in any conduct that can be characterized as overcoming the complainant through the actual application of physical force.

To the extent that the complainant's testimony regarding her prior statement can be considered as substantive evidence, it is also insufficient to support a conviction in this case. The complainant indicated in her statement that the juvenile "squeezed and rubbed" her breasts, and "touched [her] privates and ... rubbed them" despite her telling him to stop. Although these descriptions may have supported a finding that the sexual contact was not consented to, they are not sufficient to support a finding that the juvenile overcame her by the actual application of physical force. In her statement, the complainant also reported that the juvenile's conduct was "rough" and "hurting" her. However, rough, hurtful conduct is not, standing alone, among the circumstances the legislature has enumerated as a basis for a sexual assault conviction. Therefore, such evidence is insufficient to support a finding that the complainant was overcome by the application of physical force.

We have previously determined that each of the statutory variants of sexual assault listed under RSA 632–A:2, I, requires proof of an element or elements the others do not. The delinquency petition, equivalent to an indictment for the purposes of our analysis, charged the "overcoming by physical force" variant of sexual assault. Even if the evidence may have been sufficient to establish one of the other variants of sexual assault, see RSA 632–A:2, I(m) (when victim indicates consent is not freely given), considering all of the evidence and all reasonable inferences to be drawn from it in the light most favorable to the State, we conclude that no rational trier of fact could have found beyond a reasonable doubt that the juvenile committed misdemeanor sexual assault within the meaning of RSA 632–A:2, I(a), as charged under RSA 632–A:4 in the petition. Because no rational trier of fact could have found that the juvenile "overc[ame] the victim through the actual application of physical force, physical violence or superior physical strength," RSA 632–A:2, I(a), we reverse the trial court's finding of true. * * *

§ 9.04 Consent and Mistake

State v. Bunyard
133 P.3d 14 (Kan. 2006)

The opinion of the court was delivered by DAVIS, J.:

The defendant was charged with three counts of rape stemming from three separate incidents with acquaintances in 1999, 2000, and 2001. The prosecutor combined all three charges into one information filed on February 5, 2001. The defendant's motion to sever the charges was denied by the district court. He was acquitted of two of the charges but was found guilty of raping E.N.

The defendant was 21 years old when he met E.N. at a pool party at the home of a mutual friend. E.N., who was 17 years old, flirted with the defendant. She thought the defendant was "cool" so she invited him to a party at her friend's house the following night.

The defendant and friends attended the party the next night. After talking with E.N. for awhile, the defendant invited her to watch a movie in his car with another one of his friends. The defendant drove a Chrysler Sebring two-door convertible with a DVD player built in the dash. The defendant put the car's convertible top up before they began watching the movie.

After the defendant's friend left the car, the defendant and E.N. began kissing. E.N. did not object when the defendant removed her clothing. Likewise, she did not object when the defendant removed his clothing and placed a condom on his penis. However, after the defendant laid E.N. back in the seat and penetrated her vagina with his penis, E.N. said, "I don't want to do this." The defendant did not stop, replying, "Just a little bit longer." E.N. again stated that she did not "want to do this," but the defendant did not stop. E.N. testified that she unsuccessfully tried to sit up and roll over on her stomach to get away from the defendant. After 5 or 10 minutes had passed, E.N. began to cry, and the defendant stopped having sexual intercourse with her. * * *

The defendant testified that E.N. was on top of him during consensual intercourse and they were talking. E.N. asked him if he wanted a relationship and if he planned on calling her the next day. When the defendant said he was not interested in a relationship, E.N. became upset, got off of him, and told him about how she had been hurt by other guys in the past. E.N. wanted to continue kissing and wanted him to stay in the car and hold her, but the defendant did not stay in the car and told her to get dressed.

E.N. went back into the house visibly upset and told K.B. that she had been taken advantage of, that the defendant had gotten inside of her, and that she had said "no" more than once. M.B. also spoke with E.N., who was crying. M.B. testified that E.N. said, "I was raped. We had sex. I said no." E.N. did not want to report the incident to the police at that time because she did not want her parents to find out that she had been drinking.

Four days later, E.N. reported the incident to the police, and she was examined at the local hospital. The sexual assault examiner detected a cluster of abrasions consistent with blunt force trauma in E.N.'s vagina. The examiner testified that the location of the abrasions was consistent with mounting injuries. Although consensual sex could not be ruled out, the examiner testified that mounting injuries are more commonly found after nonconsensual sexual intercourse. * * *

Withdrawal of Consent After Consensual Penetration

Because we have remanded this case for a new trial on the reversed rape charge [because of prosecutorial misconduct in the closing argument], we think it advisable to assist the trial court upon remand. We therefore address defendant's third issue on the question of withdrawal of consent after consensual penetration. During its deliberations, the jury posed the following question: "If someone allows penetration, but then says no and he does not stop, does that fit the legal definition of rape? Please elaborate on the law. If there is any [to] elaborate." Outside the presence of the jury, the trial court discussed its answer with defense counsel and the State. The State asked the court to answer "yes," and defense counsel stated he would like for the answer to be "no." The court advised defense counsel that responding with a "no" would be absolutely wrong and that if its choice were between "yes" and "no," then "yes" would be the answer. [The trial judge refused to respond to the jury's question directly, only referring them back to the instructions on the elements of the offense.] * * *

Under the circumstances of this case, we conclude that the trial court's answer to a question posed by the jury was insufficient to properly instruct the jury how to consider this unique case of first impression. The problem with the trial court's response is that it failed to address the question asked by the jury.

In reaching this conclusion, our analysis begins with the following two related issues raised by the defendant: (1) Was the evidence insufficient as a matter of law to support a conviction of rape, *i.e.,* does the Kansas rape statute cover post penetration conduct, and (2) if rape can occur after consensual penetration, must the defendant have a reasonable time in which to act?

Consent Withdrawn After Penetration

The defendant argues that the Kansas rape statute does not include circumstances where consent is revoked after intercourse has begun. * * *

K.S.A.2004 Supp. 21-3502(a)(1)(A) defines rape as "[s]exual intercourse with a person who does not consent to the sexual intercourse ... [w]hen the victim is overcome by force or fear." " 'Sexual intercourse' means any penetration of the female sex organ by a finger, the male sex organ or any object. Any penetration, however slight, is sufficient to constitute sexual intercourse." K.S.A. 21-3501(1).

The defendant focuses on the phrase "[a]ny penetration, however slight, is sufficient to constitute sexual intercourse," claiming that the statute limits penetration to the initial entry of the penis or other object into the woman's vagina. While we disagree with the defendant's narrow definition of penetration, he finds support in at least two states.

Maryland and North Carolina have concluded that consent may only be withdrawn prior to the initial penetration. If consent is withdrawn after the initial penetration, the defendant cannot be convicted of rape even if the sexual acts are continued against the victim's will by force or fear. Battle v. State, 414 A.2d 1266 (Md. 1980); State v. Way, 254 S.E.2d 760 (N.C. 1979) (limiting the withdrawal of consent to multiple acts of intercourse). Neither of these courts provide any analysis or citation to authority to support their conclusions. We decline to follow Maryland and North Carolina.

The defendant's narrow definition of penetration fails to comport with the ordinary meaning and understanding of sexual intercourse, which includes the entire sexual act. Under the defendant's definition of penetration, intercourse begins and ends at the same time. Rather than limiting the definition of intercourse, the phrase "[a]ny penetration, however slight, is sufficient to constitute sexual intercourse" establishes the threshold of evidence necessary to prove that intercourse has occurred. * * * When K.S.A.2004 Supp. 21-3502(a)(1)(A) is construed in accordance with the ordinary meanings of its words, the defendant's argument fails. K.S.A.2004 Supp. 21-3502(a)(1)(A) proscribes *all* nonconsensual sexual intercourse that is accomplished by force or fear, not just the initial penetration. Thus, a person may be convicted of rape if consent is withdrawn after the initial penetration but intercourse is continued by the use of force or fear.

Our conclusion that rape may occur after the initial penetration is aligned with the majority of states that have addressed the issue of post-penetration rape. * * *

A Reasonable Time to Withdraw

The defendant contends that even if rape can occur after consensual penetration, the State failed to prove that he did not cease sexual intercourse within a reasonable time after E.N. withdrew her consent. * * * In *In re John Z*, the victim told the defendant three times that she "needed to go home," but the intercourse continued for an estimated 4 to 5 minutes after the victim first told the defendant she needed to go home. The defendant argued that in cases involving an initial consent to intercourse, the male should be permitted a reasonable amount of time in which to withdraw once the female raises an objection to intercourse. The defendant reasoned:

> "By essence of the act of sexual intercourse, a male's primal urge to reproduce is aroused. It is therefore unreasonable for a female and the law to expect a male to cease having sexual intercourse immediately upon her withdrawal of consent. It is only natural, fair and just that the male be given a reasonable amount of time in which to quell his primal urge...."

In disagreeing with this argument, the California Supreme Court found that apart from the apparent lack of supporting authority for the "primal urge" theory, nothing in the language of its statute suggested that the defendant was entitled to persist in intercourse once his victim withdrew her consent. The court went on to find that even if it was to accept the "reasonable time" argument, the defendant was given ample time to withdraw but refused despite the victim's resistance and objections. The court declined to explore or recommend instructional language governing the point in time at which a defendant must cease intercourse once consent is withdrawn.

* * * In the case of consensual intercourse and withdrawn consent, we agree that the defendant should be entitled to a reasonable time in which to act after consent is withdrawn and communicated to the defendant. However, we conclude that the jury should determine whether the time between withdrawal of consent and the interruption of intercourse was reasonable. This determination must be based upon the particular facts of each case, taking into account the manner in which consent was withdrawn. We believe this conclusion balances our rejection of the

primal urge theory per se with our recognition of the unique facts and circumstances of each individual case.

While the facts of this case may establish that the defendant's continuation of intercourse by placing the victim in fear or by forcing the victim to continue for 5 to 10 minutes was well beyond a reasonable time, we reiterate that this is a jury determination and not for the trial court or the appellate courts to decide. We, thus, conclude that the trial court had a duty to instruct the jury that post-penetration rape can occur under Kansas law and that the defendant has a "reasonable time" to respond to the withdrawal of consent.

Although we have strongly advised trial judges to follow PIK [Pattern Instructions for Kansas], we have also advised that when faced with a novel question such as the one in this case, a trial court "should not hesitate to make such modification or addition" as is not covered by the PIK instructions. The trial court in this case was presented with a question of first impression by the appellate courts of this state. Under these circumstances, the trial judge did the best he could by following the PIK instructions. However, the PIK committee had not considered the question raised in this case, and the response by the trial court, therefore, did not directly address the question raised by the jury.

We note that other courts have approved additional instructions such as the following in response to similar juror questions:

> "[I]f a couple consensually engages in sexual intercourse and one or the other changes his or her mind, and communicates the revocation or change of mind of the consent, and the other partner continues the sexual intercourse by compulsion of the party who changes his or her mind, then it would be rape. The critical element there is the continuation under compulsion.

> "If there exists consensual sexual intercourse and the alleged victim changes her mind and communicates the revocation or change of mind of consent and the other person continues the sexual intercourse by compelling the victim through the use of force then it would be sexual assault in the first degree.

> "This is not just someone withdrawing their consent but it's a withdrawal of consent communicated to the other and then sexual intercourse continues by compelling the victim through the use of force. So it's not just a withdrawal of consent, it's also a withdrawal of consent communicated to the other person and then a compelling use of force to continue sexual intercourse."

The answer given by the trial court in this case was partially correct by referring to the elements of rape. However, the complete answer in addition to setting forth the elements of rape should have indicated to the jury that rape may occur even though consent was given to the initial penetration, but only if the consent is withdrawn and communicated to the defendant, the defendant does not respond within a reasonable time, and the sexual intercourse continues where the victim is overcome by force or fear. A reasonable time depends upon the circumstances of each case and is judged by an objective reasonable person standard to be applied by the trier of fact on a case-by-case basis.

Judgment of the Court of Appeals affirming the district court is reversed. The district court is reversed, and the case is remanded for a new trial.

NOTES AND QUESTIONS

1. ***Selecting Charges.*** Rape charges can be very difficult to prove when the complainant and the defendant know one another and there is no strong forensic evidence establishing the use of force or the absence of consent. What should a prosecutor consider in the selection of charges against a defendant? The American Bar Association MODEL RULES OF PROFESSIONAL CONDUCT, Rule 3.8 provides that, "[t]he prosecutor in a criminal case shall: (a) refrain from prosecuting a charge that the prosecutor knows is not supported by probable cause." Prosecutors, however, are allowed significant discretion in selection charges. The Standards for Criminal Justice, Prosecution Function, Standard 3-3.9, states in part:

(a) A prosecutor should not institute, or cause to be instituted, or permit the continued pendency of criminal charges when the prosecutor knows that the charges are not supported by probable cause. A prosecutor should not institute, cause to be instituted, or permit the continued pendency of criminal charges in the absence of sufficient admissible evidence to support a conviction.

(b) The prosecutor is not obliged to present all charges which the evidence might support. The prosecutor may in some circumstances and for good cause consistent with the public interest decline to prosecute, notwithstanding that sufficient evidence may exist which would support a conviction.
* * *

2. ***Procedure for Bringing Charges***. Usually criminal charges start with a complaint issued shortly after arrest or with an arrest warrant and complaint issued before, and authorizing, an arrest. In some jurisdictions, a grand jury must find that there is probable cause to support every charge – or at least every felony charge. If

it so finds, it issues an indictment making those charges, though the prosecutor drafts the indictment for the grand jury's approval. If the indictment is issued, it replaces the complaint. In most jurisdictions, felony charges require a preliminary hearing to determine whether there is probable cause to support each of the charges. The preliminary hearing is an adversarial one in a public setting before a judge rather than, as with the grand jury, a secret hearing attended only by the prosecutor without the judge's or defense counsel's presence. If the preliminary hearing judge finds probable cause, he signs an "information," rather than an indictment. The information also replaces the complaint. In large prosecutors' offices, there are often assistants specially trained to handle rape and other sexual assault cases. These assistants usually draft the complaints themselves based upon the police reports.

3.   ***Eliminating Consent as an Element.*** Some states have amended their rape statutes to drop the requirement that the state prove that the victim did not consent. For example, Michigan's Criminal Sexual Conduct statute provides degrees of rape involving certain circumstances, including when "[t]he actor uses force or coercion to accomplish the sexual penetration." The statute provides examples of what constitutes "force or coercion" to include

> (i) When the actor overcomes the victim through the actual application of physical force or physical violence.

> (ii) When the actor coerces the victim to submit by threatening to use force or violence on the victim, and the victim believes that the actor has the present ability to execute these threats.

> (iii) When the actor coerces the victim to submit by threatening to retaliate in the future against the victim, or any other person, and the victim believes that the actor has the ability to execute this threat. As used in this subdivision, "to retaliate" includes threats of physical punishment, kidnapping, or extortion.

> (iv) When the actor engages in the medical treatment or examination of the victim in a manner or for purposes which are medically recognized as unethical or unacceptable.

MICH. COMP. LAWS 750.520b.

Some states eliminate consent as a defense when the perpetrator occupies a position of authority over the victim. For example, the New Hampshire Aggravated Felonious Sexual Assault statute provides:

When the actor is in a position of authority over the victim and uses this authority to coerce the victim to submit under any of the following circumstances:

(1) When the actor has direct supervisory or disciplinary authority over the victim by virtue of the victim being incarcerated in a correctional institution, the secure psychiatric unit, or juvenile detention facility where the actor is employed; or

(2) When the actor is a probation or parole officer or a juvenile probation and parole officer who has direct supervisory or disciplinary authority over the victim while the victim is on parole or probation or under juvenile probation.

Consent of the victim under any of the circumstances set forth in [this subparagraph] shall not be considered a defense.

N.H. REV. STAT. § 632-A:2(n). States that have eliminated non-consent of the victim as an element of the offense continue to recognize that consent is a valid defense to a charge. There is a split, however, regarding whether the prosecution or the defense bears the burden of showing the victim's consent. In *State v. Camara*, 781 P.2d 483 (Wash. 1989), the Washington Supreme Court held that "the removal from the prior rape statute of language expressly referring to nonconsent evidences legislative intent to shift the burden of proof on that issue to the defense." In *State v. Jackson*, 679 A.2d 572 (N.H. 1996), the New Hampshire Supreme Court concluded, "[o]nce a defendant in an aggravated felonious sexual assault case raises the defense of consent, the State must prove beyond a reasonable doubt that the victim did not consent."

4. *Form of Consent.* What constitutes sufficient consent to defend against a charge of rape? In *In the Interest of M.T.S.*, 609 A.2d 1266 (N.J. 1992), the New Jersey Supreme Court held that "any act of sexual penetration engaged in by the defendant without the affirmative and freely-given permission of the victim to the specific act of penetration constitutes the offense of sexual assault." The court tempered its holding by noting that

permission may be inferred either from acts or statements reasonably viewed in light of the surrounding circumstances. Persons need not, of course, expressly announce their consent to engage in intercourse for there to be affirmative permission. Permission to engage in an act of sexual penetration can be and indeed often is indicated through physical actions rather than words. Permission is demonstrated when the evidence, in whatever form, is sufficient to demonstrate that a reasonable person would have believed that the alleged victim had affirmatively and freely given authorization to the act.

5. ***Mens Rea for Consent.*** What should be the appropriate mental state for the element of consent in a rape case: strict liability, negligence, recklessness, knowledge, or purpose? Why? How should punishment theory of criminal law and sentencing factor in the determining the requisite level of mens rea? What is the best approach to a negligence standard: a "reasonable woman" or "reasonable person" test, a "duty of reasonable inquiry" test, one including in the circumstances of the reasonable person that he or she does not deceive himself or herself about a person's sexual desires, or some other test? Why? How does one make each of these tests real for a jury, that is, what instructions should be read to the jury to explain their task? How would cross-examination questions of the defendant by the prosecution (should the defendant choose to take the stand; under the fifth amendment privilege against self-incrimination, that person cannot be forced onto the stand) differ, if at all, under each of these tests?

6. ***Marital Exemption.*** Under the common law, a husband could not be convicted of raping his wife. The exemption was based on a statement of Lord Hale: "But the husband cannot be guilty of a rape committed by himself upon his lawful wife, for by their mutual matrimonial consent and contract the wife hath given up herself in this kind unto her husband, which she cannot retract." 1 M. HALE, THE HISTORY OF THE PLEAS OF THE CROWN 629 (S. Emlyn ed. 1778). Beginning in the 1970s, there was a movement to eliminate the exemption for marital rape, both in the legislatures and the courts, some of which found it unconstitutional. Today, "[s]tate legislatures and the courts have effectively abolished the formal marital rape exemption in all fifty states and the District of Columbia." Jessica Klarfeld, Note, *A Striking Disconnect: Marital Rape Law's Failure to Keep Up With Domestic Violence Law*, 48 AM. CRIM. L. REV. 1819 (2011).

7. ***Trial Considerations.*** Date rape trials often turn on credibility, a "he said, she said" battle about what happened. But this battle usually implicitly involves a three-part defense in the alternative, the defendant's claim being as follows: (1) she consented; (2) even if she did not consent, any reasonable man would have interpreted her "sluttish" behavior as consent; and (3) in any event, I had no idea that she did not consent and was shocked to hear her saying otherwise. Stranger rapes (the classic unknown male leaping at a woman from bushes hidden in nighttime darkness) more often turn on the question of identity — who did it, the defendant or someone else? — rather than consent.

Professor Andrew E. Taslitz has argued that there are a variety of unconscious psychological forces, rooted in our gendered preconceptions about language, that generally put most women in consent defense rape trials at a severe credibility disadvantage that has nothing to do with whether they are in fact telling the truth. Taslitz explains:

[W]hen women ... speak in public contexts, their words may not be well received. This resistance to women's words arises in part from the perception that they speak a "women's language."

Some feminist theorists have indeed posited a unique "women's language," a set of linguistic features characteristic of how women speak in most settings. Among the posited features are the use of "meaningless particles," like "my goodness"; empty adjectives expressing entirely emotional assessments, as in "It's adorable!"; and use of hedge words like "I guess" or "I think," conveying uncertainty. These features were viewed by some as learned behaviors, hallmarks of women's inferior social position....

...

Research has failed to confirm, or disconfirm, the existence of a women's speech constant across contexts. Nevertheless, research has revealed some linguistic forms that women are more likely to use than men in a wide variety of settings.... Many of these observed differences are, however, more likely due to setting, topic, role, and status. For example, those in lower-status positions (as are many women) use such politeness strategies toward those of higher status.

Even when women do not use "women's language," however, they are perceived as doing so. This perception arises because our stereotypes or "folk linguistic" beliefs about how women speak closely track the descriptions of women's language. Stereotypes lead us to ignore contrary evidence while attending to confirming evidence. Furthermore, these biases are magnified by the "fundamental attribution error," our tendency to attribute behavior more to personality than context. Consequently, when we see many women in low-status roles speaking politely, we attribute that behavior to women's essential nature rather than to their role. The resulting linguistic stereotypes resist change, as they have in American culture for more than twenty years.

One effect of perceiving women's language where it does not exist and of viewing it as typical female behavior is the self-fulfilling prophecy. Women learn that they will be ignored or disliked if they violate stereotypical norms, so they try not to deviate too much from those norms.

Although other factors, such as age, race, and class can reduce the effects of stereotypes, the effects are greatest where gender is most salient. But gender is most salient in initial encounters or where women are in the minority. Our gendered cognitive biases lessen as we get to know individuals better. Interestingly, female crime victims at trial face precisely those initial encounters (between victim and jurors) in which women are often in the minority. Moreover, the very nature of the crime of rape suggests that gender will be salient.

The effect of the real or imagined use of women's language can be devastating to a woman's credibility. Anyone using women's language is evaluated as more caring but less credible, competent, and intelligent. These evaluations are magnified when women, rather than men, are the speakers. Furthermore, the indirectness supposedly characteristic of women's language may be seen as insecure, apology as weakness. Additionally, women's language speakers use of shorter, less aggressive responses in public settings command less attention. Similarly, their giving reasons for their suggestions and arguing from their personal experience rather than abstract principle, two "feminine" strategies, are relatively unpersuasive to men. These effects are much larger in laboratory settings than in the few studies involving naturally occurring speech, but even modest effects can be decisive in criminal cases. There, defense victory requires only "reasonable doubt."

Yet women face a double bind if they violate stereotypical speech norms. Most men simply do not like aggressive women. "There is a sense in which every woman is seen as a receptionist — available to give information and help, perennially interruptible." Women who violate stereotypes may seem unlikable or unworthy to many men. Furthermore, men resist receiving information from those, like women, whom men perceive as of lower status because being lecturer rather than listener is the superior (i.e., men's) role.

In sum, women may be perceived as using women's language when they are not, a perception marking them as stupid, incompetent, and incredible. Yet too masculine a style means they will be disliked or ignored. For a woman to be seen as credible, she must walk a fine line between opposed stereotypes.

ANDREW E. TASLITZ, RAPE AND THE CULTURE OF THE COURTROOM 73-75 (1999) (endnotes omitted).

8. *Comments and Questions.* Professor Taslitz goes on to argue that these differences in linguistic perceptions are also magnified by defense lawyers' appeals to "patriarchal cultural stories," stories about proper gendered behavior that can affect jurors' credibility perceptions, often without their awareness. For example, the movie, *The Little Mermaid*, tells the story of a mermaid who must pay the price of losing her voice if she is to catch her human male love interest. She does eventually earn his affections by regaining her voice, but only because of the beauty of her song, not the content of what she has to say. On the other hand, the loud, pushy, female of the story, the "Sea Witch," who is very open about her needs and

desires, is painted as the quintessence of evil. Professor Taslitz argues that the cumulation of these many small stories in our cultural lives teaches that aggressive women, especially *sexually* aggressive ones, are for that reason alone deemed unworthy, thus less likely to be believed when the circumstances of a date go awry. Moreover, he notes, racial stereotypes can complicate matters further, and there is empirical data and theoretical prisms strongly suggesting that African-American women — largely because of stereotypes about their having active libidos — are the least likely to be believed of all rape victims, even though most rape is *intra-*racial (the one exception being rapes of Native-Americans, in which the most common alleged assailant by far is of a different race).

If Professor Taslitz is right, what can be done about it? Should experts be offered to educate jurors about their own biases? Can voir dire in jury selection help to reduce largely subconscious biases? Should the law of evidence be more receptive to evidence of prior forcible sexual activity by the male, unreceptive to evidence of prior consensual activity of the female, to combat the effect of these stereotypes? Can cross-examination rules be altered to allow women to tell more uninterrupted tales? What strategies can savvy prosecutors follow to reduce the effects of gendered language perception and to craft a truthful story that juries will find credible?

A lurking problem in finding a solution, of course, is this: even if women face an unfair credibility handicap, no matter how truthful their testimony may actually be, there surely must be times, however rare, when a woman lies. Professor Taslitz has also written about one such likely instance — the Duke University Lacrosse Players who were apparently falsely accused of rape of a dancer at a party. *See* Andrew E. Taslitz, *The Duke Lacrosse Players and the Media: Why the Fair Trial/Free Press Paradigm Doesn't Cut it Anymore*, in RACE TO INJUSTICE: LESSONS LEARNED FROM THE DUKE UNIVERSITY LACROSSE PLAYERS RAPE CASE (Michael Siegel ed. 2008). Given this danger, can reform go overboard? How can we be fair to alleged victims, do justice for the state, and still adequately protect the innocent?

Appellate opinions in this area can be especially misleading precisely because they generally arise from that subset of cases where the prosecution won and because the credibility of the prosecution witnesses is assumed on appeal. But, at trials, facts are disputed, and that means credibility disputes. If women are not believed, resulting in acquittals (from which prosecutors may not appeal because of the Double Jeopardy Clause), relatively few cases will make their way into the appellate reports. In the cases to follow, therefore, you should be attentive to how you might have interpreted the evidence had you been a juror, and in the problems to follow you will often be asked to wrestle specifically with credibility in just the way that practicing trial lawyers do.

PROBLEM THIRTY-ONE

Dakota and Riley are 18 year old high school seniors who have been dating a short time. They go to dinner and a movie, and then drink wine and beer obtained by Dakota's older brother. At the end of the evening, while driving Riley home, Dakota pulls into a dark, secluded parking area frequented by the area's teenagers, explaining to Riley that this would give them a chance to talk. Riley does not protest and, at Dakota's initiation, the two start kissing. Dakota then starts touching Riley in more intimate places, and Riley weakly protests, "No, not yet." Dakota next tells Riley, "You look beautiful, I care for you so much." Dakota again starts to touch Riley in more intimate places. This time, Riley says, "Dakota, I really like you, but I don't feel comfortable doing this." Dakota says "Don't worry, I know how to make you feel comfortable." Riley is fully aware of what is happening but feels weak and woozy from drinking. Riley is convinced that Dakota will ignore any protests, and fears that because Dakota is much larger and stronger that Dakota might use force, something Riley did not want to occur in a secluded setting. Accordingly, Riley said nothing further as Dakota proceeded to have sex, though Riley did softly cry. Dakota dropped Riley off at home, where Riley's mom was told what happened and called the police. Dakota is interviewed the next day by police detectives and confirms much of Riley's story but says Riley was crying tears of joy. Dakota says "I never would have proceeded if I thought Riley was not consenting."

1. If both Dakota and Riley are telling the truth, did Riley "consent"?

2. If Riley did not consent, did Dakota behave recklessly? Negligently? Concerning negligence, would the outcome vary based upon which negligence test is used, that is, undefined common law negligence, the reasonable person test, the duty of inquiry test, or the non-self-deceiving person test?

3. Remove the assumption that both parties are telling the truth in all respects. Are there indicators that Dakota may in fact at least have been consciously aware of a substantial and unjustifiable risk that Riley was not consenting?

4. As a prosecutor, what questions would you want to ask Dakota to determine whether the acts were performed recklessly in a if this occurred in a Model Penal Code jurisdiction? If Dakota refused to discuss the incident further on the advice of counsel, would that affect the decision whether to file charges? What questions would you ask Riley to determine whether Dakota was consciously aware of the risk of non-consent?

§ 9.05 Fraud

People v. Pham
103 Cal.Rptr.3d 366 (Cal. Ct. App. 2010)

BEDSWORTH, J.

There appears to be no limit to the ability of our species to devise new and different bad things to do to each other. Here we deal with a criminal hybridization of fraud and molestation first addressed by legislation in 2002. The issues presented appear to be of first impression in California.

Chiropractor Chi Van Pham was convicted of sexual battery by fraud (Pen.Code, § 243.4(c)) for touching the intimate body parts of his patients while purporting to examine them. * * * [There were three patients of the defendant who were victims and only identified by the court by their first names: Julie, a minor, Elsa, and Toan.]

In order to be guilty of sexual battery by fraud, the perpetrator must touch an intimate part of the victim for sexual purposes and, at the time of the touching, the victim must be "unconscious of the nature of the act because the perpetrator fraudulently represented that the touching served a professional purpose." Although Pham does not dispute he touched Julie, Elsa and Toan inappropriately while examining them, he contends there is insufficient evidence they were not conscious of the sexual nature of the touching due to any fraudulent representations he made to them. We find sufficient evidence to support Pham's convictions for sexual battery by fraud. * * *

Traditionally, the law has distinguished between two types of fraud in analyzing the issue of consent in sex crime cases, fraud in the fact and fraud in the inducement. Fraud in the fact occurs when the defendant obtains the victim's consent to perform one act, but instead engages in another act. See, e.g., *People v. Minkowski*, 23 Cal.Rptr. 92 (Cal. 1962) (defendant gynecologist obtained permission to insert a medical instrument into victim's vagina but inserted his penis instead). In that situation, consent is absent, and the defendant is guilty of sexual battery because the victim never agreed to the particular act complained of.

By contrast, fraud in the inducement takes place when the defendant makes misrepresentations to the victim in order to get her consent for a particular act, and then proceeds to carry out that very act. See, e.g., *Boro v. Superior Court*, 210 Cal.Rptr. 122 (Cal. 1985) (victim agreed to sexual intercourse because defendant falsely told her the act was necessary to treat a potentially fatal illness). In that situation, courts have historically been reluctant to impose criminal liability on the defendant since the victim consented to the particular act performed, albeit under false pretenses.

However, in 2002, the Legislature sought to expand the circumstances under which a defendant may be prosecuted for fraudulently inducing a victim to consent to sexual conduct. Now, in addition to prohibiting fraud in the fact, California law proscribes "a narrow set of circumstances involving fraudulent inducement: those in which the victim was unaware of the nature of the act due to the perpetrator's fraudulent representation that the sexual [assault] served a professional purpose." * * * The law was enacted "to close a loophole" that allowed defendants who committed sexual acts on their patients under the guise of medical treatment to escape punishment for their conduct. Falk, *Rape by Fraud and Rape by Coercion*, 64 BROOKLYN L.REV. 39(1998). In that regard, the law represents a clear "legislative judgment[ ] that fraud and coercion are totally inappropriate in certain alliances between holders of positions of trust and their patients." Id.

Pham argues he did not commit sexual battery by fraud against any of his patients because he did not expressly tell them his touching of their intimate body parts was for professional, medical purposes. However, Pham did not have to deceive his patients in such explicit terms to be guilty of fraudulent representation under Penal Code section 243.4(c). The statute does not require an express representation; it simply speaks to the situation where the defendant "fraudulently represented that the touching served a professional purpose." In keeping with the statute's intent to criminalize sexual acts committed under the guise of professional services, it only makes sense to consider the totality of the defendant's conduct—not just his verbal statements—in determining whether he fraudulently represented the nature of his actions. After all, actions often speak louder than words: "A false promise can as easily, perhaps more easily, be implied from con-duct as from language[.]" * * *

We must also be mindful of the fact that, when it comes to treating their patients, physicians occupy a position of implicit trust. A medical professional "who holds him or herself out to the public as one available to administer to the medical needs of patients through examination and treatment is burdened with the duty to act for medical purposes in dealing with patients seeking medical care. There is an inherent trust and confidence which a patient seeking medical care places in the [professional] and upon which a patient relies in allowing the [professional] access to the most intimate parts of the body." *State v. Tizard*, 897 S.W.2d 732 (Tenn. Ct. App. 1994). * * *

[I]t readily appears Pham used his position as a medical professional in order to disguise his lewd intentions and perpetrate crimes. Julie, Elsa and Toan all came to him with the expectation of receiving medical treatment for their various injuries. When they arrived at his office, they signed in and had their vital signs checked, as would be expected in a medical setting. They understood Pham would be touching and moving their bodies in various ways to diagnose and treat their injuries. In fact, they all signed consent forms which explained their treatments might be uncomfort-able. This signaled that Pham's techniques, even those that might be unsettling and anxiety-producing, were a necessary part of their treatment regimens. Pham did nothing to dispel this message. Instead, he used it as a smokescreen to obscure his true intentions.

With respect to Julie, he waited until her third treating session to commence any wrongdoing. That way, she had the experience of two normal visits on which to base her trust in Pham as a genuinely concerned medical professional. Even on that third occasion, Pham did not immediately signal his true intentions. Instead, he began treating Julie by massaging and adjusting her neck. Then he worked his way down her chest until he was massaging her breasts. And when he finally slid his hands underneath her clothing, his fondling was not overtly sexual. Rather, he felt his way around the breast, as if he were conducting a normal breast exam. In so doing, Pham continued to give the appearance his actions were medically-related. There is no evidence he displayed anything but a professional demeanor during this or any of the other exams at issue.

Unlike Julie, Elsa only saw Pham one time in his office. On that occasion, an assistant was present, and Pham checked Elsa's blood pressure and reflexes before having her lie down on the exam table. He also placed towels on her chest and waist, for the ostensible purpose of giving her privacy. However, while he was holding his stethoscope on her chest, he proceeded to slide his hand under her bra and touch her breasts. Once again, the touching was not overtly sexual in nature. Rather, he palpated Elsa's breasts, pressing down and moving his hand in a circular motion, spending only a few seconds on each breast. And while he was doing this, he asked Elsa questions about the accident that caused her injuries. These circumstances strongly suggest Pham was doing his best to give the appearance his "treatment" of Elsa was designed to serve a professional purpose.

Likewise with Toan. Pham did not start taking advantage of her until she signed a consent form allowing him to touch her chest for purposes of treating her collarbone. When he did touch her breasts and pubic region, he did so with a "tapping rub" and "patting" motion, which gave the impression the touching was medically related. And even the manner in which Pham touched Toan's buttocks left her with the impression he was merely trying to "adjust" that area of her body. Then, when Toan confronted him about his conduct, he told her he was just checking for pain.

All told, there is sufficient evidence from which the jury could reasonably conclude Pham fraudulently represented to each of the victims that his inappropriate touching served a professional purpose. Even without an express representation to this effect, the totality of the circumstances provides ample evidence of this requirement. We therefore turn our attention to the additional requirement that Pham's fraud resulted in the victims being unconscious of the nature of his acts.

The unconsciousness requirement does not require proof the victim was totally and physically unconscious during the acts in question. It simply requires proof the defendant tricked the victim into submitting to the touching on the pretext it served a professional purpose. This can be accomplished even when the victim has agreed to the act in question. So long as the victim was unaware of the "essential characteristics of the act," i.e., the sexual nature of the act itself, the unconsciousness requirement will be satisfied.

From the facts on hand, it is abundantly clear Julie was unaware of the "essential characteristics" of Pham acts at the time they occurred in 2003. She was 13. She testified she believed the intimate touching was simply part of the procedures to which she had consented. And it wasn't until two years after her treatment, when she volunteered in his office, that she began to suspect Pham of wrongdoing. Based on his kissing and coming on to her at that time, she began to question the treatment he rendered to her back in 2003. Even then, she wasn't entirely certain Pham had touched her in an inappropriate manner. Based on this evidence, the jury could easily conclude Pham's fraudulent representations rendered Julie unconscious of the sexual nature of his acts.

Elsa, 11 years older than Julie, had a different reaction to Pham's conduct. Describing her feelings when Pham touched her breasts, she testified she felt "instant shock" and was "automatically very scared." While this shows she did not expect Pham to touch her breasts, it does not necessarily prove she was aware of his sexual intentions at the time. In fact, she testified she wasn't sure what was happening at that moment. She obviously became very uncomfortable after the touching, but that could simply have been a visceral reaction to the touching itself. Her immediate reaction does not compel the conclusion she possessed a true understanding of the sexual nature of Pham's conduct.

The truth is, Elsa did not try to end the exam after Pham touched her breasts. Nor did she say anything to the assistant who was present when the touching occurred. Even after the exam was over and Pham left the room, she did not say a word to anyone in Pham's office. And she put off going to the police for several days after that. Although it is never easy for anyone to accuse a person in a position of power or authority of wrongdoing, Elsa's delay in reporting Pham's conduct does reflect a certain degree of uncertainty in her mind as to what Pham's intentions were. And, it seems clear that the context of the touching could very well have contributed to that uncertainty. Indeed, Pham's status as a medical provider, his professional demeanor, and the presence of an assistant during Elsa's exam all created the impression his actions were professionally, not sexually, motivated. Given all the circumstances surrounding the incident, the jury could reasonably find Elsa was unconscious of the sexual nature of Pham's acts at the time they were occurring.

Toan's unawareness of the essential nature of Pham's conduct is also reflected in the record. She signed a consent form permitting Pham to touch her chest area, and when Pham reached under her pants and touched her bare posterior, she believed he was trying to "adjust" her buttocks. While the touching made her somewhat uncomfortable, she did not jump to any conclusions about the matter. As a matter of fact, she didn't say anything to Pham at the time, nor did she go directly to the police. Instead, she discussed the matter with family, friends and an attorney. And at the attorney's suggestion, she ended up going back to Pham for further treatment. Her willingness to return to Pham's office suggests she was not fully cognizant of the essential characteristics of the acts that Pham performed on her.

During this return visit, Toan questioned Pham when he touched her breasts. When he said he was checking for pain, she did not question his explanation, seek to end the exam or report his conduct to the authorities. It was only after Toan's new chiropractor informed her about Pham's reputation that she finally reported Pham to the police. This indicates that while Toan came to be increasingly suspicious of Pham's conduct over time, she was not truly aware of the essential nature of his acts at the time he carried them out.

As with Julie and Elsa, we therefore conclude there is sufficient evidence from which the jury could find that Toan was unconscious of Pham's sexual intentions at the time he treated her. And because, as explained above, the evidence also shows the victims' unconsciousness was attributable to Pham's fraudulent representations—both implied and actual—we have no occasion to disturb his convictions. There is substantial evidence to support the jury's finding he committed sexual battery by fraud.

[The defendant was sentenced to seven years in prison, an enhanced sentence based in part on Julie's age.]

NOTE

A number of states make it a crime for a person who knows he or she is infected with Human Immunodeficiency Virus (HIV) to engage in sexual relations with another person without first informing that person of the presence of the condition and obtaining consent to the act. The Florida statute provides:

> It is unlawful for any person who has human immunodeficiency virus infection, when such person knows he or she is infected with this disease and when such person has been informed that he or she may communicate this disease to another person through sexual intercourse, to have

sexual intercourse with any other person, unless such other person has been informed of the presence of the sexually transmissible disease and has consented to the sexual intercourse.

FLA STAT. ANN. § 384.24(2). Note that the statute imposes an affirmative disclosure obligation on the HIV-infected person to make full disclosure before the sexual relations, so that inadequate disclosure would negate any consent. Iowa takes a different approach, making it a crime for an HIV-infected person to engage in sexual relations, and providing an affirmative defense based on consent:

It is an affirmative defense that the person exposed to the human immunodeficiency virus knew that the infected person had a positive human immunodeficiency virus status at the time of the action of exposure, knew that the action of exposure could result in transmission of the human immunodeficiency virus, and consented to the action of exposure with that knowledge.

IOWA CODE ANN. 709C.1(5).

§ 9.06 Statutory Rape

State v. Martinez
52 P.3d 1276 (Utah 2002)

DURHAM, Chief Justice:

Defendant Michael Trevor Martinez was convicted of unlawful sexual activity with a minor, a third degree felony, in violation of section 76-5-401 of the Utah Code. Defendant's conviction was upheld by the Utah Court of Appeals. Defendant appeals, arguing that the court erred when it held that unlawful sexual activity with a minor is a strict liability crime and that imposition of strict liability does not violate defendant's federal due process rights. We affirm. * * *

Defendant was nineteen years old when he had sexual intercourse with a fifteen-year-old girl. Defendant was charged with unlawful sexual intercourse in violation of section 76-5-401. Before trial, defendant filed a motion in limine to determine whether he could submit evidence in support of an affirmative defense that the victim represented herself to be seventeen years old at the time of the sexual intercourse. Defendant contended that section 76-5-401 does not impose strict liability and that he should therefore be allowed to present evidence that he did not know the victim's age. Defendant also argued that if the statute does impose strict liability, it violates federal and state due process requirements.

The trial court denied defendant's motion, relying on section 76-2-304.5 of the Utah Code which excludes the defense of mistake as to the victim's age in a prosecution for unlawful sexual intercourse. In addition, the trial court determined that neither section 76-2-304.5 nor section 76-5-401 violates due process under either the State or the federal constitution. Defendant entered a conditional guilty plea to unlawful sexual intercourse, subject to an appeal of the trial court's denial of defendant's pre-trial motion.

On appeal, the Utah Court of Appeals held that: (1) the legislature clearly intended a violation of section 76-5-401 to be a strict liability crime and expressly precluded the defense of mistake as to the victim's age; and (2) defendant's federal due process rights have not been violated because the statutory scheme reflects careful consideration of protection for minors and rationally furthers a legitimate governmental interest * * * . This court granted certiorari * * * .

Section 76-5-401 of the Utah Code governs the crime of unlawful sexual activity with a minor. On appeal, defendant argues that this statute does not impose strict liability because it fails to clearly indicate a legislative purpose to do so, and that the crime of unlawful sexual intercourse with a minor requires a culpable mental state of at least recklessness. He also argues that if section 76-5-401 does impose strict liability, it violates his federal right to due process for failing to require proof of a culpable mental state. We address each of these arguments in turn * * * .

"When interpreting statutes, our primary goal is to evince 'the true intent and purpose of the Legislature.'" * * * We discern legislative intent and purpose by first looking to the "best evidence" of its meaning, which is the plain language of the statute itself * * * When examining the statutory language we assume the legislature used each term advisedly and in accordance with its ordinary meaning * * * . Furthermore, we "avoid interpretations that will render portions of a statute superfluous or inoperative." * * *

Section 76-5-401 states in relevant part   *statute*

(1) For purposes of this section "minor" is a person who is 14 years of age or older, but younger than 16 years of age, at the time the sexual activity described in this section occurred.

(2) A person commits unlawful sexual activity with a minor if ... the actor:

   (a) has sexual intercourse with the minor ...

(3) A violation of subsection (2) is a third degree felony unless the defendant establishes by a preponderance of the evidence the mitigating

factor that the defendant is less than four years older than the minor at the time the sexual activity occurred, in which case it is a class B misdemeanor.

* * * Section 76-5-401 does not specify a culpable mental state for the crime of unlawful sexual activity with a minor. It simply says that "[a] person commits unlawful sexual activity with a minor if . . . [the person] has sexual intercourse with the minor." The sole mitigating factor provided in the statute is if the defendant can show that he or she was fewer than four years older than the victim at the time of the offense. The plain language of section 76-5-401, therefore, does not require that a defendant intend to have sexual intercourse with a minor who is fourteen or fifteen years old. The commission of the sexual act itself is sufficient to violate the statute.

* * * When a statute does not supply a mental state for proscribed conduct, further guidance is provided by section 76-2-102 of the Utah Code, which states:

> *Culpable mental state required* . . . . An offense shall involve strict liability if the statute defining the offense clearly indicates a legislative purpose to impose criminal responsibility for commission of the conduct prohibited by the statute without requiring proof of any culpable mental state.

* * * We must therefore determine whether the legislature intended to impose criminal liability for unlawful sexual activity with a minor without requiring proof that the defendant intended to engage in sexual intercourse with a fourteen or fifteen-year-old. If we find that this was the legislature's specific purpose, then the crime is one of strict liability, and proof of a culpable mental state is not required.

The plain language of section 76-5-401 does not contain a mens rea element yet we may look to the relationship between other sections of the criminal code and the section at issue for further guidance on legislative intent * * * . Section 76-2-304.5, entitled "Mistake as to victim's age not a defense," explicitly prohibits a defendant from raising mistake as to the victim's age as a defense to a violation of section 76-5-401* * * This section clearly states the legislative intent. The plain language of both section 76-2-304.5 and 76-5-401 shows that the legislature intended to impose criminal responsibility for sexual activity with a minor whether or not the defendant knew the victim's true age. Allowing the defense of mistake as to the victim's age, or requiring the prosecution to prove a mens rea for a violation of section 76-5-401 would render section 76-2-304.5 inoperative.

Defendant's statutory analysis of the strict liability question focuses on the "clearly indicates a legislative purpose" language of section 76-2-102, to the exclusion of the rest of the sentence which reads, "... to impose criminal responsibility for commission of the conduct . . . without requiring proof of any culpable mental state." That is, defendant seems to assert that clear legislative purpose cannot be discerned from the language of the statute, but that some other sign of legislative purpose is needed. However, as we have previously stated, "the fundamental rule of statutory construction is that statutes are generally to be construed according to their plain language." * * * Section 76-5-401 makes sexual intercourse with a fourteen or fifteen-year-old a violation of the statute, irrespective of defendant's knowledge of the victim's age, and section 76-2-304.5 specifically clarifies the legislature's intent regarding knowledge or mistake. We note that Utah is not unique in this regard. The majority of states do not allow mistake of age as a defense to statutory rape, and the defendant's knowledge of the victim's age is not an essential element of the crime * * * "Statutory rape, then, is commonly referred to as a strict-liability crime, meaning that the mental intent of the defendant is not important. The only inquiry is whether the act was performed on a prohibited person." * * *

Defendant argues that section 76-5-401, despite its plain language, does not clearly indicate a legislative intent to impose strict liability because general common law principles require a mens rea for criminal responsibility. Defendant fails to explain, however, why the legislature's imposition of strict liability for this particular crime would not fall within one of the recognized exceptions to the general mens rea rule, or to explain exactly why a plain language reading of the statute negates strict liability. Instead, defendant repeatedly asserts the conclusory argument that section 76-5-401 "does not clearly indicate that the Legislature intended that unlawful sexual intercourse with a minor should be a strict liability crime" and cites other factors and policy reasons the court should consider in discerning the legislature's true intent. The statute, however, is not ambiguous and we decline to read strict liability out of the statute. Unlawful sexual activity with a minor is a strict liability crime* * * .

As the court of appeals correctly stated, "[w]e simply cannot say that our legislature's determination to preclude the mistake of age defense for sexual activity with a minor fourteen or fifteen is so arbitrary as to run afoul of the Constitution." * * * Thus, section 76–5–401 does not violate federal due process.

§ 9.07 Rape Shield Laws

Commonwealth v. Sa
790 N.E.2d 733 (Mass. App. Ct. 2003)

DUFFLY, J.

The defendant was convicted by a jury of one count of aggravated rape, G.L. c. 265, § 22(a) * * *. The only issue on appeal is whether the trial judge properly invoked the rape-shield statute, G.L. c. 233, § 21B, to preclude evidence that the victim had sex with her boyfriend soon after the rape. We affirm the conviction of aggravated rape.

The jury could have found that on a Friday night in October, the seventeen year old victim from Lynn went out with friends to look for a party, ending up in Malden at a bowling alley/pool hall at about 11:00 P.M. After about an hour, the victim and two girl friends, Lonnie and Jennie, decided to leave with Jennie's boyfriend and his cousin, the defendant. The defendant offered to drive the group back to Lynn, a short ten to fifteen minutes away. The victim was the last passenger to be dropped off. She gave directions to her home, which was nearby, but the defendant passed the street to which she had directed him; he then turned left when she instructed him to turn right. The defendant continued to take wrong turns and began driving faster. During the drive, the victim became increasingly agitated and began screaming at the defendant for not following directions. Eventually, she saw that they had passed signs for Reading and Burlington. By this time, both were yelling. The defendant told the victim that because of her yelling and being mad at him, he was going to rape her. The victim said she was just upset because he would not bring her home, but the defendant told her that he "just didn't care," that he was going to rape her, and that she might never see her parents or family again.

Not far past Burlington, the defendant stopped the car, got out, and came around to the passenger side where he attempted to pull the victim from the car, saying she should get out so they could "fuck for a minute." She began crying, apologized for yelling, and asked him not do anything to her. The defendant agreed to take her home, saying, "If you don't trust me, here, I will give you my wallet so you can trust me." The victim took the wallet. After driving for about an hour, the victim saw signs for Concord and Boston. At this point the defendant said, "I could really kill you if I wanted to and nobody would know." He then pulled the car to the side of the road in a wooded area, got out, put a dark plastic bag on the back windows, and said, "All right. Let's go. Let's go." The victim began to cry and again begged to be brought home. The defendant demanded to know if she was ready, and said that he could kill her, that she would never see her family again, and that he could put her in a bag and throw her in the woods and nobody would know. Still crying, the victim eventually got into the back seat of the defendant's car, saying: "You can do whatever you want, but you know for sure, we both know that you are really raping me." The defendant removed the victim's pants and underwear, then penetrated her vaginally from behind with his penis, turned her over, climbed on top of her and twice inserted his penis into her vagina, and once entered her vagina with his fingers. The victim testified that "finally, it just came to a point where I didn't care if he was going to kill me. I didn't care what he was going to do to me." She screamed and struggled, until he stopped. As she put on her clothes he said he was "sorry" and that "he really [did]n't want to do this." She asked to go home and, following her directions, the defendant drove the victim to

Lynn without incident, stopping once on the way to permit her to use a bathroom.[3] Not wanting the defendant to know where she lived, the victim directed the defendant to her boyfriend's house, where he dropped her off at about 5:30 A.M. The victim told her boyfriend what had happened to her and asked him not to tell anyone. It was not until later that day, when a friend convinced her to report the incident to police and drove her to the Lynn police station, that she reported the crimes. She was taken to a hospital, where tests using a rape kit were performed.

The defense was consent. The defendant filed a written motion in limine before trial, pursuant to G.L. c. 233, § 21B, the rape-shield statute, seeking to introduce evidence that the victim had engaged in sexual intercourse with her boyfriend a few hours after arriving at his home.[4] The judge deferred ruling on the motion; during the trial she sustained the Commonwealth's objection to defense counsel's renewed request, made during questioning of the victim. Because the defendant objected at trial, we review to determine whether the judge abused her discretion and, if so, whether this resulted in prejudice to the defendant.

The evidence the defendant sought to elicit during questioning of the victim was that, after being dropped off at her boyfriend's house, the victim went to bed and fell asleep; upon awakening at 11:00 A.M., she and her boyfriend engaged in sexual intercourse. The defendant argued to the trial judge that the evidence was relevant because "[i]t calls into question the credibility of the complainant, not because she happened to have sex, not because she is promiscuous, but because it would not be expected behavior in that period of time after she was allegedly traumatized, sexually assaulted by my client, to have had that interaction . . . ." The judge ruled that the rape-shield statute precluded inquiry about the post-rape intercourse between the victim and her boyfriend.

A criminal defendant's right to confront a witness is not absolute. * * * A trial judge will not be overruled in determining this scope unless the defendant demonstrates an abuse of discretion.

---

[3] During this stop, the victim removed the defendant's social security card from his wallet and took down the registration number of his car.

[4] In argument to the trial judge, the defendant's attorney stated that it was undisputed that the victim and her boyfriend had made statements about having had sexual relations the morning after the event. Defense counsel first claimed that the fact of the victim's having had sex with her boyfriend was relevant to the issue of the victim's "condition" when she was subsequently examined at the hospital. The prosecutor informed the judge that the Commonwealth would not seek to introduce evidence of the hospital rape kit because the defendant did not ejaculate during his rape of the victim and because the defense was consent.

In exercising her broad discretion to control the scope of cross-examination, "a trial judge should consider the important policies underlying the rape-shield statute." *Commonwealth v. Joyce*, 415 N.E.2d 181 (Mass. 1981). Historically, a defendant was permitted to introduce evidence of a victim's sexual history because it was considered relevant to the issue of consent, on the basis that "a woman of unchaste character, having demonstrated a propensity for sexual intercourse, was more likely to consent than a virtuous woman." Burnim, *Massachusetts Rape-Shield Law — An Over-Step in the Right Direction*, 64 MASS. L. REV. 61 (1979). But "the result of this strategy was harassment and further humiliation of the victim as well as discouraging victims of rape from reporting the crimes to law enforcement authorities." *Commonwealth v. Joyce*. Indeed, the evidentiary rule was extended to permit a defendant to mount a general attack on the victim's credibility through evidence of her reputation for lack of virtue. See, e.g., *Commonwealth v. Manning*, 327 N.E.2d 715 (Mass. 1975), decided prior to passage of the rape-shield statute. In that case the court held that evidence of the complainant's poor reputation for chastity had been wrongly excluded: "[E]vidence of poor reputation for chastity, had it been admitted, could have persuaded the jury that rape did not take place, and that the complainant had testified falsely as to that. So persuaded, the jury might well have disbelieved the complainant in her further uncorroborated testimony that sodomy and unnatural acts had occurred. They might have believed, instead, that the complainant had intercourse with the defendant voluntarily, then fabricated the story of rape to provide an excuse for her return home at 5 A.M., adding the story of sodomy and unnatural acts to gain additional sympathy." As the dissent in that case observed, "The 'established law' on which the court's opinion rests is part of a legal tradition, established by men, that the complaining woman in a rape case is fair game for character assassination in open court." *Id*. (Braucher, J., dissenting).

The rape-shield law, G.L. c. 233, § 21B, enacted to prevent such harassment and character assassination of a complainant, provides as follows:

> Evidence of the reputation of a victim's sexual conduct shall not be admissible in any investigation or proceeding before a grand jury or any court of the commonwealth . . . Evidence of specific instances of a victim's sexual conduct in such an investigation or proceeding shall not be admissible except evidence of the victim's sexual conduct with the defendant or evidence of recent conduct of the victim alleged to be the cause of any physical feature, characteristic, or condition of the victim
> . . . .

G.L. c. 233, § 21B, as amended by St.1983, c. 367.

The statute does not preclude all evidence of a complainant's sexual conduct. See, e.g. *Commonwealth v. Joyce*, ("evidence of prior acts, statements or circum-stances may be relevant to show a complainant's motive to accuse falsely the defendant"). Where such evidence is relevant to show a motive to lie, the trial judge must determine whether the weight and the relevance of the evidence to the defense are sufficient to outweigh its prejudicial effect on the alleged victim.

The defendant here contends that the excluded line of questioning was necessary to attack the victim's credibility. The victim testified during trial that she was psychologically injured and traumatized by the rape. Evidence that the victim had sexual intercourse soon after the rape, and that she waited nearly twelve hours to report the rape, would, the defendant argues, tend to show that "she was not truly traumatized and psychologically injured," thus casting doubt as to whether her encounter with the defendant was nonconsensual. The defendant's reliance on *Commonwealth v. Stockhammer*, 570 N.E.2d 992 (Mass. 1991), as the primary support for this claim, is misplaced. There, the defendant sought to establish the complainant's motive to lie by showing that her parents disapproved of her being sexually active. The court concluded that the excluded testimony could explain why the complainant had waited nine months to report the rape to her parents and then did so only after an anonymous caller spoke to her father.

We think that the defendant's theory that a woman traumatized by rape would not have sex with her boyfriend soon after the event is speculative at best. In weighing the potential prejudice to the victim, the judge also could properly consider the possibility that the evidence would appeal to unfounded and antiquated biases about what a "virtuous" or "chaste" woman would be likely to do in similar circumstances.

The evidence was properly excluded because the defendant failed to show "[t]hat the theory under which he proceeds is based on more than vague hope or mere speculation." *Commonwealth v. Shaw*, 556 N.E.2d 1058 (Mass. Ct. App. 1990). The defendant's theory thus runs afoul of the rape-shield statute, which was "principally designed to prevent defense counsel from eliciting evidence of the victim's promiscuity as part of a general credibility attack." *Commonwealth v. Fitzgerald*, 590 N.E.2d 1151 (Mass. 1992). We note that the case before us stands in marked contrast to the circumstances in *Fitzgerald*, which provided a basis for asking the complainant whether she had had intercourse with anyone other than the attacker on the night of the rape. There, stains in the complainant's underwear were found to contain sperm, but the defendant argued that he could not have committed the crime because he had had a vasectomy. On appeal, the court concluded that the inquiry whether the complainant had had any other sexual partner fell outside the rape-shield statute; it was not a general attack on credibility based on the complainant's promiscuity, but rather it would have supported the defendant's theory that he was falsely accused and someone else was the perpetrator. Here, the defendant had not ejaculated during his rape of the victim and was not claiming that evidence of intercourse with her boyfriend was needed to explain a physical condition such as the presence of sperm on the victim. The evidence that the victim had sexual intercourse after the rape was not relevant to a defense theory based on consent.[6]

The defendant's unsupported claim, that a woman traumatized by being raped would necessarily avoid sexual congress with her partner after the crime, amounts to a general attack on the victim's credibility of the sort that the rape-shield statute was intended to prohibit. Even if evidence of sexual conduct were not prohibited by the specific statutory language of G.L. c. 233, § 21B, such evidence was properly excluded in this case because the role that sexuality plays in the lives of two people is so varied that the nexus between sexual activity and traumatic events is necessarily speculative. There was no abuse of discretion.

NOTE

Is a defendant's prior sexual assault relevant to a rape charge? Consider Federal Rule of Evidence 413(a):

> In a criminal case in which the defendant is accused of an offense of sexual assault, evidence of the defendant's commission of another offense or offenses of sexual assault is admissible, and may be considered for its bearing on any matter to which it is relevant.

The Rule permits the introduction of propensity evidence regarding the defendant, which would otherwise be excluded by the evidence rule. In *United States v. Blue Bird*, 372 F.3d 989 (8th Cir. 2004), the court explained:

> Rule 413 allows propensity evidence, "[e]vidence of other crimes ... to prove the character of a person in order to show action in conformity therewith." Cf. Fed.R.Evid. 404(b). Evidence of a previous attempt could lead to a valid inference about Mr. Blue Bird's testimony. If he has a propensity to seek sex with minors, then he may have been seeking sex with a minor in this case. If so, then the minor's trial testimony that Mr. Blue Bird did not make any inquiries to insure that she was above the age of consent might be deemed to be more reliable. But it is important to note that this inference depends on the propriety of the initial inference of propensity, an inference that is normally impermissible and is allowed in this case only because of the narrowly drawn exception of Rule 413.

---

[6] Admission of specific acts of sexual conduct by the victim is allowed where the acts are offered to explain the victim's physical condition subsequent to the alleged crime, such as the presence of semen or bruises in the vaginal area.

CASE STUDY FOUR

Part I

Nathaniel Lewis and C.H. were friends who met during their first year at the University. H. stated that Lewis was a "joker and a flirt" who was interested in her sexually. She responded to Lewis's advances by explaining she "wasn't that kind of person that started having sex with anybody that she just met." She stated to a friend that she was physically attracted to Lewis, but he "tried to hook up with everybody" and was not interested in the same kind of relationship as she was. One evening at 8:45 p.m., H. called Lewis and invited him to her room in the dormitory. Lewis arrived a few minutes later; they had discussed earlier in the day that Lewis would come to her room to download a computer file. H. and Lewis watched television, listened to music, and talked with K.M. while H. drank wine coolers. M. left at approximately 9:30, and H. and Lewis were alone in H.'s room. While H. and Lewis were listening to music, Lewis got up, turned off the light, and, according to H.'s statement, grabbed her, threw her on the bed, and took off all her clothes. Lewis then took off his clothes and placed a condom on his penis. H. testified Lewis repeatedly pushed her down and her legs were forced apart, while she continued to say "don't do this." Lewis then engaged in sexual intercourse with H.

After Lewis left, H. went to see the Resident Coordinator for the dormitory, who called the police. H. did not want to speak to the police initially. She was taken to the hospital, but did not want to see a rape counselor, and for the first several hours did not wish to file any charges. H. eventually agreed to see a counselor, who encouraged her to keep a diary.

The next day, after H. filed a report with the police, Lewis met with a police officer. In his statement, Lewis said that after K.M. left he turned the lights off and said to H., "Come and find me." H. found him on the bed, and he put his hand up her shirt, removed her bra, and they kissed. Together they removed H.'s sweatshirt, and then Lewis disrobed and put on a condom while H. took off the rest of her clothes. Lewis stated that H. did not say anything during intercourse. When they were done, Lewis turned on the lights, wrapped the condom in a tissue, and threw it in the trash. H. picked up the condom wrapper, threw it in the trash, and told Lewis he had to leave. H. left the room with Lewis. Lewis stopped a couple of doors down the hall to write a note on another girl's door. H. rode down the elevator with Lewis and signed him out at the front desk..

1. What considerations will be relevant to the prosecutor's decision whether to file rape charges in this case? What additional information — if any — will be helpful for making the decision, including witnesses to be interviewed and information from the victim that will be needed?

2. If the prosecutor decides to file charges, is it a permissible consideration whether the lead attorney on the case should be a male or female?

3. How should defense counsel respond if the prosecutor provides an opportunity to discuss the case before any charges are filed? If Lewis had not given a statement to the police and the condom could not be located, would it be possible to defend the charges on the ground that the government does not have sufficient evidence to prove the sexual intercourse element of the crime, aside from the victim's testimony? Is the victim's testimony sufficient without corroboration?

Part II

The prosecutor charges Lewis with one count of forcible rape. Two days before trial, Lewis receives an unmarked envelope at his home containing entries in a diary written by H. that she started at the behest of the rape counselor. One entry states:

> I can't believe the trial's only a week away. I feel guilty (sort of) for trying to get Nate locked up, but his lack of respect for women is terrible. I remember how disrespectful he always was to all of us girls in the courtyard . . . he thinks females are a bunch of sex objects! And he's such a player! He was trying to get with Holly and me, and all the while he had a girlfriend. I think I pounced on Nate because he was the last straw. That, and because I've always seemed to need some drama in my life. Otherwise I get bored. That definitely needs to change. I'm sick of men taking advantage of me . . . *and I'm sick of myself for giving in to them. I'm not a nympho like all those guys think. I'm just not strong enough to say no to them. I'm tired of being a whore. This is where it ends.*

The trial court ruled before trial that the italicized portion of the diary entry could not be introduced under the state's rape shield statute, which is identical to Massachusetts' provision. If Lewis is convicted, what argument will defense counsel make that the judge improperly excluded evidence, and how will the prosecution respond?

Chapter 10
Theft and Property Offenses

Under the common law, the basic theft offense was *larceny*, which required the government to prove the following elements: (1) a trespassory taking and (2) carrying away of (3) personal property (4) of another person (5) with intent to steal. *See* WAYNE R. LAFAVE, SUBSTANTIVE CRIMINAL LAW § 19.1 (2d ed. 2003). Other theft offenses build off this core crime, depending on whether force or fear is used (*robbery*), whether the person has lawful possession of the property and converts it to personal use (*embezzlement*), or whether title, rather than possession, was obtained by false statement of past or present fact (*false pretenses*). Another important property offense is *burglary*, a common law felony that punishes the entry into a dwelling at night with the intent to commit a felony upon entry. Unlike a theft offense, burglary punishes the entry into the home when the perpetrator intends to engage in any felony, including crimes of violence like murder and rape, and does not require that the victim suffer any loss or harm.

---

§ 10.01 Theft Offenses

The common law theft offenses were built around technical distinctions that were rooted in the agrarian economy of the time. The Vermont Supreme Court, in *State v. Brennan*, 775 A.2d 919 (Vt. 2001), discussed the development of the crime:

> As Blackstone recorded in 1771, the origin of larceny from the person can be traced to the Roman and Athenian legal systems, where "saccularii," or cutpurses, were punished more severely than ordinary thieves. 4 W. BLACKSTONE, COMMENTARIES 241 (4th ed. 1771). Following these ancient law traditions, the English Statutes at Large incorporated specifically enhanced penalties for similar acts. *See* 8 Eliz. c. 4 § 2 (1565) (removing benefit of clergy for pickpurses and cut purses convicted of "felonious taking of any money, or goods, or chattels, from the person of any other, privily without his knowledge"). The penalties were more severe than larceny "owing to the ease with which such offenses are committed, and the difficulty in guarding against them." BLACKSTONE. Thus, the offense was a compound crime, made up of the simple theft, but aggravated by an invasion of one's person.

In contrast to the private stealing done by pickpockets, Blackstone distinguished another form of larceny from the person: robbery. It is characterized by "open and violent assault" on a person where property is stolen through fear and an involuntary dispossession. Under this form of larceny from the person, the property need only be in the presence of its owner and not literally attached to the owner's body.

The crime of larceny by trick is a good example of how the law bent itself to cover situations that might otherwise fall outside the criminal proscription:

Unlike other developments in the law of theft, larceny by trick did not originate by statute. It is entirely attributable to *The King v. Pear* (*Pear's Case*), decided in 1779. In that case, Pear hired a horse with the intent to sell it and to flee with the proceeds. It appeared that because Pear had the owner's consent to possess the horse, he had not committed larceny. However, the court found that the acquisition of consent by a false promise constituted a breach of possession. This result stemmed from the theory that consent obtained by fraud did not equal true consent. Thus, larceny by trick emerged. * * *

John Wesley Bartram, Note, *Pleading for Theft Consolidation in Virginia: Larceny, Embezzlement, False Pretenses and § 19.2-284*, 56 WASH. & LEE L. REV. 249 (1999).

Many of the common law distinctions remain important. Some states have consolidated all the theft offenses in one provision. For example, the California theft statute, CAL. PENAL CODE § 484(a), provides:

Every person who shall feloniously steal, take, carry, lead, or drive away the personal property of another, or who shall fraudulently appropriate property which has been entrusted to him or her, or who shall knowingly and designedly, by any false or fraudulent representation or pretense, defraud any other person of money, labor or real or personal property, or who causes or procures others to report falsely of his or her wealth or mercantile character and by thus imposing upon any person, obtains credit and thereby fraudulently gets or obtains possession of money, or property or obtains the labor or service of another, is guilty of theft.

Maryland's consolidated statute merges the various common law offenses by providing: "Conduct described as theft in this part constitutes a single crime and includes the separate crimes formerly known as: (1) larceny; (2) larceny by trick; (3) larceny after trust; (4) embezzlement; (5) false pretenses; (6) shoplifting; and (7) receiving stolen property." MD. CODE § 7-102. The statute describes the basic theft offense as follows:

Unauthorized control over property

(a) A person may not willfully or knowingly obtain or exert unauthorized control over property, if the person:

(1) intends to deprive the owner of the property;

(2) willfully or knowingly uses, conceals, or abandons the property in a manner that deprives the owner of the property; or

(3) uses, conceals, or abandons the property knowing the use, concealment, or abandonment probably will deprive the owner of the property.

Unauthorized control over property — By deception

(b) A person may not obtain control over property by willfully or knowingly using deception, if the person:

(1) intends to deprive the owner of the property;

(2) willfully or knowingly uses, conceals, or abandons the property in a manner that deprives the owner of the property; or

(3) uses, conceals, or abandons the property knowing the use, concealment, or abandonment probably will deprive the owner of the property.

MD. CODE § 7-104(a)-(b).

In the following cases, consider how the courts incorporate the common law elements of the theft offenses into modern statutes.

A. Larceny

Bell v. United States
462 U.S. 356 (1983)

Justice POWELL delivered the opinion of the Court.

On October 13, 1978, a Cincinnati man wrote a check for $10,000 drawn on a Cincinnati bank. He endorsed the check for deposit to his account at Dade Federal Savings & Loan of Miami and mailed the check to an agent there. The agent never received the check. On October 17, petitioner Nelson Bell opened an account at a Dade Federal branch and deposited $50 — the minimum amount necessary for new accounts. He used his own name, but gave a false address, birth date, and social security number. Later that day, at another branch, he deposited the Cincinnati man's $10,000 check into this new account. The endorsement had been altered to show Bell's account number. Dade Federal accepted the deposit, but put a 20-day hold on the funds. On November 7, as soon as the hold had expired, Bell returned to the branch at which he had opened the account. The total balance, with accrued interest, was then slightly over $10,080. Bell closed the account and was paid the total balance in cash.

Bell was apprehended and charged with violating 18 U.S.C. § 2113(b). The statute provides, in relevant part:

> Whoever takes and carries away, with intent to steal or purloin, any property or money or any other thing of value exceeding $100 belonging to, or in the care, custody, control, management, or possession of any bank, credit union, or any savings and loan association, shall be fined not more than $5,000 or imprisoned not more than ten years, or both[.]

Bell was convicted after a jury trial in the United States District Court for the Southern District of Florida. * * *

In the 13th century, larceny was limited to trespassory taking: a thief committed larceny only if he feloniously "took and carried away" another's personal property from his possession. The goal was more to prevent breaches of the peace than losses of property, and violence was more likely when property was taken from the owner's actual possession.

As the common law developed, protection of property also became an important goal. The definition of larceny accordingly was expanded by judicial interpretation to include cases where the owner merely was deemed to be in possession. Thus when a bailee of packaged goods broke open the packages and misappropriated the contents, he committed larceny. *The Carrier's Case*, Y.B.Pasch. 13 Edw. IV, f. 9, pl. 5 (Star Ch. and Exch. Ch. 1473). The bailor was deemed to be in possession of the contents of the packages, at least by the time of the misappropriation. Similarly, a thief committed "larceny by trick" when he obtained custody of a horse by telling the owner that he intended to use it for one purpose when he in fact intended to sell it and to keep the proceeds. *King v. Pear*, 168 Eng.Rep. 208 (Cr.Cas.Res.1779). The judges accepted the fiction that the owner retained possession of the horse until it was sold, on the theory that the thief had custody only for a limited purpose.

By the late 18th century, courts were less willing to expand common-law definitions. Thus when a bank clerk retained money given to him by a customer rather than depositing it in the bank, he was not guilty of larceny, for the bank had not been in possession of the money. *King v. Bazeley*, 168 Eng.Rep. 517 (Cr.Cas.Res.1799). Statutory crimes such as embezzlement and obtaining property by false pretenses therefore were created to fill this gap.

The theoretical distinction between false pretenses and larceny by trick may be stated simply. If a thief, through his trickery, acquired title to the property from the owner, he has obtained property by false pretenses; but if he merely acquired possession from the owner, he has committed larceny by trick. In this case the parties agree that Bell is guilty of obtaining money by false pretenses. When the teller at Dade Federal handed him $10,080 in cash, Bell acquired title to the money. The only dispute is whether 18 U.S.C. § 2113(b) proscribes the crime of false pretenses, or whether the statute is instead limited to common-law larceny.

Bell's argument in favor of the narrower reading of § 2113(b) relies principally on the statute's use of the traditional common-law language "takes and carries away." He cites the rule of statutory construction that when a federal criminal statute uses a common-law term without defining it, Congress is presumed to intend the common-law meaning. In § 2113(b), however, Congress has not adopted the elements of larceny in common-law terms. The language "takes and carries away" is but one part of the statute and represents only one element of common-law larceny. Other language in § 2113(b), such as "with intent to steal or purloin," has no established meaning at common law. Moreover, "taking and carrying away," although not a necessary element of the crime, is entirely consistent with false pretenses.

Two other aspects of § 2113(b) show an intention to go beyond the common-law definition of larceny. First, common-law larceny was limited to thefts of tangible personal property. This limitation excluded, for example, the theft of a written instrument embodying a chose in action. Section 2113(b) is thus broader than common-law larceny, for it covers "any property or money or any other thing of value exceeding $100." Second, and of particular relevance to the distinction at issue here, common-law larceny required a theft from the possession of the owner. When the definition was expanded, it still applied only when the owner was deemed to be in possession. Section 2113(b), however, goes well beyond even this expanded definition. It applies when the property "belong[s] to," or is "in the care, custody, control, management, or possession of," a covered institution.

In sum, the statutory language does not suggest that it covers only common-law larceny. Although § 2113(b) does not apply to a case of false pretenses in which there is not a taking and carrying away, it proscribes Bell's conduct here. The evidence is clear that he "t[ook] and carrie[d] away, with intent to steal or purloin, [over $10,000 that was] in the care, custody, control, management, or possession of" Dade Federal Savings & Loan.

The legislative history of § 2113(b) also suggests that Congress intended the statute to reach Bell's conduct. As originally enacted in 1934, the Federal Bank Robbery Act, governed only robbery–a crime requiring a forcible taking. Congress apparently was concerned with "gangsters who operate habitually from one State to another in robbing banks." S.REP. NO. 537, 73rd Cong., 2d Sess. (1934); H.R.REP. NO. 1461, 73rd Cong., 2d Sess. (1934).

By 1937 the concern was broader, for the limited nature of the original Act "ha[d] led to some incongruous results." H.R.REP. NO. 732, 75th Cong., 1st Sess.,

1 (1937). It was possible for a thief to steal a large amount from a bank "without displaying any force or violence and without putting any one in fear," and he would not violate any federal law. Congress amended the Act to fill this gap, adding language now found at §§ 2113(a) and (b). Although the term "larceny" appears in the legislative reports, the congressional purpose plainly was to protect banks from those who wished to steal banks' assets–even if they used no force in doing so.

The congressional goal of protecting bank assets is entirely independent of the traditional distinction on which Bell relies. To the extent that a bank needs protection against larceny by trick, it also needs protection from false pretenses. We cannot believe that Congress wished to limit the scope of the amended Act's coverage, and thus limit its remedial purpose, on the basis of an arcane and artificial distinction more suited to the social conditions of 18th century England than the needs of 20th century America. Such an interpretation would signal a return to the "incongruous results" that the 1937 amendment was designed to eliminate.

We conclude that 18 U.S.C. § 2113(b) is not limited to common-law larceny. Although § 2113(b) may not cover the full range of theft offenses, it covers Bell's conduct here. His conviction therefore was proper * * * .

People v. Shannon
78 Cal.Rptr.2d 177 (Cal. 1998)

ORTEGA, J.

The case arose when Shannon went into a department store, took clothes from a rack, hid them in a bag, and took them to a cashier. Falsely claiming ownership of the clothes, Shannon asked to exchange them for a cash refund.

Store personnel had seen Shannon hide the clothes and knew he had stolen them from the rack. Nonetheless, the cashier completed the exchange as part of the store's plan to catch Shannon. Security agents arrested Shannon after he left the store with the money. * * *

In defense, Yamileth Santos, Shannon's fiancee, said that on July 11, 1996, she asked him to return some items for her at the store. Santos had bought these items, including two skirts and a sweater, earlier. * * *

Shannon urges us to reduce his conviction [for petty theft, a felony that triggered the California Three Strikes statute resulting in a 25-year term of imprisonment] to attempted petty theft, a misdemeanor * * * .

Shannon makes two related arguments why, as a matter of law, he committed only attempted, not completed, theft. First, Shannon argues he could not be convicted of completed theft of the skirts and sweater which he put into his bag and subsequently returned for a cash refund, because he did not remove the clothes from the store. Second, Shannon argues the theft was not completed at that point because he did not intend to permanently deprive the store of the clothes. We reject both arguments.

Theft, of which Shannon was convicted, is the unlawful taking of another's property. The crime includes larceny, embezzlement, larceny by trick, and theft by false pretenses. Larceny, larceny by trick, and embezzlement involve taking another's personal property from the owner's possession, without the owner's consent, with the intent to deprive the owner permanently of the property. Theft by false pretenses does not require that the defendant take the property; it requires that the defendant use false pretenses to induce the other to give the property to him.

The jury here was instructed only on larceny. The jury was not instructed on larceny by trick, theft by false pretenses, or embezzlement.

"The completed crime of larceny–as distinguished from an attempt–requires asportation or carrying away, in addition to the taking. The element of asportation is not satisfied unless it is shown that the goods were severed from the possession or custody of the owner, and in the possession of the thief, though it be but for a moment." *People v. Khoury*, 166 Cal.Rptr. 180 (Cal. App. Ct. 1980). However, one need not remove property from the store to be convicted of theft of the property from the store. One need only take possession of the property, detaching it from the store shelves or other location, and move it slightly with the intent to deprive the owner of it permanently. *People v. Khoury* (affirming completed theft conviction, and rejecting claim that it was only at attempt, where Khoury hid $900 worth of merchandise in a chandelier box, took it to the checkstand, and tried to pay only the much lower price marked on the box, but the salesclerk became suspicious and refused the sale, whereupon Khoury abandoned the box and its contents, walked away from the counter, and was arrested inside the store). Indeed, the standard jury instruction defining theft by larceny states: "To constitute a 'carrying away,' the property need not be actually removed from the [place] [or] premises where it was kept . . . ." Thus, Shannon's claim that he could not be guilty of completed theft unless he took the clothes outside the store is wrong.

* * * Shannon then makes a related point: the theft was not complete when he took the clothes because he did not intend to permanently deprive the store of the clothes, but only intended to take the money he would receive from the false

refund. * * * As the jury was instructed, theft requires the specific intent to permanently deprive the owner of its property. However, the intent to later restore or make restitution for the property is no defense. Likewise, "the property need not . . . be retained by the perpetrator." [*California Model Jury Instructions*] "Asportation of the property with the intention to appropriate it is sufficient to constitute larceny even though the property may subsequently be returned to the owner . . . The fact that a thief is prevented by an officer from getting away with the property, or that he may change his mind and return the property to escape prosecution for the crime, does not relieve him from the consequences of the theft . . . [T]heft may be committed when the accused persons, with a preconceived design to obtain and appropriate property by means of fraud or trickery, thereby gain possession of the property, even though they do not retain or use it for their own benefit." *People v. Post*, 173 P.2d 48 (Cal. 1946). Moreover, the prosecution need not show the defendant took the property for his own use; the intent to destroy it and thus deprive the owner of its use is sufficient.

Thus, the fact that Shannon apparently did not intend to keep the clothes, but to steal its monetary value by exchanging the clothes while falsely claiming to own them, does not alter our conclusion that the theft was complete when he put the clothes in his bag with the described intent. Shannon unquestionably intended to permanently deprive the store of money equal to the clothes' value, and thus to "use [them] for [his] own benefit." *Post.* There is no evidence that had Shannon been unable to complete the fraudulent refund, he would have abandoned the stolen clothes rather than leaving the store with them.

In any event, even if Shannon intended to abandon the clothes if his scheme failed, the theft was complete when he dropped the clothes into his bag intending to defraud the store of their monetary value. The fact that Shannon planned to get the money from the store, rather than taking the clothes and selling them to a fence or an innocent buyer, or trading them for drugs, or any of the other myriad ways in which he could have appropriated their value other than by wearing them, is irrelevant. Unlike a joyrider, who plans to use the car temporarily and then return it, Shannon intended not to unconditionally return the clothes, but to appropriate them for his purpose of selling them back. "One who takes another's property intending at the time he takes it to use it temporarily and then to return it unconditionally within a reasonable time — and having a substantial ability to do so–lacks the intent to steal required for larceny." 2 LaFave & Scott, Substantive Criminal Law § 8.5(b). Put another way, "[t]he intent to steal is an intent to deprive the possessor permanently. One who takes another's property for temporary use or concealment, with the intention of returning it, is liable in tort for damages but is not guilty of larceny." 2 Witkin & Epstein, Cal.Criminal Law, Crimes Against Property § 585.

In support, both texts cite *People v. Brown*, 38 P. 518 (Cal. 1894), which reversed a burglary conviction based on incorrect jury instructions. Brown admitted entering, intending to take his landlord's son's bicycle "to get even with the boy" for an earlier quarrel. Brown intended to return the bicycle unconditionally within a day. However, by mistake Brown took another's bicycle. Brown was caught before he could return the bicycle. The court ordered a new trial because the jury instruction stated the taking did not have to be with the intent to permanently deprive.

Shannon, of course, did not intend to return the store's property unconditionally. Instead, he intended to sell the store's own property, which he took with wrongful intent, back to it, falsely claiming to be the rightful owner. Thus, Shannon neither lacked wrongful intent nor intended to return the clothes unconditionally and cannot benefit from this defense.

In *People v. Stay*, 96 Cal.Rptr. 651 (Cal. 1971), the defendant's employees picked up retail store shopping carts, each marked with the owning store's identification, which patrons used to take their purchases home and then left on the streets surrounding the stores. Stay then contacted the stores and offered to return each store's carts for $2.50 each, although other legitimate companies returned the carts for 25 cents each. A few of the stores complied with Stay's ransom demands, while most did not. Stay removed the names and numbers from the carts he could not sell back to their owners' stores and then sold the relabeled carts to other stores. Stay was convicted of five counts of completed grand theft, some from stores that paid him for their returned carts, some from stores that refused to pay and whose carts he resold after altering them. We affirmed.

First, we rejected Stay's claim that, like the legitimate companies described above, he was acting under a statute which entitled those who returned shopping carts to their owners "without compensation" to receive "a reasonable charge for saving and taking care of the property[,]" and thus was not guilty of theft or attempted theft. Second, and dispositive of this issue, we rejected Stay's argument that he did not commit theft because he did not intend to deprive the stores of their carts permanently. In doing so, we did not distinguish between those stores that paid the ransom and got their carts back, and those that refused and never got them back because Stay sold them to others. Thus, although Stay never intended to keep the carts, but stole them intending to ransom them back to their owners or, failing that, sell them to others, we affirmed his completed theft convictions.

Although the scheme here is different, the result is the same. In neither case does it matter that the thief intends to sell the victim's property back to the victim after wrongfully stealing the property and claiming to be the rightful owner, thus ultimately stealing the victim's money rather than the property. Shannon completed the theft when he moved the clothes, thus appropriating them and intending to fraudulently resell them to the store. On this basis, the evidence supports Shannon's larceny conviction.

NOTES AND QUESTIONS

1. ***Asportation***. In *State v. Donaldson* [p. 58], the Iowa Supreme Court discussed the asportation element of larceny, and citing to the Commentary of the Model Penal Code, explained the requirement:

> "Caption," or taking, occurred when the actor secured dominion over the property of another. The element of "asportation," or carrying away, was satisfied with even the most slight change in position of the stolen object. At common law, to prove a theft, the State had to show a defendant took the property of another, i.e., secured dominion over it, and carried the property away.

2. ***Permanent Deprivation***. Larceny requires that the defendant intend to *permanently* deprive the owner/possessor of the property, rather than a temporary deprivation. A common situation is when a person — often a teenager — takes a car out joyriding without intending to keep it. In *Slay v. State*, 241 So.2d 362 (Miss. 1970), the Mississippi Supreme Court overturned the conviction because the defendant did not intend to steal the car.

> The specific intent to deprive the owner of his property is a necessary ingredient of larceny. There must be criminal intent wholly and permanently to deprive the owner of his property. It is not larceny to take a thing for a temporary purpose with the bona fide intention of returning it. Hence the taking of property with the intention of using it temporarily and with no intention of depriving its owner permanently is not larceny. So when one takes an automobile, intending only to ride or drive it somewhere and then to restore it to the possession of the owner or leave it where he may reclaim it, this is not larceny. * * *

> Slay, 18 years of age, was to report for Army duty in five days. He with two younger boys wrongfully, he admitted, took the car from the motor company lot and drove it around in Crystal Springs. They were stopped by an officer and Slay was given a ticket for driving without a license and tag, but they continued to drive around in that city. There is no evidence that they intended to take the car out of the city limits. When the marshal pursued them, the car was wrecked in making a turn within the city. The jury could consider the fact of the initial wrongful taking of the car on the issue of whether there was specific intent to deprive the owner of the property permanently. However, that was the only substantive evidence indicating a larcenous intent. The great weight of the evidence indicates that these boys, having wrongfully taken the car by an act of trespass, simply intended to drive it around town on that New Year's Eve night.

Similarly, in *State v. Schminkey*, 597 N.W.2d 785 (Iowa 1999), the Iowa Supreme Court stated, "In our search for other facts or circumstances that might reveal Schminkey's intent in taking the pickup, we find none indicating that he intended to do anything more than temporarily use the vehicle to go home or to another bar. Because Schminkey wrecked the pickup before he could dispose of it, we do not have the typical inferences that can be drawn from a defendant's actions subsequent to the taking."

3. *Continuing Trespass.* The common law element of a specific intent to steal meant that the defendant's intent at the moment of the taking determined whether the conduct was a larceny. What about the situation in which a defendant took property temporarily, and then changed his mind and decided to keep it. Is that a larceny? The common law solution was the "continuing trespass" doctrine, under which the defendant's retaining possession of the item is a trespass, and at the moment the intent to permanently hold the item the larceny is then complete. The continuing trespass doctrine also allows a state to prosecute a person for larceny when something is stolen in one state and then transported into the prosecuting state. In *Hamilton v. State*, 277 A.2d 460 (Md. Ct. Spec. App. 1971), the Maryland Court of Special Appeals held:

> Both appellants question the continuing vitality of the continuing trespass doctrine * * *. There is no question in this case but that the initial trespassory taking of the money from the bank occurred in the District of Columbia during the course of the armed bank robbery. It is equally clear that as the robbers attempted to make their escape in the getaway car, the trespass continued and that when that getaway car bearing both the robbers and the stolen goods crossed the line between the District of Columbia and the State of Maryland, a fresh caption and asportation occurred within the State of Maryland. The occurrence of a caption and asportation in Maryland, along with the other undisputed elements such as the fact that the stolen cash was the personal property of someone other than the robbers and that the robbers intended permanently to deprive the true owners of that cash, is adequate to spell out the crime of larceny in the State of Maryland.

4. *Stealing From a Thief.* As a crime against possession, the common law did not require that the victim of the larceny be a *lawful* possessor of the personal property taken by the defendant. This creates the potentially anomalous situation in which a defendant is charged with stealing from a thief. "Many modern codes expressly provide, as does the Model Penal Code, that property may be the subject of theft even though the 'victim' is a person whose interest in the property is unlawful. This is as it should be." WAYNE R. LAFAVE, SUBSTANTIVE CRIMINAL LAW § 19.4(c) (2d ed. 2003). Cases in this area usually occur when the defendant seeks to trick a person into parting with property or money after engaging in wrongdoing to obtain it. In the civil law, there is the *in pari delicto* or unclean hands defense, which means that parties whose conduct is equally wrongful cannot recover from one

another for any losses resulting from their misconduct. The same rule does not apply in criminal cases, as discussed in *United States v. Benson*, 548 F.2d 42 (2d Cir. 1977):

> It is accepted that the prostitute may be raped, the burglar's home burgled, the killer murdered and the thief a victim of larceny. * * * While it is generally held in a civil suit where both parties are guilty of criminal behavior with respect to the cause sued upon, that the court will leave the parties where it finds them and refuse to act as a referee among thieves, a criminal action is on a manifestly different footing. [The victim] is not the plaintiff here. The United States has brought a criminal proceeding against defendants alleged to have engaged in a crude swindle which induced [the victim] to travel in interstate and foreign commerce [in order to steal valuable jewels. The victim]'s gullibility or his own criminal background is not relevant to the inquiry as to whether the defendants were properly convicted * * * .

5. ***Retrieving Ill-Gotten Gains***. While a person has the right to take back their property, what about the situation in which the defendant loses property in an illegal activity, such as gambling, and then seeks to retrieve it on the ground that it was obtained illegally? Can taking property from the person who possesses it constitute a larceny? Consider the analysis of the New York Supreme Court, Appellate Division, in *People v. Coates*, 407 N.Y.S.2d 866 (N.Y. Supr. Ct. App. Div. 1978):

> [I]t is the long settled law in New York, and most other American jurisdictions, "that an individual who wins money or other consideration from another in an illegal game of chance does not acquire title to the winnings". However, the narrow question of who possesses legal title is substantially irrelevant to a prosecution for larceny. The larcenous act is no more than the wrongful taking of property from an owner thereof. Nowhere is it required that the depossessed owner also be the title holder of the property. * * * [I]t is patently absurd to suggest that violent self-help will be tolerated. The losing gambler has violated the law to as great an extent as the winner. Having voluntarily engaged in the unlawful gaming enterprise, it must be held that the loser parts with ownership upon transfer of the wagered property, and that the winner gains ownership, subject to divestment, upon taking actual possession. Nor will this principle be disputed by any gambler who has ever been favored by the luck of the roll.

6. ***Valuing the Property***. Most states have different degrees of larceny depending on the value of the property taken. For example, if the item stolen was worth more than $1,000, it may be a higher level felony punishable by a longer term of imprisonment, or the determination whether an offense is a misdemeanor or a felony might depend on the valuation of the property. Maryland provides the

following basic definition of "value" for a theft offense: "(1) the market value of the property or service at the time and place of the crime; or (2) if the market value cannot satisfactorily be ascertained, the cost of the replacement of the property or service within a reasonable time after the crime." MD. CODE § 7-103(a).

The method of valuing stolen property can be very important under recidivist sentencing statutes, such as the California Three Strikes law, which make the level of the prior offenses the determinative factor in imposing a substantial penalty enhancement upon conviction for a third or successive offense. In *People v. Medjdoubi*, 661 N.Y.S.2d 502 (N.Y. Sup. Ct. 1997), the New York Supreme Court considered whether the sales tax should be included in determining the valuation of stolen items which totaled $1,000, the dividing line between different offenses. The court provided the following analysis of valuation in deciding that the sales tax should not be considered:

The market value of stolen property is the amount which the thief would have had to pay had he purchased the goods in the market instead of stealing them. This is the appropriate standard even if the thief steals merchandise not for sale, such as free goods or gifts.

In analyzing "market value," the New York Court of Appeals has recognized two legitimate markets, the wholesale market and the retail market. The market value of property stolen from a wholesaler is the price at which a wholesaler could have sold the property. The market value of property stolen from a retailer is the price at which a retailer could have sold the property.

Both new and used property can be sold on the wholesale or retail market. The existence of a legitimate market for used goods contemplates that sales of the used items occur in the regular course of business, with some regularity and uniformity. Therefore, just as in the case of new property, where a thief steals used property from a wholesaler or retailer, the market value of such property is the amount the thief would have had to pay had he purchased the used goods in that particular used market.

The market value of property stolen from a consumer is the price of the item reduced for any depreciation or change in its condition which affected its value at the time of the crime.

No statutory language, nor Court of Appeals or Appellate Division decision, has articulated any other basis for determining the value of stolen property other than its "market value" or its "replacement cost." * * *

Sales tax does not enhance the value of property. Rather, it is itself calculated based upon the dollar value of the property. It therefore should not be used to elevate the seriousness of the charge by changing its classification and the punishment that can be imposed. This court, therefore, holds that the value of stolen property which is retail merchandise is its market value as reflected by the purchase price exclusive of any levied sales tax.

7. **_Single Larceny Doctrine_**. If a defendant takes different items from the same general location, is there a separate charge for each piece of property, or a single offense? The decision on this issue may be important when the aggregate value of the property makes the crime a felony or triggers a significantly higher sentence. The single larceny doctrine looks to the circumstances of the offense to determine whether a defendant committed multiple offenses or only one larceny.

> There is no litmus test that will determine whether a defendant's conduct constitutes a single crime or multiple crimes. When a prosecutor's policy is to charge as many offenses as possible, the inquiry takes on added significance. Is, for example, the drug trafficker who has ten packets of cocaine in his pocket guilty of one or ten counts of possession with the intent to distribute? Is the assailant who shoots his victim three times guilty of three malicious woundings or three attempts to murder or is that but one offense? As to larceny, is the person who successively carries three televisions from a store to his van guilty of three larcenies, but the thief who loads them from a dolly into his van guilty of but one offense? Is the thief who rifles through three drawers of a desk, stealing items from each drawer, guilty of one crime or three? If the thief is interrupted briefly after stealing from two drawers, but continues his thievery moments later, has he committed two crimes? Is the thief who steals numerous items from various rooms of a person's home guilty of but one larceny, whereas a thief who steals the same items from different offices in the same business complex guilty of multiple larcenies?

> In order for the single larceny doctrine to apply, the items stolen may, but do not have to, be part of the same bundle or parcel; it is sufficient if they be at the same location — that is on the "same table," or same room, or "same shop," as Lord Hale first observed. When the evidence supports a finding that the thefts were part of the same larcenous impulse or scheme and were part of a continuous act, a single larceny has occurred. The primary factor to be considered is the intent of the thief and the question to be asked is whether the thefts, although occurring successively within a brief time frame, were part of one impulse. The circumstances to be considered that will bear upon the issue are the location of the items stolen, the lapse of time between their taking, the general and specific intent of the thief, the number of owners, and whether intervening events occurred between the takings. Unless the evidence proves that two or more separate and discrete thefts occurred at separate times which were not part of the

same larcenous impulse, then thefts from the same room are but a single larceny.

Richardson v. Commonwealth, 489 S.E.2d 698 (Va. Ct. App. 1997).

8. ***From the Person***. Many states impose a higher penalty for larceny "from the person." The original prohibition in this area concerned pickpockets, who take the property directly from the victim. States have been divided on how closely to view the phrase "from the person" as requiring that the article be in physical contact with the victim at the time of the taking or whether taking an item within the vicinity of the person suffices. In *State v. Brennan*, 775 A.2d 919 (Vt. 2001), the Vermont Supreme Court reviewed a conviction for "larceny from the person" when the defendant, a hitchhiker riding in the back seat of the victim's car, took $80 from her purse without her noticing it until after he had left the car. The court noted the different approaches in this area:

> Courts in other jurisdictions have followed two major approaches to the issue raised by this case. The first approach has pursued a strict reading of the phrase "from the person." These jurisdictions have required that the stolen item is physically touching the victim at the time of theft, harkening back to the origin of the statute to punish pickpockets. Two cases show the stringency of this requirement. In *People v. Huggins*, 60 Cal.Rptr.2d 177 (Cal. App. 1997), for example, the court affirmed the conviction of grand theft "from the person" where the victim's purse was stolen as it rested on the floor at her feet. The basis of the conviction was that her foot was in contact with the purse. The court held that the victim's purpose in keeping the purse against her foot was to retain "dominion and control" over the purse and guard against purse-snatchers. Yet, in *People v. Williams*, 12 Cal.Rptr.2d 243 (Cal. App. 1992), the court reversed a conviction of grand theft from the person where a victim's purse was taken from the car seat beside her. The court held that in spite of the fact that the thief reached into the car window to grab the purse, the statute did not extend to property that had been "laid aside" from the person. The victim had hardly given up voluntary control of her purse, but the court held that actual physical contact was necessary.

> The other approach stems from jurisdictions that permit a broader reading of their statutes, holding that where property is taken from the presence or constructive control or possession of the owner, the statute is satisfied. Courts have reasoned that there is a constructive trespass on the victim's person and that the heightened risk to the victim justifies an enhanced penalty. In *Garland* [*v. Commonwealth*, 446 S.E.2d 628 (Va. Ct. App. 1992)], for instance, the defendant frightened a cashier when he reached across to steal money from the cash drawer. The cashier was not physically touching the cash drawer, but the thief's hands came within inches of hers

in order to get the money. The court held that the money was within her immediate control and custody and the thief's conduct was "of an assaultive nature." Therefore, the court affirmed defendant's from the person conviction, viewing the assault as a constructive trespass on the person.

Similarly, the Supreme Court of Rhode Island held that assaultive conduct is sufficient to justify a conviction for larceny from the person, even though the statute does not expressly include the phrase "in his presence." *State v. Shepard*, 726 A.2d 1138 (R.I. 1999). In *Shepard*, the defendant was convicted of larceny from the person, after crashing his car into the victim's car and threatening her. The defendant then "entered her vehicle without her permission, when she was still dazed from the accident and unable to retreat or withdraw" to demand compensation for the damage. He tried to grab the victim's wallet and cell phone, which were within her immediate presence. Relying in part on *Garland*, the court affirmed the conviction of larceny from the person. It concluded that the broader interpretation of from the person was more consonant with the statute's purpose: "to protect the dignity and sanctity of each person from a theft of property within that person's custody and control while that person is present physically."

The court held that "from the person" "creates a zone of protection around a person's body that warrants a higher penalty when a theft occurs within this zone." It determined, however, that the defendant's theft of the $80 did not invade the victim's zone of protection because his conduct did not have an "assaultive nature," the victim was unaware of the taking, and there was not potential risk of violence and danger to the victim.

9. ***Lost or Mislaid Property***. It may be that a person will find a valuable piece of property and decide to keep it. Is that person guilty of larceny, or does the playground adage "Finders keepers, losers weepers" apply? While that phrase may work in kindergarten — although probably not if the teacher is around — it surely does not apply in the law.

> Even assuming, *arguendo*, that defendant believed this was lost or abandoned property, it is well-established that the finder of lost property must make every reasonable effort to find the owner when he has the means to do so or else the finder exposes himself to possible prosecution. "A person who finds lost property under circumstances which give him knowledge or means of inquiry as to the true owner, and who appropriates such property to his own use, or to the use of another person who is not entitled thereto, without having first made every reasonable effort to find the owner and restore the property to him, is guilty of larceny."

People v. Francia, 585 N.Y.S.2d 157 (N.Y. Crim. Ct. 1992) (quoting *People v. Seaton*, 15 N.Y.S. 270 (N.Y. Sup.Ct. 1891)).

10. ***Breaking Bulk.*** The common law larceny rules required courts to engage in a number of legal fictions in order to hold a defendant who manifested some measure of larcenous intent liable for a criminal offense because of the peculiar elements of the crime. Perhaps the most blatant of the fictions is the so-called "breaking bulk" doctrine that permits a delivery person to be convicted of larceny rather than embezzlement. The law of embezzlement, which developed after larceny, reaches a person who has custody of property and misuses it for his or her own personal purposes without taking it from the possession of another, which would be required for larceny. In many jurisdictions, larceny was a more serious offense with a higher punishment. To reach the delivery person, the common law developed the "breaking bulk" doctrine, which has been described as follows:

> Under this doctrine, the bailee-carrier was given possession of a bale, but not its contents. Therefore, when the bailee pilfered the entire bale, he was not guilty of larceny; but when he broke open the bale and took a portion or all of the contents, he was guilty of larceny because his taking was trespassory and it was from the constructive possession of another.

3 WHARTON'S CRIMINAL LAW (1980). Thus, by removing the contents of the package, the delivery person has taken the property from the *constructive possession* of the person who entrusted it for delivery. For example, in *United States v. Mafnas*, 701 F.2d 83 (9th Cir. 1983), the court upheld the bank larceny conviction of an armored car guard for removing cash from a bag before delivering it to a bank, stating, "The later decision to take the money was larceny, because it was beyond the consent of the owner, who retained constructive possession until the custodian's task was completed." This is a legal fiction that allows a court to find that the elements of larceny have been met because the defendant did not "possess" the money in the bag despite having physical control over it and the contain which held it. To avoid the fiction of the "breaking bulk" doctrine, many states enacted statutes making it a crime for a bailee of property, who has lawful possession of it temporarily, to steal it, known as larceny by bailee.

11. ***Larceny by Trick.*** Larceny usually requites a trespassory taking of property from another person who has actual or constructive possession of it, without that person's consent. But what if a thief lies about returning property in order to induce someone to voluntarily turn over possession of the item? It is arguable that a larceny did not take place because the offender did not obtain the property by trespass. The common law dealt with this situation by recognizing a type of larceny called larceny by trick. In *Pear's Case*, 168 Eng.Rep. 208 (Cr.Cas.Res.1779), the English court concluded that a thief committed larceny by trick when he took possession of a horse by telling the owner that he intended to use it for only half a day when he planned to take it to another town and sell it. While it appeared the owner voluntarily gave possession to the thief, the consent was obtained by a lie and so did not constitute valid consent to negate the trespass.

Larceny by trick is the basis for viewing fraud as a type of larceny. In both situations the victim voluntarily gives over possession of the property in response to the misstatements of the perpetrator. Some modern fraud statutes, such as the federal mail and wire fraud provisions, 18 U.S.C. §§ 1341 and 1343, are even broader because they do not require proof that the defendant obtained possession of the property, instead reaching any "scheme or artifice to defraud." Along the same lines, they take a more expansive view of the type of property that can be the subject of the prosecution, including intangible property like copyrights and securities. Indeed, a federal statute, 18 U.S.C. § 1346, provides that a scheme to defraud includes deprivation of the intangible "right of honest services," which is far removed from the type of personal property covered by the common law offense of larceny.

PROBLEM THIRTY-TWO

Johnson received a voicemail message stating, "Your cell phone has been found and if you want it returned, you should go to the corner of 34th & Vine and ask a hotdog vendor there for an package with your name on the outside. I suggest you give the vendor an envelope with a $500 reward if you want the phone back. I'm sure it has lots of valuable information stored in it." Johnson believes that the phone fell out of a pocket earlier that morning when Johnson was inside the changing room at a local clothing store trying on some new clothes. The phone contains sale contacts related to Johnson's job as a pharmaceutical representative and personal financial information, including PINs for various bank and brokerage accounts worth over $150,000. Johnson calls the police, who set up a stakeout at the corner. A few minutes after Johnson gives an envelope with $500 to the vendor, a young male stops to speak with the vendor and takes the envelope. The police immediately arrest this individual and recover the $500. The state's larceny statute mirrors the common law, and grades the offense as a felony if the property has a value over $500 and a misdemeanor if the value is not greater than $500. The prosecutor charges one count of felony larceny of personal property with a value over $500. The phone's retail price is $659, but can be purchased for $199 with a two-year contract with the cell phone carrier. Defendant has two prior felony convictions, and if convicted of this charge will be sentenced under the state's mandatory recidivist statute to a 50-year term of imprisonment with no chance for parole. What argument(s) can defense counsel make that the felony larceny charge should be dismissed or reduced to a misdemeanor, and how will the prosecutor respond?

B. Embezzlement

Embezzlement is different from larceny because the victim entrusts the property to the defendant, and the defendant then converts it to personal use. Common types of entrustments are employees who hold or receive money or property on behalf of the employer (the bank teller or retail clerk), businesses that take in items for repair or servicing, and fiduciaries — such as lawyers — who administer or manage property on behalf of the beneficiary. In each of these situations, the person has lawful possession of the property, and then misuses the property for his own purposes. "Generally speaking, to constitute larceny there must be a wrongful taking and carrying away of the personal property of another without his consent. . . . It involves a trespass either actual or constructive. . . . The embezzlement statute makes criminal the fraudulent conversion of personal property by one . . . [who was] entrusted with and received into his possession lawfully the personal property of another, and thereafter . . . converted the property to his own use." *State v. Griffin*, 79 S.E.2d 230 (N.C. 1953).

Professor Fletcher described the rationale for the common law's development of the crimes of larceny and embezzlement as offenses not only against ownership, but also against the social order.

> It is important to realize that an act of thieving might endanger a range of interests other than wealth. In the traditional view, the thief upset the social order not only by threatening property, but by violating the general sense of security and well-being of the community; in this broader sense, theft was feared as a socially unnerving event. Similarly, the harm in improper acquisitions by employees, later punished as embezzlement, was traditionally thought to be a breach of trust. Thus, the harm in both larceny and embezzlement was primarily relational: The thief endangered the established order of the community; the embezzler breached a particular relationship of confidence with his employer. The transition to the modern conception of theft witnessed the dissolution of these relational aspects of larceny and embezzlement. Both crimes came to be seen primarily as offenses against property interests. The modern vision of the criminal law seems to be that the proper allocation of each item of property enjoys the full concern of the community; the dishonest displacement of wealth from one person to another therefore becomes a public harm. This transition in the concept of harm and in the nature of theft as a crime lay behind the nineteenth century misunderstanding of the distinctions worked out in the traditional approach to larceny.

George P. Fletcher, *The Metamorphosis of Larceny*, 89 HARV. L. REV. 469 (1976).

United States v. Lequire
672 F.3d 724 (9th Cir. 2012)

SILVERMAN, Circuit Judge:

* * * Lequire was charged with ten counts of embezzlement of insurance premiums, in violation of 18 U.S.C. § 1033(b)(1), and one count of conspiracy to commit embezzlement.

Patriot Insurance Agency, owned by former Congressman Rick Renzi and his wife Roberta and regulated by the Arizona Department of Insurance, brokers property and liability insurance through insurance underwriters at group rates to non-profit organizations. During the relevant time period, defendant Lequire was Patriot's treasurer.

After he was elected to Congress in 2002, Renzi placed Patriot in his wife's name but stayed involved with the company. Testimony established that Renzi was in charge; he instructed Patriot's staff whom to pay and when to pay them. In 2005, Renzi, with Lequire's help, formed Spirit Mountain Insurance Company. Spirit was formed as a "risk retention group," a way for similarly situated entities, like the non-profit groups for whom Patriot brokered policies, to self-insure against risk. Though licensed in the District of Columbia, Spirit was able to operate nationally. Lequire was Spirit's treasurer as well.

Spirit contracted with Risk Services, LLC to serve as captive manager for Spirit. As captive manager, Risk Services was responsible for handling Spirit's regulatory filings, accounting and financial reporting, and various legal and administrative services. Risk Services was also the conduit between Spirit and the D.C. Department of Insurance, Securities and Banking (DISB). Risk Services was independent from Spirit and Patriot, though it had one overlapping director. Neither Lequire, Renzi, nor Renzi's wife had a role in Risk Services.

Patriot and Spirit entered into a Program Administrator Agreement, an agency agreement signed by Roberta Renzi for Spirit and Lequire for Patriot. As Spirit's program administrator in Arizona, Patriot performed policy-related services for Spirit including underwriting, paying claims, and charging and collecting premiums. Pursuant to the Agreement, Patriot collected insurance premium payments from policyholders insured by Spirit and made monthly payments to Spirit.

For purposes of this appeal, the pertinent provisions of the Agreement between Patriot and Spirit are as follows:

Receipt of Funds: Accounts

A. [Patriot] shall hold all funds received by it in connection with the Agreement as a fiduciary of [Spirit]. [Patriot] shall, under no circumstances, make any personal or corporate use of such funds not authorized by this Agreement. [Patriot] may deposit said funds into its general operating account (the "Agency Account") which may include premiums due to other carriers and commissions due to [Patriot].

B. [Patriot] shall be responsible for collecting and paying to [Spirit] all premiums due on the business written pursuant to this Agreement. Failure to collect shall not operate as a defense against full payment by [Patriot] to [Spirit] of all amounts due and owing to [Spirit] for all liability assumed by [Spirit]. * * *

At Renzi's direction, Patriot promptly deposited premium checks received from its clients into Patriot's general operating account. Through July 2006, Patriot stamped premium checks it received "For Deposit Only, Patriot Insurance Agency, Inc. Trust Account," but there was no trust account. After July 2006, Patriot stopped using the rubber stamp, and continued to deposit the premium checks into its general operating account.

Patriot routinely failed to pay the premiums over to Spirit on a timely basis. Instead, Lequire, over a two-year period, transferred the premium funds to Renzi's personal account and Renzi used those funds to pay for personal expenditures. In all, Lequire transferred over $750,000 to Renzi at a time when Patriot had less in its bank accounts than it owed Spirit.

The entire time that Patriot was delinquent in its payments to Spirit, Lequire submitted accurate reports to Risk Services showing Patriot's delinquency. Risk Services then reported the delinquent payments to DISB. Even though Patriot was unabashedly delinquent in timely paying Spirit, neither Spirit, Risk Services, nor DISB ever invoked the 1.5% penalty interest clause.

A number of witnesses, several with no firsthand knowledge of the Agreement, testified regarding their personal beliefs as to the nature of Spirit and Patriot's relationship. Officials at Risk Services and DISB testified that they believed Spirit had a fiduciary relationship with Patriot and an official at DISB testified that she would not have approved a program administrator agreement without a fiduciary clause. Others opined that, although there is no Arizona statute requiring Patriot to be Spirit's fiduciary, the practice in Arizona amongst brokers is to be "trustworthy and responsible" and to treat premium funds as not their own.

After the jury found Lequire guilty of the conspiracy charge and eight of the ten embezzlement counts, Lequire moved for a judgment of acquittal pursuant to

Rule 29(c) of the Federal Rules of Criminal Procedure. Lequire argued that as a matter of law and fact there was no trust relationship between Patriot and Spirit as required for a § 1033(b)(1) violation under embezzlement. The argument was that if the money was not actually held "in trust," it was not Spirit's money, and therefore could not be embezzled from Spirit. The district court denied the motion, ruling that there was sufficient evidence to support the jury's finding that a fiduciary relationship of trust existed between Patriot and Spirit.

* * * The crime of embezzlement of insurance premiums in set forth in 18 U.S.C. § 1033(b)(1): "Whoever [ ] acting as, or being an officer, director, agent, or employee of, any person engaged in the business of insurance . . . willfully embezzles, abstracts, purloins, or misappropriates any of the moneys, funds, premiums, credits, or other property of such person so engaged shall be punished . . . ."

The statute uses the word "embezzles" without definition. However, the cases define embezzlement as "the fraudulent appropriation of property by a person to whom such property has been entrusted, or into whose hands it has lawfully come." *United States v. Eriksen*, 639 F.3d 1138 (9th Cir. 2011).

Although federal law defines embezzlement, whether a person's property is held "in trust," or is not even that person's property at all, is a question of state law. In *United States v. Lawson*, 925 F.2d 1207 (9th Cir. 1991), we looked to state law to determine whether an auctioneer holds auction proceeds as a bailee or as a debtor; if the auctioneer was a bailee he could have been guilty of embezzlement. For the same reason, here, we look to Arizona law to determine whether Patriot held the premiums "in trust" for Spirit, or merely had a contractual obligation to remit certain amounts due each month.

Both parties agree that Spirit's premiums must have been held in trust by Patriot for Lequire to be guilty of embezzlement. If they were not, the relationship was a debtor-creditor one and there could be no embezzlement. We agree with Lequire that as a matter of Arizona law, Patriot was a debtor of Spirit, not a trustee.

First of all, Arizona law does not require an insurance broker to hold funds in trust for an insurance company. Whether funds are held in trust depends on the terms of the particular contract. Here, the Agreement states that "[Patriot] shall hold all funds received by it in connection with this Agreement as a fiduciary of [Spirit]. [Patriot] shall, under no circumstances, make any personal or corporate use of such funds not authorized by this agreement." Conspicuously missing from the Agreement is any mention of "a trust," of property being "entrusted," "held in trust," of Patriot being a "trustee," or any other variant of the word.

There is no doubt that Patriot is a fiduciary of Spirit, but that does not necessarily make it a trustee. A trust is "a fiduciary relationship with respect to property." *Restatement (Third) of Trusts* § 2 (2003). However, "the trust relation-ship is one of many forms of fiduciary relationships" including: "guardian-ward, agent-principal, attorney-client, and partnership relations." We have explained, in no uncertain terms, that the two terms are not synonymous. * * * Although a trustee is always a fiduciary, a fiduciary is not always a trustee.

The main problem for the government here is that under Arizona law, when an insurance agent is allowed by contract to commingle funds in a single account and has the duty to pay over premiums to the insurance company regardless of whether the premiums have actually been collected, as a matter of law no trust relationship exists; what exists is a debtor-creditor relationship. * * *

Here * * * the Agreement allowed Patriot to commingle premium payments in its general operating account. And * * * Patriot was required to pay Spirit premiums owed regardless of whether or not they had been collected. In addition, if Patriot did not timely pay the premiums, interest would begin accruing at 1.5% per month, making the case for a debtor-creditor relationship even stronger than in either of the other two cases. If interest is due on unremitted amounts, "it becomes close to certain that the relationship is a debt rather than a trust." *Restatement (Third) of Trusts* § 5k.

* * * [T]he fact that Patriot was admittedly a fiduciary does not mean it was also a trustee. To reiterate, many—indeed most—fiduciaries are not trustees. * * * [T]he fact that the Agreement contained a clause prohibiting personal and corporate use of funds alone is insufficient to prove a trust, as opposed to it being a contractual restriction. In *Lawson*, we held that even though a statute required auctioneers to keep auction proceeds separate from personal funds, the auctioneer had a debtor-creditor relationship with the owner of the property because he could commingle the proceeds from all auctions and he was not required to remit the actual auction proceeds—just the amount of the proceeds.

Because being a fiduciary does not ipso facto create a trust relationship, the majority of the evidence the government cites—including the testimony of witnesses opining that Patriot had fiduciary and "trustworthiness" obligations towards Spirit—is irrelevant to the crucial question: whether the Agreement created a trust. * * *

The fact that for a period of time Patriot endorsed checks deposited into its general account using a rubber stamp containing the words "trust account" is of no significance. First of all, there was no separate "trust account;" it is undisputed that the funds were deposited into a commingled general account. More importantly, this case turns on the terms of the contract between the parties and not on what was, or was not, on Patriot's endorsement stamp. For example, if the Agreement had in fact created a trust, Lequire's use of an endorsement stamp claiming the funds to be his own would not have saved him.

* * * The district court also relied on Spirit Mountain's security interest in Patriot's future commissions and fees to find that Spirit had a sufficient ownership interest to sustain Lequire's embezzlement conviction. This rationale fails, however, because Spirit's security interest was in future commissions and fees, not in the premiums collected. * * *

In summary, we hold that the funds in Patriot's possession were not held in trust because the Agreement allowed for commingling, required premium payments to be paid to Spirit regardless of whether or not Patriot had collected them, and allowed Spirit to collect an interest on late premium payments. Because Patriot did not hold premium payments "in trust," Lequire cannot be guilty of embezzlement.

For the foregoing reasons, the judgment of the district court is REVERSED and the case is REMANDED for entry of judgment of acquittal on all counts.

NOTE

Similar to the adoption of embezzlement to reach situations that fell outside larceny, Parliament in the eighteenth century enacted the crime of false pretenses to address thefts involving a transfer of ownership rather than just possession. The crime of false pretenses occurs when a defendant, with the intent to defraud the owner, knowingly misrepresents a past or present fact in order to induce the owner to transfer title to the property. Both false pretenses and larceny by trick involve a misrepresentation of fact to induce another person to give over an interest in property, the two crimes are often confused. The distinction between them is based on the interest transferred in response to the misrepresentation. If a defendant acquired title to the property, then the offense is false pretenses, while if the defendant merely acquired possession then the crime would be larceny by trick.

PROBLEM THIRTY-THREE

Could the prosecutor have charged Lequire with any other theft offense? Should this conduct be prosecuted as a crime, or is it more appropriate to leave it for a civil action between the parties to the contract?

C. Receiving Stolen Property

State v. Jennings
2002 Ohio 7266 (Ohio Ct. App. 2002)

ROBERT A. NADER, J.

Appellant appeals from a judgment of the Lake County Court of Common Pleas convicting him of two counts of receiving stolen property.

On April 21, 2000, appellant was indicted on two counts of receiving stolen property, in violation of R.C. 2913.51, felonies of the fifth degree. One count was for a Citi Bank credit card and the second count was for a Bank One money card.

* * * In appellant's first assignment of error, he argues that the State failed to prove beyond a reasonable doubt that appellant received, retained, or disposed of Ms. Kay's credit card and/or money card. Appellant argues that because none of the witnesses stated that they actually observed appellant in possession of Ms. Kay's property or that they heard the three men discussing her property, the State failed to meet its burden. Further, appellant asserts that a money card does not fall within the purview of the definition of credit card set forth in R.C. 2913.71.

* * * The elements of the offense of receiving stolen property are set forth in R.C. 2913.51, which provides that "no person shall, receive, retain, or dispose of property of another knowing or having reasonable cause to believe that the property has been obtained through commission of a theft offense."

In the instant case, the record reveals that three men, one of whom was later identified as appellant, were seen running from the Fluid Regulators parking lot onto Ms. Mapes' property, on the evening of December 15, 1999. The three individuals ran into the woods where they were seen drinking Miller Gold beer, the type of beer stolen from Ms. Kay. After apprehending the men, the police discovered that one of appellant's companions was in possession of fifty-five dollars and one of Ms. Kay's withdrawal receipts and that two of Ms. Kay's credit cards were found in a jacket discarded by his companion. Appellant, who had moved approximately fifteen feet from where Officer Cueni first observed him, had Ms. Kay's bankcard and a third credit card at his feet. Although none of the witnesses attested that they observed appellant in possession of Ms. Kay's property or heard the men discussing the property, the foregoing evidence established that appellant violated R.C. 2913.51(A). Ms. Kay's property was found in an area within appellant's immediate control. Thus, viewing the evidence in a light most favorable to the prosecution, we conclude that a rational trier of fact could have found the essential elements of the crime proven beyond a reasonable doubt.

* * * Next, we will briefly address appellant's argument that money cards do not fall within the purview of type of property which enhances a receiving stolen property offense from a misdemeanor to a felony under R.C. 2913.71.

R.C. 2913.71 provides:

"Regardless of the value of the property involved and regardless of whether the offender previously has been convicted of a theft offense, a violation of section 2913.02 or 2913.51 of the Revised Code is a felony of the fifth degree if the property involved is any of the following:

(A) A credit card;

* * * A "'credit card' includes, but is not limited to, a card, code, device, or other means of access to a customer's account for the purpose of obtaining money, property, labor, or services on credit, or for initiating an electronic fund transfer at a point-of-sale terminal, an automated teller machine, or a cash dispensing machine." R.C. 2913.01(U).

Money cards are a "means of access to a customer's account" for the purpose of "initiating an electronic fund transfer at a point-of-sale terminal, an automated teller machine, or a cash dispensing machine." Therefore, money cards fall within the definition of credit card set forth in R.C. 2913.01(U). Further, like credit cards, money cards can be used to obtain hundreds of thousands of dollars in cash or merchandise. Although money cards have per diem limits with respect to the amount of cash that may be withdrawn, there is no such limitation upon how much merchandise an individual may obtain. Due to the lag time between the actual transaction and the bank's accounting, money cards can be used to withdraw funds in excess of the amount contained in an individual's bank account.

Further, in *State of Ohio v. Hendking*, 631 N.E.2d 1108 (Ohio Ct. App. 1993), the appellate court held that a closed or expired credit card fits within the statutory definition * * *. The court explained that a credit card account need not be open because an expired or canceled credit card may still be a means to access a customer's account if used at a store which "utilizes paper authorization books published monthly, rather than an electronic authorization machine." * * * Many money cards are now embossed with credit card logos and, thus, are used as credit cards. Therefore, an expired or closed money card containing a credit card logo could also be used at a store that "utilizes paper authorization books published monthly." In light of the foregoing, we cannot conclude that the trial court erred in finding money cards fall within the purview of the statutory definition of credit cards. Appellant's first assignment of error lacks merit. * * * The judgment of the Lake County Court of Common Pleas is affirmed. * * *

PROBLEM THIRTY-FOUR

Kelly was the president of the local Association of Foster Parents, a non-profit organization that aids foster parents by providing them with toys, clothing, and household goods that are donated to it. During the prior year, the AFP received over 4,000 items, and distributed many of them to local foster parents. One afternoon, a volunteer at the AFP's offices noticed Kelly taking some of the nicer items out to her car. When the volunteer asked Kelly about taking the items, Kelly responded, "I'm making a delivery on my way home." Over the next few weeks, the volunteer saw Kelly taking items with her on a regular basis. The volunteer notified the police about Kelly's conduct. An investigation revealed that Kelly had been selling a number of items donated to AFP on internet auction sites, and had given some to her family as gifts. A search of her garage turned up a large number of donated items stored there. Kelly said in an interview with the police that none of the donors gave any specific direction on how the items were to be used, and none ever inquired about them after the donation. Kelly also said that the money from selling items was used by AFP to cover its operating expenses, which includes paying her a small salary. Many of the sales were paid in cash, traveler's checks, or money orders that cannot be traced. She works full-time for AFP in her town, and has been the driving force behind its operation for years. The jurisdiction has a statute similar to the California theft provision (p. 396) that codifies the common law offenses of larceny, embezzlement, and false pretenses. On what theories can the prosecution proceed if it charges Kelly with violating the statute, and what defenses can be offered to rebut a charge?

§ 10.02 Robbery

A. Force or Threat

Commonwealth v. Powell
742 N.E.2d 1061 (Mass. 2001)

SOSMAN, J.

The defendant, Walter L. Powell, was convicted of armed robbery (G.L. c. 265, § 17), * * * . The defendant claims on appeal that the trial judge erred in denying his motion for a required finding of not guilty as to the armed robbery charge (thereby reducing it to unarmed robbery) on the ground that the object used by the defendant was not a dangerous weapon. * * *

On January 16, 1998, the victim, Theresa Campbell, was working as a cashier in a gasoline station convenience store in Plymouth. At about 10:30 P.M., when there were no other customers or employees present, the defendant entered the store and came up to the counter as if to make a purchase. He then asked the victim if she could give him the money in the cash register. The victim did not think the defendant was serious, and she jokingly told him she could not do that because she would "get in trouble." The defendant then walked around the counter and, standing directly beside the victim, told her to open the register. He also told the victim not to move because he had a gun, and he threatened to shoot the victim if she "tried anything."

The victim could see that the defendant had an object under his jacket, and he put his right hand on it a few times. She could see the very tip of the object, about one-half to one inch of it at most, protruding out the top of the jacket. The victim said it looked like the end of "two sticks coming up, like wooden sticks." The victim was not certain exactly what the object was: "I didn't know, you know, if it was a real gun, or what he had. I just knew it was an object in his jacket."

The defendant removed approximately $170 in cash from the register. As he left the store, he told the victim to follow him. The victim did so, and testified at trial that she followed the defendant's instructions because she was scared and did not know if the defendant was going to shoot her. Once outside the store the defendant, with the victim following, walked down the street and through the parking lot of a nearby school. At one point, the defendant turned around and grabbed the victim by the hands, forcing her to walk next to him. After walking for about five to ten minutes, the defendant told the victim to turn around and run back to the store. The victim returned to the store and telephoned the police.

A Plymouth police officer, after hearing a radio dispatch regarding the robbery, began searching the area for a suspect. He found a wooden object in the roadway, about 200 to 300 yards away from the store. It was a replica of a double barrel shotgun, with two wooden dowels in place of the barrels, a wood stock, and a clothespin to replicate the hammer. The replica gun was subsequently identified by the victim as the object she had seen protruding from the robber's jacket.

Three days later, the victim was stopped at a red light when she saw the defendant walk by her car. She recognized him, contacted the police immediately, and the defendant was apprehended shortly thereafter.

In order to commit the crime of armed robbery, the defendant must "be[ ] armed with a dangerous weapon" at the time of the robbery. G.L. c. 265, § 17. Thus, the Commonwealth must prove beyond a reasonable doubt that the defendant had, at the time he was in the store, an object that would qualify as a "dangerous weapon." The standard definition of "dangerous weapon" includes those items that are, by their nature, capable of causing serious injury or death, but also includes items that are used or displayed in a way such that they reasonably appear capable of causing serious injury or death. Thus, an object that is, on closer inspection, incapable of inflicting serious injury or death can still be a dangerous weapon if, at the time of the offense, it would have been reasonable to believe that it was capable of inflicting such injury. See, e.g., *Commonwealth v. Henson*, 259 N.E.2d 769 (Mass. 1970) (upholding conviction of assault by means of a dangerous weapon even though defendant's revolver had only blank cartridges); *Commonwealth v. Nickologines*, 76 N.E.2d 649 (Mass. 1948) (on charge of armed robbery, Commonwealth does not have to prove that defendant's gun was loaded); *Commonwealth v. Johnson*, 543 N.E.2d 22 (Mass. Ct. App. 1989) (victim's reasonable perception that object in defendant's pocket was gun sufficient to support conviction of armed assault with intent to rob even though object was only hairbrush); *Commonwealth v. Garafolo*, 499 N.E.2d 839 (Mass Ct. App. 1986) (defendant used toy handgun to commit armed assault with intent to rob); *Commonwealth v. Nicholson*, 477 N.E.2d 1038 (Mass. Ct. App. 1985) (armed robbery could be committed with "fake plastic gun" if "it reasonably appeared capable of inflicting bodily harm"); *Commonwealth v. Perry*, 378 N.E.2d 1384 (Mass. Ct. App. 1978) (armed robbery committed with black plastic toy pistol). See also *McLaughlin v. United States*, 476 U.S. 16 (1986) (unloaded gun displayed during bank robbery is "dangerous weapon" under Federal bank robbery statute).

Here, the judge provided the jury with a correct definition of "dangerous weapon," giving appropriate emphasis to the requirement that, if the object was not actually capable of inflicting death or serious injury, it could only constitute a dangerous weapon if it reasonably appeared capable of causing death or serious injury.[3] This instruction was consistent with case law holding that a replica or fake weapon is a dangerous weapon if the victim would, in all the surrounding circumstances, reasonably believe that the object was a real weapon.

The defendant contends that our decision in *Commonwealth v. Howard*, 436 N.E.2d 1211 (Mass. 1982), is to the contrary and that fake or toy weapons cannot qualify as dangerous weapons. Nothing in the *Howard* decision changes the standard definition of a dangerous weapon, nor does it prevent inoperable, fake, or replica weapons from being dangerous weapons. In *Howard*, the defendant threatened his robbery victim by telling her that he would "pull the trigger" if she did "anything foolish." The victim had not seen any gun or any object resembling a gun in the defendant's possession. Police arrived while the robbery was still in

---

[3] The judge's instruction included the following: "A dangerous weapon is any instrument which by nature of its construction, or the manner of it [s] use, is capable of causing grievous bodily injury or death, or could be perceived by a reasonable person as so capable.... This means it is not necessary that the instrument be actually capable of causing serious bodily harm or death, so long as it appears to a reasonable person to be capable of doing so. For example, for the purpose of establishing this element of armed robbery, an unloaded gun or a gun which cannot fire bullets can be a dangerous weapon, if the gun appears capable of causing serious bodily harm to the victim. A person who uses a toy gun or other fake weapon to commit a robbery may be convicted of an armed robbery if the victim reasonably took it to be a real gun or weapon which was capable of inflicting bodily injury."

progress, and the defendant, arrested at the scene without an opportunity to dispose of any weapon, was found to have no gun on him. The court held that, where the defendant did not have any weapon in his possession, he could not have been "armed with a dangerous weapon." The defendant's mere statement that he had a weapon, when he in fact had no form of weapon at all, would not permit the jury to conclude that the defendant was "armed" with a weapon: "[W]here a robber had no instrumentality at all, although he said he had a gun, a conviction of armed robbery is not warranted."

In that context, the court noted that the crime of armed robbery did not extend to one who was only "apparently" armed. * * * In holding that being only "apparently" armed was not sufficient, the court did not alter the underlying definition of dangerous weapon. We merely specified, consistent with the statute, that the defendant had to have some object in his possession and that, when he did not have any object at all, the defendant's statements to the victim claiming to have a weapon would not suffice.[4] Recognizing that a robber's claim to have a weapon would engender the same fear in the victim, whether the robber actually had a weapon or not, the court left it to the Legislature to determine whether the armed robbery statute should be amended to include "robbery committed while apparently armed."

In *Howard*, we reiterated the definition of dangerous weapon, requiring the Commonwealth to prove that the defendant was armed with "some instrumentality which presents an objective threat of danger to a person of reasonable and average sensibility." Where, as here, there was evidence that the defendant had an actual object in his possession, it was for the jury to determine whether that object came within the definition of dangerous weapon.

The jury were properly instructed that, in order for a fake weapon to be considered a "dangerous weapon," it would have to be "reasonable" for the victim to believe that the weapon was real or that it was capable of inflicting death or serious bodily injury. There was evidence from which the jury could conclude that it would be reasonable for the victim to believe that the object under the defendant's jacket was a gun. The defendant claimed to have a gun; there was an object under his jacket; the object was of the size and shape of a gun; and the defendant gestured at that object with his hand. The victim testified that she complied with the defendant's orders, including his command that she come with him when he left the store, because of her fear of being shot. Where it reasonably appeared, in all the circumstances, that the object in the defendant's possession was capable of inflicting serious bodily injury or death, the jury could conclude that that object was

---

[4] * * * [The court distinguished between cases where the accused might have disposed of the weapon.]

a dangerous weapon and that the robbery was therefore an armed robbery. [Conviction for armed robbery affirmed.]

NOTES AND QUESTIONS

1. *Whose Viewpoint.* The "weapon" that Powell possessed could have been used as a bludgeon, and therefore could be viewed as a dangerous weapon in that context. He did not, however, threaten the victim with that use, instead intimating that it was a firearm of some sort, and she apparently concluded that there was a possibility that it was — not an unreasonable conclusion, by the way. As the Massachusetts Supreme Judicial Court points out, just saying you have a gun is not enough. But the question remains whether the victim's view of the nature of the weapon determines whether it is dangerous, or whether the objective nature of the item governs. *Powell* adopts the victim's viewpoint as the determinative factor, asking whether the victim reasonably believed the defendant had a dangerous weapon at the time of the theft to make it an armed robbery.

2. *Defining a "Dangerous Weapon."* Some states explicitly provide for situations in which the defendant does not actually possess a firearm or other dangerous instrumentality but intimates that one is present to establish liability for armed or aggravated robbery. For example, the Oregon robbery statutes cover any person who "[r]epresents by word or conduct that the person is armed with what purports to be a dangerous or deadly weapon." OR. REV. STAT. § 164.405(1)(b). Similarly, the Colorado aggravated robbery statute includes any defendant who "possesses any article used or fashioned in a manner to lead any person who is present reasonably to believe it to be a deadly weapon or represents verbally or otherwise that he is then and there so armed." COLO. REV. STAT. § 18-4-302(d).

Other states limit the definition of a dangerous weapon to those things that are capable of inflicting death or serious bodily harm. For example, the Iowa armed robbery statute provides:

A "dangerous weapon" is any instrument or device designed primarily for use in inflicting death or injury upon a human being or animal, and which is capable of inflicting death upon a human being when used in the manner for which it was designed. Additionally, any instrument or device of any sort whatsoever which is actually used in such a manner as to indicate that the defendant intends to inflict death or serious injury upon the other, and which, when so used, is capable of inflicting death upon a human being, is a dangerous weapon. Dangerous weapons include, but are not limited to, any offensive weapon, pistol, revolver, or other firearm, dagger, razor, stiletto, switchblade knife, or knife having a blade exceeding five inches in length.

IOWA CON. ACTS § 702.7. In *Brooks v. State*, 552 A.2d 872 (Md. 1989), the Maryland Court of Appeals considered whether the use of a toy pistol was sufficient to establish a robbery "with a dangerous or deadly weapon." The court stated:

> The offense [of armed robbery] is not a new substantive crime; it is common law or simple robbery aggravated by use of a dangerous or deadly weapon. We believe the legislative purpose in prescribing an enhanced penalty for armed robbery was aimed at deterring those capable of actually inflicting death or serious bodily injury. The use of a toy gun "adds nothing extra to the bare fact that [the robber] intimidated the victim." W. LAFAVE & A. SCOTT, [CRIMINAL LAW] § 8.11(f).

> This construction of the statute, and its adoption of the objective approach, is fully consistent with the legislative language. Moreover, it avoids possible absurd results. For example, under the subjective view, a robber whose finger is extended in his or her jacket pocket to simulate a gun barrel, and who intimidates the victim by claiming to possess a gun, could be convicted of armed robbery. Although that robber would be guilty of robbery[,] it would be ridiculous to convict this individual of robbery with a dangerous or deadly weapon.

B. Timing of Use of Force

Commonwealth v. Jones
591 S.E.2d 68 (Va. 2004)

Opinion by Senior Justice ROSCOE B. STEPHENSON, JR.

* * * On February 17, 2001, Jones entered a store known as Shoe Carnival, in the City of Hampton. Bobby Ray Baker, the store manager, immediately began to watch Jones through a video camera because Jones previously had stolen merchandise from the store. Baker watched as Jones picked up shoes in each aisle of the store. Baker then walked down to the floor to watch Jones. From that vantage point, Baker saw Jones put a pair of boots in his pants and walk out of the store. Jones neither paid for the boots nor had permission to take them.

Baker followed Jones out of the store and approached him in "the [store's] parking lot." When Baker was "a little less than ten feet" from Jones, he asked Jones to return the boots. Jones denied having the boots, and Baker told Jones that he had seen Jones put the boots in his pants. At that point, Jones withdrew a firearm from a pocket of his jacket, pointed it at Baker, and said, "You better back . . . off me." Baker was frightened, and he ran and hid behind a parked vehicle. Jones then fled in a nearby car.

Robbery, a common-law offense, is defined as "'the taking, with intent to steal, of the personal property of another, from his person or in his presence, against his will, by violence or intimidation.'" *George v. Commonwealth*, 411 S.E.2d 12 (Va. 1991). We have held that, in order to establish a robbery, the violence or intimidation "must occur before or at the time of the taking." *Branch v. Commonwealth*, 300 S.E.2d 758 (Va. 1983).

Jones contends that the violence or intimidation did not precede or occur at the same time as the taking. More specifically, he asserts that he

> completed the act of petty larceny by concealing the boots in his pants. Although [the store manager] could have intervened to prevent the shoplifting, he failed to do so and allowed Jones to remove the stolen goods from the store. The record contains no evidence that Jones employed force to conceal the goods, or for that matter, to remove them from store property. Instead, . . . Jones resorted to a showing of force when [the store manager] attempted to prevent his escape.

The Commonwealth, on the other hand, summarizes its contention as follows:

> [The store manager] followed Jones out of the shoe store and approached him to retrieve the boots that Jones had taken, but for which he had not paid. While Jones' original intent may have been to commit only larceny, his intention changed to robbery. In order to accomplish the theft, Jones introduced a firearm to overcome the interference of the manager with Jones' asportation of the property. The asportation of the victim's property began when Jones picked up the boots inside the store and continued throughout the time that he pointed the gun at [the manager] and carried the boots away from [the manager's] presence.

* * * In support of their contentions, the parties rely in large measure on three of our cases. Those cases are *Pritchard v. Commonwealth*, 303 S.E.2d 911 (Va. 1983); *Durham v. Commonwealth*, 198 S.E.2d 603 (Va. 1973); and *Mason v. Commonwealth*, 105 S.E.2d 149 (Va. 1958).

In *Mason*, the accused broke a store's display window and entered the store. He picked up a portable television set about two and one-half feet from the hole in the window and handed it to a confederate who was outside the store. Just as the accused was handing the television set to his confederate, the store owner, who had been hiding behind the display window, struck the accused with a board. The accused then threw a portable radio at the owner and fired a pistol four times towards the owner. The owner testified that "'the television was out of [the accused's] arms and in the arms of [the accused's] companion before [the accused] threw the radio set and started shooting.'"

In holding that the evidence was insufficient to support a robbery conviction, we stated the following:

> Here no force was used towards [the owner] and there was no intimidation until accused had taken the television set in his arms and handed the article to a confederate who made off with it. The taking and asportation preceded both the violence, and the intimidation for neither occurred until after accused had passed the article to his companion and been struck by [the owner].
>
> The facts and circumstances unquestionably show that in time sequence the taking and asportation occurred before there was any violence or intimidation by throwing the radio or by presentation of firearms.

Unlike the present case, the accused in *Mason* had succeeded in removing the merchandise from the presence and constructive possession of the owner before the accused introduced violence toward the owner.

In *Durham*, a mother and her daughter were found stabbed to death in the daughter's home. The accused and an accomplice had broken into and entered the home with the intent to commit larceny. We reasonably inferred from proven facts that, while the thieves were in the process of carrying out their intended act, the victims appeared on the scene and surprised them. It was then that the thieves' intention "changed from the commission of larceny to robbery to accomplish their original purpose by overcoming [the victims'] interference with the taking."

In *Durham*, we stated the following:

> Where the owner of personal property, or another having custody or constructive possession of the same, interposes himself to prevent a thief from taking the property, and the force and violence used to overcome the opposition to the taking is concurrent or concomitant with the taking, the thief's action constitutes robbery.

We also said that "[a]n intent to commit robbery does not have to exist for any particular length of time. It may occur momentarily."

In the present case, Jones, like the thieves in *Durham*, originally intended to commit larceny. While Jones was in the process of carrying out that intention and the larceny was continuing, the store manager interposed himself to prevent Jones from taking the merchandise. At that time, Jones produced the firearm to overcome the manager's opposition to the taking, and his crime became robbery, not merely larceny.

Finally, in *Pritchard*, the proprietor of a gasoline service station filled the tank of the accused's car. When the proprietor asked the accused for payment, the accused produced and cocked a firearm. The proprietor ran into the station, and the accused drove away without paying for the gasoline.

Pritchard contended that he did not commit a robbery "because he presented no deadly force or intimidation to [the proprietor] until after the asportation of the stolen gasoline was complete." Pritchard claimed that the asportation occurred when the proprietor pumped the gasoline into the tank of his car. According to Pritchard, when the pumping of the gasoline ended, the proprietor had surrendered to him "control and possession" of the gasoline; thus, the taking was unaccompanied by force or violence and was merely a petit larceny.

We rejected Pritchard's contention and focused upon the distinction, in the context of larceny, between possession and custody. We held that Pritchard had committed a robbery because, when the gasoline was pumped into the car's tank, Pritchard "became a bare custodian of the gasoline" while the proprietor "remained in constructive possession [of the gasoline] pending payment." Concluding, we said the following:

> When Pritchard produced the firearm, he exerted intimidation upon [the proprietor]. This subdued [the proprietor's] ability to resist and enabled Pritchard to convert his custody into possession by carrying the goods away in violation of the condition, with the intent to steal. The use of force preceded this conversion and enabled Pritchard to obtain possession.

The rationale in *Pritchard* applies in the present case. When Jones seized and hid the boots, he had custody of them, not possession. The store manager, as he observed Jones, retained constructive possession of the merchandise. As Jones' larceny was continuing, but before his custody was converted into possession, the manager interposed himself to prevent the theft. When Jones introduced force and violence by producing the firearm, his crime was transformed into robbery.

———————

NOTE

The common law rule distinguishing robbery from larceny was the use of force no matter how slight to accomplish the taking from the person or presence of the victim. How much force is required? The Arizona Court of Appeals noted in *State v. Miguel*, 611 P.2d 125 (Ariz. Ct. App. 1980), that "the force used to merely remove the property from a victim is not the same force required by statute to support a robbery charge . . . Thus, in the instant case, the mere removal of the wallet from the victim's pocket does not constitute the element of force or threat required to support a robbery conviction." In *People v. Taylor*, 541 N.E.2d 677 (Ill. 1989), the Illinois Supreme Court considered the situation involving the removal of an item attached to the victim as a robbery:

> Sufficient force to constitute robbery may be found when the article taken is "so attached to the person or clothes as to create resistance, however slight." A person may attach an item to his or her person or clothing in such a manner that a perpetrator may not take the item without the use of force sufficient to overcome the resistance created by the attachment. The force required to overcome the physical resistance created by the attachment of an item to the person or clothing of the owner is to be distinguished from "the mere physical effort" which must occur whenever any item, not attached to the person or clothing of the owner, is transferred from one person (the owner) to another person (the taker). It will be a theft, therefore, and not a robbery, when the evidence "show[s] no more force than the mere physical effort of taking the pocketbook from [the victim's] person and transferring it to [the defendant]." When an item, which is not attached to the person or clothing of another such that resistance to its taking is created, is taken by one who, without threatening the imminent use of force, uses no more force than the mere physical effort of transferring the item from the owner to himself, then such force is not sufficient, by itself, to constitute robbery; such a taking is a theft.

PROBLEM THIRTY-FIVE

At midnight, two individuals armed with guns and with bandanas over their faces walked into the Starlight Lounge. They ordered everyone to lay down on the floor and then took a metal box containing approximately $175 from behind the counter. Ross, the only employee on duty at the time of the robbery, had taken a break to go to the restroom right before these individuals entered the Lounge. Not hearing the regular crowd noise from inside the restroom, Ross looked out of the restroom door. Ross saw everyone on the floor, and two individuals running out the front door. Ross immediately called 9-1-1, notifying the police of what was happening at the lounge. Ross did not see the faces of the individuals who ran from the lounge. Two individuals were arrested and charged with armed robbery of the Lounge. The statute prohibits "the use or threatened use of a weapon of any type against a person to take and carry away that person's property." What argument(s) can defense counsel make that the defendants did not violate the statute?

§ 10.03 Burglary

State v. Crossman
790 A.2d 603 (Me. 2002)

ALEXANDER, J.

Merle Crossman appeals from a judgment of conviction * * * upon a jury verdict finding him guilty of burglary of a dwelling, Class B, 17-A M.R.S.A. § 401 (1983) and theft, Class E, 17-A M.R.S.A. § 353 (1983). [The court sentenced Crossman to an 18-month term of imprisonment with all but five months suspended, two years probation, and imposed a restitution requirement of $ 1,053 on the burglary count. On the count of theft, Crossman was sentenced to ninety days.] Crossman challenges the sufficiency of the evidence in the record to support both charges, and particularly the evidence of entry to support the burglary charge. We find no error and affirm * * * .

Based on the evidence presented at trial, taken in the light most favorable to the State, * * * the jury could rationally find the following facts: David and Nancy Carpenter reside on Goshen Road in Winterport. Two houses from the Carpenters is a vacant house on which Peoples Heritage Bank had recently foreclosed. The bank had never given anyone permission to enter the property or remove any items from it.

On the evening of July 7, 1999, David Carpenter left his home to run an errand. On his way past the vacant home, he noticed a black Nissan pickup truck in the driveway. Carpenter knew that no one was currently living in the home. About ten minutes later, on his way back, Carpenter noticed that the truck was still in the driveway and pulled in behind it to investigate. A woman he did not recognize was standing by the truck; she told Carpenter she was thinking about buying the home. A man Carpenter later recognized as Merle Crossman then came around the corner of the house. He told Carpenter he was thinking about buying the home. Nothing appeared to be out of the ordinary about the house, and Crossman's truck bed was empty at that time. Carpenter, the woman, and Crossman then left the property.

After Carpenter returned home, he and his wife walked over to the home, a distance of about 250 to 300 feet, with flashlights. On the way, they noticed a dark pickup truck pass them on Goshen Road. When they reached the home, they noticed a blanket next to the driveway with some doors partially covered beneath it. They also noticed that some of the doors on the home were missing, including the front door and some sliding glass doors. The missing doors appeared to be the doors underneath the blanket. * * *

[The Carpenters later returned to the house a third time and heard voices in low tones and rustling, and then saw the cab of the black pickup truck near the house.] The Carpenters proceeded home again and got into their own truck. When they pulled out onto Goshen Road from their own driveway, they noticed taillights at the end of the road, but recalled that no other vehicle had gone by them. They pursued the truck, passed it, and pulled across the road in front of it to block the truck from continuing. It was the same black Nissan pickup truck they had seen earlier. The tailgate of the truck was down and the truck bed contained some doors. Nothing was covering the doors.

David Carpenter recognized the driver of the black Nissan pickup truck as Crossman. When Crossman yelled for Carpenter to move, Carpenter told Crossman that he knew what Crossman had done. Crossman made a U-turn in the road and headed in the other direction. As Crossman turned, two of the three doors in Crossman's truck bed fell into the road, including the front door and one of the sliding glass doors from the home. * * *

Carpenter notified the police of what he had seen. When he and the police returned to the vacant home later that evening, the house appeared to have been ransacked. Both the front door and the sliding glass doors were missing. Other interior doors also appeared to be missing.

In a sufficiency of the evidence challenge, we view the evidence in the light most favorable to the State to determine if a rational fact-finder could find each element of the crime proven beyond a reasonable doubt * * * The fact-finder is also permitted to "draw any reasonable inference that logically flows from the testimony or proved physical facts," to "believe some parts of witness testimony to the exclusion of others," and to "selectively accept or reject testimony and to combine such testimony in any way." * * * The elements of any crime, including entry, may be proven by circumstantial evidence * * *.

The elements of burglary are: (1) entering or surreptitiously remaining in a structure; (2) with knowledge that the actor is not licensed or privileged to do so; and (3) with the intent to commit a crime in the structure * * *. Burglary is a Class B crime if the structure entered is a dwelling place, as in this case * * *.

Crossman contends that insufficient evidence exists in the record to support the first element of burglary, entry into the home, because no witness saw him in the house and because the doors he allegedly took were exterior doors that would not require entry to remove. Entry may be proven either with direct evidence, such as an eyewitness who observes the defendant entering the structure or physical evidence proving the defendant was inside the structure, or with circumstantial evidence that indicates the defendant was inside the structure * * *.

A burglarious entry is accomplished by the intrusion into the building of any part of the body, an arm, a hand, a finger or a foot, or, in some instances, of an instrument, providing the instrument is inserted and utilized as a means of effectuating or attempting to effectuate the theft and not solely as a means of accomplishing the breaking into the building * * * . Prior cases have found a "breaking and entering" where the defendant merely moved "to a material degree something that barred the way, i.e., either a closed door or a closed window."* * *

Carpenter testified that he saw Crossman in possession of doors that Carpenter recognized as recently removed from the vacant home. In addition, the jury could have made the logical inference that the hinges of a residential door are located on the inside of a dwelling rather than the outside. Crossman's own testimony indicated that he was experienced in removing doors and that removing a door would require him to "work from both sides of the door." This evidence supports the reasonable inferences that, in his efforts to remove the doors, (1) some part of Crossman's body intruded into the home; (2) Crossman may have inserted an instrument such as a screwdriver, into the home to complete the theft of the doors; and (3) Crossman moved the doors to a material degree in order to remove them. Any one of these three reasonable inferences is sufficient to support the jury's finding that Crossman entered the vacant home. Therefore, although the State presented no direct evidence that Crossman entered the home, a reasonable inference that he entered the home is supported by the evidence * * *

NOTES

1. ***Common Law Burglary.*** Common law burglary is the (1) breaking and entering of (2) a dwelling of another (3) in the nighttime with (4) intent to commit a felony therein. It is also necessary that the state prove that the accused had the intent to break and enter in addition to the intent to commit a felony therein. It is for this reason that common law burglary is considered a specific intent crime. Most jurisdictions have removed the requirement of the act occurring at nighttime. Other crimes that jurisdictions might use when all the elements are not present are "breaking and entering" or "trespass." Some states have adopted home invasion statutes that call for increased punishment for entries into a home if it is occupied at the time or if the defendant is armed at the time of entry. In addition, many statutes have added other types of structures, such as office buildings, garages, boats, planes, and automobiles to the list of locations that can be the subject of a burglary. Expanding the law to cover a wider range of locations raises questions about burglary's historical roots as a means of protecting the sanctity of property and the privacy interests of the dweller rather than as a type of theft offense. While a burglar is often portrayed as someone breaking into a home to steal something inside, the offense covers the intent to commit any felony, including murder, rape, and aggravated assault.

2. ***Specific Intent.*** Burglary requires the specific intent to commit a crime upon entry, and that intent must be formed *before* the burglary. As described by the

Louisiana Supreme Court in *State v. Anderson*, 343 So.2d 135 (La. 1977):

> [P]roof that an accused actually committed a felony or theft is not necessary to a conviction for simple burglary; however, at the moment of his unauthorized entry, the actor must intend to commit a felony or theft therein. We have previously held, and continue to subscribe to the view, that the intent required . . . is specific criminal intent. The actor must specifically intend to accomplish certain prescribed criminal consequences — i. e., he must actively desire to commit a felony or theft within the premises at the time of his unauthorized entry.

3. ***Possession of Burglar's Tools***. Most states criminalize the possession of tools that the defendant intends to use for a burglary. The Florida statute provides: "Whoever has in his or her possession any tool, machine, or implement with intent to use the same, or allow the same to be used, to commit any burglary or trespass shall be guilty of a felony of the third degree . . . ." FLA. STAT. ANN. § 810.06. The Florida Supreme Court explained that "[w]here a person is accused of possessing 'burglary' tools, the state must prove beyond every reasonable doubt not merely that the accused intended to commit a burglary or trespass while those tools were in his possession, but that the accused actually intended to use those tools to perpetrate the crime." *Thomas v. State*, 531 So.2d 708 (Fla. 1988). The possession statute essentially punishes a person for *attempting* to commit a burglary through the use of the tools. The topic of attempt is the subject of the next Chapter.

PROBLEM THIRTY-SIX

Hayden was arrested while removing the tires from the rear of an automobile. An inspection of the car showed that Hayden had also punctured the gasoline tank from underneath with a nail and had siphoned off about two gallons of gasoline. Hayden was charged with one count of burglary under the jurisdiction's statute that provides, "Burglary consists of the unauthorized entry of any vehicle, watercraft, aircraft, dwelling or other structure, movable or immovable, with the intent to commit any felony or theft therein." Hayden did not own the car, and was not authorized to remove the tires or take the gasoline. Hayden has filed a motion to dismiss the charge on the ground that the conduct did not violate the burglary statute. What arguments will the defense make in support of the motion, and how will the prosecution respond? What if the vehicle was a pickup truck and Hayden had removed a tool chest from the bed of the truck, which was not covered?

PART FIVE
INCHOATE CRIMES AND ACCESSORY LIABILITY

Chapter 11
Attempt

§ 11.01 Generally

A. Inchoate Offenses

In most instances in which a person commits a criminal offense, the criminal objective is achieved by the perpetrator of the crime. Under limited circumstances, however, the law punishes criminal conduct when the actor fails to accomplish his or her criminal goals. As previously seen, criminal liability is predicated on both a guilty mind and a voluntary act and a causal relation between the conduct and the harm inflicted. The next three offenses explore how attempt, conspiracy and solicitation differ from specific offenses in that they attach criminal liability for conduct in which the actor does not achieve the actor's criminal purpose. Therefore, the title assigned to these crimes is "inchoate" or incomplete offenses.

When studying the major "inchoate" offenses, attempt, solicitation, or conspiracy, it is important to remember that sometimes they are not considered discrete, or separate, crimes; rather, they can attach to specific criminal offenses. For example, one can have an attempted robbery, or conspiracy to distribute cocaine, or solicitation to commit murder. Other jurisdictions may have a discrete crime such as solicitation or conspiracy. For example, the federal offense of conspiracy to defraud the government, as stated in 18 U.S.C. § 371, is unattached to a specific statute. States may also have crimes called solicitation that are not associated with other criminal statutes. That said, all three inchoate offenses have distinct requirements and definitions. In some instances they may merge with the completed crime if the actor achieves his or her criminal objective. For example, if the perpetrator achieves his or her objective there is no need to be convicted of the attempt since the substantive offense has been met. In other instances, for example, one can be convicted of conspiracy to possess cocaine and possession of cocaine. These distinctions are discussed in more detail in these three chapters.

B. Attempt

If a person takes out a gun, aims it, and then shoots and kills another, a homicide charge is a likely result, probably first degree murder. What if another person aims their gun at another but the gun misfires, or it hits the victim but does not kill — is that also a crime? The intent of the two is identical, and each caused a significant social harm. Yet, because the results are different, perhaps because of bad luck or poor aim, one is guilty of murder — and may be subject to the death penalty in many states — while the other cannot be convicted of murder because there has not been an unlawful killing. Should the second shooter also be punished? The law of criminal attempts deals with defendants who do not, for one reason or another, succeed in completing their crime. A key limitation on the scope of attempt crimes is the adage that a person is not liable for his or her evil intentions or bad thoughts. A criminal violation requires an act *coupled* with the requisite intent, and merely proving a person's intention to commit a crime is (usually) insufficient for criminal liability. The Wisconsin Supreme Court described the elements required to prove an attempt to commit a crime:

> At common law two elements were required for conduct to be deemed a criminal attempt: (1) intent to commit the crime alleged attempted; (2) some acts in furtherance of that intent. While it was generally agreed that something more than mere criminal intent was necessary and that some overt act was required, a variety of approaches was used to determine what acts would satisfy the requirements. A common purpose of all the approaches was to provide a basis for determining whether the accused had "done enough" to justify an inference of a criminal intent and to give rise to attempt liability.

State v. Berry, 280 N.W.2d 204 (Wis. 1979).

By statute, every jurisdiction punishes an attempt to commit a crime, usually with a lesser punishment than for completing the crime. For example, California provides:

> If the crime attempted is punishable by imprisonment in the state prison, the person guilty of the attempt shall be punished by imprisonment in the state prison for one-half the term of imprisonment prescribed upon a conviction of the offense attempted. However, if the crime attempted is willful, deliberate, and premeditated murder, * * * the person guilty of that attempt shall be punished by imprisonment in the state prison for life with the possibility of parole.

CAL. STAT. ANN. § 664(a); *see also* LA. REV. STAT. § 14:27(3) ("In all other cases he shall be fined or imprisoned or both, in the same manner as for the offense attempted; such fine or imprisonment shall not exceed one-half of the largest fine, or one-half of the longest term of imprisonment prescribed for the offense so attempted, or both.").

The best way to think about an attempt crime is to view the defendant's conduct as occurring along a continuum, and asking whether the evidence is sufficient to establish (a) the actus reus of the offense and (b) the mens rea. Attempt is a "specific intent" crime, meaning that the prosecutor usually must prove that the defendant intended to commit the target offense. At what point along the continuum is the defendant's conduct sufficient to establish the act and intent for an attempt charge, and for a complete attempt, is the conduct enough to infer the intent to commit the target offense?

NOTE

Some jurisdictions divide criminal attempt into two types: **complete attempt**, in which the defendant does everything possible to effect the crime but does not cause the result of the particular offense, *i.e.* killing the victim; and, **incomplete attempt**, in which the defendant stops short of completing the offense, either of his own accord or because of the intervention of a third party. The law does not distinguish between completed and incomplete attempts, treating them identically as far as proving the crime and imposing punishment. The distinction may be important, however, for determining what defenses are available to the defendant. For a complete attempt, a defendant is most likely to argue that the conduct is insufficient to show his intent to commit the alleged crime. For an incomplete attempt, the defendant can argue that his conduct is insufficient to show that he had moved beyond the preparatory stage to actually attempting to commit the crime.

§ 11.02 The Act & Intent

The classic distinction is between (mere) preparation and perpetration: a defendant is not guilty of an attempt when the conduct has not gone beyond preparation. It is therefore necessary to determine at what point the defendant crosses the line beyond mere preparation. The law has developed a number of different tests and jurisdictions vary as to which test they may apply. In *Young v. State*, 493 A.2d 352 (Md. 1985), the Maryland Court of Appeals discussed some of the different tests:

> What act will suffice to show that an attempt itself has reached the stage of a completed crime has persistently troubled the courts. They have applied a number of approaches in order to determine when preparation for the commission of a crime has ceased and the actual attempt to commit it has begun. It is at the point when preparation has been completed and perpetration of the intended crime has started that a

criminal attempt has been committed and culpability for that misde-meanor attaches. A number of text writers have discussed and evaluated the different approaches employed by the courts to resolve the problem. We find the exposition of these approaches by LaFave and Scott to be the clearest, and what follows is taken largely from their comments on "The Act" at pages 431-438 of their *Handbook on Criminal Law.*

In the "Proximity Approach" the act must be sufficiently proximate to the intended crime. But how proximate? The strictest approach is that the accused must have engaged in the "last proximate act," that is, have done everything he believes necessary to bring about the intended result. Some courts follow a less rigid formula. They deem that the act is proximate when it is indispensable to the criminal scheme. Other courts believe that an act is "proximate" when it is physically proximate to the intended crime so that there is a dangerous proximity to success.[a] The emphasis is not so much upon what the accused has done as upon what remains to be done. Thus the time and place at which the intended crime is supposed to occur take on considerable importance. * * *

"The Probable Desistance Approach" contemplates an act which in the ordinary course of events would result in the commission of the intended crime except for the intervention of some extraneous factor. Under this approach the accused's conduct must pass that point where most men, holding such an intention as the accused holds, would think better of their conduct and desist.

In "The Equivocality Approach" the act which transforms the accused's conduct from preparation to perpetration constitutes a step towards the commission of the intended crime, and the doing of the act can have no other purpose than the commission of that crime. This approach is also known as the *res ipsa loquitur* test.

"The Model Penal Code Approach" looks to § 5.01 of the Model Penal Code (Proposed Official Draft 1962) to solve the problem. Under subsection (1)(c) a person is guilty of an attempt to commit a crime if, acting with the kind of culpability otherwise required for commission of the crime, he "purposely does or omits to do anything which, under the circumstances as he believes them to be, is an act or omission constitut-

---

[a] The "Dangerous Proximity Test" is credited to Justice Oliver Wendell Holmes in his dissenting opinion in *Hyde v. United States*, 225 U.S. 347 (1912). Factors to be considered are "the nearness of danger, the substantiality of harm and the apprehension felt." State v. Reid, 679 S.E.2d 194 (S.C. Ct. App. 2009) (citing JOSHUA DRESSLER, CASES AND MATERIALS ON CRIMINAL LAW 762-63 (4th ed. 2007)).

ing a *substantial step* in a course of conduct planned to culminate in his commission of the crime." (emphasis added).

Each of these approaches is not without advantages and disadvantages in theory and in application, as is readily apparent from a perusal of the comments of various text writers and of the courts. * * *

State v. Stewart
420 N.W.2d 44 (Wisc. 1988)

SHIRLEY S. ABRAHAMSON, Justice.

* * * The court of appeals reversed the conviction of defendant Walter Lee Stewart for attempted robbery * * *. The court of appeals concluded that the trier of fact could not be convinced beyond a reasonable doubt that the defendant would have committed robbery except for the intervention of another person or extraneous factor pursuant to sec. 939.32(3).

Sec. 939.32(3), the attempt statute, provides as follows:

An attempt to commit a crime requires that the actor have an intent to perform acts and attain a result which, if accomplished, would constitute such crime and that he does acts toward the commission of the crime which demonstrate unequivocally, under all the circumstances, that he formed that intent and would commit the crime except for the intervention of another person or some other extraneous factor.

We interpret sec. 939.32(3) as follows: to prove attempt, the state must prove an intent to commit a specific crime accompanied by sufficient acts to demonstrate unequivocally that it was improbable the accused would desist of his or her own free will. The intervention of another person or some other extraneous factor that prevents the accused from completing the crime is not an element of the crime of attempt. If the individual, acting with the requisite intent, commits sufficient acts to constitute an attempt, voluntary abandonment of the crime after that point is not a defense.

* * * The only evidence at trial was the testimony of the complainant, Scott Kodanko. The complainant testified that he was waiting for a bus at about 4:30 P.M. on a Saturday, after leaving work. He was alone in a three-sided plexiglass bus shelter open to the street in downtown Milwaukee. Two men, Mr. Moore and the defendant, entered the bus shelter while a third man, Mr. Levy, remained outside.

Moore and the defendant stood one to two feet from the complainant. The complainant was in a corner of the shelter, his exit to the street blocked by the two men. Moore asked the complainant if he wanted to buy some cigarettes. The complainant responded that he did not. Moore then said, "Give us some change." When the complainant refused, the defendant said "Give us some change, man." The defendant repeated this demand in an increasingly loud voice three to four times. The complainant still refused to give the two men change. The defendant then reached into his coat with his right hand at about the waist level, whereupon Moore stated something to the effect of "put that gun away." At that point Levy, who had been waiting outside the bus shelter, entered and said to the defendant and Moore "Come on, let's go." Levy showed the complainant some money, stating, "I don't want your money, I got lots of money."

The three men left the bus shelter together and entered a restaurant across the street. A few minutes later Moore returned and made "small talk" with the complainant. The three men were arrested a short while later. It appears from the record that the complainant did not report the incident to the police. The record does not reveal who called the police.

The complainant testified that he felt threatened throughout the encounter, which lasted less than three minutes. None of the men ever touched him or raised a hand to him, and at no time did he attempt to leave the shelter.

In a bench trial, the circuit judge found the defendant guilty of attempted robbery. * * *

The defendant claims that the state failed to prove beyond a reasonable doubt that he intended to commit the crime of robbery * * * .

In *Hamiel v. State*, 285 N.W.2d 639 (Wisc. 1979), this court interpreted sec. 939.32(3) as establishing two elements for the crime of attempt: (1) an intent to commit the crime charged; and (2) sufficient acts in furtherance of the criminal intent to demonstrate unequivocally that it was improbable the accused would desist from the crime of his or her own free will. The *Hamiel* court stated the two elements of attempted robbery as follows:

> In order for the defendant to be found guilty of attempted robbery * * * it must only be shown that: (1) the defendant's actions in furtherance of the crime clearly demonstrate, under the circumstances that he had the requisite intent to commit the crime of attempted robbery; and (2) that having formed such intent the defendant had taken sufficient steps in furtherance of the crime so that it was improbable that he would have voluntarily terminated his participation in the commission of the crime.

The defendant argues that viewing the evidence in the light most favorable to the prosecution, this court must conclude that a rational trier of fact could not be convinced beyond a reasonable doubt that he intended to commit robbery. According to the defendant, all of his conduct, including his leaving the bus shelter when he did, demonstrates that he was panhandling, not attempting robbery.

Intent may be inferred from the defendant's conduct, including his words and gestures taken in the context of the circumstances. As we said in *Hamiel*, "[I]n the crime of attempt, it is primarily the acts of the accused which provide evidence of the requisite mental intent . . . The acts must . . . establish that the accused intended to commit the substantive crime."

The acts of the accused, however, "must not be so few or of such an equivocal nature as to render doubtful the existence of the requisite criminal intent." *State v. Berry*, 280 N.W.2d 204 (Wisc. 1979). When a person desists from acts that appear criminal, the intent of the actor may appear equivocal. Desistance thus raises a factual question relevant to the element of intent. As this court said in *Berry*, "Failure, if and by whatever means the actor's efforts are frustrated, is relevant and significant only insofar as it may negate any inference that the actor did in fact possess the necessary criminal intent to commit the crime in question."

With these principles in mind we examine the record to determine whether the evidence is sufficient for the trier of fact to conclude that the defendant had the requisite intent.

We conclude that the circuit judge as trier of fact could reasonably find that the defendant's repeated statement, "Give us some change," was not merely a request but a demand. Given the setting in which the statement was made, the trier of fact could reasonably find that the demand was backed by threat of force. The circuit judge could find that the defendant's reaching into his coat as Moore said, "Hey, man, put that gun away," demonstrated that the defendant intended to frighten the complainant into handing over his change. The trier of fact could reasonably believe that the defendant exploited the circumstances in order to coerce the complainant into complying with his demand for money. * * *

Model Penal Code

5.01. Criminal Attempt.

(1) Definition of Attempt. A person is guilty of an attempt to commit a crime if, acting with the kind of culpability otherwise required for commission of the crime, he:

(a) purposely engages in conduct that would constitute the crime if the attendant circumstances were as he believes them to be; or

(b) when causing a particular result is an element of the crime, does or omits to do anything with the purpose of causing or with the belief that it will cause such result without further conduct on his part; or

(c) purposely does or omits to do anything that, under the circumstances as he believes them to be, is an act or omission constituting a substantial step in a course of conduct planned to culminate in his commission of the crime.

(2) Conduct That May Be Held Substantial Step Under Subsection (1)(c). Conduct shall not be held to constitute a substantial step under Subsection (1)(c) of this Section unless it is strongly corroborative of the actor's criminal purpose. Without negativing the sufficiency of other conduct, the following, if strongly corroborative of the actor's criminal purpose, shall not be held insufficient as a matter of law:

(a) lying in wait, searching for or following the contemplated victim of the crime;

(b) enticing or seeking to entice the contemplated victim of the crime to go to the place contemplated for its commission;

(c) reconnoitering the place contemplated for the commission of the crime;

(d) unlawful entry of a structure, vehicle or enclosure in which it is contemplated that the crime will be committed;

(e) possession of materials to be employed in the commission of the crime, that are specially designed for such unlawful use or that can serve no lawful purpose of the actor under the circumstances;

(f) possession, collection or fabrication of materials to be employed in the commission of the crime, at or near the place contemplated for its commission, if such possession, collection or fabrication serves no lawful purpose of the actor under the circumstances;

(g) soliciting an innocent agent to engage in conduct constituting an element of the crime.

(3) Conduct Designed to Aid Another in Commission of a Crime. A person who engages in conduct designed to aid another to commit a crime that would establish his complicity under Section 2.06 if the crime were committed by such other person, is guilty of an attempt to commit the crime, although the crime is not committed or attempted by such other person.

Evans v. State
453 S.E.2d 100 (Ga. Ct. App.1995)

JOHNSON, Judge.

Derek Evans and Christopher Tinch appeal from their convictions, rendered by a judge sitting without a jury, of criminal attempt to enter an automobile.

Evans and Tinch claim there was insufficient evidence that they took a substantial step toward entering an automobile. "A person commits the offense of criminal attempt when, with intent to commit a specific crime, he performs any act which constitutes a substantial step toward the commission of that crime." OCGA s 16-4-1. In determining whether there was sufficient proof of a substantial step, we must review the evidence in the light most favorable to the verdict. * * * Viewed in this light, the evidence shows Evans, Tinch and Jermaine Corbitt discussed stealing stereo equipment from automobiles; they were in possession of screwdrivers, pliers and various car keys; Tinch drove the trio in his car to a mall parking lot to find a car to break into; they slowly drove through the parking lots of the mall and two other nearby shopping centers for approximately 45 minutes, but left without entering an automobile because they were being followed by a pickup truck, which they later learned was occupied by undercover police officers.

Contrary to the claim of Evans and Tinch, this evidence was sufficient to support the court's finding that they took a substantial step toward entering an automobile with the intent to commit a theft. * * * "In order to constitute the offense of attempt to commit a crime, the accused must do some act towards its commission. Commission means the act of committing, doing, or performing; the act of perpetrating. Mere acts of preparation, not proximately leading to the consummation of the intended crime, will not suffice to establish an attempt to commit it. To constitute an attempt there must be an act done in pursuance of the intent, and more or less directly tending to the commission of the crime. In general, the act must be inexplicable as a lawful act, and must be more than mere preparation. Yet it cannot accurately be said that no preparations can amount to an attempt. It is a question of degree, and depends upon the circumstances of each case. The substantial step language of OCGA s 16-4-1 shifts the emphasis from what remains to be done to what the actor has already done. The fact that further steps must be taken before the crime can be completed does not preclude such a finding that the steps already undertaken are substantial. In addition to assuring firmness of criminal purpose, the requirement of a substantial step will remove very remote preparatory acts from the ambit of attempt liability and the relatively stringent sanctions imposed for attempts. * * *

Evans' and Tinch's discussion regarding the theft of a car stereo and their possession of tools to aid in the commission of such a theft, without more, would not have amounted to an attempt to enter an automobile, but merely would have been preparatory acts not proximately leading to the consummation of the crime of entering an automobile. Evans and Tinch, however, went beyond these remote acts of preparation when they drove to the shopping center parking lots in search of a specific car to enter. Taken as a whole, the acts of Evans and Tinch were done in pursuit of their intent to enter an automobile for the purpose of stealing stereo equipment and those acts directly tended to the commission of that crime. * * *

The trial court therefore did not err in finding Evans and Tinch guilty beyond a reasonable doubt of criminal attempt to enter an automobile. * * * Judgments affirmed.

NOTES AND QUESTIONS

1. *Tests Beyond Mere Preparation.* Looking at the tests that have been used to determine whether the accused acted beyond mere preparation, which test is most favorable to the accused and which for obtaining a conviction against the accused? While the issue is usually left to the jury, there are a number of judicial decisions holding that the defendant's conduct, as a matter of law, was insufficient to prove an attempt. Consider the following factual recitation by the Florida Court of Appeals in *Robinson v. State*, 263 So.2d 595 (Fla. Ct. App. 1972), about a defendant convicted of attempted grand larceny:

> Charles S. Olesky, received a telephone call from an unknown person asking whether he wanted to purchase a stolen television set for four hundred dollars. Following the telephone call Olesky contacted the police who later kept the rendezvous established between Olesky and the caller. A police officer contacted the defendant at the meeting place and while the two men sat in an automobile the officer told defendant he had the money for the television set when in fact he only had five dollars in an

envelope. Defendant stated the television set was nearby but he wanted the money first and when the officer refused, defendant said "No man, we don't do business that way." Defendant then attempted to leave the vehicle but the officer placed him under arrest.

Is this a sufficient factual basis to uphold Robinson's conviction? The court described the applicable test this way: "The overt act must reach far enough towards the accomplishment of the desired result to amount to a commencement of the consummation. There must be some appreciable fragment of the crime committed and it must be in such progress that it would be consummated unless interrupted by circumstances independent of the will of the attempter." Based on that language, what is the likely result?

2. *Assault and Attempt*. Many jurisdictions do not define an offense of assault with intent to murder; instead, an assault with this specific intent is simply treated as "attempted murder." Some jurisdictions hold that the offense of "attempted assault" does not exist because the crime punishes an attempt to commit a battery. So how can one attempt to commit an attempt? These jurisdictions treat the offense as a simple assault, and require the government to prove that the defendant has the "present ability" to commit the assault. Present ability is similar to the perpetration requirement for an attempt crime, in that a person who does not have the present ability to cause a battery will not have reached a point where liability can be assessed for an assault.

3. *Threats*. A number of states make it a crime to make a written or verbal communication to another person that contains a threat of death or serious bodily harm, a crime similar to assault. For example, a California statute provides:

> Any person who willfully threatens to commit a crime which will result in death or great bodily injury to another person, with the specific intent that the statement, made verbally, in writing, or by means of an electronic communication device, is to be taken as a threat, even if there is no intent of actually carrying it out, which, on its face and under the circumstances in which it is made, is so unequivocal, unconditional, immediate, and specific as to convey to the person threatened, a gravity of purpose and an immediate prospect of execution of the threat, and thereby causes that person reasonably to be in sustained fear for his or her own safety or for his or her immediate family's safety, shall be punished by imprisonment in the county jail not to exceed one year, or by imprisonment in the state prison.

CAL. PENAL CODE § 422(a). Is there a crime of attempted threat? The California Supreme Court answered that question in the affirmative in *People v. Toledo*, 26 Cal.4th 221 (Cal. 2001), in which a husband during a domestic dispute told his wife would die that evening, and later made a striking motion that brought scissors very close to her neck. The court noted that "in statements made to an investigating officer, [the wife] declared that she 'was afraid that' defendant 'was going to kill her.' By contrast, when she testified at trial, [the wife] denied that she had entertained any fear of defendant on the evening in question." The jury found the defendant guilty of assault with intent to kill, not guilty of making a threat but guilty of attempted threat. In rejecting the challenge to the attempted threat conviction, the California Supreme Court held:

> [A] defendant properly may be found guilty of attempted criminal threat whenever, acting with the specific intent to commit the offense of criminal threat, the defendant performs an act that goes beyond mere preparation and indicates that he or she is putting a plan into action. Furthermore, in view of the elements of the offense of criminal threat, a defendant acts with the specific intent to commit the offense of criminal threat only if he or she specifically intends to threaten to commit a crime resulting in death or great bodily injury with the further intent that the threat be taken as a threat, under circumstances sufficient to convey to the person threatened a gravity of purpose and an immediate prospect of execution so as to reasonably cause the person to be in sustained fear for his or her own safety or for his or her family's safety.

A variety of potential circumstances fall within the reach of the offense of attempted criminal threat. For example, if a defendant takes all steps necessary to perpetrate the completed crime of criminal threat by means of a written threat, but the crime is not completed only because the written threat is intercepted before delivery to the threatened person, the defendant properly may be found guilty of attempted criminal threat. Similarly, if a defendant, with the requisite intent, orally makes a sufficient threat directly to the threatened person, but for some reason the threatened person does not understand the threat, an attempted criminal threat also would occur. Further, if a defendant, again acting with the requisite intent, makes a sufficient threat that is received and understood by the threatened person, but, for whatever reason, the threat does not actually cause the threatened person to be in sustained fear for his or her safety even though, under the circumstances, that person reasonably could have been placed in such fear, the defendant properly may be found to have committed the offense of attempted criminal threat. In each of these situations, only a fortuity, not intended by the defendant, has prevented the defendant from perpetrating the completed offense of criminal threat itself.

PROBLEM THIRTY-SEVEN

Jaidyn and Armani had been married for two years when Jaidyn moved out of the house, filed for divorce, and obtained a Personal Protection Order that prohibited Armani from coming to the apartment or the hospital where Jaidyn worked. Shortly after filing for divorce, Armani met with his neighbor Cameron and said, "My house is going to be foreclosed, so I plan to kill Jaidyn and then myself." This was at about 3:30 p.m., and Armani appeared drunk walking back to this home. At 8:30 p.m., Armani went to Cameron's house across the street and said "Tonight's the night." As they walked back to the house, Armani again told Cameron, "I am going to kill Jaidyn and myself" Once back in Armani's house, each of them drank a beer and Armani dozed off in a chair. Thinking that Armani was asleep for the evening, Cameron walked back home, but then Cameron observed Armani driving away. Cameron called the police to warn them about what Armani had said, and in turn the police contacted Jaidyn — who was working an evening shift at the hospital — and told Jaidyn to remain inside while they searched for Armani. In a parking lot near the hospital, officers spotted Armani's vehicle parked with the engine off; Armani was inside asleep. An officer opened the driver's door, woke up Armani, and told Armani to exit the vehicle. Once outside the vehicle, the officers noticed that Armani was intoxicated and they took Armani into custody. They then searched the interior of the car and found an ice pick, a box cutter, a pair of binoculars, and an open beer can. Armani was charged with attempted murder. The jurisdiction has adopted MPC § 5.01(1) defining criminal attempt. Armani files a motion to dismiss the charge for insufficient evidence that this conduct constituted an attempt to murder Jaidyn. What argument(s) will the defense make in support of the motion, and how will the prosecution respond?

§ 11.03 Mens Rea

An attempt charge requires the government to prove that the defendant acted with the specific intent to commit the target offense. Since general intent typically will not suffice, many jurisdictions hold that attempt cannot be used when the object crime is defined merely by recklessness or negligence. Some courts, however, make reference to "knowledge" as sufficient, and some jurisdictions adopt an approach tying attempt to the mens rea of the object crime, at least for some elements, requiring that the actor exhibit the degree of culpability for attempt that is required for the object offense. For a specific intent crime, the government will have to show both the intent for the offense and the intent to commit the offense. If the crime only requires proof of negligence or recklessness, can a person be guilty of attempting such a crime, e.g. attempted involuntary manslaughter? The general rule is that such a charge is impossible, as explained by the Hawaii Supreme Court in *State v. Holbron*, 904 P.2d 912 (Haw. 1995):

(1) by its very nature, a criminal attempt presupposes a desired or "intended consequence"; (2) recklessness and "desire or intention" are mutually exclusive; (3) when the elements of a criminal offense are so defined that the "consequence" of the actor's conduct is produced

recklessly, "it is impossible to conceive of an attempt"; (4) it is the essence of involuntary manslaughter "that the consequence be produced . . . recklessly"; (5) therefore, "there can be no attempt to commit involuntary manslaughter"; but, (6) "when the consequence involved in the complete crime is intended," there can be attempted voluntary manslaughter precipitated through "provocation."

Similarly, the Colorado Court of Appeals noted that, "[a]n attempt to commit criminally negligent homicide thus requires proof that the defendant intended to perpetrate an unintentional killing a logical impossibility. The words 'attempt' and 'negligence' are at war with one another; they are internally inconsistent and cannot sensibly coexist." *Colo. Court of Appeals v. Hernandez*, 614 P.2d 900 (Colo. App. 1980).

Proof of intent can be based on circumstantial evidence. [See Chap. 6]. For an attempt crime, it will often be difficult to determine what the defendant intended when the attempt is incomplete. When the defendant completes one crime, that evidence may not be sufficient to establish the intent to commit a more serious crime, as discussed in the following case.

Baldwin v. Commonwealth
645 S.E.2d 433 (Va. 2007)

G. STEVEN AGEE, Justice.

Demetrius D. Baldwin appeals from the judgment of the Court of Appeals of Virginia, which affirmed his conviction in the Circuit Court of Chesterfield County for attempted murder * * *. The sole issue in this appeal is whether the evidence was sufficient to prove the necessary intent to kill to support a conviction for attempted murder. For the reasons set forth below, we will reverse the judgment of the Court of Appeals.

* * * The evidence adduced at trial showed that on the June 16, 2004, Mark D. Bowen, a Chesterfield County police officer, observed Baldwin traveling approximately 25 miles per hour over the posted speed limit in a residential area. Bowen followed Baldwin in his police cruiser and both vehicles turned onto Route 10 before Bowen activated his emergency equipment. Baldwin brought his car to a stop on the paved right-hand turn lane of the road with a clear path in the turn lane in front of his vehicle. Bowen parked "about a vehicle and a half length" behind Baldwin, and then approached Baldwin's vehicle on foot. Bowen stopped by the "driver's side rear passenger window" and "the driver's door" of Baldwin's vehicle, keeping his "hand down on the vehicle in case [Baldwin] tried to pop the vehicle or open his door."

Bowen observed Baldwin speaking on a cellular telephone, so he tapped on Baldwin's window. Rather than acknowledging Bowen, Baldwin "put both hands on the steering wheel and turned his vehicle towards [Bowen], and then proceeded over two lanes of traffic and sped off." In order to prevent the back wheels of Baldwin's vehicle from running over his feet as the car accelerated, Bowen perceived he "had to push off the back of the car." Joined by several other police officers, Bowen then pursued Baldwin and was able to stop and arrest him approximately seven miles from the location of the initial stop.

At trial * * *, Baldwin testified he fled from the initial stop after "panick[ing]" because of an outstanding warrant for his arrest for violating the terms of his probation for a DUI conviction. Baldwin testified he last saw Bowen "[a]t the rim of [Baldwin's] car" and that he did not hear Bowen tap on the window. Baldwin also denied intending to strike Bowen with his vehicle.

After a bench trial, the circuit court convicted Baldwin of attempted murder * * * and eluding police * * *. The circuit court sentenced Baldwin to 15 years incarceration on the attempted murder conviction, with 11 years suspended. [Baldwin did not appeal his conviction for eluding police.] * * *

[Baldwin argues] that because the evidence does not show he had the specific intent to kill Bowen, he cannot be guilty of attempted murder. Baldwin contends Bowen's testimony supports the reasonable hypothesis that Baldwin merely panicked and was fleeing the scene rather than taking any action directed toward Bowen. In particular, Baldwin draws attention to Bowen's testimony that he was standing beside Baldwin's vehicle and "had to push off the back of the car so [Baldwin's vehicle's] back wheels didn't run over [his] feet." Baldwin asserts "given Officer Bowen's position beside and behind [Baldwin's] vehicle, [Baldwin] could not have even intended to run over Bowen for being in his way."

Baldwin distinguishes other vehicle-pedestrian cases in which defendants have been convicted for attempted murder based on the evidence in those cases that "the defendant[s] deliberately pointed [their] vehicle[s] toward a potential victim." Baldwin analogizes the facts in the case at bar to those in *Haywood v. Commonwealth*, 458 S.E.2d 606 (Va. Ct. App. 1995), where the Court of Appeals reversed Haywood's conviction "because the Commonwealth presented no direct evidence that Haywood in running the road blocks intended to murder the police officers and because its circumstantial evidence did not exclude a reasonable hypothesis of innocence."

The Commonwealth responds the evidence supports the factfinder's conclusion as to Baldwin's intent, which must be given deference on appeal. It contends the evidence supports the reasonable inference that "Baldwin intended to kill [Bowen] to effectuate his escape." This is so, the Commonwealth avers, because "[n]othing prevented Baldwin from 'going straight' as he pulled away," yet

Baldwin "grabbed the steering wheel with both hands, turned his car toward [Bowen] and sped away." The Commonwealth concludes the circuit court was free to weigh the credibility of witnesses and ignore Baldwin's self-serving explanation in light of Bowen's testimony supporting the conviction.

* * * [W]e find the Court of Appeals erred in affirming Baldwin's conviction for attempted murder because the evidence does not support the conclusion that Baldwin had the intent to kill Bowen with his vehicle. "[W]hile a person may be guilty of murder though there was no actual intent to kill, he cannot be guilty of an attempt to commit murder unless he has a specific intent to kill." *Merritt v. Commonwealth*, 180 S.E. 395 (Va. 1935) The Commonwealth thus had the burden of proving beyond a reasonable doubt at trial that Baldwin acted with the specific intent to kill Bowen. This, it failed to do.

Bowen and Baldwin were the only two witnesses to testify at trial. By Bowen's own account, he was standing beside and slightly behind the driver's side door when Baldwin "put both hands on the steering wheel and turned his vehicle towards me, . . . proceed[ing] over two lanes of traffic and [speeding] off, at which time [he] had to push off the back of the car so [the vehicle's] back wheels didn't run over [his] feet." And on cross-examination Bowen agreed that Baldwin "didn't put the car in reverse and try to strike [Bowen] with [the] vehicle" and that Baldwin "never tried to strike [Bowen's] vehicle with his vehicle." Bowen's testimony simply does not support the circuit court's finding that Baldwin formed the intent to kill Bowen by using his vehicle as a weapon.

The case at bar is clearly distinguished from *Coles v. Commonwealth*, 621 S.E.2d 109 (Va. 2005), and cases from the Court of Appeals affirming convictions for attempted murder in somewhat similar circumstances involving a motor vehicle as a potential weapon. In *Coles*, a case with unique facts, the Court observed:

> Important [to the conclusion that Coles formed the requisite specific intent] are the relative positions of [Coles' vehicle], [the police officer's] cruiser, and [the police officer] when the vehicles were stopped and before [Coles] accelerated [his vehicle]. [The police officer and his vehicle were located at an angle to the left and front of the defendant's vehicle.] As [the officer] was confronting the defendant, [Coles] assumed a surrender position, and [the officer] believed the pursuit had ended. . . .

> [Coles'] contention [that he was merely trying to escape] is belied by the clear evidence that [Coles] drove [his vehicle], not straight ahead where there was plenty of room to make a right turn, but swerved to the left and aimed the [vehicle] directly toward the officer and the police vehicle.

Thus, in *Coles*, the defendant "aimed [his vehicle] directly toward" the police officer, who was standing in front of the defendant's vehicle. In contrast, the evidence in the case at bar shows that Baldwin turned his car into traffic in order to flee while Bowen was standing toward the rear of the vehicle and slightly behind the driver's side door. There was no evidence that Baldwin aimed his vehicle directly toward Bowen or otherwise had any intent to inflict bodily harm on Bowen, much less that he had formed the intent to murder Bowen. Indeed, Bowen's testimony indicates that even if he had not pushed away from Baldwin's vehicle, the vehicle would at most have struck his feet. When viewed in the light most favorable to the Commonwealth, this evidence does not support the conclusion that Baldwin possessed the requisite specific intent to kill Bowen necessary to support a conviction for attempted murder.

As Baldwin contends, the facts of this case are more analogous to *Haywood*, which only supported the conclusion that the defendant was attempting to escape. Similarly, the facts before us in this case are insufficient as a matter of law to prove an intent to kill. Thus, the Commonwealth failed to prove a necessary element of the crime of attempted murder. * * *

For the reasons set forth above, we will reverse the judgment of the Court of Appeals and dismiss the indictment.

NOTES

1. ***Common Law Attempt Mens Rea.*** There are generally three *mens rea* requirements, though they are not always so clearly separately stated: first, having whatever mental state the completed crime requires; second, in addition, having the purpose to bring about the acts and any results that are elements of the completed crime; and third, merely *knowing* of the existence of any attendant circumstances that the completed crime requires. Usually, it is the second of these mental states that is most important, so we have focused on it, namely, a purpose to do acts and achieve results. But all three sorts of mental states are likely required to prove common law attempt and, under some factual situations, failure to analyze all three separately can lead to inaccurate results.

For example, with attempted burglary, a defendant may not care whether he or she breaks into a particular house at night (nighttime being an attendant circumstance element of burglary) or during the day if he or she believes the family to be on vacation, making it safe for the defendant to break in. The defendant, thus, does not have the "purpose" of committing this crime at night. But only knowledge, not purpose, is required for this nighttime element because it is an attendant circumstance. Thus, if the defendant is nevertheless aware that it is indeed nighttime when trying to break into the house to steal a television, the defendant "knows" the attendant circumstance that it is nighttime (mental state 3). That is sufficient to hold the defendant liable for attempted burglary if he or she also had the purpose of breaking and entering (the acts) and was trying to do so with the goal of committing a crime therein.

2. ***Sufficient Evidence to Infer Intent?*** Courts have struggled to explain coherently what constitutes sufficient evidence of intent to attempt a crime, but the cases are decided on their facts regarding whether there is sufficient circumstantial evidence of intent. Consider the following scenario, and then review the excerpts from the decision of the state supreme court. Is there any way to tell which is the majority and which the dissent in a case charging the defendant with attempted burglary?

> Shortly after midnight on September 23, 1981, Harold Truman was awakened by a sound at the window. Truman got up to investigate, but did not see anyone. Shortly thereafter, he heard noises at the back of the apartment, armed himself with a .38 caliber pistol and went to the back door. Seeing someone through the window of the door, Truman asked, "What are you doing here?", but received no response. The screen door latch had been pulled loose. Truman warned the individual that he would shoot, and received a profane negative in response. Since it looked as though the person was coming in the door, Truman fired his weapon. He aimed low and wounded the defendant in the leg. The gunshot awakened Sallie Talbert, who shared the apartment with Truman. After the police were called, they followed a trail of blood and located the defendant in a vacant apartment in a neighboring building.

> Defendant Ricks testified that he had been drinking with friends and relatives before going to visit Sallie Talbert. After knocking loudly and calling her name, he got ready to leave and was shot. He testified about a long association and said he helped paint the apartment. Although unaware Sallie was living with anyone, Ricks said he would have stopped by to give her a "holler" anyway. Ricks denied that Truman had spoken to him through the door and that he had responded. Several defense witnesses corroborated Ricks' account of heavy drinking and intoxication that evening.

> Truman testified that Ricks did not appear intoxicated. Two police officers corroborated this and said he had no odor of alcohol on his breath. Talbert admitted she had known Ricks for about a year but denied that he had ever been in the apartment.

The opinion by Justice Watson stated:

Ricks was unarmed, carried no burglary tools, and did not steal or attempt to steal anything. No evidence was introduced that Ricks had been involved in other similar burglaries. Ricks' attempt to enter the apartment and his response to Truman's warning do not show he intended to commit a felony or theft inside. Only evidence of intent to commit specific types of crimes is sufficient to support a conviction of attempted burglary of an inhabited dwelling. The evidence introduced by the state does not exclude reasonable hypotheses that the defendant intended to commit a misdemeanor or intended a social visit as he asserted.

The opinion by Justice Lemmon stated:

> Why would defendant break the screen door latch, rather than calling out to his "friend" for authorization to enter, unless he intended to commit a crime therein? Why did defendant not respond when Truman asked what he was doing there, unless his intent at the time of breaking the latch was to enter without authorization and commit a crime? Why did defendant hide in a vacant apartment in a neighboring building, after he ran from the door upon being shot, rather than seeking medical treatment, if he did not intend to commit a crime upon entering the building? Why did defendant claim a long association with Miss Talbert and a previous visit to the apartment to help with painting unless he was trying to cover up his criminal intent at the time of the attempted entry?

> It is extremely significant in this case that the jury flatly rejected defendant's evidence, by which he attempted to show an innocent explanation for his entry on two bases, namely (1) that he intended to visit Miss Talbert, his long-time friend, and called out for entry and (2) that he was so intoxicated that he could not have intended to commit a crime. The jury's rejection of these two explanations leaves no apparent explanation for his attempted entry other than to commit a crime inside the apartment.

The answer is available by reading *State v. Ricks*, 428 So.2d 794 (La. 1983).

3. ***Attempted Second Degree Murder***. Most jurisdictions require proof of specific intent for an attempt prosecution, so it would seem logical that a person charged with attempted murder must have intended the death of the victim, and therefore the appropriate charge is attempted first degree murder. The Florida Supreme Court, however, has adopted the position that a defendant can be convicted of attempted second-degree murder. Does this make sense? Consider the court's analysis in *State v. Brady*, 745 So.2d 954 (Fla. 1999), in which the defendant (Brady) was charged with two counts of attempted first-degree murder but the jury convicted him of attempted second degree murder for firing a gun at the intended victim in a night club but only hitting a bystander (Harrell) in the hand. The court stated:

The offense of attempted second-degree murder does not require proof of the specific intent to commit the underlying act (i.e., murder). *See Gentry v. State*, 437 So.2d 1097 (Fla. 1983). In *Gentry*, we held that the crime of attempted second-degree murder does not require proof of the specific intent to kill. Although the crime of attempt generally requires proof of a specific intent to commit the crime plus an overt act in furtherance of that intent, we reasoned: "If the state is not required to show specific intent to successfully prosecute the completed crime, it will not be required to show specific intent to successfully prosecute an attempt to commit that crime." To establish attempted second-degree murder of Harrell, the state had to show (1) that Brady intentionally committed an act which would have resulted in the death of Harrell except that someone prevented him from killing Harrell or he failed to do so, and (2) that the act was imminently dangerous to another and demonstrated a depraved mind without regard for human life. . .

. . . because Harrell was in close proximity we also believe a jury could reasonably conclude, under the evidence, that the "act imminently dangerous to others" requirement of the second-degree murder statute would also be met by the proof submitted.

Other states require proof of a specific intent to kill for the defendant to be convicted of attempted murder. In *Richeson v. State*, 704 N.E.2d 1008 (Ind. 1998), the Indiana Supreme Court explained:

[W]e think that the distance between perpetrator and victim in many attempted murder cases poses special problems of "intent ambiguity." In other attempt prosecutions, the probable or intended victim and result are often clearly indicated by the facts and circumstances surrounding the commission of the crime.

In many attempted murder cases, however, the victim, the result, or both, are more difficult to ascertain. A drive-by shooting is the paradigm problematic attempted murder case. In such cases it is often unclear whether the defendant intended to murder or to batter, whether he knew of a high probability of death or a touching, or whether he simply recklessly disregarded either. Such ambiguity carries with it the risk that the jury will fail to distinguish between levels of culpability, imposing a penalty for reckless actions, rather than for intentional or knowing ones. In order to ensure that juries sort out the higher level of culpability in attempted murder prosecutions, we construed the attempt statute * * * to require proof that the defendant intended death.

———————————

PROBLEM THIRTY-EIGHT

One evening, paramedics were called to treat Jo for chest pains. Upon entering Jo's trailer, they discovered conditions inside to be almost indescribably filthy. Garbage and refuse were scattered throughout the home, and pungent odors of urine, old fried food, and human feces permeated every corner. The paramedics further observed a baby lying in a pile of trash and dirty clothes with only the top of its head visible, and they saw two children asleep on a couch under a roach-infested blanket. Local police authorities were then summoned and they observed a pool of vomit in front of the door, filthy dishes in the kitchen, and moldy and rotten food littered throughout the trailer. The officers also found feces on the floor next to the commode in the bathroom, which was likewise exceptionally filthy. The officers contacted the Department of Children's Services, who removed the three children that night and took them to their grandmother's house. Despite living in these abhorrent conditions, however, the children appeared by all accounts to be in good health, and they did not exhibit any signs of illness or other affliction, except that one child was suffering from a cold. The parents are charged with three counts of attempted child neglect. The statute provides: "Any person who knowingly, other than by accidental means, treats a child under eighteen (18) years of age in such a manner as to inflict injury or neglects such a child so as to adversely affect the child's health and welfare commits a Class A misdemeanor; provided, however, that if the abused or neglected child is six (6) years of age or less, the penalty is a Class D felony." What argument will defense counsel make that the government cannot prove the requisite specific intent for the crime, and how will the government respond? Assume that the jurisdiction has adopted the Model Penal Code attempt statute (§ 5.01).

§ 11.04 Impossibility

1. **Definition.** In some cases the defendant's act could never result in the completion of a crime. Thus, the question becomes whether this "impossibility" serves as a defense to the crime. There are several different approaches, but they often seem indistinguishable.

   a. **Factual Impossibility.** The defendant is mistaken about the facts, but if the defendant had been correct the crime could be accomplished. The classic example used to demonstrate factual impossibility is the case of the person who attempts to steal from an empty pocket. The pickpocket is held criminally liable despite the fact that the pocket is found empty. What if, however, the defendant shoots bullets into the head of a dummy, thinking it human? The defendant could be guilty of murder if the dummy were in fact a human. The defendant is held accountable for the attempted crime because this "factual" impossibility does not negate the defendant's intent to commit the crime.

b. ***Legal Impossibility****:* In a case like the "attempted murder" of a dummy, the defense may argue that the impossibility is not factual, but rather it is legal impossibility. As a matter of law it is impossible that shooting a dummy would be the crime of murder. Some courts allow legal impossibility. Classic examples of legal impossibility are cases where "a person accepting goods which he believed to have been stolen, but which were not then 'stolen' goods was not guilty of an attempt to receive stolen goods." *People v. Jaffe*, 78 N.E. 169 (N.Y. 1906). Some would argue that legal impossibility is not really legal impossibility but, rather, a species of factual impossibility (or as some awkwardly put it — factual/legal impossibility).

c. ***"True" Legal Impossibility.*** If the person's objective had been accomplished but there would be no criminal violation, the person cannot be held criminally liable for an attempt. This is called "true" legal impossibility, in the sense that there cannot be a successful criminal prosecution nor can punishment be imposed.

2. ***Modern Approach****.* Although the common law permitted legal impossibility, but not factual impossibility, today most jurisdictions do not recognize either factual or legal impossibility. If it is a "true" legal impossibility there may be no crime for which the accused could be prosecuted and thus, there can be no prosecution. In this regard, one can say that "true" legal impossibility precludes a conviction.

One of the reasons for the widespread rejection of the factual/legal impossibility distinction is its lack of logic. Most situations can logically be construed as either factual or legal impossibility. For example, assume that Jaci wants to kill Bobbi. Jaci shoots at a blob in a bed that Jaci believes to be the sleeping Bobbi. But the blob is just sheets and pillows bunched up to look like a person. This situation could be called one of factual impossibility because had the situation been as Jaci believed it to be – that is, had Bobbi been in the bed – Jaci would have killed Bobbi, thus committing murder. But the situation also could be viewed as legal impossibility, it not being a crime (or at least not homicide) to shoot at sheets and pillows. Lawyers in jurisdictions adhering to the distinction had no choice given the unusual facts of many cases but to analogize to precedent declaring an allegedly similar situation (let us say, shooting at a dummy) to be either factual or instead legal impossibility. In such cases, and where no viable analogy was available, lawyers also had to make contestable policy arguments, for example, about whether Jaci is so dangerous (because she did try to kill a person) that no defense should be available, therefore classifying the situation as factual impossibility, or is of so little danger (being unable to distinguish sheets from persons) as to merit a defense, thus making the situation legally impossible. Lawyers in jurisdictions retaining this confusing distinction must still follow these options. The modern jurisdictions avoid the problem entirely by simply eliminating the distinction entirely.

3. ***Impossibility and Omissions***. In *People v. Likine*, 823 N.W.2d 50 (Mich. 2012), the Michigan Supreme Court held that a defendant can offer an impossibility defense when the actus reus of the crime is an omission. The defendant was charged with failing to pay court-ordered child and spousal support, and an amendment to the statute removed any intent element, rendering it a strict liability offense. Regarding the defendant's claim that he did not have the money to pay the support, the court noted that "[a]t common law, an established defense to a crime of omission is impossibility." If allowing the defense to this crime, it concluded that "a defendant cannot be held criminally liable for failing to perform an act that was impossible for the defendant to perform. When it is genuinely *impossible* for a defendant to discharge a duty imposed by law, the defendant's failure is excused." The proof of impossibility requires that "a defendant must show that he or she acted in good faith and made all reasonable efforts to comply with the family court order, but could not do so through no fault of his or her own." Would this defense be factual or legal impossibility?

Chen v. State
42 S.W.3d 926 (Tex. Crim. App. 2001)

HOLLAND, J., delivered the opinion of the unanimous Court.

Appellant was convicted in a bench trial of attempted sexual performance by a child, and he was sentenced to seven years confinement and a fine of $1000. Imposition of the seven years confinement was suspended, and appellant was placed on seven years community supervision. * * * We granted appellant's petition for discretionary review to determine "[w]hether a 47 year old male undercover officer posing as a 13 year old female for the purposes of internet communications established evidence that was sufficient, as a matter of law, to support a conviction for the offense of attempted sexual performance by a child." * * *

The evidence presented at appellant's bench trial showed that on December 13, 1996, appellant placed an advertisement on an America Online computer bulletin board stating, "A nude dancer needed for discreet pleasure. I am generous and rich. You must be very attractive and young." Detective Steve Nelson, a Dallas Police Officer working on a specialized crime task involving child exploitation, discovered the advertisement. On December 16, [1996], he e-mailed appellant back representing himself as J. Cirello and asking appellant "how young of a nude dancer [he was] looking for." Appellant replied, "I will say between 20 and 30 or as long as you have a young looking face and tender body." Detective Nelson responded that there was no one in that age range and signed the email "J. Cirello."

Appellant e-mailed again and asked, "What age are you in?" Posing as J. Cirello, Detective Nelson wrote, "If you don't care about age I am 13, looking for independence. What are you looking for?" Appellant replied that he was looking for a girl who "dares to be nude and watched by me while I am masturbating." He asked to "get together" and requested her name and location. Detective Nelson e-mailed, stating "My name is Julie." He also wrote that "Julie" had never seen a man masturbate and did not want "her" parents to find out.

During the next few e-mails, appellant asked where Julie lived and when they could get together. He expressed a desire to exchange telephone numbers. He stated that they could get to know each other first and assured Julie that he would not hurt her. "Julie" asked for his description and his phone number and stated that "it might be better if [she] calls [appellant]." "Julie" wrote that "she" had never had sex before and was a little scared. Appellant responded that "sex is [a] wonderful thing." He also later wrote that "sex is not my major object." "Julie" then expressed that "she" was possibly interested in sex "if the right person came along to explain things and help [her]." For a few more weeks, Appellant and "Julie" e-mailed each other, discussing appellant's sexual history, "Julie's" nervousness, and plans to meet in person. Appellant described his van as champagne colored.

On February 6, 1997, appellant and "Julie" began their plan to meet. Appellant assured "Julie" that he would bring protection and lubrication, so that he would not hurt her or get her pregnant. After a series of e-mails, they decided to meet at a Best Western on a Tuesday afternoon (February 11, 1997). Appellant informed Julie that he had a room reserved for that day. "Julie" wrote appellant, stating that she would be outside the lobby between 3:30 and 4:00 pm and described herself as "5-foot one inch tall with long blond hair."

The Garland Police Department set up surveillance at the Best Western. Appellant arrived at the motel in a champagne colored minivan. He initially sat in the minivan for about ten minutes. Eventually, he went in the lobby, stayed for two minutes, then came back out to his vehicle. When he got back into his minivan, the police arrested him. Appellant had a package of condoms and a tube of KY Jelly on the console of his minivan. He later gave a voluntary statement in which he admitted that he was going to show a girl how to have sex.

Detective Nelson admitted on cross-examination that he was a white male and had never been known by the name of Julie Cirello. "Julie" did not exist, and he was the author of the e-mails signed by "Julie." Appellant asked the trial court to render a verdict of "not guilty" because the State failed to prove the elements contained in the indictment. Specifically, appellant argued that the State failed to prove he attempted to induce the named complainant, Julie Cirello, to commit any acts alleged in the indictment. Additionally, he asserted that the State failed to prove that Julie Cirello was a person under the age of 18 and that the proof presented at trial was a fatal variance with the allegation in the indictment. The trial court found appellant guilty beyond a reasonable doubt as charged in the indictment.

The relevant portion of Texas Penal Code section 43.25(b) states, "A person commits an offense if, knowing the character and content thereof, he employs, authorizes, or induces a child younger than 18 years of age to engage in sexual conduct or a sexual performance." TEX. PEN.CODE ANN. § 43.25(b). "A person commits an offense, if with specific intent to commit an offense, he does an act amounting to more than mere preparation that tends but fails to effect the commission of the offense intended." TEX. PEN.CODE ANN. § 15.01. Therefore, the offense of attempted sexual performance by a child is committed if: 1) the defendant; 2) with specific intent to commit sexual performance by a child; 3) does an act amounting to more than mere preparation; 4) that tends but fails to effect the commission of sexual performance by a child. See *Yalch v. State*, 743 S.W.2d 231 (Tex. Crim. App. 1988).

This Court discussed the doctrine of legal impossibility and factual impossibility at length in *Lawhorn v. State*, 898 S.W.2d 886 (Tex. Crim. App. 1995). At that time, we stated that legal impossibility was a valid defense, while factual impossibility was not. * * *

"The distinction between factual and legal impossibility has been characterized as turning on whether the goal of the actor was deemed by the law to be a crime." 21 AM.JUR.2D CRIMINAL LAW § 178 (1999). Legal impossibility exists "where the act if completed would not be a crime, although what the actor intends to accomplish would be a crime." *Lawhorn*. It has also been described as "existing [when] what the actor intends to do would not constitute a crime, or at least the crime charged." On the other hand, factual impossibility exists when "due to a physical or factual condition unknown to the actor, the attempted crime could not be completed." In other words, factual impossibility "refers to a situation in which the actor's objective was forbidden by the criminal law, although the actor was prevented from reaching that objective due to circumstances unknown to him." 21 AM.JUR.2D CRIMINAL LAW § 178 (1999).

This Court has very few cases raising the issues of factual or legal impossibility–especially in the context of attempt crimes. The concept of factual impossibility is well-illustrated in *People v. Grant*, 233 P.2d 660 (Cal. 1951). In *Grant*, the defendant placed a homemade bomb in his suitcase for a family trip to San Diego. The defendant apparently intended for his family to be on the plane when it exploded, leaving him to collect the insurance money on their lives. The bomb discharged before the plane had been filled with people, but it was extinguished before it harmed anyone. At trial, evidence was admitted that showed if the bomb had worked properly, the plane would have crashed into the ocean. In discussing the factual impossibility of the crime, the court noted that the defendant intended to cause the destruction of his family's airplane. Even though the bomb exploded early, the defendant was still guilty of attempted murder. "[W]here a defendant is charged with an attempt to commit a crime it is immaterial whether the attempted crime is impossible of completion if, as in the present case, completion was apparently possible to the defendant who was acting with the intent to commit the crime of murder."

In applying these concepts to the instant case, we initially note that if Julie Cirello had been an actual thirteen year old, then what appellant intended to accomplish (sexual performance by a child) constituted an actual crime. Appellant's goal was to commit the offense of sexual performance by a child. Because that goal is a crime by law, the doctrine of legal impossibility is not at issue in this case. Rather, this case presents a factual impossibility scenario. Due to a factual condition unknown to appellant (that Julie Cirello did not actually exist), the offense of sexual performance by a child could not be completed. It is true that, as appellant claims, the actual offense of sexual performance by a child would have been impossible for appellant to complete; the complainant, Julie Cirello, did not physically exist. But completion of the crime was apparently possible to appellant. He had specific intent to commit the offense of sexual performance by a child, and he committed an act amounting to more than mere preparation that tended but failed to effect the commission of the offense. The State presented evidence for each of the necessary elements of attempted sexual performance by a child.

In conclusion, appellant's case does not present the doctrine of legal impossibility. The evidence presented at trial, reviewed in the light most favorable to the verdict, was sufficient for the trier of fact to reasonably conclude that appellant was guilty of attempted sexual performance by a child.

PROBLEM THIRTY-NINE

Morgan was upset that Jamie, a co-worker, received a promotion that Morgan wanted. One evening, Morgan followed Jamie home from work. After Jamie went into the apartment building, Morgan went to Jamie's car and poured motor oil on its roof and tried to light a rag. It was very windy, and the matches kept blowing out before the rag could catch fire. A neighbor of Jamie's observed what Morgan was doing and called the police, who arrived a few minutes later and placed Morgan under arrest while driving out of the parking lot after not being able to light the rag. Morgan admitted to pouring the motor oil on Jamie's car but then refused to answer any further questions from the police. Morgan is charged with attempted arson in a jurisdiction that includes automobiles in its arson statute. Morgan's lawyer files a pretrial motion to dismiss the charge on the grounds of impossibility, citing two grounds: (1) Morgan was unable to light the rag due to the high winds; (2) an expert's affidavit that the motor oil could not have been ignited by Morgan to set the car on fire. Should the court grant the motion to dismiss?

§ 11.05 Abandonment and Renunciation

States are divided on whether a person's decision to abandon a criminal attempt should relieve the person of liability. The common law did not recognize an abandonment or renunciation defense because, once the defendant's conduct crosses the line from preparation to perpetration, the crime is complete and liability should attach. In *State v. Stewart, supra.*, the Wisconsin Supreme Court explained:

> The defendant finally argues that this court should interpret sec. 939.32(3) [the attempt statute] as incorporating the affirmative defense of voluntary abandonment. He urges that recognition of the defense is good public policy. Although the traditional common law view is that voluntary abandonment is not a defense, the modern trend is toward recognition of the defense. The drafters of the Model Penal Code included a provision that voluntary abandonment is an affirmative defense. Several state legislatures have adopted the defense. Following the reasoning of the Code, Professors LaFave and Scott favor the defense, concluding that recognition of the defense tends to encourage the actor to desist and escape penalty. They further assert that a true voluntary abandonment tends to negative the dangerousness of the actor. * * *

> We conclude that if the legislature had intended voluntary abandonment to be a defense, it would have expressly said so. We do not believe this court should distort the statutory language to incorporate the defense. The public policy arguments in favor of the defense are better addressed to the legislature than to the court.

Note that a common law approach may have a defendant's abandonment as evidence that there is insufficient conduct to prove an attempt. It can also be used to infer that the accused did not have the requisite intent to attempt the object offense. But it would not be considered as a separate defense to the charge of an attempted crime.

Model Penal Code § 5.01(4) takes a different approach, recognizing explicitly a defense of renunciation:

> It is an affirmative defense to a charge of criminal attempt, solicitation or conspiracy that the person, after committing the criminal attempt, solicitation or conspiracy, prevented the successful commission of the

offense attempted, solicited or conspired, under circumstances manifesting a complete and voluntary renunciation of the person's criminal
purpose.

Within the meaning of this Article, renunciation of criminal purpose is
not voluntary if it is motivated, in whole or in part, by circumstances, not
present or apparent at the inception of the actor's course of conduct, that
increase the probability of detection or apprehension or that make more
difficult the accomplishment of the criminal purpose. Renunciation is not
complete if it is motivated by a decision to postpone the criminal conduct
until a more advantageous time or to transfer the criminal effort to
another but similar objective or victim.

As explained by the Second Circuit in *United States v. Crowley*, 318 F.3d 401 (2d
Cir. 2003):

The defense is somewhat anomalous; ordinarily, once a person has
committed acts sufficient to establish criminal liability, his repentance or
desistance from further crimes cannot absolve him from guilt. The
proposed renunciation defense was closely linked to the MPC's adoption
of the "substantial step" test for triggering attempt liability. The Code
proposed expanding the definition of attempt, permitting a defendant
under some circumstances to be found guilty of attempt for taking
preliminary steps toward committing a crime, but allowing acquittal
where the defendant can persuade the fact finder that he had indeed taken
such a step, but then had a change of heart and abandoned his efforts.

The defendant bears the burden of proof by a preponderance of the evidence to
establish the voluntary renunciation of the attempted crime. It is necessary for the
defendant to show that the abandonment is both "voluntary and complete."
Consider these concepts in the following case:

Patterson v. State
729 N.E.2d 1035 (Ind. Ct. App. 2000)

KIRSCH, Judge

* * * Around 4:00 a.m. on December 6, 1997, eighty-two year old Julia
Maciejewski was awakened by the sound of breaking glass. She went to investigate,
and found a broken window in her sunroom, glass on the floor, and blood on the
curtains. She called the police.

When the police responded to the call, they discovered Patterson at the back
of Maciejewski's house. After a chase on foot, police apprehended the bleeding

Patterson, who commented that he knew he should not have broken the window. Maciejewski identified Patterson as the man who had come to her door several days earlier looking for work shoveling snow.

Patterson was charged and convicted of attempted burglary with the intent to commit theft. He was adjudged to be a habitual offender and was sentenced to fifty years imprisonment. * * *

Patterson argues that the trial court erred in refusing to give his instruction on the defense of abandonment. The manner of instructing the jury lies within the sound discretion of the trial court. Error in the instruction of the jury will not warrant reversal unless it is of such a nature that the jury is misled regarding the law on the case. When reviewing a trial court's refusal of jury instructions, this court applies a three part test: 1) whether the instruction correctly states the law; 2) whether there was evidence in the record to support the giving of the instruction; and 3) whether the substance of the tendered instruction is covered by other instructions which are given.

Where attempt is at issue, an accused will be relieved of criminal responsibility if, subsequent to taking a substantial step towards committing a crime but prior to its consummation, he voluntarily abandoned his efforts. The defense of abandonment is available only when a defendant voluntarily abandons his effort to commit the crime and voluntarily prevents its commission. To be considered voluntary, the decision to abandon must originate with the defendant, not as a result of extrinsic factors that increase the probability of detection.

The trial court did not err in refusing to give Patterson's tendered instruction on abandonment because the evidence in the record did not support such an instruction. The evidence showed eighty-two year old Maciejewski was awakened by the sound of breaking glass. She found a flashlight and went to investigate, turning on lights as she went through the house. She found a window in her sunroom had been broken. When police responded to her call, they found Patterson still lurking behind her house. The reasonable inference from this evidence is that Patterson abandoned his attempt to enter Maciejewski's house because he was about to be discovered by her. Because his abandonment of his criminal endeavor was made in response to an extrinsic factor, namely, the probability of detection, and was not a product purely of his own volition, it does not constitute a legal defense and Patterson was not entitled to an instruction on this theory. The trial court did not err in refusing to give this instruction. See *Peak v. State*, 520 N.E.2d 465 (Ind. Ct. App. 1988) (defendant failed to establish abandonment defense where evidence showed he abandoned attempt to break into house because he was unable to break down the door and because he saw a police officer).

PROBLEM FORTY

Chris is charged with attempted possession of more than 500 grams of cocaine. The evidence at trial shows that an undercover narcotics officer agreed to supply Chris with a kilogram of cocaine for $5,000 the following evening. Chris and the agent met in a parking lot behind a pool hall. The agent gave Chris a paper bag with a glassine envelope containing cocaine from the police storage. Chris opened the envelope and tasted a small amount of the powder. He then spit on the ground and said, "This stuff is crap. What are you trying to sell me, chump?" Chris then turned and walked away, shouting, "Sell that junk somewhere else, I ain't buyin' it." At that moment, two officers hiding behind the pool hall emerged and arrested Chris. At trial, defense counsel requests an abandonment instruction. What arguments will the prosecutor make that the instruction is not supported by the evidence, and how will defense counsel respond?

§ 11.06 Criminalizing Preparatory Conduct

An attempt charge requires the government to prove criminality based on what can be inferred from the evidence regarding how a course of events would have developed and what the defendant's state of mind was in pursuing the conduct. A state legislature can, if it chooses, make certain conduct a crime that is preliminary to another offense. For example, there are statutes that make it a crime to communicate a threat, even if the threat is never received or the recipient is not harmed by the conduct. The transmission of the threat may not even rise to the level of an assault or an attempted battery, but the preparatory conduct itself can be made a criminal act so that the person can be convicted before there is a substantial step toward a more serious offense. A federal statute, 18 U.S.C. § 875(c), provides, "Whoever transmits in interstate or foreign commerce any communication containing any threat to kidnap any person or any threat to injure the person of another, shall be fined under this title or imprisoned not more than five years, or both." In *United States v. Holder*, 302 F.Supp. 296 (D. Mont. 1969), the District Court described the scope of the statute:

> Defendant's offered instruction is predicated upon his contention that the threat must reach the person threatened and be of such a nature as to have induced fear in the mind of that person. I do not so read the statute, which refers to "any threat to injure the person of another." * * * Nor is it necessary to show that the threat induced fear in the person threatened. It is sufficient to show that the threat was of such a nature as reasonably to have induced fear, even though the communication was not delivered to the person threatened.

Similarly, most states prohibit the possession of burglar's tools even though the items may have a perfectly legal use. A Florida statute provides: "Whoever has in his or her possession any tool, machine, or implement with intent to use the same, or allow the same to be used, to commit any burglary or trespass shall be guilty of a felony of the third degree . . . ." FLA. STAT. ANN. § 810.06. In *Thomas v. State*, 531 So.2d 708 (Fla. 1988), the Florida Supreme Court explained the operation of the statute:

> [T]he burglary tool statute actually describes and prohibits a crime in the nature of an attempt. In effect, it criminalizes an attempt to commit a burglary or trespass, which is discerned through the possession of tools or devices coupled with the defendant's intent to use those tools in the commission of the crime.

> * * * What constitutes a burglary tool often cannot be determined from a particular tool or device's innate characteristics, but only from the context in which it is to be used. This is to say no more than that the intent must be gleaned from the totality of the circumstances in each case. Certainly, there will be instances in which a tool or device is so peculiarly adapted to the commission of a burglary or trespass as to render the state's burden of proof relatively easy to meet. On other occasions, because of common household usage of the tool or device, the state might not be able to shoulder its burden of proving beyond a reasonable doubt the intent to commit a felony.

> We do not believe any purpose is served by requiring the trial court to determine as a matter of law whether specific tools per se are "common" or not. The only real issue is whether the actions of the accused showed he or she was preparing to use the tool to commit a burglary or trespass.

Note that a person stopped short of completing the requisite breaking and entry for a burglary while using a tool to accomplish the crime may be charged with both attempted burglary and possession of burglar's tools because the possession violation is not a lesser-included offense of burglary.

In the area of domestic violence or violence involving formerly intimate parties, the legislatures have adopted statutes to prevent threatening conduct by one person against another. Stalking statutes are an example of this type of legislation that reaches much broader conduct than more traditional statutes, even those that permit a conviction for an attempt. How far can the legislature go in defining conduct as "threatening" or "harassing"?

State v. McCarthy
980 P.2d 629 (Mont. 1999)

Chief Justice J.A. TURNAGE delivered the Opinion of the Court.

* * * The relationship between Roman [McCarthy] and Karen spans a period of approximately fifteen years. The relationship, however, was a chaotic one, and in October 1995, Karen decided to terminate it. Karen moved into a women's shelter, and shortly thereafter, obtained a temporary restraining order against Roman. This restraining order was continued as a permanent order of protection in November 1995. This protective order directed that Roman not "personally contact, telephone, or otherwise communicate, follow, harass, intimidate, threaten, annoy or disturb" the peace of Karen.

In July 1996, Roman petitioned for a restraining order against Karen, and the District Court issued a reciprocal protection order that prohibited the parties from molesting or disturbing the peace of one another, and directed that neither party "follow, harass, intimidate, telephone, touch, threaten, or contact each other by a third party at work, at school, in public or at any other place." * * *

Despite the issuance of both protective orders, Roman continued to telephone and mail letters to Karen. In November 1996, Roman was charged and convicted of stalking Karen in violation of the protective orders. He was sentenced to five years in the Montana State Prison (MSP), with two years suspended.

While incarcerated at the Gallatin County Detention Center awaiting transportation to MSP on his first stalking conviction, Roman mailed a letter to the Law and Justice Center in Bozeman, Montana, addressed to both Karen and Gloria Edwards (Gloria), one of the Gallatin County Victim Witness Coordinators who worked at the center. Gloria opened and read the letter, determined that it contained more of the "same stuff," and submitted a copy of the letter to a detective at the Bozeman police department. Gloria also contacted Karen and informed her that she had received a letter for her from Roman.

A week later, while incarcerated at MSP, Roman sent another letter directly to Karen at her home address. Following the advice of her clinical therapist, Karen did not open the letter, but instead contacted the Bozeman police department to report that Roman had again attempted to contact her by mail in violation of the protective orders.

Roman was charged by information with stalking, second offense, and tried before a jury. At the close of the State's case-in-chief and again at the close of evidence, Roman moved to have the charges against him dismissed on the grounds that two instances of attempted contact by letter were legally insufficient to support a conviction for stalking. The District Court denied both motions. Roman was found guilty and sentenced to five years at MSP, two years suspended, to run consecutively with his previous sentence. * * *

[The court rejected Roman's argument that "repeatedly" means more than two attempted contacts, holding: "We disagree that two unwanted attempts at contact with the victim is legally insufficient to support a conviction for stalking."]

Was there sufficient evidence presented at trial to support McCarthy's conviction?

We review the sufficiency of the evidence to support a jury verdict in a criminal case to determine whether, after viewing the evidence in the light most favorable to the prosecution, any rational trier of fact could have found the essential elements of the crime beyond a reasonable doubt.

Roman argues that there was insufficient evidence presented at trial from which a reasonable jury could find that Roman repeatedly harassed Karen where one of the two letters upon which his conviction rests was mailed and addressed to a third party and not to Karen directly. Moreover, Roman argues, if Karen felt harassed by the fact that he attempted to contact her through Gloria, the blame should be attributed to Gloria for reporting the letter to Karen, rather than to him for sending it.

We find this argument unpersuasive. As an initial matter, we note that the letter mailed to Gloria was addressed to both Gloria and Karen. Although Gloria did not read the contents of the letter to Karen, she did communicate to her that she had received the letter and that it was similar in content to prior correspondence from Roman. We note further that the protective order which prohibited Roman from contacting Karen via third parties was still in force at the time Roman mailed the letter to Gloria.

Section 45-5-220(b), MCA, states that stalking occurs when the stalker repeatedly harasses, threatens, or intimidates the stalked person "in person, or by phone, by mail, or by other action, device or method." Communicating through a third party whom the stalker knows is likely to relay the fact of contact, and hence produce the desired effect of harassing or intimidating the victim, constitutes an "action, device or method" of stalking. "To hold otherwise would defeat the clear purpose of the stalking statute by permitting a stalker to intimidate and harass his intended victim simply by communicating his threats to third parties who (the stalker knows and expects) will inform the victim." *State v. Rooks*, 468 S.E.2d 354 (Ga. 1996) (Sears, J., concurring).

We have employed similar reasoning in the application of an analogous statute defining the offense of intimidation by threat:

We believe that it is within the language and intent of the statute that the person who receives the threat can be different from the person who is sought to be compelled by the threat. Otherwise, for example, an individual could contact the news media threatening to take the life of a hostage if the Governor does not meet his demands, and he could not be convicted under [the intimidation] statute. But it is this very situation which the statute is aimed at outlawing.

State v. Lance, 721 P.2d 1258 (Mont. 1986).

There are a host of potential scenarios in which a stalker could communicate with the friends, family, co-workers, employers, and neighbors of the victim with the full and reasonable expectation that the form and content of such contacts will be conveyed to the victim. There is as great a likelihood, and possibly even a greater one, that such contacts would generate substantial emotional distress for the victim as contacting the victim directly because of the additional stress and embarrassment caused by the involvement of these third parties in the activities of the stalker. Such a result clearly falls within the prophylactic radius of the statute, particularly where there is a protective order in place expressly prohibiting such contact.

There is substantial credible evidence in the record from which a rational trier of fact could have found beyond a reasonable doubt that Roman's purpose in, and the ultimate effect of, sending the letter to Gloria was to harass Karen, and that Roman repeatedly harassed Karen both directly and indirectly through contact with a third party familiar to Karen. We therefore will not disturb the jury's findings on this issue.

Roman also argues that there was insufficient evidence presented at trial from which a reasonable juror could find that his attempted contacts with Karen caused her substantial emotional distress or reasonable apprehension of bodily injury or death because she never actually read the contents of either letter. In the alternative, Roman argues that in the event Karen did suffer from emotional distress as a result of the letters, such distress was not substantial or reasonable under the circumstances, since Roman was already incarcerated at the time the letters were written and Karen was merely speculating as to the probable content of the letters.

The standard for determining whether a person has suffered emotional distress or reasonably apprehended bodily injury is that of a reasonable person under similar circumstances. Gloria testified that, upon learning that Roman had again attempted to contact her, "[Karen] was real upset. She was scared." Karen testified that prior to Roman's first conviction for stalking, she would receive letters from him "almost every single day." These letters contained "threats and a lot of negative stuff about my character" that made her feel "horrible." When she received the letter Roman sent to her home address she "got really terrified" and "didn't want to open it and read what was in there . . . just didn't think I could handle reading it." Karen's therapist testified that she had instructed Karen not to open Roman's letters any more because of the distress they caused her. Finally, a detective with the Bozeman police department testified that upon receiving or learning of the letters Roman had sent from prison, Karen was equally if not more upset than she had been upon receiving his letters in the past.

The jury in this case found that Roman's efforts to contact Karen caused her substantial emotional distress or reasonable apprehension of bodily injury or death. The jury also found that given the protracted and tumultuous relationship between these two individuals, Karen's distress at receiving Roman's letters was reasonable, notwithstanding the fact that she never actually read the contents of the letters or that Roman was already incarcerated on his first stalking conviction when he sent the letters. Because we find sufficient evidence in the record to support these findings, we affirm Roman's conviction. * * *

Justice TERRY N. TRIEWEILER dissenting.

I concur with the majority's conclusion that, within the context of the stalking statute, "repeatedly" means more than once. I dissent from the majority's conclusion that there was sufficient evidence for a rational trier of fact to have found that the defendant, Roman Sonny McCarthy, committed the offense of stalking beyond a reasonable doubt. * * *

In this case, the extent of the defendant's contact with Karen was her receipt of one sealed envelope which was never opened. For purposes of the record, the contents of the sealed envelope are unknown. Based on Karen's receipt of one sealed envelope, the contents of which were unknown, the defendant was convicted of a felony punishable by five years in prison and a fine of $10,000.

The defendant may be a bad person; he may have violated protective orders which were in effect at the time of his communication; and the contents of the unopened envelope may have been offensive and frightening. However, for purposes of this case, we have to assume the envelope contained nothing because there was no evidence of the envelope's content which was disclosed to the jury. * * *

Although the extent of the defendant's direct communication with his alleged victim was the delivery of one unopened envelope, the majority concludes that the "repeatedly" requirement of the stalking statute is satisfied by the fact that Gloria Edwards, a victim's assistant in the Gallatin County Attorney's Office, also received a letter from the defendant which was addressed to both Edwards and Karen. However, the fact that it was addressed to Karen is irrelevant. It was not sent to Karen; it was not received by her; she never handled it; and she never read it.

The only reason that Karen was even aware of the letter received by Gloria Edwards was because the day after she received it, Edwards informed Karen that it had been sent. In other words, it was not the defendant who caused Karen emotional distress by sending the first letter, it was Edwards, the victim's assistant in the county attorney's office whose apparent responsibility is to help victims — not contribute to their emotional distress. If the consequence of mere knowledge of the letter was sufficiently severe to warrant punishment of up to five years in jail and a $10,000 fine, why would a victim's assistant cause the result that the law is designed to protect against?

So, according to the majority and the District Court, the State satisfied its burden of proving that the defendant purposely or knowingly caused the victim substantial emotional distress by repeatedly harassing, threatening, or intimidating her by mail, even though the substance and extent of his communications with her was the receipt of one envelope, the contents of which she was unaware, and a third party's receipt of a second envelope, the contents of which were never disclosed to her and about which she would never have known had the person employed to protect her not advised her that it had been received. This all seems to me a little like conviction by smoke and mirrors. * * *

The defendant may have had a history of intolerable conduct in his relationship and attempted relationship with Karen; however, he had already been convicted once of stalking for his prior conduct.

What was not proven in this case was that the defendant's conduct subsequent to his first conviction for stalking satisfied the elements of the offense, as set forth in § 45-5-220, MCA. The majority's flexible application of § 45-5-220, MCA, may accomplish a socially desirable result in this case; however, the precedent established expands this serious offense beyond what was ever intended by the Legislature. * * *

NOTE

If the goal of adopting stalking statutes is to prevent an attack on the victim, is stalking a form of assault? And if it is considered a form of assault, then can there be a charge of attempted stalking? Many states have rejected the crime of attempted assault, so should they also preclude a prosecution for attempted stalking on the same grounds? The Georgia Supreme Court distinguished the two crimes in *State v. Rooks*, 468 S.E.2d 354 (Ga. 1996), when it upheld a conviction for attempted aggravated stalking. The court rejected the defendant's argument that stalking is only a type of assault:

> In reversing Rooks' conviction, the court of appeals reasoned that stalking is in essence an assault. Because there is no such crime as an attempted assault, the court of appeals reasoned that attempted stalking is likewise a legal impossibility. While we agree that there is no such crime as an attempted assault, we disagree that stalking is merely an assault crime. In recent years states have begun to enact stalking laws in response to the increase in stalking behavior and the ineffectiveness of traditional criminal statutes in preventing and curtailing this behavior. Georgia's stalking law, OCGA § 16-5-90, mirrors this trend by proscribing intentional actions not covered by the assault statutes.

> Under OCGA § 16-5-90 a person commits stalking when with a specific intent he "follows, places under surveillance, or contacts another person." Aggravated stalking is the same behavior when done in violation of a judicial order prohibiting such conduct. Generally, none of these actions would constitute an assault, which requires a demonstration of violence and a present ability to inflict injury. The intent element of the stalking statute requires proof of intentional conduct that "causes emotional distress by placing such person in reasonable fear of death or bodily harm to himself or herself or to a member of his or her immediate family." This element differs from assault in two significant ways. The assault statute requires proof that the accused induced fear of an immediate violent injury. The stalking law contains no immediacy requirement. Secondly, assault requires proof that the victim perceived the threat of violent injury to himself, whereas stalking may be committed by inducing fear that the victim's family may be harmed. These differences in both the act and intent elements demonstrate that stalking is not "in essence a common law assault."

> While assault and stalking may overlap in some circumstances, the rationale for not punishing an attempted assault does not apply to an attempted stalking. In refusing to recognize the crime of attempted assault, this court stated that to attempt an assault is "to do any act towards doing an act towards the commission of the offense" and noted the absurdity and impracticality of criminalizing such behavior. To attempt to stalk, however, is to attempt to follow, place under surveillance or contact another person. It is neither absurd nor impractical to subject to criminal sanction such actions when they are done with the requisite specific intent to cause emotional distress by inducing a reasonable fear of death or bodily injury.

PROBLEM FORTY-ONE

Finley and Sidney met as freshmen in college and began dating. They were seriously involved until April of their sophomore year, when the relationship ended. Finley returned home for the summer, and said to Sidney, "I don't want to date you again." When Finley came back for the junior year, Sidney had enrolled in the same classes that Finley had signed up to take. Finley asked Sidney, "Why are you taking the these courses?" Sidney responded, "I switched my major to the same one as you." That evening, Finley saw Sidney jogging on the block where Finley lived. Finley learned from a friend that Sidney had just rented a room in a house across the street from Finley's apartment. Finley received a number of e-mails from an untraceable account with subject lines like "Slut," "Whore," and "Pig" that did not contain any message. Finley confronted Sidney about them, but Sidney denied any involvement, and said "I just want to get on with my life -- stop bugging me." At the end of the first week of classes, Finley attended the first meeting of the college's Habitat for Humanity chapter, which Finley joined as a freshman and is now serving as Treasurer. Sidney was at the meeting and said "I came because I want to help build houses for the poor." Finley filed a complaint with the local police saying that "Sidney is stalking me and I am was fearful Sidney might attack me. The local stalking statute provides, "A person commits the offense of stalking when he or she follows, places under surveillance, or contacts another person at or about a place or places without the consent of the other person for the purpose of harassing and intimidating the other person." The statute defines "harassing and intimidating" as "a knowing and willful course of conduct directed at a specific person which causes emotional distress by placing such person in reasonable fear for such person's safety or the safety of a member of his or her immediate family, by establishing a pattern of harassing and intimidating behavior, and which serves no legitimate purpose." Should the prosecutor charge Sidney with violating the stalking statute? Should the charge be stalking or attempted stalking? What argument will defense counsel make that Sidney has not violated the provision, or attempted to violate it? Does it affect the analysis if the school has a small enrollment in a town with a population of 13,000, or is a large state university located in an urban area?

Chapter 12
Solicitation

§ 12.01 Generally

Solicitation is the crime of asking another person to join in a course of criminal conduct, with the intent that the other person commit the crime or participate in its commission. Kansas has a typical statute: "Criminal solicitation is commanding, encouraging or requesting another person to commit a felony, attempt to commit a felony or aid and abet in the commission or attempted commission of a felony for the purpose of promoting or facilitating the felony." KAN. STAT. ANN. 21-3303(a). Solicitation is usually punished less severely than an attempt to commit the crime.

Solicitation must be distinguished from the situation in which one person uses another to commit a crime unbeknownst to the other person. For example, Smith may ask Jones to go into a house and remove a television that he (Smith) asserts he owns but is unable to carry. If Jones removes the television and Smith does not own it, Jones will not be liable for larceny (or burglary) if he actually believed Smith, while Smith is liable for larceny for the trespassory taking and carrying away of the television, even though he did not physically engage in the conduct. In this situation, Smith is the perpetrator of the crime and Jones is nothing more than an "innocent instrumentality."

Solicitation is similar to a criminal attempt because it is a preliminary step toward the completion of a crime that usually does not come to fruition. Indeed, nothing more need happen once the person asks another to commit the crime — their answer is irrelevant. As the Colorado Court of Appeals noted in *People v. Hood*, 878 P.2d 89 (Colo. Ct. App. 1994), "The crime of solicitation does not require that the person solicited actually commit or attempt to commit the act solicited. Once the inducement is made, with the intent to promote the underlying crime and under circumstances that corroborate that intent, the solicitation is complete even if the person solicited does nothing at all."

As will become clear in the next chapter, solicitation is preparatory to the crime of conspiracy. As a general proposition, the crime of solicitation merges into the crime of attempt and the completed offense. This means that the government cannot convict a person of both solicitation and an attempt to commit the crime. If the government cannot prove the attempt but has evidence that the defendant asked another person to engage in criminal conduct, then that can be the basis for a criminal conviction. It is usually the case that a solicitation charge will be brought when the target offense has not been completed, which frequently occurs for two reasons. First, the solicitation was not received by the recipient. The issue then is whether an undelivered (or intercepted) solicitation should constitute a crime. [See § 12.02] Second, when the solicitation is made to an undercover police officer or person who has no intention of carrying out the crime, the object of the solicitation will never occur. [See § 12.03].

Model Penal Code

§ 5.02 Criminal Solicitation.

(1) **Definition of Solicitation.** A person is guilty of solicitation to commit a crime if with the purpose of promoting or facilitating its commission he commands, encourages or requests another person to engage in specific conduct that would constitute such crime or an attempt to commit such crime or would establish his complicity in its commission or attempted commission.

(2) **Uncommunicated Solicitation.** It is immaterial under Subsection (1) of this Section that the actor fails to communicate with the person he solicits to commit a crime if his conduct was designed to effect such communication.

(3) **Renunciation of Criminal Purpose.** It is an affirmative defense that the actor, after soliciting another person to commit a crime, persuaded him not to do so or otherwise prevented the commission of the crime, under circumstances manifesting a complete and voluntary renunciation of his criminal purpose.

§ 12.02 Uncommunicated Solicitations

People v. Saephanh
94 Cal. Rptr. 2d 910 (Cal. Ct. App. 2000)

HARRIS, J.

In October and November 1997, appellant had consensual sexual intercourse with Cassandra Y. Cassandra who became pregnant and, in January 1998 while appellant was in prison, she informed appellant of her pregnancy. Appellant first asked if the baby was his and, when told it was, exclaimed, "'Oh, I've been wanting a baby for a long time.'" Cassandra and appellant spoke about the baby every week and appellant was excited.

In May 1998, while still incarcerated, appellant wrote a letter dated May 22, 1998, to his friend and fellow gang member Cheng Saechao, also known as O. Dee. In pertinent part, it stated,

> By the way loc, could you & the homies do me a big favor & take care that white bitch, Cassie for me. ha, ha, ha!! Cuzz, it's too late to have abortion so I think a miss carrage would do just fine. I aint fista pay child sport for this bull-shit loc. You think you can get the homies or home girls do that for me before she have the baby on Aug. '98.

At the time he wrote the letter, appellant was upset. He did not want to pay child support.

Vicki Lawrence, a correctional officer at Corcoran State Prison working for the investigative service unit, testified that when an indigent inmate wishes to send a letter, he puts it into a night drop for processing through the mail room where the letter is stamped for delivery. * * * The investigative unit reviews inmate correspondence placed in the institution's mail system. According to Lawrence, she opened and read the letter appellant had written. She immediately notified her supervisor, Sergeant Basinger. The letter was thus intercepted by the institution's internal investigative unit and never reached the addressee. [Saephanh was convicted for solicitation of murder.]

Appellant contends there is insufficient evidence to support his conviction for solicitation of murder because the evidence establishes that the soliciting communication was not received by the intended recipient and, in fact, establishes no one was solicited. He asserts that California's solicitation statute, section 653f, requires proof of a completed communication. He suggests a "completed communication" occurs only when the intended recipient of the communication receives it.

In *State v. Cotton* 790 P.2d 1050 (N.M. Ct. App. 1990), the defendant was convicted of two counts of criminal solicitation. While he was incarcerated in New Mexico, he wrote two letters to his wife in Indiana suggesting that she warn their daughter not to testify against defendant * * * Neither letter ever reached defendant's wife, both having landed in the hands of law enforcement. On appeal, the defendant claimed insufficient evidence to support the solicitation convictions because the letters never reached the intended recipient, the defendant's wife.

The New Mexico Court of Appeal agreed. First, it noted that New Mexico's criminal solicitation statute "adopts in part, language defining the crime of solicitation as set out in the Model Penal Code promulgated by the American Law Institute." The court distinguished New Mexico's statute from the Model Penal

Code, noting that New Mexico's solicitation statute

> specifically omits that portion of the Model Penal Code subsection declaring that an uncommunicated solicitation to commit a crime may constitute the offense of criminal solicitation. The latter omission, we conclude, indicates an implicit legislative intent that the offense of solicitation requires some form of actual communication from the defendant to either an intermediary or the person intended to be solicited, indicating the subject matter of the solicitation.

Thus, by adopting in part the Model Penal Code section defining solicitation but omitting language from that section criminalizing uncommunicated solicitations, the New Mexico Legislature intended that the New Mexico statute not criminalize uncommunicated solicitations. * * *

In *State v. Lee*, 804 P.2d 1208 (Or. Ct. App. 1991), the Oregon Court of Appeal reached a similar result. There, the defendant, while in jail, wrote letters to an acquaintance in a juvenile center outlining plans to rob a store and residence. Authorities in the juvenile center intercepted the letters, which never reached the intended recipient. The defendant was convicted of solicitation to commit robbery. On appeal, he argued lack of evidence to sustain the conviction because the letters were never received by the intended recipient.

Citing *Cotton* and apparently following its reasoning, the Oregon court noted Oregon's criminal solicitation statute "was based, in part, on the Model Penal Code." As did the court in *Cotton*, the *Lee* court noted the omission of Model Penal Code language criminalizing uncommunicated solicitations in Oregon's criminal solicitation statute. * * *

Respondent agrees no California authority has directly addressed the issue of whether one may be found guilty of solicitation where the intended recipient of the soliciting communication never received the message. Respondent notes there is a split in authorities from other jurisdictions addressing the issue.

In *People v. Lubow,* 323 N.Y.S.2d 829 (N.Y. 1971), cited by respondent, the New York court concluded that state's criminal solicitation statute included in the crime uncommunicated solicitations. The court noted the New York statute indicated one is guilty of solicitation if, with the intent another engage in criminal conduct, the defendant "solicits, requests, commands, importunes or otherwise attempts to cause such other person to engage in such conduct." The court noted New York's statute stems from the Model Penal Code. The court pointed to that portion of the New York statute stating one is guilty of solicitation if he solicits another to engage in criminal conduct, "or otherwise attempts to cause" such conduct. The court found "[t]his has the same effect as the Model Penal Code...." The court held,

[A]n attempt at communication which fails to reach the other person may also constitute the offense for the concluding clause 'or otherwise attempts to cause such other person to engage in such conduct' would seem literally to embrace as an attempt an undelivered letter or message initiated with the necessary intent."

Thus, the New York court reached a different conclusion as to the meaning of the "otherwise attempts" language in the New York statute than did the Cotton court as to the meaning of identical language in the New Mexico statute.

Does California's section 653f include in its ambit solicitations not received by the intended recipient? *Cotton* and *Lee* concluded the New Mexico and Oregon Legislatures intended their solicitation statutes to require a solicitation be received by the intended recipient for criminal liability to attach on the basis of the omission from their statutes of language contained in the Model Penal Code on which those statutes are based. Section 653f, enacted in 1929, is not based on the Model Penal Code. * * * Thus, we disagree with appellant that *Cotton* and *Lee* examined "solicitation statutes similar to California's Penal Code section 653f," at least in terms of legislative history and intent. We find *Cotton* and *Lee* unpersuasive on the issue of whether section 653f criminalizes the making of soliciting communications not received by the intended recipient.

Likewise, *Lubow* provides no guidance on the issue because in that case the court noted New York's solicitation statute stems from the Model Penal Code. The court found that the "or otherwise attempts" language in the statute was akin to subsection 2 of Model Penal Code section 5.02. Section 653f, not derived from the Model Penal Code, does not contain attempt language. * * * Section 653f, subdivision (b) provides: "Every person who, with the intent that the crime be committed, solicits another to commit or join in the commission of murder shall be punished by imprisonment in the state prison for three, six, or nine years."

The plain language of section 653f, in particular the phrase "solicits another," demonstrates that proof the defendant's soliciting message was received by an intended recipient is required for liability to attach.

Respondent nonetheless contends the harm is in the asking and suggests the crime of solicitation was complete when appellant "deposited the correspondence with the requisite criminal intent." According to respondent, solicitation has two elements, a request to do a crime and intent that it be completed. Thus, respondent asserts, "appellant's letter was the murder request and, when he dropped it off to be mailed, he possessed the requisite criminal intent, thus satisfying both the elements to criminal solicitation."

We disagree that the letter, never received by any person appellant intended to solicit, in itself constitutes a "request" as that term may be applied in interpreting section 653f. * * * The crime of solicitation defined by section 653f requires that two or more persons must be involved, at least one being necessarily a solicitor and the other necessarily being the person solicited.

We agree with appellant that solicitation requires a completed communication.

Respondent insists that even if solicitation requires a completed communication, Vicki Lawrence, the correctional officer, received the letter. In our view, this argument evades the issue of whether appellant "solicited another." Appellant did not ask Vicki Lawrence to kill anyone, or do anything for that matter. She was not a person solicited.

* * * Uncommunicated soliciting messages do not expose others to inducements to commit crimes. Nor is there a likelihood that an uncommunicated message would result in the commission of crimes. Thus, letters posted but not delivered do not give rise to the dangers from which section 653f seeks to protect society.

However, messages urging commission of a crime which are received expose individuals to invitation to crime and create a risk of criminal activity. Criminalizing completed solicitations furthers the policies of protecting individuals from exposure to inducements to commit crimes and preventing commission of the crimes solicited. Thus, a conviction for a violation of section 653f requires proof that the person solicited received the soliciting communication. One cannot "solicit another" without a completed communication. The communication is only completed when it is received by its intended recipient.

Appellant next contends he is guilty of no crime. He asserts attempted solicitation is not a crime in California because there is no reference to attempt in section 653f. He cites other criminal and non-criminal statutes containing attempt language and suggests the absence of such language in section 653f is a clear manifestation of legislative intent attempted solicitation is not a crime.

We disagree.

"Every person who attempts to commit any crime, but fails, or is prevented or intercepted in its perpetration, shall be punished where no provision is made by law for the punishment of those attempts, . . ." (§ 664)

Solicitation is a crime, and thus falls within section 664, which applies to the attempted commission of any crime. The plain language of section 664 makes clear the Legislature is aware of specific provisions regarding attempt in the context of some crimes, and it expressly applies to those crimes which do not address attempt. Attempted solicitation of murder is a crime in California.

Appellant insists that attempted solicitation cannot be a crime because, according to appellant, solicitation is an attempt crime in itself — attempted conspiracy. Appellant compares the relationship between attempt and assault to the relationship between attempt and solicitation, noting attempted assault is not a crime. * * *

It does not necessarily follow that every solicitation is an attempted conspiracy. The crime of solicitation is complete when the solicitation is made, i.e., when the soliciting message is received by its intended recipient. It is immaterial that the object of the solicitation is never consummated, or that no steps are taken towards its completion. Unlike assault, which is statutorily defined as an attempted battery, section 653f makes no mention of attempted conspiracy. * * *

Pursuant to the plain language of sections 653f and 664, attempted solicitation of murder is a crime. We will direct that appellant's conviction be modified to a conviction of attempted solicitation of murder.

NOTE AND QUESTIONS

The Rhode Island Supreme Court agreed with *Saephanh*'s interpretation of the general solicitation statute that "actual receipt of a criminal solicitation by an intended solicitee is required for liability to attach. Specifically, the phrase 'solicits another' commands this result. In the present case, defendant sought to solicit his brother to kill a woman whose testimony might have landed defendant in prison for a lengthy stay. But his brother never received the message; therefore, no solicitation was made." *State v. Andujar*, 899 A.2d 1209 (R.I. 2006). The defendant in *Andujar* sent a letter to his brother, who was living in an apartment in New York City, asking him to kill the victim of a crime who would testify at Andujar's impending trial. The letter was accidently delivered to another tenant who was a police officer, and he forwarded it to the Rhode Island authorities. The court also found that the defendant's conduct constituted an attempted solicitation, as the California Court of Appeals did in *Saephanh*. For that offense, when has the defendant's conduct reached a sufficient point that it constitutes an attempt? Would it be when Saephanh put the letter into the outgoing prison mail, when he sealed and addressed the envelope, or when he was writing it? If the Model Penal Code's substantial step analysis is used, which one of these is sufficient? Could there be an attempt under the dangerous proximity test? Given the imprecision of the tests for attempt, when that offense is coupled with solicitation it may well be impossible to determine exactly where the line is for conduct that has not moved well toward delivery of the solicitation but is thwarted for some reason, as occurred in *Saephanh* and *Andujar*. For those states that follow the Model Penal Code approach and do not require delivery of the solicitation, then an argument can be made there is no need for the offense of attempted solicitation so long as it is clear one person is requesting another person commit a crime.

§ 12.03 Distinguishing Solicitation from Attempt

State v. Disanto
688 N.W.2d 201 (S.D. 2004)

KONENKAMP, Justice.

Defendant told several people of his intent to murder his former girlfriend [Olson] and her new boyfriend [Egemo]. Unknown to defendant, his design was revealed to the authorities and they had a police officer [McCabe] pose as a contract killer to interject himself in the plan. Defendant and the "hit man" discussed the murders, wherein defendant wanted each victim shot twice in the head. He directed the feigned killer to the former girlfriend's address, gave him a picture of her, provided details on what valuables could be obtained during the killings, instructed him to kill a child witness if necessary, and issued a final command to proceed with the murders. Shortly afterwards, however, defendant communicated with an intermediary that he wanted to "halt" the murders, saying "I'm not backing out of it, I just want to put it on hold." * * *

Defendant argues that the trial court erred in denying his motion for judgment of acquittal because the State failed to offer sufficient evidence to sustain a conviction on the three counts of attempted murder. * * *

In defining the crime of attempt, we begin with our statute. SDCL 22-4-1 states that "Any person who attempts to commit a crime and in the attempt does any act toward the commission of the crime, but fails or is prevented or intercepted in the perpetration thereof, is punishable" as therein provided. To prove an attempt, therefore, the prosecution must show that defendant (1) had the specific intent to commit the crime, (2) committed a direct act toward the commission of the intended crime, and (3) failed or was prevented or intercepted in the perpetration of the crime.

We need not linger on the question of intent. Plainly, the evidence established that defendant repeatedly expressed an intention to kill Olson and Egemo, as well as Olson's daughter, if necessary. As McCabe told the jury, defendant "was a man on a mission to have three individuals murdered." [The court rejected Disanto's abandonment argument.] * * *

The more perplexing question here is whether there was evidence that, in fulfilling his murderous intent, defendant committed an "act" toward the commission of first degree murder. Defendant contends that he never went beyond mere preparation. * * * [T]he boundary between preparation and attempt lies at the point where an act "unequivocally demonstrate[s] that a crime is about to be committed." Thus, the term "act" "presupposes some direct act or movement in execution of the design, as distinguished from mere preparation, which leaves the intended assailant only in the condition to commence the first direct act toward consummation of his design." The unequivocal act toward the commission of the offense must demonstrate that a crime is about to be committed unless frustrated by intervening circumstances. However, this act need not be the last possible act before actual accomplishment of the crime to constitute an attempt.

We have no decisions on point in South Dakota; therefore, we will examine similar cases in other jurisdictions. In murder for hire cases, the courts are divided on how to characterize the offense: is it a solicitation to murder or an act toward the commission of murder? Most courts "take the view that the mere act of solicitation does not constitute an attempt to commit the crime solicited. This issue is particularly significant in a jurisdiction where any crime can be the subject of attempt but only certain crimes can be the subject of solicitation." 4 CHARLES E. TORCIA, WHARTON'S CRIMINAL LAW § 672 (15th ed. 1996). As one commentator explained, "[a]lthough in some jurisdictions solicitations are treated as indictable attempts, either by virtue of judicial decisions failing to distinguish them, or by statutory provisions, the great weight of authority is otherwise. Analytically the two crimes are distinct." Francis Bowes Sayre, *Criminal Attempts*, 41 HARV. L. REV. 821 (1928).

Typical of the cases following the majority rule is *State v. Davis*, 6 S.W.2d 609 (Mo. 1928) (superceded by statute). There, the defendant and the wife of the intended victim plotted to kill her husband to collect the life insurance proceeds and then to live together. A police officer, posing as an ex-convict, met with the defendant several times. The defendant gave the undercover officer a map showing where the husband could be found and two photographs of him. He promised to pay the agent $600, and later paid that sum. He wanted the matter handled so that the murder would appear to have been committed in the course of a robbery. Because the agent employed to commit the murder did not act toward the consummation of the intended crime, the court held that the defendant's acts amounted to no more than solicitation or preparation. Similarly, in *People v. Adami*, 111 Cal.Rptr. 544 (Cal. Ct. App. 1973), the defendant gave an undercover police officer $500, a photograph, and a written description of his wife, with instructions to kill her. The court reversed the conviction, finding that the agent, who had only pretended to agree to commit the murder, had performed no act toward the commission of the crime.

In *State v. Otto*, 629 P.2d 646 (Idaho 1981), the defendant hired an undercover police officer to kill another police officer investigating the disappearance of the defendant's wife. A divided Idaho Supreme Court reversed the attempted first-degree murder conviction, ruling that the act of soliciting the agent to commit the actual crime, coupled with the payment of $250 and a promise of a larger sum after the crime had been completed, amounted to solicitation to murder rather than attempted murder. The court in *Otto* held that "[t]he solicit[ation] of another, assuming neither solicitor nor solicitee proximately acts toward the crime's commission, cannot be held for an attempt. He does not by his incitement of another to criminal activity commit a dangerously proximate act of perpetration. The extension of attempt liability back to the solicitor destroys the distinction between preparation and perpetration." In sum, "[n]either [the defendant in Otto] nor the agent ever took any steps of perpetration in dangerous proximity to the commission of the offense planned."

Requisite to understanding the general rule "is the recognition that solicitation is in the nature of the incitement or encouragement of another to commit a crime in the future [and so] it is essentially preparatory to the commission of the targeted offense." The Idaho Supreme Court made the rather pointed observation that

> [i]t is foreseeable that jurisdictions faced with a general attempt statute and no means of severely punishing a solicitation to commit a felony might resort to the device of transforming the solicitor's urgings into a proximate attempted commission of the crime urged but doing so violates the very essence of the requirement that a sufficient actus reus be proven before criminal liability will attach.

Cases like *Davis*, *Otto*, and *Adami* are helpful to our analysis because, at the time they were decided, the statutes or case law in those jurisdictions defined attempt in a way identical to our attempt statute. Under this formulation, there must be specific intent to commit the crime and also a direct act done towards its commission, which failed or was intercepted in its perpetration. As the Missouri Supreme Court noted, "[t]his tougher language was couched in terms of preparation and perpetration, and required that'. . . the defendant must have taken steps going beyond mere preparation, by doing something bringing him nearer the crime he intends to commit.' " *State v. Molasky*, 765 S.W.2d 597 (Mo. 1989). * * *

[T]here are several courts taking the minority position that solicitation of murder can constitute attempted murder * * *.

In *Braham v. State*, 571 P.2d 631 (Alaska 1977), evidence that the defendant instructed the hired gunman to visit the intended victim in the hospital for purpose of fostering a relationship of trust and confidence was sufficient to establish the required overt act necessary to prove attempted murder requiring an act toward the commission of murder. Alaska's attempt statute at the time is almost identical to ours. The Alaska Supreme Court held that whether an act is merely preparatory or "sufficiently close to the consummation of the crime to amount to attempt, is a question of degree and depends upon the facts and circumstances of a particular case."

In *Duke v. State*, 340 So.2d 727 (Miss. 1976), the defendant solicited an employee to kill his business partner. The murder was to take place on a hunting trip. That plan failed and the defendant sought to hire another killer. An FBI agent posed as the killer and collected $11,500 from the defendant after representing to the defendant that the partner was dead. This evidence was held sufficient to sustain the conviction because the court concluded that the defendant's acts went beyond mere preparation.

In *State v. Mandel*, 278 P.2d 413 (Ariz. 1954), a woman who made a contract with two pretended accomplices to have her husband murdered, partly executed that contract by paying a portion of the consideration in advance, identified for the intended assassins the home and the car of the intended victim, pointed out a possible site for disposing of the body, and advised them on the time and place where contact could be made for the execution of the murder. The court held that she was properly convicted of attempted murder, stating, "She did everything she was supposed to do to accomplish the purpose. Had it not been for the subterfuge, the intended victim would have been murdered. Under such circumstances she cannot escape by reason of clever, elusive distinctions between preparation, solicitation and acts committed in furtherance of the design."

In *State v. Gay*, 486 P.2d 341 (Wash. Ct. App. 1971), a wife paid a $1,000 retainer to a feigned killer to assassinate her husband and agreed to pay the killer an additional $9,000 when her husband was dead. She furnished the killer with pictures of her husband so that he would kill the right man and told him about her husband's habits and where he could be found. In upholding her conviction for attempted murder, the court acknowledged that mere solicitation, which involves no more than asking or enticing someone to commit a crime, would not constitute the crime of attempt. However, the court declared that the very act of hiring a contract killer is an overt act directed toward the commission of the target crime. The court ruled that the defendant had done everything that was to be done by her to accomplish the murder of her husband. Since the feigned assassin had made all the contacts and she had no way to contact him, she could not have stopped him after the final planning. The court concluded that the defendant's attempt to murder her husband was clearly established by the following undisputed evidence: (1) the forged assignment of the insurance policy six months before she hired a man to kill her husband, (2) the payment of premiums on her husband's $50,000 life insurance policy after the divorce had commenced, without the knowledge of her husband, and (3) the hiring of the feigned assassin.

The minority view expressed in *Braham*, *Duke*, *Gay*, and *Mandel* is epitomized in the dissenting opinion in *Otto*, where it was noted that efforts to distinguish between "acts of preparation and acts of perpetration" are "highly artificial, since all acts leading up to the ultimate consummation of a crime are by their very nature preparatory." For these courts, preparation and perpetration are seen merely as degrees on a continuum, and thus the distinction between preparation and perpetration becomes blurred. * * *

We cannot convert solicitation into attempt because to do so is obviously contrary to what the Legislature had in mind when it set up the distinct categories of solicitation and attempt. Indeed, the Legislature has criminalized other types of solicitations. See SDCL 22-43-2 (soliciting commercial bribe); SDCL 22-23-8 (pimping as felony); SDCL 22-11-20 (solicitation by witnesses); SDCL 22-22-24.5 (solicitation of minor for sex); SDCL 16-18-7 (solicitation by disbarred or suspended attorney).

Beyond any doubt, defendant's behavior here was immoral and malevolent. But the question is whether his evil intent went beyond preparation into acts of perpetration. Acts of mere preparation in setting the groundwork for a crime do not amount to an attempt. Under South Dakota's definition of attempt, solicitation alone cannot constitute an attempt to commit a crime. Attempt and solicitation are distinct offenses. To call solicitation an attempt is to do away with the necessary element of an overt act. Worse, to succumb to the understandable but misguided temptation to merge solicitation and attempt only muddles the two concepts and perverts the normal and beneficial development of the criminal law through incremental legislative corrections and improvements. It is for the Legislature to remedy this problem, and not for us through judicial expansion to uphold a conviction where no crime under South Dakota law was committed.

ZINTER, Justice (dissenting).

I join the Court's legal analysis concerning the distinction between solicitations and attempts to commit murder. Therefore, I agree that Disanto's solicitation of McCabe, in and of itself, was legally insufficient to constitute an attempt to commit murder under SDCL 22-4-1. However, I respectfully disagree with the Court's analysis of the facts, which leads it to find as a matter of law that Disanto "committed [no] act toward the commission of the offense[]." In my judgment, the Court's view of the facts is not supported by the record. On the contrary, even setting aside Disanto's solicitation, he still engaged in sufficient other "acts" toward the commission of the murder such that reasonable jurors could have found that he proceeded "so far that they would result in the accomplishment of the crime unless frustrated by extraneous circumstances." *State v. Martinez*, 220 N.W.2d 530 (S.D. 1974). The intended victims were clearly in more danger then than they were when Disanto first expressed his desire to kill them.

Specifically, Disanto physically provided McCabe with a photograph of the victim, he pointed out her vehicle, and he took McCabe to the victim's home and pointed her out as she was leaving. None of these acts were acts of solicitation. Rather, they were physical act[s going] toward the commission of the murder. SDCL 22-4-1.

Although it is acknowledged that the cases discussed by the Court have found that one or more of the foregoing acts can be part of a solicitation, Disanto's case has one significant distinguishing feature. After his solicitation was completed, after the details were arranged, and after Disanto completed the physical acts described above, he then went even further and executed a command to implement the killing. In fact, this Court itself describes this act as the final command to execute the murder. Disanto issued the order: "It's a go." This act is not present in the solicitation cases that invalidate attempted murder convictions because they proceeded no further than preparation.

Therefore, when Disanto's final command to execute the plan is combined with his history and other acts, this is the type of case that proceeded further than the mere solicitations and plans found insufficient in the case law. This combination of physical acts would have resulted in accomplishment of the crime absent the intervention of the law enforcement officer. Clearly, the victim was in substantially greater danger after the final command than when Disanto first expressed his desire to kill her. Consequently, there was sufficient evidence to support an attempt conviction. * * *

NOTE

The California Supreme Court took a different approach in *People v. Superior Court (Decker)*, 157 P.3d 1017 (Cal. 2007), in finding that a defendant's solicitation of murder constituted an attempt:

Decker's plan was to get rid of his sister so that he could recover money that she owed him. He was concerned, however, that he would be considered an obvious suspect in her murder, so he sought out someone else to carry out his plan. To that end, he conducted research into the underworld of professional killers, he budgeted to pay for those services, he evaluated how and where the murder should be done, he tested the level of security around his sister's condominium, and he considered the possibility that there might be a witness and what should be done in that event. Once he met Detective Holston, who he believed was a professional assassin, they agreed Holston would kill Donna and (if necessary) her friend Hermine, they agreed on a price, and they agreed it would be done within the week. Decker provided Holston with all of the necessary information concerning his sister, her home and office, and her habits and demeanor. He also gave Holston the agreed-on downpayment of $5,000 cash. Before he did, Holston warned him, "I want you to know, once I leave here, it's done. So, you sure you want to go through with it?" Decker replied, "I am absolutely, positively, 100 percent sure, that I want to go through with it. I've never been so sure of anything in my entire life." * * *

The issue, then, is not whether "solicitation alone" is sufficient to establish an attempt but whether a solicitation to commit murder, combined with a completed agreement to hire a professional killer and the making of a downpayment under that agreement, can establish probable cause to believe Decker attempted to murder these victims. A substantial number of our sister states have held that it can. Additional jurisdictions have held that a solicitation to murder, in combination with a completed agreement to hire a professional killer and further conduct implementing the agreement, can similarly constitute an attempted murder. * * *

In finding the record sufficient to hold Decker to answer to the charges of attempted murder here, we do not decide whether an agreement to kill followed by a downpayment is always sufficient to support a charge of attempted murder. Whether acts done in contemplation of the commission of a crime are merely preparatory or whether they are instead sufficiently close to the consummation of the crime is a question of degree and depends upon the facts and circumstances of a particular case. A different situation may exist, for example, when the assassin has been hired and paid but the victims have not yet been identified. In this case, however, Decker had effectively done all that he needed to do to ensure that Donna and her friend were executed. Accordingly, he should have been held to answer to the charges of attempted murder.

PROBLEM FORTY-TWO

Robin has become addicted to crack cocaine. One evening, Robin drives to a street on which crack is sold from street corners. Driving down the street, Robin sees a young individual standing under a streetlight with a paper shopping bag. Robin pulls to the curb next to the person, rolls down the window, and says, "Yo — rock." At that moment, two police officers emerge from a van parked across the street and arrest Robin. Robin is charged with solicitation to purchase a controlled substance and attempted purchase of a controlled substance. What argument will defense counsel make to dismiss each charge, and how will the government respond?

Would it change the argument for each charge if the young individual had responded, "Thirty," whereupon Robin reached for a wallet under the front seat and officers then emerged from the van and arrested Robin? Would it change the argument for each charge if Robin pulls up to the curb, takes a $20 bill from the wallet, and holds it up to the window but does not roll it down? Would it make a difference if the statute in this jurisdiction was worded, "it is unlawful for any person to purchase, possess, or have under his or her control any controlled substance?"

Chapter 13
Conspiracy

§ 13.01 Generally

Conspiracy is an inchoate crime that protects the public from concerted criminal activity ("In union there is strength"). The crime has been described by Judge Learned Hand as "that darling of the modern prosecutor's nursery," in part because it provides significant advantages to the prosecution. The prosecution can bring together all conspirators in a single criminal trial, which can enhance the possibility of "guilt by association." In addition, prosecutors have great flexibility in choosing the venue in a conspiracy case because jurisdiction can be found wherever an overt act occurred or where the parties formed the agreement. This may enable prosecutors to choose a forum that is most convenient for prosecution witnesses and resources and, in some instances, less advantageous for the defendants because of the cost of travel and the need to hire local counsel. As described below, a conspiracy charge may increase the evidence available to the prosecutor by allowing the admission of statements made by one conspirator during the course of the conspiracy, and in furtherance of it, that would otherwise be subject to exclusion as hearsay.

Conspiracy requires an agreement between two or more people, although it is not a contract in any legal sense of the term. The agreement does not need to be in writing, does not require specific statements by the parties, and can be ascertained from evidence as slight as the nod of one's head or even what appears to be concerted activity. A conspiracy can be inferred from the "facts and circumstances of the case." The key is that the parties have an understanding as to the common purpose. Knowledge of another person's criminal purpose, without an agreement, however, is insufficient for a conspiracy.

Some conspiracy statutes require an overt act, which is some step toward completing the object of the conspiracy. An overt act need not be illegal in itself. The common law did not require an overt act, but the general federal conspiracy statute, 18 U.S.C. § 371, has as an element of the offense a conspirator must "do any act to effect the object of the conspiracy." Other conspiracy statutes, such as the drug conspiracy statute (21 U.S.C § 846), do not require an overt act and the agreement coupled with the intent are sufficient for prosecuting the crime.

A conspiracy charge can reach conduct that occurs at the earliest stages of criminal activity because the crime is complete when the defendants enter into the criminal agreement and commit an overt act (if required). Thus, prosecutors can charge a conspiracy even when actions of the conspirators never proceed as far as necessary to constitute an attempt to commit the object crime. As you proceed through this Chapter, note how in some jurisdictions, like the federal system, prosecutors are permitted to bring a conspiracy charge in addition to the underlying substantive offenses, often as a means to enhance the possibility of a conviction and possibly to increase the punishment.

MODEL PENAL CODE

§ 5.03. Criminal Conspiracy

(1) **Definition of Conspiracy**. A person is guilty of conspiracy with another person or persons to commit a crime if with the purpose of promoting or facilitating its commission he:

(a) agrees with such other person or persons that they or one or more of them will engage in conduct that constitutes such crime or an attempt or solicitation to commit such crime; or

(b) agrees to aid such other person or persons in the planning or commission of such crime or of an attempt or solicitation to commit such crime.

(2) **Scope of Conspiratorial Relationship**. If a person guilty of conspiracy, as defined by Subsection (1) of this Section, knows that a person with whom he conspires to commit a crime has conspired with another person or persons to commit the same crime, he is guilty of conspiring with such other person or persons, whether or not he knows their identity, to commit such crime.

(3) **Conspiracy with Multiple Criminal Objectives**. If a person conspires to commit a number of crimes, he is guilty of only one conspiracy so long as such multiple crimes are the object of the same agreement or continuous conspiratorial relationship.

(4) **Joinder and Venue in Conspiracy Prosecutions**.

(a) Subject to the provisions of paragraph (b) of this Subsection, two or more persons charged with criminal conspiracy may be prosecuted jointly if:

(i) they are charged with conspiring with one another; or

(ii) the conspiracies alleged, whether they have the same or different parties, are so related that they constitute different aspects of a scheme of organized criminal conduct.

(b) In any joint prosecutions prosecution under paragraph (a) of this Subsection:

(i) no defendant shall be charged with a conspiracy in any county [parish or district] other than one in which he entered into such conspiracy or in which an overt act pursuant to such conspiracy was done by him or by a person with whom he conspired; and

(ii) neither the liability of any defendant nor the admissibility against him of evidence of acts or declarations of another shall be enlarged by such joinder; and

(iii) the Court shall order a severance or take a special verdict as to any defendant who so requests, if it deems it necessary or appropriate to promote the fair determination of his guilt or innocence, and shall take any other proper measures to protect the fairness of the trial.

(5) **Overt Act**. No person may be convicted of conspiracy to commit a crime, other than a felony of the first or second degree, unless an overt act in pursuance of such conspiracy is alleged and proved to have been done by him or by a person with whom he conspired.

(6) **Renunciation of Criminal Purpose**. It is an affirmative defense that the actor, after conspiring to commit a crime, thwarted the success of the conspiracy, under circumstances manifesting a complete and voluntary renunciation of his criminal purpose.

(7) **Duration of Conspiracy**. For purposes of Section 1.06(4):

(a) conspiracy is a continuing course of conduct that terminates when the crime or crimes that are its object are committed or the agreement that they be committed is abandoned by the defendant and by those with whom he conspired; and

(b) such abandonment is presumed if neither the defendant nor anyone with whom he conspired does any overt act in pursuance of the conspiracy during the applicable period of limitation; and

(c) if an individual abandons the agreement, the conspiracy is terminated as to him only if and when he advises those with whom he conspired of his abandonment or he informs the law enforcement authorities of the existence of the conspiracy and of his participation therein.

§ 13.02 Agreement

United States v. Fitz
317 F.3d 878 (8th Cir. 2003)

HEANEY, Circuit Judge.

After a trial by jury, Edwardo Flores Fitz, also known as Victor Manuel Crespo-Garcia, was found guilty of conspiracy to distribute and possess with intent to distribute methamphetamine and possession with intent to distribute and distribution of the same, and was sentenced to two concurrent terms of 188 months imprisonment. * * * Fitz [argues] that there was insufficient evidence to support the verdicts[.] * * * After careful review of the record, we hold there was insufficient evidence to support Fitz's convictions. * * *

* * * "'In reviewing the sufficiency of the evidence to support a guilty verdict, we look at evidence in the light most favorable to the verdict and accept as established all reasonable inferences supporting the verdict.'" * * * In a conspiracy, the government must prove there was a conspiracy with an illegal purpose, that the defendant was aware of the conspiracy, and that he knowingly became a part of it. * * * Moreover, there must be evidence that the defendant entered into an agreement with at least one other person and that the agreement had as its objective a violation of law. * * * It is not necessary to prove an overt act in furtherance of a conspiracy. The conspiracy may be proved through circumstantial evidence and may be implied by the surrounding circumstances or by inference from the actions of the parties. * * * "Once the government establishes the existence of a drug conspiracy, only slight evidence linking the defendant to the conspiracy is required to prove the defendant's involvement and support the conviction." * * *

With this background, we turn to a detailed discussion of the evidence and the reasons why we conclude there was insufficient evidence to establish Fitz's guilt on either count. * * * Applying the principles outlined above and reviewing the evidence in the light most favorable to the verdict, the only evidence in the record that could be said to support the view that Fitz knowingly participated in the conspiracy was the following: Fitz, Vega, and Preciado traveled from Minneapolis to Grand Forks in a Honda Civic and a Nissan Pathfinder, in which the drugs were hidden; Fitz was observed in the presence of Preciado and Vega in Grand Forks at various locations between 6:00 p.m. and 9:30 p.m.; Fitz gave a false name when he was arrested; and Fitz was present during a recorded conversation between the confidential informant and Preciado in the Burger King parking lot in Grand Forks, in which Preciado said he wanted everything and wanted to return to the motel to discuss the matter. Thereafter, Preciado and Fitz left the parking lot in a Honda Civic when they were stopped by the Grand Forks Narcotics Task Force officers and arrested.

On the other hand, there is considerable evidence that casts into serious doubt whether Fitz knowingly participated in the conspiracy. The confidential informant never talked to Fitz. Moreover, the conversation that occurred in Fitz's presence between the confidential informant and Preciado was conducted in English, and there is no evidence in the record that shows that Fitz spoke or understands English. He was provided with an interpreter during the entire trial and the sentencing hearing. Further, there is no evidence in the record to indicate that Fitz knew there were drugs in a secret compartment in the Pathfinder's gas tank. Also, when Preciado, Vega, and Fitz first arrived in Grand Forks, a hotel room was rented in the name of Antonio Mendoza. This name was used in the past by Preciado at the same motel.

Nothing in the record indicates that Fitz had been in Grand Forks at an earlier date, and Fitz had no prior criminal record or any record of dealing in drugs * * * The confidential informant had Preciado's pager number and could reach Preciado at any time. Between June 26 and June 28, seven calls were made between the confidential informant and Preciado. There is no evidence, however, that the informant knew how to contact Fitz or ever sought to do so. There is evidence Fitz ever rode in or drove the Pathfinder. Even if Fitz had been in the Pathfinder, the methamphetamine was well hidden in the Pathfinder, and there was no evidence in the record that Fitz was aware of the existence of the drugs.

Perhaps, most importantly, the government failed to call the confidential informant as a witness even though the confidential informant was available and known only to the government. * * *

In short, while the government can prove that a conspiracy existed between Preciado and Vega, the government failed to prove that Fitz was aware of the conspiracy, or that Fitz knowingly agreed to join the conspiracy. As the government cannot prove two of the three necessary elemnets of Fitz's alleged crimes, we cannot affirm his convictions. * * *

There is no evidence in the record that would tend to show by inference or otherwise that Fitz was a knowing participant in the drug conspiracy or that he constructively possessed the methamphetamine because he was a passenger in a car that accompanied the Pathfinder from Minneapolis to Grand Forks. A verdict based on unsupported speculation cannot stand. Under these circumstances, we have no alternative but to reverse Fitz's convictions.

NOTES AND QUESTIONS

1. ***Plurality.*** Although more than one person is required for a conspiracy, it is not necessary that the government charge all parties to the agreement. It is common for the government to have unindicted coconspirator. Issues do arise as to whether a conspiracy existed when one person is convicted and the other is acquitted. Was there really an agreement here? Historically, inconsistent verdicts were impermissible, although the rule did not apply when only one person was tried for the crime. Thus, having an unindicted coconspirator would not preclude a conspiracy conviction for the other party. In recent years courts have moved away from prohibiting inconsistent verdicts where one defendant is found not guilty and another guilty of making the requisite conspiratorial agreement. Courts rely on the fact that a jury may feel particular sympathy for a defendant that could explain the inconsistent verdict. There is disagreement, however, when one of the parties to the conspiracy is a government agent. Some courts require a true agreement, something that cannot be achieved when one party is a government agent. Others, however, permit unilateral conspiracies. *See* Eric L. Muller, *The Hobgoblin of Little Minds? Our Foolish Law of Inconsistent Verdicts*, 111 HARV. L. REV. 771 (1998).

2. ***Unilateral-Bilateral Conspiracies.*** Model Penal Code § 5.03(1) does not require that there be more than one participant in the conspiracy so long as "a person" "agrees with such other person or persons" to engage in criminal conduct. This is called the unilateral theory of conspiracy, which allows for a prosecution even though no one else actually enters into an agreement, such as when an undercover officer is the second participant in the purported conspiracy. Most jurisdictions follow the traditional bilateral approach reflected in the federal conspiracy statute, 18 U.S.C. § 371, which makes it a crime when "two or more persons conspire" to commit an offense. If the other purported participant is an undercover agent, or only feigns agreement, then there is no conspiracy if these are the only two participants. But if a third person also agrees to the commission of the offense, then there would be the requisite plurality even though one person is not actually agreeing to commit the crime.

3. ***Charging Conspiracy.*** A conspiracy is not limited to the commission of a single criminal offense. For example, an agreement to sell narcotics and then to launder the money by placing in a bank account under a fictitious name would constitute at least two crimes: the drug sale and then money laundering. However, there would only be one conspiracy with multiple criminal objects. Model Penal Code § 5.03(3) addresses this issue by providing that "[i]f a person conspires to commit a number of crimes, he is guilty of only one conspiracy so long as such multiple crimes are the object of the same agreement or continuous conspiratorial relationship." It is also possible for a conspiracy to change over time, so that additional crimes could be added to the agreement, so that there is still only one conspiracy.

4. ***Wharton's Rule.*** When the crime by its very nature requires two people, courts have precluded use of conspiracy. Thus, one could not prosecute the crime of adultery as a conspiracy when the crime itself required two individuals. Wharton's Rule tends to arise in cases involving bribery, bigamy and adultery, and simple drug sales, although in recent years it has been significantly limited. In *Iannelli v. United States*, 420 U.S. 770 (1975), the Supreme Court found that Wharton's Rule only acts "as a judicial presumption, to be applied in the absence of legislative intent to the contrary." The Model Penal Code rejects Wharton's Rule on the ground that the fact a crime inevitably involves two participants is not a reason to insulate the participants from liability so long as one has the requisite intent to agree to the commission of an offense.

5. ***Unlawful Object of the Agreement***. In recent years there has been a requirement that the agreement be to commit a criminal act. This was not always the case. At common law, the agreement could be to "to do either an unlawful act or a *lawful act by criminal or unlawful means*." The object of the conspiracy need not be a single criminal act, and can encompass a continuing course of illegal acts, such as drugs distribution, prostitution, and loan sharking. In addition, the conspiracy can change to incorporate additional criminal objects so long as the members agree to the new crimes.

6. ***Overt Act.*** The drug conspiracy statute (21 U.S.C. § 846) prosecuted in the *Fitz* case does not require an overt act. It is common for federal drug conspiracy statutes not to require an overt act, allowing prosecutors to prove the conspiracy merely upon proof of the agreement and *mens rea*. In *Whitfield v. United States*, 543 U.S. 209 (2005), the Supreme Court held that the money laundering conspiracy statute did not require an overt act. The Court noted that there is "an express overt-act requirement in at least 22 [ ] current [federal] conspiracy statutes." The key to determining whether an overt act was required was whether Congress explicitly provided for it in the statute. When an overt act is required, it need not be criminal in itself, only that it be a step in the process of committing the object of the conspiracy. Otherwise innocent acts – renting a car, purchasing a weapon, or placing a telephone call – may be overt acts if they relate to the conspiracy's crime. Model Penal Code § 5.03(4) does not require proof of an overt act for serious crimes, designated as first or second degree felonies, but does for lower level offenses.

7. ***Merger.*** The majority rule is that conspiracy is a separate offense from any substantive crimes committed in the course of the conspiracy. Unlike solicitation and attempt, which merge with the target offense, conspiracy can be charged and punished in addition to any punishment for the object(s) of the conspiracy. Therefore, it is possible for a defendant to be found not guilty of a crime but guilty of a conspiracy to commit that offense because it is the agreement that constitutes the *actus reus* of conspiracy and not the actual or attempted commission of the substantive crime. The Model Penal Code's definition of the crime does not

recognize merger, and includes an agreement to attempt or solicit a crime as sufficient to prove a conspiracy.

8. ***Abandonment/Renunciation.*** Since the agreement forms the basis of the crime, if there is proof of the agreement and an overt act in furtherance of the conspiracy – assuming one is needed – then subsequent abandonment is irrelevant to whether the crime occurred. Upon entering into the agreement, and commission of an overt act, if necessary, the crime is complete. If the accused, however, abandons the agreement and withdraws from the conspiracy, avoiding criminal liability may be possible. Some courts require communicating withdrawal to all the co-conspirators or possibly even getting those who were a party to the conspiracy to cease the conspiracy. Notification to police authorities may also be required. The Model Penal Code recognizes two means for an individual to terminate participation in a conspiracy. Section 5.03(6) recognizes the defense of renunciation, which requires the conspirator to thwart "the success of the conspiracy, under circumstances manifesting a complete and voluntary renunciation of his criminal purpose." How successful does the person have to be in preventing the conspiracy from being successful? Does the renunciation defense require a conspirator to inform the authorities? Model Penal Code § 5.03(7) also recognizes that a conspiracy has ended when all conspirators abandon the criminal object of the agreement, and "such abandonment is presumed if neither the defendant nor anyone with whom he conspired does any overt act in pursuance of the conspiracy during the applicable period of limitation." An individual conspirator can also abandon the agreement, even if it continues forward with others, but "only if and when he advises those with whom he conspired of his abandonment or he informs the law enforcement authorities of the existence of the conspiracy and of his participation therein." Note that this is not a defense to conspiracy so much as a claim that by abandoning the conspiracy the person did not violate the law. Given how high the standard is for abandonment, would it be better to argue for the defense of renunciation? The Model Penal Code does not make renunciation and abandonment mutually exclusive, so a defendant could argue for both and hope that one is successful.

9. ***Burden of Proof of Withdrawal.*** Although the "government must prove the time of the conspiracy offense if a statute-of-limitations defense is raised," the defendant can be made to prove a defense of withdrawal from the conspiracy. *See Smith v. United States*, 133 S.Ct. 714 (2013).

PROBLEM FORTY-THREE

Terry is walking near the University when a car pulls up and a passenger in the back seat rolls down the window and calls out, "Hey, friend, do you know where 'University Restaurant' is?" Terry approaches the car and says, "Sorry, I've never heard of it." The rear passenger door opens and two individuals emerge. They grab Terry, throw Terry to the ground, and take Terry's backpack. The two individuals then jump back in the car and drive away. A witness to the robbery calls the police and provides the license plate number of the car. The police stop the vehicle two miles away and arrest its three occupants: Lynn, the driver, Paige, and Pat, who were passengers. When questioned, Lynn admits to ownership of the car and says that Paige and Pat were individuals that Lynn met that afternoon while playing pool. Lynn says that Paige and Pat asked for a ride to a restaurant near the University. Paige and Pat refuse to speak with the police. These three individuals are charged with robbery and conspiracy. What evidence can the prosecution cite to the jury in order to show that Lynn is guilty of conspiracy? How should the defense respond?

§ 13.03 Mens Rea

United States v. Jones
371 F.3d 363 (7th Cir. 2004)

WILLIAMS, Circuit Judge.

[Dirk Jones was convicted and sentenced to 60 months imprisonment for a conspiracy with two criminal objects: to make a false statement to a federally licensed firearms dealer, and to transfer a firearm to a resident of another state. 18 U.S.C. §§ 371, 922(a)(6), 922(a)(5).]

Early on the morning of June 20, 2001, Dennis Rock entered the Westforth Sports Shop in Gary, Indiana, with an unidentified individual and made a $200 down payment on a Norinco SKS semi-automatic assault rifle. Rock was a frequent customer at Westforth's. Between September 2000 and June 2001, Rock had purchased at least ten firearms from Westforth's, and agents from the Bureau of Alcohol, Tobacco, and Firearms (ATF) had asked the store to alert them if Rock made any more purchases. After Rock placed the down payment on the rifle and had left the store, the sales clerk called the ATF to report the transaction. ATF agents arrived at the store and hid in a back room. The government made no effort at trial to establish the identity of Rock's companion, but nevertheless argued in closing that Jones was the second man in the store.

Rock returned to Westforth's later than morning, and Jones admits that this time he was with Rock. Store surveillance cameras recorded the entire time the two men were at Westforth's. Rock and Jones spent at least half an hour in the store because the ATF had instructed the sales clerk to delay completing the transaction until additional agents could arrive. During this time, the store surveillance video showed that Rock filled out a federally required Form 4473. The video also showed that during this period Jones handled the SKS rifle briefly, spoke with Rock and the sales clerk, smoked a cigarette, looked at the display cases, and held a pistol from one of the cases for a few moments. There was no testimony about what Jones said while in the store. Once the sale was completed, the sales clerk placed the rifle in a box and Jones carried the box to Rock's car and placed it in the trunk.

The two men then drove away, and ATF agents followed. Rock drove around Gary with Jones in the car for approximately ninety minutes, making stops at a convenience store, an apartment building, and a restaurant. Rock then entered Interstate 90 and drove into Chicago, stopping in front of a Chicago Housing Authority building at 2920 South State Street. While Rock remained in the car, Jones go out and walked into the building. Approximately a minute later Rock exited his car and opened the trunk. The ATF agents testified that they believed Rock was trying to remove the rifle from the trunk, so they approached the car and arrested him. [A short time later, Jones was arrested as he left the building on South State Street, and he was then released. Seventeen months later, the government indicted Rock and Jones for conspiracy. Rock was a fugitive and Jones was tried alone on the conspiracy charge.]

The government and the defense offer widely different theories about Jones's actions on that day. The government's theory of the case was that Rock had an ongoing relationship with the man in Chicago named "Vino" or "Vince." Agent Kevin O'Malley read into evidence a redacted written confession Rock had given to the police on the day he was arrested, in which Rock describes his dealings with Vino and says that he was purchasing the SKS rifle for Vino. Agent Cynthia Carroll testified that the ATF had been investigating Rock because he had bought eleven firearms from Westforth's. Agent Carroll testified that the ATF suspected Rock of making "straw purchases" – meaning that Rock (who had a gun permit and could legally buy firearms) would purchase a gun from a store and then resell it in Chicago, possibly with Vino's assistance. The government presented no evidence that Jones was involved in any other transactions, but argued in its closing that Jones was helping Rock to carry out one of these straw purchases on June 20, and that Jones entered the housing project to find a buyer for the rifle. The version of Rock's confession read to the jury made no mention of Jones.

The defense argued instead that Jones had nothing to do with the purchase or sale of the rifle. Jones testified that he is a drug addict and that on the morning in question he wanted to go to Chicago to purchase heroin. Indeed, Jones had two previous convictions for drug offenses, and at trial he rolled up his sleeve to show the jury what are apparently extensive needle marks on his arm. He testified that he was standing on a street corner in Gary where addicts regularly go to look for rides into Chicago to buy drugs, when Rock – who was a casual acquaintance – drove up and offered to take him. According to Jones, Rock said he needed to make a stop before heading to Chicago and then went to Westforth's. Jones said he was experiencing withdrawal and wanted to get to Chicago quickly, so he went into the store to try to keep Rock from wasting time – an explanation the government disputed in its closing. When they arrived at 2920 South State Street, according to Jones, he went inside and bought heroin that he snorted while still inside. Jones also testified that this building was the location where he usually bought his heroin.

* * *

Consp[iracy] elements

In order to establish a conspiracy under § 371, the government must prove: (1) an agreement to commit an illegal act; (2) the defendant's knowing and intentional participation in the agreement; and (3) an overt act committed in furtherance of the agreement. The government may rely on circumstantial evidence to establish both the existence of a conspiracy and the defendant's involvement. But although a jury may infer facts from other facts derived by inference, "each link in the chain of inferences must be sufficiently strong to avoid a lapse into speculation." *United States v. Peters*, 277 F.3d 963 (7th Cir. 2002).

In its brief, the government lists a sequence of events it says the jury could have found without drawing any inferences. The events are: Jones talked with Rock on the morning of June 20, 2001, and entered his car; Rock entered Westforth's with another man and made a $200 deposit on a SKS rifle; Jones and Rock later entered Westforth's together; Rock paid for the rifle and filled out the necessary paperwork, and Jones placed the rifle in Rock's trunk; three hours later Rock and Jones arrived at 2920 South State Street, and Jones entered the building; approximately a minute later Rock opened his trunk and started to remove the rifle; Rock was detained; and Jones exited the building by a side door with seven or eight men. The government says this sequence "amply supports" the jury's finding that Jones participated in the conspiracy.

The government overstates the strength of its evidence. The sequence of events establishes at most that Jones was present while Rock engaged in what Rock admitted was an illegal straw purchase of a firearm. But "mere presence" while a crime is being committed is insufficient to show that a defendant acted to further a conspiracy. Even if Jones knew of Rock's plan to resell the rifle, his knowledge or approval of the illegal scheme is insufficient to sustain a conviction.

The indictment charged that Jones conspired with Rock to make a false statement to a firearms dealer because Rock stated on the Form 4473 that he was purchasing the gun form himself when in reality he was purchasing it for Vino. Jones would not have known that Rock falsified the ATF form unless he knew of Rock's plan at that point. But the government's evidence at trial that Jones was connected with – or even aware of – Vino's and Rock's scheme to resell firearms in Chicago is nonexistent. There is no evidentiary support that shows either an agreement between Rock and Jones, or Jones's knowing participation in an agreement between Rock and Vino. Rock, not Jones, filled out the form and gave the money to the clerk. Moreover, Agent O'Malley even testified that he had no probable cause to make an arrest at the time Rock and Jones left Westforth's because Rock had a valid gun permit. The government's evidence does not even establish that Jones knew that Rock committed a crime at Westforth's, much less that he participated in it.

Likewise, the fact that Jones knew Rock bought the gun does not prove that he knew that Rock planned to sell it to a nonresident of Indiana or that he played any role in the scheme. The ATF agents could only speculate as to Jones's purpose for entering 2920 South State Street, because once they arrested Rock and Jones, they made no attempt to locate any potential buyer of the rifle or to identify any of the people who left the building with Jones. Rock did not testify at Jones's trial, so he could not establish the purpose for which Jones entered the building. Jones claimed he entered the building to purchase heroin from his regular drug supplier, and the government presented no evidence to the contrary.

To further support its case, the government lists several inferences it says the jury reasonably could have drawn from the evidence. First, it says the jury could have inferred that Rock enlisted Jones to help him sell the rifle in Chicago and that Jones agreed to participate to get money for drugs. Although surely the jury could have inferred both the existence of an agreement and Jones's knowing participation had there been evidence from which to reasonably draw those inferences, * * * there was not in this case even circumstantial evidence to support either inference. The government never explained at trial how Jones was to profit from this transaction if he was to profit at all; speculation is all that the government offers now.

Adding to its speculation, the government also says that the jury could have inferred that Jones told Rock that they could sell the gun to one of his heroin suppliers at 2920 South State Street. But the only bases for suspecting that Jones told Rock he knew of a buyer for the gun is a single sentence in Rock's post-arrest confession: "My friend Duke, came with me to pickup the SKS, and that he (Duke) knew of someone in the city of Chicago that would purchase the SKS from me for a profit." The government argues that "Duke" is an alias for Dirk Jones. But the jury never saw this sentence because the parties agreed before trial that is was inadmissible. The government next argues that the jury could have inferred that Jones was the man who went into Westforth's with Rock when Rock made his down payment, that the two men left the store to finalize their plan, and that they returned to the store so Rock could complete the purchase. * * *

Finally, the government says the jury could have inferred that Jones knew Rock was going to lie on the Form 4473 about being the actual purchaser, and the pursuant to their "agreement" Jones entered 2920 South State Street to look for a buyer. These arguments again assume that Jones was aware of a conspiracy and was a knowing participant in it. The government might have obtained support for the latter point if the ATF had further investigated after detaining Jones. But the ATF did not question any of the seven or eight people who left the building at the same time as Jones and made no attempt to locate the assumed buyer of the weapon. All the government brought to trial was its speculation about the stop at the housing project.

In short, the government's evidence establishes at most that Jones was present while Rock committed two federal firearms crimes: falsifying the ATF form and driving to Chicago for the purpose of selling the SKS rifle to an out-of-state resident. The government tries to infer from his presence that Jones both knew of and knowingly participated in a conspiracy to commit those offenses. But the government's case relies on speculation with scant evidentiary support. Even though a jury may infer facts, "each link in the chain of inferences must be sufficiently strong to avoid a lapse into speculation." The government's evidence in this case required the jury to do just that. The government's case certainly casts suspicion upon Jones. But a "strong suspicion that someone is involved in criminal activity is no substitute for proof of guilt beyond a reasonable doubt." Even given the deferential standard of appellate review that applies here, we cannot say that the government met its burden.

NOTES AND QUESTIONS

1. **Specific Intent.** Conspiracy requires specific intent. One must have knowledge of the agreement and the specific intent to agree to commit the unlawful objective of the agreement. The key is whether there is sufficient proof of a defendant's knowledge of the agreement for the common criminal objective, and if that knowledge can be the basis to infer the requisite specific intent to agree. The government does not, however, have to prove that a conspirator had knowledge of all the circumstances of the agreement or knew all the participants in the conspiracy.

2. **Buyers and Sellers.** The issue of intent to agree becomes especially difficult in cases in which a conspiracy is charged between a buyer and seller. Was the transaction a "one-shot deal" or a continuing course of conduct such that the jury can reasonable infer the agreement and intent? Was there a measure of mutual trust or some evidence of a continuing relationship to establish an agreement beyond just the transaction? In *United States v. Colon*, 549 F.3d 565 (7th Cir. 2008), the Seventh Circuit overturned the conspiracy conviction of a seller of cocaine based on an alleged illegal agreement with his two suppliers. While there were six or seven transactions over a six-week period, which the government argued were "regular" purchases showing the relationship was standardized to reflect a conspiratorial agreement, that alone was not enough, as the circuit court explained:

In any event, how "regular" purchases on "standard" terms can transform a customer into a co-conspirator mystifies us. * * * The government either is confusing buying with conspiring or believes that a seller and a buyer who fail to wrangle over each sale aren't dealing at arms' length and therefore must trust each other. But "mutual trust" is already a factor in the conventional analysis of conspiracy; an act that is merely evidence of mutual trust cannot be a separate factor. And anyway repeat transactions need not imply greater mutual trust than is required in any buyer-seller relationship. If you buy from Wal-Mart your transactions will be highly regular and utterly standardized, but there will be no mutual trust suggestive of a relationship other than that of buyer and seller.

It is different if * * * a seller assists his customers in establishing the methods by which they will take delivery from him, for then he is more than just a seller; he is helping to create a distribution system for his illegal product. But the defendant in our case (a buyer, not a seller) did nothing to help Saucedo and Rodriguez establish a delivery system that would enable them to serve him, or serve him better.

The fact that in his conversations with Rodriguez, Saucedo referred to Colon as "Dude" or "Old Boy," rather than calling him by his name, is not, as the government believes, indicative of intimacy or a pre-existing relationship; it is for obvious reasons a convention in the drug trade not to refer to a customer by his real name. There were no sales on credit to the defendant, or other evidence of mutual trust or dependance, and he had no dealings with – indeed, he never met or spoke to – Rodriguez, Saucedo's unquestioned co-conspirator, although the defendant knew that they worked together. There is no suggestion that the defendant could expect to receive any part of the income that Saucedo obtained from selling cocaine to other customers.

3. *Merchants.* Does the fact that one knows about a customer's purpose to commit a crime, and if it could be prevented by refusing to sell an item crucial to its success, establish an agreement to commit the offense? *See People v. Lauria,* 59 Cal. Rptr.2d 628 (Cal. Ct. App. 1967) (the appellate court dismissed a conspiracy charge against the operator of a telephone answering service used by prostitutes to receive calls from their clientele). Should the status of the item as lawful or unlawful distinguish the basis for conspiratorial liability? Should appellate courts be especially careful in reviewing the government's evidence of an agreement when the presence of illegal drugs, weapons, or other contraband may sway the jury to return a guilty verdict on a conspiracy charge based largely on the underlying criminality? Should prosecutors be more careful when they charge conspiracy because of the potential "spill-over" effect of other charges?

4. *Knowledge as Specific Intent.* Courts rather routinely state that knowledge of a criminal plan is not sufficient to prove an intent to enter into an agreement. On the other hand, in *United States v. Falcone*, 109 F.2d 579 (2d Cir. 1940), the court stated that the intent to agree can be inferred if the defendant knows of the agreement and has a "stake in its outcome." In *Jones*, it did not appear that the defendant had any stake in Rock's plan, so his presence and apparent knowledge of the gun was insufficient to establish his intent to enter an agreement.

5. *Knowledge of Attendant Circumstances.* In *United States v. Feola*, 420 U.S. 671 (1975), the Supreme Court did not require the defendants to know that the victim was a federal officer when the charge was "assault on a federal officer." The defendants attempted to rob undercover drug agents of the money they brought to purchase drugs from the defendants. The attendant circumstance, one of jurisdiction, did not require knowledge in order to convict them of conspiracy based on the agreement to assault. The proposition that the defendants would not have robbed a DEA agent had they known the victim's identity is irrelevant to the determination of whether they entered an agreement to forcibly assault an individual who turns out to be a federal employee engaged in his duties. The agreement to engage in the wrongful conduct – an assault – is sufficient without regard to the status of the victim, which is the basis for permitting federal jurisdiction but need not be the subject of the illegal agreement. *See United States v. Boone*, 738 F.2d 763 (6th Cir. 1984) (upholding convictions of two defendants for violating § 111 for taking the purse of federal appeals court judge on a Sunday afternoon as she walked to the federal courthouse to conduct legal research for a case to be heard the next morning.)

6. *Conscious Avoidance of Knowledge*. The defendant must know that he is entering into a conspiratorial agreement. Therefore, in addition to proof of a specific intent to agree, the government must establish the defendant's knowledge that the agreement contained a criminal object. In *United States v. Svodoba*, 347 F.3d 471 (2d Cir. 2003), the Second Circuit held that a conscious avoidance instruction may be given for proving this aspect of the defendant's intent. A conscious avoidance instruction permits a jury to infer knowledge when there is sufficient evidence that the defendant was aware of a high probability of the fact the criminal object of the agreement but consciously avoided confirming that fact. The court stated:

> [W]e can see no reason why the factfinder may not rely on conscious avoidance to satisfy at least the knowledge component of intent to participate in a conspiracy. Moreover, we firmly reject [the defendant's] contention that a conscious avoidance charge may not be used in a two-person conspiracy. Whether the conspiracy is among two members or more, a defendant's conscious avoidance of knowledge of its illegal purpose may substitute for knowledge of the illegal purpose. * * *

[Defendant] contends that a two-person conspiracy requires proof that each alleged co-conspirator possessed actual knowledge of the unlawful objectives of the charged scheme – otherwise, he argues, there can be no illicit agreement. This argument presupposes that a finding of conscious avoidance stands on a lesser legal footing than a finding of actual knowledge. Our precedents, however, establish that knowledge consciously avoided is the legal equivalent of knowledge actually possessed. See e.g., *United States v. Finkelstein*, 229 F.3d 90 (2d Cir. 2000) ("one who deliberately avoided knowing the wrongful nature of his conduct is as culpable as one who knew"). The defendant's conscious avoidance of knowledge of the unlawful aims of the conspiracy thus may be invoked as the equivalent of knowledge of those unlawful aims. In the context of a two-person conspiracy, intent to participate may be shown by a finding that the defendant either knew, or consciously avoided knowing, the unlawful aims of the charged scheme and intended to advance those unlawful ends.

PROBLEM FORTY-FOUR

Paige and Pat ask Lynn if they can borrow Lynn's car to run an "errand" near the University. When Lynn asks what they plan to do, Pat says, "We need a little spending money, and you know those rich college kids always carry around more than they need. We'll just help ourselves to a little bit of it." Lynn gives them the keys to the car, but does not accompany them. If Paige and Pat rob Terry, using Lynn's car to travel to and from the crime, can Lynn be convicted of conspiracy?

PROBLEM FORTY-FIVE

Terry (from Problem Forty-Four) is an undercover federal Drug Enforcement Agency officer posing as a graduate chemistry student to infiltrate a group of students suspected of stealing chemicals from the University and operating a secret methamphetamine lab. Terry was on the way to meet with two of the students who would take Terry to the secret lab when Paige and Pat robbed Terry. Lynn, Paige, and Pat are charged with conspiracy to violate 18 U.S.C. § 111, a federal statute that makes it a crime for any person who "forcibly assaults . . . any [federal employee] while engaged in or on account of performance of official duties . . . ." Each defendant truthfully states that they did not know that Terry was an undercover DEA officer, and there was no way to know that Terry was engaged in official duties at the time. Can they be convicted of conspiracy to violate 18 U.S.C. § 111 when the agreement was only to rob someone and not assault a federal employee?

§ 13.04 Single and Multiple Conspiracies

United States v. McDermott
245 F.3d 133 (2d Cir. 2002)

OAKES, Senior Circuit Judge.

Defendant James J. McDermott appeals from a judgment entered against him in the United States District Court for the Southern District of New York following a jury trial * * * convicting him of conspiracy to commit insider trading and of insider trading * * * [T]here is insufficient evidence to support the conspiracy count, although sufficient evidence exists to support McDermott's conviction on the substantive offenses. Nevertheless, because of the variance between the single conspiracy charged in the indictment and the proof adduced at trial, we find that McDermott was prejudiced to the point of being denied a fair trial. Accordingly, we reverse the conspiracy count and remand for a new trial on the substantive counts.

The present prosecution arose out of a triangulated love affair involving the president of a prominent investment bank, a pornographic film star and a New Jersey businessman.

Until May 1999, McDermott was the president, CEO and Chairman of Keefe Bruyette & Woods ("KBW"), an investment bank headquartered in New York City that specialized in mergers and acquisitions in the banking industry. Around 1996, McDermott began having an extramartial affair with Kathryn Gannon. Gannon was an adult film star and an alleged prostitute who performed using the stage name "Marilyn Star." During the course of their affair, McDermott made numerous stock recommendations to Gannon. Unbeknownst to McDermott, Gannon was simultaneously having an affair with Anthony Pomponio and passing these recommendations to him. Although neither Gannon nor Pomponio had extensive training or expertise in securities trading, together they earned around $170,000 in profits during the period relevant to this case.

The government indicted McDermott, Gannon and Pomponio for conspiracy to commit insider trading and for insider trading on the theory that McDermott's recommendations to Gannon were based on non-public, material information. McDermott and Pomponio were tried together, but Gannon was not present. The evidence at trial concerned primarily the relationship between McDermott and Gannon and the trading activities of Gannon and Pomponio. The Government built its case against McDermott almost entirely on circumstantial evidence linking records of telephone conversations between McDermott and Gannon with records of Gannon's and Pomponio's trading activities. Telephone records revealed that McDermott and Gannon engaged in approximately 800 telephone calls during the charged period, including up to 29 calls in one day. Trading records revealed correlations between the telephone calls and stock trades. In addition to these records, the sensational highlight of the government's evidence, which formed the basis of its perjury count again Pomponio, consisted of audiotape recordings of Pomponio's SEC deposition. These tapes undermined Pomponio's defense and credibility, as they recorded him poorly telling lies, evading questions and affecting incredulous reactions.

McDermott challenges the sufficiency of the evidence to establish his convictions both for a single conspiracy to commit insider trading and for the related substantive offenses.

"[I]n order to prove a single conspiracy, the government must show that each alleged member agreed to participate in what he knew to be a collective venture directed toward a common goal. The coconspirators need not have agreed on the details of the conspiracy, so long as they agreed on the essential nature of the plan." We have frequently noted that the "essense of conspiracy is the agreement and not the commission of the substantive offense." Additionally, it is a long-standing principle of this Court's law of conspiracy that "[n]obody is liable in conspiracy except for the fair import of the concerted purpose or agreement as he understands it; if later comers change that, he is not liable for the change; his liability is limited to the common purposes while he remains in it."

Despite this well-settled law, the government here asks us to redefine a conspiracy by its purpose, rather than by the agreement of its members to that purpose. The government argues that from the perspective of Gannon and Pomponio, albeit not from McDermott's perspective, there was a unitary purpose to commit insider trading based on information furnished by McDermott. According to the government, therefore, McDermott was part of the conspiracy even though he did not agree to pass information to both Gannon and Pomponio.

* * * [W]e find that McDermott is not liable for the trades made by Pomponio. There is no record evidence suggesting that McDermott's agreement with Gannon encompassed a broader scope than the two of them. McDermott and Gannon were having an affair, and it is not obvious that it was or should have been within McDermott's frame of reference that Gannon would share stock information with others similarly situated, or even that there existed others similarly situated. We decline to hold as a matter of law that a cheating heart must foresee a cheating heart. Indeed, the only evidence that McDermott did foresee or should have foreseen Gannon passing information to Pomponio consisted of evidence suggesting that Gannon was a prostitute – evidence that the district court explicitly prohibited.

Moreover, the proof at trial established that McDermott had no knowledge of Pomponio's existence.

Accordingly, we hold that, as a matter of law, no rational jury could find McDermott guilty beyond a reasonable doubt of a single conspiracy with Pomponio to commit insider trading. The government has failed to show the most basic element of a single conspiracy, namely , and agreement to pass insider information to Gannon and possibly to another person, even if unknown. We therefore reverse the judgement of conviction on that count. [The court found sufficient evidence for a rational jury to find McDermott guilty of the substantive charge of insider trading for giving the information to Gannon for the purpose of her trading on it, but then considered the following issue:]

McDermott argues that he was prejudiced to the point of being denied a fair trial as a result of the variance between the single conspiracy charged in the indictment and the proof adduced at trial. We agree.

We begin by referring to our foregoing discussion of the sufficiency of the evidence for the conspiracy count to note that there was a variance in this case between the single conspiracy charged and the proof at trial. We review the variance for its potential prejudicial effect on McDermott's trial for the substantive counts of insider trading.

In order to reverse a conviction because of the existence of a variance, the variance must have caused the defendant "substantial prejudice" at trial. In evaluating whether a defendant has been prejudiced by a variance, we consider * * * whether there was prejudicial spillover due to a large number of joined defendants * * *.

We find here that there was prejudicial spillover due to joinder, even though there was only one defendant joined with McDermott. The fact that McDermott and Pomponio were tried together, in the absence of anyone else at the defense table, increased the prejudicial effect of Pomponio's testimony on McDermott's defense by channeling all references to a source of securities information entirely onto McDermott. Given that Pomponio and McDermott were on trial for conspiring to commit insider trading, that there was a large disparity between the government's case against Pomponio for perjury and its case against McDermott, that Pomponio could only be guilty on the substantive insider trading counts if McDermott also were guilty, and that McDermott conceded having given some public information to Gannon, the potential for spillover was substantial.

In light of this prejudice, we reverse the judgement of conviction against McDermott, and remand for new trial on the substantive counts.

NOTES AND QUESTIONS

1. *Strategy*. The government will often prove a conspiracy charge based on the interaction of the defendants, asking the jury to infer that apparently coordinated conduct demonstrates the existence of an agreement. The problem is that proof of the commission of the object is not sufficient in itself to prove the agreement. Even if there is an agreement to commit a crime, the fact that different actors committed the same crime does not prove that they entered an agreement. Because the government's proof is usually circumstantial, the courts struggle with determining the scope of an agreement, and whether all the defendants entered into a common agreement. The determination of the scope of the conspiratorial agreement may be crucial because the government is required to prove the offense it charges in its indictment or information. If it charges one conspiracy when in fact there were two separate agreements, then there may be a fatal variance between the charge and the proof adduced at trial, requiring reversal of a conspiracy conviction. In addition, if the government fails to prove that the defendants were members of the same conspiracy, then the evidence against one defendant would not be admissible against another defendant who was not a member of the conspiracy, and the prejudicial effect of that evidence may result in a reversal of a conviction for the substantive offense.

2. *Wheels and Chains*. If a drug dealer sells drugs to five different purchasers, is there a single conspiracy to sell drugs, with six people agreeing, or are there five separate conspiracies that share a common seller and target offense, but not a single agreement? Is there a single conspiracy when one person imports the drugs, a second purchases and repackages them for distribution, a third takes a portion of the imported drugs and arranges for the sales to end-users? In looking at whether there is a single conspiracy or multiple conspiracy, the courts have described how the agreement can be viewed in different ways, using the metaphors of a "wheel" conspiracy – with a hub and spokes – and a "chain" conspiracy. In *Kotteakos v. United States*, 328 U.S. 750 (1946), the Court reversed the conspiracy conviction for a wheel conspiracy involving a central "hub" figure, whose associates were the "spokes." In *Blumenthal v. United States*, 332 U.S. 539 (1947), the Court upheld a conviction involving a chain conspiracy, with several "links" leading linearly from a source; each link may not know the entire chain, but the links eventually lead back to the source. In *United States v. Payne*, 99 F.3d 1273 (5th Cir. 1996), the court discussed the problem of attaching the proper label to the conspiracy to determine whether it was a single ("chain") or multiple ("wheel") conspiracy:

> [Defendant] may be correct that the conspiracy in this case does not fit neatly into either the wheel or chain theory. He obtains no relief from the fact, however, because our Circuit has rejected such artificial categories in analyzing conspiracies. As Judge Brown said over 20 years ago, "conspiracies are as complex as the versatility of human nature and federal protection against them is not to be measured by spokes, hubs,

wheels, rims, chains or any one or all of today's galaxy of mechanical molecular or atomic forces."

3. ***Knowledge of Other Conspirators***. Courts frequently assert that the conspirators need not know one another to participate in the same agreement. Similarly, Model Penal Code § 5.03(2) provides that if a conspirator "knows that a person with whom he conspires to commit a crime has conspired with another person or persons to commit the same crime, he is guilty of conspiring with such other person or persons, whether or not he knows their identity, to commit such crime." In some conspiracies, ignorance of the exact identity of other members – especially the ringleaders – is desired to limit the damage if one or more members are arrested and cooperate with the government. To be members of the *same* conspiracy, however, each person must know that others are involved in the criminal enterprise, and that those unknown participants are a functional part of the conspiracy. While the court in *McDermott* noted that McDermott and Pomponio never met, that was not dispositive until the government failed to prove that agreement contemplated the involvement of other participants in the insider trading aside from Gannon.

4. ***When Does a Conspiracy End?*** In *Krulewitch v. United States*, 336 U.S. 440 (1949), the government tried to introduce the statement of an alleged conspirator urging a cover-up of the participation of another conspirator after they had been arrested. The government argued that any statements designed to conceal the existence of a conspiracy are part of the conspiracy, and therefore the conspiracy continues so long as it is not exposed and the later statements can be used to establish its existence. The Court rejected the government's proposed expansion of every conspiracy, stating:

> The Government now asks us to expand this narrow exception to the hearsay rule and hold admissible a declaration, not made in furtherance of the alleged criminal transportation conspiracy charged, but made in furtherance of an alleged implied but uncharged conspiracy aimed at preventing detection and punishment. No federal court case cited by the Government suggests so hospitable a reception to the use of the hearsay evidence to convict in conspiracy cases. * * * The rule contended for by the Government could have far-reaching results. For under this rule plausible arguments could generally be made in conspiracy cases that most out-of-court statements offered in evidence tended to shield co-conspirators. We are not persuaded to adopt the Government's implicit conspiracy theory which in all criminal conspiracy cases would create automatically a further breach of the general rule against the admission of hearsay evidence.

§ 13.05 Proof of the Conspiracy: Co-Conspirator Statements

A significant benefit for prosecutors proving the existence of a conspiracy is that any statements made by one conspirator during the course of the conspiracy and in furtherance of the conspiracy can be used as evidence against every other member of the conspiracy. Federal Rule of Evidence 801(d)(2)(E) provides an exception to the hearsay rule, that "a statement by a co-conspirator of a party during the course and in furtherance of the conspiracy" is admissible evidence. This expands the range of relevant evidence available to prove the existence of the conspiracy and the participation of others in it. For example, a statement by one conspirator that another person has joined the enterprise can be used to prove the second person's guilt, even though that person never said anything about the conspiracy and there may be no other evidence of the person's participation. Can the statement of one conspirator, standing alone, establish the existence of a conspiracy? Federal Rule of Evidence 801(d)(2) provides that "[t]he contents of the statement shall be considered but are not alone sufficient to establish . . . the existence of the conspiracy and the participation therein of the declarant and the party against whom the statement is offered under subdivision (E)."

United States v. Gajo
290 F.3d 922 (7th Cir. 2002)

FLAUM, Chief Judge.

A jury convicted Defendant-Appellant Bogdan Gajo of conspiracy to commit arson in violation of 18 U.S.C. § 371 * * *. Gajo appeals his conviction, challenging two evidentiary rulings related to the admission of tape recorded statements * * *. For the reasons stated herein, we affirm.

Gajo owned a business called Cragin Sausage, which sold specialty ethnic foods, beverages and cigarettes. On January 16, 1996, the building where Cragin Sausage was located caught fire and burned moderately. The fire was concentrated in the rear kitchen and storage area of Cragin Sausage. After the fire was safely extinguished, Daniel Cullen, who worked in the Fire Department's Office of Fire Investigation, examined the property and concluded that the fire was deliberately set. Traces of gasoline were present in debris samples taken from the scene, even though there was no gasoline present in the store prior to the fire. In addition, Cragin Sausage's rear southwest door, which was the only door open at the time of the fire, exhibited marks indicating that the locks had been pried off from the inside in an attempt to simulate a forced entry. * * * Only Gajo and his girlfriend, Maria Grazina Curylo, had keys to Cragin Sausage. They were also the only two people who knew the code to the store's security system, which never activated during the fire. Approximately one week after the fire, Gajo submitted an insurance claim for the damage at Cragin Sausage. Gajo later submitted a proof of loss. The insurance company eventually denied Gajo's claim * * *.

During the arson investigation, government agents examined Cragin Sausage's outgoing telephone records, which led them to an individual named Jay Smith. Agents questioned Smith, who ultimately agreed to cooperate with the government. Smith recounted that in December 1995, a former coworker named Edward Baumgart approached Smith at his place of employment (the Banks Grill) and introduced him to Gajo. According to Smith, Baumgart told him that "Gajo needed a building burned down." Smith also stated that although Gajo spoke almost exclusively in Polish, Gajo told him in English that burning down Cragin Sausage "was urgent." Gajo and Baumgart offered Smith $4,000 to set fire to Cragin Sausage, but Smith declined. [Several real estate agents testified that Gajo was desperate to sell the business, and one agent testified that Gajo suggested that the agent burn down Cragin Sausage to obtain insurance proceeds. Gajo told government agents that he left the building on Sunday at 4:00 p.m., but others testified they saw Gajo at the building the day of the fire removing boxes of liquor, which he subsequently reported missing in the fire. Gajo submitted evidence that he received a substantial settlement after the death of his wife and did not have a need for money.]

Approximately 10 months after the fire, Smith contacted Baumgart at the direction of a federal agent. Smith and Baumgart engaged in two conversations, each of which was recorded and ultimately introduced into evidence. On the first tape, Baumgart responds to Smith's probing about what he should say to an agent questioning him about the fire at Cragin Sausage. Baumgart instructs Smith to tell the investigating officer "To fuck off." In the second conversation, which occurred several minutes later, Baumgart admits introducing Gajo to Smith, but states the he does not know who burned Cragin Sausage:

SMITH: This guy you introduced me to.

BAUMGART: Uh huh.

SMITH: . . .is he going to put me in a bad spot?

BAUMGART: He's not going to put you in a bad spot, because if he would he's gonna go to jail. OK.

SMITH: Alright. OK. Alright.

BAUMGART: Cause right now he doing all he can to get -

SMITH:. . .for my benefit what was the asshole's name?

BAUMGART: Gajo.

SMITH: Gajo, alright.

BAUMGART: G, A, J, O.

SMITH: Alright.

BAUMGART: Bogdan.

Later in the second tape, Baumgart further instructed Smith about how to respond if investigating agents asked who set the fire. Baumgart stated, "Well, you, you, you weren't there. I wasn't there." Baumgart also told Smith, " You don't know a motherfuckin' thing. Neither do I." [On cross-examination, Smith made statements inconsistent with his testimony on direct examination regarding what language Gajo spoke in when discussing the arson.]

[W]e believe the district court properly admitted the tape recorded conversations between Baumgart and Smith. * * * [A] statement is not hearsay and admissible under FRE 801 (d)(2)(E) if it is made by a coconspirator "during the course and in furtherance of the conspiracy." To be admissible, then, the government must establish by a preponderance of the evidence two requirements: (1) a conspiracy existed at the time of the statements between the defendant and the declarant, and (2) the statements contributed to the ultimate goal of the conspiracy. *Bourjaily v. United States*, 483 U.S. 171 (1987). In this case, Gajo challenges whether a conspiracy existed after the fire at Cragin Sausage and whether the statements are "in furtherance of "the conspiracy's ultimate criminal objective.

We first address whether the conspiracy existed at the time of the tape recorded conversations. By the time Smith contacted Baumgart at the behest of an ATF agent, ten months had passed since the fire at Cragin Sausage. Relying on *Grunewald v. United States*, 353 U.S. 391 (1957), and its progeny, Gajo argues that the time lapse between the fire and the statements rendered the conspiracy to commit arson complete at the time of the Baumgart-Smith conversations. *Grunewald* held that the act of concealment typically is not part of a conspiracy's primary criminal objective. Once the coconspirators achieve the goals of the conspiracy, statements concerning acts of concealment (or to avoid punishment) are generally inadmissible. However, this principle does not extend easily to the arson-for-profit context. In *United States v. Xheka,* 704 F.2d 974 (7th Cir.1983), we held that the primary goal of a conspiracy involving arson is not only to destroy a building by fire, but also to obtain the insurance proceeds. In other words, unlike most other criminal conspiracies, concealment is actually one of the main criminal objectives of an arson-for-profit scheme, because it facilitates the primary objective of fraudulently acquiring insurance proceeds.

Based on the foregoing, resolution of this issue would be clear except for one additional factor. The record in this case does not reveal when Gajo's insurance company denied his claim or whether the claim remained pending at the time of the Baumgart-Smith statements. Despite this absence, there was sufficient evidence to find that the conspiracy to obtain the insurance proceeds was ongoing 10 months after the fire. First, in August 1996, Gajo gave deposition testimony in a civil lawsuit related to the fire at Cragin Sausage and Gajo's insurance claims. Second, Baumgart made at least one statement in October 1996 – "It looks like the fuckin' case is still going on" – that suggests the conspiracy was ongoing. Third, there is no dispute that at the time of the October 1996 conversations "Gajo had not yet received [the] insurance proceeds." In contrast, the only evidence that the conspiracy had ended was the parties' stipulation that the insurance company had denied Gajo's claim sometime after he submitted a proof of loss on July 3, 1996. But this stipulation lacked a specific date, rendering it irrelevant to the question of whether the conspiracy existed at the time of the tape recorded conversations. From this evidence, the district court was within its discretion to conclude that a conspiracy still existed at the time of the Baumgart-Smith conversations.

We next address whether Baumgart's statements were "in furtherance of" the conspiracy – an inquiry that requires examination of the statements' content. We consider statements to be "in furtherance of" the conspiracy when they promote the conspiracies objectives, *Bourjaily*, i.e., when the statements are "part of the information flow between conspirators to help each perform a role." In this case, Gajo objects to the admission of two statements, each of which relates to Baumgart's attempts to instruct Smith to remain quiet about the meeting between Baumgart, Smith and Gajo. Gajo submits that although the conversations reveal "an attempt to cover what had transpired at the meeting," there is no indication that Baumgart was part of the conspiracy to obtain insurance proceeds.

We decline to accept Gajo's contention that the specific mention of insurance proceeds is a necessary condition for admissibility of a coconspirator's statements in this context. In our view, Gajo's assertion ignores one of the primary objectives of the crime in this case. As we have already discussed, an arson-for-profit scheme has two criminal objectives: the destruction of a building by fire and the attainment of insurance proceeds. However, a necessary corollary to the insurance scam is that the co-conspirators must conceal their illegal conduct from law enforcement and insurance investigators. Thus, Baumgart's statements advanced the conspiracy's goal of falsely acquiring insurance proceeds, but only in the sense that concealment was a necessary predicate to achieving that criminal objective. Because Baumgart's statements reflect an attempt to avoid detection, he was furthering one of the conspiracy's goals.

§ 13.06 Conspiracy and Liability for Substantive Crimes

PROBLEM FORTY-SIX

Terry ran around a corner and out of sight of the car when Paige and Pat emerged from the car. Paige and Pat caught up with Terry after chasing Terry for two blocks. When Terry tried to resist them, Paige took out a hunting knife, stabbed Terry in the chest, and Pat then took Terry's wallet. Paige and Pat returned to the car and Lynn drove away; they were arrested a short time after the attack. Terry died later that evening from the stab wound. Is Lynn liable for the death of Terry by agreeing to the robbery? What if Lynn specifically said that Paige and Pat should not use any violence against the victim?

United States v. Walls
225 F.3d 858 (7th Cir. 2000)

ROVNER, Circuit Judge.

Daisy Walls and Sharee S. Williams were convicted after a jury trial of conspiracy to possess with intent to distribute and conspiracy to distribute substances containing cocaine. * * * Williams was also convicted of knowingly possessing a firearm as a felon in violation of 18 U.S.C. § 922(g)(1).

On April 22, 1998, Federal Express ("FedEx") identified as suspicious two packages that were purportedly shipped by the Renaissance Electrical Supply Company in Los Angeles, California, for delivery to Tascam Electrical Supply Company at 9121 S. Colfax in Chicago, to the attention of Daisy Walls. FedEx employees conducted a field test on the contents of the packages, which revealed the presence of cocaine. [FedEx notified the DEA, which placed an electronic signal device in each package and conducted a controlled delivery of the drugs.] Agent Markhart * * * donned a FedEx uniform and drove to 9121 S. Colfax in a truck with FedEx markings. Approximately fifteen undercover agents dispersed in the area surrounding the residence. Agent Markhart arrived at 9121 S. Colfax (which was private residence) * * * As he approached the residence he passed two persons standing in front of it, and one of them yelled toward the house "Mama, your package is here." Daisy Walls ("Walls") answered his knock, and he apologized for the late delivery because the packages had been scheduled for delivery the previous day. When he requested a signature for the packages, Walls turned to a male standing just inside the door, who was later identified as her son Daniel Walls, and asked him to sign. He scrutinized Markhart and declined to sign. Walls then said "I'll sign the electric company." Until that time, Walls could not have seen the address labels on the packages and Agent Markhart had not mentioned that the addressee was an electrical company. Walls then examined the packages and signed Tascam Electric, DGW. During this exchange, Markhart noticed approximately 10-15 people in the front room of the house, apparently having a party. * * *

[Williams brought the packages from Walls' house to her house at 9127 S. Colfax. When the signal from one package ceased, the agents went to the house at 9121 S. Colfax and knocked on the door. After initially being denied entry, Walls allowed the agents to enter and told them "That this was the third time she had accepted similar packages, that she did not know what it contained the first time but that she opened the second one out of curiosity and discovered it contained cocaine, and that she knew the third package contained cocaine as well. Walls told the agents that the packages belonged to Delano Target, a member of the Gangster Disciples street gang."]

After arresting Walls, the agents brought Williams into the kitchen. She declared that she had nothing to hide and gave written consent for the search of her basement apartment at 9127 S. Colfax. A search of the basement apartment revealed: A clear plastic bag containing marijuana in a dresser drawer; approximately $4000 in U.S. currency inside a basket of clothes; approximately $1000 in U.S. currency in a safe; and a box of rubber gloves, tinfoil, plastic bags, white powder, paper masks, and a digital scale, all of a type used in packaging and weighing cocaine for sale, on or near the kitchen table. In addition, the search yielded a Ravens Arms .25 caliber firearm in a dresser drawer of the bedroom. A photograph taken by the agents revealed some clothes next to the firearm, which appeared to be boxer shorts and a tie or possibly a scarf. At the DEA office, Williams acknowledged her *Miranda* rights and signed a written statement declaring that she was at Walls' house when the package arrived, that she saw the package on the table knew it contained drugs but did not know the type or quantity, and that Walls wanted the packages removed from her house and she volunteered to take them to her home. A jury convicted Walls and Williams on all charges. * * *

Williams * * * attacks her conviction for possession of a firearm as a felon under 18 U.S.C. § 922(g)(1). In order to obtain a conviction for felon-in-possession under that provision, the government must establish beyond a reasonable doubt that (1) the defendant had a previous felony conviction, (2) the defendant possessed a firearm, and (3) the firearm had traveled in or affected interstate commerce. Only the possession element is at issue here. It is well-established that possession under that statute may be demonstrated through either actual or constructive possession. Actual possession is demonstrated if a person knowingly has direct physical control over a thing at a given time. Where that direct physical contact is lacking, a defendant may nevertheless have constructive possession if she "knowingly has the power and the intention at a given time to exercise dominion and control over an object, either directly or through others." *United States v. Hunte*, 196 F.3d. 687 (7th Cir. 1999). Those means of establishing possession are uncontroversial and were pursued by the government in this case. In addition, however, the government also sought to prove the element of possession under a theory of vicarious liability premised on the Supreme Court's decision in *Pinkerton v. United States*, 328 U.S. 640 (1946). Under that theory, Williams could be found guilty of possessing the firearm as a felon even if she lacked either actual or constructive possession, as long as another member of the conspiracy possessed a gun. The government made no real effort to produce any evidence regarding the co-conspirator who possessed the firearm. Williams' defense theory, however, appeared to be that Samuel Simmons, Walls' son, was the one involved in the drug dealing and that Williams was unaware of it. The government presumably proffered the *Pinkerton* instruction for the proposition that if Williams did not possess the gun found in her apartment, the her roommate, Samuel Simmons, must have possessed it and that he was a co-conspirator because she attributed the drugs to him. Williams objected to the submission of the *Pinkerton* instruction to the jury, but the court ruled in the government's favor.

In order to properly determine the applicability of *Pinkerton* to this case, we must examine the basis for the *Pinkerton* ruling. The holding in *Pinkerton* flowed from a number of established propositions. First, a person may be convicted both for a conspiracy and a substantive offense, and "it is not material that overt acts charged in the conspiracy count were also charged and proved as substantive offenses." Second, an overt act of one conspirator may be the act of all without any new agreement specifically directed to that act. The Court then considered whether a conspirator could be found guilty of the substantive offense committed by a co-conspirator in furtherance of the conspiracy. It held that the governing principle should be the same where the overt acts in the conspiracy constitute a substantive offense, and that a conspirator could be convicted of the substantive offence committed by a co-conspirator as long as the offense was committed in furtherance of the conspiracy, fell within the scope of the unlawful project, and was reasonably foreseeable as a necessary or natural consequence of the unlawful agreement.

In accordance with that reasoning, we have held that

> the jury [asked to decide a case number under the *Pinkerton* doctrine] must be made to focus on the coconspirator's act, on whether it is a crime, on whether the coconspirator's guilt of this crime was proved beyond a reasonable doubt, and on whether it was committed in furtherance of the conspiracy in which the defendant participated.

United States v. Manzella, 791 F.2d 1263 (7th Cir. 1986). The government's use of *Pinkerton* in this case takes this one step farther in that it seeks *Pinkerton* liability based in part upon acts by a co-conspirator that did not constitute the crime. There are no allegations that a co-conspirator was guilty of violating § 922(g)(1). Instead, the government uses a cut-and-paste approach, taking the firearm possession by one conspirator, adding it to the felon status of another conspirator, and thereby creating a substantive offense for that second conspirator. It is a significant expansion of the *Pinkerton* doctrine that appears to be difficult to limit.

For instance, under such a use of *Pinkerton*, even lawful possession of a firearm by a conspirator could presumably be used to establish a § 922(g)(1) violation for a co-conspirator who is a felon. Moreover, one can easily imagine a large-scale conspiracy, in which a conspirator's possession of a firearm in California is used to obtain a felon-in-possession conviction of a co-conspirator in Illinois. This seems far afield from the purpose of the felon-in-possession prohibition, which is to "keep firearms away from the persons Congress classified as potentially irresponsible and dangerous." It is an unwarranted, and possibly unconstitutional, expansion of the *Pinkerton* doctrine. *See United States v. Castaneda*, 9 F.3d 761 (9th Cir. 1993) ("due process constrains the application of *Pinkerton* where the relationship between the defendant and the substantive offense is slight").

Finally, the felon-in-possession statute seems a particularly inappropriate vehicle for such an expanded use of *Pinkerton* liability. It criminalizes conduct that could otherwise be lawful based upon the status of the person engaging in that conduct. * * * The firearm in the hands of a non-felon (who lacks the criminal conviction that betrays a proclivity to threaten public safety) could be used to impose vicarious criminal liability on a felon (who lacks the firearm that threatens the public). The danger to the public rationale underlying the statute thus ceases to be relevant.

Theoretically, the application of *Pinkerton* here would also invite the future inverse use of the doctrine to attribute a felon's possession of a firearm to his non-felon co-conspirator. A non-felon could be deemed guilty of being a felon in possession of a firearm. That ridiculous prospect reveals the fundamental problem with extending *Pinkerton* liability to the felon-in-possession statute. Because § 922(g)(1) defines the offense in terms of the status of the individual possessing the firearm, the vicarious liability provisions of *Pinkerton* are inappropriate for such an offense. Accordingly, the district court erred in submitting the *Pinkerton* instruction to the jury on the § 922(g)(1) charge.

NOTES AND QUESTIONS

1. *Scope of* **Pinkerton.** The *Pinkerton* rule has broad implications, to all conspirators, of liability for substantive crimes committed by any conspirator, with or without the participation or even knowledge of the other conspirators, if committed during and in furtherance of the conspiracy. Under *Pinkerton*, the co-conspirator's offense must also be *reasonably foreseeable*. *Pinkerton* is a notoriously vague doctrine that permits prosecutors to attribute a number of

offenses to each member of the conspiracy regardless of that person's connection to the offense conduct. In *Pinkerton*, the Supreme Court distinguished the case in which a conspirator commits a crime that is not "in furtherance" of the conspiracy from one that "could not be reasonably foreseen." Is there ay real difference between these two requirements? Will the government's evidence that a crime is "in furtherance" of the agreement essentially demonstrate the foreseeability of that crime? How often will a crime be in furtherance but not foreseeable, or vice-versa?

2. *Rationale of the* **Pinkerton Rule.** In *State v. Coltherst*, 820 A.2d 1024 (Conn. 2003) the Connecticut Supreme Court explained the rationale for the *Pinkerton* doctrine in this way:

> We conclude that the *Pinkerton* doctrine constitutionally may be, and, as a matter of state policy, should be, applied in cases in which the defendant did not have the level of intent required by the substantive offense with which he was charged. The rationale for the doctrine is to deter collective criminal agreement and to protect the public from its inherent dangers by holding conspirators responsible for the natural and probable – not just the intended – results of their conspiracy. This court previously has recognized that "[c]ombination in crime makes more likely the commission of crimes unrelated to the original purpose for which the group was formed. In sum, the danger which a conspiracy generates is not confined to the substantive offense which is the immediate aim of the enterprise." (Internal quotation marks omitted.) *State v. Robinson*, 567 A.2d 1173 (Conn. 1989). In other words, one natural and probable result of a criminal conspiracy is the commission of originally unintended crimes. When the defendant has "played a necessary part in setting in motion a discrete course of criminal conduct" * * * he cannot reasonably complain that it is unfair to hold him vicariously liable, under the *Pinkerton* doctrine, for the natural and probable results of that conduct that, although he did not intend, he should have foreseen.

3. *Rejection of the* **Pinkerton Rule.** Many states do not accept the *Pinkerton* rule. They reject the authority to prove the defendant's guilt for a substantive offense solely on the ground that he was a member of a conspiracy and the crime was foreseeable. *See Bolden v. State*, 124 P.3d 191 (Nev. 2005); *State v. Nevarez*, 130 P.3d 1154 (Idaho Ct. App. 2005); *State v. Stein,* 27 P.3d 184 (Wash. 2001); *State ex rel. Woods v. Cohen,* 844 P.2d 1147 (Ariz. 1992); *State v. Lind*, 322 N.W.2d 826 (N.D. 1982). Model Penal Code § 2.06(3) rejects *Pinkerton* liability and limits a defendant's potential liability to substantive crimes in which the conspirator was an accomplice to that offense, discussed in the following Chapter. In *Cohen*, the Arizona Supreme Court explained how accomplice liability would work in the context of a conspiracy charge in which *Pinkerton* is not available:

It may well be an unusual conspirator who stops at the purely hypothetical agreement stage at which the conspiracy is committed, without doing something to promote the crime agreed upon and thus becoming an accomplice to it. Because of the broad reach of accomplice liability, our holding does not prevent the conviction of those who are culpable for the substantive offenses committed in furtherance of a conspiracy. It simply prevents a conspirator, who is not also an accomplice, from being held liable for a potentially limitless number of criminal acts which, though later determined to be "foreseeable," are at the time of their commission totally beyond the conspirator's knowledge and control. The conspirator, nevertheless, remains liable from the crime of conspiracy.

4. ***Proving the Conspiracy***. Note that while *Pinkerton* creates liability for every member of the conspiracy, the government is not required to charge a conspiracy to invoke the doctrine. *Pinkerton* is a rule of vicarious liability for the criminal act of other conspirators, as *Walls* discusses, and it applies regardless of whether the government actually charges the conspiracy offense. Like proof of any criminal offense, the government must establish the elements of the conspiracy beyond a reasonable doubt, so prosecutors usually charge the offense.

Chapter 14
Accomplice Liability

§ 14.01   Actus Reus

State v. Barnum
14 S.W.3d 587 (Mo. 2000)

WILLIAM RAY PRICE, JR., J.

Norma Barnum ("Appellant") was convicted of assault in the first degree, in violation of section 565.050, RSMo 1994, as an accomplice in the beating of Candis West. She appeals raising the following * * * [issue]: (1) whether the evidence was sufficient to support the conviction; * * * We affirm. * * *

At about 1:00 a.m. on August 11, 1997, fourteen-year-old Candis West snuck out of her home and went to visit her boyfriend, Brandon Srader. When she arrived at the Srader residence, Brandon was not home but Appellant, his nineteen-year-old sister, was. Candis and Appellant decided to go for a walk. When they returned at approximately 2:00 a.m., Brandon and Christina Cassidy, Jessica Griffin, Heather Belt, Travis Laster, and Michael Jackson were at the Srader home. Candis did not know Christina, Jessica, or Heather, but quickly discovered that Brandon had begun a relationship with Jessica. Candis told Christina and Heather she was upset with Brandon's involvement with Jessica.

Christina and Heather told Jessica what Candis had said. The three girls concocted a plan to take Candis somewhere and beat her up. Everyone at the house, except for Candis and Michael, was aware of the girls' intention to attack Candis. The original plan was to carry out the beating at Wal-Mart. Travis drove Brandon, Candis, Jessica, Christina, Heather, and Appellant to the Wal-Mart store where the girls used the bathroom. The attack did not begin, however, because Travis secretly told the other girls that he knew of a better spot for the beating. Travis then drove the entire group to a low-water bridge in Pettis County, Missouri.

As everyone got out of the vehicle, Christina hit Candis in the face and began pulling her hair. Candis did not fight back but instead fell to the ground. As Christina began to kick Candis, Jessica and Heather joined in. Over the course of one hour, the three girls dragged Candis by her hair over the concrete, attempted to burn her hair with a lighter, forced her to remove all her clothing, spanked her with her shoes, threw her into the water, and tossed her clothes in after her. Brandon, Travis, and Appellant stood and watched the entire assault on Candis.

At some point, Appellant, who was laughing during the beating, yelled, "yeah, yeah, let's kill her, kill her . . . run her over with the van." Eventually, Travis told Christina, Jessica, and Heather that it was time to stop. The group returned to the vehicle, leaving Candis in the water, and Christina warned Candis that if she moved, they would come back and kill her. Appellant accompanied the group as they left, making no attempt to assist Candis or get medical assistance for her.

Candis, naked and severely beaten, was eventually able to stop a passing car. The driver gave her a flannel shirt and a jacket, and drove her to the police station in Sedalia. The police briefly spoke to Candis, photographed her injuries, and called for an ambulance. Before leaving to go to the hospital, Candis gave Sgt. Mike Koenig the names and addresses of the individuals involved in the attack. Sgt. Koenig's investigation uncovered Candis' clothing and jewelry under the bridge. Travis, Appellant, and "three other white female juveniles" were arrested.

At the hospital, Candis was treated for a crushed eye bone, a broken nose, and two broken ribs. Candis was later sent by ambulance to a hospital in Columbia where more X-rays and a CAT scan were performed. Eventually, she had to have reconstructive surgery on her eye socket, and was plagued by vision problems and headaches.

Appellant was charged with the first-degree assault of Candis West under an accomplice liability theory and was tried before a jury on February 25, 1998. * * * The jury found Appellant guilty of assault in the first degree and recommended a sentence of ten years imprisonment. The court sentenced Appellant in accordance with the jury's recommendation.

The law of accessory liability emanates from statute, as construed by the courts. "A person is criminally responsible for the conduct of another when either before or during the commission of an offense, with the purpose of promoting the commission of the offense, he aids or agrees to aid or attempts to aid such other person in planning, committing or attempting to commit the offense." * * * This subsection is designed to make individuals who could not be guilty of a crime solely on the basis of their own conduct, guilty nonetheless as an accessory. * * *

Appellant argues that because she did not actively participate in the planning or actual beating of Candis, and because the attackers did not act directly on the suggestions she shouted during the attack, the evidence was insufficient to support her conviction of first-degree assault. Where there is a challenge to the sufficiency of the evidence, "the evidence together with all reasonable inferences is viewed favorably to the verdict and evidence or inferences to the contrary are ignored."
* * *

Missouri eliminated the distinction between principals and accessories in 1979, and it is now the law that all persons who act in concert are equally guilty. * * * The doctrine of accomplice liability embodied in section 562.041.1(2) "comprehends any of a potentially wide variety of actions intended by an individual to assist another in criminal conduct." The evidence need not show the defendant personally committed every element of the crime. * * *

While mere presence at a crime scene, considered alone or in combination with a refusal to interfere, is insufficient to support a conviction, "the broad concept of 'aiding and abetting' plainly encompasses acts that could be construed as 'encouragement' or its derivation." * * * Mere encouragement is enough. * * * Encouragement is the equivalent of conduct that "by any means countenances or approves the criminal action of another." * * * "Countenances or approves" includes "encouraging or exciting [a criminal act] by words, gestures, looks, or signs." * * * In fact, associating with those that committed the crime before, during, or after its occurrence, acting as part of a show of force in the commission of the crime, attempting flight from the crime scene, or failing to assist the victim or seek medical help are all factors which may be considered. * * *

The direct evidence and inferences favorable to the verdict show the evidence was sufficient to convict Appellant of assault in the first degree. It was testified that Appellant was present during the planning of the attack on Candis. It is undisputed that Appellant accompanied the attackers and Candis to Wal-Mart and to the area under the low-water bridge where the beating took place. Appellant stood and watched the entire attack, laughing. Travis Laster testified that during the beating, Appellant stated, "just kill her" and near the end of the attack, "just run her over with the van." Candis testified Appellant stated, "yeah, yeah, let's kill her, let's kill her, let's run her over with the car — or the van." Either version shows clear support and encouragement of the attack. Appellant got back in the van with the attackers when the beating ended and left Candis beaten, naked, and alone.

Appellant argues that because the three attackers did not carry out her suggestion of running Candis over with the van, that her words did not encourage them. We disagree. Appellant's statements certainly could be found by the jury to be words of general encouragement during the beating and they, combined with the other facts of Appellant's participation, adequately support the jury's verdict. * * * For the reasons stated above, we affirm the judgement (sic) of the trial court. * * *

————————————————

NOTES AND QUESTIONS

1. *Generally*. Many crimes involve multiple parties to the course of conduct, and assessing the liability of each is an important facet of the criminal law. For example, A enlists B and C to rob a bank. A plans the bank robbery, B drives the getaway car, and C enters the bank with a pistol and takes the money. What is the liability of A, B, and C for the bank robbery? Can all three be convicted of bank robbery even though only one actually entered the bank with a weapon?

> The answer is provided by a set of rules for accomplice liability. These rules require distinguishing the basis for liability through an assessment of each participant's particular role in the offense. A basic principle of accomplice liability is that the liability of one person may be derivative of the criminal conduct of another person. Under this analysis, a person who provides some aid for a crime, such as driving the getaway vehicle from a robbery or shouting encouragement to an assailant, can be convicted of the same offense as the person who actually robs the store or beats the victim. Returning to the bank robbery hypothetical above, this means that A (who planned the robbery) and B (who drove the getaway car) may be convicted of bank robbery and punished to the same extent as C (who actually robbed the bank). In other words, accomplice liability principles result in convicting A, B, and C of bank robbery, as if each had entered the bank with the pistol.

ELLEN S. PODGOR, PETER J. HENNING, & NEIL P. COHEN, MASTERING CRIMINAL LAW § 13A (2008).

2. *Common Law.* The common law categorized participants in crime by a set of complex and rigid categories:

> Persons associated in some way in the commission of a crime were classified as principals and accessories. These classifications in turn were broken down into the categories of principals in the first and second degree and accessories before and after the fact. The designation of principal in the first degree was applied to the actual perpetrator of the crime, while the characterization of principal in the second degree pertained to one who was present, either actually or constructively, at the scene of the crime assisting in some fashion the principal in the first degree. The rank of accessory before the fact was attached to one who, though not present at the scene of the offense, counseled, advised, or directed commission of the crime, while one who, knowing a crime had been committed, aided or assisted the felon in escaping capture and prosecution was denominated an accessory after the fact.

State v. Gladstone, 474 P.2d 274 (Wash. 1970).

3. ***Modern Statutory Approach.*** The modern approach used by state statutes eliminates the distinction between principals and accessories before the fact, treating them all as principals in the crime and imposing the same punishment. This approach is also used in the federal system. For example, a federal statute, 18 U.S.C. § 2(a), provides: "[w]hoever commits an offense against the United States or aids, abets, counsels, commands, induces or procures its commission, is punishable as a principal." Note that accessory liability is a means to prove a person committed a crime, but it is not a separate offense; that is, a defendant is not guilty of aiding and abetting, the person is guilty of the crime for which he provided assistance or encouragement.

4. ***Accessory After the Fact.*** Some states and the federal system have a separate criminal statute for an accessory after the fact, removing this category of conduct from principals and accomplices of the substantive offense. The federal statute provides: "[w]hoever, knowing that an offense against the United States has been committed, receives, relieves, comforts or assists the offender in order to hinder or prevent his apprehension, trial or punishment, is an accessory after the fact." The Ninth Circuit explained the distinction between aiding a crime — or conspiring to commit one–and being an accessory after the fact in *United States v. Graves*, 143 F.3d 1185 (9th Cir. 1998):

> [T]here is a critical difference between the nature of the crime of being an accessory after the fact and the nature of the crime of being either an aider and abettor or a conspirator. One who acts as an accessory after the fact does not participate in the commission of the primary offense. Instead, an accessory is one who provides assistance to the offender by helping him to avoid apprehension or prosecution after he has already committed an offense. Accordingly, an accessory does not incur liability as a principal. For this reason, the offense of accessory after the fact is considered a far less serious offense than the primary offense, and the accessory, who has not played a role in the actual commission of an offense, is considered far less culpable than one who has participated in the commission of the offense. In fact, the accessory after the fact statute specifically limits the punishment for that offense to no more than half of the punishment prescribed for the primary offense.

In *State v. Budik*, 272 P.3d 81 (Wash. 2012), the Washington Supreme Court held that the State's rendering criminal assistance statute required an affirmative act by the defendant, and mere denial of knowledge about a crime or failure to disclose information to the police was not, standing alone, sufficient to prove a conviction.

5. ***Proving Accessory Liability.*** Where the government charges only on an accomplice theory, it must prove that the person provided some assistance — common terms are "aid, abet, counsel, or encourage"— in the commission of the offense by the primary violator — the principal — and acted with the requisite

intent for the commission of the target offense. Mere presence at the scene of the crime is considered insufficient.

6. **Proving a Principal Committed a Crime.** In order to aid and abet a crime, a principal must have committed the offense. That does not, however, mean that the principal must be *convicted* of the crime. "Although a defendant may not be convicted of aiding and abetting if the guilt of the principal has not been shown, the identity of the principal is not necessary if the existence of a guilty principal is proven." *People v. Wilson*, 493 N.W.2d 471 (Mich. Ct. App. 1993). Even if the principal is not charged with the crime, a person may be convicted of aiding and abetting the offense. "The failure to prosecute or obtain a prior conviction of a principal, such as where he may have been granted immunity or pleaded to a lesser offense, does not preclude conviction of the aider and abettor, as long as the commission of the crime by a principal is proved." *United States v. Ruffin*, 613 F.2d 408 (2d Cir. 1979).

The Model Penal Code rule is, however, to the contrary, holding the accomplice liable, albeit for an attempt, even if the principal never even tries to commit the crime. Model Penal Code § 5.01(3) states:

> *Conduct Designed to Aid Another in Commission of a Crime.* A person who engages in conduct designed to aid another to commit a crime that would establish his complicity under Section 2.06 if the crime were committed by such other person, is guilty of an attempt to commit the crime, although the crime is not committed or attempted by such other person.

Thus, if A, incorrectly believing that B plans to rob a bank, anonymously leaves a gun on B's door step for B to use in the supposed robbery, but B never finds the gun and never planned to commit a robbery anyway, B is guilty of nothing but A is guilty of *attempted* robbery under the MPC. A engaged in conduct *designed* to aid another (whether he or she actually succeeds in aiding being irrelevant under the MPC) in committing the robbery, and that is all that MPC § 5.01(3) requires. By contrast, under the common law, neither A nor B would be guilty of any crime whatsoever.

7. **Acquittal of the Principal.** If a court or jury acquits the person charged as a principal, can another person be convicted of aiding and abetting that principal in the commission of the offense? The common law rule was that an acquittal of the principal prevented conviction of the accessory because, logically, no crime was committed that one could assist. As the Supreme Court explained in *Standefer v. United States*, 477 U.S. 10 (1980), this approach has been abandoned by statutory changes to the scope of accessory liability:

Because at early common law all parties to a felony received the death penalty, certain procedural rules developed tending to shield accessories from punishment. * * * Among them was one of special relevance to this case: the rule that an accessory could not be convicted without the prior conviction of the principal offender. * * * Under this rule, the principal's flight, death, or acquittal barred prosecution of the accessory. And if the principal were pardoned or his conviction reversed on appeal, the accessory's conviction could not stand. In every way "an accessory follow[ed], like a shadow, his principal." * * *

This procedural bar applied only to the prosecution of accessories in felony cases. In misdemeanor cases, where all participants were deemed principals, a prior acquittal of the actual perpetrator did not prevent the subsequent conviction of a person who rendered assistance. * * * And in felony cases a principal in the second degree could be convicted notwithstanding the prior acquittal of the first-degree principal. * * * Not surprisingly, considerable effort was expended in defining the categories–in determining, for instance, when a person was "constructively present" so as to be a second-degree principal. * * * In the process, justice all too frequently was defeated.

To overcome these judge-made rules, statutes were enacted in England and in the United States. In 1848 the Parliament enacted a statute providing that an accessory before the fact could be "indicted, tried, convicted, and punished in all respects *like the principal*." * * * As interpreted, the statute permitted an accessory to be convicted "although the principal be acquitted." * * * Several state legislatures followed suit. In 1899, Congress joined this growing reform movement with the enactment of a general penal code for Alaska which abrogated the common-law distinctions and provided that "all persons concerned in the commission of a crime, whether it be felony or misdemeanor, and whether they directly commit the act constituting the crime or aid and abet in its commission, though not present, are principals, and to be tried and punished as such." Act of Mar. 3, 1899, § 186, 30 Stat. 1282. In 1901, Congress enacted a similar provision for the District of Columbia.

The enactment of 18 U.S.C. § 2 in 1909 was part and parcel of this same reform movement. The language of the statute, as enacted, unmistakably demonstrates the point:

"Whoever directly commits any act constituting an offense defined in any law of the United States, or aids, abets, counsels, commands, induces, or procures its commission, *is a principal*." Act of Mar. 4, 1909, § 332, 35 Stat. 1152 (emphasis added).* * *

The statute "abolishe[d] the distinction between principals and accessories and [made] them all principals." *Hammer v. United States*, 271 U.S. 620 (1926). Read against its common-law background, the provision evinces a clear intent to permit the conviction of accessories to federal criminal offenses despite the prior acquittal of the actual perpetrator of the offense. It gives general effect to what had always been the rule for second-decree principals and for all misdemeanants. * * *

This history plainly rebuts petitioner's contention that § 2 was not intended to authorize conviction of an aider and abettor after the principal had been acquitted of the offense charged. With the enactment of that section, all participants in conduct violating a federal criminal statute are "principals." As such, they are punishable for their criminal conduct; the fate of other participants is irrelevant. * * *

8. ***Multiple Defendants***. In order to convict a defendant, the government must prove beyond a reasonable doubt its theory for holding the defendant liable, whether the person was acting as a principal or as an accomplice to the primary violator's conduct. In some cases, the prosecutor will not know which person among multiple defendants engaged in the actual criminal conduct, and therefore may charge a person as both the principal and for aiding and abetting the crime. A jury may return a verdict of guilty so long as the evidence supports either basis for liability because the distinction is not relevant to punishment. In *United States v. Garcia*, 400 F.3d 816 (9th Cir. 2005), the court explained:

> In the context of aider and abettor liability, there is a single crime that the defendant is charged with committing; he could commit that offense by directly performing illegal acts himself, or by aiding, abetting, counseling, commanding, inducing, or procuring the commission of the offense. Whichever, the defendant (if convicted) is liable as a principal. *See* 18 U.S.C. § 2(a) ("Whoever commits an offense against the United States or aids, abets, counsels, commands, induces or procures its commission, is punishable as a principal."). Thus, unlike the mens rea for attempts, an aider and abettor's intent regarding the substantive offense is the same intent required for conviction as a principal.

> Of course, to prove liability as an aider and abettor the government must establish beyond a reasonable doubt that the accused had the specific intent to facilitate the commission of a crime by someone else — and this is an "element" that need not be established for conviction on the underlying offense. However, as the Supreme Court pointed out in *Schad v. Arizona*, 501 U.S. 624 (1991), jurors are not required to agree unanimously on alternative means of committing a crime.

9. ***Abandonment.*** As with conspiracy and attempt, one who abandons the criminal act may not be held criminally liable. The abandonment needs to be voluntary and there must be a complete abandonment. Often it is necessary to communicate the withdrawal from the accessory activity to law enforcement.

MODEL PENAL CODE

§ 2.06. Liability for Conduct of Another; Complicity.

(1) A person is guilty of an offense if it is committed by his own conduct or by the conduct of another person for which he is legally accountable, or both.

(2) A person is legally accountable for the conduct of another person when:

(a) acting with the kind of culpability that is sufficient for the commission of the offense, he causes an innocent or irresponsible person to engage in such conduct; or

(b) he is made accountable for the conduct of such other person by the Code or by the law defining the offense; or

(c) he is an accomplice of such other person in the commission of the offense.

(3) A person is an accomplice of another person in the commission of an offense if:

(a) with the purpose of promoting or facilitating the commission of the offense, he

(i) solicits such other person to commit it, or

(ii) aids or agrees or attempts to aid such other person in planning or committing it, or

(iii) having a legal duty to prevent the commission of the offense, fails to make proper effort so to do; or

(b) his conduct is expressly declared by law to establish his complicity.

(4) When causing a particular result is an element of an offense, an accomplice in the conduct causing such result is an accomplice in the commission of that offense if he acts with the kind of culpability, if any, with respect to that result that is sufficient for the commission of the offense.

(5) A person who is legally incapable of committing a particular offense himself may be guilty thereof if it is committed by the conduct of another person for which he is legally accountable, unless such liability is inconsistent with the purpose of the provision establishing his incapacity.

(6) Unless otherwise provided by the Code or by the law defining the offense, a person is not an accomplice in an offense committed by another person if:

(a) he is a victim of that offense; or

(b) the offense is so defined that his conduct is inevitably incident to its commission; or

(c) he terminates his complicity prior to the commission of the offense and

(i) wholly deprives it of effectiveness in the commission of the offense; or

(ii) gives timely warning to the law enforcement authorities or otherwise makes proper effort to prevent the commission of the offense.

(7) An accomplice may be convicted on proof of the commission of the offense and of his complicity therein, though the person claimed to have committed the offense has not been prosecuted or convicted or has been convicted of a different offense or degree of offense or has an immunity to prosecution or conviction or has been acquitted.

PROBLEM FORTY-SEVEN

An undercover DEA agent befriends Sandy, who is reputed to be a drug supplier. The agent asks Sandy to help finance the purchase of a kilogram of cocaine. Sandy agrees to provide $20,000 in cash for the purchase, knowing that there will be a 75% profit from the eventual sale of the drugs. The agent asks Sandy to meet at 7:00 p.m. at a local motel to deliver the cash for the deal. The agent says, "[I]t's scheduled to go down at eight, so you can be long gone in case there are any problems." Sandy arrives at the motel at 7:10 p.m., and is videotaped giving the agent a leather bag that contains $20,000 in unmarked bills. Sandy leaves the room and is about to get into a car when Sandy is arrested by two DEA agents. Sandy is charged with one count of attempted possession of cocaine with intent to distribute (21 U.S.C. § 846) and aiding and abetting the crime under 18 U.S.C. § 2. What argument will defense counsel make that the government cannot establish Sandy's guilt, and how will the prosecutor respond?

§ 14.02 Mens Rea

United States v. Cruz
363 F.3d 187 (2d Cir. 2004)

MESKILL, Circuit Judge.

* * * Several years ago, a team of DEA agents worked with a paid informant to investigate the activities of Carlos Medina. Eventually, Brian Fleming, the case agent assigned by the DEA to manage the operation, directed the informant, Enrique Ramos, to meet with Medina at a Boston Market in Queens, New York and to purchase approximately 900 grams of heroin from him. In accordance with these instructions, Ramos spoke with Medina and arranged to meet him at the restaurant on December 13, 2000, for the purpose of buying the heroin.

On the Friday before this narcotics transaction took place, defendant Cruz was approached by an intermediary who apparently asked Cruz if he would assault several Ecuadorian men in exchange for $200. When Cruz agreed to do so, the intermediary arranged for a follow-up meeting with him on December 12, 2000. Medina attended this subsequent meeting and discussed the planned assault with Cruz. After Cruz affirmed his agreement to assault the Ecuadorians, he was told that he needed to return for a third meeting on December 13, 2000. However, on arriving the following day, Cruz was informed that events were not proceeding according to plan. Cruz was told that he initially needed "to watch" Medina's "back" while Medina finalized a "deal." He also learned that the so-called "deal" would be taking place at the aforementioned Boston Market.

In the interim, Fleming had assigned a surveillance unit of DEA agents to observe the Market and the surrounding area in an effort to monitor the meeting between Medina and Ramos. These agents were on hand conducting their surveillance when Cruz and his co-defendant, Luis Rodriguez, arrived at the Market in a Lincoln Town Car. According to the agents, Cruz and Rodriguez suspiciously examined vehicles in the nearby area as they approached the restaurant as if they were engaged in "countersurveillance" against law enforcement scrutiny.

Cruz and Rodriguez eventually entered the Boston Market, ordered food at the counter, and took a seat towards the side of the restaurant. Subsequently, Medina also arrived at the Market and sat at a different table with Ramos, who had arrived earlier and had been waiting for him. Ramos and Medina discussed the narcotics transaction and agreed that Medina would sell Ramos the heroin "right there." Neither Cruz nor Rodriguez had any contact with either Medina or Ramos while they were in the restaurant.

After Medina and Ramos finalized their negotiations, Medina left the Boston Market. Not long thereafter, DEA agents noted that Cruz and Rodriguez also left the

Market and drove off in the Lincoln Town Car. More than half an hour later, the agents observed the Town Car return to the Market. Medina stepped out of the vehicle's front-side passenger seat and waved towards Ramos. In response, Ramos walked over to the car, stepped inside, and sat down in the back. At that stage, he noticed that Cruz was sitting in the driver's seat. Medina eventually directed Ramos' attention towards a telephone box that had been placed in the back of the vehicle behind the driver's seat. When Ramos opened the box, he found heroin hidden inside a plastic bag within the box.

Once he saw the drugs, Ramos informed Medina that he would soon return with the money for the heroin. When he stepped out of the Lincoln Town Car, Ramos gave a pre-arranged signal to the DEA agents. The signal informed the agents that he had seen the heroin and that they should move in to effectuate arrests. After they received the signal, the DEA agents closed in on the car. They seized the heroin and arrested both Medina and Cruz.

After his arrest, Cruz made a number of statements to [DEA Agent] Tully. At Cruz's trial, Tully testified regarding the substance of these post-arrest statements. Cruz apparently told Tully that he had been at the Boston Market and in the Lincoln Town Car "to watch [Medina's] back while he did business." Cruz also told Fleming that he had not known that he had agreed to take part in a "drug deal." Rather, Cruz explained that he "knew it was some kind of a deal, but not a drug deal." Cruz subsequently reiterated to Tully that he had been asked "to watch [Medina's] back while he [did] a deal or [did] business." When Tully inquired regarding whether Cruz understood that the deal in question was a "drug deal," Cruz explained that he "knew it was a deal that was going on, but [he] didn't know what kind of deal." Cruz purportedly informed Tully that he was not certain whether he and Medina "were going to be picking up money or if [they] were going to be delivering drugs, [he] didn't know which one it was." [Cruz was convicted of possession with intent to distribute heroin in violation of 21 U.S.C. § 841 after a two-day jury trial.]

* * * In this case, the government concedes that it sought to convict Cruz of possession with intent to distribute a substance containing heroin on the basis of "an aiding and abetting theory." An aiding and abetting conviction must be premised on "more than evidence of a general cognizance of criminal activity" or "suspicious circumstances." *United States v. Samaria*, 239 F.3d 228 (2d Cir. 2001). Rather, "[t]o convict a defendant on a theory of aiding and abetting, the government must prove that the underlying crime was committed by a person other than the defendant and that the defendant acted, or failed to act in a way that the law required him to act, with the specific purpose of bringing about the underlying crime." *United States v. Labat*, 905 F.2d 18 (2d Cir. 1990). "To prove that the defendant acted with that specific intent, the government must show that he knew of the proposed crime." *Id*.

* * * [T]he record is devoid, by and large, of any evidence that Cruz knew that Medina possessed drugs or that he intended to sell drugs to Ramos. Cruz initially agreed to assault several Ecuadorians, not to assist Medina with a narcotics transaction. Although Cruz later agreed "to watch" Medina's "back" during a "deal," Tully acknowledged that Cruz informed Fleming that he did not know the deal in question was a drug deal. Moreover, Cruz later told Tully that he "didn't know what kind of deal" would be taking place. Furthermore, while Cruz was present in the Boston Market as Medina negotiated a narcotics transaction with Ramos, he did not sit at Medina's table during those negotiations; rather, Cruz sat several tables away, and Ramos cast doubt on whether the defendant could have overheard the discussions about the heroin since Ramos and Medina were "talking in a low voice." In addition, despite the government's observation that Cruz approached the Boston Market in a "surveillance conscious manner," testimony to that effect did not categorically suggest that Cruz engaged in such so-called "countersurveillance" because he knew Medina was engaged in a narcotics transaction and hoped to further the commission of that crime. Finally, although Cruz was the driver of the Lincoln Town Car in which Ramos found the heroin, there is no evidence to suggest that Cruz had been aware of the presence of narcotics in the car before Medina drew Ramos' attention to the heroin; Cruz was sitting in the driver's seat of the Lincoln Town Car whereas the heroin was hidden in the back of the vehicle inside both a telephone box and a plastic bag. The trial record does not indicate that Cruz discussed the contents of that package with Medina as they drove to the Boston Market to meet with Ramos or that he somehow managed to see the heroin hidden therein from his vantage point in the Town Car.

In essence, the trial record * * * reflects that Cruz was present at the scene of the crime and likely knew that some type of crime was being committed. * * * [T]here is little evidence in the record which suggests that Cruz knew of the specific crime Medina proposed to commit or that Cruz intended to facilitate such a crime. *Samaria.* Although the government may prove the requisite knowledge and specific intent by circumstantial evidence, that evidence must still include some indicia of the specific elements of the underlying crime. For example, such indicia could include conversations directly related to the substance of the illegal activity, possession of documents related to the crime, exercise of authority within a conspiracy, receiving a share of the profits from the deal, or explicit confirmation of the nature of the crime. Here, none of these direct indicia of intent and knowledge are present. Instead, the record encompasses little more than Cruz's statement that he would "watch [Medina's] back" and Tully's testimony linking this statement to narcotics transactions. Such a tenuous link is clearly insufficient to meet the burden imposed on the prosecution to prove guilt beyond a reasonable doubt.

Viewing all the evidence in the light most favorable to the government and drawing all permissible inferences in its favor, the most the prosecution demonstrated here with its circumstantial evidence was that Cruz acted as a lookout for

Medina. In other cases where defendants have acted as lookouts, however, we have upheld convictions only when other indicia of the elements of the underlying substantive offense including knowledge and intent have been in evidence. See *United States v. Pitre*, 960 F.2d 1112 (2d Cir. 1992) (upholding conspiracy conviction for serving as a lookout for a narcotics transaction when other evidence showed that defendants knowingly and intentionally participated in the drug conspiracy); *United States v. Torres*, 845 F.2d 1165 (2d Cir. 1988) (upholding conspiracy conviction on lookout theory when defendant was identified as the source of the drugs). Our sister circuits have also held that mere evidence the defendant acted as a lookout will not suffice to prove knowledge and specific intent. *See, e.g., United States v. Dean*, 59 F.3d 1479 (5th Cir. 1995) (finding that evidence sufficient to show that defendant was acting as a lookout was not sufficient to show that he knew what he was protecting); *United States v. Wexler*, 838 F.2d 88 (3d Cir. 1988) (finding that even though defendant acted as a lookout, absence of evidence linking defendant to the specific object of the crime was fatal to prosecution). Similarly here, * * * the government has established that Cruz was acting as a lookout for Medina but has not offered anything to directly connect Cruz to the transaction and prove the requisite knowledge and intent needed for an aiding and abetting conviction. As we have held numerous times before, the defendant's mere presence at the scene of the crime or association with wrongdoers does not constitute intentional participation in the crime, even if the defendant had knowledge of the criminal activity. Where, as here, no more direct link between the defendant's actions as a lookout and the underlying elements of the crime is offered by the government, circumstantial evidence will be insufficient to support an aiding and abetting conviction.

Thus, we conclude that the record evidence here does not support the conclusion that a reasonable factfinder could have found Cruz guilty beyond a reasonable doubt.

NOTES AND QUESTIONS

1. *Common Law*. In the common law there are two classes of mental states for accomplice liability, though they are not always stated separately: first, whatever mental state the substantive crime requires, including possible attendant circumstances; second, the *purpose* to commit the act of aiding the principal in committing the substantive crime and, in many jurisdictions, the purpose to achieve the result required by the crime. Some jurisdictions instead, however, hold the accomplice responsible for the "natural and probable consequences" (the foreseeable consequences) of the actions that he or she purposely aided, in effect making negligence, rather than purpose, the mental state for a result element.

The first mental state matters because whatever mental state the underlying crime requires for attendant circumstances will be sufficient for the accomplice to hold. Thus, to be an accomplice in a rape, an aider and abettor must have the purpose of aiding the principal in committing the acts of forcible sexual intercourse but need only have whatever mental state the particular common law jurisdiction requires for the attendant circumstances (usually that requirement is negligence) of the acts being done with a woman who is not the principal's wife. Likewise, the jurisdictional variation on the second mental state matters because those jurisdictions requiring purpose for acts and results would, for example, hold someone who purposely aids a principal, with the goal of his or her committing only a bank robbery, but where the principal in fact kills someone, guilty only of the robbery but not of the murder under an accomplice liability theory. This would be so because the purported accomplice did not want to kill anyone but only to rob them. But jurisdictions extending liability to the "natural and probable consequences" of purposeful action would likely hold the aider liable for both bank robbery and murder on an accomplice liability theory because, depending on the facts, it may have been foreseeable that the robbery would result in someone's death, however much that result was not intended by the aider.

Even in a jurisdiction requiring *purpose* to aid both actions *and* results, the case outcome can be affected (concerning the crime of homicide only) by the interaction of accomplice liability rules with the felony murder rule. Thus in the same hypothetical above of only having the purpose of aiding a robbery but someone nevertheless dies, the accomplice is guilty of the felony of robbery under accomplice liability principles. But the felony murder rule makes an accomplice in the underlying felony strictly liable for any resulting death, provided that all the other requirements of the felony murder rule (inherent dangerousness, merger, agency v. proximate cause) have been met.

A few jurisdictions find *knowledge* that you are aiding a principal to commit a *serious* (but not a minor) crime by providing the principal with goods and services a sufficient *mens rea* concerning commission of the act of aiding, though the traditional rule is to the contrary, namely, that knowledge that you are aiding is never enough; a purpose to aid is required. Even under this traditional rule, however, purpose can be inferred from knowledge plus additional circumstantial evidence of purpose.

2. *Model Penal Code Comparison*. The Model Penal Code language seems to require the accomplice to have the purpose of aiding the principal *both* in committing the act elements of the underlying substantive crime and concerning the accomplice's attitude toward the attendant circumstances of that crime; most states so interpret the Model Penal Code. Under this approach, aiding another to break into a third party's home to steal their T.V. set with the purpose that the principal break in and take the T.V. but with complete indifference to whether the entry took place during day or nighttime (assuming that the state's burglary statute required

nighttime as an element) would not be guilty of burglary on an accomplice liability theory because he or she did not have the purpose that the entry occur at night, nighttime again being an attendant circumstance element.

The Model Penal Code drafters' comments, however, state that they were undecided whether purpose or whatever mental state was required by the underlying crime should suffice for accomplice liability as to attendant circumstance elements (but all agree that purpose is required as to act elements). Some states do in fact resolve this ambiguity by only requiring the accomplice to have the same mental state for attendant circumstances as is true for the underlying crime. Under this approach, it would not automatically defeat accomplice liability for the accomplice immediately above to have lacked the purpose that entry to a third party's home happen during the presence of the attendant circumstance of it being nighttime. If that particular state's burglary statute permitted a lesser mental state than purpose as to the nighttime attendant circumstance element *for the completed crime*, then that same mental state as to that attendant circumstance would also suffice in determining whether someone can also be held liable as an accomplice to the burglary.

For result elements, however, the Model Penal Code clearly does require only whatever mental state the underlying crime requires for that result so long as the accused was an accomplice in any underlying crime that led to that result. (*see* Model Penal Code § 2.06(4)). Thus, if a defendant was an accomplice in bank robbery but did not want anyone to die, yet the principal fatally shot a bank clerk who initially refused to turn over the money, the robbery accomplice can also be an accomplice to some form of homicide — even though he or she fervently hoped that no one would die. If the accused *knew* that death would result, he or she could be convicted of a knowing murder; if he or she was consciously aware of a substantial and unjustifiable risk of someone's dying during the robbery (*i.e.*, recklessness), then the conviction could be for manslaughter; and if thoroughly unaware of such a risk but should have been so aware, the accused could be convicted of negligent homicide. In *Commonwealth v. Roebuck*, 32 A.3d 613 (Pa. 2011), the Pennsylvania Supreme Court stated, "[I]t certainly is possible for a state legislature to employ complicity theory to establish legal accountability on the part of an accomplice for foreseeable but unintended results caused by a principal. Indeed, this was the express design of the American Law Institute's widely influential Model Penal Code."

3. *Scope of Aiding and Abetting Liability*. While the person who aids and abets a crime must act with the requisite mens rea, can that person be guilty of a greater offense than the perpetrator of the crime? Consider *People v. McCoy*, 108 Cal. Rptr. 2d 188 (Cal. 2001), in which McCoy testified that he fired from a moving car into a group of men in self-defense because he believed he had been shot at by them earlier in the day. When the shooting occurred, McCoy was accompanied by Lackey, who also shot at the group of men. One person died from their shooting,

and the fatal bullet was traced to McCoy's gun. Each was convicted of first-degree murder. The court of appeals reversed McCoy's murder conviction because it found the judge improperly instructed the jury on the defense of "imperfect self-defense" that would negate his specific intent, thereby allowing a verdict of voluntary manslaughter. The court of appeals did not reverse Lackey's conviction, however, and he appealed to the California Supreme Court on the ground that he could only be liable for the same crime as the principal, and not a greater offense. The California Supreme Court rejected that argument, holding:

It is important to bear in mind that an aider and abettor's liability for criminal conduct is of two kinds. First, an aider and abettor with the necessary mental state is guilty of the intended crime. Second, under the natural and probable consequences doctrine, an aider and abettor is guilty not only of the intended crime, but also "for any other offense that was a 'natural and probable consequence' of the crime aided and abetted." *People v. Prettyman*, 58 Cal. Rptr. 2d 827 (Cal. 1996). Thus, for example, if a person aids and abets only an intended assault, but a murder results, that person may be guilty of that murder, even if unintended, if it is a natural and probable consequence of the intended assault. * * *

Except for strict liability offenses, every crime has two components: (1) an act or omission, sometimes called the actus reus; and (2) a necessary mental state, sometimes called the mens rea. This principle applies to aiding and abetting liability as well as direct liability. An aider and abettor must do something and have a certain mental state.

We have described the mental state required of an aider and abettor as "different from the mental state necessary for conviction as the actual perpetrator." *People v. Mendoza*, 77 Cal. Rptr. 2d 428 (Cal. 1998). The difference, however, does not mean that the mental state of an aider and abettor is less culpable than that of the actual perpetrator. On the contrary, outside of the natural and probable consequences doctrine, an aider and abettor's mental state must be at least that required of the direct perpetrator. * * *

Aider and abettor liability is thus vicarious only in the sense that the aider and abettor is liable for another's actions as well as that person's own actions. When a person "chooses to become a part of the criminal activity of another, she says in essence, 'your acts are my acts. . . .'" Joshua Dressler, *Reassessing the Theoretical Underpinnings of Accomplice Liability: New Solutions to an Old Problem*, 37 HASTINGS L.J. 91(1985). But that person's own acts are also her acts for which she is also liable. Moreover, that person's mental state is her own; she is liable for her mens rea, not the other person's. * * *

We thus conclude that when a person, with the mental state necessary for an aider and abettor, helps or induces another to kill, that person's guilt is determined by the combined acts of all the participants as well as that person's own mens rea. If that person's mens rea is more culpable than another's, that person's guilt may be greater even if the other might be deemed the actual perpetrator.

4. *Timing*. When is a person an accessory to the crime, as opposed to being an accessory after the fact? The key determinant is the point in time when the individual provides the assistance to the principal with the requisite mens rea. For example, in *People v. Cooper*, 282 Cal. Rptr. 450 (Cal. 1991), the California Supreme Court held that providing assistance in fleeing from a robbery after all acts constituting the offense have occurred renders the defendant liable only as an accessory after the fact:

> A primary rationale for punishing aiders and abettors as principals — to deter them from aiding or encouraging the commission of offenses — is not served by imposing aider and abettor liability on a getaway driver in a robbery if that person was unaware of the robbery until after all of the acts constituting robbery, including the asportation, had ceased. Such a driver is powerless to either prevent the robbery, or end the acts constituting the robbery if such acts have already ceased. Although the law should also deter the getaway driver from helping the robbers escape from justice after commission of the crime has ended, this goal is appropriately served by the threat of liability as an accessory after the fact. Thus, in determining liability as an aider and abettor, the focus must be on the acts constituting the robbery, not the escape.

In *Cooper*, the defendant, who drove the vehicle into which the robbers jumped after two others knocked over an 89-year old woman and stole her wallet, claimed that he did not know about the crime until after he saw the others commit it, so that his intent to provide assistance and supplying of that assistance took place *after* the commission of the robbery. In contrast, if one has knowledge of the crime and participates as a getaway driver to that crime knowing that the crime is being committed, one can be considered a principal to the crime. In the common law, getaway drivers and lookouts were considered principals in the second degree. (p. 524, Note 2).

5. *Liability for Greater Offenses*. In *State v. Ivy*, 350 N.W.2d 622 (Wisc. 1984), the Wisconsin Supreme Court described how a person aiding and abetting a crime can be held liable for a more serious offense.

> [A] defendant could be liable for aiding and abetting the armed robbery even though he or she did not actually know that the person or persons who

directly committed the armed robbery were armed with a dangerous weapon.

Robbery is itself a violent crime involving the taking of a person's property against his or her will by the threat or actual use of force. Because threatened or actual force is involved in a robbery, there are myriad factual situations in which it would be reasonable to find that an armed robbery that occurred was a natural and probable consequence of robbery. For example, if a person intends to rob an armored money truck, it is likely that the person would have to use a weapon during the robbery in order to successfully accomplish the robbery. Similarly, if a person intends to rob a bank or business that is guarded by armed security guards, it is likely that the person would have to use a weapon to successfully effectuate the robbery. If a defendant in either example intended to aid the crime of robbery but actually knew that the person who directly committed the robbery planned to rob an armored money truck, or actually knew that the perpetrator planned to rob a bank guarded by armed security guards, and an armed robbery actually occurred, the defendant conceivably could be liable for the commission of the armed robbery even though he or she did not actually know that the person directly committing the robbery was armed with a dangerous weapon. Under those circumstances, the armed robbery could be considered a natural and probable consequence of robbery and, given the facts the defendant actually knew about the robbery he or she intended to assist, he or she would at least be on notice of the likelihood that the person who directly committed the robbery would be armed with a dangerous weapon and might use that weapon. Just as it [is reasonable] to infer intent on the part of the defendant to assist in the commission of the crime that actually occurred, it would be reasonable in the above examples to infer knowledge on the part of the aider and abettor that the principal was armed with a dangerous weapon.

6. *Capital Punishment.* The Supreme Court held in *Enmund v. Florida*, 458 U.S. 782 (1982), that a defendant who drove the "getaway" vehicle used in an armed robbery, but who did not otherwise participate in the robbery that resulted in the murder of two victims, could not receive a sentence of capital punishment for murder on the basis of being an accomplice to the felony that resulted in the deaths. The Court stated,

[I]t is for us ultimately to judge whether the Eighth Amendment permits imposition of the death penalty on one such as Enmund who aids and abets a felony in the course of which a murder is committed by others but who does not himself kill, attempt to kill, or intend that a killing take place or that lethal force will be employed. We have concluded, along with most legislatures and juries, that it does not.

In *Tison v. Arizona*, 481 U.S. 137 (1987), the Court upheld imposition of the death penalty on two defendants convicted of felony murder for their role in assisting the escape of prisoners by providing weapons that were used to murder a family during the course of the escape. It stated, "[S]ubstantial participation in a violent felony under circumstances likely to result in the loss of innocent human life may justify the death penalty even absent an 'intent to kill.'" Thus, the degree of the accomplices participation in the crime that results in death determines whether the capital punishment can be imposed even when the person did not directly cause the death.

7. *Natural and Probable Consequences Doctrine*. Many states permit a conviction for aiding and abetting a crime under the natural and probable consequences doctrine. For example, a Minnesota statute provides that an accomplice "is also liable for any other crime committed in pursuance of the intended crime if reasonably foreseeable by the person as a probable consequence of committing or attempting to commit the crime intended." MINN. STAT. ANN. 609.05(2). In rejecting this doctrine in *Sharma v. State*, 56 P.3d 868 (Nev. 2002), the Nevada court stated:

> To be convicted of an attempt to commit a crime in Nevada, the State must show, among other things, that the accused committed an act with the intent to commit that crime. Under the natural and probable consequences doctrine, however, an accused may be convicted upon a far different showing, i.e., that the charged crime, although not intended, was nonetheless foreseeable. As the Supreme Court of New Mexico observed in rejecting the doctrine for similar reasons, the doctrine thus "allows a defendant to be convicted for crimes the defendant may have been able to foresee but never intended." [*State v. Carrasco*, 946 P.2d 1075 (N.M. 1997).]

> This court has repeatedly emphasized that, under Nevada law, "[t]here is no such criminal offense as an attempt to achieve an unintended result." We have also reasoned that "[a]n attempt, by nature, is a failure to accomplish what one intended to do." Because the natural and probable consequences doctrine permits a defendant to be convicted of a specific intent crime where he or she did not possess the statutory intent required for the offense, we hereby disavow and abandon the doctrine. It is not only "inconsistent with more fundamental principles of our system of criminal law," but is also inconsistent with those Nevada statutes that require proof of a specific intent to commit the crime alleged.

Liability under the natural and probable consequences doctrine is similar to that of the conspirator who is being held criminally liable under the *Pinkerton* doctrine for substantive offenses committed in furtherance of the conspiracy. The jury's determination of the scope of liability for the person who aids and abets the principal requires careful jury instructions. In *People v. Culuko*, 92 Cal. Rptr. 2d 789 (Cal. Ct. App. 2000), the court stated:

> In our view, merely instructing the jury to determine whether murder was the natural and probable consequence of the "act" aided and abetted could hurt more than it helps. The jury could take this too broadly, as meaning the "act" the perpetrator actually performed — in the Supreme Court's example, assault with a steel pipe — even if the aider and abettor could not reasonably foresee it. Contrariwise, the jury could also take it too narrowly, as limiting it to some "act" that the aider and abettor actually intended. Thus, if it found the aider and abettor intended to facilitate an assault with a knife, but the perpetrator actually committed an assault with a steel pipe, the jury might erroneously conclude that murder was not the natural and probable consequence of the assault aided and abetted.

> We believe the best way to convey the crucial legal principle is by an entirely separate instruction. Here, the trial court gave such an instruction. It explained: "In determining whether the crime of murder was a natural and probable consequence, you must determine whether a reasonable person in the [d]efendant's position would have known that the crime was a reasonably foreseeable consequence of the act aided and abetted. In making this determination, you must consider those circumstances which the defendant knew, taking into account all the facts and circumstances surrounding the particular defendant[']s conduct."

> This instruction was adequate. It prevented the jurors from finding Culuko guilty of murder, merely because she aided and abetted Garcia's commission of felony child abuse, if it was unforeseeable that Garcia would commit murder as a result. At the same time, it allowed the jurors to find Culuko guilty of murder if she did aid and abet Garcia's commission of felony child abuse, and if it was foreseeable that Garcia would commit murder as a result. Moreover, it did not erect an artificial requirement that Culuko had to intend and encourage Garcia to deliver the fatal punch to the abdomen. It could be sufficient that she intended and encouraged Garcia to brutalize the baby any way he chose, as long as murder was a foreseeable result.

8. ***Innocent Instrumentality.*** When a person uses another individual to commit a crime for them, and the person being used does not have the requisite mens rea for the commission of the crime, the person being used to commit the crime is likely an innocent instrumentality. The person who uses this individual to commit the crime is the principal, even though he or she may not be present at the scene of the crime. If, however, the person being used was aware of a high probability that they were being used, but deliberately avoided confirming this suspicion, they can be held liable as a principal as they were willfully blind.

CASE STUDY FIVE

Dwight decides he wants to kill his boss, Michael, because he was not promoted to Assistant Regional Manager at their restaurant supply company. Dwight calls Stan, a high school friend with combat experience, about "helping" with a little problem he has with his boss. Dwight tells Stan that he wants his boss killed in a way that will make it appear to be a drive-by shooting by a local drug gang. Dwight offers to pay Stan $10,000 to do the shooting. Stan tells Dwight that he'll need to get someone to help him as the driver.

The next day, Stan contacts Ryan, a buddy from his military days, to see if he'd be interested in "helping me out with a little dirty work, nothing as dangerous as what we did in the old days." Ryan asks what he needs to do, and Stan says, "Just do a little drivin' and don't ask questions." Stan then tells Dwight, "I've got a wheel man, so that's all taken care of. I'll get us a car that we can ditch. When do you want this thing to go down." Dwight tells Stan that Michael is taking a yoga class on Thursday evenings, and the session ends around 9:00 p.m. Dwight and Stan drive to the yoga studio to look around to see the best place to do the drive-by shooting. The parking lot next to the studio leads into a narrow alley from which the cars then emerge onto a small residential street. Stan tells Dwight that he'll be waiting on the street when Michael's car emerges from the alley and pull up next to him for the shooting.

On the following Thursday, Michael calls in sick to the office. Dwight contacts Stan and tells him that he'll have to wait until the following week. Stan calls Ryan and says, "It's off for tonight because our guy won't be where we need him to be. It's on for next Thursday." The following Monday, Ryan calls Stan and says, "Look Stan, I can't help you, I gotta keep my nose clean, so you'll have to scare this guy yourself." Stan decides that he will do the job himself so that he won't have to share the money with anyone else. On the next Thursday, Stan steals a car and drives it to the street near the yoga studio. As Michael's car emerges from the alley, Stan pulls up next to it, fires three shots, and then drives away quickly. The bullets strike the car but miss Michael. When Michael comes into the office the next morning, Dwight is shocked to see him.

Two weeks after the shooting, Dwight is passed over again by Michael for the Assistant Regional Manager position. Enraged at this continued slight, Dwight contacts another high school friend, Pam, and asks her if she knows anyone "who can do a little dirty work for me." When Pam asks what he wants, Dwight replies, "I need someone who can make a guy disappear." Pam says she'll have a friend of hers give Dwight a call. That evening, Pam speaks with Jim, who she knows spent time in prison. She says, "I've got a friend who needs someone to do a little something off the record. I figured that since you're out of a job, you might want to get in touch with him." Unknown to Pam, Jim is a confidential informant for the police working to infiltrate a local drug ring. A few days later, Pam tells a friend about Dwight's request and says "Dwight is so delusional, he would never do anything to hurt someone."

With his police supervisor's permission, Jim contacts Dwight to see what he wants done. Dwight explains that he wants Michael killed. Jim agrees to do it for $15,000 — half up front and half after the job is completed — and says that he can arrange for it to look like an accident so no one will be suspicious. Jim calls Pam and says, "I spoke with your friend Dwight, and he's gonna pay me ten grand to do some work for him. I figure I owe you something for sending me the work because I really need the cash." Pam says, "Well, if you want to drop off some money for me, that would be great, but you don't have to."

The following week, Jim explains to Dwight how he will make it look like someone forced Michael's car off the road and into a ditch, and will rig the gas tank in Michael's car to explode. Jim has no intention of causing Michael any harm, and is making up the story. Dwight says, "Look, I want to come along to see for myself. The last guy I hired to do this screwed it up." Jim says he doesn't need any company while he does his work, to which Dwight replies, "If I'm not there the deal is off and we're finished." Jim reluctantly agrees, and they decide to do it the following Thursday when Michael is driving home from the yoga studio through a wooded area near his condo.

On Thursday evening, Jim and Dwight follow Michael as he leaves the yoga studio. Jim's police supervisor has arranged to have officers in the wooded area where he said the killing would take place so that they can intercept Jim's car and arrest Dwight. Michael is not aware of the plan because the police determined Michael would not be able to keep the plan secret to ensure there is sufficient evidence to arrest Dwight for attempted murder. As they drive through the wooded area, two police cars block the road, and Michael and Jim both come to a stop. When Dwight sees what's happening, he jumps from the car and runs toward Michael screaming, "I'm gonna get you myself." When Dwight is about 20 feet from him, Michael takes out a concealed weapon he bought after the first attack, points it at Dwight, and shoots. The bullet misses Dwight but hits Jim — who is chasing after Dwight — in the head, killing him instantly. Dwight and Michael are arrested. Stan is arrested on different charges and gives a statement recounting the involvement of Dwight and Ryan in the earlier shooting; he agrees to plead guilty and testify against them. All of Jim's conversations with Dwight and Pam are recorded, and Pam is arrested.

Discuss the potential charges that can be filed against Dwight, Ryan, Pam, and Michael from the course of conduct described above. Be sure to discuss (1) the most serious crimes that can be charged, including any lesser-included offenses, (2) what evidence the prosecution can use to prove its case, and (3) potential defenses the defendants can raise. The state's murder statute is identical to California's homicide provision [see p. 281], and the state's courts follow the majority common law rules in interpreting its criminal laws.

PART SIX
DEFENSES

Chapter 15
Defenses

§ 15.01 Generally

Once the prosecution concludes presenting its evidence in its case-in-chief, the defense counsel can request that the court dismiss the charges because there is insufficient proof of the crime. This is called a motion for a judgment of acquittal or directed verdict. Some maintain that it is obligatory for counsel to make this motion. This is in part because the motion can serve to preserve the right to challenge the sufficiency of the prosecution's evidence should an appeal be necessary. In *Oxendine v. State*, (p. 181) the court reviewed the state of the evidence as of the close of the government's case-in-chief, and found it was insufficient to support the prosecution's theory of causation to establish the homicide charge.

In contrast, other courts note that there may be circumstances where it is not imperative to make this motion. In the Supreme Court opinion of *Evans v. Michigan*, 133 S.Ct. 1069 (2013), the Court noted that "nothing obligates a jurisdiction to afford its trial courts the power to grant a midtrial acquittal, and at least two States disallow the practice." The Court cites to a Nevada statute (NEV.REV.STAT. § 175.381(1) (2011)) and Louisiana case (*State v. Parfait*, 693 So.2d 1232, 1242 (La. Ct. App. 1997)).

If the motion for acquittal is made, the judge decides whether a reasonable juror, drawing all inferences in favor of the prosecution, could find the defendant guilty of the offense. If so, then the case will continue and the defendant may, but need not, present evidence to rebut the charge. Even if the judge denies the directed verdict motion, the defendant can still dispute the sufficiency of the prosecution's evidence.

The defense has the option to present additional defenses to the jury, but is under no obligation to do so. Professor Robinson summarizes the different types of criminal law defenses:

The term "defense" is commonly used, at least in a casual sense, to mean any set of identifiable conditions or circumstances which may prevent a conviction for an offense. Current law recognizes a surprising variety of such possible bars to conviction, from amnesia to withdrawal. Upon examining the functions of and the rationales supporting these rules and doctrines, five general categories become apparent. They may be termed: failure of proof defenses, offense modification defenses, justifications, excuses, and nonexculpatory public policy defenses.

Failure of proof defenses are nothing more than instances where, because of the "defense," the prosecution is unable to prove all the required elements of the offense, the objective conduct, circumstance, and result elements and their corresponding culpability requirements. Offense modifications are similar in that they essentially modify or refine the criminalization decision embodied in the definition of the particular offense. The remaining three groups of defenses — justifications, excuses, and nonexculpatory public policy defenses — are general defenses; they theoretically apply to all offenses, even when the required elements of an offense are satisfied. They represent principles of exculpation or defense which operate independently of the criminalization decision reflected in the particular offense. A justified actor engages in conduct that is not culpable because its benefits outweigh the harm or evil of the offense; an excused actor admits the harm or evil but nonetheless claims an absence of personal culpability; and an actor exempt under a nonexculpatory public policy defense admits the harm or evil and his culpability but relies upon an important public policy interest, apart from blamelessness, that is furthered by foregoing the defendant's conviction.

Paul H. Robinson, *Criminal Law Defenses: A Systematic Analysis*, 82 COLUM. L. REV. 199 (1982).

§ 15.02 The Right to Present a Defense

Beaty v. Commonwealth
125 S.W.3d 196 (Ky. 2003)

Opinion of the Court by Justice COOPER.

On November 8, 2000, Logan County Deputy Sheriff Jimmy Phelps observed a white Chevrolet erratically weaving from side to side on the highway. Upon stopping and approaching the vehicle, Phelps detected a strong odor of anhydrous ammonia. Appellant was the driver of the Chevrolet; his girlfriend, Marion Ann Hanks, was in the front passenger seat. Phelps asked Appellant to exit the vehicle, and as he did so, Phelps observed that he was unsteady on his feet. Appellant failed the field sobriety tests and was arrested and charged with DUI. KRS 189A.010(1).

Because the breath test was negative, Phelps concluded that Appellant was under the influence of a substance other than alcohol. Appellant refused to submit to a blood or urine test at a local hospital.

A search incident to the arrest revealed substantial evidence of illegal drug activity. In a bag concealed in the area of his groin, Appellant possessed three small bags of marijuana, a bag of cocaine, a set of scales, and other assorted drug paraphernalia. When Hanks was asked to exit the vehicle by another officer, she attempted to hide under the vehicle a bag containing marijuana and rolling papers. Officers found marijuana seeds in the front seat, open containers of beer and gin, and, in the glove compartment, a prescription pill bottle containing crack cocaine and bearing the name "Kenneth Huskey," who, as explained infra, was the boyfriend of the vehicle's owner.

The back seat and trunk of the vehicle contained a methamphetamine laboratory. * * *

The vehicle was owned by Hanks's friend, Pamela Kuhl. Appellant and Hanks testified that they had borrowed the car merely to do laundry and were ignorant of the contents of the back seat and trunk. Hanks claimed that the car was always messy and that she had not noticed the equipment in the back seat. Kuhl, and Kuhl's boyfriend, Kenneth ("Spook") Huskey, testified that the car was empty when they loaned it to Hanks in the early afternoon of November 8, 2000.

Appellant was indicted on nine counts [including manufacturing methamphetamine, possession of a controlled substance in the first degree, and possession of anhydrous ammonia in an unapproved container with the intent to manufacture methamphetamine.]

* * * Appellant contends that he was denied his Due Process right to present a defense to the methamphetamine-related offenses by exclusion of evidence that Pamela Kuhl, the owner of the vehicle, had a motive to commit the offenses. His theory was that Kuhl believed that Hanks and Huskey were secret paramours and, after discovering the affair, Kuhl contrived to loan Hanks the mobile methamphetamine laboratory in order to incriminate Hanks and eliminate her as a rival for Huskey's affections. Kuhl normally loaned her car to Hanks to drive her daughter to school, so Kuhl would have assumed that Hanks would be the driver on November 8, 2000. However, the scheme went awry. Appellant ended up as the driver, and though the trap was set for Hanks, it ensnared Appellant instead.

The Commonwealth called Kuhl as a rebuttal witness, and Appellant attempted to develop this theory on cross-examination. Specifically, Appellant attempted to elicit testimony from Kuhl about her alleged jealousy of Hanks and to introduce a document written by Kuhl illustrating her belief that Huskey and Hanks had engaged in sexual relations. The trial court sustained the Commonwealth's objection to the admission of this evidence. [The court also excluded a document and cross examination.]

Appellant contends that the document and cross-examination, both evincing Kuhl's jealousy, should have been admitted * * * substantively as probative of his defense theory that it was Kuhl, not appellant, who placed the methamphetamine laboratory and materials in the car. * * *

"The right of an accused in a criminal trial to due process is, in essence, the right to a fair opportunity to defend against the State's accusations." *Chambers v. Mississippi*, 410 U.S. 284 (1973). This right, often termed the "right to present a defense," is firmly ingrained in Kentucky jurisprudence, *e.g.*, *Rogers v. Commonwealth*, 86 S.W.3d 29 (Ky. 2002), and has been recognized repeatedly by the United States Supreme Court. An exclusion of evidence will almost invariably be declared unconstitutional when it "significantly undermine[s] fundamental elements of the defendant's defense."

Appellant's only defense to the methamphetamine-related charges was that Kuhl was the perpetrator. Likewise, in *Chambers* * * * the unconstitutionally excluded evidence was probative of the defendant's theory that a third person was the actual perpetrator of the charged offense. For the same reasons expressed in *Chambers* * * *, we have been adamant that a defendant "has the right to introduce evidence that another person committed the offense with which he is charged." * * * A trial court may only infringe upon this right when the defense theory is "unsupported," "speculat[ive]," and "far-fetched" and could thereby confuse or mislead the jury.

Federal courts have also specifically recognized the importance of the defendant's right to produce evidence that a third party (or "aaltperp," i.e., "alleged alternative perpetrator." This term was coined by Professor David McCord in his article, *"But Perry Mason Made It Look So Easy!": The Admissibility of Evidence Offered By a Criminal Defendant To Suggest That Someone Else Is Guilty*, 63 TENN. L. REV. 917, 920 (1996). * * *), actually committed the crime. * * * However, evidence is not automatically admissible simply because it tends to show that someone else committed the offense. * * * In a homicide case, a defendant is not entitled to parade before the jury every person who bore some dislike for the victim without showing that the "aaltperps" at least had an opportunity to commit the murder. * * *

In the same way, evidence of opportunity alone is insufficient to guarantee admissibility. * * * Simply showing that the "aaltperp" was at the scene of the crime, without also showing some connection between the "aaltperp" and the crime, will generally not be allowed. * * *

A defendant who is able to offer evidence of both motive and opportunity by an "aaltperp," however, is in a different position. As Professor McCord notes, appellate courts have almost invariably reversed when proffered evidence of both motive and opportunity has been excluded by the trial court. * * *

* * * Appellant did attempt to offer a defense to the methamphetamine-related charges: that Kuhl planted the methamphetamine-related products in the vehicle without his knowledge. The [ ] testimony and document support this theory by substantiating Kuhl's jealousy of Hanks and her worry that Hanks would "break up" Kuhl's relationship with Huskey. The document also illustrated Kuhl's affection for scheming, evidenced by her admissions on the cardboard document that "[w]e were trying to 'set him up,' and 'we planned it." 'The jury was aware, of course, that Kuhl had the opportunity to place the drugs in her own vehicle. However, without evidence of her motive for doing so, Appellant's defense was left in shambles.

[The Court reversed the charges related to the methamphetamine laboratory and remanded for a new trial.]

NOTES

1. **_Constitutional Rights._** There is a constitutional right guaranteed to those accused of crimes to confront witnesses against them. A defendant also has the right to present a defense, which includes the right to present witnesses on his or her behalf. In *Washington v. Texas*, 388 U.S. 14 (1967), the Supreme Court stated:

> The right to offer the testimony of witnesses, and to compel their attendance, if necessary, is in plain terms the right to present a defense, the right to present the defendant's version of the facts as well as the prosecution's to the jury so it may decide where the truth lies. Just as an accused has the right to confront the prosecution's witnesses for the purpose of challenging their testimony, he has the right to present his own witnesses to establish a defense. This right is a fundamental element of due process of law.

2. **_Evidence Rule Restrictions._** In *Holmes v. South Carolina*, 547 U.S. 319 (2006), the Court examined "whether a criminal defendant's federal constitutional rights are violated by an evidence rule under which the defendant may not introduce proof of third-party guilt if the prosecution has introduced forensic evidence that, if believed, strongly supports a guilty verdict." Justice Alito, writing the Court's opinion, emphasized the importance of "a criminal defendant's right to have 'a

meaningful opportunity to present a complete defense.'" The Court, finding no "legitimate end" in this particular State evidence rule to allow it to deprive the defendant of this right, held that the defendant should not be precluded by a State's evidence rule from being allowed to produce evidence that he had been framed and that a third-party was guilty of the crime.

3. *Affirmative Defenses.* An affirmative defense is one offered by a defendant that does not dispute the element of the offense, such as whether the acts constituting the crime took place, that the defendant is the one who engaged in the activity, or that the defendant intended the particular conduct or result. Instead, this type of defense offers a rationale for the conduct, such as a justification or an excuse, to persuade the jury that the person should not be held responsible for the actions. In *State v. Cohen*, 568 So.2d 49 (Fla. 1990), the Florida Supreme Court described affirmative defenses this way:

> An "affirmative defense" is any defense that assumes the complaint or charges to be correct but raises other facts that, if true, would establish a valid excuse or justification or a right to engage in the conduct in question. An affirmative defense does not concern itself with the elements of the offense at all; it concedes them. In effect, an affirmative defense says, "Yes, I did it, but I had a good reason."

Model Penal Code § 1.12(3) provides that "[a] ground of defense is affirmative * * * when: (c) it involves a matter of excuse or justification peculiarly within the knowledge of the defendant on which he can fairly be required to adduce supporting evidence." The defense of renunciation of the conspiracy is an example of a defense that is considered "peculiarly within the knowledge of the defendant." Model Penal Code § 1.12(4)(a) also provides that "the burden of proving the fact is on the prosecution or defendant, depending on whose interest or contention will be furthered if the finding should be made . . . ." As a general matter, the prosecution is not required to negate the defense before it is offered by the defendant because it does not go to the sufficiency of the government's proof of the crime. On the other hand, a defendant does not have to offer his or her own evidence to establish an affirmative defense, so that one can be raised by evidence presented by either side.

4. *Inconsistent Defenses*. As long as the defendant offers sufficient evidence to support a defense, there is no problem with bringing forth inconsistent defenses. In *United States v. Trujillo*, 390 F.3d 1267 (10th Cir. 2004), the court stated:

> "[A] defendant is entitled to an instruction as to any recognized defense for which there exists evidence sufficient for a reasonable jury to find in his favor." *Mathews v. United States*, 485 U.S. 58 (1988). "Even if the defendant denies one or more elements of the crime, he is entitled to an entrapment instruction whenever there is sufficient evidence from which

a reasonable jury could find entrapment." *Id*. We have embraced the proposition in reiterating that a criminal defendant "is entitled to instructions on any defense, including inconsistent ones, that find support in the evidence and the law and failure to so instruct is reversible error." *United States v. Abeyta*, 27 F.3d 470 (10th Cir. 1994).

Although *Mathews* involved an entrapment defense, we have not limited its holding solely to cases involving entrapment. Indeed, in *Abeyta*, the trial court perceived a "claim of self defense preclude[d] defendant from arguing that he was too drunk to act with specific intent. If he acted intentionally to defend himself, we are told, it just 'doesn't fit' to think him too drunk to appreciate the import of his actions." We observed that argument overlooked the fact defendant is entitled to instructions on "any defense, including inconsistent ones," with evidentiary support.

5. ***Client Perjury.*** If a lawyer knows the client intends to lie on the witness stand to avoid being found guilty, can the lawyer permit the client to testify or reveal the possible perjury to the court? The Supreme Court gave one answer to that question in *Nix v. Whiteside*, 475 U.S. 157 (1986), a case in which the defendant claimed his lawyer was ineffective because he threatened to tell the judge that the defendant intended to lie in his testimony. The Court stated:

> It is universally agreed that at a minimum the attorney's first duty when confronted with a proposal for perjurious testimony is to attempt to dissuade the client from the unlawful course of conduct. *Model Rules of Professional Conduct*, Rule 3.3, Comment; Wolfram, *Client Perjury*, 50 S.CAL.L.REV. 809 (1977). A statement directly in point is found in the commentary to the Model Rules of Professional Conduct under the heading "False Evidence": "When false evidence is offered by the client, however, a conflict may arise between the lawyer's duty to keep the client's revelations confidential and the duty of candor to the court. Upon ascertaining that material evidence is false, the lawyer *should seek to persuade the client that the evidence should not be offered* or, if it has been offered, that its false character should immediately be disclosed." *Model Rules of Professional Conduct*, Rule 3.3, Comment (1983) (emphasis added).

> The commentary thus also suggests that an attorney's revelation of his client's perjury to the court is a professionally responsible and acceptable response to the conduct of a client who has actually given perjured testimony. Similarly, the Model Rules and the commentary, as well as the Code of Professional Responsibility adopted in Iowa, expressly permit withdrawal from representation as an appropriate response of an attorney when the client threatens to commit perjury. * * *

The essence of the brief amicus of the American Bar Association reviewing practices long accepted by ethical lawyers is that under no circumstance may a lawyer either advocate or passively tolerate a client's giving false testimony. This, of course, is consistent with the governance of trial conduct in what we have long called "a search for truth." The suggestion sometimes made that "a lawyer must believe his client, not judge him" in no sense means a lawyer can honorably be a party to or in any way give aid to presenting known perjury.

Some courts take the approach that the lawyer whose client intends to commit perjury should simply call the defendant to the witness stand and let him or her testify in a narrative approach, with the lawyer not asking questions. The narrative approach allows the client to tell his or her story without the lawyer partaking in presenting the false testimony. In *People v. Johnson*, 72 Cal.Rptr.2d 805 (Cal. 1998), the California Supreme Court opted for the narrative approach, under which the client testifies but the lawyer may not rely on that testimony in making an argument to the jury regarding the client's guilt. The court stated:

> None of the approaches to a client's stated intention to commit perjury is perfect. Of the various approaches, we believe the narrative approach represents the best accommodation of the competing interests of the defendant's right to testify and the attorney's obligation not to participate in the presentation of perjured testimony since it allows the defendant to tell the jury, in his own words, his version of what occurred, a right which has been described as fundamental, and allows the attorney to play a passive role.

> In contrast, the two extremes — fully cooperating with the defendant's testimony and refusing to present the defendant's testimony — involve no accommodation of the conflicting interests; the first gives no consideration to the attorney's ethical obligations, the second gives none to the defendant's right to testify. The other intermediate solutions — persuasion, withdrawal and disclosure — often result in no solution, i.e., the defendant is not persuaded, the withdrawal leads to an endless chain of withdrawals and disclosure compromises client confidentiality and typically requires further action.

> We disagree with those commentators who have found the narrative approach necessarily communicates to the jury that defense counsel believes the defendant is lying . . . [T]he jury may surmise the "defendant desired to testify unhampered by the traditional question and answer format." Because the defendant in a criminal trial is not situated the same as other witnesses, it would not be illogical for a jury to assume that special rules apply to his testimony, including a right to testify in a narrative fashion. We do not believe the possibility of a negative

inference the defendant is lying should preclude the use of the narrative approach since the alternative would be worse, i.e., the attorney's active participation in presenting the perjured testimony or exclusion of the defendant's testimony, neither of which strikes a balance between the competing interests involved.

The danger that the defendant may testify falsely is mitigated by the fact that the defendant is subject to impeachment and can be cross-examined just like any other witness. The jury is no less capable of assessing the defendant's credibility than it is of any other witness.

Does the narrative approach convey the impression that the lawyer is incompetent for not relying on the defendant's testimony in the closing argument? Will the jury speculate as to why the lawyer remains passive during the defendant's testimony, which is often the key point in a criminal trial?

The National Association of Criminal Defense Lawyers (NACDL) rejects the narrative approach. In a complex opinion that requires full study of the entire opinion, the NACDL relies on the "constitutional privilege against self-incrimination and the constitutional right to the effective assistance of counsel" in stating that: "[i]f the lawyer is unable to dissuade the client or to withdraw, the lawyer may not assist the client to improve upon the perjury, but must maintain the client's confidences and secrets, examine the client in the ordinary way, and to the extent tactically desirable, argue the client's testimony to the jury as evidence in the case." Realizing that "no ethics opinion can guarantee a safe harbor in difficult cases," the NACDL further advises defense counsel "to proceed carefully, with full knowledge of the applicable ethical rules of the jurisdiction and, ideally, with the advise of counsel."

6. ***Fruits and Instrumentalities of Crime***. When a defendant tells the attorney where the fruits of a crime are, is the attorney required to disclose the location to the authorities? In the well-known case *People v. Belge*, 372 N.Y.S.2d 798 (N.Y. Co. Ct. 1975), Robert Garrow told his two attorneys, Francis Belge and Frank Armani, where the bodies of two young women he murdered could be found; Garrow had been charged with murdering another victim, and had not been charged with killing the two women. The attorneys viewed the location of the bodies to ascertain whether Garrow was telling the truth, but did not otherwise disturb them. Belge and Armani did not disclose the whereabouts of the two victims immediately, but it came out at trial. The lawyers were later charged with the crime of violating a public health law by not reporting the location of the bodies to allow for an immediate burial. The charges were dismissed because the information from Garrow was protected by the attorney-client privilege. What if the attorneys had moved the bodies? In *People v. Meredith*, 631 P.2d 46 (Cal. 1981), the California Supreme Court held that the attorney-client privilege did not apply when a lawyer's investigator took the victim's wallet from a trash can behind the defendant's

apartment after the defendant told his lawyer that it was there. The court held that by removing the evidence, the lawyer interfered with the government's ability to locate the evidence, and therefore the lawyer could be required to reveal the location of the wallet. The statement by the client to the attorney about the location of the wallet remained protected by the privilege. When a lawyer comes into possession of the fruits or instrumentalities of a crime, the attorney-client privilege does not shield that evidence from having to be turned over to the authorities. *See In re Ryder*, 263 F.Supp. 360 (E.D. Va. 1967).

§ 15.03 Alibi Defense

State v. Deffebaugh
89 P.3d 582 (Kan. 2004)

The opinion of the court was delivered by GERNON, J.

Charles R. Deffebaugh, Jr., appeals his conviction for one count of selling cocaine. Deffebaugh's conviction resulted from a controlled purchase of two rocks of cocaine by a police informant who was cooperating with the Coffeyville police to avoid prosecution for a DUI.

Before sending the informant to purchase the cocaine, the Coffeyville police searched the informant to verify that she had no drugs on her person or in her car. An officer attached a listening device under the informant's clothing so officers could monitor the controlled purchase. After recording the serial number for each bill, an officer gave the informant $30 for purchasing cocaine.

The informant drove to a house that Coffeyville police had been observing for drug activity and parked her car along the curb. Officers followed the informant to the location of the purchase and observed the transaction from a distance to avoid being detected. Four black males approached the informant's car. The officers were too far away to visually identify the men, but Detective Robson recognized two voices over the audio transmitter, one being that of Calvin Shobe.

The informant, who was not familiar with any of the men at her car, provided the officers with a description of the man named "Jimmie" who had taken her money and given her two rocks of cocaine. Based on the informant's description, Detective Robson prepared two photo lineups and showed them to the informant within 24 hours of the controlled purchase. The informant did not select any of the pictures in the first photo array but selected Deffebaugh's photo from the second photo array without hesitation.

Within 24 hours of the controlled purchase, Detective Robson obtained a search warrant for the house associated with the controlled purchase. When the warrant was executed, the police found Deffebaugh and 10 other black males in the house, along with cash, cocaine, and guns. Deffebaugh claimed ownership of some of the money found on the floor, including one of the marked bills from the controlled purchase.

At trial, Deffebaugh called Shobe to testify that Shobe was present at the controlled purchase but Deffebaugh was not there. The State objected to Shobe's testimony, claiming that Deffebaugh failed to give notice of an alibi defense. The trial court prohibited Shobe from testifying that Shobe was present at the controlled purchase but that Deffebaugh was not there. * * *

The State argues that the trial court correctly prohibited Shobe from testifying regarding Deffebaugh's presence at the drug sale. The State contends that Shobe's testimony falls squarely under K.S.A. 22-3218, which requires a defendant to provide notice before offering evidence of an alibi. To resolve this issue, we must interpret K.S.A. 22-3218. * * *

K.S.A. 22-3218 provides in pertinent part:

(1) In the trial of any criminal action where the complaint, indictment or information charges specifically the time and place of the crime alleged to have been committed, and the nature of the crime is such as necessitated the personal presence of the one who committed the crime, and the defendant proposes to offer evidence to the effect that he was at some other place at the time of the crime charged, he shall give notice in writing of that fact to the prosecuting attorney except that no such notice shall be required to allow testimony as to alibi, by the defendant himself, in his own defense. The notice shall state where defendant contends he was at the time of the crime, and shall have endorsed thereon the names of witnesses he proposes to use in support of such contention.

(4) Unless the defendant gives the notice as above provided he shall not be permitted to offer evidence to the effect that he was at some other place at the time of the crime charged.

Although the defense does not generally have to disclose the names of defense witnesses prior to trial, the disclosure of alibi witnesses is an exception to that rule. The purpose of K.S.A. 22-3218 is to protect the State from last minute, easily fabricated defenses. The notice requirement allows the State to investigate and call rebuttal witnesses if necessary.

Kansas case law has not addressed the question of what is an alibi subject to the notice provisions of K.S.A. 22-3218. Dicta in prior Kansas cases has established two definitions for "alibi" without relying on or interpreting the language of K.S.A. 22-3218. In *State v. Pham*, 675 P.2d 848 (Kan. 1984), this court distinguished an alibi defense from a general denial by noting that "[a]n alibi places the defendant at the relevant time in a different place than the scene involved and so removed therefrom as to render it impossible for the accused to be the guilty party." This definition for "alibi" relied on *Black's Law Dictionary*.

Dicta in other Kansas cases provides a broader definition for alibi taken from PIK Crim. 52.19, which noted that an instruction is not necessary for the alibi defense because it "is not an affirmative defense, as is entrapment or insanity; it consists only of evidence showing that the defendant was not present at the time or place of the crime." *State v. Peters*, 656 P.2d 768 (Kan. 1983) (concluding that courts need not instruct on alibi as an affirmative defense).

K.S.A. 22-3218 is ambiguous. In the first sentence, the statute defines alibi as "evidence to the effect that [the accused] was at some other place at the time of the crime charged." By using the phrase "to the effect that," the legislature does not limit alibi evidence to direct testimony but includes evidence that raises an inference that the accused was at some other place. The State is relying on this inference as the basis for its argument that Shobe's proposed testimony is alibi evidence. Even though there is no direct evidence of where Deffebaugh was at the time of the drug sale, Shobe's testimony that Deffebaugh was not there infers that Deffebaugh was at some other place.

The State's argument, however, overlooks the language in the second sentence of the statute, which provides that "[t]he notice shall state where defendant contends he was at the time of the crime, and shall have endorsed thereon the names of witnesses he proposes to use in support of such contention." K.S.A. 22-3218. This sentence appears to limit alibi evidence to direct evidence that the defendant was at another specific place. Otherwise, the defendant cannot state where he contends he was in the notice.

The Court of Appeals resolved the ambiguity in K.S.A. 22-3218 by placing more emphasis on the second, more specific sentence in 22-3218(1). It concluded that Shobe was not an alibi witness under K.S.A. 22-3218 because Shobe could not testify regarding Deffebaugh's specific whereabouts at the time of the drug sale. Instead of treating Shobe as an alibi witness, the Court of Appeals concluded that Shobe was an eyewitness and so his identity and testimony did not have to be disclosed prior to trial. Based on that analysis, the Court of Appeals reversed Deffebaugh's conviction, holding that the trial court erroneously prohibited Shobe from testifying as an eyewitness. We agree with the Court of Appeals.

The Court of Appeals decision is supported by a historical analysis of the word "alibi." * * * In Latin, the meaning of alibi is literally "somewhere else." The word "alibi" was first used in the English language in the legal context as an adverb meaning "elsewhere." By the end of the 18th century, the word "alibi" was used as a noun meaning a "plea of being elsewhere at the time of a crime." AYTO, DICTIONARY OF WORD ORIGINS, 17 (1st Paperback ed.1993).

* * * Two states have addressed facts similar to those in this case. In [*People v.*] *Fritz*, 417 N.E.2d 612 (Ill. 1981), the Illinois Supreme Court reversed the defendant's conviction for indecent liberties with a child. The trial court had ruled that the defendant was attempting to introduce alibi testimony without proper notice. The alleged offense occurred in the home that the defendant shared with his wife, and the wife testified that the defendant was not home when the offense allegedly occurred. The *Fritz* court distinguished between attempting to prove that the defendant was at some other definite place and attempting to prove that the defendant was not at the scene of the crime. In determining that the wife's testimony was not an alibi, the *Fritz* court stated: "[A] defendant may introduce the testimony of an occurrence witness that the witness did not see the defendant at the time and place in question. Such testimony is elicited to rebut the State's case. It is not designed to establish that a defendant was at any other definite place."

In *State v. Volpone*, 376 A.2d 199 (N.J. Super. Ct. App. Div. 1977), the defendant was charged with assault and battery following a fight involving baseball bats. At his trial, the defendant attempted to introduce testimony from one of the fight participants that the defendant was not there when the fight occurred. The trial court excluded the testimony because the defendant had not provided the statutory notice of an alibi defense to the prosecution. The appellate court concluded that the exclusion was improper and ordered a new trial.

The *Volpone* court relied on the purpose of the notice statute — eliminating the surprise from alibi testimony during trial. According to the Volpone court, the State knows that it must prove that the defendant was present at the scene of the crime. Consequently, the State's investigation encompasses the premise that the defendant was present, and the State is not surprised by evidence that the defendant was not present at the scene of the crime. However, the State cannot investigate evidence that the defendant was in another definite place unless the defendant provides notice of where he claims to have been in advance of trial. Because the State was not surprised by the participant's testimony that the defendant was not there during the fight, the testimony was not for the purpose of an alibi, but was merely a rebuttal of the State's evidence placing the defendant at the scene. * * *

Although the statutory language [in the Kansas statute] is different, we agree with the analysis of the *Fritz* and *Volpone* courts. In this case, the State knew it had the burden of proving that Deffebaugh was present when the drug sale occurred. To meet its burden, the State introduced eyewitness testimony from the informant who performed the controlled buy identifying Deffebaugh as the person who sold her cocaine. Detective Robson observed the drug transaction and knew that there were four black males present at the informant's car. Detective Robson also recognized Shobe's voice on the audiotape made during the transaction. Shobe was one of the

11 men arrested when the search warrant was issued and Deffebaugh was arrested. The State knew that Shobe was present at the drug transaction. The State had an opportunity to interview Shobe when he was arrested with Deffebaugh. The record, however, does not establish whether the State interviewed Shobe regarding the drug transaction before Deffebaugh's trial. These facts do not support the conclusion that Shobe's testimony as an eyewitness was a surprise to the State or that the State needed time to investigate Shobe's statement. Consequently, there is no reason to exclude Shobe's eyewitness testimony simply because he would have testified that Deffebaugh was not there.

When the statutory language of K.S.A. 22-3218 is considered as a whole and interpreted so as to be consistent, harmonious, and sensible, the statute requires a defendant to provide notice when he or she intends to introduce evidence that he or she was at some other specific place during the time of the crime. K.S.A. 22-3218 does not require a defendant to provide notice when he or she intends to introduce eyewitness testimony regarding his or her presence at the scene of the crime. This interpretation is consistent with the ordinary usage of the word "alibi" and the purpose of the statute. The broader interpretation asserted by the State does not harmonize the language of the statute, consider the ordinary usage of the word "alibi," or incorporate the legislative purpose behind the statute's enactment. Accordingly, we affirm the Court of Appeals decision reversing the district court's interpretation of K.S.A. 22-3218 and remand the matter for a new trial.

NOTES AND QUESTIONS

1. *Alibi Instructions.* The defendant may be required by statute to provide notice to the government of an intent to present an alibi defense. For example, the Federal Rules of Criminal Procedure, Rule 12.1, provides that "[a]n attorney for the government may request in writing that the defendant notify an attorney for the government of any intended alibi defense. The request must state the time, date, and place of the alleged offense." The defense is then given fourteen days to respond, and the federal rule explicitly provides what must be included in the defendant's notice of alibi. When the defense presents an alibi, the court will often provide an explicit alibi instruction to the jury that states that the government is required to prove that the defendant was present at the time and place of the charged crime and that if there is a reasonable doubt as to whether the defendant was at this time and place of the crime, then the jury should find the defendant not guilty.

2. *Sufficient Evidence to Instruct on Alibi.* A claim that the government has not proven the defendant is the person who committed the crime is not the same as an alibi defense, and the court need not give the jury an alibi instruction absent some

evidence that the defendant was elsewhere when the crime occurred. The Delaware Supreme Court described when an alibi instruction is appropriate in *Gardner v. State*, 397 A.2d 1372 (Del. 1979):

> As a threshold consideration, of course, before an instruction is required there must be some credible evidence to establish an alibi defense. If a Trial Judge is satisfied that there is some credible evidence showing that the defendant was elsewhere when the crime occurred, then a determination must be made whether an instruction is required. In those circumstances, if a defendant requests an instruction on alibi, we think one should be given; and any doubt should be resolved in favor of giving the instruction.

3. ***Ethical Issues in Presenting an Alibi Defense***. Lawyers are bound by the ethics rules of the state in which they are admitted and practice. These rules require, among other things, that the lawyer keep client communications and information gained during the course of representation confidential and not reveal that information without a prior waiver by the client. At the same time, lawyers also owe certain duties to the courts, one such duty can come into play when a client wishes to present an alibi defense that involves some false testimony or evidence. The American Bar Association (ABA) has adopted the Model Rules of Professional Conduct that serves as a guide for the states in adopting their rules. ABA Model Rule 3.3(a) provides:

> A lawyer shall not knowingly :

> (1) make a false statement of material fact or law to a tribunal;

> (2) fail to disclose a material fact to a tribunal when disclosure is necessary to avoid assisting a criminal or fraudulent act by the client;

> (3) fail to disclose to the tribunal legal authority in the controlling jurisdiction known to the lawyer to be directly adverse to the position of the client and not disclosed by opposing counsel; or

> (4) offer evidence that the lawyer knows to be false. If a lawyer has offered material evidence and comes to know of its falsity, the lawyer shall take reasonable remedial measures.

Michigan Ethics Committee Opinion CI-1164 (1987)

A client charged with armed robbery has confidentially admitted the crime to his attorney. The client proposes to call some friends as witnesses at the trial who will give truthful testimony that the client was with them at the time of the crime. Relying on the detectives' notes to help him recall the time, the victim testified at the preliminary examination that the robbery occurred at the same hour and time to which the friends will testify. The client explains the time coincidence by admitting to counsel that he stole the victim's watch and rendered him unconscious so that the victim's sense of time was incorrect when relating the circumstances of the robbery to the investigating detectives. Client and lawyer have decided that the client will not testify at the trial.

The lawyer asks whether it would be ethical for the lawyer to subpoena the friends to trial to testify that client was with them at the alleged time of the crime.

[Michigan Code of Professional Responsibility] MCPR DR 7-101 requires counsel to represent the client zealously. A defense lawyer may present any evidence that is truthful. If the ethical rule were otherwise it would mean that a defendant who confessed guilt to counsel would never be able to have an active defense at trial.

The danger of an opposite approach is that sometimes innocent defendants "confess guilt" to their counsel or put forth a perceived "truthful" set of facts that do not pass independent scrutiny. Many crimes have degrees of guilt, as in homicide, where the "true facts" go to the accused's intent; something a jailed defendant may not be in a reflective mood to assess. Criminal defense counsel are not sent to the jail's interview room to be their client's one person jury and they certainly are not dispatched to court to be their client's hangman. Our society has made the decision to permit a person charged with a crime to make full disclosure to his counsel without fear that, absent the threat of some future conduct (such as a threat to kill a witness), the lawyer will not disclose the information so provided.

The role of criminal defense counsel is to zealously defend the client within the boundaries of all legal and ethical rules. Therefore, if the information confidentially disclosed by the client were to prevent counsel from marshaling an otherwise proper defense, the client would, in effect, be penalized for making the disclosure. Such a policy, over a long run, would tend to cause future defendants to fail to disclose everything to their lawyer; the result would be that they would receive an inadequate defense. Such an approach would be fundamentally inconsistent with the implicit representation made to defendants as a part of procedural due process that they may disclose everything to their lawyer without fear of adverse consequences.

It is the prosecution's responsibility to marshall relevant and accurate testimony of criminal conduct. It is not the obligation of defense counsel to correct inaccurate evidence introduced by the prosecution or to ignore truthful evidence that could exculpate his client. Although the tenor of this opinion may appear to risk an unfortunate result to society in the particular situation posed, such an attitude by defense counsel will serve in the long run to preserve the system of criminal justice envisioned by our constitution.

MCPR DR 7-102(A)(4) prohibits counsel from using perjured testimony or "false evidence," but it is perfectly proper to call to the witness stand those witnesses on behalf of the client who will present truthful testimony. The testimony of the friends will not spread any perjured testimony upon the record. The client indeed was with the witnesses at the hour to which they will testify. The victim's mistake concerning the precise time of the crime results in this windfall defense to the client.

In CI-394 the Committee reviewed a situation where there were tire marks at the scene of the crime. Defendant, after being charged with a crime, altered the tire treads on his car. An expert witness, retained by the defense, was misled when he examined the evidence of the tire tracks. We there opined that the defense lawyer could not ethically present evidence through an expert witness when the expert's opinion was based upon a set of circumstances where the client tampered with the evidence. To do so would perpetrate a fraud upon the court. The situation with the friends as alibi witnesses in the instant case does not involve tampering with evidence. One cannot suborn the truth.

We said in CI-634 that it is axiomatic that the right of a client to effective counsel does not include the right to compel counsel to knowingly assist or participate in the commission of perjury or the creation or presentation of false evidence. Thus, where truthful testimony will be offered, it seems axiomatic that a defendant is entitled to the effective assistance of counsel in presenting evidence, even though the defendant has made inculpatory statements to his counsel.

Counsel must never be a party to presenting perjury to a court. However, it must be remembered that litigation involves the independent testing by an impartial trier of fact of perceptions of events recalled by human beings. The civil lawyer enjoys the luxury of being able to scrutinize testimony many months before trial by propounding written interrogatories to witnesses and by deposing them on the record before a court reporter. The criminal lawyer does not enjoy this advantage; he goes into the courtroom with, at best, an educated guess at what witnesses for the prosecution may testify and a hope that his own witnesses will not be intimidated into giving testimony different than what he has been led to believe they would. When a witness in a civil case testifies about a daytime event at work he may be expected to have a clear recall of the event. In contrast a witness in a criminal case often testifies about events that occur in the dark of night, diminishing the witnesses' ability to observe. Sometimes a witness will have abused a controlled substance contemporaneous with making his observations, dulling the witnesses' ability to perceive. In practically all criminal cases involving violence the witness is frightened and shocked so that his ability to accurately recall events is affected. Therefore a criminal lawyer must be especially sensitive to the requirement of truthful testimony that Canon 7 places upon him. This burden is more difficult to shoulder than the neat bundle of interrogatories and depositions carried to trial by the civil lawyer.

It should be mentioned that it is appropriate for the lawyer to discuss these concerns with the client. The lawyer must guard against the natural human reaction in a desperate situation (eyewitness testimony to crime with mandatory prison sentence) to become so enamored of an unique defense opportunity that, in contemplating the small tree, he fails to see the forest. It is the convicted client who does the time, not the lawyer. An alibi defense in the instant case may be foolish; the lawyer has a responsibility to counsel his client accordingly. Defendants in serious criminal cases usually are willing to grasp at straws if their lawyer, by word or deed, suggests there is a chance at acquittal using such evidence. It may be in the best interest of the client not to present the alibi defense and, instead, negotiate for a guilty plea to a lesser offense. That evidence could ethically be presented does not mean that it should be. Obviously if the complaining witness gives positive identification of his assailant and if there is other inculpatory evidence, a jury may give very short shrift to the testimony, however true, of defendant's friends.

In the glare of the ethical question, counsel should not be blinded to the difficulty of his client's cause. All the evidence should be weighed and evaluated before deciding to go forward with an alibi defense. This thoughtful consideration of the client and his situation is the mark of a lawyer with high standards of integrity, appropriate discretion, and absolute honesty.

PROBLEM FORTY-EIGHT

Gardner is charged with first-degree murder in the death of Jean. At trial, Gardner testified to being out drinking at a bar on the evening in question, and that upon returning home found Jean severely beaten and in a semiconscious state. Gardner ran to a near-by hospital and persuaded two individuals there to help to bring the victim to the hospital where Jean was pronounced dead on arrival at 1:10 a.m. The doctor estimated that the victim had been dead for an hour, thus placing the time of death at approximately 12:05 a.m. Gardner arrived at the hospital a little after 1:00 a.m. The medical examiner testified that the victim died within a few minutes after receiving the injuries. Although Gardner did not know the exact time when returning home to find Jean, Gardner testified that when leaving the bar it "was about ready to close." A witness for the defense testified that Gardner left the bar "not too much before it closed" at 1:00 a.m., although the witness did not recall the exact time and did not recall seeing Gardner in the bar the entire time. A second defense witness testified to leaving the bar between 12:35 a.m. and 12:45 a.m. in the defendant's car, but this person first met Gardner just a few minutes before leaving.

A. How should the court rule on defense counsel's motion to give the jury an alibi instruction?

B. Prior to trial, counsel meets with Gardner and determines that Gardner may have a defense to the crime due to being quite drunk the night of the killing. An intoxication defense would permit a jury to find the defendant did not act with the requisite intent for first-degree murder, but Gardner could be convicted of second degree murder. Can defense counsel advance both defenses — alibi and intoxication? What are the risks in arguing the two defenses, and the potential benefits?

§ 15.04 Justifications and Excuses

Historically, defenses were divided into justifications and excuses. In *Adams v. State*, 228 P.2d 195 (Okla. Crim. App. 1951), the Court of Criminal Appeals of Oklahoma stated in distinguishing between justifiable and excusable homicide:

> Justifiable homicide is the taking of human life under circumstances of justification, as a matter of right, such as self-defense, or other causes set out in the statute. Excusable homicide is where death results from a lawful act by lawful means, accomplished accidentally or by misfortune or misadventure, or so accomplished with sufficient provocation, with no undue advantage and without unnecessary cruel treatment.

Courts have moved away from distinguishing between justification and excuse. This is in part because it is difficult conceptually to distinguish between these two types of defenses, even though the distinction is easily stated. Professor Berman explained the difference in this way: "[a] justified action is not criminal, whereas an excused defendant has committed a crime but is not punishable." Mitchell N. Berman, *Justification and Excuse, Law and Morality*, 53 DUKE L.J. 1 (2003). Consider also the analysis offered by Professor Milhizer:

> Perhaps the clearest expression of justification and excuse within the criminal law is as general or affirmative defenses. When operating in this fashion, justification and excuse provide an exculpatory rationale for

finding an actor not guilty, even if he has engaged in all the conduct, possessed the state of mind, and caused the harm otherwise necessary to constitute a crime. These defensive theories, as traditionally understood, exonerate based on principles that are broader than the facts of a particular case, because of the manner in which they appropriately apply to the facts of a particular case. Justification and excuse defenses thus involve applying the general to the specific, in order to make a principled judgment as to whether a given defendant ought to be stigmatized as a criminal and punished accordingly.

Although justification and excuse thus operate similarly in a procedural sense, they are, as discussed in greater detail later in this article, rudimentarily different in terms of their substance. Justification defenses focus on the act and not the actor — they exculpate otherwise criminal conduct because it benefits society, or because the conduct is in some other way judged to be socially useful. Excuse defenses focus on the actor and not the act — they exculpate even though an actor's conduct may have harmed society because the actor, for whatever reason, is not judged to be blameworthy. Accordingly, a mother would be justified–and thus be in no need of an excuse — for trespassing into a hardware store to appropriate tools to rescue her son trapped in a house fire; she would be excused — but not justified — for robbing the store at the behest of her son's kidnapper in exchange for her son's safe return. Society has determined through its criminal justice system that a mother does not deserve to be stigmatized or punished in either circumstance.

Eugene R. Milhizer, *Justification and Excuse: What They Were, What They Are, and What They Ought to Be*, 78 ST. JOHN'S L. REV. 725 (2004). Does the distinction make a difference when the outcome is usually the same — a "not guilty" verdict? Most defense lawyers, and probably every acquitted defendant, care little for the niceties of the theory, but the distinction does make a difference when trying to articulate the viability of the defense in circumstances outside the normal case. Consider whether the justification defenses offered in the following case demonstrates that the defendant should not be found guilty of the offense because the result produced a social benefit, and hence was justified.

State v. Sedlock
882 So.2d 1278 (La. Ct. App. 2004)

EZELL, Judge.

On April 29, 2003, the Defendant, Steven Russell Sedlock, was charged in a bill of information with * * * cruelty to juveniles, a violation of La.R.S. 14:93. * * *

On February 2, 2004, the Defendant waived his right to trial by jury, the matters were consolidated for trial, and a bench trial commenced. After presentation of the evidence, the trial court found the Defendant guilty of * * * cruelty to juveniles. * * *

The Defendant is the father of J.T., the victim in this matter. J.T. was a fourth grade student at Grand Lake School on April 7, 2003. On that day, the assistant principal, Jacqueline Holmes, called J.T.'s parents to inform them that he had been sent to the office due to disciplinary problems. J.T.'s parents had a conference with Ms. Holmes, and the Defendant then checked J.T. out of school. When leaving the office, the Defendant kicked J.T. in the buttocks and then kneed him in the back. Ms. Holmes was concerned about J.T.'s well-being, so she called the police. Deputy Larry Broussard responded to Ms. Holmes' call and then went to the Defendant's residence. While at the Defendant's residence, Deputy Broussard observed various injuries to J.T. and arrested the Defendant. * * *

The Defendant argues that his actions were justified as punishment for J.T.'s behavior at school. "Justification can be claimed when the conduct is reasonable discipline of minors by a parent." *State v. Comeaux*, 319 So.2d 897 (La. 1975). In *State v. Barnett*, 521 So.2d 663 (La. Ct. App. 1988), the defendant was convicted of attempted cruelty to juveniles after spanking his child with a belt. On appeal, the defendant argued the evidence was insufficient to establish the intent element of the crime. Additionally, he argued he was justified in spanking his son and the real issue was whether or not his exercise of discipline was reasonable. The defendant testified that he spanked his child with a dress belt and was not angry when he did so. He quit spanking the child when he noticed red marks on the child's buttocks. The victim's cousin observed the spanking, and when asked whether the defendant's actions exceeded the ordinary realm of a spanking, said no. Photographs taken eight hours after the spanking depicted severe bruises on the child's buttocks and thighs. A physician who examined the child on the day of the spanking testified that he had bruises all over his body and that the bruises on one area of his leg were overlapping and were too numerous to count. The court concluded that the spanking inflicted on the victim was intentional mistreatment which caused pain and suffering exceeding the bounds of reasonable discipline.

We find that the evidence proved beyond a reasonable doubt that the spanking Defendant administered upon J.T. caused pain and suffering that exceeded the bounds of reasonable discipline and was, therefore, not justified.

PETERS, J., dissenting.

I respectfully disagree with the majority opinion in this matter insofar as it affirms the defendant's conviction of cruelty to a juvenile. In my opinion, the State of Louisiana failed to establish the defendant's guilt beyond a reasonable doubt.

It is abundantly clear to me that J.T. required some degree of discipline. He had already failed the fourth grade once and was well on his way to failing a second time. The record reveals that J.T.'s attitude toward his educational and behavioral obligations left much to be desired, and this attitude had existed for an extended period of time. Thus, the defendant was faced with the task of, in some manner, redirecting J.T.'s attention to his shortcomings at school–both from an academic and a behavioral perspective. I do not disagree with the conclusion that the defendant's disciplinary measures were excessive. The question is whether they crossed the line into criminal activity. * * *

The trial record establishes that the defendant has a criminal history. It also seems to establish that the defendant's motivation in punishing his child was to impress upon J.T. his father's desire that J.T. not repeat his father's mistakes. The punishment's emphasis was on the importance of education, not the defendant's desire to impose physical punishment. I do not condone the defendant's imposition of punishment in this case. In fact, I agree with the trial court and the majority that the punishment imposed on J.T. did not fit the offense he committed. However, I cannot conclude that it reached a level such that it constituted a criminal offense. While the defendant could benefit from parenting classes, I do not believe that La.R.S. 14:93 was intended to apply to such a situation, especially given the fact that the defendant could actually lose his parental rights for this conviction.

Additionally, by finding the defendant guilty of the felony offense of cruelty to a juvenile, this court sends a chilling message to parents that corporal punishment may well be a path to criminal prosecution. This opinion clearly establishes that this punishment is not only not acceptable for J.T.'s behavior, but that it is also criminal. Should it be within our province to draw a line to state specifically the acceptable parameters of discipline for certain behaviors? I would think not and would reverse the conviction.

PROBLEM FORTY-NINE

A state statute provides a justification defense for the imposition of discipline on a child in the following circumstance:

(1) The actor is the parent or guardian or other person similarly responsible for the general care and supervision of a minor, or a person acting at the request of the parent, guardian, or other responsible person, and:

(a) The force is employed with due regard for the age and size of the minor and is reasonably related to the purpose of safeguarding or promoting the welfare of the minor, including the prevention or punishment of the minor's misconduct; and

(b) The force used is not designed to cause or known to create a risk of causing substantial bodily injury, disfigurement, extreme pain or mental distress, or neurological damage.

Would the defendant in *Sedlock* be able to establish this defense?

§ 15.05 Cultural Defenses

People v. Romero
81 Cal. Rptr. 2d 823 (Cal. Ct. App. 1999)

WISEMAN, J.

In an ever-increasing trend, this murder case arises from an all-too-familiar formula: one party commits a relatively minor "infraction" which quickly escalates into street violence and then death or serious injury. Many of us can relate to this phenomenon by reflecting upon our own experience behind the wheel of a car when a driver cuts too close to your vehicle, and "road rage" sets in.

The roots of this case are planted in a simple street scene. A group of men were crossing the road when Alex Bernal sped around the corner in his vehicle, and had to quickly brake. Words were exchanged, threats were hurled, and moments later Bernal was dying with a knife wound to his heart.

What makes this case unusual is defense counsel's attempt to introduce expert testimony on the sociology of poverty, and the role of honor, paternalism, and street fighters in the Hispanic culture. Although interesting, we conclude the trial court correctly decided this evidence was irrelevant to 1) whether defendant actually believed he was in imminent danger of death or great bodily injury; and 2) whether such a belief was objectively reasonable. In the words of the trial court, we are not prepared to sanction a "reasonable street fighter standard." The judgment is affirmed. * * *

Defendant testified that when Bernal came around the corner in the car, he yelled, "Slow down, fool." After Bernal parked and got out of his car, he and defendant began fighting. Defendant separated from the group and approached the driver because he felt he had to protect his younger brother. The fighting stopped, and defendant started to walk away. Bernal then struck him from behind. At this point defendant retrieved a knife from an unknown person, and began swinging it at Bernal to scare him away. As defendant swung the knife, Bernal was backing up. Defendant testified, "I had to stop him. From there, I didn't think of nothing else, you know." Bernal kicked at defendant a couple times, and defendant swung the knife at him. His only intention was to stop Bernal, who was kicking toward him. Defendant, however, admitted, "I can't say that I was scared." Defendant felt he had to stop Bernal from getting past him. However, he said, "I can't explain me doing what I did to him . . . ." Defendant acknowledged stabbing Bernal in the heart, but claimed he was attempting to stab Bernal in the leg. While admitting responsibility for Bernal's death, defendant maintained he never intended anyone to die.

Defendant testified he never saw Bernal with any weapons. He admitted Bernal never did or said anything to give defendant a reason to think Bernal was out to get his brother. When asked what caused him to think he had to stab Bernal to protect his brother, defendant responded: "I don't know where my brother was standing, who was doing what, where. All I know I couldn't let [Bernal] get there." "I can't let him pass me." "All I know is to stop that guy."

Other defense witnesses testified to Bernal's drinking problem, his temper, and his violent past. One witness, James Howard, testified that in 1979, his passenger/friend had thrown a shot glass at Bernal's car. In retaliation, Bernal shot Howard's car with a shotgun.

Defendant contends the trial court erred by ruling that the proposed testimony of Martin Sanchez Jankowski, a sociology professor, was irrelevant and inadmissible. According to defense counsel, Professor Jankowski had authored a book and numerous articles on the subject of street violence, and was an expert in Hispanic culture. We reject the claim of error and, in any event, find defendant was not prejudiced by the court's ruling. [The court summarized the law of self-defense, which requires that the person respond to an unlawful, imminent threat of death or serious bodily harm before using deadly force to resist. See Chap. 16].

According to defense counsel, Professor Jankowski's expertise deals with the sociology of poverty. He would testify that (1) street fighters have a special understanding of what is expected of them; (2) for a street fighter in the Hispanic culture, there is no retreat; (3) the Hispanic culture is based on honor, and honor defines a person; and (4) in this culture a person "would be responsible to take care of someone," i.e., defendant had a strong motivation to protect his younger brother. Stated differently, "He's the eldest male. He would assume a paternalistic role whether he wanted to or not. Something is expected of him."

Given the law, we conclude the testimony of Professor Jankowski was irrelevant to whether defendant actually believed he was in imminent danger of death or great bodily injury, and whether such a belief was objectively reasonable. We are unsure what defendant means by his reference to the sociology of poverty, and how it might affect his actual beliefs and the objective reasonableness of those beliefs. Similarly, even if we assume street fighters have a special understanding of what is expected of them, and that this is something with which the jurors are not acquainted, why is it relevant? Are street fighters expected to kill every person they fight with, regardless of the circumstances? If so, does this expectation replace or relax the legal requirement that before deadly force may be used a person must actually fear imminent death or great bodily injury? As noted by the trial court, "Then you're creating a separate standard for what you call street fighters." No authority or case law has been cited which supports a separate standard, and we decline to adopt one here.

In the same vein, whether a person should or should not retreat from a "street fight," has no bearing on whether that person may lawfully use deadly force. A decision not to retreat from a physical confrontation and a decision to kill are two separate acts and involve different mental exercises. The laws governing self-defense recognize these distinctions and apply different rules to these legal concepts. * * * While defendant attempted to blur the distinctions between the laws governing self-defense, the trial court correctly did not.

The evidence regarding honor, like evidence of street fighter mentality, is not relevant to whether deadly force was warranted under the circumstances. Is there honor in killing an unarmed man, and assuming that in defendant's mind it was the honorable thing to do, how does this relate to self-defense? Clearly, the question of defendant's honor was irrelevant to whether defendant was in actual fear of death or great bodily injury, and whether his fear was objectively reasonable.

Finally, even if defendant had a strong motivation to protect his younger brother, this does not answer the question of why it was necessary to use deadly force. Self-defense and defense of another are both recognized in the law. However, as with the legal concept that one need not retreat, motive is only part of the question. Assuming defendant was justified in using force to defend himself and/or to protect his brother, the question of whether he could use deadly force was a separate issue. Any expert testimony regarding honor, tradition, street mentality, culture, paternalism, poverty or sociology simply was irrelevant.

People v. Minifie, 56 Cal. Rptr. 2d 133 (Cal. 1996), does not help defendant's argument. There, the court held it was error for the trial court to have excluded evidence that the defendant (who shot a man that knocked him down and threatened to hit him with a crutch) had been threatened by members of a group who Minifie believed were associated with the victim. Unlike in Minifie, the testimony excluded in this case had nothing to do with a prior threat received by defendant from someone he associated with the victim. Minifie is not analogous to the issue here-the propriety of excluding sociological evidence.

Similarly, *People v. Davis*, 47 Cal. Rptr. 801 (Cal. 1965), does not help defendant. There, the evidence excluded was testimony from independent witnesses of prior incidents where the victim allegedly attacked other persons, sometimes with a knife. In this case, defendant was permitted to, and did, present evidence of prior acts of violence by the victim. Thus, no error under the Davis rationale occurred. * * *

Finally, defendant relies on *People v. Vu*, 278 Cal. Rptr. 2d 153 (Cal. Ct. App. 1991), for his contention that the exclusion of Professor Jankowski's testimony was error. There the court found the exclusion of an expert's testimony to be harmless error. The expert witness, a psychologist, was to testify about the effects of stress on perception to show that defendant's actual view of events may have differed from reality due to stress and preconceived expectations about what might happen. The defendant had testified he started to leave the apartment where his archenemy lived, after hearing someone call out to remove a gun and grenade. As he entered an alley, the victim, Cong Phan, and another man followed him. When he heard someone mention taking out a gun, and fearing he would be shot, he turned and shot Cong Phan. The court held the expert testimony was admissible "because defendant claimed he honestly believed Cong Phan was trying to hurt him." The expert testimony "would have supported defendant's argument that stress and expectations caused him to honestly perceive a threat where no threat was intended or apparent to others at the scene." However, since the jury rejected the charge of attempted murder and convicted the defendant of voluntary manslaughter on the theory of imperfect self-defense, the defendant was not prejudiced by the exclusion of the expert's testimony.

Putting aside the question of whether *Vu* was correctly decided, it is distinguishable. Here, unlike in *Vu*, defendant did not testify he was in imminent fear for his life at the time he stabbed Bernal. Thus, whatever stress he was under or expectation he had when he first started fighting with Bernal changed after it became obvious Bernal was not armed. Any preconceived notion defendant may have had about Bernal having a gun disappeared when Bernal fought by simply kicking into the air, and defendant could see he was unarmed. Under these circumstances, either defendant accidentally stabbed Bernal in the heart while attempting to stab his leg, as defendant testified, or he intentionally stabbed Bernal in the heart with malice aforethought, as established by the prosecution. Either way, defendant was not in fear of imminent death or great bodily injury when he stabbed Bernal. Although only defendant knows what his actual motivation was for stabbing Bernal, even his own testimony indicates it was not fear.

Further, no sociological expert could have provided this missing mental state of defendant's actual subjective state of mind at the time he stabbed Bernal. Therefore, even assuming Professor Janskowski could provide relevant testimony about street fighting, Hispanic honor and paternalism, its exclusion was harmless. Absent evidence that defendant was in fear of imminent death or great bodily injury, the jury had no evidentiary basis from which to conclude that defendant subjectively had an actual but unreasonable fear which negated malice afore-thought. Thus, it is not reasonably probable that but for exclusion of the proffered evidence, defendant would have received a more favorable result.

NOTES AND QUESTIONS

1. *Cultural Defenses and Existing Defenses*. In some cases a cultural defense will not need to be addressed because the accused will be able to present an argument that fits under a defense that has already been accepted by the legislature or courts of the State. For example, do the facts in the *Romero* case sound similar to a claim of self-defense? (*See* Chap. 16).

2. *Religious Defenses*. Should a defendant be able to have the jury consider religious beliefs as a defense to the criminal charge? Consider this issue as raised in *Nguyen v. State*, 520 S.E.2d 907 (Ga. 1999):

> Appellant sought to introduce expert evidence on appellant's Vietnamese religious beliefs, values and cultural traditions in support of her justifica-tion defense. The expert testimony proffered by the defense showed the loss of status, humiliation, and possible adverse spiritual consequences to appellant and her family from her husband's failure to maintain appellant's proper position in the household. However, there was no evidence that individuals sharing appellant's cultural background would believe themselves to be in danger of receiving any physical harm as a result of such loss of status and disrespectful treatment.

> While we can envision rare situations in which such evidence might be relevant to assist the jury in understanding why an accused acted in the way he or she did, that situation is not present in this case. Accordingly, while we disapprove the language in the Court of Appeals' opinion to the extent it holds that evidence of a criminal defendant's cultural back-

ground is never relevant, we find no abuse of the trial court's discretion in ruling that the cultural evidence proffered by appellant was not admissible here.

3. ***When Should a Cultural Defense Be Raised***. In *State v. Williams*, [p.321], the defendants, members of an Indian tribe, were convicted of manslaughter in the death of their child for not promptly seeking medical care. Would a cultural defense have been proper in this case? Consider here the following congressional finding, "that an alarmingly high percentage of Indian families are broken up by the removal, often unwarranted, of their children from them by nontribal public and private agencies and that an alarmingly high percentage of such children are placed in non-Indian foster and adoptive homes and institutions." *See* 25 U.S.C. § 1901 (1978).

4. ***Gay Panic***. Should courts allow a defendant on trial to assert a defense that he or she was provoked to commit the crime because of the victim's sexual orientation or gender identity? The American Bar Association's Criminal Justice Section passed a resolution endorsing the position of the LGBT community calling for a prohibition of this defense. The resolution must now pass the ABA House of Delegates and will be presented at the August 2013 meeting. A June 3, 2013, Press Release of the National LGBT Bar Association states:

> Gay and trans "panic" defense tactics ask a jury to find that a victim's sexual orientation or gender identity is to blame for the defendant's excessively violent reaction. The perpetrator claims that the victim's sexual orientation or gender identity not only explain – but excuse – their loss of self-control and subsequent assault of an LGBT individual. By fully or partially acquitting the perpetrators of crimes against LGBT victims, these defenses imply that LGBT lives are worth less than others.

PROBLEM FIFTY

One evening, a 13-year old female is brought to the hospital emergency room with severe stomach pain. A doctor determines that she is 3 months pregnant. When the doctor questions this female and her mother about the pregnancy, the doctor learns that she is married to a 16-year old. The doctor reports the pregnancy — as required by state law — to the Family and Child Services Agency (FCSA). An FCSA investigator determines that this young woman and the 16-year old male were married one year earlier in a religious ceremony in the United States, and the marriage had been arranged by their parents when both were young children living in Yemen. The families moved to the United States three years earlier. In the

Yemeni culture, a woman can be married once she menstruates. The young woman's mother was married when she was 12, and the young man's mother was 13 when she married. The young woman informs the FCSA investigator through a translator that she is happy with her mate, and that they live with his parents. The parents of both state that they will assist with the child care when the baby is born, and they have sufficient resources to support the 13 and 16 year old until they finish school and begin to work in the family business, which is quite successful. The FCSA investigator turns the information over to the prosecutor. Should this young man be charged with statutory rape, which in the jurisdiction carries a mandatory sentence of life imprisonment when the victim is under 14 and the statute does not contain a marital exception? Should the parents be charged with aiding and abetting statutory rape?

Chapter 16
Defending Self, Others, and Property

§ 16.01 Self-Defense

The most widely-accepted justification defense is self-defense, that a person may use force to resist another who seeks to cause that person harm. There are limitations on the defense, most importantly that the person asserting self-defense not be the aggressor in causing the threatened harm — one may not provoke another and then use that threat as an excuse to inflict bodily harm.

The Texas Court of Criminal Appeals explained the scope of the self-defense doctrine in *Boget v. State*, 74 S.W.3d 23 (Tex. Crim. App. 2002):

> Self-defense is popularly thought of as the natural right of individuals to act in concert against the threat of others. The assumption is that there is a natural right to preserve oneself from any kind of threat made against person or property with whatever force seems necessary at the time. As Blackstone said of self-defense:
>
> > Both the life and limbs of a man are of such high value, in the estimation of the law of England, that it pardons even homicide if committed se defendo, or in order to preserve them. For whatever is done by a man, to save either life or member, is looked upon as done with the highest necessity or compulsion. [1 WILLIAM BLACKSTONE, COMMENTARIES 130.] * * *
>
> [S]elf-defense has generally been limited to situations in which the defendant is charged with an assaultive crime. This is largely because the rules of self-defense evolved from the law on homicide. The connection of self-defense to assaultive crimes is clear in light of the fact that even some modern penal codes limit discussion of self-defense to the sections on homicide and assault and battery. This factor weighs against extending self-defense to offenses other than offenses against the person.

The common law of self-defense can generally be described as requiring the following to justify conduct that would otherwise be criminal: (1) the defendant is threatened with the use, or threat of the imminent use, of (2) unlawful (3) force (4) that does or could cause physical injury and (5) which a reasonable person would believe could not be avoided without the use of physical force, and the actor (6) defends by using only a reasonable amount of force and (7) was not responsible for the situation that prompted the need to use such force. Note that self-defense provides a "complete defense" to the charge, which means the defendant is found not guilty if the elements are established. In some cases the same evidence may be used to satisfy more than one element of the defense. For example, the reasonableness determination will often depend on the amount of force threatened.

The Arizona self-defense statute is typical of state efforts to codify the defense that draws on many of the common law requirements:

A. [A] person is justified in threatening or using physical force against another when and to the extent a reasonable person would believe that physical force is immediately necessary to protect himself against the other's use or attempted use of unlawful physical force.

B. The threat or use of physical force against another is not justified:

1. In response to verbal provocation alone; or

2. To resist an arrest that the person knows or should know is being made by a peace officer or by a person acting in a peace officer's presence and at his direction, whether the arrest is lawful or unlawful, unless the physical force used by the peace officer exceeds that allowed by law; or

3. If the person provoked the other's use or attempted use of unlawful physical force, unless:

(a) The person withdraws from the encounter or clearly communicates to the other his intent to do so reasonably believing he cannot safely withdraw from the encounter; and

(b) The other nevertheless continues or attempts to use unlawful physical force against the person.

ARIZ. REV. STAT. § 13-404.

People v. Goetz
497 N.E.2d 41(N.Y. 1986)

WACHTLER, C.J.:

A Grand Jury has indicted defendant on attempted murder, assault, and other charges for having shot and wounded four youths on a New York City subway train after one or two of the youths approached him and asked for $5. The lower courts, concluding that the prosecutor's charge to the Grand Jury on the defense of justification was erroneous, have dismissed the attempted murder, assault and weapons possession charges. We now reverse and reinstate all counts of the indictment. * * *

The precise circumstances of the incident giving rise to the charges against defendant are disputed, and ultimately it will be for a trial jury to determine what occurred. We feel it necessary, however, to provide some factual background to properly frame the legal issues before us. Accordingly, we have summarized the facts as they appear from the evidence before the Grand Jury. We stress, however, that we do not purport to reach any conclusions or holding as to exactly what transpired or whether defendant is blameworthy. The credibility of witnesses and the reasonableness of defendant's conduct are to be resolved by the trial jury.

On Saturday afternoon, December 22, 1984, Troy Canty, Darryl Cabey, James Ramseur, and Barry Allen boarded an IRT express subway train in The Bronx and headed south toward lower Manhattan. The four youths rode together in the rear portion of the seventh car of the train. Two of the four, Ramseur and Cabey, had screwdrivers inside their coats, which they said were to be used to break into the coin boxes of video machines.

Defendant Bernhard Goetz boarded this subway train at 14th Street in Manhattan and sat down on a bench towards the rear section of the same car occupied by the four youths. Goetz was carrying an unlicensed .38 caliber pistol loaded with five rounds of ammunition in a waistband holster. The train left the 14th Street station and headed towards Chambers Street.

It appears from the evidence before the Grand Jury that Canty approached Goetz, possibly with Allen beside him, and stated "give me five dollars." Neither Canty nor any of the other youths displayed a weapon. Goetz responded by standing up, pulling out his handgun and firing four shots in rapid succession. The first shot hit Canty in the chest; the second struck Allen in the back; the third went through Ramseur's arm and into his left side; the fourth was fired at Cabey, who apparently was then standing in the corner of the car, but missed, deflecting instead off of a wall of the conductor's cab. After Goetz briefly surveyed the scene around him, he fired another shot at Cabey, who then was sitting on the end bench of the car. The bullet entered the rear of Cabey's side and severed his spinal cord.

All but two of the other passengers fled the car when, or immediately after, the shots were fired. The conductor, who had been in the next car, heard the shots and instructed the motorman to radio for emergency assistance. The conductor then went into the car where the shooting occurred and saw Goetz sitting on a bench, the injured youths lying on the floor or slumped against a seat, and two women who had apparently taken cover, also lying on the floor. Goetz told the conductor that the four youths had tried to rob him.

While the conductor was aiding the youths, Goetz headed towards the front of the car. The train had stopped just before the Chambers Street station and Goetz went between two of the cars, jumped onto the tracks and fled. Police and ambulance crews arrived at the scene shortly thereafter. Ramseur and Canty, initially listed in critical condition, have fully recovered. Cabey remains paralyzed, and has suffered some degree of brain damage.

On December 31, 1984, Goetz surrendered to police in Concord, New Hampshire, identifying himself as the gunman being sought for the subway shootings in New York nine days earlier. Later that day, after receiving *Miranda* warnings, he made two lengthy statements, both of which were tape recorded with his permission. In the statements, which are substantially similar, Goetz admitted that he had been illegally carrying a handgun in New York City for three years. He stated that he had first purchased a gun in 1981 after he had been injured in a mugging. Goetz also revealed that twice between 1981 and 1984 he had successfully warded off assailants simply by displaying the pistol.

According to Goetz's statement, the first contact he had with the four youths came when Canty, sitting or lying on the bench across from him, asked "how are you," to which he replied "fine." Shortly thereafter, Canty, followed by one of the other youths, walked over to the defendant and stood to his left, while the other two youths remained to his right, in the corner of the subway car. Canty then said "give me five dollars." Goetz stated that he knew from the smile on Canty's face that they wanted to "play with me." Although he was certain that none of the youths had a gun, he had a fear, based on prior experiences, of being "maimed."

Goetz then established "a pattern of fire," deciding specifically to fire from left to right. His stated intention at that point was to "murder [the four youths], to hurt them, to make them suffer as much as possible." When Canty again requested money, Goetz stood up, drew his weapon, and began firing, aiming for the center of the body of each of the four. Goetz recalled that the first two he shot "tried to run through the crowd [but] they had nowhere to run." Goetz then turned to his right to "go after the other two." One of these two "tried to run through the wall of the train, but *** he had nowhere to go." The other youth (Cabey) "tried pretending that he wasn't with [the others]" by standing still, holding on to one of the subway hand straps, and not looking at Goetz. Goetz nonetheless fired his fourth shot at him. He then ran back to the first two youths to make sure they had been "taken care of." Seeing that they had both been shot, he spun back to check on the latter two. Goetz noticed that the youth who had been standing still was now sitting on a bench and seemed unhurt. As Goetz told the police, "I said '[you] seem to be all right, here's another,'" and he then fired the shot which severed Cabey's spinal cord. Goetz added that "if I was a little more under self-control *** I would have put the barrel against his forehead and fired." He also admitted that "if I had had more [bullets], I would have shot them again, and again, and again." * * *

[After being extradited from New Hampshire to New York, the first grand jury indicted Goetz on gun charges, but did not indict him for attempted murder. With new evidence, the case was presented to a second grand jury, which indicted him on "four charges of attempted murder, four charges of assault in the first degree, one charge of reckless endangerment in the first degree, and one charge of criminal possession of a weapon in the second degree."]

On October 14, 1985, Goetz moved to dismiss the charges contained in the second indictment alleging, among other things, that the evidence before the second Grand Jury was not legally sufficient to establish the offenses charged, * * * and that the prosecutor's instructions to that Grand Jury on the defense of justification were erroneous and prejudicial to the defendant so as to render its proceedings defective. * * * [New evidence was thereafter obtained from a journalist claiming that "Cabey had told him in this interview that the other three youths had all approached Goetz with the intention of robbing him."]

The court, after inspection of the Grand Jury minutes, first rejected Goetz's contention that there was not legally sufficient evidence to support the charges. It held, however, that the prosecutor, in a supplemental charge elaborating upon the justification defense, had erroneously introduced an objective element into this defense by instructing the grand jurors to consider whether Goetz's conduct was that of a "reasonable man in [Goetz's] situation". The court * * * concluded that the statutory test for whether the use of deadly force is justified to protect a person should be wholly subjective, focusing entirely on the defendant's state of mind when he used such force. It concluded that dismissal was required for this error because the justification issue was at the heart of the case.

[The court] also concluded that dismissal and resubmission of the charges were required * * * because the *Daily News* column and the statement by the police officer to the prosecution strongly indicated that the testimony of Ramseur and Canty was perjured. Because the additional evidence before the second Grand Jury, as contrasted with that before the first Grand Jury, consisted largely of the testimony of these two youths, the court found that the integrity of the second Grand Jury was "severely undermined" by the apparently perjured testimony.***

Penal Law article 35 recognizes the defense of justification, which "permits the use of force under certain circumstances" * * * Penal Law § 35.15 (1) sets forth the general principles governing all such uses of force: "[a] person may *** use physical force upon another person when and to the extent he *reasonably believes* such to be necessary to defend himself or a third person from what he *reasonably believes* to be the use or imminent use of unlawful physical force by such other person" (emphasis added).

Section 35.15 (2) sets forth further limitations on these general principles with respect to the use of "deadly physical force": "A person may not use deadly physical force upon another person under circumstances specified in subdivision one unless (a) He *reasonably believes* that such other person is using or about to use deadly physical force *** or (b) He *reasonably believes* that such other person is committing or attempting to commit a kidnapping, forcible rape, forcible sodomy or robbery" (emphasis added).* * *

Because the evidence before the second Grand Jury included statements by Goetz that he acted to protect himself from being maimed or to avert a robbery, the prosecutor correctly chose to charge the justification defense in section 35.15 to the Grand Jury * * * The prosecutor properly instructed the grand jurors to consider whether the use of deadly physical force was justified to prevent either serious physical injury or a robbery, and, in doing so, to separately analyze the defense with respect to each of the charges. He elaborated upon the prerequisites for the use of deadly physical force essentially by reading or paraphrasing the language in Penal Law § 35.15. The defense does not contend that he committed any error in this portion of the charge.

When the prosecutor had completed his charge, one of the grand jurors asked for clarification of the term "reasonably believes." The prosecutor responded by instructing the grand jurors that they were to consider the circumstances of the incident and determine "whether the defendant's conduct was that of a reasonable man in the defendant's situation." It is this response by the prosecutor — and specifically his use of "a reasonable man" — which is the basis for the dismissal of the charges by the lower courts. As expressed repeatedly in the Appellate Division's plurality opinion, because section 35.15 uses the term *"he* reasonably believes", the appropriate test, according to that court, is whether a defendant's beliefs and reactions were "reasonable *to him.*" Under that reading of the statute, a jury which believed a defendant's testimony that he felt that his own actions were warranted and were reasonable would have to acquit him, regardless of what anyone else in defendant's situation might have concluded. Such an interpretation defies the ordinary meaning and significance of the term "reasonably" in a statute, and misconstrues the clear intent of the Legislature, in enacting section 35.15, to retain an objective element as part of any provision authorizing the use of deadly physical force.

Penal statutes in New York have long codified the right recognized at common law to use deadly physical force, under appropriate circumstances, in self-defense. * * * These provisions have never required that an actor's belief as to the intention of another person to inflict serious injury be correct in order for the use of deadly force to be justified, but they have uniformly required that the belief comport with an objective notion of reasonableness. The 1829 statute, using language which was followed almost in its entirety until the 1965 recodification of the Penal Law, provided that the use of deadly force was justified in self-defense or in the defense of specified third persons "when there shall be a reasonable ground to apprehend a design to commit a felony, or to do some great personal injury, and there shall be imminent danger of such design being accomplished" * * * [The court went through the various revisions to the statute].

In 1961 the Legislature established a Commission to undertake a complete revision of the Penal Law and the Criminal Code. The impetus for the decision to update the Penal Law came in part from the drafting of the Model Penal Code by the American Law Institute, as well as from the fact that the existing law was poorly organized and in many aspects antiquated. * * * While using the Model Penal Code provisions on justification as general guidelines, however, the drafters of the new Penal Law did not simply adopt them verbatim.

The provisions of the Model Penal Code with respect to the use of deadly force in self-defense reflect the position of its drafters that any culpability which arises from a mistaken belief in the need to use such force should be no greater than the culpability such a mistake would give rise to if it were made with respect to an element of a crime. * * * Accordingly, under Model Penal Code § 3.04 (2) (b), a defendant charged with murder (or attempted murder) need only show that he *"[believed]"* that [the use of deadly force] was necessary to protect himself against death, serious bodily injury, kidnapping or [forcible] sexual intercourse" to prevail on a self-defense claim (emphasis added). If the defendant's belief was wrong, and was recklessly, or negligently formed, however, he may be convicted of the type of homicide charge requiring only a reckless or negligent, as the case may be, criminal intent. * * *

The drafters of the Model Penal Code recognized that the wholly subjective test set forth in section 3.04 differed from the existing law in most States by its omission of any requirement of reasonableness. * * * The drafters were also keenly aware that requiring that the actor have a "reasonable belief" rather than just a "belief" would alter the wholly subjective test. * * *

New York did not follow the Model Penal Code's equation of a mistake as to the need to use deadly force with a mistake negating an element of a crime, choosing instead to use a single statutory section which would provide either a complete defense or no defense at all to a defendant charged with any crime involving the use of deadly force. The drafters of the new Penal Law adopted in large part the structure and content of Model Penal Code § 3.04, but, crucially, inserted the word "reasonably" before "believes."

The plurality below agreed with defendant's argument that the change in the statutory language from "reasonable ground," used prior to 1965, to "he reasonably believes" in Penal Law § 35.15 evinced a legislative intent to conform to the subjective standard contained in Model Penal Code § 3.04. This argument, however, ignores the plain significance of the insertion of "reasonably." Had the drafters of section 35.15 wanted to adopt a subjective standard, they could have simply used the language of section 3.04. "Believes" by itself requires an honest or genuine belief by a defendant as to the need to use deadly force. * * * Interpreting the statute to require only that the defendant's belief was "reasonable to *him*," as done by the plurality below, would hardly be different from requiring only a genuine belief; in either case, the defendant's own perceptions could completely exonerate him from any criminal liability.

We cannot lightly impute to the Legislature an intent to fundamentally alter the principles of justification to allow the perpetrator of a serious crime to go free simply because that person believed his actions were reasonable and necessary to prevent some perceived harm. To completely exonerate such an individual, no matter how aberrational or bizarre his thought patterns, would allow citizens to set their own standards for the permissible use of force. It would also allow a legally competent defendant suffering from delusions to kill or perform acts of violence with impunity, contrary to fundamental principles of justice and criminal law.

We can only conclude that the Legislature retained a reasonableness requirement to avoid giving a license for such actions. * * * The conclusion that section 35.15 retains an objective element to justify the use of deadly force is buttressed by the statements of its drafters. The executive director and counsel to the Commission which revised the Penal Law have stated that the provisions of the statute with respect to the use of deadly physical force largely conformed with the prior law, with the only changes they noted not being relevant here. * * * Nowhere in the legislative history is there any indication that "reasonably believes" was designed to change the law on the use of deadly force or establish a subjective standard. To the contrary, the Commission, in the staff comment governing arrests by police officers, specifically equated "[he] reasonably believes" with having a reasonable ground for believing * * *

Statutes or rules of law requiring a person to act "reasonably" or to have a "reasonable belief" uniformly prescribe conduct meeting an objective standard measured with reference to how "a reasonable person" could have acted * * *.

Goetz also argues that the introduction of an objective element will preclude a jury from considering factors such as the prior experiences of a given actor and thus, require it to make a determination of "reasonableness" without regard to the actual circumstances of a particular incident. This argument, however, falsely presupposes that an objective standard means that the background and other relevant characteristics of a particular actor must be ignored. To the contrary, we have frequently noted that a determination of reasonableness must be based on the "circumstances" facing a defendant or his "situation" * * * Such terms encompass more than the physical movements of the potential assailant. As just discussed, these terms include any relevant knowledge the defendant had about that person. They also necessarily bring in the physical attributes of all persons involved, including the defendant. Furthermore, the defendant's circumstances encompass any prior experiences he had which could provide a reasonable basis for a belief that another person's intentions were to injure or rob him or that the use of deadly force was necessary under the circumstances.

Accordingly, a jury should be instructed to consider this type of evidence in weighing the defendant's actions. The jury must first determine whether the defendant had the requisite beliefs under Section 35.15, that is, whether he believed deadly force was necessary to avert the imminent use of deadly force or the commission of one of the felonies enumerated therein. If the People do not prove beyond a reasonable doubt that he did not have such beliefs, then the jury must also consider whether these beliefs were reasonable. The jury would have to determine, in light of all the "circumstances," as explicated above, if a reasonable person could have had these beliefs.

The prosecutor's instruction to the second Grand Jury that it had to determine whether, under the circumstances, Goetz's conduct was that of a reasonable man in his situation was thus essentially an accurate charge. It is true that the prosecutor did not elaborate on the meaning of "circumstances" or "situation" and inform the grand jurors that they could consider, for example, the prior experiences Goetz related in his statement to the police. We have held, however, that a Grand Jury need not be instructed on the law with the same degree of precision as the petit jury. * * *   This lesser standard is premised upon the different functions of the Grand Jury and the petit jury: the former determines whether sufficient evidence exists to accuse a person of a crime and thereby subject him to criminal prosecution; the latter ultimately determines the guilt or innocence of the accused, and may convict only where the People have proven his guilt beyond a reasonable doubt * * * Here, [ ] Canty and Ramseur have not recanted any of their Grand Jury testimony or told the prosecutor that they misunderstood any questions. Instead, all that has come to light is hearsay evidence that conflicts with part of Canty's testimony. There is no statute or controlling case law requiring dismissal of an indictment merely because, months later, the prosecutor becomes aware of some information which may lead to the defendant's acquittal. * * * Accordingly, the order of the Appellate Division should be reversed, and the dismissed counts of the indictment reinstated.

NOTES AND QUESTIONS

1. ***Trial and Subsequent Civil Action.*** The jury that heard Goetz's case acquitted him of attempted murder, assault, and endangerment. It convicted him only of the weapons violation. A civil suit was later filed against him by the victims of the shooting. The jury in the civil case awarded Cabey 43 million dollars.

> Goetz expressed no remorse for shooting Cabey — or the three other young black men he thought were about to rob him. "I tried to lay down a pattern a fire," he told the jury of four blacks and two Hispanics. "I was trying to get as many of them as I could." And yes, just before he shot Cabey, he told him: "you don't look so bad — here's another."

Viewpoints - This Time, Subway Vigilante's Victim Was Himself, Newsday, Apr. 25, 1996, at A58.

2. ***General Principles of Self-Defense.*** The general principles for using self-defense are: (a) necessity, (b) proportionality, and (c) reasonable belief. What is considered a necessity? If the threat to the individual is not immediate then the use of force is usually not considered necessary. Will this preclude a battered spouse from killing the one who is harming him or her when they are sleeping? This issue is considered in § 16.02. What might be considered proportional? Should the same standards used for provocation in voluntary manslaughter be used to determine whether one can use self-defense?

3. ***Objective or Subjective Approach.*** What arguments can be made for using a (a) strictly subjective test, (b) a subjective test using a reasonable person from the perspective of the accused, or (c) strictly an objective test? Typically, which test would made it easier for the prosecution in presenting a case for conviction, and which test would likely be the defense's preference? Generally, courts use the standard of a "reasonable person in the actor's situation." For example, the Kansas Supreme Court directed that the following language for an objective standard be used in a jury charge for self-defense:

> A person is justified in the use of force against an aggressor when and to the extent it appears to him and he reasonably believes that such conduct is necessary to defend himself or another against such aggressor's imminent use of unlawful force. A reasonable belief implies both a belief and the existence of facts that would persuade a reasonable man to that belief.

State v. Simon, 646 P.2d 1119 (Kan. 1982).

4. ***The Reasonableness of the Belief.*** The defendant asserting self-defense must actually hold the belief (subjective), and it must be a reasonable belief of an

imminent and unlawful harm (objective). How should the jury determine whether the defendant actually held that belief, and whether it was reasonable? The Maryland Court of Appeals discussed the analysis in *State v. Marr*, 765 A.2d 645 (Md. 2001):

> The objective standard does not require the jury to ignore the defendant's perceptions in determining the reasonableness of his or her conduct. In making that determination, the facts or circumstances must be taken as perceived by the defendant, even if they were not the true facts or circumstances, so long as a reasonable person in the defendant's position could also reasonably perceive the facts or circumstances in that way. If the fact or circumstance relied upon by the defendant to justify a belief of imminent danger or the need to use deadly force to meet that danger is so improbable that no reasonable person in the defendant's position would perceive it to be the case, the jury cannot be directed to assume that fact or circumstance in judging the reasonableness of the defendant's conduct, for that would skew the whole analysis of reasonableness.

> A belief, as to either imminent danger or the amount of force necessary to meet that danger, is necessarily founded upon the defendant's sensory and ideational perception of the situation that he or she confronts, often shaded by knowledge or perceptions of ancillary or antecedent events. The perception that serves as the impetus for responsive action may be incorrect for a variety of reasons, ranging from ignorance of relevant facts that, if known, would put the situation in a different light, to distortions in sensory perceptions, to judgmental errors in the instantaneous assimilation and appreciation of the apparent situation. The fact that the defendant's perception is incorrect does not necessarily make it unreasonable; human beings often misunderstand their surroundings and the intentions of other people. A defendant who is suddenly grabbed by another person at gunpoint may reasonably believe that the person is an assailant intending to do him immediate and grievous bodily harm, even though, in fact, the person is a plain clothes police officer possessing a valid warrant and properly, though forcibly, attempting to arrest him. Similarly, the defendant, confronted by a person with a gun, may reasonably, though incorrectly, believe that the gun is real or is loaded, when, in fact, it is not. In those kinds of circumstances, the jury would have to determine the reasonableness of the defendant's conduct in light of his reasonable, though erroneous, perception. If, however, on Halloween, the defendant confronts a costumed stranger on the street and shoots him in the honestly held belief that the stranger is a menacing alien from Mars intent upon his immediate destruction, the jury is not entitled to judge the reasonableness of the defendant's conduct on the assumption that the victim was, in fact, an alien from Mars intent on harming the defendant.

5. *Reasonable Man or Woman?* Should the sex of the defendant be a relevant consideration in determining the reasonableness of the use of deadly force? In *State v. Wanrow*, 559 P.2d 548 (Wash. 1977), the court stated:

> The second paragraph of instruction No. 10 contains an equally erroneous and prejudicial statement of the law. That portion of the instruction reads:
>
>> However, when there is no reasonable ground for the person attacked to believe that His person is in imminent danger of death or great bodily harm, and it appears to Him that only an ordinary battery is all that is intended, and all that He has reasonable grounds to fear from His assailant, He has a right to stand His ground and repel such threatened assault, yet He has no right to repel a threatened assault with naked hands, by the use of a deadly weapon in a deadly manner, unless He believes, And has reasonable grounds to believe, that He is in imminent danger of death or great bodily harm.
>
> In our society women suffer from a conspicuous lack of access to training in and the means of developing those skills necessary to effectively repel a male assailant without resorting to the use of deadly weapons. Instruction No. 12 does indicate that the "relative size and strength of the persons involved" may be considered; however, it does not make clear that the defendant's actions are to be judged against her own subjective impressions and not those which a detached jury might determine to be objectively reasonable. The applicable rule of law is * * * :

>> If the appellants, at the time of the alleged assault upon them, as reasonably and ordinarily cautious and prudent men, honestly believed that they were in danger of great bodily harm, they would have the right to resort to self-defense, and their conduct is to be judged by the condition appearing to them at the time, not by the condition as it might appear to the jury in the light of testimony before it.
>
> The second paragraph of instruction No. 10 not only establishes an objective standard, but through the persistent use of the masculine gender leaves the jury with the impression the objective standard to be applied is that applicable to an altercation between two men. The impression created — that a 5'4" woman with a cast on her leg and using a crutch must, under the law, somehow repel an assault by a 6'2" intoxicated man without employing weapons in her defense, unless the jury finds her determination of the degree of danger to be objectively reasonable — constitutes a separate and distinct misstatement of the law and, in the context of this case, violates the respondent's right to equal protection of the law. The respondent was entitled to have the jury consider her actions in the light

of her own perceptions of the situation, including those perceptions which were the product of our nation's "long and unfortunate history of sex discrimination." *Frontiero v. Richardson*, 411 U.S. 677 (1973). Until such time as the effects of that history are eradicated, care must be taken to assure that our self-defense instructions afford women the right to have their conduct judged in light of the individual physical handicaps which are the product of sex discrimination. To fail to do so is to deny the right of the individual woman involved to trial by the same rules which are applicable to male defendants.

6. *Self-Defense and Race:* **Goetz Revisited.** Goetz was white and his shooting victims were all African-Americans. Much discussion about the *Goetz* case at the time and since the jury's verdict has centered around a variety of scenarios concerning Goetz's potential racism. The assailants who succeeded in hospitalizing Goetz several years before he was charged in the shooting were also African-Americans. One scenario speculates that Goetz was as angry as he was, expressing a desire to hurt all four young men, because the earlier incident had fostered or confirmed in Goetz a hatred of African-Americans. A somewhat less nefarious scenario posits that Goetz either consciously or subconciously feared African-American males, especially young ones, perhaps because of pre-existing beliefs or because of being victimized by black assailants. Accordingly, he over-reacted because he assumed grave danger based entirely on the color of the skin of the youths whom he believed were confronting him in the subway car.

These scenarios raise important issues about the proper basis for criminal liability, the proper ground for defenses, and the degree to which we should tolerate apparent inconsistencies in the law. For example, under a purely subjective approach, shooting because of conscious racial hatred would still not constitute self-defense. But consciously shooting because you perceive yourself in grave danger of imminent harm primarily, or in significant part, because of the race of your victim would be a defense. That might mean that blacks will face more danger of assault from fearful whites than whites will face from any source, or at least the law might create incentives toward that result. The law would also, in a sense, validate racial stereotyping by allowing it to be used to exculpate offenders. A reasonable belief approach might do better on this score if courts conclude that it is "unreasonable" to rely on racial stereotyping as the basis for self-defense. Of course, this would turn on a normative judgment that such stereotyping is wrong.

7. *Stereotypes and Reasonableness.* What if a court defined "reasonableness" as what most people would think? Or what if the term "reasonable" is undefined? Would most people suffer from stereotypes? What if no conscious stereotyping were involved but subconscious stereotyping was at work? How would an attorney prove subconscious beliefs? Should a consciously well-meaning but self-deluded (i.e., unaware of his subconscious biases) fearful shooter be said to be acting "reasonably"? In *Goetz* itself, the Court claimed to be establishing a reasonable

belief test. Did it really do so? Should it have thought about these issues of racial prejudice in crafting its rule? If one favors a reasonable belief test to avoid problems of racial bias, what impact might that have on battered spouses who kill their batterers and then raise self-defense? Should an objective test apply to both the battered spouse and Goetz? Whichever position is staked out on each of these questions, consider how one would draft proposed jury instructions and what sort of evidence one would seek (and where might it be found?) of an offender's conscious or subconscious racial biases and whether they were at work in the case at hand?

8. ***Aggressor Status.*** The status of the accused as aggressor precludes a claim of self-defense. Why are aggressors not afforded the right to use self-defense? If a person withdraws from the situation and is no longer the aggressor, one may then regain a right to self-defense.

9. ***Burden of Proof.*** The common law rule was that self-defense must be proven by the defendant under the preponderance standard. Almost every state has abandoned that approach, and now requires the defendant to meet the initial burden of producing evidence to establish self-defense, and then the prosecution must demonstrate the lack of self-defense beyond a reasonable doubt for the jury to convict. In *Martin v. Ohio*, 480 U.S. 228 (1987), the Supreme Court upheld Ohio's common law approach that placed the production and persuasion burden on the defendant, finding that it did not violate a defendant's due process right under *Winship* so long as the government must still prove the elements of the offense beyond a reasonable doubt. It is important to remember that jurisdictions do not necessarily treat all defenses the same way that they treat self-defense. For example, most jurisdictions place the burdens of production (some evidence) and persuasion (usually meaning by a "preponderance of the evidence") on the defendant for affirmative defenses. Thus the burden of proving entrapment usually lies with the defendant to prove that he or she was entrapped by a preponderance of the evidence. For some defenses, the defendant has the burden of production but, if he or she meets it, the state has the burden of persuasion in disproving the defense beyond a reasonable doubt. For example, a mistake of fact defense in a common law rape case argues that the defendant was reasonably mistaken in believing that the alleged victim consented. If the jury believes that he or she was reasonably mistaken, then the state cannot prove the mental state for rape beyond a reasonable doubt. Once the defendant offers some evidence that he or she was mistaken, the state must prove beyond a reasonable doubt that the accused was in fact not mistaken. The Model Penal Code places only the burden of production on the defendant, not the burden of persuasion, for both most failure of proof and most affirmative defenses, *unless* the provision on the particular defense expressly states otherwise. Entrapment illustrates this last point, where the Code's provision expressly declares that the burden of proving entrapment lies with the defendant by a preponderance of the evidence.

10. **Retreat Rule**. A minority of the states require a defendant to retreat to a place of safety, if one is reasonably available, before using deadly force. The idea is that self-defense, especially when it involves deadly force, should be a last resort. The retreat rule does not require a person to place himself or herself in any danger, and the avenue of escape must be reasonably available to the person. If such a means to avoid the confrontation is available, then self-defense may not be offered and the person can be held liable for the harm to the victim. Consider the court's statutory analysis of the retreat requirement in the following:

State v. Sandoval
156 P.3d 60 (Or. 2007)

GILLETTE, J.

Defendant appealed his conviction after a jury trial on a charge of intentional murder, contending that the trial court improperly instructed the jury to the effect that a person is justified in using deadly force in self-defense to defend against imminent use of deadly force by another only if there is no opportunity to escape and no other means of avoiding the combat. We allowed defendant's petition for review and now conclude that the instruction was an incorrect statement of Oregon law * * *.

Defendant shot and killed his ex-wife's domestic partner, Whitcraft. The two men had a history of combative and sometimes physically violent interactions. The shooting occurred on a road that both men frequently traveled. When the police arrived on the scene, defendant described the following sequence of events: Whitcraft had driven by on the road as defendant was about to turn onto it; after defendant turned onto the road behind Whitcraft, Whitcraft stopped his truck and backed it into defendant's truck; Whitcraft then turned and aimed a pistol at defendant; defendant grabbed a rifle that he was carrying in his own vehicle (both men kept guns in their vehicles), opened the door of his truck and fired a single shot at Whitcraft. Investigators determined that the shot had entered Whitcraft's skull behind his left ear, killing him instantly. Police later found Whitcraft's loaded and cocked pistol under Whitcraft's body.

At trial, the state rejected defendant's version of the events and offered evidence that defendant had essentially ambushed Whitcraft — provoking him until he stopped his truck, training a rifle on him until he reached for his gun, and then shooting him in the head. At the close of trial, the court gave a series of jury instructions that were drawn from Uniform Criminal Jury Instructions:

A person is justified in using physical force upon another person to defend himself from what he reasonably believes to be the use or imminent use of unlawful physical force. In defending, a person may only use that degree of force which he reasonably believes to be necessary.

The burden of proof is on the state to prove beyond a reasonable doubt that the defendant did not act in self-defense.

* * * There are certain limitations on the use of deadly physical force. The defendant is not justified in using deadly physical force against another person in self-defense unless he reasonably believed that the other person was using or about to use unlawful deadly physical force against him and/or committing or attempting to commit a felony involving the use or threatened imminent use of physical force against a person.

Even in the situation where one of these threatening circumstances is present, the use of deadly physical force is justified only if it does not exceed the degree of force which defendant reasonably believes to be necessary in the circumstances.

Over defendant's objection, the court then gave an additional special instruction that the prosecution had requested:

The danger justifying the use of deadly force must be absolute, imminent, and unavoidable, and a necessity of taking human life must be actual, present, urgent and absolutely or apparently absolutely necessary. There must be no reasonable opportunity to escape to avoid the affray and there must be no other means of avoiding or declining the combat.

* * * [T]hat instruction apparently was based, not on the statutes discussed below, but on this court's 1982 opinion in *State v. Charles*, 647 P.2d 897 (Or. 1982). The jury subsequently found defendant guilty of intentional murder with a firearm, apparently rejecting defendant's claim of self-defense.

On appeal, defendant assigned error to the trial court's decision to give the special instruction. As noted, the Court of Appeals affirmed without opinion. Petitioner then sought review by this court, and we allowed his petition to consider whether the "duty to retreat" instruction that the trial court gave is a correct statement of Oregon law.

The answer to that question resides in the criminal statutes that define the concept of self-defense for purposes of Oregon law. Two merit discussion. The first, ORS 161.209, describes when the use of physical force for self-defense is "justified" and, thus, lawful:

Except as provided in [another statute, not pertinent to this case] and [ORS] 161.219, a person is justified in using physical force upon another person for self-defense or to defend a third person from what the person reasonably believes to be the use or imminent use of unlawful physical force, and the person may use a degree of force which the person reasonably believes to be necessary for the purpose.

The cross-referenced statute, ORS 161.219, deals specifically with the use of deadly physical force. It provides:

Notwithstanding the provisions of ORS 161.209, a person is not justified in using deadly physical force upon another person unless the person reasonably believes that the other person is:

(1) Committing or attempting to commit a felony involving the use or threatened imminent use of physical force against a person; or

(2) Committing or attempting to commit a burglary in a dwelling; or

(3) Using or about to use unlawful deadly physical force against a person.

* * * On a purely textual level, ORS 161.219 contains no specific reference to "retreat," "escape," or "other means of avoiding" a deadly confrontation. Neither, in our view, does it contain any other wording that would suggest a duty of that kind. Instead, it sets out, in straightforward terms, a set of circumstances that justify a person's use of deadly force (a reasonable belief that another person is using or about to use deadly force against a person) and does not purport to interpose any additional requirements beyond those circumstances.

The state contends that a duty to retreat nonetheless is implied by what it describes as a "necessity" concept that it asserts is at the heart of both ORS 161.219 and the basic self-defense statute, ORS 161.209. However, the state does not explain its construction in terms of the specific wording of either ORS 161.209 or ORS 161.219. It simply states, without further elaboration, that the central nature of a concept of necessity is "demonstrate[d]" in "the text of the interrelated statutes," i.e., ORS 161.219 and ORS 161.209.

The state may be relying on the fact that the latter statute contains the word "necessary." However, assuming that ORS 161.209 is relevant to our inquiry, it is clear that the reference to "necessary" in that statute pertains to the degree of force, which a person threatened with unlawful force reasonably believes to be required for the purpose of self-defense or defense of another. That wording assumes a right to meet unlawful force with some level of force and does not suggest that a decision to retreat or otherwise forego the use of the otherwise permissible level of force might be required in some circumstances.

Neither are we persuaded that a duty to retreat may be derived from the requirement in ORS 161.209 that an attacker's use of unlawful physical force be present or "imminent." That requirement speaks solely to the timing of the threat; it is not concerned with the nature of the threatened person's response. In short, nothing in the wording of ORS 161.219 itself, or in its broader counterpart, ORS 161.209, suggests that persons who reasonably believe that another person is about to use deadly physical force against them must calculate whether it is possible to retreat from that threat before they use deadly physical force in self-defense.

The state argues that this court's decision in *Charles* is relevant at this stage of our analysis as part of the statute's context. The state asserts, specifically, that *Charles* interpreted ORS 161.219 as imposing a duty of retreat on those who would rely on a self-defense theory to justify their own use of deadly force against another. The state then asserts that Charles is precedent that binds us here.

The state's reliance on *Charles* is understandable. In that case, this court rejected a defendant's claim that the trial court had erred in refusing to instruct a jury that a person has no duty to retreat before using deadly force to defend against an imminent use of deadly force by another. The court there stated that such an instruction would be contrary to "the Oregon cases, [which] require a defendant * * * to avoid the threatened danger where it is possible to do so without sacrificing his own safety." The problem with that pronouncement, however, is that the court based that decision entirely on its analysis of "the Oregon cases," while the right of self-defense is set out in the two statutes previously discussed.

Indeed, the entire analytical flow of the *Charles* opinion is distinctly odd: The court did not examine the wording of either ORS 161.209 or ORS 161.219 at all. Instead, the court set out the wording that the Oregon Criminal Law Commission had proposed to the legislature regarding the use of deadly force as part of the final draft of the proposed 1971 Criminal Code, which wording explicitly imposed a duty of retreat to avoid the necessity of using deadly force. Then, after noting that the 1971 legislature had rejected that wording, the court cited a view expressed in the Oregon Criminal Law Commission's Commentary to the 1971 Code to the effect that "the statute probably was not necessary" because of existing Oregon case law. Then, without discussing at all the fact that the Oregon legislature had adopted statutes on the subject, the court concluded, inexplicably, that "Oregon case law * * * controls the subject." The court then went on to discuss its prior cases (and to conclude that they did not support the defendant's claim that Oregon does not recognize a "duty of retreat").

Although, from our present perspective, it seems surprising that this court would attempt to answer the question presented in *Charles* without resort to the controlling criminal statutes, that is precisely what the *Charles* court did. The court's analysis did not focus on or even consider the words of the statutes that we now recognize to be pivotal. Neither did the court conclude, as the state suggests, that the drafters of ORS 161.219 had decided to "continue" the "common-law rules" as explicated in the various self-defense cases that preceded the enactment of that statute. *Charles*, therefore, has nothing to contribute to our present effort, which is to discern what the legislature intended with respect to the "duty of retreat" question.

Without *Charles*, we are left with our initial impression of the statute: It sets out a specific set of circumstances that justify a person's use of deadly force (that the person reasonably believes that another person is using or about to use deadly force against him or her) and does not interpose any additional requirement (including a requirement that there be no means of escape). That impression is not altered by the requirement in ORS 161.209 that the use of deadly force be present or "imminent," or by the same statute's reference to "the degree of force which the person reasonably believes to be necessary." We conclude, in short, that the legislature's intent is clear on the face of ORS 161.219: The legislature did not intend to require a person to retreat before using deadly force to defend against the imminent use of deadly physical force by another.

It follows from the foregoing that the trial court erred in giving the instruction in question. The state contends, however, that, even if that is so, the error was harmless, because the facts and legal theories that the parties presented to the jury simply did not involve any question of retreat or whether use of deadly force was unavoidable. Rather, the state argues, the factual dispute before the jury focused solely on the question of whether Whitcraft had resorted to his weapon first. The state contends that, under those circumstances, there was little likelihood that the disputed instruction affected the outcome of the case.

We disagree with the state's assessment. A jury presented with the disputed instruction would assume that it had some relevance to the case before it. Even if the state never specifically made the argument, and even if its factual case was not geared to that issue, the jury still would be likely to hear the instruction as requiring it to find that defendant had had no opportunity to retreat from or otherwise "avoid the affray" before it could accept defendant's self-defense theory. With that erroneous impression in mind, the jury may have rejected defendant's self-defense claim based on a finding that defendant could have driven away when he saw Whitcraft backing toward him (or, even better, when he first saw Whitcraft drive by). In short, there is every likelihood that the erroneous instruction affected the verdict. The error was not harmless. * * *

———————————

NOTES AND QUESTIONS

1. *Necessity*. The Oregon Supreme Court rejects the lower court's analysis of "necessity" in self-defense as requiring the retreat rule. But the Michigan Supreme Court viewed necessity as the basis for applying the retreat rule, stating: "If it is possible to safely avoid an attack then it is not *necessary*, and therefore not permissible, to exercise deadly force against the attacker." *People v. Riddle*, 649 N.W.2d 30 (Mich. 2002). Should a person who could easily avoid a physical confrontation — especially a deadly one — be required to take that route rather than using deadly force, or is one's personal integrity and right to resist force sufficient to justify the use of force that could harm or kill an assailant?

2. *No Duty to Retreat Instruction*. If a state does not impose the retreat rule, then a defendant may be entitled to a jury instruction that he or she is not required to retreat if the issue arises during trial. In *Dukes v. States*, 568 S.E.2d 151 (Ga. Ct. App. 2002), the Georgia Court of Appeals stated:

> The rule in Georgia is that if the person claiming self-defense was not the original aggressor there is no duty to retreat. Where self-defense is the sole defense, and the issue of retreat is raised by the evidence or placed in issue, the defense is entitled to a charge on the principles of retreat * * *. In order for a charge on no duty to retreat to be required, the issue of retreat must be raised by the evidence or placed in issue. A trial court's failure to charge the jury on retreat has been found to be reversible error when the prosecution has raised the issue when questioning witnesses or in closing arguments.

3. *"Stand Your Ground" Statutes*. A few states go even farther in creating statutes that allow individuals to "stand their ground." Florida's statute is illustrative, especially in light of the highly publicized shooting of the teenager Trayvon Martin at the hands of neighborhood watch activist George Zimmerman. The statute has a few prominent features: first, it states that "[a] person who is not engaged in an unlawful activity and who is attacked in any other place where he or she has a right to be has no duty to retreat and has the right to stand his or her ground and meet force with force, including deadly force if he or she reasonably believes it is necessary to do so to prevent death or great bodily harm to himself or herself or another or to prevent the commission of a forcible felony." West's F.S.A. § 776.013(3). Another provision of the statute creates a presumption of reasonable fear of "imminent peril of death or great bodily harm to himself or herself or another" if an intruder unlawfully and forcefully enters or attempts to enter "a dwelling, residence, or occupied vehicle." West's F.S.A. §776.013(1)(a). Finally, the Florida Supreme Court held in *Dennis v. State*, 51 So. 3d 456 (2010), that the part of the statute that provides immunity from criminal prosecution for a person who justifiably uses deadly force (§776.032)) authorizes the trial judge to dismiss

a criminal prosecution at the pretrial stage if the defendant shows by a preponderance of the evidence that immunity from prosecution attaches.

4. ***The Castle Doctrine***. Even in those jurisdictions that require retreat before using deadly force, a person need not withdraw in their own home, or in the area immediately adjoining it — called the "curtilage." The rationale for the Castle Doctrine has been explained:

> Regardless of any general theory to retreat as far as practicable before one can justify turning upon his assailant and taking life in self-defense, the law imposes no duty to retreat upon one who, free from fault in bringing on a difficulty, is attacked at or in his or her own dwelling or home. Upon the theory that a man's house is his castle, and that he has a right to protect it and those within it from intrusion or attack, the rule is practically universal that when a person is attacked in his own dwelling he may stand at bay and turn on and kill his assailant if this is apparently necessary to save his own life or to protect himself from great bodily harm.

40 AM.JUR.2d Homicide § 163.

5. ***Co-Ownership***. The common law retreat rule does not apply when an intruder attempts to invade a home, but what about a situation in which both parties to the affray are lawfully present? Most instances of domestic violence occur inside the home, and both parties may have a right to be present. Jurisdictions that recognize the retreat rule do not impose it in this situation, as explained by the Ohio Supreme Court in *State v. Thomas*, 673 N.E.2d 1339 (Ohio 1997):

> In Ohio, one is not required to retreat from one's own home when attacked by an intruder; similarly one should not be required to retreat when attacked by a cohabitant in order to claim self-defense. Moreover, in the case of domestic violence, as in the case sub judice, the attacks are often repeated over time, and escape from the home is rarely possible without the threat of great personal violence or death. The victims of such attacks have already "retreated to the wall" many times over and therefore should not be required as victims of domestic violence to attempt to flee to safety before being able to claim the affirmative defense of self-defense.

MODEL PENAL CODE

§ 3.04. Use of Force in Self-Protection

(1) Use of Force Justifiable for Protection of the Person. Subject to the provisions of this Section and of Section 3.09, the use of force upon or toward another person is justifiable when the actor believes that such force is immediately necessary for the purpose of protecting himself against the use of unlawful force by such other person on the present occasion.

(2) Limitations on Justifying Necessity for Use of Force.

　(a) The use of force is not justifiable under this Section:

　　(i) to resist an arrest that the actor knows is being made by a peace officer, although the arrest is unlawful; or

　　(ii) to resist force used by the occupier or possessor of property or by another person on his behalf, where the actor knows that the person using the force is doing so under a claim of right to protect the property, except that this limitation shall not apply if:

　　　(A) the actor is a public officer acting in the performance of his duties or a person lawfully assisting him therein or a person making or assisting in a lawful arrest; or

　　　(B) the actor has been unlawfully dispossessed of the property and is making a re-entry or recaption justified by Section 3.06; or

　　　(C) the actor believes that such force is necessary to protect himself against death or serious bodily injury.

　(b) The use of deadly force is not justifiable under this Section unless the actor believes that such force is necessary to protect himself against death, serious bodily injury, kidnapping or sexual intercourse compelled by force or threat; nor is it justifiable if:

　　(i) the actor, with the purpose of causing death or serious bodily injury, provoked the use of force against himself in the same encounter; or

　　(ii) the actor knows that he can avoid the necessity of using such force with complete safety by retreating or by surrendering possession of a thing to a person asserting a claim of right thereto or by complying with a demand that he abstain from any action that he has no duty to take, except that:

(A) the actor is not obliged to retreat from his dwelling or place of work, unless he was the initial aggressor or is assailed in his place of work by another person whose place of work the actor knows it to be; and

(B) a public officer justified in using force in the performance of his duties or a person justified in using force in his assistance or a person justified in using force in making an arrest or preventing an escape is not obliged to desist from efforts to perform such duty, effect such arrest or prevent such escape because of resistance or threatened resistance by or on behalf of the person against whom such action is directed.

(c) Except as required by paragraphs (a) and (b) of this Subsection, a person employing protective force may estimate the necessity thereof under the circumstances as he believes them to be when the force is used, without retreating, surrendering possession, doing any other act that he has no legal duty to do or abstaining from any lawful action.

(3) Use of Confinement as Protective Force. The justification afforded by this Section extends to the use of confinement as protective force only if the actor takes all reasonable measures to terminate the confinement as soon as he knows that he safely can, unless the person confined has been arrested on a charge of crime.

§ 3.09. Mistake of Law as to Unlawfulness of Force or Legality of Arrest; Reckless or Negligent Use of Otherwise Justifiable Force; Reckless or Negligent Injury or Risk of Injury to Innocent Persons

(1) The justification afforded by Sections 3.04 to 3.07, inclusive, is unavailable when:

(a) the actor's belief in the unlawfulness of the force or conduct against which he employs protective force or his belief in the lawfulness of an arrest that he endeavors to effect by force is erroneous; and

(b) his error is due to ignorance or mistake as to the provisions of the Code, any other provision of the criminal law or the law governing the legality of an arrest or search.

(2) When the actor believes that the use of force upon or toward the person of another is necessary for any of the purposes for which such belief would establish a justification under Sections 3.03 to 3.08 but the actor is reckless or negligent in having such belief or in acquiring or failing to acquire any knowledge or belief that is material to the justifiability of his use of force, the justification afforded by those

Sections is unavailable in a prosecution for an offense for which recklessness or negligence, as the case may be, suffices to establish culpability.

(3) When the actor is justified under Sections 3.03 to 3.08 in using force upon or toward the person of another but he recklessly or negligently injures or creates a risk of injury to innocent persons, the justification afforded by those Sections is unavailable in a prosecution for such recklessness or negligence towards innocent persons.

§ 3.11. Definitions

In this Article, unless a different meaning plainly is required:

(1) "unlawful force" means force, including confinement, that is employed without the consent of the person against whom it is directed and the employment of which constitutes an offense or actionable tort or would constitute such offense or tort except for a defense (such as the absence of intent, negligence, or mental capacity; duress; youth; or diplomatic status) not amounting to a privilege to use the force. Assent constitutes consent, within the meaning of this Section, whether or not it otherwise is legally effective, except assent to the infliction of death or serious bodily injury.

(2) "deadly force" means force that the actor uses with the purpose of causing or that he knows to create a substantial risk of causing death or serious bodily injury. Purposely firing a firearm in the direction of another person or at a vehicle in which another person is believed to be constitutes deadly force. A threat to cause death or serious bodily injury, by the production of a weapon or otherwise, so long as the actor's purpose is limited to creating an apprehension that he will use deadly force if necessary, does not constitute deadly force.

(3) "dwelling" means any building or structure, though movable or temporary, or a portion thereof, that is for the time being the actor's home or place of lodging.

PROBLEM FIFTY-ONE

Ramie and Charlie exchanged harsh words at a nightclub. After the club closed (in the early morning hours), Ramie, along with friend Tomi, left the club and went to a nearby automobile. Ramie entered the driver side of this car and Tomi was in the passenger seat as they started to depart the area. Just as they were about to leave, Charlie, who was in the immediate vicinity at this time, came over to Ramie's automobile. Charlie attempted to enter Ramie's car but was pulled away by a friend, Billie. Charlie, however, eventually escaped Billie's grasp and started to enter the vehicle on the driver's side where Rami was seated. Tomi, who held a permit to carry a concealed weapon, had a handgun on the front seat of the automobile. Ramie and Charlie "tussled" within the interior of the vehicle. Billie tried to pull Ramie from the vehicle again but before this could happen Charlie was shot and killed by passenger Tomi. After this incident, Tomi stated, "I was attempting to strike Charlie with the handgun when it discharged."

Tomi has been indicted for first-degree murder. Does Tomi have a self-defense argument in a traditional jurisdiction? If the incident occurred in Florida, should the trial court grant Tomi's motion to dismiss based on the state's "Stand Your Ground," statute?

§ 16.02 Battered Spouse Syndrome

Bonner v. State
740 So. 2d 439 (Ala. Crim. App. 1998)

McMILLAN, Judge.

The appellant, Barbara Bonner, appeals from her conviction for manslaughter, a violation of § 13A-6-3, Code of Alabama 1975. She was sentenced to 15 years' imprisonment. That sentence was split, and she was ordered to serve 2 years, followed by five years' probation.

The appellant contends that the trial court committed reversible error in refusing to allow her to introduce expert testimony concerning the "battered women syndrome." The trial court found that the relevance and materiality of the proffered testimony failed to outweigh its prejudicial effect on the jury.

"Battered spouse" syndrome has increasingly gained recognition in Alabama and in courts throughout the country. * * * The New Jersey Supreme Court, for example, found an expert's testimony on the subject of battered spouse syndrome "essential to rebut the general misconceptions regarding battered women" because this testimony "is aimed at an area where the purported common knowledge of the jury may be very much mistaken, an area where jurors' logic, drawn from their own experience, may lead to a wholly incorrect conclusion, an area where expert knowledge would enable the jurors to disregard their prior conclusions as being common myths rather than common knowledge." *State v. Kelly*, 478 A.2d 364 (N.J. 1984). The Alabama Supreme Court has reached the same conclusion in *Ex parte Haney*, 603 So. 2d 414 (Ala. 1992):

Expert testimony regarding the battered woman syndrome can be admitted to help the jury not only to understand the battered woman syndrome but also to determine whether the defendant had reasonable grounds for an honest belief that she was in imminent danger when considering the issue of self-defense.

Expert testimony on the battered woman syndrome would help dispel the ordinary lay person's perception that a woman in a battering relationship is free to leave at any time. The expert evidence would counter any 'common sense' conclusions by the jury that if the beatings were really that bad the woman would have left her husband much earlier. Popular misconceptions about battered woman syndrome would be put to rest, including the beliefs that the women are masochistic and enjoy the beatings and that they intentionally provoke their husbands into fits of rage * * * .

In this case, the trial court engaged in a relatively extensive colloquy with defense counsel regarding the relevancy and materiality of the expert's proffered testimony. Defense counsel informed the trial court that the expert was a social worker who had a master's degree and who regularly counsels battered women. Defense counsel further stated, in an offer of proof, that although the expert had never counseled the appellant, he was not offering the expert's testimony to show that the appellant suffered from any syndrome but rather to show the "psychological coping mechanisms of battered women and why they don't leave home and how they try to protect themselves." The trial court sustained the State's objection to the offer of proof because: (1) the proper factual predicate had not been laid to justify the testimony; and (2) the testimony would tend to confuse the jury because the homicide in this case occurred during a period of confrontation and the appellant was arguing self defense. In so ruling, the trial court stated, "I'm not going to allow [the testimony] until such time as the facts of the relationship are placed into evidence and we haven't had that yet." The trial court further found that "the confusion from allowing the proffered testimony into evidence outweighed the probative value of [the] testimony ... in light of the facts of the case, which is a self-defense case, where the victim is alleged to [have been] actively beating on the defendant at the time he was stabbed."

After examining the record, we hold that the trial court erred in disallowing the appellant's offer of expert testimony. First, the record reveals that a proper factual predicate was established to justify the introduction of the expert testimony. Before the appellant's offer of proof, evidence was presented during the State's case-in-chief and by defense witnesses who testified that the appellant's husband, Curtis Bonner, subjected her and her children to mental and physical abuse before and during their marriage. During direct examination by the State, Officer Robert Jackson of the Frisco City Police Department testified that on several occasions he responded to "911" emergency calls made by the appellant as a result of physical beatings by the victim. Evidence was presented that the physical violence escalated during the couple's marriage. Defense witnesses, including the appellant's 10-year-old son and 9-year-old niece, testified that at least three times a month the victim would beat the appellant with his fists and push her into the wall. They also testified that the victim had fired a gun at the appellant and had beaten her with the gun barrel. Both children testified that there were times when the appellant fought back, and that she had, on two occasions, stabbed the victim. The appellant's son testified that on the night of the killing, the victim had been drinking and was beating the appellant. He testified that she "started blocking" his assault and then grabbed a knife and stabbed the victim. Evidence was presented that throughout their marriage the appellant requested the Department of Human Resources to provide legal aid to enable her to divorce the victim. However, the victim would apologize for his behavior and persuade her not to divorce him. The record indicates that the State countered the appellant's claim of self-defense by arguing that she continued in the allegedly abusive relationship with the victim, thereby creating an inference that she was not afraid of the victim.

However, generally, a battered woman "is or has been in an intimate relationship with a man who repeatedly subjects or subjected her to forceful physical and/or psychological abuse." LENORE WALKER, THE BATTERED WOMAN SYNDROME 203 (1984).

> The violence associated with this type of relationship is neither constant nor random. Instead, it follows a pattern. Dr. [Lenore] Walker identified a three-stage cycle of violence. The first stage is the 'tension building' phase, during which small abusive episodes occur. These episodes gradually escalate over a period of time. The tension continues to build until the second stage — the acute battering phase — erupts. During this phase, in which most injuries occur, the battering is out of control. Psychological abuse in the form of threats of future harm is also prevalent. The third phase is a calm, loving period during which the batterer is contrite, seeks forgiveness, and promises to refrain from future violence. This phase provides a positive reinforcement for the woman to continue the relationship in the hope that the violent behavior will not recur. The cycle then repeats itself.

> In sum, the battered woman feels "trapped in a deadly situation." Caught in this cycle, she sometimes strikes back and kills.

PAUL C. GIANNELLI AND EDWARD J. IMWINKELREID, SCIENTIFIC EVIDENCE, § 9-3, pp. 268-73 (2d. ed. 1993).

The trial court erred in concluding that expert testimony on battered woman syndrome was unnecessary and that it would tend to confuse the jury in cases where the killing occurs during a confrontation, i.e., a situation where the killer might claim self-defense. In 1991, approximately 75% of cases using expert testimony on battered spouse syndrome involved situations where the killing occurred during a confrontation. *See* Holly Maguigan, *Battered Women and Self-Defense: Myths and Misconceptions in Current Reform Proposals*, 140 U. PA. L. REV. 379, 396-97 (1991).

> The use of syndrome evidence generates substantial confusion regarding the jurisprudential bases for the defense. Specifically, many courts approach these claims as rooted in excuse theory — as opposed to justification–or create some hybrid of the two. However, self-defense claims are based entirely upon a theory of justification. Thus, someone who kills in self-defense is not morally culpable because society considers this act to be justified. Upon sober refection, society has concluded that this action was correct under the circumstances. The theory of battered woman syndrome adheres closely to this justification rationale; in fact, the syndrome so closely parallels the law of self-defense that its basic parameters appear to be controlled more by legal convenience than by psychological observation or theory.

> When battered woman syndrome testimony is offered, many courts construe the defense as partly or wholly based upon principles of excuse. Indeed, some jurisdictions have placed syndrome testimony within such legal categories as diminished capacity or insanity. Even when courts interpret the theory as one grounded in justification, they invariably describe the defendant as 'suffering' from the syndrome, as though it were a medical malady. This "mental disability" perspective has important ramification for the law as well as for battered women defendants.

Faigman & Wright, *The Battered Woman Syndrome in the Age of Science*, 39 ARIZ. L. REV. 67 (1997) * * * .

> Allowing the defense the opportunity to present expert testimony on the syndrome and the characteristics of a battered woman would not have confused the jury but instead would have given the jury and the trial court information beyond the understanding of the average layperson. Additionally, the introduction of expert testimony may have provided clarification on the issue of self-defense, i.e., whether the appellant acted reasonably under the circumstances.

> Because the appellant laid a sufficient factual predicate to warrant introduction of the proffered expert testimony and because the expert testimony was relevant to the issue of self-defense, the judgment of the trial court is reversed and this cause remanded to that court for proceedings consistent with this opinion. REVERSED AND REMANDED * * * .

NOTES AND QUESTIONS

1. ***Expert Testimony***. When a defendant advances a defense based on prior battering, defense counsel frequently calls an expert witness to explain the effects of an abusive relationship on a person, and why that person does not leave the relationship and instead tolerates the abuse. The Michigan Supreme Court explained the requirements for the admission of such evidence in *People v. Christel*, 537 N.W.2d 194 (Mich. 1995):

> [E]xpert testimony regarding the battered woman syndrome is admissible only when it is relevant and helpful to the jury in evaluating a complainant's credibility and the expert witness is properly qualified.

> Generally, battered woman syndrome testimony is relevant and helpful when needed to explain a complainant's actions, such as prolonged endurance of physical abuse accompanied by attempts at hiding or minimizing the abuse, delays in reporting the abuse, or recanting allegations of abuse. If relevant and helpful, testimony regarding specific behavior is permissible. However, the expert may not opine whether the complainant is a battered woman, may not testify that defendant was a batterer or guilty of the instant charge, and may not comment on the complainant's truthfulness. Moreover, the trial court, when appropriate, may preclude expert testimony when the probative value of such testimony is substantially outweighed by the danger of unfair prejudice.

2. ***Imperfect Self-Defense.*** Some states recognize two forms of self-defense, regular or perfect self-defense and imperfect or partial self-defense. Imperfect self-defense arises when an "actual, subjective belief on the part of the accused that he/she is in *apparent* imminent danger of death or serious bodily harm from the assailant, requiring the use of deadly force, is not an objectively reasonable belief." In *State v. Smullen*, 844 A.2d 429, 440 (Md. 2004), the court stated:

> Unlike perfect or complete self-defense, imperfect self-defense does not constitute a justification for the killing and does not warrant an acquittal. Its only effect is to negate the element of malice required for a conviction of murder and thus reduces the offense to manslaughter. A person laboring under the honest subjective belief that he/she was, indeed, in apparent imminent danger of death or serious bodily harm and that the force used was necessary to meet the danger cannot be found to have acted out of malice. * * *

> "[T]he only substantive difference between the two doctrines, other than their consequences, is that, in perfect self-defense, the defendant's belief that he was in immediate danger of death of serious bodily harm or that

the force he used was necessary must be objectively reasonable. In all other respects, the elements of the two doctrines are the same." (citations omitted)

3. ***Battered Children's Syndrome.*** In *State v. Smullen*, 844 A.2d 429, 446-50 (Md 2004), the court stated:

> The battered child syndrome has an earlier origin and had a different initial purpose. It was first described by Drs. C. Henry Kempe, Frederic N. Silverman, Brandt F. Steele, William Droegemueller, and Henry K. Silver in *The Battered Child Syndrome,* 181 JAMA 105 (1962) as "a clinical condition in young children who have received serious physical abuse." * * * The syndrome posited by the authors had nothing whatever to do with a self-defense argument by a parent-killing child, but focused entirely on identifying child abuse. * * *

> Most appellate courts that have considered these syndromes have quite properly regarded them as in the nature of novel scientific theories and thus have subjected them to analysis under [evidence standards applicable to admission of testimony under new scientific theories]. Despite the early reluctance by the courts, especially in non-confrontational settings * * * there is an increasing judicial acceptance of the syndrome based on its medical or psychological credentials. * * * Clearly, the syndrome described by Dr. Kempe has become well-accepted in both the medical and legal community. More important, the psychological aspects of that syndrome are in harmony with the psychology of the battered spouse syndrome, which has independently gained wide acceptance in the psychological and legal communities. * * * [W]e think it more appropriate simply to conclude that the elements of the battered spouse syndrome that can help to explain why a battered woman may perceive imminent serious harm from conduct that would not likely be regarded as imminently threatening by someone else and may regard her conduct as necessary to meet that threat apply equally with respect to battered children.

4. ***Battered Person Syndrome.*** Would it be easier to recognize a battered person syndrome? In *State v. Smullen*, 844 A.2d 429, 450 (Md. 2004), the court refused to recognize a battered person syndrome, and stated:

> Although we are not prepared at this point to recognize a battered *person* syndrome, because we know not where that may lead, we do hold that the battered spouse syndrome, as recognized in § 10-916, applies as well to battered children. The underpinnings of that application, we believe, have been generally accepted in the psychological and legal communities and are therefore reliable. For convenience, we shall continue to refer to the "battered child syndrome," as that has become the term of art, but we

conceive of it simply as part of an expanded scope of the statutory battered spouse syndrome.

Id. at 450.

5. ***Self-Defense and Cultural Defenses***. In reconsidering the case of *People v. Romero* [p. 567], could the defense have successfully raised a claim of self-defense?

PROBLEM FIFTY-TWO

Judy shot and killed her spouse, John, who was lying on a bed in a rear bedroom. A later autopsy revealed that there were three gunshot wounds to the head that caused his death. An autopsy also revealed that John had a .12 blood alcohol level when he died. Judy told the police that John had been beating her all day and ordered her to lie down on the floor while he slept on the bed. After her husband fell asleep, the defendant took her grandchild who was staying at her house to her mother's house. Judy took a pistol from her mother's purse and walked back to her home. She pointed the pistol at the back of John's head while he was sleeping, but it jammed the first time she tried to shoot him. She fixed the gun and then shot her husband in the back of the head three times as he lay sleeping. After one shot, Judy saw that he was still breathing, so she then shot him twice more in the back of the head. Judy told the police that she shot John because "I took all I was going to take from him."

Judy's counsel wants to present evidence at trial showing a long history of physical and mental abuse by John. At the time of the killing, Judy and John had been married almost twenty-five years and had several children. John began drinking and abusing her about five years after they were married. The physical abuse consisted of slapping, punching and kicking her, striking her with various objects, and throwing glasses, beer bottles and other objects at her. Judy described other specific incidents of abuse, such as John putting her cigarettes out on her, throwing hot coffee on her, breaking glass against her face and crushing food on her face, leaving her with several scars. John did not work and forced her to make money by being a prostitute at a local truck stop. John made fun of her for being a prostitute, and would beat her if she resisted going to the truck stop or if he was unsatisfied with how much money she made. He regularly referred to her as a "dog," "bitch" and "whore," and sometimes would make Judy eat pet food out of the pets' bowls and bark like a dog. During the years of abuse, John threatened numerous times to kill Judy and to maim her in various ways.

On the day of the shooting, the police arrested John for drunk driving while he was driving Judy home from the truck stop, and after Judy bailed him out he was particularly abusive. The police were called to the house that evening, and Judy complained that John had been beating her all day and "I can't take it anymore." The officers advised her to file a complaint, but Judy said she was afraid that John would kill her if she had him arrested. The officers said they needed a warrant before they could arrest John, and then they left.

Judy told the police after the killing that she was too afraid of her husband to press charges against him or to leave him. She said that she had left their home several times, but John always found her, brought her home and beat her. Asked why she killed her husband, Judy replied:

> Because I was scared of him and I knowed when he woke up, it was going to be the same thing, and I was scared when he took me to the truck stop that night it was going to be worse than he had ever been. I just couldn't take it no more. There ain't no way, even if it means going to prison. It's better than living in that. That's worse hell than anything.

A. What crime, if any, should the prosecutor charge against Judy? If she is charged with first-degree murder, what argument(s) will defense counsel make to have the evidence of the victim's abuse admitted at trial, and for what purpose? Should defense counsel argue for imperfect self-defense?

B. What might be the defense presented if Judy had awakened John the first time she attempted to fire the gun, and upon seeing her point the weapon at him, John reaches for his own weapon on the night-stand next to the bed and shoots Judy, killing her? If John were charged with murder for the death of Judy, can he successfully offer a claim of self-defense? Should evidence of his long-term abuse of her be admitted to show his intent, or would it be too prejudicial?

§ 16.03 Defense of Others

State v. Cook
515 S.E.2d 127 (W. Va. 1999)

DAVIS, Justice:

* * * [Brenda S. Cook is forty years old and is married to Gerald Cook. Since 1979, the Cooks have lived in a trailer home on Dover Hollow Road near Moorefield, West Virginia. The Cooks had significant difficulties with one of their neighbors, Homer Buckler, who was a huge man, standing 6'4" and weighing in excess of 300 pounds. The problems with Mr. Buckler arose over a fence the Cooks erected along their property on Hickory Ridge Road. On May 7, 1997,

Buckler began throwing rocks from the fence at Mr. Cook and the two began to argue. Mrs. Cook saw them arguing and came outside with a shotgun, which she then discharged once into the air. Buckler then began beating Mr. Cook, who was unable to resist. Mrs. Cook tried to pull Buckler off her husband, and when Buckler pushed her away, she shot him once. Buckler died a short time later, and Mrs. Cook was charged and convicted of second-degree murder and sentenced to a 25-year term of imprisonment. The trial court instructed the jury on defense of others as a justification for Mrs. Cook's conduct, but the jury rejected the defense. On appeal, Mrs. Cook argued that the jury's verdict was unsupported by the evidence and that she was entitled to an acquittal as a matter of law.]

* * * The controlling issue in this case requires this Court to determine whether the evidence was sufficient to sustain a conviction for second degree murder. Mrs. Cook contends that the state failed to establish beyond a reasonable doubt that she did not act in defense of another, her husband, in causing the death of Mr. Buckler * * * .

The basic premise underlying the doctrine of defense of another (also called defense of others) is that a person is justified in using force to protect a third party from unlawful force by an aggressor. The defense of another doctrine closely parallels the common law doctrine of self-defense.* * * In *State v. Saunders*, 330 S.E.2d 674 (W.Va. 1985), we pointed out that "the right to defense of another usually falls under the rubric of self-defense. One simply steps into the shoes of the victim and is able to do only as much as the victim himself would lawfully be permitted to do." The broad parameters of the defense of another doctrine were articulated by this Court over one hundred years ago in the case of *State v. Greer*, 22 W. Va. 800, 819 (1883), wherein we held that the right of defense of another may be exercised in defense of a family member:

> What one may lawfully do in defense of himself — when threatened with death or great bodily harm, he may do in behalf of a brother; but if the brother was in fault in provoking an assault, that brother must retreat as far as he safely can, before his brother would be justified in taking the life of his assailant in his defense of the brother. But if the brother was so drunk as not to be mentally able to know his duty to retreat, or was physically unable to retreat, a brother is not bound to stand by and see him killed or suffer great bodily harm, because he does not under such circumstances retreat. It is only the faultless, who are exempt from the necessity of retreating while acting in self-defense. Those in fault must retreat, if able to do so; if from the fierceness of the attack or for other reasons they are unable to retreat, they will be excused by the law for not doing so. * * *

Our cases have succinctly articulated the development and scope of the doctrine of self-defense and the use of deadly force under it. However, we have not had occasion to thoroughly discuss the defense of another doctrine. The facts of the instant case require that we fully explore this doctrine's principles.

1. Initial limitations on the doctrine of defense of another. The application of the common law doctrine of defense of another was very limited in its earliest beginnings. The doctrine was imposed only as a defense when a homicide occurred in defense of a member of one's family. Under the common law, "the privilege of using [deadly] force . . . did not include authority for intervenors to protect third persons who were strangers to the intervenor."* * * Blackstone theorized that the defense actually arose out of the right to protect one's property. Blackstone noted that, at common law, one's acquired rights of property encompassed his wife, child, parent, or servant. 3 WILLIAM BLACKSTONE, COMMENTARIES ON THE LAW OF ENGLAND, ch.1, § 8(2) (1916). * * *

The initial limitation of the doctrine to one's family eroded with time as courts began to extend the doctrine to allow for the defense of strangers. * * * The expansion of the doctrine to include strangers brought with it a theory of potential liability. This theory was called the "alter ego" rule. The alter ego rule held that a defendant using deadly force to defend a person who was not entitled to use deadly force would be held criminally liable. * * *

2. Development of reasonable belief standard. The alter ego rule worked a considerable hardship upon defendants who unknowingly intervened to aid third parties who were not privileged to use self-defense. In such situations, the intervenor was criminally liable for any injury or death he or she caused. * * * Many jurisdictions began to reject the alter ego rule, to a large extent, because of the position taken by the American Law Institute's Model Penal Code, § 3.05 (1985). The Model Penal Code adopted the "reasonable belief" rule, which provided that an intervenor who acts in defense of another is not liable if his or her actions were reasonable under the circumstances. Under this rule, a defendant may be legally justified in killing to defend another, even if the intervenor acted under a mistaken belief as to who was at fault, provided his or her belief was reasonable. * * *

In this Court's review of its past decisions, decisions of other jurisdictions and commentaries, the doctrine of defense of another may be succinctly articulated. We therefore hold that to establish the doctrine of defense of another in a homicide prosecution, a defendant must show by sufficient evidence that he or she used reasonable force, including deadly force, in a situation where the defendant had a reasonable belief of the lawfulness of his or her intervention on behalf of another person who was in imminent danger of death or serious bodily harm from which such person could save himself/herself only by using force, including deadly force, against his or her assailant, but was unable to do so. We will now proceed to examine the key elements of the doctrine of defense of another.

1. *Burden of proof.* The doctrine of defense of another is an affirmative defense. This Court, as well as the United States Supreme Court, has made clear that "a defendant can be required to prove the affirmative defenses that he asserts." * * *

2. *Amount of force.* A defendant asserting the defense of another must show that the force used was reasonable. This requirement is also known as the "proportionality" rule.* * * That is "a person may use only that force which is necessary in view of the nature of the attack; any use of excessive force is not justified and a homicide which results therefrom is unlawful." * * * This principle of law is taken from the doctrine of self-defense. Our Court has previously held that the amount of force that can be used in self-defense is that normally one can return deadly force only if he reasonably believes that the assailant is about to inflict death or serious bodily harm; otherwise, where he is threatened only with non-deadly force, he may use only non-deadly force in return. * * * Therefore, the reasonable force standard is appropriate for the doctrine of defense of another.

3. *Reasonable belief that intervention was lawful.* The "reasonable belief" standard of intervention emphasizes what the intervenor believes about the circumstances, as opposed to what are the actual circumstances. An Alabama court has ruled that the reasonable belief standard "shifts the emphasis to [the] defendant's reliance on reasonable appearances rather than exposing him to the peril of liability for defending another where appearances were deceiving and there was no actual imminent danger." * * * Similarly, this Court has previously ruled that "the reasonableness of [a defendant's] belief and actions in using deadly force must be judged in the light of the circumstances in which he acted at the time and is not measured by subsequently developed facts." * * * The reasonableness of an intervenor's belief is determined by both a subjective and an objective inquiry. * * * In other words, the "actor must actually believe that [another] is in danger and that belief must be a reasonable one."* * * Insofar as the reasonable belief standard is used by this Court for self-defense, it is an appropriate standard for the doctrine of defense of another.

4. *Level of danger.* An intervenor is not obliged to use deadly force in defense of another, unless the third party is in imminent danger of death or serious bodily harm. This "simply means that an intervenor cannot act until the party whom the intervenor is defending is immediately threatened."* * * This criterion is no different from that which this Court uses in the context of self-defense. We have held that a person who reasonably believes he or she "is in imminent danger of death or serious bodily harm * * * has the right to employ deadly force in order to defend himself." * * * The imminent danger standard is appropriate for the doctrine of defense of another, as it is consistent with the requirement for using deadly force in self-defense. * * *

Mrs. Cook asserted the defense of another doctrine at trial. The trial court gave an adequate instruction of the law regarding the defense to the jury * * * Mindful of the jury's province over the evidence presented on the issue of defense of another, this Court will not permit an injustice to occur because a jury failed to adequately understand the evidence presented at trial. This is such a case.

1. *Mr. Cook was privileged to use deadly force in self-defense.* The facts of the case viewed in the light most favorable to the prosecution, clearly illustrate that Mr. Buckler stopped his truck in front of the Cooks' residence and began throwing rocks onto their property. The rocks had been placed by the Cooks near their property line fence. There was no evidence to indicate that the rocks were unlawfully situated alongside their property. Mr. Cook approached Mr. Buckler and asked him to stop removing the rocks and throwing them further onto his property. Mrs. Cook observed the two men, while in her home, and became afraid for her husband's safety. The testimony was that Mrs. Cook grabbed a shotgun and fired into the air hoping Mr. Buckler would get back into his truck and leave them alone.

Mr. Buckler was not deterred by the gunshot. In contrast, he continued to yell and curse at Mr. Cook. Mrs. Cook moved quickly to her husband's aid. The record supports that both Mr. and Mrs. Cook tried to reason with Mr. Buckler, but to no avail. When Mrs. Cook informed Mr. Buckler that she had called the police, he became incensed and renewed a previous threat to kill them if they had again called the police. At this point, Mr. Cook retreated. He began to walk away from Mr. Buckler. This Court long ago held that "to reduce homicide in self-defense to excusable homicide, it must be shown that the [defendant] was closely pressed by the other party, and retreated as far as he conveniently or safely could, in good faith, with the honest intent to avoid the violence of the assault." * * *

Mr. Buckler followed Mr. Cook, grabbed Mr. Cook and spun him around. At this juncture, the evidence demonstrates that Mr. Buckler's conduct of grabbing and spinning Mr. Cook was hostile and constituted a battery. Exercising his right to self-defense, Mr. Cook took a swing at the aggressor, Mr. Buckler. * * * A person "may only use non-deadly force where he is threatened only with non-deadly force." * * *

One swing in self-defense was attempted by Mr. Cook. Mr. Buckler immediately threw his 6'4" frame upon Mr. Cook's 5'6" frame, knocking him to the ground. Mr. Buckler began to beat Mr. Cook with unrestrained blows throughout his body. Two critical observations are required at this point. First, based upon the testimony of the witnesses, Mr. Cook was unable to free himself from the relentless blows to his body by Mr. Buckler. Second, because of the great size and strength difference between the two men, Mr. Cook was legally at liberty to use force, including deadly force, to defend himself from the vicious and relentless blows by Mr. Buckler as Mr. Cook faced real and imminent danger of great bodily harm or death from the massive blows being inflicted upon him by Mr. Buckler.

2. *Mrs. Cook was privileged to use deadly force in defense of her husband.* The evidence is clear. When Mr. Buckler began beating Mr. Cook, it was not possible for Mr. Cook to resort to the use of deadly force, or any type of force, to defend himself, because of the enormous size of Mr. Buckler. Mr. Cook was defenseless. Although we have clarified the doctrine of defense of another in this opinion, the law in this State has long been that a person has the right to repel force by force in the defense of his * * * family * * * and if in so doing he uses only so much force as the necessity, or apparent necessity, of the case requires, he is not guilty of any offense, though he kill his adversary in so doing * * * Therefore, when Mrs. Cook saw that her husband was defenseless, as he laid curled on the ground absorbing every violent blow Mr. Buckler hurled at his body, the law permitted her to intervene.

Mrs. Cook testified that she became afraid and believed that her husband would be killed by Mr. Buckler. This Court has previously ruled that "the reasonableness of [a defendant's] belief and actions in using deadly force must be judged in the light of the circumstances in which he acted at the time and is not measured by subsequently developed facts." * * * The reasonable belief standard "is composed of an objective element, *i.e.*, a reasonable belief that force is necessary, and a subjective element, *i.e.*, an actual belief that force is necessary."* * * Moreover, "a person may use only that force which is necessary in view of the nature of the attack; any use of excessive force is not justified and a homicide which results therefrom is unlawful." * * *

Mrs. Cook did not initially resort to deadly force when she came to the aid of her husband. In fact, Mrs. Cook hurled her body into the onslaught and tried to pull Mr. Buckler from her husband. This degree of force, while reasonable, proved to be inadequate. Mr. Buckler knocked Mrs. Cook aside, ripping open her shirt. He then returned to beating Mr. Cook. At this point, Mrs. Cook stepped squarely into the shoes of her husband and used the degree of force her husband, if able to do so, was privileged to use. Mrs. Cook fired the shotgun only wanting to shoot Mr. Buckler in his arm to stop him from killing her husband. The evidence shows that just as the shot was fired, Mr. Buckler raised his right arm to again hit Mr. Cook. As he did so the bullet landed under his right armpit — stopping him cold. Mrs. Cook did not fire a second shot. She reloaded the shotgun when it appeared that Mr. Buckler was going to get up and again start fighting. These facts support the conclusion that Mrs. Cook used only that degree of force which was reasonably necessary to defend her husband.

In the face of this overwhelming evidence of defense of another, the State presented testimony by Mr. Buckler's son to try and counter the facts presented by

Mr. and Mrs. Cook and corroborated by three eyewitnesses. * * * [The Court then described this testimony].

In view of the foregoing, the conviction and sentence in this case is vacated and the case is remanded for entry of a judgment of acquittal. The defendant is ordered to be released. * * * Vacated and Remanded. * * *

WORKMAN, J., concurring:

I write separately only to emphasize that it is the rare and exceptional case in which I would embark on overturning a jury verdict in a case which appears otherwise to have been fairly tried. * * * It is the compelling application of the law to the facts presented to the jury that leads me to the ultimate conclusion that there was an insufficiency of the evidence to support the Appellant's conviction in this case.

NOTE

The policy rationale for the disintegration of the "act-at-peril" or alter ego rule is so that individuals will be encouraged to assist others in need and yet not expose themselves to criminal liability in the process. In *Alexander v. State*, 447 A.2d 880 (Md. Ct. Spec. App. 1982), Judge Lowe stated:

In the decade that commenced with the assassination of President Kennedy, climaxed with the creation of this Court, and concluded with the marriage of Tiny Tim, violence proliferated, partly because police were constitutionally hobbled in controlling a rebellious reaction and partly because citizens were reluctant — or afraid — to become "involved" in deterring that violence. This reticence seemed to emanate less from fear of physical harm than from the potential consequences of a legal aftermath. Representative was the 1964 New York homicide of Catherine "Kitty" Genovese, who was viciously ravaged and repeatedly stabbed while onlookers turned their backs to avoid witnessing the butchery, and neighbors closed their doors and windows to shut out her screams of anguish until her suffering was finally ended by the murderer. Witnesses who were interviewed excused their indifference by noting that the law did not protect a protector from criminal assault charges if the one he aids was initially in the wrong, however misleading appearances may have been. *See People v. Young*, 183 N.E.2d 319 (N.Y. 1962). The onlookers hesitated to become involved in the fracas at their legal peril. Even if their hearts had been stout enough to enter the fray in defense of a stranger being violently assaulted, the fear of legal consequences chilled their better instincts. * * *

Perkins' [CRIMINAL LAW (2nd ed. 1969)] preferred position better fulfills our contemporary social needs by merging the encouragement of crime prevention with the privilege of defending others. * * *   Maryland [ ] appears to have been in the forefront in safeguarding the right which Blackstone recognized as a legal adjunct of natural instincts, and in adopting what Perkins recommends as the more "enlightened view."

> "Subject to the familiar limitations as to the degree of force permitted, one who is himself free from fault may intervene and use force to protect an innocent victim of intended crime.   And under the sound view he is protected by the usual mistake-of-fact doctrine and may act upon the situation as it reasonably seems to be."   Perkins, *supra* at 1021.

MODEL PENAL CODE

§ 3.05. Use of Force for the Protection of Other Persons

(1) Subject to the provisions of this Section and of Section 3.09, the use of force upon or toward the person of another is justifiable to protect a third person when:

(a) the actor would be justified under Section 3.04 in using such force to protect himself against the injury he believes to be threatened to the person whom he seeks to protect; and

(b) under the circumstances as the actor believes them to be, the person whom he seeks to protect would be justified in using such protective force; and

(c) the actor believes that his intervention is necessary for the protection of such other person.

(2) Notwithstanding Subsection (1) of this Section:

(a) when the actor would be obliged under Section 3.04 to retreat, to surrender the possession of a thing or to comply with a demand before using force in self-protection, he is not obliged to do so before using force for the protection of another person, unless he knows that he can thereby secure the complete safety of such other person; and

(b) when the person whom the actor seeks to protect would be obliged under Section 3.04 to retreat, to surrender the possession of a thing or to comply with a demand if he knew that he could obtain complete safety by so doing, the actor is obliged to try to cause him to do so before using force in his protection if the actor knows that he can obtain complete safety in that way; and

(c) neither the actor nor the person whom he seeks to protect is obliged to retreat when in the other's dwelling or place of work to any greater extent than in his own.

§ 3.08. Use of Force by Persons with Special Responsibility for Care, Discipline or Safety of Others

The use of force upon or toward the person of another is justifiable if:

(1) the actor is the parent or guardian or other person similarly responsible for the general care and supervision of a minor or a person acting at the request of such parent, guardian or other responsible person and:

(a) the force is used for the purpose of safeguarding or promoting the welfare of the minor, including the prevention or punishment of his misconduct; and

(b) the force used is not designed to cause or known to create a substantial risk of causing death, serious bodily injury, disfigurement, extreme pain or mental distress or gross degradation; or

(2) the actor is a teacher or a person otherwise entrusted with the care or supervision for a special purpose of a minor and:

(a) the actor believes that the force used is necessary to further such special purpose, including the maintenance of reasonable discipline in a school, class or other group, and that the use of such force is consistent with the welfare of the minor; and

(b) the degree of force, if it had been used by the parent or guardian of the minor, would not be unjustifiable under Subsection (1)(b) of this Section; or

(3) the actor is the guardian or other person similarly responsible for the general care and supervision of an incompetent person and:

(a) the force is used for the purpose of safeguarding or promoting the welfare of the incompetent person, including the prevention of his misconduct, or, when such incompetent person is in a hospital or other institution for his care and custody, for the maintenance of reasonable discipline in such institution; and

(b) the force used is not designed to cause or known to create a substantial risk of causing death, serious bodily injury, disfigurement, extreme or unnecessary pain, mental distress, or humiliation; or

(4) the actor is a doctor or other therapist or a person assisting him at his direction and:

(a) the force is used for the purpose of administering a recognized form of treatment that the actor believes to be adapted to promoting the physical or mental health of the patient; and

(b) the treatment is administered with the consent of the patient or, if the patient is a minor or an incompetent person, with the consent of his parent or guardian or other person legally competent to consent in his behalf, or the treatment is administered in an emergency when the actor believes that no one competent to consent can be consulted and that a reasonable person, wishing to safeguard the welfare of the patient, would consent; or

(5) the actor is a warden or other authorized official of a correctional institution and:

(a) he believes that the force used is necessary for the purpose of enforcing the lawful rules or procedures of the institution, unless his belief in the lawfulness of the rule or procedure sought to be enforced is erroneous and his error is due to ignorance or mistake as to the provisions of the Code, any other provision of the criminal law or the law governing the administration of the institution; and

(b) the nature or degree of force used is not forbidden by Article 303 or 304 of the Code; and

(c) if deadly force is used, its use is otherwise justifiable under this Article; or

(6) the actor is a person responsible for the safety of a vessel or an aircraft or a person acting at his direction and:

(a) he believes that the force used is necessary to prevent interference with the operation of the vessel or aircraft or obstruction of the execution of a lawful order, unless his belief in the lawfulness of the order is erroneous and his error is due to ignorance or mistake as to the law defining his authority; and

(b) if deadly force is used, its use is otherwise justifiable under this Article; or

(7) the actor is a person who is authorized or required by law to maintain order or decorum in a vehicle, train or other carrier or in a place where others are assembled, and;

(a) he believes that the force used is necessary for such purpose; and

(b) the force used is not designed to cause or known to create a substantial risk of causing death, bodily injury, or extreme mental distress.

PROBLEM FIFTY-THREE

Nate is selling drugs on a street-corner one evening when he is approached by Charles, who asks to purchase a small quantity of drugs. After receiving the money from Charles, Nate begins to remove the drugs from his pocket. At that point, Charles shouts, "Let's take him down." Suspecting that Charles is an undercover officer, Nate shoves Charles to the ground and runs behind a house across the street and down an alley, with Charles in pursuit. After a three block chase, Charles corners Nate in a closed alley, removes a gun from a holster, and shouts, "Get down on the ground now!" As Charles is pointing his gun at Nate, Priscilla, another drug dealer, looks down the alley and sees Nate on the ground with Charles standing over him pointing the gun. Nate sees her and shouts, "Please help me, this guy's trying to rip me off." Priscilla runs down the alley and shouts, "Let him go." Charles continues to point the gun at Nate and responds, "Get back." Priscilla takes a gun out of her purse and shoots at Charles, wounding him. Police officers arrive a few moments later and arrest Priscilla; Nate flees back up the alley and is never apprehended. Charles is an undercover narcotics officer. Priscilla is charged with assaulting a law enforcement officer. At trial, defense counsel requests that the judge instruct the jury on defense of others. How should the court rule on the request?

----

§ 16.04 Defense of Property

Gatlin v. United States
833 A.2d 995 (D.C. Ct. App. 2003)

REID, Associate Judge:

Appellants Brenda Gatlin * * * and Mary A.T. Anigbo, employees of a District of Columbia charter school at the time of their arrests, appeal their convictions on various charges growing out of confrontations and altercations with a newspaper reporter [Ms. Ferrechio], a photographer, and two police officers, on the premises of the school. [Gatlin and Anigbo were found guilty of assaulting the reporter, photographer, and the officers. The defendants argued that the trial judge improperly refused to consider their claim of defense of property in the non-jury trial.]

The evidence in this case showed that on December 3, 1996, at approximately four o'clock in the afternoon, Ken McIntyre, Metro Editor at the *Washington Times*, called 911. After identifying himself, he stated: "One of our reporters has been attacked and beaten at a school. We would like you to go out there and meet her there." He reported that the school was "Langley Junior High" and that the reporter, who was "very shaken up," would meet the police * * * . [The evidence at trial was that Dr. Anigbo, the principal of the school, ordered that Ms. Ferrechio be forcibly removed from the school because she had been speaking to students without permission and refused to turn over her notebook. Dr. Anigbo claimed that the notepad on which the reporter was writing was hers and that she merely took back her own property.] * * *

After learning that a *Washington Times* reporter had been assaulted at a school, the Director of Photography at the newspaper sent Clifford Owen, a photographer, to "make sure" that Ms. Ferrechio was "okay." Mr. Owen was instructed "to document any injuries [Ms. Ferrechio] has and what happened]." He met Ms. Ferrechio at North Capitol and Season Streets "a few minutes after four o'clock." * * *

Officer Poe arrived at the corner of North Capitol and Season around 4:35 p.m. He spoke with Ms. Ferrechio whom he described as "very upset." He then drove to the Langley Junior High School, accompanied by Ms. Ferrechio, in his marked police cruiser. * * * Officer Best, responding to a police radio directive, soon arrived on the scene in his marked police cruiser. After the two officers conferred, Officer Best "led the way" into the school through the front door. Although Dr. Anigbo, the principal of the school, testified that her practice was "[to keep the [school] door locked, to admit a visitor only if the visitor rang the bell, and to make sure an adult admitted any such visitor, Mr. Owen observed that the center door "was unlocked and . . . open a couple of inches." The officers entered the foyer and proceeded to the main office, followed by Mr. Owen [and] Ms. Ferrechio. The area in the main office where everyone congregated was relatively small.

As he approached the counter in the main office, "Officer Best asked who was the principal," and Dr. Anigbo replied: "I'm the principal but I'm mad, [I] don't want to talk to you." While Officer Best engaged Dr. Anigbo in conversation, Mr. Owen concentrated on getting pictures of those who reportedly attacked Ms. Ferrechio. He informed Ms. Ferrechio that his instructions from the Washington Times were to get pictures of those who assaulted her, and that "it's real important" that he do so. He asked if she "could identify anybody who had assaulted her" at the school. Ms. Ferrechio expressed concern about getting her notebook back but eventually identified the person who assaulted her as "the secretary and she has short hair." Upon seeing someone who fit the description, Mr. Owen said "very loudly," "Is this the woman who assaulted you? I need to get her picture." Mr. Owen quickly took three pictures of the woman with short hair, later identified as Ms. Gatlin.

The picture-taking sparked a reaction from the school staff. Officer Best testified that as Dr. Anigbo finished speaking, "a flash went off, the principal and staff jumped up and went towards the door where the flash had come from." Officer Poe asserted that when "the photographer and reporter entered the office . . . the principal and staff went berserk." Both officers saw Ms. Gatlin * * * and Dr. Anigbo move towards the photographer and reporter. The three women were "screaming . . . [and] running towards the photographer and the reporter. Ms. Gatlin . . . had the lead." "The staff started screaming stop taking pictures, you shouldn't be in here. . . ." Officer Poe saw "Ms. Gatlin [s]winging at [Ms.] Ferrechio and [Mr.] Owen." * * *

The officers were standing between the school staff and the *Washington Times* personnel. The women continued to push and shove the officers back toward the door of the principal's office. Officer Best asserted that Dr. Anigbo pushed and shoved him in his "chest and shoulder area," and that Ms. Smith also pushed him in the "[c]hest and shoulder area." Officer Best saw Dr. Anigbo push Officer Poe "[w]ith enough strength to get him out of the office into the hallway." * * *

After the government completed its case-in-chief, counsel for Dr. Anigbo raised the defense of property defense, as the trial court was considering the defense motion for judgment of acquittal. * * *

At the next day of the trial, before the defendants presented their cases, the trial court rejected the defense of property defense. As to the assault count involving Ms. Ferrechio, the trial court reasoned that "each of those assaults sweep within them allegations of conduct in the main office, that viewed in the light most favorable to the Government was not aimed at [ejecting] a trespasser but in getting a notebook at a minimum." With regard to the assault of Mr. Owen, the court stated: "I just think that on these facts this doctrine cannot common-sensically have any application." The trial judge added: "The long and short of it is that it just cannot be that one can resort to force in a matter of moments while the police are standing there." Moreover, "it [was not] clear [to the trial judge] that Mr. Owen was asked to leave before physical steps were taken." And, concerning the assaults charged with respect to Officers Best and Poe, the trial judge said: "[I]t goes without saying it seems to me that you can't use [this doctrine of self help with regard to trespassers on your property] as to the police, that you can't, certainly not on the facts such as these, where the police have been present on your property for a matter of time less than five minutes, use physical force to eject them in the course of a criminal investigation from the property." * * *

In essence, Dr. Anigbo and Ms. Smith contend on appeal that the trial court abused its discretion in denying their motion for a new trial because the court did not properly consider their defense of property defense. They maintain that complainants "Ferrechio, Owen, Poe and Best consistently testified that they refused to leave the [Garvey Charter School] when instructed." And, they assert that: "If this had been a jury trial and the [c]ourt had refused to instruct a jury on an affirmative defense raised by the evidence, the error would certainly be deemed harmful and reversible." The government primarily argues that the trial court considered and properly rejected the defense of property defense and did not abuse its discretion in denying appellants' motion for a new trial.

* * * [I]n *Shehyn v. United States*, 256 A.2d 404 (D.C. 1969), the court articulated the basic principle governing the defense of property defense: "It is well settled that a person may use as much force as is reasonably necessary to eject a trespasser from his property, and that if he uses more force than is necessary, he is guilty of assault." Furthermore, the District's criminal jury instruction no. 5.20 provides, in part:

> A person is justified in using reasonable force to protect his/her property from trespass or theft when s/he reasonably believes that his/her property is in immediate danger of an unlawful trespass or taking and that the use of such force is necessary to avoid the danger . . . . *Rule*

> The defendant is not required to prove that s/he acted in defense of his/her property. If evidence of defense of property is present, the government must prove beyond a reasonable doubt that the defendant did not act in defense of his/her property. If you find that the government has failed to prove beyond a reasonable doubt that the defendant did not act in defense of property, you must find the defendant not guilty.

This instruction comports with similar instructions codified in most states. *See* LAFAVE, SUBSTANTIVE CRIMINAL LAW § 10.6, vol. 2 (2003) ("One is justified in using reasonable force to protect his [or her] property from trespass or theft, when he [or she] reasonably believes that his [or her] property is in immediate danger of such an unlawful interference and that the use of such force is necessary to avoid that danger.").

We turn now to an application of the defense of property defense to the charged assaults * * * against Officers Best and Poe inside the main office or its doorway, during the second entry into the Garvey Charter School on December 3, 1996. The trial court's rejection of the defense where police officers are conducting a criminal investigation is consistent with a trend on the part of some jurisdictions. As LaFave reports in his treatise: "[S]ome courts, by analogy to the modern rule disallowing force to resist an unlawful arrest, have held force is inappropriate against a police officer's seizure of property." *Id.* § 10.06(a). In deviating from the common law rule allowing a person to resist an unlawful arrest forcibly, one court determined "that this rule is no longer consistent with the needs of modern society and should be abrogated." *Commonwealth v. Moreira*, 447 N.E.2d 1224 (Mass. 1983). The court "conclude[d] that in the absence of excessive or unnecessary force by an arresting officer, a person may not use force to resist an arrest by one he knows or has good reason to believe is an authorized police officer, engaged in the performance of his duties, regardless of whether the arrest was unlawful in the circumstances."

In New Hampshire, a state which codified the common law rule allowing the reasonable use of force to defend one's property, the Supreme Court declared that there are limits to the common law rule:

> To say that a statute designed to permit and condone self-help as a way of protecting oneself from the actions of tort-feasors, wrongdoers, and run-of-the-mill miscreants authorizes the use of force against a police officer discharging his duties in the removal of an automobile from disputed turf is to stretch the statute past the breaking point.

State v. Haas, 596 A.2d 127 (N.H. 1991). Similarly, in the case before us, application of the common law defense of property defense to preclude proper police investigation of criminal allegations within the common, public areas of a school building is inconsistent with society's larger interest in the fair and timely administration of its criminal laws. Consequently, we hold that where, as here, the police have entered the common, public areas of a school building without excessive force to investigate a criminal complaint, school personnel who have been charged with assault of one of those police officers within the school, are not entitled to the defense of property defense. We also hold that a school employee, such as Ms. Gatlin, who has been charged with assault of a newspaper photographer within the school may not rely on the defense of property defense where the employee is able to seek the assistance of police officers who are on the scene to protect the integrity of the school building. Consequently, we conclude that the trial court did not abuse its discretion in denying the new trial motion of appellants relating to the charged assaults of Officers Best and Poe, and photographer Owen.

We turn now to the assault charged against Ms. Gatlin and Dr. Anigbo with respect to Ms. Ferrechio's first entrance into the Garvey Charter School on December 3, 1996. Criminal jury instruction no. 5.20 specifies in pertinent part that: "The defendant is not required to prove that [he] acted in defense of [his] property." Rather, "[i]f evidence of defense of property is present, the [burden is on the] government [to] prove beyond a reasonable doubt that the defendant did not act in defense of [his] property."

The record does not show that the trial court made comprehensive factual findings and credibility determinations, relevant to the defense of property defense and Ms. Ferrechio's first entry into the Garvey Charter School, at the end of the presentation of all evidence, although it made some findings at the close of the government's case-in-chief. Nevertheless, based upon our review of the record and transcripts before us, we are satisfied that even if the defense of property defense arguably was available to Dr. Anigbo and Ms. Gatlin when Ms. Ferrechio first entered the school and encountered Dr. Anigbo, their use of force was unreasonable. Even assuming, without deciding, that upon seeing Ms. Ferrechio, Dr. Anigbo said: "[W]hat are you doing here? I have no appointment with you. Why are you interviewing my students? Get out, I want you out," she almost immediately demanded the notebook in Ms. Ferrechio's hands. By her own testimony, Dr. Anigbo told Ms. Ferrechio, "you're not going out of here with my note pad, give me back my note pad," and then "reached for the note pad and snatched it out of [Ms. Ferrechio's] hand." This action, as the trial court concluded, was not directed at removing a trespasser but at retrieving a notebook, and Dr. Anigbo had no right to use any force to obtain possession of the notebook since the trial court found that it did not belong to her. Indeed, Dr. Anigbo did not claim that the notebook was hers when Officer Taylor remarked: "Well, ma'am, regardless of what someone had written in their (sic) notebook, you had no right to take that from anybody."

Even assuming that Dr. Anigbo reasonably believed that the note pad was hers, and that the school personnel were entitled to eject Ms. Ferrechio from the school, the record shows that the amount of force used to accomplish that goal was not reasonable, even taking into account the trial court's statement that Ms. Ferrechio "may have exaggerated the size and veracity (sic) of the attack upon her." As we declared in *Shehyn*: "It is well settled that a person may use as much force as is reasonably necessary to eject a trespasser from his [or her] property, and that if he [or she] uses more force than is necessary, he [or she] is guilty of assault." In summary, even if the defense of property defense arguably was available to Dr. Anigbo, and recognizing that in that case, the burden of proof shifted to the government to disprove the defense, we are satisfied that the trial judge could find beyond a reasonable doubt that Dr. Anigbo and Ms. Gatlin were guilty of the assault on Ms. Ferrechio.

NOTES AND QUESTIONS

1. ***Deadly Force***. The general rule is that deadly force may not be used to defend one's property. Does this fit the general theme of self-defense's proportionality rule? Note below the exceptions provided by the Model Penal Code.

2. ***Defense of Habitation.*** Some courts distinguish between defense of property and defense of habitation. There are varying approaches to whether one may use deadly force in defense of one's home. The earliest common law permitted use of deadly force, but many have moved away from that approach. Consider the Model Penal Code approach below:

MODEL PENAL CODE

§ 3.06. Use of Force for Protection of Property

(1) Use of Force Justifiable for Protection of Property. Subject to the provisions of this Section and of Section 3.09, the use of force upon or toward the person of another is justifiable when the actor believes that such force is immediately necessary:

> (a) to prevent or terminate an unlawful entry or other trespass upon land or a trespass against or the unlawful carrying away of tangible, movable property, provided that such land or movable property is, or is believed by the actor to be, in his possession or in the possession of another person for whose protection he acts; or

> (b) to effect an entry or re-entry upon land or to retake tangible movable property, provided that the actor believes that he or the person by whose authority he acts or a person from whom he or such other person derives title was unlawfully dispossessed of such land or movable property and is entitled to possession, and provided, further, that:

>> (i) the force is used immediately or on fresh pursuit after such dispossession; or

>> (ii) the actor believes that the person against whom he uses force has no claim of right to the possession of the property and, in the case of land, the circumstances, as the actor believes them to be, are of such urgency that it would be an exceptional hardship to postpone the entry or re-entry until a court order is obtained.

(2) Meaning of Possession.   For the purposes of Subsection (1) of this Section:

(a) a person who has parted with the custody of property to another who refuses to restore it to him is no longer in possession, unless the property is movable and was and still is located on land in his possession;

(b) a person who has been dispossessed of land does not regain possession thereof merely by setting foot thereon;

(c) a person who has a license to use or occupy real property is deemed to be in possession thereof except against the licensor acting under claim of right.

(3) Limitations on Justifiable Use of Force.

(a) Request to Desist.   The use of force is justifiable under this Section only if the actor first requests the person against whom such force is used to desist from his interference with the property, unless the actor believes that:

(i) such request would be useless; or

(ii) it would be dangerous to himself or another person to make the request; or

(iii) substantial harm will be done to the physical condition of the property that is sought to be protected before the request can effectively be made.

(b) Exclusion of Trespasser. The use of force to prevent or terminate a trespass is not justifiable under this Section if the actor knows that the exclusion of the trespasser will expose him to substantial danger of serious bodily injury.

(c) Resistance of Lawful Re-entry or Recaption.   The use of force to prevent an entry or re-entry upon land or the recaption of movable property is not justifiable under this Section, although the actor believes that such re-entry or recaption is unlawful, if:

(i) the re-entry or recaption is made by or on behalf of a person who was actually dispossessed of the property; and

(ii) it is otherwise justifiable under Subsection (1)(b) of this Section.

(d) Use of Deadly Force.   The use of deadly force is not justifiable under this Section unless the actor believes that

(i) the person against whom the force is used is attempting to dispossess him of his dwelling otherwise than under a claim of right to its possession; or

(ii) the person against whom the force is used is attempting to commit or consummate arson, burglary, robbery or other felonious theft or property destruction and either:

(A) has employed or threatened deadly force against or in the presence of the actor; or

(B) the use of force other than deadly force to prevent the commission or the consummation of the crime would expose the actor or another in his presence to substantial danger of serious bodily injury.

(4) Use of Confinement as Protective Force. The justification afforded by this Section extends to the use of confinement as protective force only if the actor takes all reasonable measures to terminate the confinement as soon as he knows that he can do so with safety to the property, unless the person confined has been arrested on a charge of crime.

(5) Use of Device to Protect Property. The justification afforded by this Section extends to the use of a device for the purpose of protecting property only if:

(a) the device is not designed to cause or known to create a substantial risk of causing death or serious bodily injury; and

(b) the use of the particular device to protect the property from entry or trespass is reasonable under the circumstances, as the actor believes them to be; and

(c) the device is one customarily used for such a purpose or reasonable care is taken to make known to probable intruders the fact that it is used.

(6) Use of Force to Pass Wrongful Obstructor. The use of force to pass a person whom the actor believes to be purposely or knowingly and unjustifiably obstructing the actor from going to a place to which he may lawfully go is justifiable, provided that:

(a) the actor believes that the person against whom he uses force has no claim of right to obstruct the actor; and

(b) the actor is not being obstructed from entry or movement on land that he knows to be in the possession or custody of the person obstructing him, or in the possession or custody of another person by whose authority the obstructor acts, unless the circumstances, as the actor believes them to be, are of such urgency that it would not be reasonable to postpone the entry or movement on such land until a court order is obtained; and

(c) the force used is not greater than would be justifiable if the person obstructing the actor were using force against him to prevent his passage.

PROBLEM FIFTY-FOUR

Dana was behind on payments for furniture and a television obtained from Rent-A-Vision, a "rent-to-own" store. Dana had received notices that the items would be repossessed, but Dana failed to make the payments. One afternoon two Rent-A-Vision store employees — Kim and LaFleur — went to Dana's house to take back the items. When they pulled their truck, which did not have any markings on the side, into the driveway at Dana's house, they spoke with Dana's teenage daughter. After telling the daughter that they were there to take some furniture, the daughter told them to come into the house while she got Dana. When Dana came downstairs and saw Kim and LaFleur lifting up a couch obtained from Rent-A-Vision, Dana screamed, "Get out of my house, you darn thieves." After putting down the couch, Kim explained that they were lawfully repossessing the items. Dana told the two individuals to leave the house, and they refused and began to pick up the couch again. Dana then tried to push the couch back to the floor, and Kim tried to move Dana back by hitting Dana with a shoulder while holding on to one end of the couch. Dana grabbed a wrought-iron fire poker and struck Kim on the leg and arm. Pursuant to company policy, Kim and LaFleur left Dana's house and called the local police, who arrested Dana for assault with a deadly weapon. What defense(s) should counsel for Dana pursue at trial, and how will the prosecutor respond?

§ 16.05 Arrest

State v. Johnson
954 P.2d 79 (N.M. Ct. App. 1998)

BOSSON, Judge.

This case involves the fatal shooting of Abel Gallegos, who broke into a vehicle, stole a car stereo, and was in the process of driving away when he was shot and killed by Aaron Johnson, a friend of the owner of the vehicle. Johnson was refused a jury instruction on the defense of justifiable homicide when stopping a fleeing felon, and he appeals on that sole issue. We affirm the ruling of the district court. We hold as an issue of first impression under New Mexico law that deadly force by a private citizen in apprehending a suspected fleeing felon is subject to standards of reasonableness that were not present in this case. * * *

On April 20, 1995, Steve Haddox and Aaron Johnson, along with Matt Neel and others, were at a party at an apartment complex located in a residential area of Albuquerque. At around 10:30 or 11:30 p.m. a friend told Haddox and Johnson that someone was breaking into Neel's Suzuki automobile. Haddox, Johnson, and Neel went to the parking lot of the apartment complex and saw someone — later identified as Abel Gallegos — run from the Suzuki, get into a waiting car, and start to speed off. The window of the Suzuki had been broken, and the car stereo was missing. Haddox and Johnson then each produced handguns and fired eleven shots at the car, fatally wounding Abel Gallegos. Haddox and Johnson returned to the party, and Haddox told people there that he may have hit someone. Two officers of the Albuquerque Police Department were nearby, heard shots, and saw the Gallegos car speeding away with its lights off. The officers stopped the car and found Gallegos shot through the heart. Another bullet was also found lodged in the car. No weapons were found in the car or on any of the occupants. The officers questioned Haddox and Johnson, who admitted to the shooting and gave their weapons to the police. Neither Haddox nor Johnson asserted that he had acted in self-defense. The bullet that killed Gallegos was fired from Johnson's gun, and the bullet found lodged in the car was from Haddox's gun.

Defendants were charged with second degree murder and various other crimes in indictments returned by the Bernalillo County Grand Jury. They each entered pleas of guilty to the lesser included offense of involuntary manslaughter, * * * . Each reserved the right to appeal the district court's refusal to give a justifiable homicide instruction, which would have permitted the jury to find that the death of Abel Gallegos was justified if Defendants were attempting to make a citizen's arrest of a fleeing felon. [Haddox withdrew his appeal.] * * *

New Mexico's statute on justifiable homicide in a case of a citizen's arrest has remained essentially unchanged since Territorial times. * * * , provides that homicide by a private citizen is justifiable "when necessarily committed in attempting, by lawful ways and means, to apprehend any person for any felony committed in his presence, or in lawfully suppressing any riot, or in necessarily and lawfully keeping and preserving the peace."

Defendant interprets this subsection to mean that a citizen attempting an arrest may use that amount of force reasonably believed necessary to apprehend the felon. Thus, under this analysis, a citizen may use deadly force and even kill a suspected felon to prevent him from fleeing, regardless of whether the suspect is armed or considered dangerous, or whether the arresting citizen is placed in fear of bodily harm. Indeed, this interpretation of Section 30-2-7(C) would allow a citizen to use deadly force no matter how passive or nonviolent the suspected felony might be (e.g., embezzlement, forgery, tax or welfare fraud), and regardless of other external circumstances like time and place (e.g., populated area when people are out and about). Simply put, Defendant would be guided by one measure only: any means necessary to prevent the suspect from fleeing.

To support his interpretation of the statute, Johnson argues that case law in New Mexico applies the justifiable homicide defense to the apprehension of all fleeing felons. * * * Relying on *Alaniz v. Funk*, 364 P.2d 1033 (N.M. 1961), Defendant claims that a private citizen or a police officer may use deadly force to stop a fleeing felon regardless of whether the felony is considered serious or not.

Alaniz was a wrongful death action against an acting deputy sheriff who attempted to prevent the escape of a man accused of having stolen rifles. * * *

Alaniz today would be limited by the holding of the United States Supreme Court in *Tennessee v. Garner*, 471 U.S. 1 (1985). Garner involved a lawsuit filed under 42 U.S.C. § 1983 by the family of an unarmed fleeing house burglar, who was killed by a police officer attempting to stop him. * * * Finding the killing of an unarmed fleeing suspect unreasonable under the Fourth Amendment, the Court stated that "it is plain that reasonableness depends on not only when a seizure is made, but also how it is carried out." * * * The *Garner* Court emphasized that the use of deadly force under such circumstances "frustrates the interest of the individual, and of society, in judicial determination of guilt and punishment." * * * The Court observed that although the apprehension of criminals was a goal of the state, the Court was "not convinced that the use of deadly force is a sufficiently productive means of accomplishing [that goal] to justify the killing of nonviolent suspects." * * * Thus, the Court required that officers have probable cause to believe that they or others are threatened with serious harm before the use of deadly force could be constitutionally reasonable under the Fourth Amendment.

In *Garner*, as in the current case, the defendants argued that the common-law rule "allowed the use of whatever force was necessary to effect the arrest of a fleeing felon." * * * The Court rejected that argument, observing that, historically, many crimes that are now felonies were only misdemeanors, and that in the past most felonies were punishable by death. * * * Thus, the common-law felony rule applied to the most severe class of crimes, most of which by definition would pose a threat of harm to an arresting officer or others (e.g., murder, suicide, manslaughter, burglary, arson, robbery, rape, larceny, sodomy, and mayhem). * * * The Court also declared:

> There is an additional reason why the common-law rule cannot be directly translated to the present day. The common-law rule developed at a time when weapons were rudimentary. Deadly force could be inflicted almost solely in a hand-to-hand struggle during which, necessarily, the safety of the arresting officer was at risk.

* * * This is clearly not the case today, and as the *Garner* Court noted, "changes in the legal and technological context mean the rule is distorted almost beyond recognition when literally applied."

Thus, the classification of a crime as a misdemeanor or a felony is far different today than in Territorial times, and New Mexico law on warrantless arrests by police officers has reflected this change. * * *

After the United States Supreme Court's ruling in *Garner*, the New Mexico legislature amended NMSA 1978, Section 30-2-6 (1989), thereby limiting the use of deadly force by law enforcement officers. Apparently tracking the *Garner* opinion, the legislature added subsection 30-2-6(B) which states:

> For the purposes of this section, homicide is necessarily committed when a public officer or public employee has probable cause to believe he or another is threatened with serious harm or deadly force while performing those lawful duties described in this section. Whenever feasible, a public officer or employee should give warning prior to using deadly force.

Thus, the legislature has now limited the use of deadly force by police officers, effectively mooting the opinion in *Alaniz*. It is now clear that under today's standards of "necessarily committed * * * by lawful ways and means," Defendant's actions, if performed by a police officer, would never be tolerated. The remaining question is whether private citizens are permitted to use lethal force when the police, despite their greater training and expertise, cannot.

There is nothing in New Mexico case law that would support such an anomaly. To the contrary, New Mexico case law analyzing analogous situations applies a standard of objective reasonableness. New Mexico has applied the same reasonableness standard to the use of force permitted in a citizen's arrest as that permitted in self-defense: "the privilege of citizen's arrest, as well as self-defense, is limited to the use of reasonable force." * * * In the context of deadly force, "reasonable" means that the actor be in fear of proportionate harm or force against him. * * * This Court recently affirmed a trial court's refusal to give a jury instruction on the use of deadly force in defense of others because "there was no evidence tending to satisfy the reasonableness prong of the deadly force test." * * * This puts the use of deadly force by a private citizen in the protection of others on a parallel with the use of deadly force by law enforcement officers. The citizen is not given more latitude to use deadly force as Defendant would suggest for himself in this case. * * *

New Mexico surely does not stand alone in narrowly confining the use of force to stop a fleeing felon by lawful ways and means. Case law from Arizona supports the view that the use of lethal force in attempting a citizen's arrest should be restricted to felonies that reasonably create a fear of great bodily injury. . . . Additionally, in the recent case of *Prayor v. State*, 456 S.E.2d 664, 666 (Ga. Ct. App. 1995), the Court of Appeals of Georgia held that deadly force is limited to self-defense or situations in which it is necessary to prevent a forcible felony. The Ohio Court of Appeals in *State v. Pecora*, 622 N.E.2d 1142 (Ohio Ct. App. 1993), held that the use of deadly force was prohibited unless it is necessary to prevent escape and there is probable cause to believe the suspect poses a significant threat of death or physical injury to the arresting person or others. The *Pecora* court stressed that the rights of citizens are no greater than those of police officers. * * * In California, the use of deadly force by private citizens has been limited to crimes that were felonies at common law, such as nighttime burglaries of residences.* * * And the Supreme Judicial Court of Massachusetts has adopted the Model Penal Code, Section 3.07, which imposes on private citizens the standards of force applicable to peace officers when making an arrest. * * *

* * * Although we agree that the current case is not based on the Fourth Amendment, we are unpersuaded by Defendant's reference to judicial decisions of South Carolina. We find the public policy informing the reasoning of the Supreme Court in *Garner* to be highly relevant to the current facts. Whether the individual pursuing an unarmed felon is a police officer or a person attempting to make a citizen's arrest, we adhere to the policy that "it is not better that all felony suspects die than that they escape." * * * Like the United States Supreme Court, we believe the apprehension of criminals to be a goal of the state, but we are "not convinced that the use of deadly force is a sufficiently productive means of accomplishing [that goal] to justify the killing of nonviolent suspects." * * * More importantly, we believe the New Mexico legislature is equally persuaded and has so indicated in the language of Section 30-2-7(C). * * *

Because there was no evidence that Defendant could satisfy such a justification for the use of deadly force, the trial court properly refused the requested instruction. Accordingly, the judgment and sentence of the trial court is hereby affirmed. * * *

MODEL PENAL CODE

§ 3.07. Use of Force in Law Enforcement

(1) Use of Force Justifiable to Effect an Arrest. Subject to the provisions of this Section and of Section 3.09, the use of force upon or toward the person of another is justifiable when the actor is making or assisting in making an arrest and the actor believes that such force is immediately necessary to effect a lawful arrest.
(2) Limitations on the Use of Force.

  (a) The use of force is not justifiable under this Section unless:

(i) the actor makes known the purpose of the arrest or believes that it is otherwise known by or cannot reasonably be made known to the person to be arrested; and

(ii) when the arrest is made under a warrant, the warrant is valid or believed by the actor to be valid.

(b) The use of deadly force is not justifiable under this Section unless:

(i) the arrest is for a felony; and

(ii) the person effecting the arrest is authorized to act as a peace officer or is assisting a person whom he believes to be authorized to act as a peace officer; and

(iii) the actor believes that the force employed creates no substantial risk of injury to innocent persons; and

(iv) the actor believes that:

(A) the crime for which the arrest is made involved conduct including the use or threatened use of deadly force; or

(B) there is a substantial risk that the person to be arrested will cause death or serious bodily injury if his apprehension is delayed.

(3) Use of Force to Prevent Escape from Custody. The use of force to prevent the escape of an arrested person from custody is justifiable when the force could justifiably have been employed to effect the arrest under which the person is in custody, except that a guard or other person authorized to act as a peace officer is justified in using any force, including deadly force, that he believes to be immediately necessary to prevent the escape of a person from a jail, prison, or other institution for the detention of persons charged with or convicted of a crime.

NOTE

A Nevada statute provides: "A private person may arrest another: 1. For a public offense committed or attempted in his presence. 2. When the person arrested has committed a felony, although not in his presence. 3. When a felony has been in fact committed, and he has reasonable cause for believing the person arrested to have committed it." NEV. REV. STAT. § 171.126. The Nevada Supreme Court interpreted the statute as overturning the common law right of deadly force to effect an arrest in *State v. Weddell*, 43 P.3d 987 (Nev. 2002), stating:

> Given our legislature's evident disapproval of the fleeing-felon doctrine, and given our concern that the rationale for the rule at common law no longer exists, and given the abandonment of this common law rule in other states, we hold that, in securing or attempting an arrest under NRS 171.126, a private person may only use the amount of force that is reasonable and necessary under the circumstances. Further, we hold that the use of deadly force is, as a matter of law, unreasonable, unless the arrestee poses a threat of serious bodily injury to the private arrestor or others. Like the affirmative defense of self-defense, the State bears the burden to prove that the use of deadly force was not reasonable and necessary.

PROBLEM FIFTY- FIVE

Morgan owns a construction business in Deal City. Late one evening, a person whom Morgan believes is Leslie was a passenger in a late-model SUV that drove into the parking lot at Morgan's company offices. Not recognizing the vehicle, Morgan asked Casey, an employee of the company, to find out who was in the automobile. As Casey approached the SUV, it accelerated, then turned and struck Casey lightly. The passenger rolled down the window and asked if Casey knew where Jodi, Morgan's daughter, could be found. Casey ran away and the SUV left the parking lot. Morgan called the police and reported a partial license plate number. The next day, Jodi told Morgan that Leslie was looking for her regarding an alleged drug transaction. Morgan went and looked up Leslie's address and, provided it to a detective at the local Sheriff's Office. Unsatisfied with the detective's response, Morgan drove to the address and, recognizing the SUV that hit Casey the previous evening, called the police. After fifteen minutes no officers had arrived. Morgan observed Leslie leaving the house and walking toward the SUV. Morgan drove a car behind the SUV to prevent it from leaving, got out of the car and took out a pistol. Morgan pointed the gun at Leslie and said, "Put your hands on the SUV's hood." Leslie turned and ran, at which point Morgan shot at Leslie several times but missed. Morgan is charged with assault with a deadly weapon. Under the common law, can Morgan use deadly force to apprehend Leslie? Is Morgan's conduct reasonable under the New Mexico statute?

Chapter 17
Necessity and Duress

Common law historically distinguished between the defenses of duress and necessity. Duress was said to excuse criminal conduct where the actor was under an unlawful threat of imminent death or serious bodily injury, which threat caused the actor to engage in conduct violating the literal terms of the criminal law. While the defense of duress covered the situation where the coercion had its source in the actions of other human beings, the defense of necessity, or choice of evils, traditionally covered the situation where physical forces beyond the actor's control rendered illegal conduct the lesser of two evils. Thus, where A destroyed a dike because B threatened to kill him if he did not, A would argue that he acted under duress, whereas if A destroyed the dike in order to protect more valuable property from flooding, A could claim a defense of necessity. Modern cases have tended to blur the distinction between duress and necessity.

United States v. Bailey, 444 U.S. 394 (1980).

§ 17.01 Necessity/Choice of Evils

People v. Fontes
89 P.3d 484 (Colo. App. 2004)

Opinion by Judge GRAHAM.

Defendant, Jesus Bernardo Fontes, appeals the judgment of conviction entered on a jury verdict finding him guilty of forgery, * * * criminal impersonation, * * * and misdemeanor theft. We affirm.

Defendant was arrested after he presented a false identification card to a convenience store clerk and attempted to cash a forged payroll check in the amount of $454.75. At trial, his wife testified for the prosecution and stated that defendant had intended to use the money from the check to buy food for the couple's children.
* * *

The court refused defendant's request for a choice of evils instruction, and it also refused to let him present any evidence that his concern for his children's welfare compelled his crimes.

Defendant contends that the trial court erred by refusing his request to instruct the jury on the affirmative defense of choice of evils and by refusing to accept the argument as a general defense. We disagree.

Choice of evils is a statutory defense applicable when the alleged crimes were necessary as an emergency measure to avoid an imminent public or private injury that is about to occur by reason of a situation occasioned or developed through no conduct of the actor and which is of sufficient gravity to outweigh the criminal conduct. The defendant must offer proof of the sudden and unforeseen emergence of a situation requiring his or her immediate action to prevent an imminent injury.

An affirmative defense such as choice of evils provides a legal justification for otherwise criminally culpable behavior. A defendant who asserts an affirmative defense admits the doing of a charged act, but seeks to justify the act on grounds deemed by law to be sufficient to avoid criminal responsibility.

A defendant who has a reasonable legal alternative as a means to avoid the threatened injury is foreclosed from asserting a choice of evils defense. Moreover, a defendant who seeks to assert a choice of evils defense must offer evidence that the criminal conduct at issue did not exceed that reasonably necessary to avoid the impending injury.

Before instructing the jury on the choice of evils defense, the trial court must look at the evidence in the light most favorable to the defendant and determine whether the facts could justify the crimes charged. On appeal, we must determine as a matter of law whether defendant's offer of proof, considered in the light most favorable to him, is substantial and sufficient to support the statutory defense.

As part of his offer of proof, defendant indicated that his three children, who ranged in age from sixteen months to eleven years, suffered from serious health problems. On the date the crimes occurred, the children had not eaten for more than twenty-four hours, and three different food banks had turned down defendant's requests for food. Defendant feared that a lack of food would exacerbate his children's health problems and lead to malnutrition and death.

The trial court refused to give a choice of evils instruction, finding that defendant failed to establish an imminent threat of injury to his children and that he did not show that he could not have pursued other legal alternatives for obtaining food. We perceive no error.

While we are not without sympathy for the downtrodden, the law is clear that economic necessity alone cannot support a choice of crime. Although economic necessity may be an important issue in sentencing, a choice of evils defense cannot be based upon economic necessity. *See State v. Moe*, 24 P.2d 638 (Wash. 1933)(unemployed workers who marched on a commissary and stole groceries could not raise the defense of economic necessity); *see also People v. McKnight*, 626 P.2d 678 (Colo. 1981)(to rely on the choice of evils defense, defendant must show that he or she had no reasonable alternative except to commit the crime charged).

Further, Colorado law requires that the defendant show a direct causal connection between the action taken and the harm sought to be prevented. Here, the trial court properly ruled by implication that the causal link was absent. This ruling finds support in the record from the circumstances of forgery and the relatively large amount of the forged instrument.

We conclude that defendant's offer of proof did not entitle him to assert a choice of evils defense, and the trial court did not err by refusing to give a choice of evils instruction to the jury and by refusing to allow defendant to use the theory as a general defense.

MODEL PENAL CODE

§ 3.02. Justification Generally: Choice of Evils.

(1) Conduct that the actor believes to be necessary to avoid a harm or evil to himself or to another is justifiable, provided that:

(a) the harm or evil sought to be avoided by such conduct is greater than that sought to be prevented by the law defining the offense charged; and

(b) neither the Code nor other law defining the offense provides exceptions or defenses dealing with the specific situation involved; and

(c) a legislative purpose to exclude the justification claimed does not otherwise plainly appear.

(2) When the actor was reckless or negligent in bringing about the situation requiring a choice of harms or evils or in appraising the necessity for his conduct, the justification afforded by this Section is unavailable in a prosecution for any offense for which recklessness or negligence, as the case may be, suffices to establish culpability.

NOTES AND QUESTIONS

1. *Assessing the Harm*. One of the most difficult issues in determining the scope of the necessity defense is how to calculate the different harms from the two (or more) possible courses of conduct. Professor Parry notes that such an assessment is involved in any analysis of necessity:

> As a practical matter, necessity usually will include some assessment of harms. The crux of a necessity claim is that the defendant engaged in one course of action, and thereby violated the law and caused a harm, in order to prevent or avoid a result he or she believed was undesirable or more harmful. Moreover, necessity defendants usually claim their conduct was justified — that it was correct and even desirable conduct — because it maximized social welfare (often, of course, by minimizing the harm to aggregate social welfare). Given the need to compare possible outcomes and to determine whether the conduct was correct — not to mention the fact that a harm has occurred — it is understandable that courts tend to focus on consequences rather than, for example, the defendant's choices or character.

John T. Parry, *The Virtue of Necessity: Reshaping Culpability and the Rule of Law*, 36 HOUS. L. REV. 397 (1999).

2. *Queen v. Dudley and Stephens.* Recall *Queen v. Dudley and Stephens* in Chapter 1. Do the defendants meet the requirements for the choice of evils defense? Does it matter if the jurisdiction had used a common law or Model Penal Code § 3.02 basis?

3. *Burden of Proof.* States may adopt statutes that have similarities to necessity defenses. Consider the issue of who bears the burden of proof in the following case that explores the affirmative defense of emergency.

Geljack v. State
671 N.E.2d 163 (Ind. Ct. App. 1996)

STATON, Judge.

    Kenneth J. Geljack, Jr. appeals his conviction for operating a motor vehicle while his driving privileges were suspended. Geljack raises one issue on appeal which we restate as: whether IND.CODE § 9-30-10- 18 (1993) is unconstitutional because it imposes upon the defendant the burden of proof when establishing his affirmative defense of an emergency.

* * * Geljack was adjudged an habitual traffic offender in December 1992 and had his driving privileges suspended for ten years beginning January 1993. In July 1994, Geljack was a passenger in a car with his wife and daughter when his wife observed that the car's brakes appeared to be failing. They were on their way to keep a doctor's appointment which the wife had made. In spite of the apparent brake problem with the car, Geljack's wife and daughter kept their doctor appointment. While his wife and daughter were at the doctor's office, Geljack decided to drive the car to a nearby brake shop instead of having it towed by a wrecker. In route to the brake shop, the car's brakes completely failed causing Geljack to run a red light. This running of the red light attracted the attention of a nearby Elkhart police officer. Geljack was arrested and charged with operating a motor vehicle while his privileges were suspended. After his trial and conviction, he brings this appeal.

Geljack's defense consisted of arguing that an emergency existed within the meaning of IC 9-30-10-18 (1993), thereby excusing driving while suspended. Specifically, Geljack asserted that it was necessary for him to drive to the brake shop as he did not want his wife and daughter to ride in the car for fear of the brakes failing. The trial court instructed the jury on the emergency defense by quoting IC 9-30-10-18 which reads:

> In a criminal action brought under section 16 or 17 of this chapter, it is a defense that the operation of a motor vehicle was necessary to save life or limb in an extreme emergency. The defendant must bear the burden of proof by a preponderance of the evidence to establish this defense.

Geljack argues that this section unconstitutionally places the burden of proof of establishing this defense on a criminal defendant.

Geljack correctly argues that the burden of proving all elements of a criminal offense beyond a reasonable doubt rests with the State. This ultimate burden of persuasion never shifts to the defendant, and the raising of an affirmative defense does not relieve the State of its ultimate burden of proof. However, while the State is ultimately responsible for proving every element beyond a reasonable doubt, the State does not bear the burden of negating all affirmative defenses that justify or excuse conduct which would otherwise be criminal. Thus "there is a difference between affirmative defenses that establish separate and distinct facts in mitigation of culpability and affirmative defenses that negate an element of the crime." *Ward v. State*, 438 N.E.2d 750 (Ind. 1982). The difference is that it is only unconstitutional to place the burden of persuasion for an affirmative defense on the defendant when proving the defense becomes tantamount to requiring the defendant to negate an element of the crime. *See Fowler v. State*, 526 N.E.2d 1181 (Ind. 1988) (cannot require defendant to prove intoxication since intoxication negates mens rea element of crime). Therefore, we must determine whether the emergency defense negates an element of operating a motor vehicle while privileges are suspended.

The elements of operating a motor vehicle while privileges are suspended are (1) operating a motor vehicle, (2) while driving privileges are suspended, and (3) the defendant knew his driving privileges had been suspended as the result of his habitual traffic offender status. The existence of an emergency which threatens life or limb would not negate any of these three elements. Even if an "emergency" within the meaning of IC 9-30-10-18 existed, a defendant would still have committed the offense of driving while privileges were suspended, but his guilt would be excused under the circumstances. In other words, the conduct would still be criminal, but justified. Thus, the emergency defense is one which mitigates culpability as opposed to a defense which negates an element of the crime. See Ward, supra. Accordingly, we conclude that IC 9-30-10-18 does not unconstitutionally impose upon the defendant the burden of establishing the affirmative defense of an emergency.

§ 17.02 Civil Disobedience

United States v. Maxwell
254 F.3d 21 (1st Cir. 2001)

SELYA, Circuit Judge.

Defendant-appellant Raul Maxwell-Anthony (Maxwell) entered United States Navy property on the Puerto Rican island of Vieques without authorization. Following a bench trial, the district court found Maxwell guilty of violating 18 U.S.C. § 1382 and sentenced him to thirty days in prison for this Class B misdemeanor. Maxwell appeals. We affirm.

The United States Navy maintains a naval installation known as Camp Garcia on the island of Vieques, Puerto Rico, and periodically conducts military training operations there. Pursuant to regulations promulgated by the Department of the Navy, Camp Garcia is a "closed" base, meaning that entry by members of the general public requires permission from the commanding officer * * * . Camp Garcia contains a "live impact area," historically used by the Navy for live-fire artillery and bombardment exercises. The Navy's presence on Vieques spans some sixty years, and these exercises have sparked numerous protests. * * *

The political controversy attendant to the Navy's use of Vieques recently reached a fever pitch. In the calendar year 2000, approximately 400 persons were prosecuted for protest-related trespasses. * * * Maxwell joined this effort: the authorities arrested him three times in quick succession (June 1, June 13, and June

21, 2000) for entering Camp Garcia without the permission of its commanding officer.

The June 13 arrest which underlies this appeal came about after Maxwell peacefully approached a naval security officer inside the north fence line of the base, identified himself as a protester, and asked for a bottle of water. In the wake of this arrest, the government charged Maxwell, by means of a one-count information, with violating a statute which reads in pertinent part:

> Whoever, within the jurisdiction of the United States, goes upon any military, naval, or Coast Guard reservation, post, fort, arsenal, yard, station, or installation, for any purpose prohibited by law or lawful regulation . . . shall be fined under this title or imprisoned not more than six months, or both.

18 U.S.C. § 1382. * * *

Maxwell filed a pretrial motion, accompanied by an exegetic offer of proof, reflecting his desire to present affirmative defenses based upon necessity and international law. The government objected and the district court ruled, as a matter of law, that the proposed defenses could not be maintained because of the lack of a proper predicate. *United States v. Maxwell-Anthony*, 129 F.Supp.2d 101 (D.P.R. 2000). * * *

His cardinal contention is that such a ruling in limine unconstitutionally renders the statute a "strict liability" offense. This contention mischaracterizes the district court's ruling.

The district court did not hold that affirmative defenses to section 1382 were categorically barred. To the contrary, the court entertained the possibility that a necessity defense could be interposed. It then made a case-specific judgment, examining Maxwell's offer of proof and concluding that it was insufficient to permit him to carry his entry-level burden of adducing competent proof of necessity (and, therefore, that no useful purpose would be served by allowing the assertion of that defense at trial). * * * So viewed, Maxwell's "strict liability" contention is a red herring. The question before us is not whether necessity ever can be a proper defense to a section 1382 charge in the protest context, but, rather, whether Maxwell showed that he could muster some evidence of a viable necessity defense. We turn now to that question.

A necessity defense, like other justification defenses, allows a defendant to escape responsibility despite proof that his actions encompassed all the elements of a criminal offense. * * * The necessity defense requires the defendant to show that he (1) was faced with a choice of evils and chose the lesser evil, (2) acted to prevent imminent harm, (3) reasonably anticipated a direct causal relationship between his acts and the harm to be averted, and (4) had no legal alternative but to violate the law. * * *

Although Maxwell did not formally structure his proffer around these four elements, his presentation is congruent with them. It runs roughly as follows: the grave risks triggered by the deployment of Trident nuclear submarines are a far greater evil than the commission of a criminal trespass designed to stop their deployment; harm was imminent in that Maxwell suspected that at least one Trident submarine already was present in the waters off Puerto Rico to participate in the training exercises; he reasonably believed that his disruption of the exercises would lead to dispersion of the Trident submarine(s); and, having previously taken a wide variety of political actions to no avail, he had no practical alternative but to break the law. The government maintains that Maxwell failed to provide sufficient evidence on each and all of the four components of the defense. We assume, for argument's sake, that Maxwell carried the entry-level burden of production on the first component ("lesser of two evils"). We specifically address Maxwell's proffer on the remaining three components.

1. Imminent Harm. Assuming, favorably to Maxwell, that the deployment of Trident submarines in waters near Puerto Rico constitutes a harm, Maxwell had the burden of showing its immediacy. After all, the term "imminent harm" connotes a real emergency, a crisis involving immediate danger to oneself or to a third party. * * * The record contains no evidence to support Maxwell's naked averment that the harm he feared was imminent. Moreover, even if Maxwell could have shown that a nuclear submarine was close at hand, it is doubtful that the mere presence of such a vessel, without some kind of realistic threat of detonation, would suffice to pose an imminent harm. * * *

2. Reasonable Anticipation of Averting Harm. Maxwell argues that he reasonably believed that his disruption of the naval exercises at Camp Garcia would effect the exodus of any Trident submarines that were in the vicinity. A reasonable anticipation of averting harm, however, requires more than seeing ghosts under every bed. In this case, Maxwell's anticipation is pure conjecture, not reasonable belief.

A defendant must demonstrate cause and effect between an act of protest and the achievement of the goal of the protest by competent evidence. * * * He cannot will a causal relationship into being simply by the fervor of his convictions (no matter how sincerely held). * * * We have combed the record in this case and find nothing to indicate any linkage between the Navy's exercises at Camp Garcia and the presence of Trident submarines in Puerto Rican waters. Equally as important, we find nothing to indicate that the movement of such vessels likely would be influenced by the temporary disruption of the exercises. On this record, then,

Maxwell could not reasonably have anticipated that his act of trespass would avert the harm that he professed to fear.

3. *Legal Alternatives.* To succeed on a necessity defense, a defendant must show that he had no legal alternative to violating the law. * * * This makes perfect sense: the necessity defense does not arise from a defendant's choice of a preferred course of action from among a universe of possible courses of action (some legal, some not), but from an emergent crisis that, as a practical matter, precludes all principled options but one. * * * In other words, the defendant's act must be necessary, not merely desirable.

In the case at hand, Maxwell testified at trial to the many avenues he has explored to further nuclear disarmament (e.g., participating in letter-writing campaigns, attending a nonproliferation treaty conference, and taking part in demonstrations). His level of commitment is laudable, but the panoramic range of his activities clearly demonstrates that he has many legal options for advancing his political goals. * * * The fact that Maxwell is unlikely to effect the changes he desires through legal alternatives does not mean, ipso facto, that those alternatives are nonexistent. * * * Accepting such an argument would be tantamount to giving an individual carte blanche to interpose a necessity defense whenever he becomes disaffected by the workings of the political process.

Our conclusion that Maxwell had legal alternatives to violating the law finds ample support in the case law. Without exception, the decided cases teach that a defendant's legal alternatives will rarely, if ever, be deemed exhausted when the harm of which he complains can be palliated by political action. * * * The case at hand falls well within this general rule.

* * * Based on our de novo review of Maxwell's proffered evidence, we find as a matter of law that he could not have satisfied his entry-level burden of producing competent evidence on any of the last three elements of the necessity defense. Consequently, we uphold the district court's preclusion of that defense. A fortiori, the court properly excluded the expert testimony offered in support of that defense.

Maxwell's final plaint concerns the district court's rejection of his international law defense. This affirmative defense hinges on Maxwell's claim that the deployment of Trident submarines is a "war crime," giving him the privilege of breaking domestic law to stop it. When asked to identify the source of this privilege, he points to decisions by the international tribunal that presided over the trials of Nazi war criminals in Nuremberg after World War II * * *.

The district court held that the decisions of the Nuremberg tribunal did not shield Maxwell from the consequences of his acts * * * . Maxwell is not the first to attempt to import the Nuremberg defense into our criminal law. Confronted with such an attempt, the Eighth Circuit explained that the Nuremberg defendants undertook acts that were required by domestic law but violated international law. * * * The Nuremberg tribunal held that the defendants could not escape responsibility for these acts by pointing to their domestic law obligations; they had a privilege under international law to violate domestic law in order to prevent the ongoing crimes against humanity that their country was perpetrating through them. * * * We echo this explanation.

Because Maxwell was under no compulsion to violate international law, his attempt to cloak himself in the Nuremberg mantle fails. Under his formulation, an individual gains the privilege to violate domestic law simply by being a citizen of a nation that possesses nuclear weapons. This is a quantum leap beyond the frontier of the classic Nuremberg defense — and one that we refuse to undertake.

In our view, an individual cannot assert a privilege to disregard domestic law in order to escape liability under international law unless domestic law forces that person to violate international law. * * * Maxwell does not argue that he was put in such a position by the government, nor could he. For this reason, the district court properly rejected his international law defense. * * *

We need go no further. Maxwell was on notice of the rules for entry onto Navy bases in Puerto Rico, yet deliberately entered Camp Garcia without authorization. His arguments that the district court erred in rejecting his proffered affirmative defenses and/or in its evidentiary rulings are forcefully presented but, in the end, unpersuasive. His conviction for violating 18 U.S.C. § 1382 must, therefore, be * * * Affirmed.

NOTES AND QUESTIONS

1. ***Direct and Indirect Civil Disobedience***. In cases of civil disobedience, courts distinguish between "direct" and "indirect" civil disobedience, with a different standard being used to determine the applicability of the necessity defense. For example, in *United States v. Montanes-Sanes*, 135 F.Supp. 2d 281 (D. Puerto Rico 2001), a case with facts similar to the *Maxwell* case, the District Court stated:

> Indirect civil disobedience was defined as "violating a law or interfering with a government policy that is not, itself, the object of protest." "Direct civil disobedience, on the other hand, involves protesting the existence of a law by breaking that law or by preventing the execution of that law in a specific instance in which a particularized harm would otherwise follow." This case clearly falls under the first category. In this case the

defendant, Jose Montanes-Sanes, is alleged to have illegally entered into Camp Garcia in Vieques for the purpose of protesting the use of the island-municipality by the U.S. Navy for training. Therefore, the illegal act committed was trespass. However, the Defendant was not protesting the trespass statute, but rather the Navy presence in Vieques.

The Ninth Circuit found that in instances of indirect civil disobedience, the necessity defense is inapplicable per se because "the real problem... is that litigants are trying to distort to their purpose an age-old common law doctrine meant for a very different set of circumstances. What these cases are really about is gaining notoriety for a cause — the defense allows protestors to get their political grievances discussed in a court-room." Such is not a legitimate purpose for the application of the defense.

2. *The Role of the Court.* What type of gatekeeping role should the court play in deciding whether to permit a defendant to mount a civil disobedience form of necessity defense? The question raises the underlying tension inherent in the legal system when the matter is one of legality versus conscience, as discussed by Professor Quigley:

As a policy matter, the law of the necessity defense in civil disobedience trials pits significant concerns about protecting law and order against serious concerns about social justice, dissent, and individual freedom. The decisions of courts, federal much more so than state, show judges engaging in unpersuasive verbal contortions trying to avoid giving the law of necessity the simple direct meaning of its words in civil disobedience cases. While there are many examples where juries get to hear the necessity defenses of protestors and, as a result, find them not guilty, judges often make pre-trial determinations that juries will not hear evidence of necessity in protest cases.

William P. Quigley, *The Necessity Defense in Civil Disobedience Cases: Bring in the Jury*, 38 NEW ENG. L. REV. 3 (2003).

PROBLEM FIFTY-SIX

Jean, a college honor student, is upset with the continual flaws in security at airports. Jean writes to the Transportation Security Administration (TSA) and the Federal Bureau of Investigation (FBI) to express concerns, but receives no reply. Jean, therefore, decides to smuggle box cutters onto different airplane flights that Jean takes. Jean places the box cutters in the rest rooms of four different airplanes during the next month of traveling. Jean then notifies the TSA and FBI as to what was done. Can Jean use a necessity defense? Does Jean's conduct fall within acceptable limits to civil disobedience?

§ 17.03 Duress

State v. Harvill
234 P.3d 1166 (Wash. 2010)(en banc)

STEPHENS, J.

Joshua Frank Lee Harvill challenges his conviction for unlawful delivery of cocaine, arguing that he produced sufficient evidence at trial to entitle him to a jury instruction on the defense of duress. The trial court refused to give the duress instruction on the ground that evidence of an explicit threat was necessary, whereas Harvill's evidence showed only an implicit threat. Because this was an error of law and was not harmless, we reverse the court below and remand for a new trial.

Joshua Frank Lee Harvill sold cocaine to Michael Nolte in a controlled buy organized by the Cowlitz County Sheriff's Office. Harvill was arrested after the transaction and charged with unlawful delivery of cocaine. At trial, Harvill admitted his participation in the transaction and relied solely on the defenses of duress and entrapment. Specifically, Harvill claimed that he sold cocaine to Nolte because he feared that, if he did not, Nolte would hurt him or his family.

Harvill testified that he received 9 or 10 calls from Nolte in the days leading up to the controlled buy in which Nolte insisted that Harvill get Nolte some cocaine. Nolte would say, "You gotta get me something," or "You better get me some cocaine," and his tone was aggressive. * * * But, Harvill could not recall Nolte ever saying "or else" or words to similar effect. Harvill received four more calls on the day of the transaction, the last two while he was at Chuck E. Cheese's restaurant with his family. Harvill claimed that he was afraid that Nolte would immediately come to Chuck E. Cheese's and drag him or one of his family members outside and hurt one of them if Harvill refused to get Nolte some cocaine. * * *

Harvill and Nolte had known each other for several years. Nolte was 5 feet 10 inches and weighed 200 pounds. * * * Harvill was 5 feet 5 inches and weighed about 140 pounds. * * * Harvill was afraid of Nolte, he testified, because he saw Nolte daily at work, where Nolte would brag about how he had once smashed another man's head with a beer bottle, causing brain damage. * * * Harvill also knew that Nolte had previously grabbed a gun from another man and then stabbed him. * * * Nolte and Harvill's brother had wrestled once and Nolte nearly broke Harvill's brother's arm.* * * Harvill asserted that Nolte used steroids and that he feared what Nolte was capable of. * * *

Harvill requested a jury instruction on duress, so that he could argue the defense during closing argument. * * *The trial court denied the instruction on the ground that Nolte never voiced any actual threat to Harvill. * * * Rather, Harvill's fear of Nolte stemmed from his knowledge about Nolte's behavior, which the trial court held was insufficient to establish duress as a matter of law. * * *

The jury convicted Harvill, and he appealed. * * * The Court of Appeals assumed, without deciding, that the trial court erred by refusing the duress instruction but concluded that any error was harmless. * * * We granted review.

Duress is an affirmative defense that must be established by a preponderance of the evidence. * * * The defendant must prove that

(a) he participated in the crime under compulsion by another who by threat or use of force created an apprehension in his mind that in case of refusal he or another would be liable to immediate death or immediate grievous bodily injury; and (b) such apprehension was reasonable upon his part; and (c) he would not have participated in the crime except for the duress involved.

A defendant "is entitled to have the jury instructed on [his] theory of the case if there is evidence to support that theory. Failure to so instruct is reversible error." * * *

The question comes down to whether the duress statute requires an explicit threat or whether an implicit threat that arises from the circumstances will suffice. At trial and again on appeal, the State emphasized that Nolte never told Harvill to get him drugs "or else," arguing that the absence of this phrase or similar words confirms that no express or implied threat occurred. * * * But, the lack of an "or else" proves only that there was no direct threat. The statutory definition of threat sweeps more broadly. *See* RCW 9A.04.110(27) (defining "threat" as "to communicate, directly or indirectly the intent ... [t]o cause bodily injury" (emphasis added)). Determining what counts as an indirect communication of intent to cause physical harm depends on the totality of the circumstances. * * *

The history of the duress statute supports this view. Washington codified the common law duress defense as part of a comprehensive criminal code passed in 1909. * * * The 1909 code did not define "threat," so its ordinary meaning applied. * * * The ordinary meaning of the term "threat" in 1909 was broad enough to include implied threats arising from the circumstances. * * * It is therefore no surprise that later codifications of the statute defined "threat" in terms of both direct and indirect communications. *See* RCW 9A.04.110(27). By including "indirect" in the definition of threat, the legislature preserved the duress statute's recognition of both explicit and implicit threats.

Properly defining "threat" to include both explicit and implicit threats serves the purpose of the duress statute. The statute is concerned with the "lesser of two evils." * * * Faced with danger to his or another's safety, the defendant is excused for choosing the lesser evil of perpetrating a crime, unless the crime involves killing an innocent person, which is never the lesser of two evils. * * * The defendant forfeits his excuse if by his own fault he necessitates his Hobson's choice. * * * So long as the defendant's perception of the implicit threat is reasonable under the circumstances, he is put to the choice between two evils through no fault of his own and should be allowed to argue the defense. * * *

[D]uress is a defense only where it is shown that the threats of one person have created in the mind of another a reasonable apprehension of instant death or grievous bodily harm. "Mere fear or threat by another is not sufficient to constitute a defense." * * *

In sum, the trial court appeared to reject Harvill's duress instruction because Nolte never explicitly threatened Harvill. But there is no legal authority that requires a "threat" to be an explicit threat. The text, history, policy, and judicial interpretations of the duress statute indicate that an implicit threat arising indirectly from the circumstances can suffice to establish a threat. Accordingly, we hold that the trial court abused its discretion when it refused Harvill's duress instruction based on an erroneous view of the law. * * * Assuming error, the Court of Appeals nevertheless affirmed Harvill's conviction because it held that the trial court's error was harmless. It reasoned that, in rejecting Harvill's entrapment defense, the jury necessarily would have rejected Harvill's duress defense. This conclusion is unsupported. The elements of duress differ from those of entrapment. Irrespective of any finding on entrapment, the jury could have found Harvill not guilty on the basis of duress because he testified that he reasonably perceived Nolte's requests for drugs as an implicit threat, and Nolte's testimony substantiated important facts underlying Harvill's testimony. Whether Harvill's fear was reasonable and whether he would have sold cocaine to Nolte absent his fear was at the heart of the parties' contest below. Perhaps the jurors would have dismissed Harvill's testimony as a patent fiction, but the trial court's failure to instruct them on duress never gave them that chance. We decline to consider this error harmless. * * * We reverse the Court of Appeals' decision affirming Harvill's conviction and remand for a new trial.

MODEL PENAL CODE

§ 2.09. Duress

(1) It is an affirmative defense that the actor engaged in the conduct charged to constitute an offense because he was coerced to do so by the use of, or a threat to use, unlawful force against his person or the person of another, that a person of reasonable firmness in his situation would have been unable to resist.

(2) The defense provided by this Section is unavailable if the actor recklessly placed himself in a situation in which it was probable that he would be subjected

to duress. The defense is also unavailable if he was negligent in placing himself in such a situation, whenever negligence suffices to establish culpability for the offense charged.

(3) It is not a defense that a woman acted on the command of her husband, unless she acted under such coercion as would establish a defense under this Section. [The presumption that a woman acting in the presence of her husband is coerced is abolished.]

(4) When the conduct of the actor would otherwise be justifiable under Section 3.02, this Section does not preclude such defense.

NOTES AND QUESTIONS

1. *Distinguishing Duress and Necessity.* What factors distinguish the duress and necessity defenses? Is it possible to use both of these defenses in the same trial? The original distinction was that a necessity defense applied when a natural force required the person to engage in criminal conduct to avoid harm, while a human threat triggered a duress defense. According to Professor Robinson, this distinction has been abandoned for the most part:

> Perhaps reflecting the weakness of the previous distinction — a natural versus a human source of the threat — it has frequently been replaced with what is essentially the justification-excuse distinction. One defense, termed "choice of evils" under new codes, now serves to exculpate justified conduct no matter what the source, while another, termed "duress," excuses a pressured or coerced actor no matter what the source. These reformulated defenses previously treated as necessity and coercion are cleanly categorized by the proposed scheme.

Paul H. Robinson, *Criminal Law Defenses: A Systematic Analysis*, 82 COLUM. L. REV. 199 (1982).

2. *Strict Liability Crimes.* Is duress a defense when the crime is strict liability? In *State v. Rios*, 980 P.2d 1068 (N.M. Ct. App. 1999), the question was whether the defendant could argue duress in a DWI case, a strict liability crime in the State of New Mexico. The defendant, who was leaving a bar at closing time, claimed that he was "threatened with violence by an angry mob" and drove the car away slowly from the bar as a result of this threat. The court stated:

A defendant pleading duress is not attempting to disprove a requisite mental state. Defendants in that context are instead attempting to show that they ought to be excused from criminal liability because of the circumstances surrounding their intentional act. * * *

The State argues that permitting the defense of duress in DWI cases would lead to an explosion of "fabricated" or "pretextual defenses." We consider this concern unfounded for the reason that pretextual defenses will fall of their own weight. * * *

The duress defense is "[a]mong the oldest principles of criminal law." We consider its wholesale foreclosure more troubling than the possibility that DWI defendants may attempt to lay a plausible factual foundation for a duress defense. On this point, we note the dissenting comments of Justice Stein of the New Jersey Supreme Court:

> A conviction for driving while intoxicated (DWI) ordinarily is not an occasion for hand-wringing about issues of fundamental fairness and due process. . . . But once in a great while a DWI case comes along that presents facts so bizarre and remote from the public policy underlying the law that even a Court as committed as this one to the strict enforcement of the drunk-driving statutes can pause to make certain that no injustice has been done.

State v. Fogarty, 607 A.2d 624 (N.J. 1992) (Stein, J., dissenting). We agree with Justice Stein's observation. The requirement of proving criminal intent has been read out of certain statutory offenses. This Court, however, should not read into a statute a prohibition of common-law defenses to which a defendant may rarely but justifiably be entitled.

3. ***Duress and Homicide***. The common law rule of duress did not permit the defense for a homicide charge. As the Oklahoma Court of Criminal Appeals explained in *Long v. State*, 74 P.3d 105 (Okla. Crim. App. 2003) :

> Equally clear is the common law limitation of the defense as stated by Blackstone, that when the harm contemplated by the defendant is greater than, or equal to, the threatened harm, "he ought rather to die himself than escape by the murder of an innocent." 4 W. BLACKSTONE, COMMENTARIES 30.

> It is generally accepted that duress is not a defense to taking the life of an innocent person. As stated at WHARTON'S CRIMINAL LAW, 15th Edition, § 52: "At common law . . . a defendant is not allowed to take the life of an innocent third person even when he is ordered to do so under a threat of instant death."

Any other rule is simply repugnant to nearly universal standards of decency developed over many decades of human experience. Oklahoma has specifically delineated those legally acceptable justifications and excuses for homicide * * * . Duress is neither an excuse for nor a justification of homicide under Oklahoma law.

4. ***Burden of Proof.*** The court in *Rios* followed the majority rule that the defendant bears the burden of proof to establish the defense of duress. The Ninth Circuit explained the reason for placing the burden on the defendant in *United States v. Dominguez-Mestas*, 929 F.2d 1379 (9th Cir. 1991):

When, as here, a defense of duress does not involve refutation of any of the elements of the offense we conclude that it is proper to place the burden of proving that defense by a preponderance of the evidence on the defendant. To require the government to prove beyond a reasonable doubt the absence of duress would create a standard that would be nearly impossible to satisfy. In many cases, as in the case before us, the sole evidence of duress is the testimony offered by the defendant. Often, as here, those to whom the defendant refers either cannot be located or are outside the United States and not subject to subpoena power. In such cases, the government cannot possibly meet its burden of proving the absence of duress beyond a reasonable doubt. Even if the government is effective in impeaching the credibility of the defendant, it may not meet its burden of proving the absence of duress.

Finally, requiring the government to prove the absence of duress beyond a reasonable doubt would create a potential for abuse. Because it is extremely difficult for the government to prove the absence of duress beyond a reasonable doubt, a burden which is heightened in the context of border cases, the standard invites a defendant to tell a tale of duress, thereby placing a nearly insurmountable burden on the government. While we cannot permit practical considerations to override constitutional protections, they are appropriately taken into account in formulating rules of federal practice. Thus, we decline to impose upon the government the burden of proving the absence of duress beyond a reasonable doubt.

5. ***Following Orders.*** In some cases defendants have argued that they should not be held liable because they were just "following orders." The Rome Statute for the International Criminal Court considers this defense to one of the four international crimes covered under the Statute and states:

Article 33 – Superior orders and prescription of law

1. The fact that a crime within the jurisdiction of the Court has been committed by a person pursuant to an order of a Government or of a

superior, whether military or civilian, shall not relieve that person of criminal responsibility unless:

(a) The person was under a legal obligation to obey orders of the Government or the superior in question;

(b) The person did not know that the order was unlawful; and

(c) The order was not manifestly unlawful.

2. For the purposes of this article, orders to commit genocide or crimes against humanity are manifestly unlawful.

PROBLEM FIFTY-SEVEN

Jess drove an SUV packed with 52.20 kilograms of marijuana from another country into the United States. Jess made it no further than the Immigration and Customs Enforcement booth before falling under suspicion from the border inspectors, who brought a drug-detector dog over to the SUV. The dog indicated that there were drugs, and a search revealed thirty-six packages of marijuana hidden in the vehicle. The government charged Jess with importation of marijuana. Jess denied neither the act nor the intent; rather, Jess told an attorney of being forced by drug traffickers to smuggle the marijuana. Jess, a citizen of the other country who was a resident alien living in the United States, gave the attorney the following account:

While driving my father's car, I struck a black BMW in the parking lot of a pharmacy in my home country. Three well-dressed men piled out of the BMW and angrily confronted me. I apologized and offered either to pay for the damage in a few weeks or to accompany them right then to my father's place, where we could retrieve some money immediately. The men were armed, and scared off a police officer who entered the parking lot; they refused my offer. Instead, by threat, they required me to "do a job" for them. I took the phone they provided and returned to the United States. When the call came, I returned to this other country, met the three men, and proceeded to the border, followed all along by several tracking vehicles. I never told law enforcement of the threats because I believe the authorities in my home country are corrupt and cannot protect my family.

Jess's father, sister, and a family friend offered support for Jess's statement. Although Jess did not speak of the threats prior to the arrest, Jess's father stated that Jess was very pale and quiet after returning from the accident and that suspiciously well-dressed men had come to their home approximately a week later. Jess's sister, with whom Jess lives in the United States, testified that Jess was uncharacteristically quiet in the days prior to the smuggling attempt. The family friend testified to seeing the altercation in the parking lot. Is there sufficient evidence for the court to give the jury a duress instruction? Would it change the analysis if Jess had a conviction two years earlier for a nearly identical smuggling episode at the same border crossing?

Chapter 18
Entrapment

§ 18.01 Generally

People v. Maffett
633 N.W.2d 339 (Mich. 2001)

CORRIGAN, C.J. [dissenting from denial of leave to appeal.]

* * * The entrapment defense developed in the United States in the late nineteenth and early twentieth centuries. The prevailing view in the nineteenth century was that government inducement provided no defense to a criminal charge. A number of state courts condemned the practice of entrapment (i.e., government-manufactured crime), but "few actually held that the entrapment entitled the defendant to an acquittal." Marcus, *The Development of Entrapment Law*, 33 WAYNE L. REV. 5, 11 (1986). The criticism of government inducement generally occurred in obiter dictum.

In 1879, the Texas Court of Appeals held, for the first time ever, that an entrapped defendant could not be convicted of the charged crime. *See O'Brien v. State*, 6 Tex.App. 665 (1879). In *O'Brien*, the defendant had been convicted of bribery for attempting to pay a sheriff's deputy for a prisoner's release from the jailhouse. The parties disputed whether the defendant or the deputy first suggested the idea for the bribe. The trial court instructed the jury that this fact was irrelevant, as long as the defendant eventually agreed to pay a bribe. The Texas Court of Appeals reversed, explaining that it would be "not within the spirit" of the bribery statute to convict the defendant of bribery if the deputy originated the criminal intent and joined the defendant in the commission of the crime "merely to entrap the defendant." The court also observed that it was unable to find "any adjudicated case" in support of its holding.

Thirty-six years later, the Ninth Circuit Court of Appeals became the first federal court to bar a criminal conviction on grounds of entrapment in *Woo Wai [v. United States*, 223 F. 412 (9th Cir. 1915)]. Relying on *O'Brien*, and on dicta from five other state cases, the court explained that "a sound public policy can be upheld only by denying the criminality of those who are thus induced to commit acts which infringe the letter of the criminal statutes." Most remaining federal circuits soon after recognized some form of the entrapment defense. *See Sorrells v. United*

States, 287 U.S. 435 (1932) (citing cases). One representative case of the era, *Butts v. United States*, 273 F. 35 (8th Cir. 1921), provided the following rationale for the doctrine:

> The first duties of the officers of the law are to prevent, not to punish crime. It is not their duty to incite to and create crime for the sole purpose of prosecuting and punishing it. Here the evidence strongly tends to prove, if it does not conclusively do so, that their first and chief endeavor was to cause, to create, crime in order to punish it, and it is unconscionable, contrary to public policy, and to the established law of the land to punish a man for the commission of an offense of the like of which he had never been guilty, either in thought or in deed, and evidently never would have been guilty of if the officers of the law had not inspired, incited, persuaded, and lured him to attempt to commit it.

The early entrapment cases demonstrate that entrapment was not a traditional common-law justification or excuse defense based on the defendant's culpability. Rather, it arose from the burgeoning idea that punishing defendants for criminal violations "manufactured" by the government was offensive to public policy (or, in the case of *O'Brien* offensive to the "spirit" of the criminal law).

Two rival theories dominate the law of entrapment today. The federal courts and a majority of states have adopted the "subjective" view of entrapment. The subjective view focuses primarily on the defendant's "disposition" before the offense. The Model Penal Code, most legal commentators, and a minority of states favor the "objective" view of entrapment. The objective view focuses primarily on the nature of the police conduct before the crime. Each theory has its genesis in *Sorrells*, the first United States Supreme Court decision to adopt the entrapment defense. The majority opinion in *Sorrells*, authored by Chief Justice Hughes, set forth the theoretical basis for the subjective view. A separate opinion of Justice Roberts did the same for the rival objective view.

§ 18.02 Subjective Predisposition

Jacobson v. United States
503 U.S. 540 (1992)

Justice WHITE delivered the opinion of the Court.

On September 24, 1987, petitioner Keith Jacobson was indicted for violating a provision of the Child Protection Act of 1984 (Act), * * * which criminalizes the knowing receipt through the mails of a "visual depiction [that] involves the use of a minor engaging in sexually explicit conduct * * * ." 18 U. S. C. § 2252(a)(2)(A).

Petitioner defended on the ground that the Government entrapped him into committing the crime through a series of communications from undercover agents that spanned the 26 months preceding his arrest. Petitioner was found guilty after a jury trial. The Court of Appeals affirmed his conviction, holding that the Government had carried its burden of proving beyond reasonable doubt that petitioner was predisposed to break the law and hence was not entrapped.

Because the Government overstepped the line between setting a trap for the "unwary innocent" and the "unwary criminal," *Sherman v. United States*, 356 U.S. 369, 372 (1958), and as a matter of law failed to establish that petitioner was independently predisposed to commit the crime for which he was arrested, we reverse the Court of Appeals' judgment affirming his conviction. * * *

In February 1984, petitioner, a 56-year-old veteran-turned-farmer who supported his elderly father in Nebraska, ordered two magazines and a brochure from a California adult bookstore. The magazines, entitled Bare Boys I and Bare Boys II, contained photographs of nude preteen and teenage boys. The contents of the magazines startled petitioner, who testified that he had expected to receive photographs of "young men 18 years or older." * * *

The young men depicted in the magazines were not engaged in sexual activity, and petitioner's receipt of the magazines was legal under both federal and Nebraska law. Within three months, the law with respect to child pornography changed; Congress passed the Act illegalizing the receipt through the mails of sexually explicit depictions of children. In the very month that the new provision became law, postal inspectors found petitioner's name on the mailing list of the California bookstore that had mailed him Bare Boys I and II. There followed over the next 2 1/2 years repeated efforts by two Government agencies, through five fictitious organizations and a bogus pen pal, to explore petitioner's willingness to break the new law by ordering sexually explicit photographs of children through the mail. * * *

By March 1987, 34 months had passed since the Government obtained petitioner's name from the mailing list of the California bookstore, and 26 months had passed since the Postal Service had commenced its mailings to petitioner. Although petitioner had responded to surveys and letters, the Government had no evidence that petitioner had ever intentionally possessed or been exposed to child pornography. The Postal Service had not checked petitioner's mail to determine whether he was receiving questionable mailings from persons — other than the Government — involved in the child pornography industry. * * *

At this point, a second Government agency, the Customs Service, included petitioner in its own child pornography sting, "Operation Borderline," after receiving his name on lists submitted by the Postal Service. * * * The letter invited petitioner to send for more information. It also asked petitioner to sign an affirmation that he was "not a law enforcement officer or agent of the U. S. Government acting in an undercover capacity for the purpose of entrapping Far Eastern Trading Company, its agents or customers." * * * Petitioner was arrested after a controlled delivery of a photocopy of the magazine.

When petitioner was asked at trial why he placed such an order, he explained that the Government had succeeded in piquing his curiosity. * * *

* * * There can be no dispute about the evils of child pornography or the difficulties that laws and law enforcement have encountered in eliminating it.*** Likewise, there can be no dispute that the Government may use undercover agents to enforce the law. "It is well settled that the fact that officers or employees of the Government merely afford opportunities or facilities for the commission of the offense does not defeat the prosecution. * * *

In their zeal to enforce the law, however, Government agents may not originate a criminal design, implant in an innocent person's mind the disposition to commit a criminal act, and then induce commission of the crime so that the Government may prosecute. * * * Where the Government has induced an individual to break the law and the defense of entrapment is at issue, as it was in this case, the prosecution must prove beyond reasonable doubt that the defendant was disposed to commit the criminal act prior to first being approached by Government agents. * * *

Thus, an agent deployed to stop the traffic in illegal drugs may offer the opportunity to buy or sell drugs and, if the offer is accepted, make an arrest on the spot or later. In such a typical case, or in a more elaborate "sting" operation involving government-sponsored fencing where the defendant is simply provided with the opportunity to commit a crime, the entrapment defense is of little use because the ready commission of the criminal act amply demonstrates the defendant's predisposition. *See United States v. Sherman*, 200 F.2d 880, 882 (2d Cir. 1952). Had the agents in this case simply offered petitioner the opportunity to order child pornography through the mails, and petitioner — who must be presumed to know the law — had promptly availed himself of this criminal opportunity, it is unlikely that his entrapment defense would have warranted a jury instruction. *Mathews v. United States*, 485 U.S. 58 (1988).

But that is not what happened here. By the time petitioner finally placed his order, he had already been the target of 26 months of repeated mailings and communications from Government agents and fictitious organizations. Therefore, although he had become predisposed to break the law by May 1987, it is our view that the Government did not prove that this predisposition was independent and not the product of the attention that the Government had directed at petitioner since January 1985. * * *

The prosecution's evidence of predisposition falls into two categories: evidence developed prior to the Postal Service's mail campaign, and that developed during the course of the investigation. The sole piece of preinvestigation evidence is petitioner's 1984 order and receipt of the Bare Boys magazines. But this is scant if any proof of petitioner's predisposition to commit an illegal act, the criminal character of which a defendant is presumed to know. It may indicate a predisposition to view sexually oriented photographs that are responsive to his sexual tastes; but evidence that merely indicates a generic inclination to act within a broad range, not all of which is criminal, is of little probative value in establishing predisposition.

* * * Furthermore, petitioner was acting within the law at the time he received these magazines. Receipt through the mails of sexually explicit depictions of children for noncommercial use did not become illegal under federal law until May 1984, and Nebraska had no law that forbade petitioner's possession of such material until 1988. Neb. Rev. Stat. § 28-813.01 (1989). Evidence of predisposition to do what once was lawful is not, by itself, sufficient to show predisposition to do what is now illegal, for there is a common understanding that most people obey the law even when they disapprove of it. This obedience may reflect a generalized respect for legality or the fear of prosecution, but for whatever reason, the law's prohibitions are matters of consequence. Hence, the fact that petitioner legally ordered and received the Bare Boys magazines does little to further the Government's burden of proving that petitioner was predisposed to commit a criminal act. This is particularly true given petitioner's unchallenged testimony that he did not know until they arrived that the magazines would depict minors. * * *

Law enforcement officials go too far when they "implant in the mind of an innocent person the *disposition* to commit the alleged offense and induce its commission in order that they may prosecute." *Sorrells* (emphasis added). Like the *Sorrells* Court, we are "unable to conclude that it was the intention of the Congress in enacting this statute that its processes of detection and enforcement should be abused by the instigation by government officials of an act on the part of persons otherwise innocent in order to lure them to its commission and to punish them." * * * When the Government's quest for convictions leads to the apprehension of an otherwise law-abiding citizen who, if left to his own devices, likely would have never run afoul of the law, the courts should intervene.

Because we conclude that this is such a case and that the prosecution failed, as a matter of law, to adduce evidence to support the jury verdict that petitioner was predisposed, independent of the Government's acts and beyond a reasonable doubt, to violate the law by receiving child pornography through the mails, we reverse the Court of Appeals' judgment affirming the conviction of Keith Jacobson. * * * *It is so ordered.*

Justice O'CONNOR, with whom The Chief Justice and Justice KENNEDY join, and with whom Justice SCALIA joins except as to Part II, dissenting.

Keith Jacobson was offered only two opportunities to buy child pornography through the mail. Both times, he ordered. Both times, he asked for opportunities to buy more. He needed no Government agent to coax, threaten, or persuade him; no one played on his sympathies, friendship, or suggested that his committing the crime would further a greater good. In fact, no Government agent even contacted him face to face. The Government contends that from the enthusiasm with which Mr. Jacobson responded to the chance to commit a crime, a reasonable jury could permissibly infer beyond a reasonable doubt that he was predisposed to commit the crime. I agree. * * *

The Court, however, concludes that a reasonable jury could not have found Mr. Jacobson to be predisposed beyond a reasonable doubt on the basis of his responses to the Government's catalogs, even though it admits that, by that time, he was predisposed to commit the crime. The Government, the Court holds, failed to provide evidence that Mr. Jacobson's obvious predisposition at the time of the crime "was independent and not the product of the attention that the Government had directed at petitioner." * * * In so holding, I believe the Court fails to acknowledge the reasonableness of the jury's inference from the evidence, redefines "predisposition," and introduces a new requirement that Government sting operations have a reasonable suspicion of illegal activity before contacting a suspect. * * *

NOTES AND QUESTIONS

1. *Issue of Fact or Law?* The Supreme Court's decision in *Jacobson* found that as a *matter of law* that Jacobson had been entrapped. Issues of intent, however, are usually left to the trier of fact, and so the jury should weigh the credibility of the witnesses and determine whether the defendant was predisposed to commit the crime. The Florida Supreme Court explained in *Munoz v. State*, 629 So.2d 90 (Fla. 1993), the interplay between the judge and jury in applying the state's entrapment statute (FLA. STAT. ANN. § 777.201), which provides that "[t]he issue of entrapment shall be tried by the trier of fact:"

> The * * * question under the subjective test is whether the entrapment evaluation should be submitted to a jury. Section 777.201 directs that the issue of entrapment be submitted to the trier of fact. Such direction is consistent with the subjective evaluation of entrapment because the two factual issues above ordinarily present questions of disputed facts to be submitted to the jury as the trier of fact. However, if the factual

circumstances of a case are not in dispute, if the accused establishes that the government induced the accused to commit the offense charged, and if the State is unable to demonstrate sufficient evidence of predisposition prior to and independent of the government conduct at issue, then the trial judge has the authority to rule on the issue of predisposition as a matter of law because no factual "question of predisposition" is at issue. See, e.g., *Jacobson*. Such a ruling could be proper even when the government presents evidence of prior convictions. We reject any construction of section 777.201 that would require such an issue of law to be submitted to a jury. Under the constitution of this state, juries, as the finders of fact, decide factually disputed issues and judges apply the law to the facts as those facts are found by the jury. To construe section 777.201 as mandating that the issue of entrapment is to be submitted to a jury for determination as a matter of law would result in an unconstitutional construction that would violate article I, section 9, of the Florida Constitution. Consequently, we construe section 777.201 as requiring the question of predisposition to be submitted to a jury when factual issues are in dispute or when reasonable persons could draw different conclusions from the facts. In certain instances, however, as illustrated by * * * *Jacobson*, the trial judge and appellate courts clearly have the authority to rule on the issue as a matter of law. To hold otherwise would violate procedural due process.

2. ***Admitting the Crime.*** As a type of excuse defense, entrapment usually requires that the accused admit to committing the crime, and offer the government's improper inducement of the crime as an excuse for not holding him or her responsible for its commission. In *United States v. Mathews*, 485 U.S. 58 (1988), the Supreme Court held "that even if the defendant denies one or more elements of the crime, he is entitled to an entrapment instruction whenever there is sufficient evidence from which a reasonable jury could find entrapment." In other words, a defendant could argue that he did not have the requisite intent for the crime, or even if he did, he was entrapped by the government. The Court also rejected the government's argument that allowing a defendant to advance inconsistent defenses effectively sanctioned perjury:

> We do not think that allowing inconsistency necessarily sanctions perjury. Here petitioner wished to testify that he had no intent to commit the crime, and have his attorney argue to the jury that if it concluded otherwise, then it should consider whether that intent was the result of Government inducement. The jury would have considered inconsistent defenses, but petitioner would not have necessarily testified untruthfully.

> We would not go so far as to say that charges on inconsistent defenses may not on occasion increase the risk of perjury, but particularly in the

case of entrapment we think the practical consequences will be less burdensome than the Government fears. The Court of Appeals in *United States v. Demma*, 523 F.2d 981 (9th Cir. 1975) (en banc), observed:

> Of course, it is very unlikely that the defendant will be able to prove entrapment without testifying and, in the course of testifying, without admitting that he did the acts charged . . . . When he takes the stand, the defendant forfeits his right to remain silent, subjects himself to all the rigors of cross-examination, including impeachment, and exposes himself to prosecution for perjury. Inconsistent testimony by the defendant seriously impairs and potentially destroys his credibility. While we hold that a defendant may both deny the acts and other elements necessary to constitute the crime charged and at the same time claim entrapment, the high risks to him make it unlikely as a strategic matter that he will choose to do so.

3. *Assessing Predisposition.* What factors should a court use in assessing predisposition? Consider the factors used by the Eighth Circuit in the case of *United States v. Dion*, 762 F.2d 674 (8th Cir. 1985):

(1) whether the defendant readily responded to the inducement offered;

(2) the circumstances surrounding the illegal conduct;

(3) the state of mind of a defendant before the government agents make any suggestion that the defendant shall commit a crime;

(4) whether the defendant was engaged in an existing course of conduct similar to the crime for which the defendant is charged;

(5) whether the defendant had already formed the design to commit the crime for which the defendant is charged;

(6) the defendant's reputation;

(7) the conduct of the defendant during negotiations with the undercover agent;

(8) whether the defendant has refused to commit similar acts on other occasions;

(9) the nature of the crime charged;   .

(10) the degree of coercion which the law officers contributed to instigating the transaction relative to the defendant's criminal background.

4. ***Entrapment and Racial Profiling***. Should consideration of an entrapment defense include, when applicable, whether the accused was targeted because of his or her race? A claim of discriminatory prosecution is almost impossible to establish because prosecutors are not required to give reasons for why a person has been selected for prosecution, and courts seldom will allow a defendant to obtain discovery of the prosecutor's reason for deciding to prosecute one person (or crime) rather than another without clear evidence of an discriminatory reason. In *United States v. Armstrong*, 517 U.S. 456 (1996), the Supreme Court explained the standard for discovery in federal cases advancing a discriminatory prosecution claim:

> A selective-prosecution claim is not a defense on the merits to the criminal charge itself, but an independent assertion that the prosecutor has brought the charge for reasons forbidden by the Constitution. Our cases delineating the necessary elements to prove a claim of selective prosecution have taken great pains to explain that the standard is a demanding one. These cases afford a "background presumption," that the showing necessary to obtain discovery should itself be a significant barrier to the litigation of insubstantial claims.

> A selective-prosecution claim asks a court to exercise judicial power over a "special province" of the Executive. The Attorney General and United States Attorneys retain "broad discretion" to enforce the Nation's criminal laws. *Wayte v. United States*, 470 U.S. 598 (1985). They have this latitude because they are designated by statute as the President's delegates to help him discharge his constitutional responsibility to "take Care that the Laws be faithfully executed." U.S. CONST., Art. II, § 3. As a result, "[t]he presumption of regularity supports" their prosecutorial decisions and, "in the absence of clear evidence to the contrary, courts presume that they have properly discharged their official duties." *United States v. Chemical Foundation, Inc.*, 272 U.S. 1 (1926). In the ordinary case, "so long as the prosecutor has probable cause to believe that the accused committed an offense defined by statute, the decision whether or not to prosecute, and what charge to file or bring before a grand jury, generally rests entirely in his discretion." *Bordenkircher v. Hayes*, 434 U.S. 357 (1978).

> Of course, a prosecutor's discretion is "subject to constitutional constraints." *United States v. Batchelder*, 442 U.S. 114 (1979). One of these constraints, imposed by the equal protection component of the Due Process Clause of the Fifth Amendment, is that the decision whether to

prosecute may not be based on "an unjustifiable standard such as race, religion, or other arbitrary classification," *Oyler v. Boles*, 368 U.S. 448 (1962). A defendant may demonstrate that the administration of a criminal law is "directed so exclusively against a particular class of persons . . . with a mind so unequal and oppressive" that the system of prosecution amounts to "a practical denial" of equal protection of the law. *Yick Wo v. Hopkins*, 118 U.S. 356 (1886).

In order to dispel the presumption that a prosecutor has not violated equal protection, a criminal defendant must present "clear evidence to the contrary."

§ 18.03 Objective Approach

MODEL PENAL CODE

§ 2.13. Entrapment.

(1) A public law enforcement official or a person acting in cooperation with such an official perpetrates an entrapment if for the purpose of obtaining evidence of the commission of an offense, he induces or encourages another person to engage in conduct constituting such offense by either:

(a) making knowingly false representations designed to induce the belief that such conduct is not prohibited; or

(b) employing methods of persuasion or inducement that create a substantial risk that such an offense will be committed by persons other than those who are ready to commit it.

(2) Except as provided in Subsection (3) of this Section, a person prosecuted for an offense shall be acquitted if he proves by a preponderance of evidence that his conduct occurred in response to an entrapment. The issue of entrapment shall be tried by the Court in the absence of the jury.

(3) The defense afforded by this Section is unavailable when causing or threatening bodily injury is an element of the offense charged and the prosecution is based on conduct causing or threatening such injury to a person other than the person perpetrating the entrapment.

People v. Moore
2007 WL 2609506 (Mich. Ct. App. 2007)

PER CURIAM.

Following a bench trial, defendant was convicted of two counts of delivery of a controlled substance. * * *

Defendant was charged and convicted following a sale of Vicodin and Xanax pills to Jason Vandine on June 7, 2005. Vandine, working as an informant for the Office of Monroe Narcotics Investigations (OMNI), contacted defendant about purchasing Vicodin and Xanax pills. On June 7, 2005, the men met at a gas station and defendant sold 25 Vicodin and 29 Xanax pills to Vandine for $120.

* * * Michigan has adopted the objective test of entrapment. *People v. Juillet*, 439 475 N.W.2d 786 (Mich. 1991). "Under this test, the focus is on the nature of the police conduct." *People v. Mulkey*, 396 N.W.2d 514 (Mich. App. 1986). A defendant is entrapped if (1) the police engaged in impermissible conduct that would induce a law-abiding citizen to commit a crime in similar circumstances or (2) the police engaged in conduct so reprehensible that it cannot be tolerated. Our Supreme Court has articulated the following factors that are relevant in determining whether police engaged in impermissible conduct:

> (1) whether there existed appeals to the defendant's sympathy as a friend, (2) whether the defendant had been known to commit the crime with which he was charged, (3) whether there were any long time lapses between the investigation and the arrest, (4) whether there existed any inducements that would make the commission of a crime unusually attractive to a hypothetical law-abiding citizen, (5) whether there were offers of excessive consideration or other enticement, (6) whether there was a guarantee that the acts alleged as crimes were not illegal, (7) whether, and to what extent, any government pressure existed, (8) whether there existed sexual favors, (9) whether there were any threats of arrest, (10) whether there existed any government procedures that tended to escalate the criminal culpability of the defendant, (11) whether there was police control over any informant, and (12) whether the investigation was targeted. [*People v. Johnson*, 647 N.W.2d 480 (Mich. 2002)]

When law enforcement officials do no more than present the opportunity to commit the crime, there is no entrapment. Whether a defendant was entrapped is decided on a case-by-case basis, based on the totality of the circumstances. The trial court did not clearly err by finding that the defendant was not entrapped. Defendant and Vandine were not friends, but only acquaintances. They were regularly together every other week over a two-year period. Defendant sold Vandine drugs on occasion over that time period. At most, Vandine contacted defendant two times a week for four weeks about purchasing Vicodin and Xanax. Given their prior relationship, it cannot be concluded that Vandine exerted excessive pressure. Moreover, the price of the pills paid to defendant was not exorbitant. The pills were sold for the same value received on the street. And, defendant knew that Vandine would use the Vicodin and Xanax for recreational purposes. The record does not reveal improper appeals to defendant's sympathy, inducements that would make the crime unusually attractive to a law-abiding citizen, government pressure, sexual favors, or threats of arrest. Based on these factors, the trial court's finding that defendant was not entrapped was not clearly erroneous.

Defendant sets forth three arguments to explain his position that the trial court erred in finding that he was not entrapped. Defendant first argues that the trial court failed to recognize that Vandine exploited his friendship with defendant. An individual may be entrapped if the police or the police informant appeal to the defendant's sympathy and friendship to induce him to commit a crime. In *People v. Soper*, 226 N.W.2d 691 (Mich. App. 1975), the officer, a childhood friend of the defendant, renewed his friendship with the defendant after the defendant was released from prison and then claimed to be a heroin addict in order to get the defendant to purchase heroin for him. We held that the police officer exploited his friendship with the defendant and, thus, entrapped the defendant. However, in the present case, defendant and Vandine were not childhood friends. They were mere acquaintances, who knew each other for two years and who, according to Vandine, spent time together approximately twice a month. Moreover, when Vandine approached defendant about purchasing the Vicodin and Xanax pills, he did not beg for them. Although Vandine told defendant that he needed the pills for pain purposes, the record revealed that defendant knew that Vandine would also use the pills for recreational purposes. Based on these facts, the trial court's failure to specifically address the issue whether Vandine exploited his friendship with defendant does not make the trial court's finding that defendant was not entrapped clearly erroneous.

Second, defendant argues that the trial court failed to consider the pressure Vandine exerted on defendant. An individual may be entrapped if police continually pressure the defendant into committing a crime. In *People v. Duis*, 265 N.W.2d 794 (Mich. App. 1978), we held that the defendant was entrapped when the informant, a friend of the defendant, visited defendant's house three times and called him two times in one day about purchasing LSD. We concluded that this was of the type of pressure that would induce an innocent person to commit a crime. Likewise, in *People v. Rowell*, 395 N.W.2d 253 (Mich. App. 1986), we held that the defendant was entrapped when the informants frequented a park two to three times a week to find the defendant and asked him to sell them drugs up to three times a day. In the present case, defendant testified that Vandine only called him two times a week for a month before June 7, 2005, about purchasing Vicodin and Xanax pills. The contact was not excessive given the previous interactions between defendant and

Vandine. Further, Vandine never went over to defendant's house to ask about purchasing the pills. Based on these facts, the trial court's failure to specifically address the issue whether the pressure exerted by Vandine on defendant was of the type that would induce an innocent man to commit a crime does not make the trial court's finding that defendant was not entrapped clearly erroneous.

Third, defendant argues that the trial court failed to consider the lack of police supervision over Vandine's activities. An individual may be entrapped if police fail to exert control over an informant. There is no evidence in the record that OMNI supervised Vandine's contact with defendant before the June 7, 2005 telephone call. However, in deciding whether defendant was entrapped, we must look at the totality of the circumstances. Looking at the totality of the circumstances, we are not left with a definite and firm conviction that the trial court erred in concluding that defendant was not entrapped.

NOTES

1. ***Minority Approach***. The objective approach to entrapment is a minority approach, despite its acceptance in the Model Penal Code. How does the analysis used in the *Moore* case differ from that used by the Court in *Jacobson* [p. 654]?

2. ***Outrageous Government Conduct***. In some cases "outrageous government conduct" is considered a separate defense from entrapment. Like "objective entrapment" it is premised on the conduct of the police. In order to be successful with this defense, courts require the police conduct to rise to a level of being a due process violation. *See Williams v. United States*, 705 F.2d 603 (2d Cir. 1983) (rejecting both entrapment and outrageous government conduct defenses in a case of a Senator charged as part of Operation Abscam).

PROBLEM FIFTY-EIGHT

Undercover Police Officer Riley, pretending to be a drug addict, walks up to Kerry's automobile in a restaurant parking lot. Officer Riley and Kerry had not previously met. Officer Riley says to Kerry, "Do you know where I can score some hard?" Kerry was aware that the Officer was looking for crack cocaine. Kerry said to Officer Riley, "Sorry, but I am not into drugs, you'll have to go elsewhere." Officer Riley is persistent and says to Kerry, "I really need the stuff. Can you at least help me get some?" Kerry, feeling sorry for what he thinks is a drug addict, decides to assist. Officer Riley gets in the car and instructs Kerry to go to a house three miles down the road. Officer Riley then gave Kerry $20 dollars and said, "the guy in that house will sell you some crack, but he doesn't trust me, to sell it directly to me." Kerry questions this, but decides he needs to get home so he goes up to the house with the $20 and asks the house owner for the crack for his friend in the car. Immediately upon receiving a small container he leaves and returns to his car. Kerry is immediately arrested by several police officers.

 Does Kerry have a basis for requesting an entrapment instruction at his trial? Should this be entrapment as a matter of law, or should the issue go to the jury? Does it matter whether the jurisdiction has adopted the subjective or objective test? Would it change the analysis if Kerry had a conviction the year before for possession of marijuana?

Chapter 19
Insanity and Diminished Capacity

§ 19.01 Competency to Stand Trial

Medina v. California
505 U.S. 437 (1992)

Justice KENNEDY delivered the opinion of the Court.

* * * It is well established that the Due Process Clause of the Fourteenth Amendment prohibits the criminal prosecution of a defendant who is not competent to stand trial. * * * Based on our review of the historical treatment of the burden of proof in competency proceedings, the operation of the challenged rule, and our precedents, we cannot say that the allocation of the burden of proof to a criminal defendant to prove incompetence "offends some principle of justice so rooted in the traditions and conscience of our people as to be ranked as fundamental." *Patterson v. New York* [cite]. * * * Historical practice is probative of whether a procedural rule can be characterized as fundamental. * * * The rule that a criminal defendant who is incompetent should not be required to stand trial has deep roots in our common-law heritage. Blackstone acknowledged that a defendant "who became 'mad' after the commission of an offense should not be arraigned for it 'because he is not able to plead to it with that advice and caution that he ought,'" and "if he became 'mad' after pleading, he should not be tried, 'for how can he make his defense?'" * * *

By contrast, there is no settled tradition on the proper allocation of the burden of proof in a proceeding to determine competence. Petitioner concedes that "the common law rule on this issue at the time the Constitution was adopted is not entirely clear." * * * Discerning no historical basis for concluding that the allocation of the burden of proving incompetence to the defendant violates due process, we turn to consider whether the rule transgresses any recognized principle of "fundamental fairness" in operation. * * * Respondent argues that our decision in *Leland v. Oregon*, 343 U.S. 790 (1952), which upheld the right of the State to place on a defendant the burden of proving the defense of insanity beyond a reasonable doubt, compels the conclusion that § 1369(f) is constitutional because, like a finding of insanity, a finding of incompetence has no necessary relationship to the elements of a crime, on which the State bears the burden of proof. * * * This analogy is not convincing, because there are significant differences between a claim of incompetence and a plea of not guilty by reason of insanity. * * *

In a competency hearing, the "emphasis is on [the defendant's] capacity to consult with counsel and to comprehend the proceedings, and . . . this is by no means the same test as those which determine criminal responsibility at the time of the crime." * * * If a defendant is incompetent, due process considerations require suspension of the criminal trial until such time, if any, that the defendant regains the capacity to participate in his defense and understand the proceedings against him. * * * The entry of a plea of not guilty by reason of insanity, by contrast, presupposes that the defendant is competent to stand trial and to enter a plea. Moreover, while the Due Process Clause affords an incompetent defendant the right not to be tried, * * * we have not said that the Constitution requires the States to recognize the insanity defense. * * *

Under California law, the allocation of the burden of proof to the defendant will affect competency determinations only in a narrow class of cases where the evidence is in equipoise; that is, where the evidence that a defendant is competent is just as strong as the evidence that he is incompetent. * * * Our cases recognize that a defendant has a constitutional right "not to be tried while legally incompetent," and that a State's "failure to observe procedures adequate to protect a defendant's right not to be tried or convicted while incompetent to stand trial deprives him of his due process right to a fair trial." * * * Once a State provides a defendant access to procedures for making a competency evaluation, however, we perceive no basis for holding that due process further requires the State to assume the burden of vindicating the defendant's constitutional right by persuading the trier of fact that the defendant is competent to stand trial. * * *

In our view, the question whether a defendant whose competence is in doubt may waive his right to a competency hearing is quite different from the question whether the burden of proof may be placed on the defendant once a hearing is held. * * * Although an impaired defendant might be limited in his ability to assist counsel in demonstrating incompetence, the defendant's inability to assist counsel can, in and of itself, constitute probative evidence of incompetence, and defense counsel will often have the best-informed view of the defendant's ability to participate in his defense. * * * While reasonable minds may differ as to the wisdom of placing the burden of proof on the defendant in these circumstances, we believe that a State may take such factors into account in making judgments as to the allocation of the burden of proof. * * * The judgment of the Supreme Court of California is Affirmed.

Justice O'CONNOR, with whom Justice SOUTER joins, concurring in the judgment.

I concur in the judgment of the Court, but I reject its intimation that the balancing of equities is inappropriate in evaluating whether state criminal procedures amount to due process. * * * After balancing the equities in this case, I agree with the Court that the burden of proof may constitutionally rest on the defendant. * * * The main concern of the prosecution, of course, is that a defendant will feign incompetence in order to avoid trial. If the burden of proving competence rests on the government, a defendant will have less incentive to cooperate in psychiatric investigations, because an inconclusive examination will benefit the defense, not the prosecution. A defendant may also be less cooperative in making available friends or family who might have information about the defendant's mental state. States may therefore decide that a more complete picture of a defendant's competence will be obtained if the defense has the incentive to produce all the evidence in its possession. The potentially greater overall access to information provided by placing the burden of proof on the defense may outweigh the danger that, in close cases, a marginally incompetent defendant is brought to trial. Unlike the requirement of a hearing or a psychiatric examination, placing the burden of proof on the government will not necessarily increase the reliability of the proceedings. The equities here, then, do not weigh so much in petitioner's favor as to rebut the presumption of constitutionality that the historical toleration of procedural variation creates * * * .

Justice BLACKMUN, with whom Justice STEVENS joins, dissenting.

Teofilo Medina, Jr., may have been mentally incompetent when the State of California convicted him and sentenced him to death. One psychiatrist testified he was incompetent. Another psychiatrist and a psychologist testified he was not. Several other experts testified but did not express an opinion on competence. Instructed to presume that petitioner Medina was competent, the jury returned a finding of competence. For all we know, the jury was entirely undecided. I do not believe a Constitution that forbids the trial and conviction of an incompetent person tolerates the trial and conviction of a person about whom the evidence of competency is so equivocal and unclear. I dissent. * * *

The right to be tried while competent is the foundational right for the effective exercise of a defendant's other rights in a criminal trial. "Competence to stand trial is rudimentary, for upon it depends the main part of those rights deemed essential to a fair trial, including the right to effective assistance of counsel, the rights to summon, to confront, and to cross-examine witnesses, and the right to testify on one's own behalf or to remain silent without penalty for doing so." . . In the words of Professor Morris, one of the world's leading criminologists, incompetent persons "are not really present at trial; they may not be able properly to play the role of an accused person, to recall relevant events, to produce evidence and witnesses, to testify effectively on their own behalf, to help confront hostile witnesses, and to project to the trier of facts a sense of their innocence." * * *

This Court's cases are clear that the right to be tried while competent is so critical a prerequisite to the criminal process that "state procedures *must be adequate* to protect this right." * * * "The failure to observe procedures adequate to protect a defendant's right not to be tried or convicted while incompetent to stand trial deprives him of his due process right to a fair trial."* * * In other words, the Due Process Clause does not simply forbid the State to try to convict a person who is incompetent. It also demands adequate *anticipatory, protective procedures* to minimize the risk that an incompetent person will be convicted. Justice Frankfurter recognized this in a related context: "If the deeply rooted principle in our society against killing an insane man is to be respected, at least the minimum provision for assuring a fair application of that principle is inherent in the principle itself." * * * Anticipatory protective procedures are necessary as well because "we have previously emphasized the difficulty of retrospectively determining an accused's competence to stand trial." * * *

I consider it no less likely that petitioner Medina was tried and sentenced to death while effectively unable to defend himself. That is why I do not share the Court's remarkable confidence that "nothing in today's decision is inconsistent with our longstanding recognition that the criminal trial of an incompetent defendant violates due process." * * * I do not believe the constitutional prohibition against convicting incompetent persons remains "fundamental" if the State is at liberty to go forward with a trial when the evidence of competency is inconclusive. Accordingly, I dissent.

NOTES AND QUESTIONS

1. *Competency vs. Insanity.* Competency to stand trial differs from insanity. It is usually a pre-trial determination in which a court ascertains if the accused (a) has the capacity to consult with his or her attorney "with a reasonable degree of understanding of the proceedings," and (b) whether the accused understands the proceedings against him or her. Competency is premised upon the requirement of due process in proceeding against an individual charged with a crime. If one does not understand the proceedings, then one is not competent to stand trial.

2. *Civil Commitment for Incompetency.* If a defendant is deemed incompetent to stand trial, criminal proceedings against him cannot proceed until he regains competency. If a defendant suffers from a mental condition that renders her unlikely to retain competency in the "foreseeable" future, she cannot remain

incarcerated indefinitely. In *Jackson v. Indiana*, 406 U.S. 715 (1972), the Supreme Court held that a person may not be held "more than the reasonable period of time necessary to determine whether there is substantial probability that he will attain... capacity in the near future." Otherwise, she must be released from confinement or committed under civil proceedings.

3. ***Ethical Issues***. Does the concurring opinion in *Medina* assume that the accused benefits when there is a finding of incompetence? Can a finding of incompetence require additional time in a facility than if the accused had proceeded to trial and been sentenced? Consider cases where an individual is charged with a misdemeanor. If the maximum sentence for the crime might be six months, but if the accused is sent to a mental facility and will likely spend three years there, will the accused work to assist in a finding of incompetence? Consider the predicament placed upon defense counsel when such a result might occur. Is defense counsel zealously representing the client when they proceed for a determination of incompetency knowing that their client will receive additional time within a facility if such a finding is made. The ABA Standards on Mental Health provide defense counsel with some guidance when tackling these questions of professional responsibility.

4. ***Mental Health and Criminal Justice.*** Mental health issues are a serious problem in the criminal justice system. Professor Richard E. Redding notes that:

> The prevalence of mental disorders among persons with criminal justice system involvement is staggering. Each year about 700,000 adults with serious mental illness come into contact with the criminal justice system. Justice Department statistics indicate that sixteen percent of jail and prison inmates have a serious mental illness, but these estimates rise to 35% when they include less serious disorders. About 70% of those admitted to correctional facilities have active symptoms of serious mental illness, making the Los Angeles, Cook County (Chicago and surrounding suburbs), and Rikers Island (New York City) jails the largest mental hospitals in the country. Indeed, a recent study in Michigan found that 31% of its prison population required psychiatric care. The largest study to date, sampling 3,332 inmates in New York prisons, found that 80% had severe disorders requiring treatment and another 16% had mental disorders requiring periodic mental health services. * * *

> Clearly, attorneys representing criminal defendants will encounter many clients who suffer from one or more mental disorders. Extrapolating from data on the prevalence of mental disorders among jail and prison inmates, as well as data on the frequency with which defense attorneys have concerns about their client's mental health status, permits the conclusion that many clients will have diagnosable mental disorders. The most common serious mental disorders among criminal defendants include

schizophrenia, bipolar disorder (formerly known as manic depression), mania, major depression, personality disorders (particularly antisocial, narcissistic, and borderline disorders), and neuropsychological abnormalities. Common but less-serious disorders include attentional disorders, post-traumatic stress disorder, and anxiety disorders. Substance abuse and dependence is also quite common in this population.It is not surprising, therefore, that forensic mental health issues (e.g., concerns about representing mentally ill clients, competence to stand trial, and the use of mental health evidence in sentencing) frequently arise in criminal practice.

Richard E. Redding, *Why It Is Essential to Teach About Mental Health Issues In Criminal Law (And a Primer on How to Do It)*, 14 WASH. U.J.L. & POL'Y 407 (2004) (citations omitted).

MODEL PENAL CODE

§ 4.04. Mental Disease or Defect Excluding Fitness to Proceed.

No person who as a result of mental disease or defect lacks capacity to understand the proceedings against him or to assist in his own defense shall be tried, convicted or sentenced for the commission of an offense so long as such incapacity endures.

§ 4.06. Determination of Fitness to Proceed; Effect of Finding of Unfitness; Proceedings if Fitness Is Regained [; Post-Commitment Hearing].

(1) When the defendant's fitness to proceed is drawn in question, the issue shall be determined by the Court. If neither the prosecuting attorney nor counsel for the defendant contests the finding of the report filed pursuant to Section 4.05, the Court may make the determination on the basis of such report. If the finding is contested, the Court shall hold a hearing on the issue. If the report is received in evidence upon such hearing, the party who contests the finding thereof shall have the right to summon and to cross- examine the psychiatrists who joined in the report and to offer evidence upon the issue.

(2) If the Court determines that the defendant lacks fitness to proceed, the proceeding against him shall be suspended, except as provided in Subsection (3) [Subsections (3) and (4)] of this Section, and the Court shall commit him to the custody of the Commissioner of Mental Hygiene [Public Health or Correction] to be placed in an appropriate institution of the Department of Mental Hygiene [Public Health or Correction] for so long as such unfitness shall endure. When the Court,

on its own motion or upon the application of the Commissioner of Mental Hygiene [Public Health or Correction] or the prosecuting attorney, determines, after a hearing if a hearing is requested, that the defendant has regained fitness to proceed, the proceeding shall be resumed. If, however, the Court is of the view that so much time has elapsed since the commitment of the defendant that it would be unjust to resume the criminal proceeding, the Court may dismiss the charge and may order the defendant to be discharged or, subject to the law governing the civil commitment of persons suffering from mental disease or defect, order the defendant to be committed to an appropriate institution of the Department of Mental Hygiene [Public Health] * * * .

§ 19.02 Insanity

Clark v. Arizona
548 U.S. 735 (2006)

Justice SOUTER delivered the opinion of the Court.

The case presents two questions: whether due process prohibits Arizona's use of an insanity test stated solely in terms of the capacity to tell whether an act charged as a crime was right or wrong; and whether Arizona violates due process in restricting consideration of defense evidence of mental illness and incapacity to its bearing on a claim of insanity, thus eliminating its significance directly on the issue of the mental element of the crime charged (known in legal shorthand as the mens rea, or guilty mind). We hold that there is no violation of due process in either instance.

In the early hours of June 21, 2000, Officer Jeffrey Moritz of the Flagstaff Police responded in uniform to complaints that a pickup truck with loud music blaring was circling a residential block. When he located the truck, the officer turned on the emergency lights and siren of his marked patrol car, which prompted petitioner Eric Clark, the truck's driver (then 17), to pull over. Officer Moritz got out of the patrol car and told Clark to stay where he was. Less than a minute later, Clark shot the officer, who died soon after but not before calling the police dispatcher for help. Clark ran away on foot but was arrested later that day with gunpowder residue on his hands; the gun that killed the officer was found nearby, stuffed into a knit cap.

Clark was charged with first-degree murder * * * for intentionally or knowingly killing a law enforcement officer in the line of duty. * * *

In presenting the defense case, Clark claimed mental illness, which he sought to introduce for two purposes. First, he raised the affirmative defense of insanity, putting the burden on himself to prove by clear and convincing evidence that "at the time of the commission of the criminal act [he] was afflicted with a mental disease or defect of such severity that [he] did not know the criminal act was wrong." Second, he aimed to rebut the prosecution's evidence of the requisite mens rea, that he had acted intentionally or knowingly to kill a law enforcement officer.

The trial court ruled that Clark could not rely on evidence bearing on insanity to dispute the mens rea. The court cited *State v. Mott*, 931 P.2d 1046 (Ariz. 1997), which "refused to allow psychiatric testimony to negate specific intent," and held that "Arizona does not allow evidence of a defendant's mental disorder short of insanity . . . to negate the mens rea element of a crime."

As to his insanity, then, Clark presented testimony from classmates, school officials, and his family describing his increasingly bizarre behavior over the year before the shooting. Witnesses testified, for example, that paranoid delusions led Clark to rig a fishing line with beads and wind chimes at home to alert him to intrusion by invaders, and to keep a bird in his automobile to warn of airborne poison. There was lay and expert testimony that Clark thought Flagstaff was populated with "aliens" (some impersonating government agents), the "aliens" were trying to kill him, and bullets were the only way to stop them. A psychiatrist testified that Clark was suffering from paranoid schizophrenia with delusions about "aliens" when he killed Officer Moritz, and he concluded that Clark was incapable of luring the officer or understanding right from wrong and that he was thus insane at the time of the killing. In rebuttal, a psychiatrist for the State gave his opinion that Clark's paranoid schizophrenia did not keep him from appreciating the wrongfulness of his conduct, as shown by his actions before and after the shooting (such as circling the residential block with music blaring as if to lure the police to intervene, evading the police after the shooting, and hiding the gun).

At the close of the defense case consisting of this evidence bearing on mental illness, the trial court denied Clark's renewed motion for a directed verdict grounded on failure of the prosecution to show that Clark knew the victim was a police officer. The judge then issued a special verdict of first-degree murder, * * *. The sentence was life imprisonment without the possibility of release for 25 years.

[In the first part of the opinion, the Court upheld the validity of Arizona's definition of insanity as "whether a mental defect leaves a defendant unable to understand what he is doing." In the second part of the opinion, the Court considered the defendant's challenge to the exclusion of the evidence regarding his diminished capacity as negating proof beyond a reasonable doubt that he had the requisite mens rea for first degree murder.]

Clark's second claim of a due process violation challenges the rule adopted by the Supreme Court of Arizona in *State v. Mott*. This case ruled on the admissibility of testimony from a psychologist offered to show that the defendant suffered from battered women's syndrome and therefore lacked the capacity to form the mens rea of the crime charged against her. * * * The state court held that testimony of a professional psychologist or psychiatrist about a defendant's mental incapacity owing to mental disease or defect was admissible, and could be considered, only for its bearing on an insanity defense; such evidence could not be considered on the element of mens rea, that is, what the State must show about a defendant's mental state (such as intent or understanding) when he performed the act charged against him.

Understanding Clark's claim requires attention to the categories of evidence with a potential bearing on mens rea. First, there is "observation evidence" in the everyday sense, testimony from those who observed what Clark did and heard what he said; this category would also include testimony that an expert witness might give about Clark's tendency to think in a certain way and his behavioral characteristics. This evidence may support a professional diagnosis of mental disease and in any event is the kind of evidence that can be relevant to show what in fact was on Clark's mind when he fired the gun. Observation evidence in the record covers Clark's behavior at home and with friends, his expressions of belief around the time of the killing that "aliens" were inhabiting the bodies of local people (including government agents),[27] his driving around the neighborhood before the police arrived, and so on. * * *

Second, there is "mental-disease evidence" in the form of opinion testimony that Clark suffered from a mental disease with features described by the witness. As was true here, this evidence characteristically but not always comes from professional psychologists or psychiatrists who testify as expert witnesses and base their opinions in part on examination of a defendant, usually conducted after the events in question. The thrust of this evidence was that, based on factual reports, professional observations, and tests, Clark was psychotic at the time in question, with a condition that fell within the category of schizophrenia.

Third, there is evidence we will refer to as "capacity evidence" about a defendant's capacity for cognition and moral judgment (and ultimately also his capacity to form mens rea). This, too, is opinion evidence. Here, as it usually does, this testimony came from the same experts and concentrated on those specific

---

[27] Clark's parents testified that, in the months before the shooting and even days beforehand, Clark called them "aliens" and thought that "aliens" were out to get him. One night before the shooting, according to Clark's mother, Clark repeatedly viewed a popular film characterized by her as telling a story about "aliens" masquerading as government agents, a story Clark insisted was real despite his mother's protestations to the contrary. And two months after the shooting, Clark purportedly told his parents that his hometown, Flagstaff, was inhabited principally by "aliens," who had to be stopped, and that the only way to stop them was with bullets.

details of the mental condition that make the difference between sanity and insanity under the Arizona definition. In their respective testimony on these details the experts disagreed: the defense expert gave his opinion that the symptoms or effects of the disease in Clark's case included inability to appreciate the nature of his action and to tell that it was wrong, whereas the State's psychiatrist was of the view that Clark was a schizophrenic who was still sufficiently able to appreciate the reality of shooting the officer and to know that it was wrong to do that. * * *

It is clear that *Mott* itself imposed no restriction on considering evidence of the first sort, the observation evidence. We read the *Mott* restriction to apply, rather, to evidence addressing the two issues in testimony that characteristically comes only from psychologists or psychiatrists qualified to give opinions as expert witnesses: mental-disease evidence (whether at the time of the crime a defendant suffered from a mental disease or defect, such as schizophrenia) and capacity evidence (whether the disease or defect left him incapable of performing or experiencing a mental process defined as necessary for sanity such as appreciating the nature and quality of his act and knowing that it was wrong). * * *

The third principle implicated by Clark's argument is a defendant's right as a matter of simple due process to present evidence favorable to himself on an element that must be proven to convict him. As already noted, evidence tending to show that a defendant suffers from mental disease and lacks capacity to form mens rea is relevant to rebut evidence that he did in fact form the required mens rea at the time in question; this is the reason that Clark claims a right to require the factfinder in this case to consider testimony about his mental illness and his incapacity directly, when weighing the persuasiveness of other evidence tending to show mens rea, which the prosecution has the burden to prove.

As Clark recognizes, however, the right to introduce relevant evidence can be curtailed if there is a good reason for doing that. "While the Constitution . . . prohibits the exclusion of defense evidence under rules that serve no legitimate purpose or that are disproportionate to the ends that they are asserted to promote, well-established rules of evidence permit trial judges to exclude evidence if its probative value is outweighed by certain other factors such as unfair prejudice, confusion of the issues, or potential to mislead the jury." *Holmes v. South Carolina*, 547 U.S. 319 (2006). And if evidence may be kept out entirely, its consideration may be subject to limitation, which Arizona claims the power to impose here. State law says that evidence of mental disease and incapacity may be introduced and considered, and if sufficiently forceful to satisfy the defendant's burden of proof under the insanity rule it will displace the presumption of sanity and excuse from criminal responsibility. But mental-disease and capacity evidence may be considered only for its bearing on the insanity defense, and it will avail a defendant only if it is persuasive enough to satisfy the defendant's burden as defined by the terms of that defense. The mental-disease and capacity evidence is thus being channeled or restricted to one issue and given effect only if the defendant carries the burden to convince the factfinder of insanity; the evidence is not being excluded entirely, and the question is whether reasons for requiring it to be channeled and restricted are good enough to satisfy the standard of fundamental fairness that due process requires. We think they are.

The first reason supporting the *Mott* rule is Arizona's authority to define its presumption of sanity (or capacity or responsibility) by choosing an insanity definition, and by placing the burden of persuasion on defendants who claim incapacity as an excuse from customary criminal responsibility. No one, certainly not Clark here, denies that a State may place a burden of persuasion on a defendant claiming insanity. And Clark presses no objection to Arizona's decision to require persuasion to a clear and convincing degree before the presumption of sanity and normal responsibility is overcome.

But if a State is to have this authority in practice as well as in theory, it must be able to deny a defendant the opportunity to displace the presumption of sanity more easily when addressing a different issue in the course of the criminal trial. Yet, as we have explained, just such an opportunity would be available if expert testimony of mental disease and incapacity could be considered for whatever a factfinder might think it was worth on the issue of mens rea. As we mentioned, the presumption of sanity would then be only as strong as the evidence a factfinder would accept as enough to raise a reasonable doubt about mens rea for the crime charged; once reasonable doubt was found, acquittal would be required, and the standards established for the defense of insanity would go by the boards.

Now, a State is of course free to accept such a possibility in its law. After all, it is free to define the insanity defense by treating the presumption of sanity as a bursting bubble, whose disappearance shifts the burden to the prosecution to prove sanity whenever a defendant presents any credible evidence of mental disease or incapacity. In States with this kind of insanity rule, the legislature may well be willing to allow such evidence to be considered on the mens rea element for whatever the factfinder thinks it is worth. What counts for due process, however, is simply that a State that wishes to avoid a second avenue for exploring capacity, less stringent for a defendant, has a good reason for confining the consideration of evidence of mental disease and incapacity to the insanity defense.

It is obvious that Arizona's *Mott* rule reflects such a choice. The State Supreme Court pointed out that the State had declined to adopt a defense of diminished capacity (allowing a jury to decide when to excuse a defendant because of greater than normal difficulty in conforming to the law). The court reasoned that the State's choice would be undercut if evidence of incapacity could be considered for whatever a jury might think sufficient to raise a reasonable doubt about mens rea, even if it did not show insanity. In other words, if a jury were free to decide how much evidence of mental disease and incapacity was enough to counter evidence of mens rea to the point of creating a reasonable doubt, that would in functional terms be analogous to allowing jurors to decide upon some degree of diminished capacity to obey the law, a degree set by them, that would prevail as a stand-alone defense.

A State's insistence on preserving its chosen standard of legal insanity cannot be the sole reason for a rule like *Mott*, however, for it fails to answer an objection the dissent makes in this case. An insanity rule gives a defendant already found guilty the opportunity to excuse his conduct by showing he was insane when he acted, that is, that he did not have the mental capacity for conventional guilt and criminal responsibility. But, as the dissent argues, if the same evidence that affirmatively shows he was not guilty by reason of insanity (or "guilty except insane" under Arizona law), also shows it was at least doubtful that he could form mens rea, then he should not be found guilty in the first place; it thus violates due process when the State impedes him from using mental-disease and capacity evidence directly to rebut the prosecution's evidence that he did form mens rea.

Are there, then, characteristics of mental-disease and capacity evidence giving rise to risks that may reasonably be hedged by channeling the consideration of such evidence to the insanity issue on which, in States like Arizona, a defendant has the burden of persuasion? We think there are: in the controversial character of some categories of mental disease, in the potential of mental-disease evidence to mislead, and in the danger of according greater certainty to capacity evidence than experts claim for it.

* * * It bears repeating that not every State will find it worthwhile to make the judgment Arizona has made, and the choices the States do make about dealing with the risks posed by mental-disease and capacity evidence will reflect their varying assessments about the presumption of sanity as expressed in choices of insanity rules. The point here simply is that Arizona has sensible reasons to assign the risks as it has done by channeling the evidence.[45]

---

[45] Arizona's rule is supported by a further practical reason, though not as weighty as those just considered. As mentioned before, if substantial mental-disease and capacity evidence is accepted as rebutting mens rea in a given case, the affirmative defense of insanity will probably not be reached or ruled upon; the defendant will simply be acquitted (or perhaps convicted of a lesser included offense). If an acquitted defendant suffers from a mental disease or defect that makes him dangerous, he will neither be confined nor treated psychiatrically unless a judge so orders after some independent commitment proceeding. But if a defendant succeeds in showing himself insane, Arizona law (and presumably that of every other State with an insanity rule) will require commitment and treatment as a consequence of that finding without more. It makes sense, then, to channel capacity evidence to the issue structured to deal with mental incapacity when such a claim is raised successfully.

Arizona's rule serves to preserve the State's chosen standard for recognizing insanity as a defense and to avoid confusion and misunderstanding on the part of jurors. For these reasons, there is no violation of due process * * *, and no cause to claim that channeling evidence on mental disease and capacity offends any principle of justice so rooted in the traditions and conscience of our people as to be ranked as fundamental.

NOTES AND QUESTIONS

1. *Abolishing Insanity.* Four states have abolished the insanity defense. Does using the evidence that would be used to present an insanity defense, to negate the mens rea, sufficiently permit the accused to explain their mental disease or defect? Will allowing the evidence to negate mens rea, in some instances, permit a wider range of evidence to the submitted to the jury than might be presented with an insanity defense? For example, will presenting evidence to negate the mens rea permit a defendant to show that he or she did not know what they were doing even though they did not suffer from a mental disease or defect? Will claims of temporary delusional states that negate intent be permitted, that might not be allowed if insanity were used as the basis for presenting the defense?

2. *Policy Rationale.* Why do most states permit the use of an insanity defense? What is the policy rationale behind having a defense of insanity?

3. *Mens Rea.* Should the use of an insanity defense preclude the defense of a lack of mens rea? Consider the position of the Model Penal Code that offers the insanity defense and also the use of this evidence to negate the mens rea. In § 4.02(1) it states: "Evidence that the defendant suffered from a mental disease or defect is admissible whenever it is relevant to prove that the defendant did or did not have a state of mind that is an element of the offense." Many states, however, will not allow evidence that relates to insanity to be offered to negate mens rea. As seen in *Clark v. Arizona,* the Supreme Court upheld an Arizona statute that precluded a defendant from offering evidence related to his insanity from being considered by the jury as undermining the government's proof of his mens rea for the offense if he did not meet the test for insanity.

4. *Different Insanity Tests.* Courts use different tests for determining whether the accused should be found insane. In *State v, Searcy,* 798 P.2d 914, 917 n.3 (Idaho 1990), the court discussed the different tests as follows:

> One of the earliest formulations of the insanity defense and one still in use in as many as sixteen states is the *M'Naghten* rule. This rule is stated as follows:

[T]o establish a defense on the ground of insanity, it must be clearly proven that, at the time of the committing of the act, the party accused was labouring under such a defect [of] reason, from disease of the mind, as not to know the nature and quality of the act he was doing; or, if he did know it, that he did not know he was doing what was wrong.

M'Naghten's Case, 8 Eng.Rep. 718, 722 (1843).

Another test broadens the scope of the *M'Naghten* rule to include those who knew that their actions were wrong but who, as a result of a "disease of the mind," were unable to exercise control over their actions. This "irresistible impulse" test is used to supplement the *M'Naghten* rule in approximately five states.

Many states follow a variation of the American Law Institute (ALI) test which is a combination of the M'Naghten Rule and the "irresistible impulse" test. The ALI standard reads:

(1) A person is not responsible for criminal conduct if at the time of such conduct as a result of mental disease or defect, he lacks substantial capacity either to appreciate the criminality (wrongfulness) of his conduct or to conform his conduct to the requirements of the law.

(2) As used in this article, the terms "mental disease or defect" do not include an abnormality manifested only by repeated criminal or otherwise anti-social conduct.

American Law Institute, Model Penal Code (Proposed Official Draft, 1962), § 4.01, at p. 74. Among those states which follow the ALI test, some favor the word "wrongfulness" instead of "criminality." Still others remove the word "substantial."

New Hampshire is the only state which follows the *Durham* rule or "product" test. As set forth in *Durham v. United States*, 214 F.2d 862, 874-875 (D.C. Cir. 1954), "a defendant is not criminally responsible if his unlawful act was a product of mental disease or defect."

Three other states have adopted unique standards drawing in part from the cognitive rightwrong language of the *M'Naghten* rule and the "irresistible impulse" test while adding other considerations, such as "prevailing community standards" and "legal and moral aspects of responsibility."

See generally I. Keilitz & J.P. Fulton, *The Insanity Defense and its Alternatives: A Guide for Policymakers, Institute on Mental Disability and the Law, National Center for State Courts* (October 1983).

What are the pros and cons of each of these tests? For example, the *M'Naghten* test fails to include a volitional element. The irresistible impulse test fails to include defects that accrue from brooding or long term illness. Some claim that the *Durham* test limits the jury decision to the medical evidence offered at trial. In light of the extensive criticism of each of these different tests, which test best meets the policy considerations of criminal law, namely punishment theories?

5. *International Law.* Which insanity test was selected for the Rome Statute of the International Criminal Court? It reads as follows:

Article 31 – Grounds for excluding criminal responsibility

1. In addition to other grounds for excluding criminal responsibility provided for in this Statute, a person shall not be criminally responsible if, at the time of that person's conduct:

(a) The person suffers from a mental disease or defect that destroys that person's capacity to appreciate the unlawfulness or nature of his or her conduct, or capacity to control his or her conduct to conform to the requirements of law; * * *

6. *Mental Disease or Defect.* Many of the definitions of insanity are premised upon a showing of a "mental disease or defect." How does one define this term for purposes of insanity? Should one use a psychiatric or medical definition? In *United States v. Murdoch*, 98 F.3d 472 (9th Cir. 1996), District Judge Wilson in a concurring opinion stated:

There is little guidance as to when a psychiatric condition falls within the scope of § 4243's mental disease or defect. The courts have expressed reluctance in relying on medical categories and labels in determining the limits of legal insanity. * * * Such reluctance is warranted. "What definition of 'mental disease or defect' is to be employed by courts enforcing the criminal law is, in the final analysis, a question of legal, moral and policy–not of medical–judgment. * * *

Among the states, there have been mixed results on the issue. At least two states have categorically excluded personality disorders from the definition of mental disease or defect. Cal. Penal Code § 25.5; Or. Rev. Stat. § 161.295. Others exclude certain types of personality defects, disorders, or abnormalities, most commonly those of the antisocial subcategory. Ala. Code § 13A-3-1; Ariz. Rev. Stat. Ann. § 13-502; Ill. St.

Ch. 720 § 5/6-2; Ind. St. 35-41-3-6; Me. Rev. Stat. Am. Tit., 17 -A, § 39; Tenn. Code Ann. § 39-11-501; Utah Code Ann. § 76-2-305. At the opposite end of the spectrum, Alaska has adopted an extraordinarily broad definition of mental disease or defect which would seem to encompass all personality disorders. Alaska Stat. § 12.47.130 (3) (mental disease or defect means a disorder of thought or mood that substantially impairs judgment, behavior, capacity to recognize reality, or ability to cope with the ordinary demands of life). In those states which have chosen to exclude personality disorders from serving as the basis for a verdict of not guilty by reason of insanity, there seems to be a desire to guard against turning every personality quirk into a "mental disease or defect" through the imprimatur of a psychiatric category. * * * "

7. *Affirmative Defense.* In many states, insanity is an affirmative defense and the burden of proof is on the defendant. The Model Penal Code in § 4.03(1) states, "[m]ental disease or defect excluding responsibility is an affirmative defense." In §4.03(2) it provides:

> Evidence of mental disease or defect excluding responsibility is not admissible unless the defendant, at the time of entering his plea of not guilty or within ten days thereafter or at such later time as the Court may for good cause permit, files a written notice of his purpose to rely on such defense.

8. *Guilty But Mentally Ill.* Several states have moved away from the verdict of "not guilty by reason of insanity" to using a verdict of "guilty but mentally ill." Some attribute this shift in the law to the result in the prosecution of John Hinckley, Jr., who was charged with attempt to kill President Reagan in 1981 and was found not guilty by reason of insanity. Under the "guilty but mentally ill" finding, the accused goes initially to a hospital facility and when (or if) the person is cured, they are then sent to prison to complete the sentence. In response to the verdict in the Hinkley prosecution, Congress revised federal insanity law in 1984 in the Insanity Defense Reform Act to permit the defense only if the defendant "was unable to appreciate the nature and quality or the wrongfulness of his acts" due to a mental disease or defect, and the defendant bears the burden of proof by clear and convincing evidence. 18 U.S.C. § 17.

9. *Deific Decree.* What about a defendant who knows the difference between right and wrong, but believes he or she has been ordered by God (or some deity) to engage in conduct that constitutes a crime — is that person insane? Under the cognitive test of insanity, the answer should be no because the person knows that, under human law, the act is wrong, but engages in the conduct anyway because of a higher calling. Courts deal with this variant of insanity under the "deific decree" exception, as discussed in the following decision.

State v. Turgeon
120 Wash. App. 1050 (Wash. Ct. App. 2003) (Unpublished)

GROSSE, J.

A deific decree jury instruction may condition an insanity finding on whether God's command destroyed the defendant's free will to distinguish right from wrong. Therefore, as here, an otherwise rational defendant who murders another, allegedly following a direct command from God, is not legally insane if the command did not overcome his cognitive ability to tell right from wrong. We affirm.

Christopher Turgeon claims that he is able to predict events and that he regularly receives messages from God. Because of this, he has devoted his life to teaching, prophesying, and confronting others with their sins. In 1991, Turgeon formed a Bible study ministry called "Ahabah Asah," which he later renamed "the Gatekeepers." In 1996, Turgeon allegedly received a message from God that it was time to declare war against the government. The Gatekeepers attempted to advance this mission by robbing and defrauding businesses that it perceived to be sinful. Turgeon and the Gatekeepers also acted according to God's will by exacting judgment on people, particularly those who left the group.

Dan Jess was once a member of the Gatekeepers. After leaving the group, Jess allegedly called Turgeon a "false prophet" and said that he would "stop at nothing" to stop him. In March 1998, during a Gatekeepers meeting, God allegedly told Turgeon that "Dan must be killed." Another group member, Blaine Applin, allegedly received a similar message. The Gatekeepers agreed that Turgeon and Applin must kill Jess.

In preparation for the murder, Turgeon and Applin obtained camouflage clothing and wiped fingerprints off the shell casings that they planned to use. The men drove from their home in California to Jess' home in Washington. Turgeon testified that, on the way to Washington, he asked God to make them take an unscheduled stop if killing Jess was not God's will. Instead, the two men saw seven rainbows, leading them to believe that God blessed their mission. In the early morning of March 29, 1998, Applin knocked on Jess' door, and when Jess answered, Applin shot him multiple times. Turgeon operated as a lookout and drove the getaway car. Turgeon and Applin confessed to the crime but asserted the insanity defense, arguing that God commanded them to murder Jess. The two men received a joint trial. The jury convicted both men of first degree murder. [The court affirmed Applin's conviction in a separate opinion.] * * *

To be considered legally insane, Turgeon must establish by a preponderance of the evidence that, at the time of the act and as a result of mental disease or defect, he was unable to perceive the nature and quality of the act or was unable to tell right from wrong with reference to the act. Turgeon may also establish insanity if he knew the criminal act was wrong but believed, as a result of mental defect, that God commanded the act. [*State v. Crenshaw*, 798, 659 P.2d 488 (Wash. 1983).] This is known as the deific decree exception. In this case, the trial court gave a general instruction about the insanity defense, followed by this deific decree instruction:

> A defendant is also not guilty by reason of insanity if you find that each of these elements has been proved by a preponderance of the evidence:
>
> (1) At the time of the acts charged the defendant had a mental disease or defect; and
>
> (2) As a result of that mental disease or defect, the defendant had a delusion that he had received a direct command from God to do the acts; and
>
> (3) The defendant did the acts because of that direct command; and
>
> (4) The direct command destroyed the defendant's free will and his ability to distinguish right from wrong.

Turgeon challenges this instruction, arguing that the court should have instead instructed:

> If you find that the defendant believed, because of mental disease or defect, that he was acting under the direct command of God he may be found not guilty by the reason of insanity only if you find, by a preponderance of the evidence, that his belief prevented the defendant from comprehending the act with which he is charged was morally wrong or prevented the defendant from perceiving the nature and quality of the act with which he is charged.

According to Turgeon, the court's rejection of the latter instruction in favor of the former denied him a fair trial.

First, Turgeon argues that the trial court erred by refusing to define wrongfulness in terms of moral wrong. But we have already resolved this issue, as Turgeon's co-defendant, Blaine Applin, presented an identical claim to this court. After examining the relevant case law, we concluded that no definition of wrongfulness should ordinarily be given in legal insanity jury instructions.[8] We further concluded that the trial court's instruction was neutral, allowed both parties to argue their theories of the case, and made the relevant legal standard "manifestly apparent to the average juror." Turgeon now asks this court to reconsider its decision in *Applin*, claiming that it misstates the relevant case law. To the contrary, *Applin* provides a correct statement of Washington law.

Turgeon nevertheless argues that his proposed instruction was necessary to correct expert testimony presented at trial. Several psychologists and psychiatrists testified, and Turgeon argues that their varying recitations of the legal insanity standard were contradictory and misleading. Drs. Lee Gustafson and Doyle Brock spoke of legal wrong, while Dr. G. Preston Sims spoke of moral wrong. Drs. Samuel Etchie, Murray Hart, and Gregory Leong testified about the standard using both legal and moral terms. But the experts stated that they were only explaining their understanding of the insanity standard, and Turgeon was still able to argue his theory of the case in closing argument.

Trial testimony was not misleading or contradictory, and the court did not err by rejecting Turgeon's proposed deific decree instruction.

Turgeon next argues that the court's reference to "free will" in its deific decree instruction misstated the appropriate standard. As we recognized in *Applin*, the role of free will in deific decree instructions has been a source of confusion and debate. The Supreme Court introduced the notion in *Crenshaw*. In illustrating the deific decree exception, the court hypothesized about a mother who killed her child only because God ordered her to do so: "Although the woman knows that the law and society condemn the act, it would be unrealistic to hold her responsible for the crime, since her free will has been subsumed by her belief in the deific decree."

The court again mentioned free will in *Cameron*, stating that considerable evidence existed from which the jury could conclude that the defendant's "free will had been subsumed by [his] belief in the deific decree." In *State v. Rice*, the court stated that case law makes it "clear that a defendant following deific commands qualifies as insane only if his free will has been subsumed by his belief in the deific decree." While the Supreme Court has spoken of free will only in passing, this court closely examined the issue in *State v. Potter*.

---

[8] [*See*] *Crenshaw* ("as a general rule no definition of wrong should accompany an insanity defense instruction"); *State v. Cameron*, 674 P.2d 650 (Wash. 1983) (a trial court should not define wrongfulness in purely legal terms); *State v. Rice*, 757 P.2d 889 (Wash. 1988) (defendant did not qualify for a deific decree defense because he showed no evidence that his free will had been subsumed); *State v. Potter*, 842 P.2d 481 (Wash. 1992) (free will language in deific decree instructions must refer to the cognitive test).

In *Potter*, the defendant argued that the trial court erred by not instructing the jury that, if it found the defendant's free will was subsumed by the deific command, it need not reach the wrongfulness issue. This court disagreed, stating that free will is not related to the volitional ability to control one's behavior but rather the cognitive ability to tell right from wrong. In other words, a court may instruct the jury that the defendant is legally insane if his cognitive ability to distinguish between right and wrong was destroyed by a delusion that God commanded the act. Volitional control is irrelevant.

Here, the trial court did not instruct that the loss of volitional control was required. It stated that Turgeon was legally insane if, among other things, the direct command from God "destroyed [his] free will and his ability to distinguish right from wrong." According to Turgeon, this instruction caused the State to misinterpret the concept of free will to involve irresistible impulse or, in other words, volitional control. Specifically, Turgeon points out that, during closing arguments, the State said the defendants were not "zombies," or "robots," or "characters out of Invasion of the Body Snatchers." But the State made these statements while discussing the defendants' ability to distinguish right from wrong and thus the statements comport with Potter.

The trial court's instruction did not improperly inject the notion of irresistible impulse as Turgeon suggests. While the instruction would have conformed more obviously with *Potter* if it had instead required the jury to find that the direct command from God had destroyed the defendant's free will to distinguish between right and wrong, the instruction still accurately reflects *Crenshaw, Cameron,* and *Rice*. In addition, the instruction permitted Turgeon to argue his theory of the case. The trial court did not misstate the deific decree standard.

We further note that it is awkward to apply the insanity defense to someone like Turgeon. Turgeon is not like the defendants in *Crenshaw*, [(defendant had a history of psychiatric-related hospitalizations and decapitated his wife because he suspected her of being unfaithful; he afterwards chatted with the motel manager over a beer)] *Cameron*, [(defendant was a paranoid schizophrenic who stabbed his stepmother over 70 times because he thought she was an agent of Satan; defendant was later found wandering the streets in women's clothes)] or *Rice*, [(defendant with schizoid and paranoid features brutally murdered two adults and two children because he thought they were Communists)] and the traditional insanity defense is likely inapplicable to Turgeon because he is not insane in the traditional sense; he does not suffer from mental disease.

The trial court's deific decree instruction referred to "a direct command from God." Turgeon now argues that the State, during closing arguments, contended that a command is "direct" only if the defendant received it audibly. Turgeon claims that this statement constituted prosecutorial misconduct because it misstates the law. But the State never made this statement. Instead, its argument suggested that the defendant had to receive a direct order from God, rather than a general religious thought. Turgeon's prosecutorial misconduct claim fails.* * * Affirmed.

PROBLEM FIFTY- NINE

Jo established a religious cult settlement in a remote jungle area outside the U.S. He convinced U.S. citizens to move to this settlement as a place where they would not be subject to U.S. law enforcement. After several months of living in this settlement, he convinces everyone to commit suicide saying that this is an order from God. Almost everyone in the settlement acts according to Jo's preaching and takes their own lives. U.S. authorities, who came to this settlement looking for Ari, a young teenager who ran away from a home in the U.S., arrive to find many individuals deceased, including Ari. Jo is charged with the Assisted Suicide of Ari in a state court in the U.S. that has such a statute. Jo's attorney presents an insanity defense and requests that the court give a deific decree instruction. How should the court rule on this issue?

§ 19.03 Diminished Capacity

People v. Carpenter
627 N.W.2d 276 (Mich. 2001)

YOUNG, J.

* * * The events giving rise to defendant's convictions took place in the early morning of July 9, 1995. After attending a dance at a local community hall, complainants Audrey Thomas and Aron Blakely returned to Thomas' home in Saginaw at approximately 2:00 a.m.

Thomas and Blakely were sitting in the family room when Thomas heard the doorbell ring. Thomas discovered that defendant was at the door. Defendant demanded to be let in, yelling that Blakely should "come on out" and that Thomas was his "woman." When Thomas refused to admit him, defendant eventually crashed through a window. Defendant produced a handgun and fired two shots in the general direction of Thomas and Blakely. Neither was hit. Blakely then announced that he was leaving. As defendant opened the door for him, defendant struck Blakely in the face with his fist. Although defendant initially walked out the front door with Blakely, he immediately returned to the house where he confronted Thomas, striking her head with the butt of his gun. The blow apparently caused the gun to discharge a third time. Blakely heard the shot and went next door to call the police.

Defendant eventually fled the scene and drove to his nearby home. He immediately called Thomas and threatened her. Several police officers arrived at defendant's home a short time later. A stand-off ensued, during which defendant threatened to shoot himself and any officers who attempted to enter the house. Saginaw Police Sergeant Terri Johnson-Wise established telephone contact with defendant and spoke with him several times. She testified that defendant was yelling and screaming initially, and that when he calmed down he began talking about demons and "money that was stolen from him."

At some point, defendant asked for some heart medication that was in his truck. Saginaw Police Officer Daniel Kuhn lured him to a window by offering to give defendant his medication. When Officer Kuhn tried to grab defendant through the open window, defendant got free and slammed the window on Officer Kuhn's fingers. Defendant eventually allowed the officers to enter and he was placed under arrest. He was subsequently charged with first-degree home invasion [and] two counts of assault with intent to commit murder * * *.

At his bench trial, defendant presented a diminished capacity defense. In addition to several lay witnesses that testified that he had been drinking before the incident and that he appeared intoxicated, defendant presented a report from Kingswood Hospital, where he had been treated approximately a month after the incident. The report described him as being "delusional" and indicated that he suffered from organic brain damage. The report further described his conduct upon admission to the hospital:

> He stated that his son had been killed in April 1995 and "they had broken into my computer." He says that he has special forces that are guarding him; that people are stealing money from his son's records. He also hears voices telling him that people are looking and laughing at him. . . . He is afraid that someone is trying to poison him. He talks of the organization that is manipulating him and that someone has put "voodoo dolls" on him.

Defendant also presented expert testimony from Dr. Michael Abramsky, a board-certified clinical and forensic psychologist. Dr. Abramsky testified that defendant's bizarre behavior at the time of the shooting and ensuing standoff "suggests that he was mentally ill at the time" and that defendant's drug-induced organic brain damage, combined with his ingestion of alcohol and various prescription drugs, was the likely cause not only of his behavior but his claimed loss of memory of the incident. In sum, Dr. Abramsky believed that defendant suffered from diminished capacity and that he therefore could not formulate a specific intent.

In rebuttal, the prosecution presented the testimony of Dr. George Watson of the Center for Forensic Psychiatry. Although he acknowledged defendant's apparent organic brain damage, Dr. Watson did not believe defendant to be obviously and acutely psychotic. Instead, on the basis of his clinical interview, Dr. Watson believed "that the possibility of Mr. Carpenter exaggerating appeared to be more likely * * * ."

In a comprehensive written opinion, the trial court issued its findings. * * * Regarding the two counts of assault with intent to commit murder, the court found that the prosecution had failed to prove that defendant intended to kill either victim. Instead, the court found that the evidence only supported a finding of guilt on the lesser offense of felonious assault. Finally, the trial court found defendant guilty as charged of * * * first-degree home invasion * * * .

The court proceeded to address and reject defendant's diminished capacity defense:

 The court does not find that the defendant has supported his burden of proof of diminished capacity by a preponderance of the evidence. His actions seem very "goal oriented" . . . all suggest very goal oriented actions consistent with the capacity to form a specific intent.

* * * In affirming defendant's convictions and sentences, the Court of Appeals rejected defendant's argument that the trial court erred in shifting the burden to defendant to prove his claim of diminished capacity by a preponderance of the evidence. * * *

In Michigan, the insanity defense has been governed by statute since 1975 * * * . Legal insanity is an affirmative defense requiring proof that, * * * as a result of mental illness or being mentally retarded as defined in the mental health code, the defendant lacked "substantial capacity either to appreciate the nature and quality or the wrongfulness of his or her conduct or conform his or her conduct to the requirements of the law." Importantly, the statute provides that "the *defendant* has the burden of proving the defense of insanity by a preponderance of the evidence." * * *

As defined by our Court of Appeals, the so-called "diminished capacity" defense allows a defendant, even though legally sane, to offer evidence of some mental abnormality to negate the specific intent required to commit a particular crime * * * . "The theory is that if because of mental disease or defect a defendant cannot form the specific state of mind required as an essential element of a crime, he may be convicted only of a lower grade of the offense not requiring that particular mental element." * * *

This Court has several times acknowledged in passing the concept of the diminished capacity defense. * * * However, we have never specifically authorized its use in Michigan courts. * * * We agree with defendant that there is no indication in § 21a that the Legislature intended to make diminished capacity an affirmative defense. However, that is only because, as explained below, the Legislature's enactment of a comprehensive statutory scheme concerning defenses based on either mental illness or mental retardation demonstrates the Legislature's intent to preclude the use of *any* evidence of a defendant's lack of mental capacity short of legal insanity to avoid or reduce criminal responsibility by negating specific intent. * * *

Since its inception in the United States, the diminished capacity defense has been the subject of much debate. At present, there is a wide divergence of views among the states concerning the admissibility of evidence of mental illness short of insanity. *See generally* 1 ROBINSON, CRIMINAL LAW DEFENSES, § 64(a). A common criticism is that the subtle gradations of mental illness recognized in the psychiatric field are of little utility in determining criminal responsibility. * * * Theoretically the insanity concept operates as a bright line test separating the criminally responsible from the criminally irresponsible. The diminished capacity concept on the other hand posits a series of rather blurry lines representing gradations of culpability.

We need not join the affray because we agree with the prosecution that our Legislature, by enacting the comprehensive statutory framework described above, has already conclusively determined when mental incapacity can serve as a basis for relieving one from criminal responsibility. We conclude that, through this framework, the Legislature has created an all or nothing insanity defense. Central to our holding is the fact that the Legislature has already contemplated and addressed situations involving persons who are mentally ill or retarded yet not legally insane. As noted above, such a person may be found "guilty but mentally ill" and must be sentenced in the same manner as any other defendant committing the same offense and subject to psychiatric evaluation and treatment. * * * Through this statutory provision, the Legislature has demonstrated its policy choice that evidence of mental incapacity short of insanity cannot be used to avoid or reduce criminal responsibility by negating specific intent. * * *

[The court found no due process violation in precluding this evidence.]

* * * [T]he insanity defense as established by the Legislature is the sole standard for determining criminal responsibility as it relates to mental illness or retardation. Consequently, we affirm the decision of the Court of Appeals on this alternative basis. * * *

KELLY, J. (dissenting).

* * * Today, the majority creates a rule per se prohibiting an accused from introducing evidence that, because of mental abnormality or illness, he lacked the specific intent to commit the crime. Under my view of controlling United States

Supreme Court authority, this exclusion denies an accused his due process right to present a defense.* * *

NOTES AND QUESTIONS

1. *Specific Intent vs. General Intent.* The court in *Carpenter* states that diminished capacity might be considered a defense in some jurisdictions, but even then only when it negates the specific intent of the crime. The Tennessee Court of Criminal Appeals, in *State v. Phipps*, 883 S.W.2d 138 (Tenn. Crim. App. 1994), described the scope of the diminished capacity claim in this way:

> As is sometimes the case, determining what diminished capacity is not is a helpful starting point. It is not an absolute or affirmative defense. Though frequently confused, diminished capacity is not synonymous with diminished responsibility. The distinctions are significant. Diminished capacity most often refers to evidence negating the mens rea element of a crime, such as premeditation or malice. A second type of diminished capacity allows a defendant to show a lack of not only the specific intent required to commit the offense, but a lack of total capacity to form any mens rea as well. Because only extraordinary circumstances exist in which a defendant would not have the capacity to form any mens rea, this type of diminished capacity is more academic than functional. In either form, however, diminished capacity is never used as a justification or an excuse for a crime. Rather, it is an attempt to prove that the defendant, incapable of the requisite intent of the crime charged, is innocent of that crime but may well be guilty of a lesser one. * * *

> Equally distinguishable and significantly different from diminished capacity and diminished responsibility is the insanity defense which focuses on the defendant's responsibility for his criminal acts and, if established, acquits and excuses the defendant from punishment. A defendant pleading diminished responsibility does not seek relief from punishment by justification or excuse, but seeks to be punished for a lesser offense which he generally admits committing. In contrast, diminished capacity focuses on a defendant's capacity to commit a specific intent crime, and, if established, does not excuse punishment, but results in punishment instead for the general intent crime defendant was capable of committing. Evidence to demonstrate such a lack of specific intent is not equivalent to evidence to establish diminished responsibility or insanity.

> Thus, a defendant claiming diminished capacity contemplates full responsibility, but only for the crime actually committed. Diminished capacity is based on the presentation of evidence aimed at negating specific intent.

What would be the rationale for permitting diminished capacity to negate specific intent but not general intent crimes? Would this result in the person who commits the more egregious offense being given the greatest possibility of having a defense?

2. *Three Approaches.* There are three possible ways that courts can approach the diminished capacity defense: (a) permit its use as a separate defense; (b) not permit its use as a separate defense but allow evidence only to the extent that it negates the mens rea; (c) not permit it as a separate defense but allow evidence of diminished capacity when it rises to the level of insanity. What are the pros and cons of each of these approaches? Which of these approaches best reflects the policy consider-ations upon which criminal law is based? The West Virginia Supreme Court endorsed the mens rea negation approach in *State v. Joseph*, 590 S.E.2d 718 (W. Va. 2003), and explained how the doctrine works:

> [T]he diminished capacity defense is available in West Virginia to permit a defendant to introduce expert testimony regarding a mental disease or defect that rendered the defendant incapable, at the time the crime was committed, of forming a mental state that is an element of the crime charged. This defense is asserted ordinarily when the offense charged is a crime for which there is a lesser included offense. This is so because the successful use of this defense renders the defendant not guilty of the particular crime charged, but does not preclude a conviction for a lesser included offense.

3. *Partial Responsibility.* Some courts have developed a partial responsibility defense to reduce a murder charge to manslaughter. Some contend that the Model Penal Code has adopted this view in permitting murder to be reduced to manslaugh-ter when there is a showing "of extreme mental or emotional disturbance for which there is reasonable explanation or excuse." Consider this issue as it arose in the case of *State v. Melendez*, 811 A.2d 261 (Conn. App. Ct. 2002):

> Finally, the defendant claims that the court should have instructed the jury on the defense of extreme emotional disturbance* * *. The defendant argues that he was upset by the argument over the dogs and that his repeating of "don't disrespect my father" while shooting showed his agitated state.
>
> Extreme emotional disturbance . . . is . . . an affirmative defense upon which the burden of persuasion rests on the defendant. * * * "To sustain his burden of establishing extreme emotional disturbance by a preponder-ance of the evidence, the defendant must persuade the trier of fact that: (1) the emotional disturbance is not a mental disease or defect that rises to the level of insanity as defined by the penal code; (2) the defendant was exposed to an extremely unusual and overwhelming state, that is, not mere annoyance or unhappiness; and (3) the defendant had an extreme

emotional reaction to it, as a result of which there was a loss of self-control, and reason was overborne by extreme intense feeling, such as passion, anger, distress, grief, excessive agitation or other similar emotions." * * *

On the basis of our review of the record and transcript, we conclude that the defendant has failed to sustain his burden of production. The defendant's counsel admitted to the court that he had failed to put on evidence in that regard. Because there was insufficient evidence regarding the defendant's emotional state, the court properly did not instruct the jury on manslaughter founded on an extreme emotional reaction defense.

We conclude, therefore, that because the defendant's state of mind was not sufficiently in dispute, the court did not improperly fail to instruct the jury on lesser included offenses because the jury could not reasonably have found the defendant innocent of murder, but guilty of manslaughter in the first degree under any of the proffered theories.

4. ***Federal Law***. Consider the following from *United States v. Pohlot*, 827 F.2d 889 (3d Cir. 1987):

The entire structure of the Congressional debate suggests that Congress did not intend to bar evidence of mental abnormality to prove a lack of mens rea. After a jury acquitted John S. Hinckley of attempting to kill President Reagan, there was widespread support in Congress, in the Administration and in medical and legal professional organizations for some reform of the insanity defense. Many members of Congress wished to preserve some affirmative insanity defense but to delete the "volitional prong" of the Model Penal Code approach, * * * and to shift the burden of proof. Other members of Congress, backed by the Justice Department, wished to abolish the insanity defense altogether. Even those favoring abolition, however, wished to preserve the defendant's right to use psychiatric evidence to prove lack of mens rea, and their bills explicitly did so. * * *

Eventually, the abolition approach did not triumph. Congress preserved a limited affirmative insanity defense. It did so, however, not because of doubts about the use of evidence to negate mens rea, but rather because it felt that concerns about the dangers of an insanity defense were overstated and because abolition "would alter that fundamental basis of Anglo-American criminal law: the existence of moral culpability as a prerequisite for punishment." * * * In light of this legislative history, it would be ironic to view the acceptance of an affirmative insanity defense as a rejection of psychiatric evidence on mens rea. * * *

We do not decide the constitutionality of any Congressional attempt to bar evidence of mental abnormality from the issue of mens rea. The constitutional issues are sufficiently substantial, however, that we are unwilling to create a rule of evidence that would raise them in the absence of explicit Congressional direction. * * * For all the foregoing reasons, we therefore reject the government's contention that the Insanity Defense Reform Act either explicitly or implicitly bars a defendant from introducing evidence of mental abnormality on the issue of mens rea. * * *

Although we reject the government's broader argument, the Senate Report makes clear that § 17(a) does preclude defenses akin to partially diminished capacity or diminished responsibility. * * * The Senate Report indicates disapproval in this context not just of the creation of actual technical defenses but also of presenting the jury with "needlessly confusing psychiatric testimony." * * *

In light of the strong danger of misuse, we join other circuits that have directed district courts to examine proffered psychiatric testimony carefully "to determine whether the proof offered is grounded in sufficient scientific support to warrant use in the courtroom, and whether it would aid the jury in deciding the ultimate issues." * * * As this case shows, however, expert psychiatric evidence is not the only evidence of mental abnormality bearing on mens rea, for a defendant or other witnesses may testify about mental abnormality. Courts should also be careful in deciding whether to issue jury instructions or to permit defense arguments directing the jury to consider whether any evidence of mental abnormality negates mens rea. Notions of intent, purpose and premeditation are malleable and at their margins imprecise. But the limits of these concepts are questions of law. District courts should admit evidence of mental abnormality on the issue of mens rea only when, if believed, it would support a legally acceptable theory of lack of mens rea. In deciding such a question, courts should evaluate the testimony outside the presence of the jury. * * *

5. *International Law.* The issue of diminished responsibility is not unique to the United States, and has arisen in international tribunals. In the Ad Hoc Tribunal for the Former Yugoslavia (ICTY), the court was faced with the issue of whether diminished capacity would constitute a defense. In examining the origins of this doctrine, as well as the laws of other countries the appeals chamber court in *Prosecutor v. Delalic et.al,* Case No. IT-96-21-A, Judgment, ¶ 586 (Int'l Crim. Trib. for the Former Yugoslavia Feb. 20, 2001) stated:

The partial defence of diminished responsibility originated in Scotland in the 19th century. It was developed there by the courts as a means of avoiding murder convictions for those offenders who were otherwise liable for murder but who did not satisfy the restrictive test for the defence of insanity, but whose mental state was nevertheless impaired.

The subsequent English statute, enacted in 1957, provided the model for largely identical legislation in some common law countries. In most (if not all) such countries, the legislation, by reducing the crime from murder to manslaughter, permitted the sentencing judge to impose a sentence other than the relevant mandatory sentence for murder, which was either death or penal servitude for life. The partial defence is in effect, then, a matter which primarily provides for mitigation of sentence by reason of the diminished mental responsibility of the defendant. A recent review of the partial defence of diminished responsibility in Australia concluded that, notwithstanding the abolition of mandatory sentences for murder, the partial defence should be maintained in order to assist in the sentencing process.

6. *Capacity.* Diminished capacity is not the same as incapacity resulting from age. States often recognize immaturity of the accused and transfer the individual to juvenile court. Consider the Model Penal Rule regarding immaturity:

MODEL PENAL CODE

§ 4.10. Immaturity Excluding Criminal Conviction; Transfer of Proceedings to Juvenile Court.

(1) A person shall not be tried for or convicted of an offense if:

(a) at the time of the conduct charged to constitute the offense he was less than sixteen years of age [, in which case the Juvenile Court shall have exclusive jurisdiction]; or

(b) at the time of the conduct charged to constitute the offense he was sixteen or seventeen years of age, unless:

(i) the Juvenile Court has no jurisdiction over him, or

(ii) the Juvenile Court has entered an order waiving jurisdiction and consenting to the institution of criminal proceedings against him.

(2) No court shall have jurisdiction to try or convict a person of an offense if criminal proceedings against him are barred by Subsection (1) of this Section. When it appears that a person charged with the commission of an offense may be of such an age that criminal proceedings may be barred under Subsection (1) of this

Section, the Court shall hold a hearing thereon, and the burden shall be on the prosecution to establish to the satisfaction of the Court that the criminal proceeding is not barred upon such grounds. If the Court determines that the proceeding is barred, custody of the person charged shall be surrendered to the Juvenile Court, and the case, including all papers and processes relating thereto, shall be transferred.

NOTE

Model Penal Code § 210.3(1)(b) [p. 308] permits a reduction from murder to manslaughter when "[t]he defendant acted under the influence of extreme emotional disturbance for which there was a reasonable explanation or excuse, the reasonableness of which is to be determined from the viewpoint of a person in the defendant's situation under the circumstances as the defendant believed them to be. * * * ." Unlike a claim of insanity, which seeks to link the mental illness to the particular crime, the Model Penal Code approach focuses on the reasonableness of the disturbance that affects the defendant that permits a jury to find the defendant guilty of the lesser-included offense of manslaughter.

PROBLEM SIXTY

Lynn was charged with second-degree murder in the beating death of Dana. In 2004, while Lynn was serving in the Army in Afghanistan, Lynn's spouse, Mani, become involved romantically with Dana. Within a month of Lynn's return from Afghanistan, Mani moved out of their house and began living with Dana. Lynn does not deny beating Dana to death. Lynn testifies to going to Dana's house to wait for Mani to return from work in the hope of convincing Mani to come back. At some point, Lynn approached the house and saw Dana watching television through a window. Lynn knocked on the screen door and entered the house. Dana jumped up, threw a glass at Lynn, and ran out a side door to a car. Lynn thought Dana was going to leave, but Dana returned to the house with a large stick in hand. Lynn felt threatened by Dana's holding the stick, grabbed Dana, and a struggle ensued. Although Lynn had no clear memory of the events that followed, Lynn admitted to having struck many blows to the body and head of Dana. Lynn remembered moving the body and being in a car with the body.

Lynn testified about experiences as a soldier in Afghanistan, including killing a young Taliban soldier. Soldiers who served with Lynn testified about the constant tension they experienced during their experiences and the anxiety caused by Taliban attacks. Four experts testified as to Lynn's mental condition. All four experts agreed that Lynn was competent to stand trial and was not legally insane at the time of the murder. The experts also agreed that Lynn suffered from depression and post-traumatic stress syndrome and they all concurred that Lynn was not faking these symptoms.

Dr. A testified that the depression was "of a sufficient level to significantly affect Lynn's thinking, reasoning, judgment, and emotional well-being," and that the "components of post-traumatic stress disorder may have lessened the threshold or made Lynn more sensitive to defense and protection." Dr. A says that this increased the likelihood of Lynn over-reacting to a real or perceived threat. Dr. B agreed that anxiety was sufficient to significantly affect Lynn's reasoning. Dr. C, testifying for the defense, stated that Lynn was unable to make a rational decision to murder someone. Dr. D, a psychologist, agreed with the other experts that Lynn suffered from depression, severe anxiety, and post-traumatic stress syndrome.

A. Defense counsel requests a diminished capacity instruction in a jurisdiction that has no case law or statute approving or disapproving of this defense. What arguments can the defense make to support the request for this jury instruction, and how will the prosecution respond?

B. If the jurisdiction has adopted the Model Penal Code's extreme mental or emotional disturbance, to reduce a murder charge to manslaughter, has Lynn met the threshold requirement to give such a jury instruction?

C. What arguments would be made if Lynn had been charged with first-degree murder?

Chapter 20
Intoxication

§ 20.01 Involuntary Intoxication

Miller v. Florida
805 So.2d 885 (Fla. Dist. Ct. App. 2001)

DAVIS, Judge.

John Robert Miller challenges his convictions for burglary with a firearm, shooting into a building, and discharging a firearm in public. He argues that the trial court improperly denied his motions for judgment of acquittal, improperly excluded certain testimony, and erroneously instructed the jury on the intoxication defense. Although we affirm the trial court on the first two issues without discussion, we agree that the trial court improperly instructed the jury. Accordingly, we reverse Miller's convictions for armed burglary and shooting into a building.

An admitted heroin user, Miller went to the Parental Awareness and Responsibility (PAR) clinic seeking treatment for his addiction and enrolled in a methadone program. After a number of months, Miller decided he wanted to be free of all drugs, including methadone. He attempted to get off the methadone through the PAR clinic but was unsuccessful. He then turned to Neuraad, a clinic that offered a different type of treatment called opiate detoxification. Under this program, intense doses of numerous toxic drugs are introduced into the patient's system, following which the patient is sedated with anesthesia. The patient then sleeps during the period that his or her body undergoes the physical manifestations of withdrawal, thus greatly reducing the patient's conscious awareness of the most acute symptoms of withdrawal.

Miller checked into the Neuraad clinic on a Tuesday morning. The staff administered the medications and the anesthesia. Some twenty-seven hours later he was released, still under the influence of significant amounts of medication and with prescriptions for additional medication. Within three hours of his release, Miller went to the PAR clinic. When he arrived, the clinic was closed for the day. Upset that he could not get in, Miller shot the lock off of the gate. He walked around the building, shooting into it several times. He then broke a window and climbed inside. He ultimately surrendered to the police when they entered. Miller was charged with shooting into a building, burglary with a firearm, and aggravated assault.

699

At trial, Miller raised the defenses of insanity and intoxication. He argued that because of the drugs that Neuraad had given him, he did not have the capacity to distinguish between right and wrong and, thus, was legally insane when he arrived at the PAR clinic. In the alternative, he argued that due to the drugs, he did not have the ability to form the specific intent to commit the offenses of armed burglary and shooting into a building. The trial court properly found that the evidence supported instructing the jury on both defenses.

Miller's trial counsel requested, and the trial court gave, both the standard instruction on insanity and the standard instruction on voluntary intoxication. However, Miller's counsel also presented the court with two proposed instructions on involuntary intoxication. Although one of the proposed instructions was an accurate statement of law, the trial court accepted neither and chose instead to give the jury an instruction of its own design, which failed to adequately instruct the jury. Accordingly, we must reverse. * * *

At the outset, we observe that there is a crucial distinction between the defense of insanity and that of intoxication. A successful insanity defense results in the defendant's acquittal of all charges on the theory that one cannot be held criminally responsible for acts that he or she did not know were wrong. * * * By contrast, a successful intoxication defense results in an acquittal of specific intent crimes only, not general intent crimes. * * * The rationale is that although an intoxicated defendant may know the difference between right and wrong, he or she may not be able to form the specific intent required to commit certain offenses.

The issue here is whether the intoxication defense applies where the intoxication is involuntary, but does not rise to the level of legal insanity. When intoxication is voluntary, it is considered to be a defense to specific intent crimes. However, where the intoxication is involuntary, it typically has been raised in an attempt to prove an insanity defense rather than an intoxication defense. The definition of insanity has been expanded to include those situations in which a person could not distinguish right from wrong as the result of an involuntarily-induced intoxicated state. * * *

If one who willingly and purposely consumes intoxicants to the point that he is unable to form a specific intent is to be excused from guilt of a specific intent crime, why should one who has unknowingly consumed the intoxicant be denied the same relief? * * *

In this case, it is clear that the jury rejected the insanity defense and concluded that Miller knew the difference between right and wrong. However, it is not clear what the jury concluded in regard to the intoxication defense. As instructed, if the jury concluded that Miller was involuntarily intoxicated, it could not consider the intoxication defense at all; it was limited to the insanity defense. That is, it is not clear whether the jury found Miller had the requisite intent or, instead, found he lacked the requisite intent but also found his intoxication was involuntary, and, under the erroneous instruction, the intoxication defense did not apply.

Because the instruction was misleading and misinformed the jury as to the applicable law, we reverse Miller's convictions on the specific intent crimes and remand for a new trial on the charges of burglary with a firearm and shooting into a building. Reversed and remanded.

NOTE

At common law, voluntary intoxication was not a defense to general intent crimes, but could negate the mens rea in specific intent crimes. In contrast, involuntary intoxication was a complete defense to the crime. Designations of specific intent crimes and general intent crimes are not applicable under the Model Penal Code.

MODEL PENAL CODE

§ 2.08. Intoxication

(1) Except as provided in Subsection (4) of this Section, intoxication of the actor is not a defense unless it negatives an element of the offense.

(2) When recklessness establishes an element of the offense, if the actor, due to self-induced intoxication, is unaware of a risk of which he would have been aware had he been sober, such unawareness is immaterial.

(3) Intoxication does not, in itself, constitute mental disease within the meaning of Section 4.01.

(4) Intoxication that (a) is not self-induced or (b) is pathological is an affirmative defense if by reason of such intoxication the actor at the time of his conduct lacks substantial capacity either to appreciate its criminality [wrongfulness] or to conform his conduct to the requirements of law.

(5) Definitions. In this Section unless a different meaning plainly is required:

(a) "intoxication" means a disturbance of mental or physical capacities resulting from the introduction of substances into the body;

(b) "self-induced intoxication" means intoxication caused by substances that the actor knowingly introduces into his body, the tendency of which to cause intoxication he knows or ought to know, unless he introduces them pursuant to medical advice or under such circumstances as would afford a defense to a charge of crime;

(c) "pathological intoxication" means intoxication grossly excessive in degree, given the amount of the intoxicant, to which the actor does not know he is susceptible.

NOTES AND QUESTIONS

1. *Unexpected Results.* Defendants will sometimes take two (or more) different intoxicants, which can lead to an unexpected result, such as extreme intoxication, that would not be caused by either one alone. Even if both are ingested voluntarily, the intoxicating effect is not considered involuntary, as the Pennsylvania Superior Court explained in *Commonwealth v. Smith*, 831 A.2d 636 (Pa. Super. Ct. 2003):

Pennsylvania law is consonant with the Model Penal Code's definition and would not characterize intoxication produced by the voluntary consumption of a prescription drug and alcohol as "involuntary" even if that consumption was without knowledge of a synergistic effect. Here, * * * the evidence merely established that Appellant drank alcohol without regard to the effects of its combination with medication she was taking. Thus, even assuming the proffered defense is viable, these facts alone cannot establish involuntary intoxication.

2. *Knowledge of the Intoxicating Effect.* The states are divided whether a person who takes a prescription medication knowing that a potential side-effect will be extreme intoxication can raise the involuntary intoxication defense when the impairment arises. Consider the analysis of the Wisconsin Court of Appeals in *State v. Gardner*, 601 N.W.2d 670 (Wis. Ct. App. 1999):

The State acknowledges that the effects of prescription medication may constitute involuntary intoxication, but urges us to add the requirement that the defendant must not know of the intoxicating effect. We acknowledge that ample case law supports this position. The rationale is that if the defendant knows of the intoxicating effect prior to taking the medication, then the intoxication is rendered voluntary. See *City of Minneapolis v. Altimus*, 238 N.W.2d 851 (Minn. 1976). We see no reason to so limit the defense. Even if forewarned of the intoxicating effect of a prescription drug, a person should have recourse to the defense if the drug renders him or her unable to distinguish between right and wrong. When faced with a medical condition requiring drug treatment, the patient hardly has a choice but to follow the doctor's orders. Intoxication resulting from such compliance with a physician's advice should not be deemed voluntary just because the patient is aware of potential adverse side effects. We agree with the Texas courts' formulation of when the defense is available. "The involuntary intoxication defense is limited to (1) the defendant's unawareness of what the intoxicating substance is; (2) force or duress; or (3) medically prescribed drugs taken according to prescription." *Shurbet v. State*, 652 S.W.2d 425 (Tex. Ct. Crim. App.1982). We note that this does not include cases where a patient knowingly takes more than the prescribed dosage, or mixes a prescription medication with alcohol or other controlled substances. Neither would the defense be available to one who voluntarily undertakes an activity incompatible with the drug's side effects.

3. ***Burden of Proof.*** The defendant can be required to bear the burden of proof with respect to affirmative defenses. Will this shift in burden be applicable to cases of both voluntary and involuntary intoxication? Consider this issue as raised in *Commonwealth v. Collins*, 810 A.2d 698 (Pa. Super. Ct. 2002):

> In this case, we determine whether the trial court erred when it instructed the jury that the defendant must prove the affirmative defense of intoxication by a preponderance of the evidence. Jennie Collins appeals the judgment of sentence imposed following her conviction of Driving Under the Influence of a Controlled Substance (phencyclidine or PCP). She contends that the trial court's jury instruction on involuntary intoxication improperly placed the burden of proof on the defendant and violated Section 301 of the Pennsylvania Crimes Code. We hold that the trial court rightly placed the burden of proof for the affirmative defense of involuntary intoxication on the defendant and conclude, accordingly, that the trial court properly instructed the jury. Accordingly, we affirm the judgment of sentence. * * *

> Collins also asserts that the trial court erred when it instructed the jury that the law required Collins to prove the affirmative defense of intoxication by a preponderance of the evidence. * * * It is well established that "an accused in a criminal case is clothed with a presumption of innocence." * * * The Commonwealth bears the burden of proving guilt beyond a reasonable doubt as to every element of the crime * * * . The Commonwealth's failure to maintain this burden of proof will result in the acquittal of the accused * * * . This Court has long held that the burden of proving an affirmative defense that relieves the accused of criminal responsibility, but does not negate an element of the offense charged may

be placed on the defendant. * * * Thus, when a defense is asserted that relates to the defendant's mental state or information that is peculiarly within the defendant's own knowledge and control, the general rule is that the defendant has the burden of proving the defense by a preponderance of the evidence. * * *

The record indicates that the trial judge informed the jury of the elements of the crime charged and the Commonwealth's burden of proof, and instructed the jury that Collins had the burden of proving the affirmative defense of involuntary intoxication by a preponderance of the evidence * * * . The record also documents that the trial judge clearly admonished the jury that it had to find that the Commonwealth had met its burden of proof on the charge of driving under the influence, before considering the involuntary intoxication defense. * * * Thus, we find that the trial court's jury instructions adequately apprised the jury of the applicable law and analytical framework.

4. *Eliminating Intoxication as a Defense*. Ten states have rejected intoxication as a defense to any crime. For example, Delaware provides: "[t]he fact that a criminal act was committed while the person committing such act was in a state of intoxication, or was committed because of such intoxication, is no defense to any criminal charge if the intoxication was voluntary." 11 DEL.CODE. § 421. In *Montana v. Egelhoff*, 518 U.S. 37 (1996), the Supreme Court upheld the constitutionality of a Montana statute, MT. CODE ANN. § 45-2-203, providing that "[a] person who is in an intoxicated condition is criminally responsible for his conduct and an intoxicated condition is not a defense to any offense and may not be taken into consideration in determining the existence of a mental state which is an element of the offense * * * ." Justice Scalia, writing for a four-justice plurality, found that the statute did not violate the defendant's due process right because the rule only prohibited the jury from hearing certain evidence that did not affect the state's burden to prove all the elements of the crime beyond a reasonable doubt:

There is, in modern times, even more justification for laws such as § 45-2-203 than there used to be. Some recent studies suggest that the connection between drunkenness and crime is as much cultural as pharmacological — that is, that drunks are violent not simply because alcohol makes them that way, but because they are behaving in accord with their learned belief that drunks are violent. This not only adds additional support to the traditional view that an intoxicated criminal is not deserving of exoneration, but it suggests that juries — who possess the same learned belief as the intoxicated offender–will be too quick to accept the claim that the defendant was biologically incapable of forming the requisite mens rea. Treating the matter as one of excluding misleading evidence therefore makes some sense.

Justice Ginsburg, in an opinion concurring in the judgment that upheld the Montana law, stated that if "it is within the legislature's province to instruct courts to treat a sober person and a voluntarily intoxicated person as equally responsible for conduct — to place a voluntarily intoxicated person on a level with a sober person–then the Montana law is no less tenable under the Federal Constitution than are the laws, with no significant difference in wording, upheld in sister States." Justice O'Connor's dissenting opinion found that the statute denied the defendant the right to offer a defense to the charge:

> Our cases establish that due process sets an outer limit on the restrictions that may be placed on a defendant's ability to raise an effective defense to the State's accusations. Here, to impede the defendant's ability to throw doubt on the State's case, Montana has removed from the jury's consideration a category of evidence relevant to determination of mental state where that mental state is an essential element of the offense that must be proved beyond a reasonable doubt. Because this disallowance eliminates evidence with which the defense might negate an essential element, the State's burden to prove its case is made correspondingly easier. The justification for this disallowance is the State's desire to increase the likelihood of conviction of a certain class of defendants who might otherwise be able to prove that they did not satisfy a requisite element of the offense. In my view, the statute's effect on the criminal proceeding violates due process.

5. ***Pathological Intoxication***. The Model Penal Code provides a definition of pathological intoxication and tells when it can be a defense. *See also* Tim Feulner, Note, *The Minotaur Defense: The Myth of the Pathological Intoxication Defense*, 49 AM. CRIM. L. REV. 1969 (2012).

§ 20.02 Strict Liability Crimes

State v. Hammond
571 A.2d 942 (N.J. 1990)

HANDLER, J.

The issue presented by this appeal is whether involuntary intoxication, as defined under the New Jersey Code of Criminal Justice, can be a defense to a drunk-driving charge under the State's Motor Vehicle Act. The Motor Vehicle Act prohibits the operation of a motor vehicle "while under the influence of intoxicating liquor, . . . or . . . with a blood alcohol concentration of 0.10% or more . . . in the defendant's blood." * * * The New Jersey Code of Criminal Justice provides generally that intoxication can constitute an "affirmative defense" if it deprives the defendant of the "capacity either to appreciate [the] wrongfulness [of his or her conduct] or to conform his [or her] conduct to the requirements of the law." * * *

We now hold that motor vehicle violations are not offenses under the Code of Criminal Justice, and hence the Code's provisions, including the involuntary intoxication defense, do not apply to a defendant charged with operating a motor vehicle under the influence of intoxicating liquor in violation of the Motor Vehicle Act.

The defendant, Theodore Hammond, had a small dinner party at his home on May 31, 1985. While he was cooking dinner, a friend, Joe Hovanec, made him a mixed vodka drink, which he drank at about nine o'clock. At dinner, defendant and his three friends shared a bottle of wine, of which defendant testified he drank one and a half to two glasses.

After dinner, Hammond and his friends decided to visit the new home of one of the party, Henry Spence. At Spence's house, at around midnight, defendant asked for some fruit juice. Spence testified that as a practical joke he prepared a mixture of cranberry juice and vodka, concocted in such a way as to disguise any taste of alcohol. Spence stated he learned this trick from bartenders at the restaurant where he worked. Defendant stated that he did not know Spence had put vodka in the juice. He drank two cups of this mixture at Spence's home, and another cup in the car on the way to a bar, consuming approximately ten to twelve ounces of vodka. Defendant testified that he was not "feeling well" at that point, but felt obligated to proceed to the bar since he had agreed to meet Hovanec there. Spence drove Hammond's car to the bar.

According to the defense testimony, at the bar Hovanec bought Hammond a beer which he did not drink. Since Hammond said he felt sick, and Spence had left the bar, Hovanec offered Hammond a ride home. But Hammond refused the ride. At trial, he stated he felt he "was being held together with something. ... And if I could get home before I unglued, I'd be okay." Defendant also stated that "it was beginning to storm, and I just had to get home."

At 2:27 a.m. on Route 31 in Hopewell Township, Officer William Reading observed a vehicle that, he reported, was going slowly then suddenly accelerating, braking excessively, drifting between lanes, and using the right turn signal to turn left. At one point the vehicle almost hit a tree, then continued to move erratically. The officer signaled the car to pull over and stop. On exiting the car defendant stumbled, grabbing the car door for support as he fell. The police report indicates that Hammond could hardly walk, had bloodshot eyes, slurred his speech, and smelled of alcohol.

In the ensuing conversation defendant reportedly told the officer he was very sorry, that he had made a mistake, that he does not drink, and that this was a "one time shot" for him. Defendant also told the officer he had had a beer to drink, which contradicts the record, including defendant's own testimony. Breathalyzer test results were .20 at 3:20 a.m., and .21 at 3:28 a.m.

At the Municipal Court hearing, Hammond, Spence and Hovanec testified for the defense. It was stipulated that Officer Reading would have testified to the information contained in the police report. It was further stipulated that an expert witness for the defense, Dr. Zylman, would have testified "that the defendant could . . . imbibe 10, 11, or 12 ounces . . . (of the cranberry-vodka mixture) over a period of an hour and a half or two hours in separate drinks, without tasting the vodka portion of the drinks so as to be aware that the drinks contain an alcoholic beverage."

The court found defendant guilty, giving credence to the police report, as well as defendant's statements to the officer that he had had beer, but discounting as incredulous the testimony that Spence wandered off, letting his friend Hammond drive himself home after having spiked his juice. The court stated further:

[T]here is no question that involuntary intoxication is a defense, and would have applied in this case had the court concluded factually that the defendant consumed this substance without his knowledge.

Hammond was given the statutorily minimum sentence for a violation of N.J.S.A. 39:4-50, including a $250 fine, twelve to forty-eight hours at an Intoxicated Driver Resource Center and loss of his driving privileges for one hundred eighty days. The court stayed the sentence pending appeal.

Defendant appealed his conviction to the Law Division. The court found that the record indicated beyond a reasonable doubt that defendant had operated his vehicle while intoxicated and thus was guilty of violation of N.J.S.A. 39:4-50. The court found there was "no need . . . to consider [the argument] . . . that the defendant was, in fact, involuntarily intoxicated." The court added, however, that it did not "endorse or accept the Municipal Court's statement . . . that involuntary intoxication is a defense to the drunk driving statute."

Defendant again appealed his conviction raising the involuntary intoxication defense, among other issues that are no longer contested. The Appellate Division reversed the judgment of conviction, holding that the involuntary intoxication defense can apply to a violation of N.J.S.A. 39:4-50, and remanding the matter to the Law Division for a retrial consistent with its determination. We granted the State's petition for certification and denied defendant's cross-petition. * * *

In addressing the issue whether involuntary intoxication as defined by the Code can be applied as an affirmative defense to the motor vehicle violation of driving while intoxicated, the Court must determine initially whether a violation of the Motor Vehicle Act constitutes an "offense" within the meaning of the Code of Criminal Justice. If it does, then, as the Appellate Division explained, several provisions of the Code, including the defense of involuntary intoxication, could apply in the prosecution of the DWI offense. * * *

[The court discussed how the statute and legislative history did not intend to include motor vehicle offenses under the criminal code.]

[I]ntoxication is not a defense unless it establishes a reasonable doubt as to the existence of an element of the offense . . . [Since driving under the influence] . . . is not subject to the provisions of . . . the criminal code requiring a 'culpable mental state' . . . [and] the only elements of the offense charged are operating a motor vehicle and being under the influence of intoxicating liquor while doing so, it follows that intoxication . . . cannot establish a reasonable doubt as to the existence of any element of the . . . offense. * * *

The Code further specifies that involuntary intoxication is an affirmative defense if by reason of such intoxication the actor at the time of his conduct lacks . . . capacity either to appreciate its wrongfulness or to conform his conduct to the requirement of law. * * *

The Appellate Division believed these provisions could be applied to drunk driving and, as noted, would be consistent with general Code requirements of culpability and voluntariness; indeed, it felt that if the involuntary intoxication defense did not apply to drunk driving, that motor vehicle offense would be based solely on "strict liability," a construction that should be avoided under the Code. * * * However, driving under the influence has generally been considered an absolute liability offense requiring no culpable mental state, including knowledge of one's intoxication. * * *

Moreover, it is settled that under our motor vehicle provisions for drunk driving, it is the objective state of intoxication that is crucial, * * * , provided intoxication is correlated with the operation of the motor vehicle * * * . The antecedent circumstances resulting in intoxication are relevant only in terms of their probative bearing on whether the driver was intoxicated while operating the motor vehicle. * * * The Legislature has thus made it clear that once drivers become intoxicated and operate a motor vehicle, it does not matter how they became intoxicated or whether they realized they were intoxicated or believed they could overcome the effects of intoxication. * * * The interjection of "involuntariness" or lack of knowledge as an excuse would be wholly discordant with the liability envisioned by the statute. The application of the involuntary intoxication defense would be anomalous: the more drunk the driver is, the less culpable he or she would be. * * *

It is well to recapitulate the evolution of the drunk driving statute on this point. The aim of the statute has moved from the driver's subjective state of intoxication or personal tolerance to alcohol, including the individual circumstances surrounding the manner in which the driver became intoxicated, to an objective one. * * * Because of the difficulty of determining when a person was actually "under the influence," the Legislature, in 1951, enacted N.J.S.A. 39:4-50.1, establishing a presumption that with a .15% blood alcohol level, a defendant is intoxicated.* * * That presumption was rebuttable, serving to reduce but not eliminate the relevance of subjective intoxication. * * * In 1977, amendments were enacted that lowered the presumption of intoxication to .10% blood alcohol level. * * * And, in 1983 the Legislature made driving with a .10% blood alcohol level a *per se* offense. The purpose and effect of these amendments were to eventually eliminate evidence of subjective intoxication, * * * The Legislature has thus made crystal clear that intoxication objectively determined by a breathalyzer test coupled with the operation of a motor vehicle constitutes the offense of drunk driving. * * * The judgment of the Appellate Division is reversed and the sentence imposed by the Law Division is reinstated.

§ 20.03 Actus Reus

United States v. Hernandez-Hernandez
519 F.3d 1236 (10th Cir. 2008)

GORSUCH, Circuit Judge.

At a bar in Palomas, Mexico, Alfredo Hernandez-Hernandez, a Mexican citizen twice deported from the United States, consumed a sufficient amount of alcohol and marijuana to blackout. The next thing he knew, Mr. Hernandez was in the United States without any recollection how he got there and, in short order, arrested for illegally reentering the country.

* * * According to Mr. Hernandez, he consumed more than a fifth of a quart of liquor, as well as some marijuana, at a bar in Palomas and promptly blacked out. When Mr. Hernandez regained his faculties, he found himself in the United States and confronted by a United States Border Patrol Agent. In response to the agent's questions, Mr. Hernandez admitted that he was a Mexican national and acknowledged that he had no documentation allowing him to be legally present in the United States. * * *

Rather than simply deporting him again, this time authorities indicted Mr. Hernandez for violation of 8 U.S.C. § 1326(a) and (b), and, more specifically, under the provision making it unlawful to be "found in" the United States illegally after a prior deportation.[1] In pre-trial proceedings, the government filed a motion in

---

[1] 8 U.S.C. § 1326(a) provides: [A]ny alien who (1) has been denied admission, excluded, deported, or removed or has departed the United States while an order of exclusion, deportation, or removal is outstanding, and thereafter (2) enters, attempts to enter, or is at any time found in, the United States, * * * shall be fined under Title 18, or imprisoned not

limine, seeking to exclude from trial any evidence that Mr. Hernandez might present regarding his voluntary intoxication. Mr. Hernandez opposed the government's motion, arguing that he should be allowed to show that "he has absolutely no memory of taking any actions to illegally cross the border" and "does not know whether his subsequent presence in the United States was voluntary and knowingly made. If [he] was brought to the United States and dumped on the United States side while he was passed out, clearly such an act would be a viable and acceptable defense to the crime charged." In aid of this argument, Mr. Hernandez proffered not just his own testimony but also offered Dr. Orrin McCleod, who sought to testify that Mr. Hernandez's history of alcoholism caused him to suffer "intoxicant amnesia" from the consumption of large amounts of alcohol, and Eugenio Vergara-Sosa, a fellow detainee who was prepared to testify that Mr. Hernandez was highly intoxicated and disoriented the day of his arrest.

The district court granted the government's motion and excluded Mr. Hernandez's proffered evidence. The court reasoned that Section 1326 creates only a "general intent" crime, that as a rule voluntary intoxication is not a defense to such crimes, and that Mr. Hernandez's evidence amounted to little more than an effort to effect an end-run around this rule. [Hernandez-Hernandez entered a guilty plea conditioned on his right to appeal the trial court's ruling excluding the evidence.]

Mr. Hernandez [argues that] his proffered proof bears on the mens rea element of the crime. But the mens rea required to secure a Section 1326 conviction for being unlawfully "found in" the United States is limited. In the past, we admit, the mental elements associated with Section 1326 were sometimes shrouded by reference to vague concepts like "general" and "specific" intent. But in this area, as in many others, we have sought to follow the thrust of modern American jurisprudence and clarify the required mens rea, often by reference to the Model Penal Code's helpfully defined terms, rather than persist in employing opaque common law labels that sometimes blur the line between distinct mental elements.

Accordingly, fully twenty years ago, we announced that the only mens rea required to establish a violation under Section 1326's provision prohibiting those previously denied the right to be in the United States from "enter[ing]" the country is a showing "that the defendant's acts were intentional. No intent to break the law — whether characterized as 'specific intent' or 'general criminal intent' — must be proved." [In a more recent case,] we added that this same intent — "the intent to do the act of entering the country"— will suffice to support a conviction under Section 1326's provision, now before us, making it unlawful to be "found in" the United States after a prior deportation.

---

more than 2 years, or both.

For his part, Mr. Hernandez, although contending that his intoxication has a relationship to the necessary mens rea, does not argue that his alcohol — and drug-induced blackout is sufficient to negate the limited mens rea required by the statute. To the contrary, he "has maintained since this issue has arisen that the Government is correct that voluntary intoxication is not a defense to this crime," and that voluntary intoxication provides a defense only when "specific" intent — or, a bit more precisely, an intent to do something more than just the physical act the crime requires — is necessary.

Instead, while the mens rea required under Section 1326 is limited, Mr. Hernandez emphasizes that, under the theory the government pursued in this case, it does require at least an intent to undertake the physical act that results in the defendant crossing the border. And Mr. Hernandez argues that, because of his blackout, there is a "complete vacuum in his memory," so that it is possible he was abducted and did not enter the United States of his own volition. * * *

In approaching this argument, * * * an alien's presence in the United States gives rise to a natural, common sense inference that his or her presence was intentional in the very limited, Section 1326 sense. After all, those crossing the border usually do so intending their own physical actions. Still, this inference can be overcome; while most border crossings are surely intentional in the Section 1326 sense, neither can we deny that the trafficking of human beings against their will across international boundaries is a reality. But to dispel the inference, the alien would have to demonstrate that one of the speculative possibilities of involuntary entry had actually taken place. And our test for assessing the relevance of evidence seeking to dispel this inference, as always, turns on whether the proffered proof makes a "fact that is of consequence to the determination of the action more probable or less probable." FED.R.EVID. 401.

So, Mr. Hernandez was surely entitled to produce evidence making it "more probable" that he was taken across the border against his will. The problem is that Mr. Hernandez's proof in this case does no such thing. An ordinary intoxication defense, where permissible, is relevant only because it makes it less likely the defendant possessed the mental state the government is required to prove. Here, however, Mr. Hernandez does not seek to argue that his intoxication would have negated the requisite mens rea under Section 1326. Instead, he wishes to offer his intoxication as evidence that his lack of memory is credible, and it is his lack of memory, Mr. Hernandez submits, that goes to the requisite mental state. Because he cannot remember anything after he blacked out, Mr. Hernandez seems to suggest, anything is possible. Maybe he was kidnapped. Maybe he was dragged across the border by a drinking pal. Maybe someone was playing a practical joke and transported him in a catatonic state into the United States. The difficulty lies in the fact that Mr. Hernandez's lack of memory leaves equally open the possibility that he walked across the border under his own steam. Or hitched a ride. Or paid to be driven. Simply put, Mr. Hernandez's proof does not make it any more or less likely that he was (innocently) carried across the border against his will or (culpably) intended the physical actions that transported him to the United States.

Had Mr. Hernandez's proffer included any evidence suggesting that he was taken across the border against his will, that would be one thing. But inviting the jury to guess about the mode of Mr. Hernandez's arrival in the United States based on the absence of proof (a "complete vacuum in his memory") is another, and the district court properly ruled it out of bounds. Relevant evidence does not include the suggestion of speculative possibilities.

The Fifth and Sixth Amendment right to produce witnesses on one's behalf, while fundamental, does not extend to irrelevant (or immaterial) matters. The testimony excluded here simply was not relevant to any fact at issue in the defense Mr. Hernandez pursued-making it neither more nor less probably true. Accordingly, the district court's decision to exclude it was appropriate.

NOTES AND QUESTIONS

1. *Alcohol and Crime.* The role of alcohol in all types of crimes is especially important. Consider the following Bureau of Justice Statistics report, *Crime Characteristics* (2004):

> About 1 million violent crimes occurred in 2002 in which victims perceived the offender to have been drinking at the time of the offense. Among those victims who provided information about the offender's use of alcohol, about 30% of the victimizations involved an offender who had been drinking.

> Two-thirds of victims who suffered violence by an intimate (a current or former spouse, boyfriend, or girlfriend) reported that alcohol had been a factor. Among spouse victims, 3 out of 4 incidents were reported to have involved an offender who had been drinking. By contrast, an estimated 31% of stranger victimizations where the victim could determine the absence or presence of alcohol were perceived to be alcohol-related.

> For about 1 in 5 violent victimizations involving perceived alcohol use by the offender, victims also reported they believed the offender to have been using drugs as well.

2. *Intoxication and Mistake.* What if a person is voluntarily intoxicated, and then engages in a crime and argues a mistake of fact defense based on the intoxication?

This is not strictly an intoxication defense, but it has many of its hallmarks because the intoxication may cause the mistake, or at least contribute to it:

> It is worth mentioning the close relationship between the intoxication defense and the mistake of fact defense, both of which represent a failure to prove the mental state required by the criminal offense. A mistake of fact could be caused by the perpetrator's voluntary intoxication. For example, a man may be mistaken as to whether or not the woman consented to sexual intercourse due to his voluntary consumption of alcohol. Nevertheless, there is an important distinction between these two defenses because the person who voluntarily produces the condition that brings about the unreasonable act is considered more culpable than the person who fails to assess the situation correctly because of factors outside of his control.

Valerie M. Ryan, Comment, *Intoxicating Encounters: Allocating Responsibility in the Law of Rape*, 40 CAL. W. L. REV. 407 (2004).

3. ***Intoxication and Murder.*** In *Wheeler v. United States*, 832 A.2d 1271 (D.C. 2003), the defendant argued that the trial judge erred in not giving his requested instruction on intoxication as a defense to second-degree murder. In affirming the conviction, the court stated that "[t]he trial judge instructed the jury on voluntary intoxication as a defense to first-degree murder, but, on the basis of prevailing case law, refused to give the same instruction as to second-degree murder." The court noted that:

> The leading case on intoxication in this jurisdiction is *Bishop v. United States*, 107 F.2d 297 (D.C. Cir. 1939). There the U.S. Court of Appeals reviewed the common law authorities and held that, although voluntary intoxication "may negative the ability of the defendant to form the specific intent to kill, or the deliberation and premeditation necessary to constitute first degree murder, in which event there is a reduction to second degree murder," it "may not reduce murder to voluntary manslaughter, nor permit an acquittal of murder." "[V]oluntary immediate drunkenness," in particular, "is not admissible to disprove [the element of] malice" integral to the crime of murder. * * *

PROBLEM SIXTY-ONE

Vica was highly intoxicated when in an accident in a National Forest. Vica failed field sobriety tests given by two U. S. Park Rangers. The Park Rangers then placed Vica under arrest and attempted to put Vica in the back of their vehicle.

Vica began to struggle and attempted to pull away from one of the Rangers, pulling the Ranger down to one knee and causing an abrasion on the leg. After the Park Rangers secured Vica in the vehicle, Vica then stated to the Rangers, "I'm going to mess with you; if I get a shot at you, well dammit I'll kill you, I will; and I'm going to cut your head off." A short time later, Vica said to the Rangers, "I will put a bullet straight in your f*****' head. The sheriff won't always be in office and 15 years later I'll walk up on you. I'm going to drive you'ans all straight to h***." Vica is charged with one count of violating 18 U.S.C. § 111(a)(1), and two counts of violating 18 U.S.C. § 115. The statutes provide:

> § 111:Whoever forcibly assaults, resists, opposes, impedes, intimidates, or interferes with [any officer or employee of the United States or of any agency in any branch of the United States Government, or any person assisting such an officer or employee] while engaged in or on account of the performance of official duties . . . shall, where the acts . . . constitute only simple assault, be fined . . . or imprisoned not more than one year, or both.

> § 115:Whoever threatens to assault, kidnap, or murder, a United States official, a United States judge, a Federal law enforcement officer, or an official whose killing would be a crime under [18 U.S.C. § 1114], with intent to impede, intimidate, or interfere with such official, judge, or law enforcement officer while engaged in the performance of official duties, or with intent to retaliate against such official, judge, or law enforcement officer on account of the performance of official duties, shall be punished
> . . . .

For which of these offenses can Vica offer a defense of voluntary intoxication?

CASE STUDY SIX

Mo has a new friend named Jo, who told Mo that a person named Switch had a bullet with Mo's name on it. Said Jo: "Switch heard that you've been going out with 'E.' Didn't you know that the two of them have been going out together?" Switch was 6'2" tall and about 220 pounds of muscle. Mo had seen Switch around the neighborhood and knew who Switch was but had never spoken to Switch nor heard much about Switch until this very moment. Mo was about 5'10" tall and about 170 pounds and didn't work out much. Mo had just met Jo a few weeks ago playing darts in a local bar. The two had played darts and pool on two or three occasions since, and Mo had taken a liking to Jo. Mo did not carry a weapon but Jo said that Mo could get one from Andi, who hung out at the local bar.

Mo tracked Andi down at the bar. The two talked awhile, and Mo had about three boilermakers. Mo now got up the courage to ask Andi about the gun. Andi said, "I could make a trade: the gun for some cocaine." Mo offered to pay cash for the gun, but Andi refused, even when Mo said, "I don't use the stuff and am not sure I can get some quickly enough." Andi said, "If you'd rather face Switch without a weapon, that's your business." Mo relented and said "I'll be back in a moment and returned to Jo to explain the situation. Jo gave some coke to Mo, saying, "We'll settle up later. After all, we're friends, right?" Mo went back to the bar, asked to see the gun first, so Andi pulled it from the jacket pocket just enough to be seen, then replaced it. Mo handed over the coke. Just at that moment, Switch entered the bar, striding quickly toward Mo, saying, "I need to talk to you." Mo reacted quickly, plucking the gun from Andi's pocket, turning, and firing, killing Switch instantly with a single bullet to the heart. Andi, who turned out to be an undercover police officer, wrestled Mo to the ground and arrested Mo.

Switch, it turns out, was a member of a pacifist religious group that had recently set up a small church in the area with the goal of reducing neighborhood crime. Switch had converted to pacifism after teenage years involved in violent crime and a subsequent stint as a Navy Seal. Switch had been working to set up neighborhood watch groups and had been cooperating with the police and arranging for area residents to report suspicious activity to Switch, who forwarded the information to the police but without passing on the informants' names. Switch's work was having some success, seriously irking a local gang boss, Wilson Fisk. Jo was one of Fisk's on-the-street drug dealers and owed Fisk some money. Fisk had a subordinate tell Jo that Jo was to arrange for Switch's quick departure from this world. If Jo succeeded, all debts would be forgiven. If not, Jo would instead be the one to visit the other side. That conversation took place yesterday, and the subordinate gave Jo until midnight today to do the deed. Switch died exactly one hour before that deadline. Jo knew everyone in the neighborhood and knew that Andi was an undercover officer who carried a loaded weapon for Andi's own protection. Jo had gotten Switch to go to the bar by telling Switch that Mo was there and was in the process of threatening some of Switch's co-religionists to silence them from cooperating with the police. Switch was a committed pacifist but still had a temper and could blow up (though usually only by using loud and angry language) if Switch felt that a mission was being threatened.

Mo had no criminal record and had been employed successfully for the past ten years as a furniture salesman. Mo was usually a model employee. However, Mo had long been taking medication for paranoid schizophrenia. Although the medication was generally remarkably effective, Mo's paranoia was most likely to flair, and occasionally did flair, when Mo suspected infidelity, for Mo was a very jealous person. Mo's paranoia could result in hallucinations and delusions (respectively hearing or seeing things that were not there or persisting in beliefs despite inadequate evidence supporting them or even all the evidence undercutting them).

Mo is arrested on charges of homicide and distribution of a controlled substance. Jo is also arrested on these two charges.

1.   (a) Of what types of homicide (murder, manslaughter, degrees of each) and on what theories might Mo be convicted? What defenses might defense counsel raise? What is the likely success of each of these prosecution and defense arguments, if one assumes that each side with the relevant burden of persuasion can indeed prove the facts above? How might the answers to these questions differ depending on whether one is in a common law or Model Penal Code jurisdiction?

(b) Drop the assumption that the facts recited above can be proven. What witnesses should the prosecution and the defense respectively call to prove their cases and why? Are there gaps in the proof, that is, things that one just does not know that would help one side or the other? If so, what investigation should each side do, how, and why? What sorts of questions should be asked of the witnesses on cross-examination by the opposition to undercut the witness' credibility? Consider evidentiary issues that might arise in proving each crime or defense and what responses might be available.

(c) Will Mo have any defense(s) if charged with possession of a controlled substance, and what is the likelihood that Mo will succeed in escaping liability? Why? What witnesses will each side call on these questions?

2.   Now assume that Jo is on trial and answer questions 1(a)-(c) above but as to Jo rather than Mo.

INDEX